PSYCHOLOGY IN
COMMUNITY SETTINGS

Clinical, Educational, Vocational, Social Aspects

Seymour B. Sarason, Kenneth S. Davidson, and Burton Blatt
THE PREPARATION OF TEACHERS, 1962

Seymour B. Sarason, Kenneth S. Davidson, Frederick F. Lighthall,
Richard R. Waite, and Britton K. Ruebush
ANXIETY IN ELEMENTARY SCHOOL CHILDREN, 1960

PSYCHOLOGY IN COMMUNITY SETTINGS

Clinical, Educational, Vocational, Social Aspects

SEYMOUR B. SARASON

MURRAY LEVINE

I. IRA GOLDENBERG

DENNIS L. CHERLIN

EDWARD M. BENNETT

Yale University

JOHN WILEY & SONS, INC.

New York · London · Sydney

With respect and appreciation we dedicate this book
to the staff and goals of

Community Progress Inc. (CPI)

The New Haven Regional Center for Mental Retardation

and to the many school teachers, principals
and administrative personnel with whom
our Clinic has so closely worked.

Acknowledgments

This book is about the origins and activities of the Psycho-Educational Clinic in the Department of Psychology at Yale, a service, training, and research facility that represents a new departure for our department and a marked change in the thinking and practices of those of us involved in the Clinic. It is no exaggeration to say that our lives have been so changed that it is hard for us to remember clearly what we did before the Clinic's existence. Because we feel that we have learned a lot and have been given an opportunity to venture forth in relatively unfettered ways not always possible for others who may have wished to do so, it is more than a token gesture on our part to express our thanks to those individuals and agencies who helped us in diverse ways. To Claude Buxton, who was the chairman of our department at the time, we owe a special debt of gratitude not only for his belief in what we were going to attempt but also because he helped steer our plans through the academic maze so that we could do what we wanted to do.

Unfortunately, the number of teachers, principals, and other school administrators who have been helpful to us is so vast that it defies individual acknowledgment here. School personnel in general do not receive the recognition they merit, and it is cause for regret that our indebtedness to so many is so great that it would require several pages to express our thanks to each of them.

Much the same situation exists in relation to Community Progress Inc. (CPI) and the New Haven Regional Center for Mental Retardation. Here, however, the help and cooperation we received from three individuals were of proportions that require special mention. It is with profound thanks, therefore, that we acknowledge our indebtedness to Mitchell Sviridoff, the head of CPI, George Bennett, CPI Director of Manpower, and Stanley Meyers, Director of the New Haven Regional Center. The dedication of this book is testimony to the respect we have for the accomplishments of these individuals and their staffs, and it also expresses our feelings about the school personnel with whom we have worked.

In the beginning phases of our work Dr. Michael Kahn, Dr. Lyn Carlsmith, and Dr. Esther Sarason were of inestimable help to us both in terms of developing services and of sharing with us the burden of doubts and anxieties one expects but still hopes to avoid in any new venture. In later phases we benefited from the participation of Dr. Frances Kaplan, Dr. Donald McIntyre, and Dr. Albert Myers and the continued affiliation of Esther Sarason. We are also grateful for the different ways in which Mrs. Kate McGraw has been professionally helpful to us in our work in schools.

To our students, past and present, we say thanks for their independence of mind, enthusiasm, intimidating brightness, and friendship. When we felt that we had justified our existence to our students, we knew we had passed some kind of acid test.

We have long believed that two of the most unstudied mental-health problems in our society are parking and secretaries. We studied but did not solve the parking problem, but we did solve the secretary problem in the person of Anita Miller, whose brightness, efficiency, and capacity for work have made us the object of the envy of our colleagues. For what she has contributed to the Clinic and our mental health we are indeed grateful.

S.B.S.
M.L.
I.I.G.
D.L.C.
E.M.B.

Contents

PSYCHOLOGY IN
COMMUNITY SETTINGS

Clinical, Educational, Vocational, Social Aspects

Chapter 1

Introduction

The decision to write a book, like any other form of motivated behavior, is determined by a variety of factors. In our case three major goals influenced our decision. First, we wanted to convey some of the historical-professional considerations that caused us to alter our own professional way of functioning. Although we discuss them primarily in terms of clinical psychology, the historical-professional considerations we describe are central to all of the mental health professions. It is no exaggeration to say that at the present time all of the mental health professions are confronted with problems of orientation and role which, when and however resolved, will be associated with important changes in the relationship of these professions to the larger society of which they are a part. We could say, in fact, that the current ferment in the mental health fields has developed because of their relatively parochial view of the needs of our society. When matters of public policy and societal needs, on the one hand, conflict with professional orientation on the other, we have the conditions for legitimate controversy and the possibility of change.

A second major goal in writing this book was to describe certain settings in which the mental health fields have been conspicuous by their absence, so that the reader may make a judgment for himself whether such settings can remain peripheral to the mental health fields. The size of this book is due primarily to our desire to convey, via clinical, anecdotal, and detailed descriptions, a feeling for the nature of these settings and their obvious importance to the professional or layman concerned with clinical and preventive approaches in mental health planning and programs. For the most part what we attempt to say is not new. We are by no means the first to be aware of these settings, either in terms of their needs and nature or of their lack of a meaningful relationship to the mental health fields. The justification for describing our experience is that it has been of a depth that may

1

allow us to transmit matters to the reader in a more compelling way than heretofore.

The third major goal was to describe how we at the Psycho-Educational Clinic carried out ways of working in these settings; for example, how to get into the settings, the variety of ways in which it is possible to function, the clinical and preventive functions to be performed, and the kinds of accomplishments and failures to expect. In a truly personal sense this goal was initially most important to us because, in response to "what do you do?"—and this was the most frequent question put to us—we found that a short answer was impossible. The most satisfying answer contained example after example of what we do—but not many questioners had the time to listen to more than a few examples. The descriptions of what we do are not presented because we are certain that what we do is the best way of meeting the problems in the particular setting, but rather as a basis for discussion. We hope that as more and more people begin to work in these settings we will see the problem of professional action more comprehensively and be better able to formulate questions and develop relevant methodologies for evaluation. This book would, of course, never have been written if we did not feel that there was face validity to many of the things we have done. However, at the present time it is our opinion that more important than what *we* may have accomplished is whether we have described the settings in a way that makes clear the many things that need to be accomplished.

In keeping with our goals, Part I of this book is devoted to those historical-professional considerations that influenced our thinking and actions. Our discussion centers around clinical psychology, but we cannot take up clinical psychology without taking up its relation to psychiatry, psychiatric social work, and other professions. It would have been beyond the scope of this book to present these considerations with the historic detail they merit. Training programs tend not to give the student an historical perspective which can act as a corrective against the tendency to assume that all good thinking and ideas are modern phenomena. A detailed history of these issues is very much needed, not only to tell us where we have been but as a guide to where we may be going.

Part II is concerned with the different ways in which our clinic has functioned *in* the schools as well as in the clinic with children from the schools with which we are affiliated. In the appendix we present transcripts of teacher-discussion groups, still another service we developed as a result of our school experiences. The reasons leading up to the formation of these groups are covered in Chapter 14.

Part III is concerned with our involvement in some of the activities of Community Progress, Inc. (CPI), a local social action agency with nationwide influence. Many of the inner-city programs now being stimulated and supported by federal programs had some aspect of their beginning in the early activities of CPI. In many ways CPI can be viewed as one of the first and most comprehensive community mental health programs in the country, though it was not so labeled, and mental health personnel did not participate in its activities until after it had become a going and ever-growing program. As shown in Part III, our clinic was intimately involved in two of CPI's programs: the Neighborhood Employment Centers and the work crews, neither title conveying the types or seriousness of the human problems with which these programs deal or the kinds of challenge they present to the traditionally trained mental health worker.

Part IV describes our relationship with the New Haven Regional Center, which reflects a new concept in service to mentally retarded individuals and their families. This part differs from the others, if only because the Center was just ready to open its doors when this book was submitted for publication. It was precisely because the Center did not have its own facilities and possessed only a skeleton staff that it was important to some of our purposes to establish a close relationship with it. However, the fact that the Center had obligations to a wide variety of families even before it opened, provided what was for us an invaluable means to present and implement ideas relevant to clinical and organizational problems, an opportunity not ordinarily available. The brevity of this part of the book in no way reflects a judgment about its potential significance. We may note here that the Regional Center provided us with a means for bringing together aspects of our work in the schools and CPI.

It should be said at this point that the activities of the Psycho-Educational Clinic reflect a number of different purposes, one of the most important of which is the development of a research program concerned with two broad questions: how do we determine, understand, and describe the culture of the school setting, and related to that, how do we introduce change into an ongoing social system? Although we touch on and discuss aspects of these questions, they are not the main focus of this book. In a real sense this book is a prologue to the study of questions that will occupy us in the coming years. They are not easy questions—and we are not at all certain that they are well formulated—but they are the kinds of questions that must be pursued if the knowledge we have gained about human behavior is to be applied in non-self-defeating ways. These questions take on added significance in these times when there is ever-increasing pressure to apply knowledge in new ways to new and old settings.

PART I

HISTORICAL AND PROFESSIONAL ORIGINS OF THE PSYCHO-EDUCATIONAL CLINIC

Chapter 2

The Mental-Health Professions and the
Aftermaths of World War II

It has been noted time and again in the course of history that wars produce profound effects on the societies involved. World War II has proved to be no exception to the rule. There is scarcely an aspect of our society that does not reflect our involvement in the last war. For example, the issues and problems with which we are confronted in education, race relations, population growth, and governmental responsibility reflect social processes that were either exacerbated or produced by World War II. That the lives of the millions of individuals who directly or indirectly participated in the war effort were forever affected in large or small ways needs no documentation. What tends to be forgotten or overlooked is that the effects on the war generation had consequences not only for the lives of subsequent generations but for governmental policy and action that by their nature produced further consequences for everyone. Nowhere is this more clear than in the mental-health field.

With America's involvement in the war two problems came to the fore with compelling urgency. The first and most immediate problem was to anticipate and plan for the care of a staggering number of individuals who would become one or another kind of casualty during the course of the war. The second problem was to plan for the enormous increase in facilities that would be required if the government was to discharge its legal and moral responsibilities honorably to veterans in the postwar period. Involved were hundreds of thousands of individuals and billions of dollars, and a large portion of each would be concerned with the treatment and care of psychiatric casualties. The difficulty of the problem was not made easier by the speed necessary for planning and action. (It should be said at this point that however much we may regret some of the consequences of what was done, the over-all effort deserves the highest praise from the lay and professional person.)

In regard to the problem of psychiatric casualties during and after the war it was immediately apparent that the relevant professional personnel existed in numbers woefully short of what was required. It would be more correct to say that during the war years there was acute awareness of the lack of professional personnel to meet the immediate problems, but it was hoped that the manpower problem would be discernibly improved in the postwar period. This hope, as we show later, was only partly realized in regard to the veteran population and, to the extent that it was realized, markedly retarded efforts to move in new directions to meet the mental-health problems in other sections of our society. In any event, the major governmental problem during and after the war was recruiting and training personnel in the mental-health field, that is, psychiatrists, psychiatric social workers, and clinical psychologists.

The manpower problem was most acute in clinical psychology because this field, for all practical purposes, did not exist before World War II. We mean by this that training programs in clinical psychology did not exist in our universities before the war. Students did not enter graduate departments of psychology in order to become clinical psychologists. There was no formalized clinical program involving course requirements, practicum, and internship. There were a few clinical centers to which psychologists could go for field experience but these centers had no relationship to university departments. Graduate departments might have courses in "tests and measurements" and in abnormal psychology but they were not viewed as being part of any kind of professional training. It is unlikely that examination of course offerings in all prewar graduate departments of psychology would reveal a single example either of a course in psychotherapy or a supervised experience in psychotherapy. It would be correct to characterize American psychology before World War II as "academic," but this would not convey the fact that it was also anticlinical in orientation. The Ph.D. was treasured as a symbol of scholarly and research performance untainted by practical or professional considerations.

It should not be surprising that American psychology, lacking as it did a meaningful background in a tradition of clinical service, would be particularly dependent on and influenced by the other mental-health professions at that point when training in clinical psychology was brought into the universities. The absence of a clinical tradition in psychology was only one, and not the most important, reason for such a dependent role. The most important reason resided in the manner in which those responsible for planning and action conceived of the nature of mental illness and its consequences for professional responsibility. This is not to suggest that these planners devised new conceptions from which they drew new conclusions about professional practice and responsibility. What happened was a natural continuation of the tradition that mental health, like physical health, was primarily the concern and responsibility of the medical profession. Such terms as "psychiatric or neuropsychiatric casualties" reflected accurately what was at that time the actual view and prevailing practice, that "mentally ill" individuals looked for help to the physician with a specialty in psychiatry. Before, during, and for a short period after World War II there was hardly a challenge to the conception that mental illness was by its nature a medical problem. At this point in our discussion it is not necessary to examine or challenge this conception of mental illness. What is important is to emphasize that in actual practice it was the psychiatrist who assumed leadership and responsibility in this area. Society was and should have been, so to speak, thankful that some profession devoted itself to a problem area in which other professional groups had little or no interest and responsibility.

The conception of mental illness as a medical problem and the actual leadership role of the psychiatrist were basic considerations in planning for the treatment and care of the hundreds of thousands of veterans who were or would become "psychiatric" casualties. There was clear recognition that other professions (clinical psychology, psychiatric social work) were necessary to help meet the problem, but this was in the context of a view and a tradition of professional practice which we have already described. Let us now turn to an examination of the consequence of this context for clinical psychology, a field which had short and thin roots in the soil of American psychology.

THE ROLE OF THE GOVERNMENT

From the vantage point of twenty years after World War II it is perhaps necessary to labor the obvious point that sources of money play a fateful role in the lives of individuals and professions. As the war began to draw to a close, and in the years thereafter, the Veterans Administration—faced as it was with the overwhelming task of building facilities and professions at the same time that it had to care for thousands upon thousands of individuals—had appropriated to it large sums of money. Never before did a government agency have so much money to devote to training programs in the universities. The result was that many graduate departments of psychology tied in their new training programs in clinical psychology to the VA needs and settings. Money was made available for support of graduate students and (in diverse ways) for faculty salaries. An additional factor contributing to the university-VA relationship was the far-from-healthy financial position of the university during and shortly after the war period. Responsiveness to a social need, a particular source of governmental support, university receptivity—these were the interacting factors that proved to have a crucial influence on psychology in general and clinical psychology in particular.

THE SETTING FOR CLINICAL TRAINING

The tie with the VA immediately restricted programs in clinical psychology to two types of setting, that is, the hospital and the outpatient clinic. This restriction reflected not only the traditional conception of mental illness as a medical problem and responsibility but also the places in which psychiatrists most frequently dealt with the problems. It is true that the new hospitals were built, wherever possible, near medical schools and not in the middle of nowhere as had been the case before the war. It is also true that the new hospitals were splendidly equipped and were frequently centers of intellectual ferment and research activity. These admirable developments, however, could not change the fact that the clinical psychology trainee's view of mental health and psychopathology was limited by the nature of the setting in which he trained and worked. There is no setting that does not impose a limitation of view or perspective on those who participate in it. The limitation becomes a handicap to the extent that a participant is unaware of it or assumes without evidence that it is not serious. In the new programs in clinical psychology there was insufficient awareness that the hospital and clinic setting imposed severe limitations on what could be observed, understood, and done in regard to those under such care, and as important, in regard to those individuals outside the clinical or hospital situation who felt in need of some kind of personal help. Physical setting and unquestioning acceptance of professional tradition are among the most formidable obstacles to change and attainment of a broad perspective toward one's work.

THE PATIENT POPULATION

The most obvious, and one of the most serious, limitations of the placement of clinical psychology training programs in VA facilities was in the purpose for which these facilities were built, that is, to care for a certain range of patients. There were, to be sure, some female veterans who came to these facilities, but for all practical purposes the patient population was male; more specifically, males who had been through a war experience and could or would not avail themselves of other types of community mental-health facilities, private or public. It is very likely, therefore, that there were clinical psychologists who, in the course of their training, had little or no clinical experience with children, adolescents, or adult women. It is not necessary to labor the point that the VA population seriously lacked range and variety for the purposes of training in clinical psychology, assuming that the over-all purposes of the program went beyond training for work with a restricted population in a certain type of physical setting.

THE NATURE OF PROFESSIONAL SKILLS

The two major clinical skills the psychology intern was expected to understand and perform were diagnostic testing and psychotherapy. In the decade after the war far more attention was devoted to training in psychodiagnostics than in psychotherapy (individual or group) because the former, in contrast to the latter, was represented as a special skill and interest of psychologists. The development and application of psychological tests for many different purposes in different settings were part of the tradition of American psychology. Psychotherapy had little or no part in this tradition and was a professional skill considered to be the special province of the psychiatrist. For a variety of reasons this neat division of skills, based on tradition among other things, soon began to disappear—at least it began to be questioned vigorously. At the same time that the clinical psychologist sought and obtained greater psychotherapeutic skill and experience his interest in and his view of the importance of his psychodiagnostic role lessened. It is not relevant to our present purposes to pass judgment on this development. What is relevant is that it reflects acceptance of the view that psychotherapy was *the* major way in which mental illness should be approached and ameliorated. It should be no surprise that by tying itself rather exclusively to psychiatry and the traditional type of psychiatric setting clinical psychology became increasingly involved with the prime technique employed in those settings. This development was not in itself "bad." What should have been a source of concern was the narrowness of perspective toward the over-all mental-health problem in our society which was unwittingly imposed on the developing field of clinical psychology.

In the decade following the war a number of people seemed to believe that the most important step that could be taken to meet the problem in our society was a crash program in the training of psychotherapists. Two reality factors made this belief and hope quite untenable. The first was the variable efficacy of the different psychotherapies and the absence of meaningful research to serve as a guide for understanding therapeutic success and failure. The second was that the universities could not train psychotherapists in numbers sufficient to meet what was thought to be society's needs. Reality was persuasive in helping clinical psychology confront the dangers of tying itself to *a* way of helping people.

PROFESSIONAL DEPENDENCE AND RESPONSIBILITY

The close relationship between clinical psychology and psychiatry—a relationship initially fostered heartily by both fields—had decisive consequences for the sense of professional identity of the clinical psychologist. In large measure these consequences arose from the reality that the psychiatric setting, as the label implies, was one in which the psychiatrist had administrative responsibility and in which he was to exercise leadership. It was not only that mental illness or disturbance was conceived of as a medical problem, but also that there were in fact certain therapeutic procedures (e.g., drugs, electric shock) which by law only the physician-psychiatrist could perform. In such a setting clinical psychology could not function or develop as an independent profession, but rather as one of several professions ancillary to the medical one.

The dependence of the clinical psychologist on the psychiatrist was further reinforced, particularly in the decade after the war, by the fact that in the psychotherapeutic area there were relatively few psychologists with the degree of training and skill necessary to assume the role of supervisor. This made his dependence clear not only to the clinical psychologist, but also to the psychiatrist, to whom this state of affairs was as it should be. A further factor facilitating this development was the psychology intern's experience in and relationship to his "home base," that is, the graduate department of psychology in which clinical psychology was something new and by no means well integrated with the more traditional areas. More important than youth was the tendency on the part of these departments to view clinical staff and students—who appeared to them to be more interested in helping people and "doing good" than in doing research—as less worthy than other types of psychologists and potentially a divisive and dangerous influence. Bluntly and briefly, the clinical student came from a setting in which he was often made to feel like a second-class citizen and entered a setting in which for other reasons this feeling was reinforced. It also needs to be said that the clinical student tended to be poorly prepared for this transition in terms of professional preparation, theoretical issues and orientation, and interprofessional problems and practices.

These developments, which we have by necessity described in broad generalizations and not in historical detail, could not be other than crucial factors in the development of a sense of professional identity. In some instances there was little or no conflict in accepting an important but secondary role in the psychiatric setting. There were people to be helped and research to be done, and these activities could be a source of satisfaction, particularly if others in the setting recognized and rewarded such activities. In other instances, and our guess is in a majority of all instances, there was engendered a sense of professional inferiority compounded of frustration, anger, and resignation. Some clinical psychologists literally left this arena of work, some returned to the universities where they had varying degrees of relationship to the clinical program, others shifted to settings that permitted them wider scope in clinical functioning, and others (in increasing numbers) turned to private practice which by its nature requires professional independence and the acceptance of total responsibility for what one does in work with patients.

It is important to emphasize that one of the consequences of this "identity crisis"—and for a field as young as clinical psychology such a term seems particularly appropriate—was the recognition by some that there was a good deal more to the mental-health field than could be observed, handled, and studied in the traditional psychiatric setting. This recognition was frequently independent of considerations of professional pride, power, and status, and it should not be thought that clinical psychologists were alone in perceiving the provincialism of this setting in regard to mental-health problems not seen in the hospital, clinic, or private office. There were some in all the mental-health professions, as well as among those responsible for public policy and action, who saw the need for changing or breaking with traditions of training, practice, and setting. The public schools, juvenile delinquency, cultural deprivation, the complexities of integration and racial conflict, the consequences of the increasing numbers of aged people, and the relative absence of preventive programs in mental health—these were some of the psychological problems and issues that required thought and personnel and for which the traditional clinic and hospital with their pattern of practice and training were by no means appropriate solutions. This statement cannot be construed as a criticism of the psychiatric clinic and hospital, because by intent these settings were not meaningfully concerned with these other problems, issues, and settings that in one way or another posed or contained serious problems of psychological disturbance and adjustment. Their relative neglect, however, was in part a function of the narrowness in training and outlook of the mental-health professions. To the extent that a governmental agency such as the Veterans Administration attracted, supported, and trained mental-health personnel, it markedly reduced the number of such personnel available for work in other settings with different problems. Perhaps because clinical psychology was in a formal sense part of the psychiatric setting for a relatively brief period of time, in addition to its dissatisfactions with its dependent role in these settings, it was easier for it than for other fields to move in new directions.

THE CLINICAL MODEL

The final consequence to be discussed of the relatively exclusive alliance in the postwar years between clinical psychology and the psychiatric setting is probably the most subtle at the same time that it may be the most important in determining the course and nature of new programs and directions. We refer here to a habit or way of thinking that is easily but implicitly learned in the course of clinical training: that is, the clinician, who plays an essentially passive role, does not seek out the individual or the problem, but deals only with those that are brought to him in his clinical setting. At this point he does the very best he can, on the basis of whatever skills and knowledge he possesses, to be helpful. He applies his knowledge and skill to what literally confronts him and tends not to think of applications to other individuals and settings.

When we consider how difficult it is and how long it takes to deal clinically, in an effective way, with particular individuals in a particular setting, it is not surprising that we can lose sight of the possibilities that the traditional clinical model may not be the only or the best way of dealing with the problem area, that in other settings the role of the clinician may have to be altered (e.g., in terms of initiative and activity), or that aspects of the theory which gives rise to a particular type of clinical functioning may be in error. For example, when we look at the controversies within and among psychiatric settings about the nature, conduct, and goals of psychotherapy—controversies that involve differing conceptions of clinical behavior and responsibility—it should be clear that there is no *one* clinical model compellingly appropriate to mental-health problems.

What concerns us most about the consequences of clinical training is the tendency to regard one's own way of functioning as the best way and to describe variants of the model in pejorative terms. This tendency in itself would not be so difficult to combat if it were not so frequently accompanied by strong opposition to the initiation of new programs based on a different type of clinical intervention.

We have attempted to indicate some of the factors facilitating a close relationship between modern clinical psychology and the psychiatric setting, and some of the consequences of this tie for this newly developing field. In emphasizing the role of the Veterans Administration in discharging its responsibilities it was not our intention to be critical. In characterizing the psychiatric setting as we did it was, again, not with the aim of derogating its goals, procedures, or efficacy. Our discussion was intended to make two points: social needs and pressures have markedly affected clinical psychology as we know it today; and in responding to these real and legitimate needs and pressures there has been insufficient awareness of the limitations that clinical psychology has imposed on itself by the nature of its response.

We do not doubt that clinical psychology benefited a great deal from its tie to the psychiatric setting, and nothing that we have said or will say should be interpreted as suggesting that this tie should be completely severed. If for no other reason (and there are other reasons), the tie between clinical psychology and the psychiatric setting exposed the clinical psychologist to the intricacies, perplexities, and difficulties of the helping process in which the clinician's thoughts, feelings, and overt actions were important variables. This exposure influenced the thought and actions of several generations of clinical psychologists, and to the extent that the training programs were based in universities they had an inevitably broad influence. Nevertheless, according recognition to benefits does not obviate the reality of limitations and the need to face them.

DISSATISFACTION AND FERMENT IN THE
MENTAL-HEALTH PROFESSIONS

It would be quite a mistake if the impression were created in the reader that dissatisfaction with and awareness of the limitations of the traditional psychiatric setting were peculiar to a newly emerging profession striving to develop a sense of identity and independence. To be disabused of such an impression it is necessary only to study the publications of the Joint Commission on Mental Health and Illness which was set up in 1955 by a congressional act that called for "an objective, thorough, nationwide analysis and re-evaluation of the human and economic problems of mental illness." The Joint Commission's final report, "Action for Mental Health," was transmitted to Congress in 1961. It is not necessary to go into detail about the surveys and studies that were the basis for the conclusions and recommendations put forth by the Joint Commission. In one sense it may be said that the major achievement of the Joint Commission was to bring into the national consciousness in a clear and compelling way what had for some years before been obvious to a variety of professional and lay people. The staggering extent of the mental-health problem, the inadequacy of numbers of professionally trained personnel, the limitations of exclusive dependence on the hospital, clinic, and private-practice setting, the pressing importance of becoming involved in nonpsychiatric and nonmedical settings, the need to explore use of and training for subprofessional groups, the consequences of the neglect of a truly preventive approach—these were some of the findings and recommendations which gave an impetus and a base to those who wished to venture in new directions. The report contributed a certain amount of cohesion to the scattered voices and groups who, because of their small numbers, inadequate financial resources, or lack of a strong or prestigeful organizational base, had been a negligible factor in the mental-health field. When, as was inevitable, congressional legislation and appropriations made possible the implementation of some of the Joint Commission's recommendations, this signaled the end of an era and tradition. We are still too near these new developments to evaluate how sharp a break with tradition they represent or to what extent they achieve their purposes. Traditions do not, as perhaps they should not, change easily, and the tendency to cloak traditional concepts and practices with the garments of new phrases and slogans must be anticipated. For example, to say that a new mental-health program is *community*-oriented, whereas in fact those involved are functioning in much the same way (albeit in newer and bigger surroundings) with the same kinds of viewpoint, as was traditionally the case, is not basic change. That more people may be receiving help in a greater variety of clinics and hospitals is not to be lightly dismissed; it is also no cause for enthusiasm for those who believe that the traditional way of providing service is but one way of meeting some problems.

On the other hand, because something is clearly new in intent and practice, it does not follow that it is worthwhile. Newness should not be confused with validated change. To rebel against a tradition is not in itself a virtue and this may be one of the reasons why those holding to tradition react skeptically to innovations. Another reason, of course, is the tendency to fear the new and the unfamiliar.

THE 1965 CONFERENCE ON THE PROFESSIONAL PREPARATION OF CLINICAL PSYCHOLOGISTS

It is hard to underestimate the ferment and controversy taking place in the mental-health fields in general and in clinical psychology in particular. Traditional conceptions and practices are being challenged, professional roles are changing, and in the next ten years we shall witness a wide variety of innovations that will markedly affect, among other things, the nature of professional training. It is hard to be sure of anything except that things will change. Nowhere is this better illustrated than in the forces giving rise to the 1965 Conference on the Professional Preparation of Clinical Psychologists, sponsored by the National Institute of Mental Health and the American Psychological Association. The present book was being submitted for publication at the time this conference was being held, but we did have an opportunity to read all of the position papers prepared for it. We can only hope that the final report faithfully represents the diversity of points of view contained in these papers. The published preconference materials (American Psychological Association, 1965) do give an overview of the issues with which this conference was to be confronted. Within the last few years there have been an astonishing number of publications which in different ways suggest that we are at the end of one professional era in the mental-health field and at the beginning of another. In our bibliography we have starred those publications that we think will give the reader a more detailed picture of the controversies and their origins than is contained in the present chapter.

We have in this chapter attempted to convey in brief fashion some of the factors contributing to the rapid rise of numerous university-based programs in clinical psychology, the significances and limitations of their near-exclusive tie to traditional settings and models of practice, and the social forces and needs that create ferment and an atmosphere conducive to change. In Chapter 3 we shall try to particularize these points by describing how we, in a particular department in a particular community, experienced the developments over the last twenty years and the steps we took to implement the lessons we learned.

Chapter 3

The Psycho-Educational Clinic:
Background Factors

This chapter concerns itself with a presentation of ideas and experiences which over a period of two decades have resulted in the development of a training and research facility markedly different from that which had existed in our clinical training program. The decision to start such a facility, the Psycho-Educational Clinic, was made in 1961. The theoretical conceptions, professional experiences, and social forces which the clinic reflects have, of course, a much longer history. As in all biography, what follows in this chapter suffers from incomplete recall, distortions based on the need to present a coherent story, and the requirements of discretion in regard to the feelings of others. Like all published research (Taylor, 1959), our story probably sounds far more rational and sober than the true picture would reveal.

THE BOULDER CONFERENCE

In 1949 the American Psychological Association and the National Institute of Mental Health sponsored a conference on graduate education in clinical psychology (Raimy, 1950). The Boulder Conference, as it came to be known, played a most important role in shaping the future of clinical psychology because it promulgated new ideas and even more because it reflected what were then the dominant views in the field.[1] Many issues were taken up at this conference, but among the

[1] Shakow's recent (1965) article contains a brief but authoritative discussion of the considerations which led to the Boulder Conference, as well as to those convened at Stanford (Strother, 1956) and Miami (Roe, 1959). Since Shakow probably played a more important role than any other individual in shaping modern clinical psychology, his unhappiness with developments as he now sees them deserves close scrutiny, particularly because of his view that part of the past and current professional problems in clinical psychology reflect forces within rather than outside psychology—a caveat that should have a sobering

18

most important were the content of clinical training and the setting in which it was to be obtained. How these issues were resolved is given in the following:

In the original wording of a proposition relating to standards for field training, there was reference to "close and continuous supervision by clinical psychologists, psychiatrists, and social workers" throughout the "internship" period. Following debate lasting over several days, a relatively satisfactory agreement was reached in regard to the need for internship experience in a psychiatric setting. The following proposition was approved 60 to 10 during the last days of the Conference:

"It is the responsibility of the Department of Psychology to make for each student a substantial field placement in an agency in which adequate supervision is provided and in which the staff consists of qualified clinical psychologists, psychiatrists, and social workers."

How much or how long "substantial" is, was not defined. There is no doubt, however, that the spirit of the resolution recognizes the importance of an "internship" experience in a psychiatric setting where intensive experience with the psychiatrically "sick" can be obtained. Even those students planning work primarily in educational or vocational settings presumably cannot be excused from obtaining such experiences, even though another "substantial" portion of their field work is spent in school, vocational, or counselling settings.

One of the authors of the present book was a participant in the conference and can personally attest to some of the content of the "debate lasting over several days." A very small minority argued strongly against the requirement that clinical training had to take place in a

---

effect on those who feel that in and of themselves new programs are answers to some basic problems. As Shakow well puts it:

"What kind of profession do we want? What we get depends to a great extent on whether we pay attention to our own inadequacies and are mainly concerned about getting the best training program, or whether we look elsewhere, using the natural tendency to project our difficulties. For one interested in psychodynamics, the situation is pathetic. Koch's defensive "scientism," accompanied as it is by a condescension to clinical psychology, is pervasive. At the same time, the inferiority feelings of clinical psychologists toward the "experimentalists," and their so ready acceptance of a relatively low status, is appalling, whether this is expressed by acceptance or defensive hostility. It is unnecessary to emphasize what this does to the self-image of the clinical psychologist as psychologist, and indirectly of psychology.

We will not have a generation of upstanding clinical psychologists until these symptoms disappear in psychology and until there are sufficient models of adequate teachers in all areas who clearly and effectively represent their own particular areas of interest."

psychiatric setting. It was the thought of this minority that such a requirement would unduly restrict the scope and training of the clinical psychologist and that the field as a whole would be hamstrung in an effort to explore other settings in which a preventive orientation was likely to be more adequate in meeting the over-all needs of our society.[2] To this minority there seemed no compelling reason why placement in a psychiatric setting should be mandatory and placement elsewhere optional unless the assumption was made that the traditional clinical-psychiatric model was indisputably superior to any other model that an emerging mental-health profession could adopt. It was this assumption that was unsuccessfully challenged, not on the grounds that it was wrong, but that it was unproved and therefore not a basis for a field to put, so to speak, all its eggs in one basket. Although students could receive training in other settings, it was clear then that the bulk of clinical students would receive all of their training in the psychiatric setting: it had funds to pay students, and the opinion of most of the participants at the conference was that the psychiatric setting was indeed the best one for training purposes. These two factors made it unlikely that training programs would develop their own facilities in order to explore new problems and practices.

The significance of the relatively exclusive tie between clinical psychology and the psychiatric setting is best seen in the fact that in the conference report the only clinical technique to which a whole chapter was devoted was psychotherapy, the major clinical technique used in the psychiatric setting. This emphasis reflected among other things an orientation that in essence tied a field to *a* setting and *a* technique, an orientation that guaranteed conflict between clinical psychologists and psychiatrists. The heat subsequently generated by that conflict tended to create in the antagonists the view that psychotherapy was man's only weapon in the mental-health field.

Debates and discussion at the Boulder Conference tended almost always to center on important substantive issues about which legitimate differences could be expected. A close reading of the conference will reveal that many of the issues presently the concern of clinical psychology were then recognized with varying degrees of clarity. For example, the following statement leaves little to be desired as an example of broadness of thinking in relation to an important problem in practice and research:

[2] In recent years, both within psychology and psychiatry, the necessity of taking seriously the preventive approach for practice, training, and research has been raised again with clarity and urgency. This has been well discussed by Bower (1963), Caplan (1963), Eisenberg (1962), and Eisenberg and Gruenberg (1961).

Admitting the present impossibility of arriving at a definite statement about the therapeutic process, the group nonetheless agreed to the following proposition as a working definition. (It was taken from the 1947 Report of the APA Committee on Training in Clinical Psychology.)

"Psychotherapy is defined as a process involving interpersonal relationships between a therapist and one or more patients or clients by which the former employs psychological methods based on systematic knowledge of the human personality in attempting to improve the mental health of the latter."

A number of eyebrows were raised at the clause "based on systematic knowledge of the human personality"; but in a developing field of knowledge, pious hopes must sometimes fill gaps in acceptable theory.

Such a working definition suggested a number of questions about areas of application. Is vocational counseling therapy? Remedial education? Speech correction? Retraining of the physically handicapped? In view of currently divergent definitions in the literature and in practice, there was surprisingly unanimous agreement that the basic principles of psychotherapy are probably applicable over the entire field of psychological disturbance and defect. Their application may vary with the type of disturbance or defect presented, but the principles themselves should be fundamental in conception. Such a solution, of course, skirts the issues of whether persons engaged in vocational counseling or remedial reading should be qualified therapists in all areas and whether they should be called psychotherapists.

What seemed to be insufficiently recognized at the conference was the unlikelihood that a student in a clinical program would ever have experience in vocational counseling, remedial education, speech correction, or retraining of the physically handicapped.[3] In short, research on the general applicability of basic principles of psychotherapy would not be done if only because the student lacked the experiences necessary to become aware of the problem and its diverse implications. Then, as now, psychotherapy is as psychotherapists do, and since they almost always practice in the psychiatric setting or private office other types of helping situation are not regarded as involving psychotherapy—a good example of definition on the basis of phenotypic rather than genotypic characteristics. Although the problem was well posed at the conference, it was ignored in subsequent developments.

---

[3] One of the major consequences of the direction in which clinical training went after World War II was that the fields of clinical and counseling psychology drifted apart, an unfortunate development in light of the broader orientation and more diverse settings that characterized the practice of counseling psychology. This development is well discussed in the report of the Greystone Conference on the professional preparation of counseling psychologists (Thompson and Super, 1964).

Why it would be ignored could have been predicted by the following statement in the conference report:

One of the most perplexing and difficult questions in regard to training clinical psychologists in psychotherapy relates to the problem of interprofessional relationships, particularly with psychiatry and psychiatric social work. Chapter 13 deals with the general problems of interprofessional relations. The Conference paid particular attention to Report No. 10 (July, 1949) of the Group for the Advancement of Psychiatry, entitled "The Relation of Clinical Psychology to Psychiatry." Several members were present from the Group for the Advancement of Psychiatry Committee as well as from the APA Committee on the Relation of Psychology to Psychiatry, which had met with its counterpart committee of the American Psychiatric Association. Both sources indicated that relations between the two professions are undergoing considerable improvement and that in most local situations amicable working collaboration is in effect. However, many issues still remain as open questions, since the relative newness of clinical psychology as a profession has raised doubts of its adequacy in the clinical situation. There are even legal aspects, since the laws (as well as the professions) fail to define the limits of mental health or the methods of treatment that are controlled by law. Considerable confusion still remains on matters that call for definition. For example, the present Conference defined psychotherapy as applying to remedial work as well as to interview treatment of "sick" persons. The GAP Report No. 10 apparently differentiates between clinical psychology as a profession dealing with "counseling, vocational guidance, and retraining" and as a profession related to psychiatry.

Our experience in the years following the Boulder Conference confirmed a number of misgivings about the direction in which clinical psychology was going. For one thing, it quickly became apparent that clinical psychology was almost exclusively an auxiliary profession in the psychiatric setting, a development unduly restricting the clinical psychologist in practice and research. Related to this was a morale problem; that is, the feeling on the part of many clinical students that they were subordinate professionals exercising functions not always viewed by themselves and others as of much significance. As a result, the student began to derogate his diagnostic role and to seek to establish himself on a par with the psychiatrist in the psychotherapeutic role, the status function in the setting. Equally important was the quick extinction in many of the desire to do research in the setting, and research training was the most distinctive way in which the student differed from those in the other fields. Research in the clinical setting is never easy, particularly if the researcher truly respects the rights and interests of patients. However, for many research problems involving issues basic to practice it is necessary to have a degree of control over, or for flexibility to exist within, the setting. This was frequently not the case and posed for many the choice of doing trivial research or not doing any at all. In any event, students quickly saw the difficulties of doing research in a setting in which they were in a subordinate role and in which there was a clash of traditions as to what constituted good research.

To those who are responsible for a training program in clinical psychology the morale of their students is not a problem to be avoided, particularly if the sources of the problem play into the biases of the clinical staff. It was our experience that the morale problem was fairly general across the country and far from being a particular problem in a particular university. As we might have expected, the reaction to the morale problem has taken two major forms. The first is seen in the increasing frequency with which clinical psychologists have left the psychiatric setting to engage in private practice, a development restricted primarily to our very large urban areas where mental-health workers were already heavily concentrated. The second form is reflected in the movement of a number of clinical psychologists to settings other than psychiatric ones, particularly the school setting. It would be incorrect to view the second development as a flight from an inhospitable setting to one in which to gratify the need for independence. This element undoubtedly exists, but it is far overshadowed by a lesson well learned, and one adumbrated in the Boulder report, that the traditional psychiatric setting is only one of the places in which it is possible to meet and deal with mental-health problems, and it remains to be seen whether the traditions of that setting are adequate for viewing and meeting the problems in their most important aspects.

THE SCHOOL SETTING

Before starting the Psycho-Educational Clinic we had extensive experience—clinical and research, formal and informal—in various educational settings for children and teachers. In our experience in institutions for problem children several impressions and facts quickly forced themselves on us. Among the most obvious was that existing institutions, public and private, were grossly inadequate to meet the needs (and demands) of families and social agencies. The disparity between the number of children in the institution and the number for whom the institution was considered the placement of choice was little short of impossible. Experiencing the problem was not made easy by the realization that the most difficult problem children suffered institutionalization, that effectiveness of therapeutic programs was by no means a source of professional enthusiasm, and that the families from which these children came were either a contributing factor to the child's problems or had been pathologically affected by the child's condition. The "numbers" problem was cause for despair when considered only in terms of children and a cause for gloom when looking at the problem in terms of families. It is perhaps fortunate that the nature of institutions tends to dull us to the larger social context in which problems are imbedded. This tendency, we must quickly add, accounts in part for the selective factor that determines the professional people who remain in the setting for very long.

A conclusion to which many professional people in institutions for problem children come, although it tends not to be stated with the force and clarity it deserves, is that many children are institutionalized long after that point in time when their problems were first recognized. The seriousness might have been misevaluated earlier or, for one reason or another, intervention had been lacking or inadequate. Of particular interest to us at this point is that in the bulk of these cases there was no doubt that the problems of these children were clearly apparent early in their school careers and that appropriate recognition and intervention in the school setting might have made institutionalization far from inevitable (Sarason, 1964). We are not maintaining either that the school was derelict in its duty or that the problems were caused by the school. The fact is that the schools did not and do not possess the resources that allow effective intervention. This fact, however, does not lessen the significance of the conclusion that institutionalization frequently reflected the failure or lack of community resources of which the school was a most important one from the standpoint of prevention and intervention.

Our view of the school setting was not determined only by our experiences in and with institutions for children. In fact, it was our institutional experience that forced us over time to become involved, for clinical and research purposes, with the public-school setting and teacher-training programs.[4] This involvement resulted in some firmly held convictions.

[4] There is no doubt that in recent years there has been a renewed interest in the potentialities of school psychology in the early diagnosis and management of problems as well as in preventive programs. Among the most important contributions are those of Passow (Ed., 1963), White and Harris (1961), and the series of papers by Kipfer (1961), Morse (1961), McNeill (1961), and Cutler (1961) constituting a workshop held at the 1960 meeting of the American Orthopsychiatric Association.

1. The schools contain a large number of children whose difficulties in learning and social living are of a degree of seriousness that precludes progress over time in accord with their particular age and social groups. For example, we became aware that a surprising number of children in elementary schools had repeated at least one grade and that in many instances the grade repetition was not a function of poor intellectual potential. We endeavored to obtain published data on the

TABLE 1

NUMBER OF CHILDREN IN GRADES 1 AND 2 IN ONE COMMUNITY WHO REPEATED ONE OR MORE GRADES

School	Grade 2 Boys ($N = 36$)	Grade 2 Girls ($N = 27$)	Grade 1 Boys ($N = 14$)	Grade 1 Girls ($N = 11$)
A	2	0	1	1
B	3	6	3	2
C	4	4	1	2
D	4	5	3	2
E	5	2	1	1
F	4	1	2	1
G	1	1	0	0
II	4	2	1	1
I	2	1	1	0
J	3	2	0	1
K	1	2	1	0
L	3	1	0	0
	36	27	14	11
Repeaters as % of total N of same set in that grade	$\dfrac{36}{168} = 21\%$	$\dfrac{27}{179} = 15\%$	$\dfrac{14}{157} = 9\%$	$\dfrac{11}{166} = 7\%$

incidence of grade repetition, but our efforts were fruitless. School systems and the state education agencies apparently do not collect or publish such data. We were able to collect them for the total population in two grades in a rather large, middle-class, suburban school system, predominantly white in race and not containing what are ordinarily thought of as slums. The data in Table 1 are based on a large sample of children who in 1958–1959 were in first and second grades and were subsequently followed through the elementary-school grades. These data reveal that when the study began 21% of the second-grade boys and 15% of second-grade girls had already repeated either kindergarten or grade 1. The smaller percentages for the first-grade sample reflect the fact that at that time they had less opportunity to repeat a grade than the second-grade children. Although there is variability from school to school, it is quite clear that a sizable number of children have, for one reason or another, been unable to progress normally in school. Children who repeat grades do not, of course, exhaust the group of those who very clearly manifest patterns of behavior and feeling that force us to view their futures with much concern.

2. As a group, teachers are acutely aware that in any one classroom there will be a handful of children whose rate of learning and/or pattern of behavior and feeling are puzzling, self-defeating, or uninfluenceable. What we came increasingly to appreciate was how frequently the teacher felt she did not know how to begin to understand these children and felt inadequate, guilty, and frustrated because her approach and procedures had no discernible positive effects. Even if we assume that the teacher was wrong in her conception of these children, it would merely serve to underscore the significant point that teachers have to take action, and frequently do so with subjective feelings of inadequacy and puzzlement, followed by the perception of objective failure. Using our own judgment as a criterion, we found ourselves frequently agreeing with the teacher's evaluation of the seriousness of the problem and her perception of the failure consequent to her actions; and frequently disagreeing with the choice of and rationale for action. At the same time, we were aware of several children in the class whom we considered serious problems but who were not so regarded by the teacher. The teacher could be counted on to become aware of the child who was not learning or who was interfering in an obvious way with the teacher's pedagogical efforts; that is, the teacher is aware of the *disturbing* child far more than she is of the disturbed one.

3. There is no group that is more aware than teachers of the difficulties and problems they face in the classroom and the inadequacy of their training for understanding and handling these problems. Teacher-training programs have no more discerning critics than classroom teachers. We did not become aware of this in our early experiences in the schools, but only after a relationship of mutual trust had developed between teachers and ourselves. It seems that in recent decades there have not been many who ruled themselves out, on the basis of lack of knowledge and competence, as critics of education. It is not surprising, therefore, that teachers should be wary of presenting publicly their strongly held criticisms of their own training (Sarason, 1963) and should view an inquiring outsider as an enemy until he proves himself otherwise.

4. Most schools lack the kind, quantity, and quality of personnel who could provide teachers with the help they need in understanding and coping with problem children *in the school setting*. The practice of referring children to outside mental-health facilities runs up against certain obstacles and limitations: (a) the referral process is usually protracted, (b) the child is frequently put on a waiting list, (c) the relationship between the school and the outside agency is a very distant one, usually as a result of clinic practice and orientation, and (d) change in the child's status as a result of psychotherapeutic intervention is slow. In the meantime the child is in a classroom with a teacher who frequently feels inadequate to the problem and who is kept uninformed about what is going on elsewhere with the child, because the clinic has no meaningful relationship to the teacher who has to cope with the child. Our experience clearly indicated that knowledge by the teacher that a child was being seen in a mental-health clinic sometimes resulted in a "hands-off" policy that was frequently antitherapeutic for child, teacher, and other children. As frequent were the self-doubts of teachers about the appropriateness of what they were or were not doing; that is, the fear that they were doing the wrong thing and the feeling that they needed guidance for the sake of the child.

5. The training of those in the mental-health professions is markedly inadequate both in terms of information about the nature of the school setting and clinical experience within it. Training in these fields, as we indicated in Chapter 2, is almost exclusively within the traditional clinic and hospital setting, and such parochialism has built a wall between them and the schools which has limited the effectiveness of both. The ignorance of those in the mental-health professions about children in school, the culture of the schools, the problems of teachers, and the training of various school personnel is staggering. Ignorance would be bad enough if it were not so often masked by distorted conceptions, derogation of school personnel, and professional arrogance. There is much about schools that the informed mental-health professional can criticize and be very much concerned about. If such criticisms and concerns do not reflect a sincere understanding and desire to help, the wall between the school and the mental-health professions becomes higher. It is by no means clear that the present training of those in the mental-health fields fits them to operate competently and effectively in schools. We concluded early in our experience that training programs in these fields would have to change if they were to make an effective contribution in a setting that in present programs is foreign territory (Sarason, Blatt, and Davidson, 1962).

We do not think it necessary to labor the point that the schools contain a fair number of problem children and that what happens to them in school, regardless of where, outside the school, the problems originate, makes a difference in their lives. It would indeed be nice if the school were not confronted with so many children with problems in learning or problem behavior that may or may not intrude into the learning situation. The facts, however, are otherwise and give no support to the conception that a school is a place in which children learn academic skills and content and in which a teacher devotes herself to guiding a narrowly conceived learning process. To say that the role of the teacher is to inform and guide the "intellectual" part of the mind is as true and uninformative as to say that the job of the parent is to rear his child well. Our experience has forced us to the view that such statements characterize the thinking of many mental-health professionals and accurately reflect their ignorance of what actually goes on in the school setting. When such ignorance is dispelled by first-hand experience of a systematic kind, the true state of affairs is at first discouraging, but this too can be dispelled by the recognition that under appropriate conditions much can be done in the "here and now" within the setting to prevent big problems from becoming impossible ones, to prevent small problems from becoming bigger, and even to prevent certain problems from occurring.

What we have said so far about our experiences in the school setting has been about schools in general. Our account would be incomplete without some comments about our inner-city schools, those slum and near-slum schools in or near the center of our cities. In recent years the popular press and literature, particularly in relation to the issues involved in school integration, have done a good job of describing the deplorable characteristics of the inner-city schools: "blackboard jungle," "dens of mental-health iniquity," "educational cancers," "breeding ground of social problems" are some of the phrases used to describe these schools. The one point we have to make is that the traditional mental-health facilities have had some, albeit peripheral, relation to so-called middle-class schools, but they tend to have no contact with the inner-city schools. There have been many reasons for this but the following example, the spirit of which can be illustrated by numerous cases, may indicate one of the most troublesome reasons:

Example 1. A teacher in an inner-city school became quite concerned at a marked change of behavior in a girl whom she liked a great deal and who was an adequate third-grade student. The teacher had known that the child's father was in the army in Korea, there were two younger siblings at home, the mother had been forced to move twice in the past six months either for failure to pay the rent or because she created disturbances in relation to various men who visited her. Whereas the child had previously been polite and engaging she had now become moody, hostile toward other children, uninterested in her school work, and on several occasions had to be sent to the principal's office because of fights with older boys. The teacher was puzzled and concerned and felt that something needed to be done and she was quite aware that there were no resources to draw on in the school system. She talked the matter over with a friend who suggested she contact a local child-guidance clinic. The teacher did call the clinic and was informed that they had recently closed intake. The sense of urgency which the teacher felt must have come across in the telephone conversation because the teacher was told that the mother of the child should be told to call for an appointment. The teacher replied that it was her opinion that the mother would not follow through on the suggestion but that the teacher would be willing to bring the child for whatever number of visits would be necessary. The teacher was told that this was not acceptable clinic practice and that the mother would have to bring the child. The teacher contacted the mother and, as the teacher expected, there was no follow through.

This anecdote, one among many, is presented to illustrate the contention that traditional clinic practice is frequently not appropriate for inner-city children whose family structures are loose, disorganized, and not dependable in terms of clinic practices. We are not criticizing clinic practice, but we are indicating that the requirement that one member of the family must take responsibility for, and become involved in, the treatment of the child automatically rules out many inner-city children from clinic services.[5] It is understandable that a clinic may not wish to change its practices and orientation or to set up new services. What is less understandable is that the mental-health professions have felt no responsibility for becoming involved in new ways in areas that contribute disproportionately to the mental-health problems of the community. In regard to inner-city children we may

---

[5] It should be noted that the attrition rate in psychiatric clinics for children is disturbingly high. In a study of 1813 children admitted to eleven outpatient psychiatric clinics in Philadelphia, Tuckman and Lavell (1959) found that 31 per cent of the cases were terminated by patient or parent during or at the end of the intake phase. "Irrespective of phase, the overall attrition rate (patient or parent termination of clinic contact) was 59 per cent of all clinic admissions." There was, of course, variation among clinics, and it does not necessarily follow that some of the cases who terminated did not in some way benefit from the contact. Gordon's (1965) discussion emphasizes the seriousness of the problem and, in addition, suggests that clinic practices present serious obstacles to lower class patients, a suggestion clearly in line with our own experiences. Two particularly incisive papers in the practices and outlook of child guidance clinics are those by Caplan (1964) and Gray (1964), two "working papers in community mental health" from the Laboratory of Community Psychiatry at the Harvard Medical School.

say that the mental-health professions have been concerned, when they have been concerned at all, about adapting these children to their own orientation and practice rather than adapting professional knowledge and skill to the problems of these children in the contexts in which they become manifest and in which the possibility of meaningful intervention exists. When we view this problem in the context of our discussion in Chapter 2 on the limitations in scope and practice of traditional training in the mental-health professions, it is not surprising that these professions should be unfamiliar with schools in general and inner-city schools in particular.

A study relevant to the point we are making is illustrated by Hassler's (1965) survey of psychiatric residents in 22 approved training centers in Massachusetts, one of the major training areas in the United States.

Each of the 22 approved training centers within the state was contacted, and a listing was obtained of all persons in formal psychiatric training who had at least one year of experience. The list included 158 possible respondents from all fields of training (general psychiatry, child psychiatry, research, and the like) and from all training settings (public or private hospitals or clinics as well as university programs). After one follow-up mailing 120 individuals had completed and returned the questionnaire; consequently the study had a return rate of 76 per cent.

Table 2 contains data on how the psychiatric residents report the distribution of their training. Two things are noteworthy in this table. First, the school is not a "training area," although it is conceivable (but not likely) that some minimal exposure to schools is obtained in the training area of "consultation theory and techniques." Second, there is very little exposure in such areas as "community organization or knowledge of community agencies," "public health principles or techniques," or "concepts of allied social sciences." What is heartening is that Hassler reports other data that indicate a strong desire on the part of the psychiatric residents for more exposure to these neglected areas. However the fact remains that Hassler's data, as well as our own experiences with psychiatric residency programs, leave little doubt that currently the psychiatric resident has little opportunity to gain a meaningful exposure to the school and the complexity we call a community.

THE PROBLEMS OF THE INNER CITY

The inner-city school is but one place in which we can observe the consequences of social disorganization and the manufacturing of new

TABLE 2

CURRENT TRAINING TIME AS REPORTED BY PSYCHIATRIC RESIDENTS
(PER CENT DISTRIBUTION) (FROM HASSLER, 1965)

1 person = 0.8%

Training Areas	1 Much Time	2 Some Time	3 Little Time	4 No Time	5 No Response
1. Intensive depth psychotherapy	59.1	25.8	9.2	5.0	0.8
2. Consultation theory and techniques	13.3	39.2	32.5	15.0	—
3. Clinical diagnostic skills	34.2	52.5	11.7	0.8	0.8
4. Concepts of allied social science	1.7	19.2	55.8	22.5	0.8
5. Clinical research	6.7	16.7	29.2	45.8	1.7
6. Administration	22.5	16.7	32.5	28.3	—
7. Experience in training and teaching	5.0	31.7	35.8	25.8	1.7
8. Short-term or crisis therapy	12.5	31.7	35.0	20.8	—
9. Psychopharmacology or chemotherapy	10.0	24.2	43.3	20.8	1.7
10. Community organization or knowledge of community agencies	0.8	16.7	54.1	28.3	—
11. Clinical neurology	3.3	12.5	23.3	60.8	—
12. Epidemiology or ecology	—	—	25.0	74.1	0.8
13. Action research or program evaluation	1.7	5.8	12.5	79.1	0.8
14. Public-health principles or techniques	—	—	18.3	81.6	—
15. Neuroanatomy or neurophysiology	—	10.0	11.7	78.3	—
16. Mental-health education	0.8	3.3	33.3	61.6	0.8
17. Knowledge of individual psychodynamics	75.8	17.5	6.7	—	—
18. Knowledge of family or group psychodynamics	24.2	49.1	22.5	4.2	—

problems. We have only to spend a little time in our public institutions (reformatories, prisons, and detention homes) and various social agencies (state and city welfare departments and family agencies) to become aware of the scope and severity of the human problems of the inner-city population. Until recently these problems and their interrelationships were not in what could be called national awareness. Such terms as "inner city," "war on poverty," "community mental health" have only recently gained popular usage and reflect recognition of a previous absence of attempts to provide an attack on, and to think preventively about, a particular complex of social problems.

The fact that the mental-health professions had little meaningful contact with the inner-city population reflected, among other things, the view that the problems of these groups were primarily social, economic, and vocational in nature and that until these "causes" were attacked there was little that the mental-health professions could do, given their clinical orientation and practices. There is, of course, a good deal of truth to this view of etiology, but what seemed to be overlooked was that this view was probably equally valid for the social groups with which the mental-health professions had the most clinical contact. The mental-health professions work primarily in large urban centers with middle- and upper-class individuals whose problems also reflect social, economic, and vocational factors. This fact, however, has not been used as a basis for inaction on the part of these professions. The neglect of the inner-city population in our experience reflects two factors. The first is that the mental-health professions have not been sufficiently aware of how their thinking and practices have reflected their own social backgrounds, economic needs, and vocational training. The second, stemming from the first, is the tendency to use a different "psychology" when thinking about or working with an inner-city individual compared with the typical middle-class person. What has long disturbed us is the tendency for the mental-health worker to approach and work with the inner-city individual in the manner of the self-fulfilling prophecy, that is, we act in ways that will ensure our proving the validity of our preconceptions.

Although there was no doubt in our minds that the mental-health professions could make a significant contribution to the problems of the inner-city population, we were equally convinced, and as federal monies became available for inner-city programs we became concerned, that they lacked the knowledge, flexibility, and understanding that allow us to adapt to new problems and minimize the possibility that new problems will be transformed to make them conform to familiar modes of thinking and practice. For example, as a result of federal legislation and appropriation of funds, a tremendous expansion of "community" mental-health facilities is currently taking place. In large part this expansion involves building additional clinics, expanding old ones, and developing new types of clinics (such as the multipurpose one) in contrast to those that serve either children or adults. These facilities are needed and will undoubtedly provide more services to more people. However there is legitimate concern that these facilities, contained as they frequently are in or around medical centers and oriented as they are to traditional conceptions of giving help, will not reach the inner-city population to a greater extent than before. It is not only a matter of where these clinics are located or the types of service provided *in* the clinic, but whether the inner-city population will come to the clinic in the manner traditional clinic practice requires.

In the training of research workers, regardless of field, the student is frequently told that the nature of the problem dictates the methodology and that he must avoid the error of adapting the problem to the requirements of the methodologies familiar to the student. Our experience in the past led us to the conclusion that insofar as inner-city individuals were concerned the mental-health professions were committing this error. Because training programs in these fields are not discernibly different from those in the past in terms of content areas, skills, and setting, we cannot look with undiluted enthusiasm on efforts to train more people in more of the traditional settings.

We do not wish to convey the impression that our past concerns about the lack of meaningful relationships between the mental-health setting and the inner-city population reflected superior knowledge on our part or a clear conception of what should be done in training and in practice. We felt a vague sense of social responsibility; unease with the parochialism of psychiatric settings in regard to range of approaches and populations served; dissatisfaction with the neglect of ideas and programs aimed at prevention, and the failure to participate meaningfully and spontaneously in programs specifically designed to change and influence the behavior of inner-city groups in the areas of housing, work programs, preschool projects, and job corps. In regard to the last point, we should note here our experience in several communities in which the mental-health professions had little or no relation to community programs specifically designed to change the thinking and behavior of large groups of people. Such changes involved psychological issues, techniques, and conceptions toward which these professions could have contributed much if they were a meaningful part of the programs.

PROFESSIONAL PRECIOUSNESS

We have characterized the mental-health professions as parochial, by which we mean their restricted knowledge of and exposure to the larger society of which they are a part, the application of knowledge and skill primarily in the clinic, or hospital, or private office setting, and the restricted social class range of the populations served. We recognize that there are many within these professions who may disagree strongly with this characterization and who view efforts to change the nature and model of clinical training as well-intentioned but misguided ventures that will result only in poorer services and public and professional disillusionment. At this stage of the game we can only say that these expectations may turn out to be true, yet we must also say that such pessimism always precedes changes in and challenges to the existing order and cannot serve as a defense for the status quo.

One of the most serious consequences of the parochialism of the mental-health professions is what we would call professional preciousness: the tendency to view what they are and do as unique, and to believe that they are the only ones who "truly" understand, grapple with, and effect changes in individuals beset with problems in living and adjustment. We do not have to look at the attitudes of mental-health professionals toward outside groups and individuals to illustrate the nature and consequences of preciousness. In Chapter 2 we indicated that for a number of decades psychotherapy was considered a skill or a practice only the psychiatrist could perform. During that time all sorts of arguments were presented to support the position that psychotherapy should be restricted to those who were physician-psychiatrists. For example, from the outset of the child-guidance movement there was a clear differentiation among the functions of the clinic team: the psychiatric social worker did casework, the psychologist did testing, and the psychiatrist was responsible for the treatment.[6] There are few clinics today, for children or adults, that adhere in practice to these differentiations, although in a number of places much is made of the fact that role changes are permissible as long as a psychiatrist is in some kind of directing role. In any event, a large number of nonpsychiatrists, in clinics and in private practice, engage

---

[6] In discussing the problem of waiting lists, Heyder (1965) describes how the clinic of which he is the director has eliminated waiting lists and how in order to do so it is necessary to deal with overlearned attitudes of the professional staff. It is interesting that in order to eliminate the waiting lists he considers it necessary (among other things) almost to eliminate differences among the clinic team:

"The psychiatrist has to become a more astute diagnostician, accept the potentialities of other professions and communicate to the patient confidence in the nonmedical therapists. The psychologist is under pressure to increase his skill in psychotherapy and to minimize the routine use of long tests. The psychiatric social worker is challenged to develop psychotherapeutic skills and shorter, more pointed consultations. The custom of "taking social histories" ought to be abandoned in favor of immediate therapy which produces social information as a byproduct. The staff should be held accountable for results but not for methods. At times the team aspect of treatment should be bypassed."

in psychotherapy and there is not the slightest evidence that the quality of what they do is less than what the psychiatrist does. There are differing opinions about this turn of events but no evidence, a situation that guarantees the continuation of fruitless controversy.

It has been our impression that once the psychologist and social worker won the professional battle of psychotherapy they adopted equally as precious an attitude as the psychiatrist earlier had taken that no individual or group should practice psychotherapy unless it were clinical psychologist, psychiatric social worker, or psychiatrist. Preciousness became the luxury of those who had arrived.

Our interest here, however, is in the attitude of the mental-health professions toward other groups whose labels and work settings put them outside the fold; for example, guidance workers, vocational and physical rehabilitation personnel, speech therapists, and those involved in various forms of educational remediation. In general, mental-health workers look on these other groups as lesser trained professionals or technicians the nature of whose work is in principle less complex and demanding of psychological understanding and skill than that required of the mental-health worker. In practice this attitude is frequently but by no means always justified. What tends to be overlooked is that there is confusion between the level of practice of these groups and the complexity of the problems with which they are faced. Our own experience has convinced us that these groups face problems as demanding of psychological skill and understanding as those with which the mental-health worker ordinarily deals. We have found this conclusion to be inordinately difficult for the mental-health worker to consider seriously, let alone accept, for at least two reasons. The first is implied in the conception that unless we have received the kinds of training that mental-health workers obtain we cannot be effective in bringing about changes, superficial or marked, in the mental-health status of people with problems. The very phrase "mental-health professions"—referring primarily to psychiatric social workers, psychiatrists, and clinical psychologists—connotes that those not included in the label are in some way lesser professional citizens, however much their professional lives are concerned with effecting changes in the psychological status of those suffering from disordered living and development.

The second reason is that mental-health workers simply have no knowledge of or exposure to the practice of other groups. The typical training program does not expose the mental-health worker to the problems in the setting in which these other groups work. Ignorance resulting from lack of exposure has had the unfortunate consequence of being unfair to the ignored and distorting the perspective and limiting the potential contribution of the mental-health professional. This situation is certainly not helped by the tendency, perhaps inevitable, for each to regard his profession as the chosen one and therefore to justify preciousness.

We are not maintaining that everybody is a mental-health worker and that boundaries between fields should be forthwith and indiscriminately eradicated. We are also not maintaining that all existing groups are equal by virtue of their motivation or desire to help others. Our point is that by their parochialism and preciousness the mental-health professions have little appreciation of the psychological problems with which other professional groups are coping and therefore have not in any meaningful way participated in their training or in the settings in which they work. A particularly good example is the attitude of the clinical psychologist toward the school psychologist. It must first be noted that school psychological personnel (who far outnumber clinical psychologists) receive their training in schools of education and not, as in the case of clinical psychologists, in graduate departments of psychology. On the basis of this fact alone anyone familiar with the university culture could predict that the clinical psychologist would look on the school psychologist as someone really not deserving of the title of psychologist. There is no gainsaying that the training of the school psychologist tends to be briefer, less clinically oriented, and narrower than that of the clinical psychologist. In addition to pointing to inadequacies of training, clinical psychologists can get quite upset about the quality of psychological practice in the school setting, and we have to state on the basis of our past experience our opinion that there is justice in this complaint. It is, however, frequently found in a context of discussion that reveals clearly that school psychologists face and cope with problems no less thorny and important than those of clinical psychologists, although the latter find it much easier to criticize practices and inadequacies than to recognize the seriousness of the problems with which the former must deal. Despite these complaints, graduate departments of psychology have, with few exceptions, successfully resisted efforts to orient their clinical training program to settings other than the traditional psychiatric one. In most instances they have been equally successful in avoiding communication with personnel and students in the school psychology program. In our view purity has been maintained and preciousness reinforced at the expense of broadening of scope, quality of practice, and extension of services. As important as these consequences, however, is the lost opportunity to develop research programs in the school setting that will give us a better understanding of how this subculture in our society influences all who are part of it and how such understanding can serve as a basis for introducing changes that cannot help affecting whatever it is we mean by mental health. Ignorance of the school culture has not in the past been a barrier to many mental-health workers offering suggestions for change and practice that, however well intentioned, showed their lack of familiarity with the complex setting called the school.

We know that in recent years there has been increasing awareness in the mental-health professions of the imprisoning consequences of parochialism and preciousness. We can only hope that this awareness may become manifest in training programs in which traditions are strongest and change most difficult. The force of academic traditions is strong enough to prevent changes from occurring quickly.

MENTAL SUBNORMALITY

Since the pre-World War II period it has become fashionable, and even academically respectable, to be involved in problems of mental subnormality. This change is due largely to the leadership provided by parent groups, the personal significance of the problem for the late President Kennedy, and the availability of federal funds for facilities, training programs, and research. That the mental-health professions played little or no role in this change requires no comment beyond what we have said here and in earlier writings (Sarason, 1959). What is important is that mental subnormality has come into national focus in a way that emphasizes how much of a community is involved in one way or another with this problem area. The enormity of the problem in the inner-city population, the significance of it in racial issues, the basis it has provided for many school and preschool programs, the popular use of terms like "cultural deprivation," "war on poverty"— all of these in one way or another, directly or indirectly, reflect an increasing awareness of the degree to which mental subnormality is a community problem. There is scarcely a community agency that does not cope with some aspect of mental subnormality.

Although we do not equate the spending of money or development of new programs with progress, we are of the opinion that many of the new developments in the field of mental subnormality have had desirable consequences, primarily in the development of educational facilities and programs. But in at least two respects these new programs and services fall short of the mark. The first concerns the relative neglect—particularly when a child is severely defective—of the disruptive consequences of his condition on other members of the family. There are a number of reasons for this, but chief among them is the tendency to focus almost all the attention on "the patient." In marked contrast is the practice of the child-guidance clinic, which bases its operations on a concern with the family. This orientation stems from a set of theoretical conceptions about development and behavior change too rarely utilized in work with the mentally subnormal. However, child-guidance clinics tend not to work with the mentally subnormal; they do not regard it as central to their focus and refer such cases elsewhere. This is another example of the dimensions of a profession being defined by practice and tradition and not by where the problems exist. As a consequence, mental subnormality in its more severe forms tends to be handled in settings in which the child is the main, if not sole, focus.

The second respect in which newer developments have fallen short of their mark concerns the quality of diagnostic services and program planning in the schools, particularly in the inner-city schools. On the verbal level, at least, we have heard much over the years about the inadequacy of the IQ as a basis for action in the individual case; that is, the IQ is a score which has to be interpreted in the light of a whole host of factors before action is taken that will affect the life of an individual. To take a stand against such a caution is to be for sin and against virtue. It has been our experience, however, that in actual practice test scores too frequently *do* determine drastic changes in program, such as placement in a special class. This would be bad enough were it not also frequently the case that the transfer is handled in a manner that seems to assume that the child does not need to be prepared for the change. Time and again we have seen children transferred to a special class without warning or discussion in much the same way as parents not telling a child he is going to the hospital until he is in the car and on the way there. In our experience this is certainly not because those who are responsible for such practices are cruel people. But it does reflect a lack of understanding and clinical sophistication which in turn reflect the inadequacies of the psychological training of principals, teachers, and school psychological personnel.

We have in the last two decades trained a number of clinical psychologists in the intricacies of psychological diagnosis and treatment of problems typically found in psychiatric settings. These settings are comforting and protective in that they rarely require the practitioner physically to appear and work in other, unfamiliar settings. It is not necessary to go out and look for problems, because there is no dearth of work in the clinic or private office and, more subtly, because the clinical model reinforces the tendency to deal only with what is literally brought to our attention. If the mental-health professions take seriously the concept of community mental health, training programs will be required that will bring closer together the traditions of the clinic and those of the public-health movement. The field of mental subnormality, representing as it does a vast number of individuals and a complex of psychological problems in living and adjustment, remains as it has in the past the rejected child of the mental-health professions. It is mistakenly presumed to lack the fascination and challenge of psychotherapy, to provide the clinician with insufficient satisfaction for having helped another human being with personal problems, and to contain in principle a set of problems not primarily psychological in nature. There is a germ of truth in these assertions as long as the focus is on the child, particularly the severely defective one. These assertions are patently absurd when the focus turns to the family as a social-psychological unit that affects and is affected by the subnormal child. In any event, to the extent that the mental-health professions continue to regard mental subnormality as peripheral to their focus and as the responsibility of other groups and agencies, they effectively and arbitrarily insulate themselves from a set of psychological problems to which their clinical contribution is potentially great.

Professions define for themselves the scope and manner of their practice, and this is as it should be. They must, however, constantly guard against the possibility that their definitions are remaining static, their values unexamined, and their satisfaction with how things are stronger than their reaction to their conception of how things ought to be. Over the years we have found ourselves forced to the conclusion that the tendency of the mental-health professions to restrict their practice to certain problems and social classes has no warrant in psychological theory, no defense in logic, no basis in research, and no justification on a number of criteria of social responsibility. We should make clear that this statement refers not to what these professions do but to the justifications ordinarily put forth for restricting their scope to certain problems and social classes.

We have in this chapter presented some ideas and experiences that led us into the activities and areas to be described in the remainder of this book. Lest our position, obviously critical of the existing professional order and establishment, be misconstrued, it may be clarifying if we indicate what we have *not* been saying.

Although this chapter might be interpreted as a plea for a kind of psychological imperialism in which the mental-health professions would exert a directing control over a large number of professional groups involved with psychological problems of diverse sorts and seriousness, to assert or to imply such a plea would be as indulgent of fantasies of omniscience as it would be self-defeating in reality. What we have attempted to make clear is that the mental-health professions have insulated themselves from other professional groups that are equally concerned with problems of psychological diagnosis and adjustments; an insulation that makes difficult, if not impossible, the kind of professional collaboration that enlarges horizons, increases the quality of services, and gives rise to new conceptualizations and research. Ultimately the most adequate psychological theory will be judged in part on the basis of the range of phenomena to which its applicability can be demonstrated. The insulation of the mental-health professions guarantees, in our opinion, that the theories they generate will have only limited utility and will unduly restrict the range of practices to which they give rise. It is our view that, as the mental-health professions begin to understand better a wider range of problems and settings, the nature of psychological theorizing and practice will become more complex and productive than now appears to be the case. Rather than advocating a kind of psychological imperialism, our position is that the mental-health professions have much to learn and to understand about human behavior and problems in settings now alien to their thinking and experience. The psychologist can be an unwitting prisoner of the clinic in much the same way as other psychologists have been imprisoned in the rat laboratory (Beach, 1950).

Neither did we intend to suggest in this chapter that clinical psychology should completely sever its tie to the psychiatric setting and venture forth in search of a new identity. It would not be consistent to counteract one form of parochialism by another. What aspects of traditional training are necessary, if any, as we move into unfamiliar settings and problems, is an empirical question. What seems absolutely essential is that training programs be changed so that they meaningfully expose the student to a greater variety of problems and settings than is now the case, in order to maximize the possibility that more of the coming generations of clinicians will move in new directions and serve as a force for continued change. We shall have to steer a course that avoids the dangers of the assumption that change is a virtue in itself and the equal dangers flowing from smugness in our ability to reproduce students who are identical to ourselves.

Finally, we must make clear that in emphasizing the parochialism of the mental-health professions we are not aligning with "community mental health" as that is reflected in the Community Mental Health

Act of 1963 and in programs reflecting that legislation. We have more to say about this in a later chapter. Suffice it to say here that this legislation, suggesting as it does psychiatric leadership and the development of facilities in traditional settings, gives promise of helping more of the same kinds of people in more of the same kinds of ways. This is "good," but we see no clear reasons why it should be called community mental health. The change in labels means little change in function or scope. Certainly the exposure of students in the mental-health professions to the complexities of the concept of a "community" and how these complexities bear on mental health and mental illness is severely lacking, especially compared to that which the sociologist and anthropologist frequently receive, a fact that allows us to suggest that these behavioral scientists may do a far better job than the mental-health worker in giving leadership to new programs.

The problems and issues discussed in this chapter have converged to move us in the direction of developing a facility that would be a vehicle by means of which we could, on a clinical level, learn about the process of helping in what were for us primarily new settings or new roles in old settings. In the next chapter we turn to some of the special problems we encountered or anticipated in developing the Psycho-Educational Clinic.

Chapter 4

The Psycho-Educational Clinic:
Problems Encountered or Anticipated

Our decision to develop a new clinical facility, explore new ways of rendering service, and provide a basis for initiating various research programs presented us with a number of problems. Before discussing some of the major ones, we must state briefly those considerations that guided our planning and actions. Again we caution the reader, particularly the young one, not to interpret our discussion as reflecting an approach in which our goals, near and far, were clear or the processes of implementation merely a matter of labor, organization, and patience. That this could not be the situation was guaranteed by our general purpose to explore new settings or new ways of rendering help. But one other factor of which we were aware stemmed from a research interest that would permeate all we would do. This interest was in the form of the question: how may change be introduced into an ongoing social system? It was amusing as well as somewhat paradoxical that before studying this question in a variety of settings we first had to answer the question in our own academic setting in which change in the form of a Psycho-Educational Clinic had to be brought about. Our pilot study, so to speak, involved ourselves and a particular kind of setting, that is, a department of psychology having certain traditions, values, and goals. Bringing about such change reflected a simple lesson in principle that later was illustrated in our work in other and phenotypically different settings. We refer here to the principle that where there is a situation of mutual trust, in the sense that there is awareness of an identity of values and goals, however different the means by which one is guided or the backgrounds of those involved, the setting is capable of change. Consequently, because there was this type of situation there were no serious problems in developing the kind of service and research facility we had in mind.

We now turn to those considerations that guided our planning and actions.

1. We would not duplicate any existing facility or develop services to settings already being provided. We were aware that we could justify our professional existence merely by providing more of the same services that already existed, for there is no community without need of more than it already has.

2. We wanted to work in settings in such a way that what we did had the clear possibility of serving one or both of two functions: that potentially serious problems could be anticipated and mitigated and that the effects of our efforts could be transferred by those involved to other individuals and problems. Put in another way, our aim was that the payoff for our efforts would be not only in terms of a single problem or instance but hopefully also in terms of other individuals and instances which the individuals involved (e.g., a teacher) would encounter.

3. A most important consideration was that we had to be part of, and intimately know, the setting in which our services would be rendered. We wished to avoid the consultant role which does not provide the opportunity to observe first-hand the context in which the problem manifests itself. For any problem presented to us it was crucial that we be able to observe the social context in which the problem was perceived, because it was this context that would be the object of change. Over the years we had learned that although the consultant role could be a valuable one, it was frequently limited by the fact that the consultant's knowledge of the problem was based on verbal reports that were incomplete or partly in error. The problem is identical to that in psychotherapy in which the verbal report of the patient distorts or misrepresents in one way or another events and relationships external to the therapeutic relationship. In setting the criterion that we had to be able to observe the context in which a problem was being manifested, we assumed that we would gain a truer picture of the situation that could serve as a basis for suggested change relevant to and effective in that context. This, of course, meant that our relationship to the setting would have to be of a kind that would permit—and in the eyes of others make mandatory—easy access to the setting. Rather than consultants, we would be participant observers.

A consequence was that we expected most of our activities to be away from our own departmental setting. When viewing the helping role as requiring intimate knowledge and observation of the social context in which problems are manifested, and, in addition, as focusing on the possibilities of change in that particular context, it is obvious that relatively little time can be spent in the office.

4. As a clinic we wished to provide services, in an administrative sense, to settings and not to individuals. In other words, we did not wish to be open to the public, as is usually the case in clinical settings, but rather to any individual *within* those settings with which we had formal relations. For one thing, as we already have said, our focus was not an individual in *our* setting but in *his* setting. By taking this focus and its methodological implications we assumed that we might be able to help the individual in such a way that the principles involved could be transferred in that setting to helping individuals not brought to our attention.

5. We wanted our activities to be in one or another way concerned with problems of children and youth as they manifest themselves in an educational setting. We were aware that the public school is only one of these settings and that there were other settings in our community seriously involved with the various consequences of failure in the public-school setting. This was particularly true in New Haven in regard to inner-city children for whom a variety of educational and vocational programs was developed away from the public-school setting. Our past clinical experience had made it clear to us that many of the problems we encountered in work with the mentally subnormal individual away from the public-school setting were originally discernible in the public-school setting but handled in ways that increased the seriousness of the problems and made later adjustment more difficult for child and family. In other words, it is in the public schools that the great majority of these problems is first detected, but the ways in which they are handled make it necessary for other community agencies to develop programs to cope with these problems. We do not blame the public schools, because so frequently they lack the knowledge, personnel, and programs necessary to cope adequately with the problems. In our opinion certain community agencies have had to develop various educational programs for a wide variety of children for whom there had been inadequate programs in the public schools. Our belief that this need not have been the case—or that it need not continue to be the case to the extent that it is—was perhaps most important in steering our attention to a variety of educational settings and programs for children and youth. Thus our interest in educational settings was based on the conviction that they contained the potential for influencing and molding children and youth to prevent or minimize the occurrence of patterns of attitude and behavior that interfere with productive learning and growth.

6. Intimately related to what we have just discussed was that we hoped to concentrate our efforts in those educational settings primarily concerned with inner-city children. As we indicated in Chapter 3, the inner-city population contributes disproportionately to almost every type of mental-health problem but is under-represented in the population availing themselves of mental-health services. This is particularly true of children and youth. It was our aim to determine to what extent the educational setting could become a more effective vehicle for prevention and intervention. To some readers it may appear that our goal was to transform the educational setting into a social agency in which academic learning would become either a secondary function or only one of several equal functions. That this was not our aim will become clear later in this chapter. What needs to be said at this point is that our previous experience with inner-city schools indicated that to the extent that these schools conceived their function to be solely educational, in the narrow, classroom sense of that word, they tended to exacerbate rather than minimize the number and seriousness of learning problems.

7. In whatever setting we worked we would not only attempt to deal with the problems presented to us but we would actively look for and be concerned with other problems not brought to our attention. It was basic to our thinking that any problem reflected factors in the particular setting in which it was discerned, even though the etiology of the problem may have had roots elsewhere (e.g., the family context). Consequently we had to be concerned with the setting not only in relation to a particular individual but also in relation to other individuals in that setting. As soon as we assume that any setting—however good or bad it may be judged—differentially elicits or presents difficulties to those within it, it becomes necessary for those with a helping orientation to focus not only on an individual but on the culture of the setting as well. To the extent that we focus on individuals, we may lose sight of the role of the larger context in creating problems and therefore be restricted in the amount of help we can give. It was our expectation that we would rarely, if ever, be asked to focus on the setting, but rather on individuals or limited problems within it. Therefore we considered it essential that we look on each individual problem as an instance illuminating the ways in which the larger social context could be a source of problems and the nature of the changes that would be required in order to reduce the incidence or severity of problems. It could be said, although we find these differentiations of little significance, that to the extent that we focused on the individual we were clinicians and to the extent that we were con-

cerned with setting, organization, and process of institutional change we were more like anthropologists, sociologists, or industrial psychologists.

THE THORNIEST PROBLEM

The first and thorniest problem we encountered in implementing the Psycho-Educational Clinic stemmed from several interacting factors. On the one hand, no one was asking for our services, a strange and somewhat amusing situation for clinical psychologists who, like other types of clinician, generally feel overwhelmed by the demands on their time. On the other hand, although we had ideas about the types of setting in which we wanted to become involved and about the kind of help we wanted to render, we were acutely aware that the shape of our activities would be determined by the settings in ways we could not anticipate. We were like salesmen who are not at all sure of what kinds of products they are selling to what kinds of customers. We felt kinship to the anthropologist who, before going to a foreign culture, learns as much about it as possible—knowing full well that when he gets there he will have much more to learn and unlearn.

One of the real dangers in being in such a situation of ambiguity (and anxiety) is that it can unwittingly facilitate the tendency to transform what is strange to that with which one is familiar, that is, to adapt the strange settings to traditional and highly practiced ways of thinking and acting. Resisting this tendency was not made easy by the knowledge that the settings in which we wanted to work would expect, and in reality need, such services traditionally associated with the role of the clinical psychologist as diagnostic testing, individual therapy, and consultation of a traditional sort.

We considered this problem as the thorniest one because, to the extent that we were not constantly and acutely aware of it, we ran the risk of defeating our aim of venturing in new ways within old and new settings. In addition, in light of our research goal of studying processes of change in ongoing social systems, we who were part of the vehicle for change had to have firmly in mind what we wanted to accomplish.

THE PROBLEM OF RESEARCH AND SERVICE

The competing requirements of research and service in a single agency have always been troublesome, and frequently one of the two activities becomes dominant. Our own inclinations as well as the traditions of our department gave great weight to research activity and precluded that this activity would play a secondary role in the Psycho-Educational Clinic. The danger was rather one of subjugating service, or unduly restricting it, to research needs. In one sense we were fortunate in that our over-all research interest in the process of change in ongoing social systems required that we develop services for the settings we wanted to study. Although the development of new services was of great importance to us in its own right, it was equally true that we viewed these services as a way of providing an entry into the setting. It soon became apparent, as others before us could have told us, that developing meaningful clinical services can be a fantastically difficult and time-consuming task, in the course of which the perspective can unwittingly change. This possibility is particularly facilitated when the clinical activity as such is stimulating, exciting, and a constant source of challenge.

Although we firmly believed that research and service would be co-equal in our activities and that services were essential for making the research activity possible and meaningful, our awareness that intentions are but intentions and that means effect ends produced a kind of nagging uneasiness in us. This was not for us an idle problem because in discussions with others, particularly those from grant-giving agencies, the question of how research and service activities would be related kept coming up. The fact that we could describe neither the specifics of our proposed research nor the details of our future services —because both depended on our getting into settings in order to be able to determine whether we were asking the right questions and thinking realistically about services—was a sore point for many people and, therefore, for us. It was sometimes hard for us to determine whether our reluctance, indeed our inability, to commit ourselves to a detailed statement of our future research and service was a form of defense or a reflection of what we thought was reality. Needless to say, we preferred to think that the problem was as real as the state of our ignorance and that the former would be clarified as our experience in settings grew.

As is often the case, reality rather than previous knowledge helped provide us with at least a partial answer to the problem of the relationship between service and research. It was in connection with our initial contacts with educational settings, particularly the elementary school, that we began to see that *the process of offering and giving help allowed us to see aspects of the setting that we would never see if we were not in the helping role.* For the purposes of our over-all research interest in processes of change in ongoing social systems we could no longer view clinical services merely as ways of gaining entry into the setting, or as means for introducing change, but rather as essential to a comprehensive view of the culture of the setting in which we were working. Put another way, the response to a helping service, the attempts to utilize and integrate it into existing patterns, the questions it raises about administration and authority, the challenge such a service inevitably presents to the existing order—these are aspects of the setting that can be seen with a degree of force and clarity not likely to be matched by other ways of studying the setting. Service, therefore, was a necessary tool, the response to which provided data of varying sorts that could then serve as a basis for describing the dimensions along which the setting was organized. The content of the method for the purposes of our over-all research goal was less important than the fact that it involved us in a helping relationship *within* the setting. Viewed in this way each clinical contact became an example illuminating one or more dimensions along which the setting was organized.

It has to be emphasized that our initial contacts with the educational setting, particularly the public school, forced on us the realization that a prior research question had to be answered before we could hope to study the general question of processes of change in ongoing social systems. The question might be put as follows: could we get to that point in a setting where what we did and said made a difference in that others acted on the basis of what we said or did? Unless this question could be answered in the affirmative, we could neither develop services nor proceed with research.

The question was not primarily whether what we did clinically was good or bad, but rather whether we had and could continue to have an effect. Involved here, of course, was the matter of the services offered and the manner in which they were presented and carried out. To the extent that we could become a meaningful part of the setting, the first problem in the research would be resolved at the same time that it said something about the services. That this book has been written testifies to our belief that this first step had been successfully accomplished. Primarily, however, this book is addressed to the nature of the services and their possible effectiveness.

THE PROBLEM OF PERSPECTIVE

It was clear that we were going to develop services in relation to certain settings and that this would be an absorbing task, but at the same time we had to discriminate between short- and long-term goals. We viewed the short-term goal as trying and developing any means that gave promise of rendering a useful service in the settings in which we were involved. In adopting such a view, we had to anticipate varying degrees of success either in terms of individuals or changes in organizational structure, processes, and aims. We were concerned that we could be so taken up with the short-term goals that we would lose sight of the long-term goal of how to use our experiences as a basis for programs that ultimately and ideally would eliminate the need for our kinds of service. For example, we knew we would be working with teachers in relation to a variety of problems, and we would encounter different obstacles that would account, in part at least, for the success or failure of our efforts. What we had to learn to keep in mind was that we had to view each instance, successful or not, as bearing on the question of how teacher-training programs could be changed to make our kinds of service less necessary or more effectively used. In other words, the payoff for our efforts would not only be how much help we could render in our day-to-day clinical role but how we could utilize our experiences for developing future training and educational programs that would serve a more preventive or public-health role.

The importance of keeping the long-term goals in mind is not only to be able to see day-to-day activities from a broader perspective but also to make it more likely that programs and activities can change in the direction of the long-term goals. It is all too easy (and understandable) for clinical facilities to become so absorbed and overwhelmed with current problems and programs that they have neither the time nor the attitudinal set to consider and implement long-term objectives. Not being sure that it is possible to get through a day is not conducive to thinking about tomorrow.

Basic to our way of thinking was that the most important obligation of the clinician, aside from helping others to the best of his knowledge and ability, is to conduct his activities so that he may identify sources of success and failure—a statement of virtuous intent that founders so frequently on issues of self-protection and selective perception. There were two reasons why this problem took on crucial significance for us. Since we anticipated that we would experience failure in certain aspects of our work in certain settings—because we would be trying to develop new services in new or old settings—it would be all too easy to blame failure on the setting and minimize our contribution; for example, to blame failure on lack of cooperation and strong resistance to change rather than on our manner of presentation, impatience, and faulty understanding of the other person's frame of reference. The second reason this problem was of importance to us involved the relationship between identification of sources of failure and our long-term goals. If our long-term goal was to develop training and educational programs to serve a preventive or public-health function, and these programs would reflect evaluation of our activities in meeting short-term objectives, the adequacy with which we evaluated these activities was of primary significance. To the extent that we misjudged these activities we ran the risk of developing the wrong kinds of programs in the future.

We have presented the problem of perspective because we have considered it as something that had to become part of our everyday thinking and not a luxury to be experienced every now and then; that is, whatever we did not only had bearing on what we were doing in the here and now but, just as important, on what we might do at some other time.

In Chapter 5 we turn to a description and discussion of our activities in the school setting, one of the three major settings in which our clinic operates. In discussing each of these settings, our primary aim is to describe as objectively and comprehensively as possible what we have done, why we have done it, and the problems encountered.

PART II

THE SCHOOLS

Chapter 5

The Approach to the Schools

Our approach to the schools was facilitated by our involvement over a period of years in various research projects in elementary schools in the New Haven area. As a consequence, we met and talked with superintendents of schools, principals, and teachers. Fortunately for us, the major research in which we had been engaged concerned the relationship between anxiety and performance in elementary-school children (Sarason et al., 1960; Sarason, Hill, & Zimbardo, 1964; and Hill & Sarason, in press) and this research was regarded by school personnel as "practical and necessary" in comparison to other psychological research in the schools, which was regarded as tangential, if not irrelevant, to the needs and problems of teachers and children. It was also true that, aside from the research, we were interested in observing and understanding the nature of schools and classrooms and its relation to the learning and behavior of children. In other words, we were not only researchers but interested and sympathetic listeners and bystanders.

The services our clinic developed in the elementary schools were determined not only by the knowledge we gained in the course of conducting a longitudinal study over the elementary school years. It will be recalled from Chapter 3 that over the years some of us had worked in special educational settings and in addition had taught in various colleges of education. In different ways these experiences were put to use by the need to develop and present to the schools a kind of service which promised to fill a felt need. More correctly stated, over the years we had become increasingly aware of certain factors in the school setting that presented to us the outlines of the required services: the nature of the service was as much a result of the problem as we experienced it over the years as it was the result of a deliberate thinking-through process at a particular time. In order to understand better how we approached the school, we shall discuss briefly those considerations and observations that determined the types of service we were prepared to offer.

FACTORS DETERMINING THE NATURE
OF THE SCHOOL SERVICE

When a clinical psychologist, or some other mental-health worker, becomes truly familiar with a particular school, he may be struck, as we were, by the differences between relationships among colleagues in his clinical setting and those that tend to exist among school personnel. For example, in almost all clinical settings the case conference is the major vehicle by means of which colleagues share experiences and viewpoints. In fact, as has been facetiously remarked by many people, so much time is frequently devoted to case conferencing as to suggest the possibility that it may be a defense against seeing patients. The point, of course, is that the case conference is a valuable training device for staff as well as interns. This vehicle for sharing experiences and problems is rarely utilized in the school setting. Teachers are essentially alone with their problems, not necessarily because they prefer it that way, but primarily because it is not part of the traditions of the school setting for the staff to meet, present, and critically evaluate their different problems and the ways they handle them. Why this is so need not detain us at this point; what is important is recognition that case conferencing is distinguished by its absence in most schools. This is not to say that there are no staff members (e.g., the principal or various kinds of supervisors) who presumably should exercise leadership in this respect or who are available on an individual basis to a teacher. The fact is that teachers tend to have no one with whom they can discuss questions and problems without such a discussion reflecting the constrictions and inhibitions inherent in a relationship between a superior and a subordinate.

In recent years there have been increasing numbers of mental-health workers introduced into school systems, frequently in the role of consultants who usually meet with teachers in small groups. Teachers have generally voiced four different types of reaction to their contacts with them:

1. A mixture of gratitude and surprise that someone from the mental-health professions comes to discuss with them the problems they are experiencing.

2. The discussions are worthwhile in that the teachers gain a more comprehensive view of child behavior and development.

3. A major limitation of the discussions is that it is frequently not clear to the teachers either how the content of the discussions are relevant to the classroom or how the principles discussed can be or should be implemented in the classroom.

4. Related to this, consultants tend to lack a knowledge or appreciation of the complexities faced in managing a large group of children.

It is in connection with this last reaction that many teachers have voiced the hope that the mental-health worker could spend time in the classroom observing both teacher and problem child so that his suggestions would have the kind of concreteness the teacher feels she needs. As one teacher put it, "The next time somebody tells me that the child needs individual attention I'll scream. That's what I try to do. What I want to know is what I should do and if I'm doing it the right way." The attitudes reflected in this statement have been sensed by many consultants who, understandably, shy away from a degree of specificity that may satisfy a teacher's need *at that moment* but also may be harmful because they do not know the child or the teacher *in her role as teacher*. It should not be surprising, therefore, that both teachers and mental-health consultants tend to experience their relationship as worthwhile at the same time that they recognize its limitations and even dangers.

Particularly bothersome to the mental-health consultant has been the tendency on the part of teachers to seek direction from and to become dependent on the consultant. There has been a real question how much of this dependency reflects a difficult reality situation and how much of it is a defensive reaction that seeks to shift responsibility for action onto other people—a question that troubles the consultant and is essentially unanswerable as long as he is not in a position to observe and know the teacher in her classroom role. This issue can be seen again in a somewhat different form in the relationship between teacher and school psychologist. Too often the school psychologist is one whose primary, if not sole, responsibility is to conduct psychological examinations as they may be requested by teachers. Because the school psychologist is usually overwhelmed by referrals (and has little time to spend in classroom observation when it is expected or permissible—and it is by no means always expected or permitted), it becomes important to determine why these referrals are made, whether they are made because the teacher has a question for which testing is appropriate or are symptomatic of the tendency to ask someone else to think through a problem which the teacher in principle should do. The answers are not easy to determine. Often the referral to the school psychologist does not reflect a clear formulation of the problem but rather an unclear plea for help for which testing is not compellingly appropriate. At times, too, the referral is a routine gesture made by the teacher before she has given any thought to the nature of the problem or the appropriateness of the referral, that is, testing is viewed as a kind of laboratory procedure that should be available to as many children as possible. In any event, the nature of the communication and relationship between teacher and school psychologist tends to frustrate both of them; the school psychologist because he feels his efforts are not recognized or appropriately used and the teacher because she has not had the kind of help she feels she needs. We could present dozens of reports by school psychologists that would justify the teacher's criticism. We could present as many examples to illustrate inappropriate referrals by teachers and, more important, inappropriate actions based on misinterpretation of the psychological report.

The situations we have been describing become somewhat more understandable when we recognize that the training of teachers is woefully deficient in preparing them for the use of different kinds of services and consultants, particularly in the mental-health area. In the absence of such preparation it should not be surprising that the relationship between teachers and mental-health workers is so often a troubled one. Unfortunately many consultants have not been so aware as they should be that to the teacher the consultant is an unfamiliar professional person to whom they have few guidelines for deciding how he can and should be used. In point of fact we can assume that many teachers have unrealistic conceptions about the consultant, the extent of his knowledge, the nature of his training, and his techniques of help. It is not unusual for the mental-health consultant to be asked "to see the child" or to "talk to the child," the implication being that he possesses techniques for change of a somewhat magical nature. It has, in our opinion, been a mistake for the mental-health worker to view such attitudes as only reflecting something about the motivations, personality dynamics, and capabilities of teachers. Though these are undoubtedly factors, we must see them in the context of the training and experience of teachers that poorly prepares them to understand and effectively use psychological principles underlying behavior and processes of change (Sarason, Davidson, & Blatt, 1962). However, as we indicated in Chapter 3, we must also recognize that the training and experience of the mental-health consultant does not equip him to understand the background of teachers, the types of problem they encounter in the classroom, and the kinds of help teachers feel they need (Sarason, 1963).[1]

A variant of this problem involves the relationship between school personnel and the child-guidance clinic. Many, if not most, of the cases coming to the child-guidance clinic reflect problem behavior in the school setting, and frequently the school has recommended to the parents that they seek outside help for their child. In those cases in which the child is accepted by the clinic for evaluation and treatment we find several types of reaction or expectation on the part of school personnel, particularly the teacher. The first is the expectation that *now* something is being done and change will take place in the near future, an expectation, of course, that is all too frequently unrealistic. This serves to emphasize the point made earlier about the lack of understanding on the part of teachers about the ways in which mental-health people work and the problems they have in bringing about change. A second reaction of the teacher is puzzlement about why the clinic does not seek her out either to utilize her knowledge about and problems with the child or to help guide her in managing the child in the classroom. Again we see how the reaction of the teacher reflects her unfamiliarity with child-guidance clinic procedures and therapeutic orientation, particularly in relation to the problems of confidentiality. The fact remains that the teacher feels left out of things and uncertain or in conflict about how she should react to the child. We have seen numerous instances in which knowledge that the child is being seen in a clinic has resulted in a "hands-off" policy by the teacher, a policy productive of more problems than it resolves.

However the child-guidance clinic justifies the distance between it and the teacher, we cannot overlook or underestimate the significance of the fact that what happens to the child in school has effects not only in school and in the home but in the clinic as well. This is particularly true in cases of learning problems in which the more a child falls behind the pace of his class the more difficult the therapeutic task be-

---

[1] Morse (1961) has summarized our own position in his conclusions stemming from experiences in a service-research program in school mental health:

"(1) There will never be enough specialists to handle all of the school problems. (2) Some of the impact of mental health on schools has been negative and a re-evaluation is in order. (3) Present training designs are inadequate to give teachers diagnostic and management skills. (4) The specialist's present functioning frequently does not seem in keeping with the over-all educational milieu. A new orientation must be developed. (5) The perceptions of the teacher concerning the teacher role and its complications offer a useful point of beginning."

comes and the greater the likelihood that the child's problems will become more generalized. Therapeutic progress with children is neither that effective nor that quick to justify the assumption that the daily experience of a child in school can be viewed as tangential to the focus of the therapeutic endeavor. As in the case of the home, to which the clinic devotes a great deal of investigative and counseling time, the child is involved in school in a variety of significant relationships and is confronted with tasks and adaptations all of which shape his present and future development. Teachers are aware of this point and it underlies their reactions of puzzlement, anger, and rejection at being left out of the clinic's activities with child and family. In recent years child-guidance clinics have reached out more frequently to school personnel, but even here the focus has been not on what help can be provided to the teacher but rather on gaining information useful to the clinic in its work with a particular child.

We have attempted to describe aspects of teachers' attitudes and verbalized needs in relation to problem children as they have been expressed to us over the years. It has not been our intention in this discussion to pass judgment on these aspects but rather to indicate how teachers react to their experiences with problem children and to those professional individuals in and out of the school setting who are also concerned with these children. We have stressed the feelings and reactions of teachers because over time they became increasingly important and influential in our thinking about the kinds of services we felt needed to be developed by our Clinic in relation to the school setting. As we shall show later, our earlier experiences with teachers in different settings forced to our attention two questions. First, how and to what extent could we develop a helping service to teachers in relation to the management of children in the classroom situation? Second, what would be the effectiveness of a therapeutic relationship with a child in a clinic setting in which the central focus was the child in school?

In developing services in relation to the school, we have been influenced not only by the attitudes and reactions of teachers but also by several conclusions based on our own observations and experiences. The first and most important of these conclusions was that the role of the teacher in influencing, managing, and guiding the behavior of children was of enormous significance. This conclusion may be regarded as a glimpse of the obvious but it is intended to emphasize that a teacher—wittingly or unwittingly, for good or for bad—shapes the behavior of children. A second and related conclusion was that differences among teachers made dramatic differences in the lives of children. Stated otherwise, we rarely saw a problem child in a classroom for whom there was not another teacher in that school who could handle him in ways productive of learning and personal change. It seemed from our observations to be far too simple to "explain" such differences among teachers by such adjectives as good or bad, labels that conveyed a germ of truth at the same time that they helped emphasize the unwarranted and unfair assumption that a teacher should be equally effective with all types of children. A third major conclusion to which our observations led us was that, as a group, teachers had a potential for change in attitudes and practices that under appropriate conditions would discernibly increase their effectiveness as stimulators and molders of productive change in children.

It was these three major conclusions that, together with the previously discussed reactions of teachers to problem children and mental-health workers, influenced the nature of the services we wanted to provide and the steps we took to introduce them into the elementary schools. In the following section we take up in detail how and in what ways we approached the schools, that is, how we went about solving the "port of entry" problem.

THE PORT-OF-ENTRY PROBLEM

Once we had decided the types of service we wanted to provide, we approached the superintendents of the school systems in which we wanted to start. This approach was facilitated by our previous acquaintance with these individuals. In each instance we requested (as we anticipated the superintendent would require) the opportunity to discuss our proposed services with the principals of the schools in which we wanted to begin. In addition, and on the assumption that the principals were willing for us to work in their schools, we also asked that we be permitted to describe our services to the teachers in each of the schools. Our presentation to the teachers differed in no way from that for the superintendents and principals, and we give here a summary of the standard presentation or "set speech" to teachers at a faculty meeting:

For a number of years some of us in the Department of Psychology at Yale have been engaged in different research projects involving elementary schools. In addition to our experiences in the elementary schools, some of us have long been interested in various aspects of special education and in the preparation of teachers. As a consequence, we became increasingly interested in the day-to-day problems facing schools in general and teachers in particular. Let me say right off that there are two conclusions to which we have come. The first is that anyone who teaches in the public schools for less than $15,000 per year ought to have his head examined. The second conclusion is that a law ought to be passed making it mandatory for each parent to teach a class by himself for a day each year. Although these recommendations may not solve all problems, they would certainly help bring about changes that all of us would agree are necessary. All of this is by way of saying that our experiences have given us an understanding of what is involved in teaching and managing a large group of children, each of whom is a distinct character, for several hours each day over a period of 10 months. It is not flattery but rather strong conviction underlying the statement that the classroom teacher performs one of the most difficult tasks asked of any professional person. It would indeed be nice if all a teacher had to do was to teach. You know, and I know, that a teacher is a parent, a social worker, a psychologist, and a record-keeping clerk. Hopefully there is time to teach once the duties associated with these other roles are discharged. We are living at a time when everyone seems to be an expert on the schools and ignorance seems to be no barrier to articulating strong opinions. There is no doubt, as I am sure you will agree, that there is much one can criticize about schools, but there is also no doubt that unless one understands what a school is like and what it is faced with in its day-to-day operation the benefits we would like to see from these changes will not be so great as they should be.

One of the most staggering problems facing our society concerns the degree of serious maladjustment in many people. One has only to look at the size and number of our mental hospitals, psychiatric clinics, reformatories, and the like to begin to grasp how enormous a problem this is. We are talking about millions of people and billions of dollars. What needs to be stressed is that in the foreseeable future we will have neither the personnel nor the facilities to give these troubled people the quality of treatment they need. In all honesty I must also say that for many of these people our knowledge and treatment procedures leave much to be desired.

As a result of our experiences, we at the Psycho-Educational Clinic in the Yale Department of Psychology have come to two conclusions: first, far too little is being done either to try to prevent the occurrence of problems or to spot them at those points in the individual's life where with a little effort a lot may be accomplished. Second, if we believe what we say, we ought in a very limited kind of way to attempt to see what we can do. I do not have to emphasize to a group of elementary-school teachers the significance of a preventive approach to problems in the early grades. As I am sure all of you know as well as, if not better than I, you are faced daily with children whose behavior, learning difficulties, and inter-personal relations (with you or other children) arouse in you concern, bewilderment, anger, and a lot of other reactions. On the basis of all the talks and meetings we have had over the years with teachers there would seem to be in any one classroom of 25 children anywhere from three to six children about whom the teacher is concerned in the sense that she has a question about their academic learning and personal adjustment in the school setting.

What do we propose to do? It is easier for me to tell you what we do *not* intend to do. For one thing, we do not intend to come into a school in order to see how many problem children we can refer out to various agencies. There is no doubt that you know a lot of children who could utilize the services of a child-guidance clinic or family service society. To come in with the intent of referring them out is both unfair and unrealistic because these agencies, particularly the child-guidance clinics, are overwhelmed with cases and generally have long waiting lists. *Even if the child-guidance clinic could take the child on, it would take them quite a while to get to first base with the child and in the meantime you still have that child in your class.* Treatment procedures are neither that quick nor effective to allow you to expect that *your* difficulties with the child are over once you know he is being seen in a clinic. The question we have asked of ourselves is how can we be of help to the teacher in the here and now with whatever questions and problems she raises with us. In short, we want to see how we can be of help within the confines of the school.

It is not our purpose to come into a school to sit and talk to teachers, however helpful and interesting that might be. When we say we want to be helpful in the here and now within the confines of the school, we mean that in addition to talking with the teacher about a child *we have to be able to observe that child in the context of the classroom in which the problem manifests itself.* For help to be meaningful and practical it must be based on what actually goes in the classroom setting. For example, it is in our experience of no particular help to a teacher to be told that a child needs individual attention, a need which differentiates him not at all from the rest of us. What a teacher wants to know is when, how, and for what goals this "individual attention" will occur, and this requires a first-hand knowledge of what is going on.

We do not view ourselves in the schools as people to whom questions are directed and from whom answers will be forthcoming. Life and the helping process are not that simple. We have no easy answers, but we have a way of functioning that involves us in a relationship to the teacher and the classroom and that together we can come up with concrete ideas and plans that we feel will be helpful to a particular child. We are not the experts who can come up with solutions even though we have no first-hand knowledge of the context in which the problem has been identified.

I hope I have made clear that when we say we want to help it means that we want to talk to the teacher, observe in the classroom, talk again to the teacher, and together come up with a plan of action that with persistence, patience, and consistency gives promise of bringing about change. It is not a quick process and it is certainly not an easy one.

I cannot state too strongly that we are not coming into the schools with the intent of criticizing or passing judgment on anyone. *We are nobody's private FBI or counterintelligence service. We are not the agent of the principal or some other administrative officer.* In fact, we are in no way part of the administrative hierarchy or power structure of the school system. We have no special strength or power except that which flows from our being able to establish a situation of mutual trust between teachers and ourselves. To the extent that we can demonstrate to you by our manner, gesture, and verbalization that we want to help, to that extent we make the development of this mutual trust more likely and quickly to occur.

There is one aspect of the way we function that I think needs some elaboration. I have already told you why it is essential for us, if our efforts are to be maximally useful, that we spend time in the classroom. Another reason this is essential resides in the one advantage we have over the teacher, i.e., we do not have the awesome responsibility of having to handle a large group of young characters five days a week for several hours each day, a responsibility that makes dispassionate observation and clear thinking extraordinarily difficult. We can enjoy the luxury of being in the classroom without the responsibility of the teacher for managing and thinking about 25 or more unique personalities. We do not envy you although I am quite sure that you will envy us for not having your responsibilities. It is precisely because we are "free" that we can observe what is going on in a way not usually possible for a teacher.

In order for us to help in a school it is crucial that we know that school as a physical entity and as a kind of social organization. Consequently, we usually make the request that for the first six weeks or so we visit classrooms and get to know you and what you do in the different grades without any obligation to get involved with any problem. A school and a classroom are not simple settings and it takes several weeks until we get the feeling of familiarity. We will be here on certain days of the week so that you can count on when we will be here. We try to spend a day and a half a week in each school.

We do not know to what extent we can be of help to you. We do not present ourselves as experts who have answers. We have much to learn about this helping process. If our previous work with teachers is any guide, the type of service we want to develop is one that they feel they need. The only thing we can guarantee you is that we want to learn and to help. We have much to learn from you, and together we may be able to be of help to children in school.

This summary contains, with one exception to be noted later, the essentials of our thinking and proposed practices. Following the presentation there was a discussion period in which teachers asked questions, which afforded us an opportunity to restate how and why we wanted to operate in the elementary school. The reactions of the teachers reflected, as we expected, a number of attitudes and concerns. When we say "as we expected," we refer to the fact that our familiarity with the school setting had given us some understanding of a school culture that had traditions, dynamics, and goals of its own, which, to those within that culture, set it apart from the rest of the community. The idea that the school is a subculture in our society was most influential in determining what we wanted to do, the way in which we would present ourselves, and the kinds of problems we could expect to encounter in trying to become part of the setting. In earlier years we had a number of opportunities to witness how attempts to introduce an innovation into the schools had foundered because of a lack of understanding of the complexities of the school culture. What we have termed the "port-of-entry problem" is in principle no different from that which confronts the anthropologist who wants to understand and become part of a foreign culture or the social scientist who wants to study the dimensions along which a particular social system, large or small, is organized and understandable. Basic to our thinking was the idea that to the extent that our knowledge of the school culture was limited or wrong, becoming part of the setting would be a problem and would interfere with our attempts to change.[2] Neither in the psychotherapeutic interaction nor in a particular subculture are the possession of laudable goals and the desire to help guarantees that change will occur. That the road to hell is paved with good intentions is a caveat applicable to the scientist as well as the moralist.

The following are the most frequent attitudes and reactions encountered in the discussion that succeeds our presentation:

1. As we expected, the initial reaction tended to be one of wariness. We were aware that we would be regarded as ivory-tower kinds of people from a university not viewed as particularly involved or concerned with the community. It was common knowledge that several years before the university had eliminated its department of education and that the president who initiated the action had taken a dim view of the status and quality of public education and teacher training institutions. In other words, there was no good basis in reality for the teachers to believe that we could do what we said we wanted to do or that our motivations were as well-intentioned as we claimed. For us to have expected otherwise would have meant that we subscribed to the magic of words.

2. Despite the wariness there was recognition that the type of service we described was a very necessary one that ought to be given a

---

[2] In a brief and very interesting paper concerned with the relation between Indian clients and the Bureau of Indian Affairs, Leon (1965) illustrates the generality of the point we are discussing.

chance to work. This is not to say that this recognition was voiced by a majority of the teachers or in an unqualified enthusiastic manner, but we could usually count on a few teachers to verbalize their need for this kind of service. Since the principals were always present at the meetings with teachers, and schools vary markedly in terms of the relationship between principal and teachers, we expected that the nature, scope, and freedom of discussion would in some ways reflect these relationships, particularly because the description of our proposed role could be seen as supplanting or overlapping with the responsibilities of the principal.

3. Related to the last point were questions bearing on possible conflicts between our functions and those of existing special services; for example, school psychologists, social workers, and reading specialists. What was most instructive and interesting about these questions was that at the same time they indicated that our proposed service was not being performed by existing personnel there was concern that the classroom teacher might lose the good will of those personnel with whom she had a relationship. Our response was that the teacher had to decide for herself to whom to take a particular problem and that it was not our intention to supplant or overshadow any existing help available to her. We stressed that the questions being raised were completely understandable to us and that similar questions would be raised by other types of school personnel. It would, we said, be our responsibility to demonstrate in practice our aim to provide a distinctive service that would add to and not take away from existing services.

If nothing else, the meeting with the teachers served the purpose of making clear to us that our job of becoming a meaningful part of the school could not be expected to be an easy one, not only because we were "foreigners," but because the school is a very complex organization in which traditions, clarity of roles, and degrees of responsibility are among the dominant factors. We stress this because there is a tendency among clinicians (as well as a lot of other people) to expect that a well-intentioned offer to help should be greeted with enthusiasm and to look to personality dynamics for an explanation when such enthusiasm is not forthcoming. Although personality dynamics undoubtedly entered into the reactions of each of the teachers, it is equally true that their reactions reflected their knowledge of and experiences in the school culture; that is, the realities of the day-to-day functioning of the social system we call a school.

It should be recalled that in Chapter 4 we indicated that our overall research aim of understanding and studying the school culture could best be accomplished if we could be in some kind of service relationship to the schools. We assumed that the response to an offer of help, as well as the problems that arise in implementing such help, would bring to the fore aspects of the school culture that would lead us to those variables crucial to an understanding of how and why a school is organized as it is. The reactions of the teachers to our initial presentation supported this assumption. For example, it became clear to us in the discussion period that the wariness of the teachers was not only a response to a stranger or to something novel but also to the expectation that in one way or another they would be the recipients of some sort of criticism. We had anticipated such a reaction and in our presentation had emphasized that we shared with the teachers the view that it was all too easy to direct criticism at schools in general and teachers in particular. In a couple of instances, teachers used the discussion period to express the feeling that they were much more the recipients of criticism than any form of praise or support. The discussion period made it plain that the reaction of wariness indicated not only personality but reality factors as well, a conclusion that prevented us from perceiving the situation as one explainable by a concept such as "resistance."

Our entry into the schools was made more difficult by a factor that was also a source of strength, the fact that our coming into the schools was perceived by the teachers as a decision already made by superintendents or principals, and the teachers had no alternative but to go along. This, in point of fact, was usually the case, not because higher-echelon personnel had presented a directive to the teachers but because they indicated that what we were offering gave promise of being helpful: the teachers were put in the position of being unable to turn down our services without publicly rejecting the opinions of their policy-making superiors. We were aware that this situation (not unusual in complex social systems) facilitated our physical entry into the school but could interfere with our becoming a meaningful part of it. Here again we can see how the reactions of teachers must be viewed not only in terms of personality factors but in terms of the social realities or context of which they are aware and a part.

It is not our purpose here to describe and discuss the school culture and the ways in which it affects change, personality, and goals. Although much that is in this book bears on the nature of the school culture, it is a problem of such theoretical and methodological complexity that it warrants separate treatment and further experience. Our purpose here has been to indicate that entry into the schools is a difficult task which can become impossible and self-defeating if we are not acutely aware that the attitudes and behavior of those in the setting reflect personality-cognitive factors on the one hand and what may be termed the social-cultural realities of the setting on the other hand. Just as the university professor can be flabbergasted at how little a public school teacher may understand about the college culture, the teacher has similar reactions in relation to the professor. That the university professor was once an elementary school pupil and the school teacher was once a college student are obviously inadequate bases for mutual understanding of each other's setting.

The task of presenting our ideas to the teachers and gaining their overt cooperation was a relatively easy step preliminary to the difficult one of developing a situation of mutual trust with teachers in relation to their classroom setting. By mutual trust we mean that point in a relationship at which there is give and take in discussion relatively unencumbered by feelings of suspicion, wariness, and evasion. Because the attainment of such a relationship is not easy, in the following section we focus on the early weeks of our work in a school, an extremely trying period, somewhat fateful for the course of future work.

THE EARLY WEEKS

In our initial presentation to the teachers we indicated that in order to be maximally helpful it was necessary in the early weeks for us to visit classrooms and talk to teachers, and to become familiar with the setting without the feeling of obligation to help in any way; that is, to get a feeling for the setting as a physical and social entity. The teachers knew on what days we would be in the school, and ordinarily we were there for one and a half days each week.

It was (and is) standard procedure that on each day we first checked in with the principal, an explicit recognition that the principal was in charge of the school and had the responsibility for whatever went on there. We assumed, and experience confirmed, that we might be regarded by the principal as wanting to infringe, wittingly or unwittingly, on his prerogatives as administrator and policy maker for that setting. We also assumed that, unlike anyone else coming into the school, we were not part of the power and administrative structure of the school system and that this would present a problem of utilizing us or of relating to us in an administrative sense. In addition, because we had stressed that our focus would be on the classroom setting, we could anticipate the principal's expectation that in the course of our observations and in discussions with teachers we would become aware of matters, personal and professional, that might reflect unfavorably on the principal. Just as it is unrealistic to expect a teacher to like and to be equally effective with all children in her class, it is unrealistic to expect that the relationships of a principal with his staff would be unmarred by tension, hostility, and personal antagonisms. Principals, like teachers, *do* vary in personal and professional effectiveness and it would be foolhardy in the extreme to approach the school as if it were a happy family.

These considerations indicate that the port-of-entry problem begins with the person who is in charge of the port, that is, the principal. In our early relationship with the principal there were three points that we endeavored to make clear about our role.

1. We were quite thankful that we were not in the principal's position of being responsible for any and all problems occurring in the school, implementing educational policies of the school system (particularly in inner-city schools), coping with shortages of materials and special personnel, and preparing the diverse records and reports that consume much of a principal's time. We tried to convey what we actually felt: the principal's job is far from easy, and we had no desire to assume any of its responsibilities. It was our hope that to the extent that we could be helpful to teachers in relation to their classroom problems we would be rendering a service to the principal.

2. Our relationship with teachers necessarily had to be confidential if they were to feel free to discuss any problems with which they thought we could help. We were aware, we said, as we were sure the principal was aware, that to the teacher the principal was one who had to pass judgment on the teacher and from time to time take actions which affected teachers. Unless confidentiality was respected we could be similarly perceived and our usefulness would come to an end.

3. We wished to be helpful to the principal in whatever ways possible, but at this stage of our work it was clear that the principal could be extremely helpful to us in giving us an understanding of this particular school. We had much to learn about it and the system of which it was a part and it was our earnest hope that the principal would contribute to our learning.

As might be imagined, our relationships with principals in the early weeks varied considerably from one in which we were given a blank check to one in which wariness compounded of anxiety, hostility, and suspicion was dominant. The most difficult task was to keep two things constantly in mind: there were dangers for us in both types of extreme reaction, and our conception of our role and goal had to be the controlling factor in our own overt reactions. It was extremely difficult to avoid reacting positively and with relief to a principal who greeted us warmly and told us to do whatever we wanted; it was equally difficult to avoid reacting negatively to a principal who made it quite clear that we were not particularly welcome.

By far the most trying aspect of these early weeks involved our observational activities in the classroom. The difficulty here was less in the reception accorded us by teachers than in our own reactions to our new professional role in a new setting. Part of the difficulty stemmed from the fact that almost all of our clinical experiences had been in the modal type of psychiatric setting in which the techniques of help were relatively clear and the procedures of intake and disposition grounded in a relatively well-defined tradition. In such a setting we know our roles, the basis for working with other clinic personnel, and the types of problems addressed. Coming from such a background into a classroom that will be the focus of our efforts is not, and should not be, an affectless experience. Aside from the relative unfamiliarity of the setting and the myriad things to be observed, we quickly experience with some concern the question how we *can* help within the confines of the classroom. Although we had previously spent a great deal of time in scores of classrooms in connection with our research activities, and the classroom was far from an unfamiliar setting, our perception of it and of ourselves in relation to it underwent rapid change when confronted with the goal of developing a helping service within the confines of that setting. We did not know how this helping role would develop, the obstacles we would encounter, and the limitations that the nature of the setting would impose on the variety of ways we might help.

In these early weeks it was by no means easy to sit in each classroom for an hour or more with no particular focus except to "soak in" what was going on. The observer's attention strays from child to child; questions arise about the significance of their behaviors and interactions; he becomes puzzled about the criteria by which a particular behavior is judged to be unusual for that setting; he experiences all kinds of questions about the motivation of the children for learning and the interest value of the materials and tasks presented to them; and, finally, he is concerned about how long it should take to feel secure about his understanding of the classroom and the factors that determine its atmosphere and, consequently, the means by which it can be changed. Needless to say, he also experiences a variety of reactions to the teacher that are no less varied, emotional, and personal than those toward parents met for the first time in the typical clinical setting. With some teachers he immediately gets the feeling "you can work with her," whereas with others he reacts with quiet despair about the possibilities of change. The apparently psychologically minded teacher elicits joy; the "sergeant-type" evokes anger and criticism. The warm personality is *good;* the "cold personality" is *bad.* What makes the situation so difficult for the observer is not the spontaneous reaction to the teacher but the knowledge that first impressions tend to be true *and* false, that he must suspend judgment, that he must lend every effort to learn to understand the teacher in her terms, and that to an undetermined extent the teacher's behavior involves a reaction not only to the observer's personality but to the teacher's perception of the observer's role.

To the clinically trained reader the gamut of reactions we have described should occasion no surprise because the dynamics of the helping role should not be expected to be radically different from one setting to another. What made these initial weeks so trying was our awareness that we had placed ourselves in the position of helping without being able to fall back on traditions and guidelines as to how or to what extent we could be of help. It is not easy when we know that we have to prove ourselves in a situation in which the process and criteria of proof are, to begin with, relatively unknown or unclear.

Although we have emphasized the difficult aspects of the initial weeks, there were several considerations we constantly kept in mind because we considered them crucial in that we assumed, to the extent that they were reflected in our behavior, that our entry into the school would be facilitated and the nature of our role in it gradually clarified. The first of these considerations was the conviction that there is no more taxing task than to teach a group of 25 or more youngsters, who differ among themselves in a variety of ways, for several hours each day over a ten-month period. Taken seriously, this conviction prevents us from making hasty judgments about teachers or talking to them in ways that convey an underestimation of what is involved in teaching. More important, perhaps, is that this conviction forces us to view what might be considered the negative characteristics of a teacher as, in part at least, reflecting a reaction to the difficult, demanding, and even debilitating aspects of teaching. A second consideration which governed our language and actions was the wish to learn how we could help. We truly did not have ready answers to questions and our job was to find out how we could work *with* teachers on whatever problems they were experiencing in the classroom. We were secure about our motivations, realistic about the difficulties, uncertain about how things would go, and eager to learn through success and failure. A third consideration we had constantly to bear in mind in the early weeks was the necessity of being clear about our time perspective. The establishment of mutual trust takes time; it should not be expected to proceed in a straight-line, upward fashion, and this time perspective was probably as central to the thinking of teachers about us as it was on our part in relation to them.

THE INITIAL BREAKTHROUGH

At some point in the early weeks "something happens" that provides the opportunity to demonstrate willingness to try to help, however difficult the occasion and high the probability of failure. The following event took place in the third of the early weeks in one of the inner-city schools:

During his first visit to a first-grade class, the staff member assigned to this school immediately became aware of Eddie,[3] an eight-year-old boy. He was wandering around the room, never interacted with another child, and did not respond to any of the teacher's verbal attempts to have him take his seat or to engage in any of the ongoing activities. During the middle of the visit the teacher came over to the observer and began telling him about Eddie: he had been excluded the previous year from school and was now back on a half-day basis. She indicated that what the staff member was observing was not quite representative of Eddie's behavior because he was usually more hyperactive, more diffusely hostile and destructive, and far less easy to manage. Essentially her approach was to leave him to his own devices with the hope that she could get through the morning without a struggle. During two subsequent visits the observer had an opportunity to see the more representative behavior. During the third week the observer was in another classroom when a child walked in with the message to the observer that the principal would like him to come down quickly to the room in which Eddie was a pupil. The observer had no idea what the message was about and was not prepared for the scene he encountered: Eddie was curled up on the floor in a very constricted fashion, clutching a toy, and every now and then violently kicking his leg toward whoever was standing near him. The teacher reported that Eddie had been in a particularly ugly mood that morning, began to destroy what other children were doing, picked up objects and threw them around, and reacted more and more violently to the verbal and physical attempts of the teacher to restrain him. The mother had already been called to come and take Eddie home. The teacher, principal, and children stood anxiously and helplessly around Eddie, fascinated as well as frightened by this magnificent display of temper—reactions shared by the observer. Two things become apparent to the observer: he was called to come because he was a male and a psychologist (and what are psychologists for?), and it was necessary to remove the boy from the classroom until the mother came for him. When the psychol-

[3] This and all following names have been changed.

ogist knelt to try to talk to Eddie, the boy curled up into more of a human ball and began to propel himself away by energetic thrusts. After a couple of minutes of the tender-loving-care approach the psychologist grasped the boy and carried him from the room. The boy struggled violently and attacked the psychologist who continued to talk quietly to him at the same time that he indicated that he did not want to punish or hurt him but just wanted him to sit quietly on the psychologist's lap so that both could talk about what had happened. The battle went on for at least half an hour until the mother arrived. (The boy lived three houses from the school and it took the mother approximately one hour to make the trip.) The psychologist accompanied the mother and boy to their home and remained there for another hour.

The consequence of this event was that in the eyes of the school's personnel the psychologist no longer seemed to be an ivory-tower academician who could not or would not immerse himself in the many difficult problems of the school. As one teacher put it several months later: "You *saw* what we are faced with in this school and you *did* something."

In the early weeks in another school a staff member was in a kindergarten class in which a child was having an extremely difficult time separating from the mother. The child sat in the room sobbing silently and unable to participate in any activity. That morning the principal had told the mother that she could no longer take the child to the classroom but would have to leave her at the school door where the teacher met the children. Previously the child had created a scene whenever the mother left the classroom, and it was felt that this created problems for the other children. On this occasion the psychologist departed from her role as visitor-observer and asked the teacher if it would be appropriate for her to talk with the child. The teacher was more than glad and the psychologist went over to the child, spoke with her, and then took her for a walk and explored the school building, during which they talked some more. After the walk they returned to the room. The psychologist said she would be back in school the next day and would drop in to say hello. She left the room, after which the child began to engage wholeheartedly in the ongoing activities. The next day the psychologist did drop in to say hello and observed the child happily engaged in play.

Needless to say, the psychologist's response was not due to any foreknowledge that her intervention would have quick results but rather to the conviction that something should be done for the child, it being clear that the teacher either did not know how to approach the child or even if she should approach the child. It seemed clear to the psychologist that the teacher was upset by the child's sobs and that departing from her role as observer would not be viewed negatively by the teacher, a decision extremely dangerous and difficult to make in the early weeks. In any event, the actions of the psychologist had the consequence of facilitating her acceptance by school personnel as someone "who knows how to handle children." This type of acceptance is by no means an unmixed blessing: it reinforces the hope or expectation that psychologists have a certain kind of magic, an expectation that can only produce future problems.

The two examples given are somewhat atypical as illustrations of how events in the early weeks of work in a school facilitate acceptance, in smaller or larger measure, by school personnel. The more usual process of acceptance begins with a relationship with one or two teachers —and it is rarely more than that—who reach out for help. These early requests for help are also not to be put in the category of unmixed blessings because they are at least of two kinds: those requests that reflect a desire to work *with* the psychologist and those that reflect the hope that the teacher can now *transfer* problems to the psychologist. In any event, we can usually count on some teacher to reach out for help, and the manner of the response to the request as well as the course of the relationship with that teacher are matters of which other teachers become aware. This is not to say that the particular teacher acts as a reporter of details to the other teachers, but rather that the establishment of a working relationship with a teacher is inevitably perceived by the other teachers. (The goldfish-bowl nature of the school is a fact of life that has its positive as well as negative aspects.) The teacher with whom an initial working relationship is established does talk to other teachers, and discussion among teachers begins to shape the behavior and attitudes of these teachers toward the psychologist. What deserves particular emphasis is our opinion that what one teacher conveys to the others has less to do with whether any change has been effected in a child (or in the teacher) than with the teacher's perception of the psychologist's degree of motivation to understand and help, his acceptance of the teacher as an equal, and the clarity with which he makes clear his own limitations in knowledge and tentativeness of his thinking and approach. Thus in the early weeks the major concern of teachers is whether they can "talk" with the psychologist and not whether they or the children will receive help. This, of course, is precisely the major concern of the psychologist in regard to the teachers and central to the objective of developing a situation of mutual trust.

In subsequent chapters we present numerous examples of our work in the schools, examples that testify to our having been able to establish in many schools those kinds of relationships that facilitated the development and acceptance of our services. It will be apparent to the reader that many of them could not have occurred had we not success-fully handled the port-of-entry problem. We must point out at this time that although we were successful in the large majority of schools with which we initiated an affiliation there were some schools with which the affiliation had to be terminated. These examples are dis-cussed in Chapter 14.

It was by no means easy to decide how best to organize our school material to convey clearly to the reader the ways in which we worked and the problems encountered. Some of the problems lend themselves to meaningful categorization, whereas others have a degree of spec-ificity, or a degree of infrequency, that makes grouping difficult and possibly misleading. After much thought we decided to choose and group case material in ways that would give the reader a picture of several things: the nature of our relationships with school personnel, the kinds of problems with which teachers are confronted, the manner in which teachers respond to and are affected by these problems, our own perception of problems and issues, and aspects of the school cul-ture that have to be considered in the development of comprehensive mental-health programs in the school setting. All of the material in these chapters is taken from our work *in* the schools. In a later chapter we discuss similar material in the context of our work with individual children at our Clinic.

Chapter 6

Teaching Is a Lonely Profession

Although a teacher is in a room throughout the entire day with 20 or more children, teaching is basically a lonely profession. A teacher presents material to children, and she may correct their work. On occasion, she may share a child's ambitions, his fantasies, or his worries, but it is rare that a teacher has the opportunity to discuss her problems or her successes in teaching with anyone else. There is certainly no formal structure for the discussion of the day-to-day concerns of the classroom. By and large, faculty meetings are devoted to issues of policy and to matters of general concern to the school. Depending on the school and the principal, faculty meetings may offer greater or lesser opportunities for open interchange of ideas. In one school general faculty meetings were not held. In another the meetings consisted almost entirely of the principal reading dicta and memoranda coming from supervisory personnel, from the PTA, or from the superintendent and the board of education. Teachers have nothing equivalent to the case conference in a clinic or social agency.

With some exceptions, subject-matter supervisors seem to be generally disliked by many of the teachers. Either they do not come to the schools at all, or when they do come they bring new materials which are, in effect, handed down to the teachers. Sometimes the new materials are useful, but teachers tend to feel subject-matter supervisors are primarily concerned with seeing that their subject-matter area receives adequate coverage in the teacher's day. The teacher sometimes feels she must continually squeeze more and more into the day without being able to take the time to do what she feels is important. First-grade teachers feel that reading is the most important subject they teach, but supervisory personnel are continually making demands for the inclusion of science, social studies, fine arts, and other subjects. One teacher in an inner-city school, struggling with a difficult upper-grade class, said the only comment she received from a supervisor who visited her class was that one child was chewing gum! Another said she was told she must improve the discipline in her class, but no one told her what to do. By and large the teachers do not seem to feel that supervisors are aware of or interested in their problems, and they resent the frequent recommendation coming from supervisors that *teachers* need in-service training. At a faculty meeting at which a training series was announced a teacher passed a note around the room asking why there was no in-service training for supervisors.

For various reasons the principals do not usually serve as confidantes for the teachers. Principals evaluate the teachers. A teacher is free of the threat of losing her position once she attains tenure, but until that time she feels that her situation depends on the principal's judgment, and she is not likely to take her problems to him. Even after a teacher attains tenure, she is evaluated by the principal. Promotions or regular salary increments are frequently dependent on the principal's approval.

Principals do not usually define their own jobs as including helping teachers work out solutions to problems faced in the classroom. In some cases principals are so busy with other duties they never get to the classrooms. In one school the principal regularly handles issues initiated by parents by defending the teacher to the parent, criticizing the teacher for inadequate handling of the problem, and then changing the child's class or program. On other occasions a principal may be very helpful in arranging for the services of the school psychologist or the school social worker but rarely views a request for help from the teacher as a request *to him* for help in managing the problem. From the definition of the situation and the relationship between the principal and the teacher the principal does not usually serve as the person a teacher turns to for purposes of thinking out loud.

It is surprising, but teachers tend not to talk to each other about their children except for superficial comments about a child's brightness or their difficulty in handling him. A teacher rarely consults a child's former teacher for help. Each teacher seems to believe the deficiencies she finds in a child have been caused by inadequate teaching on the preceding level. Clearly, if the former teacher did a poor job, there is no sense in consulting her. Similarly, a teacher does not dare to approach next year's teacher to offer advice, because by tradition next year's teacher inevitably will feel this year's teacher has been at fault. This is not to say that teachers do not cooperate with one another in managing children. They frequently do, and very effectively, but such cooperation occurs informally, and the opportunity is limited by the attitudes of the principal as well as the atmosphere in the school.

Lunch-hour conversation is rarely about children. A few teachers have lunch-hour duties and have no opportunity to confer with colleagues. Others feel the need for a break and will leave the building. In some schools the teachers' lounge is so small it serves no useful purpose. During the lunch hour teachers get together in small groups, but they tend to discuss husbands, clothes, grandchildren, curtains, and recipes. Less often are the informal contacts concerned with questions of managing children. Educational developments may receive some attention when the teachers exchange ideas about how to introduce new materials received from a supervisor, but there seems to be little spontaneous discussion or concern with education as such. It is certainly not because problems do not arise or that teachers' feelings do not become involved with their children. Even in the best of our suburban schools teachers have their concerns about their children. On one occasion a teacher reported having nightmares about a child at the same time the child's mother reported that the child was having nightmares about his teacher. A teacher who has a pupil who seems to be fearful of her is pained. Teachers want to do a good job with their children, and when a child does not seem to be learning the teacher can develop considerable guilt and anxiety. Moreover, in a system that relies heavily on achievement tests to evaluate the goodness of the teaching program, a pupil who is not learning may even become a threat to the teacher because he will pull down her class average.

In inner-city schools the problems are compounded. Because the pressures are greater the teachers respond with stress symptoms. One school seemed to have something like an informal tranquilizer club, with members going to each other for Miltown and Librium. Many reported visiting physicians because of tension symptoms. Children who are stubborn, provocative, or disruptive sometimes provoke rage reactions in the teachers. In other instances neglected children arouse feelings of pity and helplessness. Although the sense of stress is related to the total situation, often the most prominent element in the situation is the behavior of one or two children who are particularly difficult for the teacher to handle or to tolerate.

Except for complaints, and with some notable exceptions, teachers do not consult one another for help with problems. This is all the more surprising because in those instances in which mutual help is arranged in informal fashion it is highly effective. A kindergarten class was a frequent repository for several children who had difficulty remaining in their own classes or who for one reason or another either refused to go or were not wanted on trips. A first-grade teacher who had good rapport with a difficult second-grade child took him into her room when his class had a substitute teacher. Other similar examples can be described.

In inner-city schools each teacher has her share of problems, and there is little need for someone to take on more. Moreover, in some situations the value system is such that each teacher is expected to handle her own problems. A teacher would never ask for help because it would be an admission of inadequacy. In some situations teachers are suspicious of one another, and a request for help is sometimes interpreted as an attempt to dump or unload a problem. In consequence, except in isolated instances, teachers do not consult each other or share their problems in managing children to any extent. It is as if each is supposed to manage her own situation without calling on anyone else for advice.

Spouses may sometimes serve as listeners and advisors, but it is our impression that such an avenue is not available to many teachers. Male teachers frequently have additional jobs. Being fathers, they are concerned with their own families. Their wives may have enough to talk about concerning their own children to be unable to be sympathetic listeners. Married women may or may not have husbands who are interested. Many teachers seem to be married to small businessmen who put in long hours. A husband who has no familiarity with the teaching situation may not be able to contribute to a discussion effectively. In a few instances we have come across teachers who said they welcomed the opportunity to talk to someone about their children because after all these years their husbands were no longer interested in listening.

In this situation the consultant, who has no evaluative function and who does not stand in a competitive relationship to the teacher, is one person who can break through the loneliness of the situation. Even when a teacher is handling a problem effectively he can serve by recognizing her competence and sharing the accomplishment with her. Moreover, it must be recognized that teaching is an exhausting profession in the sense that the teacher is constantly called on to give, and she does not often receive much in return. Of course, there is the sense of accomplishment in seeing a child grow, but the accomplishment is insufficient in and of itself to serve as the day-by-day replenishment for what is given out. Each of us wants a certain amount of approval, appreciation, and admiration, but the teacher requires such nutriment because she is constantly called on to give of herself to others. Sometimes the consultant's major function is simply to observe, encourage, and approve the teacher's effort.

Example 1.[1] The first encounter between Mrs. S. and P. took place on the last day of the school year, when the children went to their new classes to meet their next year's teachers. P., an eight-year-old Negro girl in the third grade, walked up to Mrs. S. and said, "I don't like you. I don't want to be here." Mrs. S., a veteran of 37 years of teaching, much of it in inner-city schools, without batting an eyelash, replied, "That's all right with me. I didn't ask for you, and you can go right in and tell the principal."

Mrs. S. later told the consultant she thought about that child through much of the summer, partly dreading the encounter, but also looking forward to it because Mrs. S. is a person with a masterful understanding of children and how to relate to them. Throughout the school year the consultant's contacts with the child were limited to a few sessions for psychological testing, two interviews with the child's mother, and occasional contacts with the child in the classroom when he came to visit. As a consequence of his contacts with the child, the consultant was able to tell the teacher that the child was of normal intelligence, and he elaborated on his observation that the child was walled off from affective contact with others. She needed to develop trust in an adult, and she seemed to need to be shown off as a worthwhile person. In this instance the suggestions were never translated into any specific program for the child because the teacher did not seem to need such specific direction. (The consultant did manage to see the teacher almost every week, if only for a few minutes.) The minimal activity of the consultant in relation to the child is here emphasized because his predominant service was as an observer and as an approver of the teacher's truly magnificent efforts with this child.

Mrs. S. noted that P. would often come into school in a bad mood in the mornings, and that when she was in a bad mood she would be aggressive, would steal from other children, and would refuse to work. Mrs. S. made it a point to greet P. at the door when she came in each morning. Whenever she noted that the child seemed angry, she would tell her she was not permitted in the room until she washed the anger from her face. She would then send her down to the lavatory literally to wash her face. On occasion, when this treatment did not serve to change the child's mood, Mrs. S. would tell her that she could see that the anger was deep within P. on that day, and she would make arrangements for the child to help with tasks

---

[1] Elsewhere we discuss the formation of teacher discussion groups, and in the Appendix we present the verbatim transcripts of four such meetings. Many of the issues to be discussed and illustrated in the present and subsequent chapters are also contained in the transcripts, sometimes with a clarity and poignancy not always found in our examples. In terms of our aim to convey to the reader certain aspects of the school culture, the transcripts in the Appendix will be found by the reader to be unusually illuminating.

around the room or she would let her go to the kindergarten next door after she had completed a minimum of school work.

When in a bad mood, the child would sometimes copy work from another child next to her. Mrs. S.' attitude about copying was as follows: "If she is copying the work, she has some chance of learning it and she is complying with my demands. Why should I start a fight with her about a moral issue which has no meaning to her at this time?"

Mrs. S. always maintained classroom decorum with this child, calling her down as necessary, letting her know when she had misbehaved, but always tempering the negative aspects of the relationship by giving the child something concrete following a session in which she had cause to discipline her. Mrs. S. always insisted the child speak politely to her, calling her by name, and saying "Excuse me" when she interrupted a conversation. Whenever the consultant was present, Mrs. S. would call P. up to the front of the room to show off her paper or to do some work on the blackboard. Both consultant and teacher would praise her for such efforts, but the teacher also would make it a point to review some of the difficult behavior she had experienced with P. while P. was there. At the end of such a review she would give the child a hug, sometimes a cookie or some other little favor, and express her confidence that P. was coming along and would continue to come along.

Mrs S. had no qualms about giving this child extra privileges or extra attention as she felt necessary. For example, the child indicated she would like to do her work on the blackboard. The teacher explained she could not let her do the work on the blackboard before the other children finished their work because they would copy from her, but after the others finished she could do her work on the blackboard if she chose to do so. With time, Mrs. S. increased her demands on the child, making certain privileges contingent upon her completing her school work. For example, she made P. a "student teacher" who could assist the kindergarten teacher but only if she finished her work. When the child wanted to change her seat to be next to the brightest girl in the class, Mrs. S. recognized that P. wanted to identify with that child. Not only did she permit the change of seat, but she interpreted the child's desire to be like the other girl to the child, telling her she could also be a good student.

It was not until early spring that the effort really began to pay dividends for the teacher and for the child. By then, a great deal, but by no means all, of the child's aggressive and negativistic behavior dropped out. She became much more docile in class, and she was working effectively. Her reading and writing improved considerably, and her arithmetic became quite good. Her motivation toward work had changed so that she would actually ask to be permitted to stay after school so that she could get a head start on her work for the next day. At one point the little girl made a Mother's Day card for her teacher in which she spontaneously expressed her love for the teacher. The teacher showed the card to the consultant with a manner that seemed to combine her pleasure, her pride, and her humility in receiving the tribute from the child. It may have been enough for the teacher to have received the hand-made card, but it also seemed to add to its value for her to show it to the consultant and to others. At another time the teacher shared an incident with the consultant in which the child had asked her how to spell the word "beat." Later she discovered that the girl had sent a note to her neighbor saying, "I'll beat your ass after school." The teacher enjoyed the way in which the girl had used her to help write the note. The consultant was properly appreciative at the good-humored way in which the teacher dealt with the incident and the way in which she reported it. Each time there was a new development the teacher was able to use the consultant to show off her accomplishment, and the consultant expressed his very honest amazement, his pleasure, and his very real admiration at the accomplishment. It was not until the end of the year was near that the consultant raised the possibility of additional help for the child. The issue was raised with the teacher because she did not feel she could do anything about the child the following year when she was no longer in her class. She felt it would be important for the child to promote her. At this time the consultant raised the issue of next year with the child, and with her mother, pointing out that the child's progress was due entirely to the teacher's remarkable efforts with her. Mother and child were told that we fully anticipated her progress would continue, but she would have to adapt to a new teacher whom she might or might not like so well as her present teacher. The consultant then arranged for a graduate student, who would be interning the following year, to begin developing a relationship with her while the school situation was still highly positive. The relationship with the graduate student was not initiated until very close to the end of the year. For the teacher the beginning of therapy was helpful, not because she needed help with the child but because it expressed the consultant's feeling about how important her work had been with the child. It also was a concrete indication that the child would not simply be forgotten and the teacher's efforts gone for no purpose.

Throughout the year the consultant had very few important clinical contacts with the child. True, he was hovering in the background, and the child was aware of his interest, but it was the child's relationship with the teacher that clearly was critical. The consultant also made no specific suggestions to the teacher about handling the child. He listened to what the teacher reported, sympathized when she complained about the effort the child required, and enthused when she had positive progress to report. Sometimes when the teacher innovated her own technique, for example reflecting and interpreting the child's feelings of anger through the concrete medium of asking her to wash the anger from her face, the teacher looked to the consultant who gave her reassurance that her technique was effective. When one morning the child finally told the teacher that she was angry on entering the classroom the consultant was able to interpret the change as a highly positive indication of the effectiveness of what the teacher was doing. His main function was one of supporting the teacher's efforts by sharing and appreciating her accomplishments. As the teacher expressed it to the consultant, "You're like my pick-me-up, like a cocktail in the afternoon."

Numerous other examples in which the consultant served as the source of approval and as a person who shared accomplishment can be cited. A kindergarten teacher who excitedly called out to the consultant across the hall that her silent child had talked for the first time expressed the joy in sharing accomplishment with a colleague very vividly. Another, who proudly told how she had solved a problem with one child herself by arranging that he spend half days in the kindergarten and half days in her first grade, wanted and received approval from the consultant for her efforts. It is perfectly clear the teacher wants and deserves support and approval for a good job well done. As indicated, in most instances there is no formal channel for receiving the recognition, because few people are aware of how a teacher handles given problems. By definition, if a teacher is handling a problem herself, it is not a problem. That no one knows how well she is doing, except the child, is an unfortunate accident of the structure of the teaching situation and of customs that dictate that teachers do not discuss their problems or their techniques with each other, and of an implicit competitive attitude existing among teachers.

The teacher's desire for approval may sometimes become a difficulty in the relationship with the consultant. The consultant may not relate well to the particular teacher, or in fact he may not feel that the teacher is handling a situation particularly well. It is sometimes difficult to disguise these feelings or to maintain the therapeutic attitude of trying to understand the other person's viewpoint. For some teachers who are highly sensitive and who expect criticism from authority even relatively innocent questions or remarks from the consultant can lead to hurt feelings and anxious moments. The consultant's efforts to have the teacher reflect on her own experience with a child can also create anxious moments. Teachers do not share the mental-health worker's assumption that their own feelings are involved in the relationship with a child, and questions directed toward eliciting the teacher's affective involvement with a child can be quite threatening because they imply to the teacher that somehow she is wrong in the way she feels.

Example 2. A teacher had referred a sixth-grade boy for psychological examination because she felt he was a potential murderer. In discussing the boy with the consultant, the teacher pointed out that there was nothing she could put her finger on to substantiate that the boy was hostile, but she could see it in his eyes. Psychological testing revealed an introverted youngster of good intelligence and in good contact with reality. There was nothing in the testing to substantiate a view of the boy as a potential murderer, although, of course, evidence from testing is far from conclusive. The consultant continued to follow the boy with the teacher. On several occasions when the consultant visited the classroom the boy participated as much as one might expect a quiet, careful, proud boy to participate with a rather outspoken, lively, somewhat excitable teacher. The teacher continued to feel that he was hostile toward her and that he was passively resistant, deliberately holding back from giving anything to her.

At one conference between teacher and consultant the teacher was expressing her sense of frustration and anger in working with the boy. She spoke about how she felt like smashing him because of what she took to be his sullen, defiant, angry, suspicious resistance of her. The consultant sensed the teacher was overreacting to this boy and attempted to call the over-reaction to her attention. The consultant felt he had had a rather positive working relationship with the teacher, but apparently he overestimated the strength of the relationship or he was clumsy in reflecting his view back to her. When the teacher reacted quite defensively to a comment about her feelings toward the boy, the consultant backed away by offering her an intellectual explanation of how people who worked with others frequently found their own feelings were involved. The teacher seemed to accept his explanation, but for several weeks afterwards, half in jest and half seriously, she would make some remark to the consultant about how he was trying to find out if she was crazy and if she was the one who needed help.

Example 3. A teacher had referred a child for evaluation because he was not working well in her classroom. In trying to have the teacher elaborate on her perception of the problem, the consultant asked the teacher how she felt about the child. The teacher stiffened slightly at the question and repeated her previous description of the child. Shortly after the referral was made the boy's mother came to school to appeal for help because of his behavior at home and because she and her husband were on the verge of separating. Because it seemed to be a crisis situation, the consultant immediately assigned the graduate student who was doing the psychological evaluation to work with the child in psychotherapy. The consultant and graduate student stayed in close touch with the teacher and by the time testing was completed, and a report was ready, the three had developed a good working relationship. At the very beginning of the meeting the teacher asked if it would be all right if she said something. Given assent, the teacher expressed her anxiety and resentment of the consultant's question about how she felt about the child. From her viewpoint the question implied that either she was at fault in the child's problem or that she had teacher's pets in her class. Both alternatives were threatening and insulting to her. When she expressed her feelings, the consultant was able to thank her for clearing the air, and he then was able to explain that his question was part of his diagnostic procedure.

The consultant was grateful to the teacher for bringing up the issue because it might otherwise have been a block to communication. In the school culture provision may be made for individual differences, but apparently the mores are such that the teacher may not permit herself to feel differently about different children. She accepts the assumption of the classroom that a teacher is equally effective with all children in her room, despite the reality that she and each of the children have different personalities.

Sometimes the consultant may not make a direct suggestion concerning management of a child because he is not certain of what to do, because he feels the teacher is not the sort of person who would accept the suggestion he would make in the situation, or because he feels on philosophical grounds that the teacher can best be helped to work out her own solutions to the problems. The view that a teacher can work out her own solutions may lead the consultant to ask the teacher what she thinks ought to be done when she asks for help, despite the fact that the request for help comes at a point when the teacher is at her wit's end with a child. Even though the consultant may attempt to be quite reassuring, the teacher may experience his efforts as a form of criticism of her.

Example 4. A teacher referred a third-grade child who seemed bright and came from a large family with a young mother who seemed overwhelmed by her responsibilities and unable to keep her children really clean and well fed. Classroom observation suggested the child was somewhat compulsive, stubborn, slow, and a daydreamer. He would do well on a test in which the teacher was face to face with him and in which the presentation of material was paced, but he could not work alone. The teacher found she could get him to work only by constantly reminding him to get on with what he was doing or by staying near him, but otherwise he would do nothing. When she asked the consultant for further suggestions, he had a tendency to turn the question back to her. After some weeks had gone by the teacher began complaining more and more that nothing was happening with the child and that he was getting worse, although observation did not reveal any striking change in his behavior. Finally, the teacher stated that the consultant's visits made her exceedingly anxious. She felt as if he expected her to help the child and to report progress to him, but she did not know what to do, did not see progress, and she experienced the consultant's visits as making demands on her which made her feel as if she were responsible for the child's failure. As one consequence of the interaction, the teacher seemed to experience the child as a burden and a threat, which made it more difficult for her to reach out to him.

All teachers experience strong feelings of liking, anger, and despair in relation to some of their children. A conscientious teacher may sometimes go well beyond what anyone would require of her to try and work effectively with a child in her class. Sometimes in her efforts to help the teacher may go beyond the limits of tradition and do so with excellent judgment, timing, and considerable success. Nonetheless, the very fact that she does something unconventional can be anxiety-provoking. The consultant may be the one person with whom it is possible to discuss the problem, either because of the content of the problem or because he has no direct concern with the administrative rules and regulations of the school.

Example 5. A girl of about 12 who may have been a borderline psychotic and who revealed exceedingly poor judgment on occasion reached menarche without having received any information from her mother or any instruction about how to care for herself. One day she began bleeding in class and became quite excited and gleeful. The teacher, an exceptionally cool, resourceful, and intuitive person, immediately took the girl aside, took a sanitary pad and belt which she kept in her desk for emergencies, and took the girl to the teacher's lavatory. There she instructed the girl in how to care for her person and in how to use the belt and pad. She told her something about the menstrual cycle and was able to caution her about being somewhat more circumspect about her person.

The teacher related the incident to the consultant a day or so after it had happened. She had done the most reasonable thing she could do, particularly since she was the one who had an effective relationship with the child, and because the school nurse was not present in the building. She had succeeded in her efforts with the girl, but in relating the issue she indicated that she had gone well beyond what would usually be expected of a teacher, and she had handled a problem at best delicate, and even taboo, in the school. On the one hand she seemed confident and pleased that she had acted as she did, but on the other hand she was somewhat concerned about the incident, and she welcomed the opportunity to share it with the consultant.

Probably the most difficult situations arise when the teacher is concerned about managing an aggressive, negativistic, and provocative child. Sometimes the provocation seems relatively mild from the point of view of an outsider, but the child may touch off near-violent feelings in the teacher. In considering the way in which feelings are expressed, the consultant must remember he is working with women who tend to be more freely expressive and self-revealing than men. Nonetheless, the consultant's relationship to the teacher may permit the cathartic expression of rather intense emotions.

Example 6. A first-grade child was a saucy and mincing young lady who would sometimes move slowly and deliberately in rather theatrical fashion, making everyone wait on her. She also did not do her work in class, tending to daydream away her time, or complain that she was too tired. The consultant and teacher both knew that the little girl had experienced much illness in her family and that, in fact, in her own household she was a little prima donna. The teacher, a highly competent individual who shared some of the child's prima donnishness, found herself reacting almost with rage to this little girl. One afternoon, seeing the consultant in the building, she asked for a conference, during which she expressed the frustration and anger she felt with the little girl. After having permitted herself the rather uninhibited expression of her feelings, the teacher found herself amazed at the intensity of her reaction to the child and expressed guilt and shame about the situation. The consultant was able to be quite supportive of her in the situation, and throughout the rest of the term the teacher never again felt quite so distressed as she had on this one occasion.

In some instances teachers may be under strain from sources other than the classroom. Just as a child may bring problems from home to school, so may the teacher. A difficult child might not ordinarily trouble a teacher, but when the teacher is experiencing stress from other problems a difficult day with a child may be just enough to make "her cup run over."

Example 7. A highly competent teacher who was usually willing to work over long periods of time with difficult youngsters was loudly complaining about one little girl she had in her class. The child was very difficult to handle, being provocative and negativistic, and tending not to do anything correctly until the teacher insisted in a sharp and firm tone that she do what she was requested to do. The teacher not only complained to the consultant, but apparently she was expressing her feelings to a number of others in a way that led others to remark that she seemed under some unusual strain. The consultant listened while the teacher expressed her feelings of anger, her disgust with the little girl's dirty habits, and her wish to be rid of her. The teacher seemed overwrought, and at that point the consultant merely listened.

The following day the teacher seemed considerably more composed. Because he had a long-standing and mutually respectful relationship with the teacher, in what he meant to be a kidding way he asked the teacher if she were more rational today. The teacher responded in kind with kidding about her right to complain and to blow her stack. Whenever she saw the consultant throughout the day, at lunch or in the hallway, she made some remark about being more rational. Although she was able to accept the consultant's comment as he meant it, she was also somewhat distressed by what he had said. The following week the teacher indicated that there had been a death in her family, that she had been traveling out of town, and that she and her family were exhausted. The consultant's remark had distressed her, but it also served to make her aware of the degree to which she was displacing emotion into the classroom.

There is no question that teaching in an inner-city school is difficult. Frustration arises not only because many children are unresponsive or disruptive in the classroom situation but also because failure to have children respond as the teacher wishes strikes at her sense of competence. A new teacher may feel incompetent because she sees others handle the class well, or an old hand may feel incompetent because her class does not meet given standards. Schools have curricula and they have achievement tests. Having most of her children master the curriculum for the grade is the teacher's sign of achievement. Having most of her children meet or exceed grade norms on an achievement test is another form of feedback to the teacher that she is doing a good job. In many inner-city schools a substantial number of children will not meet these particular criteria of achievement. That the criteria are more or less arbitrary and that they represent average grade levels raised by the contribution from wealthier areas in which children typically score a year or more above grade norms is irrelevant to the teacher. From her position, if her children do not achieve grade norms either in terms of the curriculum or in terms of achievement tests, she may feel that she has failed and is inadequate as a teacher. Some teachers respond to this situation by attributing responsibility to the children or to the home. Although those who do project responsibility may defend against a feeling of inadequacy, the lack of feedback provided by children's classroom achievement is still present and contributes to poor morale. Others experience feelings of guilt or inadequacy and may respond with personal suffering or by attempting to drive the children. That there is usually no channel for expressing the feeling of inadequacy may contribute to its perpetuation.

Example 8. A teacher had referred a child for psychological examination because she suspected the child was slow. The child never volunteered anything in class and when called on did not seem to know what was going on. When the referral process started, the teacher chided the consultant because a previous written report had been delayed. Actually it was rather unimportant. The consultant and teacher had interviewed the parent of the child in question and had on several occasions discussed the findings and the recommendations in conference, the first one coming immediately after the testing was completed. A second interview had been completed with the child's mother to interpret the findings to her. Not much change had occurred in that case, partly because the child needed far more than that particular classroom could provide. On one occasion when the teacher continued to harp on the previous report, evidently attempting to make the consultant feel as if he had failed, the consultant expressed his annoyance at the teacher's remarks. He reminded the teacher of the previous conferences around the child, admitted not much had happened as a consequence of them, but he did not blame the teacher for failing with the child. He then asked her what her concern was about the report. Sensing the consultant's annoyance and recognizing that she had indeed overemphasized the importance of the written report, the teacher indicated how badly she felt when she could not help a child. The written report was evidence to her of the child's deficiencies and absolved her from feeling any blame for the child's failure to learn. She went on to express how she felt under pressure and how inadequate she felt when she could not achieve a desired result with her class. The teacher, a woman of 50 or so, with a normal-school education, said she became so discouraged at times that she wanted to quit. However, she felt she could do nothing else except take in laundry if she did quit, graphically expressing her feeling about herself in the situation. Her response to her feeling of guilt and the desire to give up and quit was to drive herself and her children harder and harder. Her conscience would not let her relax and ease up on a child who needed more support than censure. The consultant and teacher were able to talk about her sense of conscience and her tendency to try to force work from given children. Coming back to the child who was to be tested, the teacher and the consultant were able to work out a plan based on the principle of catching more flies with sugar than with vinegar. The teacher then worked very successfully with the child and later expressed her sense of satisfaction at the child's progress.

The process of becoming a teacher involves a series of academic and practical experiences that are both evaluated and supervised. Prospective teachers must complete a specified amount of course work and a period of student- or practice-teaching before being considered eligible or qualified to enter the teaching profession. Although there is a disproportionate amount of time spent on academic work, compared with practical experience (the period of time allotted to practice teaching usually consists of several weeks), the structure of the process utilized in training elementary school teachers is not too dissimilar from that employed in the training of clinical psychologists. In both professions prospective candidates must complete a specified amount of academic work as well as an "internship" period in which they are given the opportunity to practice their "trade" under the supervision and guidance of more experienced professionals. To be sure, differences exist between the professions in terms of the quality and intensity of the supervision available to the novice as well as in the duration of the formal period of apprenticeship. Structurally, however, both training processes have as their focus the preparation and training of professionals in a series of supervised and coordinated academic and practical experiences.

When the formal requirements of the course of study have been successfully completed and the teaching certificate has been granted, the role of "teacher" is assumed in a very real, immediate, and practical sense. Unless they wish to devote full time to advanced study, they usually are placed in teaching positions commensurate with their areas of specialization (in this case, elementary school). When this placement is made, the new teachers become members of a school faculty and assume the privileges and responsibilities of the professional. Although they do not achieve tenure on assuming a position as a faculty member (tenure usually is withheld for a period of approximately three years), the new teachers participate in almost all of the professional activities in which their colleagues are engaged. Most important, they are given "their own" classes and assume the responsibility for teaching the youngsters and for dealing with whatever problems arise in conjunction with the learning process. It is at this point that they become intimately involved in the teaching process and are confronted with the complexities and implications of the teaching situation and the teaching role. They now experience what it means to be a teacher on a daily basis and the manner in which being a teacher involves them in activities only partly defined by past experiences and training.

For many new teachers the sudden awareness of the complexity and range of their responsibilities comes as a rude awakening. They often must begin to function in areas and in ways for which they may feel they have been inadequately prepared. They must meet with parents, deal with the administration, and interact with their children along dimensions and in contexts they may not have experienced previously. They often must begin to function as applied psychologists and social workers as well as classroom teachers. In summary, new teachers are placed in situations in which the experience of teaching becomes embedded in an ongoing context that by its very nature is new and probably more complex than originally anticipated.

Under these conditions we might imagine that new teachers would require and have available even more ongoing support and supervision than heretofore had been the case. Unfortunately, the reverse is most often true. New teachers are not the beneficiaries of any continuous and formal supervisory relationship once they assume their positions as faculty members. In most cases the amount of supervision decreases and assumes the nature of periodic and infrequent visits by a roving supervisor who has neither the time nor the responsibility for maintaining a close and supportive relationship. More often than not teachers must seek guidance and help elsewhere and cannot rely on a supervisor to furnish such counsel, and fellow teachers have enough responsibilities and problems of their own.

One of the major problems confronting new teachers who feel somewhat overwhelmed by the responsibilities and complexities of full-time teaching is that, indeed, few resources are available within the school setting to meet their needs for an ongoing-in-service training period. Although they may turn to other teachers or to administrative personnel for such aid, there is little likelihood that they will receive supervision to the degree and extent they may feel is necessary. They are left essentially alone and must rely on their own resources and on whatever help they can derive from observing more experienced teachers.

Our work in the public schools has made us painfully aware of just how alone a teacher can feel within the school setting. This is true of all teachers, but it is particularly apparent in new or first-year teachers. For them the characteristic aloneness of the teacher is a relatively new experience, very different from their experiences as students in training. This, in and of itself, is not bad if we view independence of action and thought as fundamental requirements of the creative teacher. What does make the sudden aloneness a matter of concern is the way in which it occurs, the conditions under which it arises. In the first place, the aloneness occurs immediately and dramatically and without benefit of a period of transition in which they can be introduced systematically into the teaching situation. Second, they must deal with this aloneness in a period of time when they are confronted with a teaching situation that may bear very little relation to the kinds of supervised teaching experiences that had been available in the past.

New teachers respond to this sudden experience of aloneness in very different ways, depending both on the nature of their previous practice-teaching experiences and on the kinds of people they are as individuals. For some the situation is experienced as a welcome challenge, as a baptism of fire that has as its function the ritualistic completion of the process by which an individual symbolically and practically enters the teaching profession. For others the situation becomes a period of extreme stress and apprehension, a period characterized by the sudden realization of their essential aloneness and isolation in a situation which—despite its degree of similarity to or difference from previously experienced teaching situations—is infinitely more complex and anxiety-provoking than had been imagined.

What first-year teachers need most is someone to assume the function of providing a stable, supportive, and ongoing relationship—a relationship they can depend on to carry them through the transition period between the time of receiving the professional degree and the time they begin to experience themselves with a degree of professionalism. They need someone who will help them bridge the gap between their student days and their days as "real" teachers.

Example 9. Miss L., a first-year teacher in the public schools, approached her new teaching situation with all the enthusiasm and optimism of someone entering a new and coveted role. She had been looking forward to her first kindergarten class with a great deal of anticipation and youthful exuberance. As a person, Miss L. was a bright, sensitive, and eager young woman to whom teaching long had been the most important professional goal in her life. She had studied hard, done extra work on her own, and tried to prepare herself for the teaching situation in every possible way available to her within the structure of her professional training. The payoff was relatively soon in coming. From the first day of school she had fallen in love with her class, and they, in turn, had responded to her in very similar fashion. Her class was a lively, moving, and exciting place for both the students and the teacher.

After a few weeks it became relatively clear to both the teacher and ourselves that all was not sweetness and light in the kindergarten classroom. Although the vast majority of her children were enjoying school and doing quite well in class, a few children did not seem able to make the transition from home to school and the necessary adjustment in an adequate or satisfactory manner. A few of the children responded to the new situation in a markedly anxious, nervous, and frightened way. Their feelings and fears about the new situation often resulted in behavior that was disorganized and disorganizing, behavior that upset the normal routine and functioning of the class. The teacher was fully prepared for the fact that some children would have a more difficult time adjusting to the new situation than others, that they would do things and say things that both reflected their difficulties, yet had to be dealt with if the teacher were to maintain her control of the class. Consequently, the teacher was not terribly upset over the disruptive behavior manifested by most of the children who were experiencing entrance into the schoolroom situation with a high degree of difficulty. She felt that in time, with the proper amount of strength coupled with gentleness and understanding, she could help these children to deal with their difficulties and make a more satisfactory adjustment to the kindergarten setting. Indeed, time proved her to be correct. With the exception of one child she was able to deal with the difficulties experienced by the children who were having a hard time settling down.

The one child who could not or would not respond to the teacher's efforts at integrating her into the classroom situation was as veritable a terror as could be imagined. She was a little girl who apparently was unable to inhibit or control her tendency to act out in ways that were often frightening and dangerous. From the moment she came into the classroom in the morning to the time she left at noon she was virtually uncontrollable. She could not remain seated for any length of time and continually interrupted the class quiet periods by running around the room and forcibly intruding herself into the lives of the other children. With very little or no provocation she would strike out at the other children, push the little boys, tear up someone's paper, or pull another girl's hair. She did these things with an air of frantic movement, almost as if some internal stimuli were forcing her to act abruptly, immediately, and with little regard for the welfare of whomever she came in contact with. Often, either before or after such an assault, she would scream in a high-pitched shrill voice. Her behavior was extremely frightening, apparently to herself as well as to the other children.

From the teacher's point of view the behavior was also quite frightening. The little girl was terrorizing the other children and, in the process, was exhibiting the kind of behavior that made the teacher quite anxious. Miss L. was concerned over the welfare of the other children and feared that they might be physically or emotionally hurt by their encounters with the disturbed girl. Although she very much wanted to try to understand and help the little girl, she also felt a great responsibility to the other children in her classroom. Similarly, from her own point of view, she did not wish to allow a child to "run my classroom or control me."

As we indicated previously, however, the teacher was the kind of person who would not give up easily, especially when she perceived herself in a challenging situation with respect to a child. Consequently, she was not so prone as some other—perhaps more experienced, wiser, more hardened, or less exuberant—teachers might have been to try immediately to exclude the troublesome child from the classroom situation.

Although she was quite concerned with the prospect of losing control of her classroom, she was equally concerned with exploring any and all possibilities before resorting to exclusion as a means of handling the situation.

It is extremely important that the reader fully understand the predicament with which the teacher was faced. She was a first-year teacher, and control of her class was an important and realistic concern. She could expect that her roving supervisor would show up soon without giving the teacher the benefit of any advance notification. From the teacher's point of view the supervisor would evaluate her proficiency and performance mainly in terms of how well she was able to lead, supervise, and control her students. Another factor that weighed heavily on the teacher's mind was the anxiety-provoking nature of the little girl's classroom behavior. The behavior looked bizarre, frightening, and dangerous; and the teacher was not at all sure, even if she tried to work with the child within the classroom setting, that she would be able to help her. The behavior, as the teacher put it, was "an awful lot different from anything I've ever seen or had to deal with in either my practice teaching or observational experience." Still another factor in the situation was the teacher's feeling that she would not like to undertake anything with respect to the troubled child that would decrease or detract from the amount of time she had to devote to all the other children. She recognized the needs of the little girl but also felt that she had a responsibility to the other members of her class. Finally, there was the challenge: the teacher saw the child's condition as one that required a sensitive and talented person who could utilize the classroom situation as an appropriate context for therapeutic interventions. The teacher's feelings were, to say the very least, ambivalent. More than anything else, however, Miss L. was concerned with how she would be evaluated if she chose to "stay with it."

We shared the teacher's dilemma. She had made us acutely aware of the evaluative context that surrounded the new teacher. We now could understand the pressures under which she was functioning. A poor evaluation could have drastic consequences for her professional future. If the supervisor felt that the teacher could not maintain control of her class, her evaluation of the teacher would reflect this state of affairs, and such an evaluation could bode nothing but ill for the teacher's future career.

Miss L.'s concern with the implications of a "poor control of her class" evaluation was, as far as the present case was concerned, a very realistic one. In our discussions about the troubled child and in our conferences with the child's parents we had come to the conclusion that the behavior being exhibited by the child was somewhat understandable in the light of the girl's past experiences. For this little girl we both felt that going to school was being experienced, among other things, as a liberation from bondage, as a kind of freedom that never had been experienced in the past. This is not to suggest that we attributed all of the behavior to this variable, for much of what we had seen appeared too bizarre and too involved to be attributed to nothing but a child's experience of a new-found personal freedom. Nonetheless, from what we had been able to gather about the child's home environment we had reason to believe that much of the pressured hyperactivity and aggressive intrusiveness we were seeing was the child's way of exploring—of almost luxuriating in—a situation that brought with it a promise of greater personal freedom and expansiveness. The behavior was diametrically different from what the parents reported as characteristic of the child in the home situation. The home was a quiet, rigid, and austere one, a place in which "children are to be seen and not heard." Expansiveness was not tolerated, and the pervading atmosphere of the home was one in which noise was almost sinful. The more we learned about the child and the home, the more we felt what we were observing in the classroom was a child's sudden emergence from the confines of a long-enforced period of silence and restrictiveness.

After discussing the situation with the teacher, we both agreed that one of the most important learning experiences the child could have in kindergarten was the experience of finding out that there was a great area of acceptable and possible behavior between the two poles of complete restriction and anarchic freedom, that not all rules are irrational, unexplained, and limiting, and that the limits set on certain behaviors were not always arbitrary. We felt it important that the girl begin to experience structure as a condition that facilitated the appropriate expression of feelings and ideas in the classroom situation. We also agreed that in order for this to take place we would have to permit and tolerate a greater amount of acting out by the child, an amount greater than one might permit and tolerate from a child who had not been reared under conditions so oppressive and constricting.

When we had come to this conclusion, we still were confronted by the fact that if the teacher tolerated or allowed such acting out in front of her supervisor (and we knew that sooner or later the supervisor would be showing up) she would be laying herself wide open for a critical and possibly damaging series of professional evaluations. The teacher would be alone and extremely vulnerable before a supervisor who might not share her ideas or feelings about the situation, a supervisor who might be much more concerned with the control a new teacher exercised over her class than with the teacher's attempts to utilize the classroom situation as a therapeutic context for a particular child.

We felt it important that if the teacher did undertake the difficult task of helping this child she should not undertake it alone or experience herself as abandoned in the situation. We therefore raised with the teacher the possibility that we undertake the experiment as a joint venture between us, that we work together in the process of providing the little girl with the kinds of experiences we felt were necessary to help the child. We felt, however, that if we were to become involved in the situation we should commit ourselves to going the entire way with the teacher. From our point of view this meant several things. First, it meant that we would work with the teacher in the classroom each time we came to the school. We would work with the child and assist the teacher in any way that we could to ease the burdens that would be hers in the situation. Second, it meant that we also would function as a sort of buffer between the teacher and the supervisor. In this context we felt it important that the teacher not have to face the supervisor alone or be forced to explain her actions to the supervisor without the benefit of the presence of her accomplice in the setting. We would function as the consulting psychologist who would assume the burden of responsibility before the supervisor.

The teacher felt that under these conditions she would be more than willing to try to work with the child in the classroom rather than to take the easy way out by referring the child elsewhere for help. She felt that by really working together we could help the child and, at the same time, provide her with a learning experience of her own. More than anything else, however, the teacher no longer felt alone in the situation and as threatened by the supervisor who soon would be arriving on the scene. She would inform her supervisor of the situation and have the supervisor call us if we were not physically present in the classroom at that particular time. We would be working with the teacher; we would be sharing her anxieties; we would serve as the professional buffer between herself and her roving supervisor; and, hopefully, we would be sharing her joy in the accomplishment of a task which now appeared to be feasible.

The loneliness of the teaching profession is probably never more distressfully experienced than by new teachers who are suddenly confronted with thirty inner-city youngsters for the first time. Only rarely will another experienced teacher step forward with useful assistance. From other supervisors and curriculum assistants advice tends to be excessively general or tangential to the daily problems of the new teacher. Thus one supervisor told an inexperienced teacher with discipline problems to modulate her voice, and a consulting psychiatrist told another new teacher to use her sixth sense. Psychologists from our clinic tend to know the local school culture more than such supervisors and make time for detailed, repeated observation in the new teacher's classroom. We are, moreover, independent of the school system and exercise no evaluative function over the teacher. Our confidential relationship to new teachers therefore facilitates a low-anxiety, honest give-and-take with them in which we can learn about their loneliness and try to meet some of their needs.

A recurrent preoccupation of new teachers, in our experience, is their lack of confidence in organizing their classrooms in accordance with their own convictions and ideals when the prevailing school culture operates differently. Specifically, new teachers worry a great deal about how they can cope with their principal's disapproval of their own style of running the classroom. Thus in one school the principal categorically opposed any free play or recess period for children beyond kindergarten, even though the new teachers had found a fifteen-minute midmorning respite helpful in controlling their children and relaxing them. In another school the new teachers had been told by the principal to avoid discussing racial questions with the children, for there was enough dangerous protest in society without overwhelming the classroom with it as well. Such unreasonable pronouncements by a principal can be extremely demoralizing for a new teacher who may perceive herself as being deprived by such directives of effective instructional and disciplinary procedures. In such cases we have counseled teachers to re-examine their own positions and those of their principals carefully; if they believed themselves in the right, they were advised to stick up for their position politely but firmly. A kind of authoritative support was lent them by the psychologist whose attitude was not one of contempt for the principal's authority but one of respect for the professional dignity of the individual teacher.

Example 10. A weekly meeting was held at the Clinic by the psychologist for the teachers inexperienced in teaching inner-city children at a particular junior high school. The group met continuously for two years; of the original four teachers, two remained at the school during the second year when they were joined in the group by four other new teachers. The group had the dual purpose of allowing teachers to present problem children on whom they desired advice and of providing a forum in which teachers could discuss more general instructional and disciplinary concerns. The psychologist's role as leader was flexible; at times he was relatively inactive while stimulating the expression of feeling and opinion by the teachers; at times he more directly interpreted the ongoing behavior of the group or commented on the teachers' approach to the questions at hand. The general tenor of the group was informal and freely expressive, everyone being on a first-name basis, but little time was spent on pleasantries and chatter. The group meetings supplemented the in-school consultation provided by the psychologist who limited membership to relatively new teachers with the blessing of the principal who excused the teachers from remaining after school so that they might attend the meetings. During the first five or six meetings in each of the two years the new teachers chose not to discuss particular children, focusing instead on their difficulties with the principal, an older man who made their lives miserable from time to time. Under the cloak of confidentiality, the female teachers railed at length against their principal's episodic criticisms of them in front of their children and brusque barging into the classroom to teach a lesson for a few minutes while they stood by flabbergasted. They objected to the principal's old-school emphasis on the children's motionless silence, cleanliness, and stilted politeness. They also objected to the not-too-subtle intolerance of the principal of the unstable home conditions and parents of their children. They described themselves as being in a perpetual state of embarrassment, resentment, and fear over their principal's visits to the classroom and encounters in the hall. In the course of these beratings of the principal the psychologist initially encouraged the teachers to ventilate their feelings, and the teachers took heart in the congruence of feeling among their number. Then the psychologist encouraged the teachers to consider reasons for the principal's behavior, suggesting that they were under as much obligation to understand and even influence his behavior as they were with disturbed children. Every attempt to puzzle out the causes of their principal's behavior was underlined by the psychologist, and soon the teachers were acknowledging the diffi-

culties of their principal and even his assets which were in reality not absent
His panicky reaction to stresses placed on him by his own supervisors and
the press of certain school crises were elucidated by the teachers. His
begrudging witness to the deterioration over years of the community around
his school was noted by the teachers as an understandable factor in his
hostility. His fear of a real give-and-take conversation with his teachers was
also discussed. The group decided to reflect on his injunctions in the future
and if they found them unacceptable they would politely but firmly stand
their ground. The psychologist highlighted the way in which the teachers
had allowed their professional dignity to lay fallow amidst their understandable insecurity and fearful respect of authority. The teachers agreed to
concert their efforts in demanding humane treatment as well as praising the
principal whenever he was genuinely correct or helpful. The principal was
subsequently told by them individually at the time of a recurrence that a
teacher and her class are hurt by public criticisms. The teachers also
complimented the principal on the stable disciplinary tone he had set in the
school. Good-natured firmness was the rule. In a matter of weeks the
principal's behavior in relation to the new teachers with rare exceptions
became more civilized. The teachers also applied two further rules in
working with the principal. First, they no longer complained to him about
slow learners or disruptive children, for they had come to see how this could
only stimulate in their limited principal the wish to unload such children
in a special class in order to reduce class size. Instead they worked their
problems through with the group and the consulting psychologist, for the
protection of the child and themselves. Second, they derived from their
handling of the principal a model for psychological functioning with their
own children in the classroom: rather than condemn a problem and suffer
smoldering feeling, try to understand it and influence it with a variety of
encouraging and standing-ground techniques. Now that they were making
progress in liberating themselves from their principal's yoke, the new
teachers became less sarcastic about him, and they reported enjoying both
their classroom freedom and, ironically, their principal considerably more.
Subsequent group meetings centered on the teachers' educational and
emotional questions.

It has been our intent in this chapter to show that teachers come
face to face with highly difficult problems that elicit strong feelings
and require thoughtful decisions. The social structure of the elementary school is such that teachers have little opportunity to air some of
their feelings or to think out loud with others who are familiar with
the teaching situation and who may be able to help them to think of
new and different ways of approaching the critical psychological problems they face daily. As we have tried to indicate, the teaching situation is a lonely one, and one that requires that the teacher give
constantly. There is little in the teaching situation that serves to re-

plenish the daily depletions in demanding work with children. The loneliness is probably more pronounced in inner-city schools, where the number of problems is greater in the classroom and where teachers are aware that the school is a social arena in which they are under constant criticism. Because the situation is a lonely one, the support the consultant can provide is important if he does nothing more than share the problem with the teacher.

The contents of this chapter may have given the reader some inkling of how staff members function in the schools. In subsequent chapters we focus more explicitly on the consultant's activities and try to give as detailed a picture as we can of what actually transpired. The events are described as we saw them happen or as they were described to us by teachers, principals, parents, and children. We have, of course, in all instances introduced disguises and changes, as necessary, to protect confidences and to avoid embarrassment to anyone.

Chapter 7

Helping to Change the Teacher's Perception of a Problem

Teachers, no less than psychologists, are both the beneficiaries and the victims of their own perceptual and cognitive activity. In the process of teaching, teachers form judgments about their children and tend to act toward them in ways consistent with these judgments. A teacher, with very little help and under the most difficult of circumstances, must evolve hypotheses about many children and their problems. This in itself, given the conditions under which most teachers work, is a difficult task. However, once the teacher has evolved some idea of the nature of a child's difficulties she will usually deal with that child in ways consistent with the hypotheses. Many times the teacher will be correct in her perceptions, and her behavior toward a particular child will be both relevant and helpful. At other times, however, she may evolve a more or less inaccurate picture of a child, one that is more a reflection of the conditions under which it was formed than it is of the nature and content of the child's difficulties. Once these impressions have been formed, it becomes extremely difficult not to act in ways that reinforce these perceptions. When these situations occur, the teacher responds—or fails to respond—to the child in terms of her ideas about the nature of the child's difficulties, and it is sometimes very difficult for her to alter her initial impressions.

We have become aware how often limited amounts of knowledge and information are available to teachers with respect to their pupils. Consequently, one of the ways in which we have been functioning in the schools has been to work with teachers in examining the conditions and assumptions involved in making judgments about children and, wherever it has appeared to be relevant and helpful, to help the teacher reorganize her perception of a child and his problems.

THE "HANDS-OFF" PHENOMENON

Once a child has been diagnosed as emotionally disturbed, or if a teacher is aware that a child is under treatment, she has a distinct tendency to feel she is either unable or unqualified to deal with the problem the child presents in the classroom. She is concerned lest she do something harmful to the child or is flustered by the knowledge that she is dealing with someone who may be different. In the absence of continued direction from the clinic, or from the therapist who is working with the child, the teacher's tendency is to minimize her contact with the child. Minimizing contact rarely helps and often may be positively harmful to the child, to the classroom, and to the teacher's mental health because she places herself in a situation in which she feels powerless. This tendency to avoid dealing with an emotionally disturbed child we call the "hands-off" phenomenon.

Example 1. The consultant had been working with a ten-year-old boy who had a history of being a troublemaker in the neighborhood since he was very small. He had been under fairly good control in the school until he was placed in a classroom with a first-year teacher who did not know how to deal with him. On a diagnostic visit to the classroom the consultant observed that the boy had little respect for the teacher's authority. He was openly defiant of her, playing to other boys in the class who enjoyed his antics, and at times refusing to do his work. The teacher was distressed, and the boy's school work was rapidly becoming poorer.

Because this child and several others were falling behind in their work, the principal arranged for an experienced male teacher to take the group of fifth graders for arithmetic while the new teacher continued to have the children for all other subjects. The consultant was aware of the changed arrangements, but because he had complete confidence in the male teacher's ability to work with the boy and to control him (he had worked with him previously on other cases) the consultant was lax in seeking a conference with the teacher until several weeks had passed. When the consultant finally stopped by to talk to the teacher, he discovered, much to his surprise, that the boy was not working in the male teacher's class either. When asked what was happening, the male teacher stated he was getting angrier and angrier at the boy's defiant and insolent manner, but he felt he could not interfere at all because he knew the consultant had been working with the boy and his original teacher. At this point, the consultant told the male teacher simply to use his instincts as a teacher in working with the boy. The teacher thereupon adopted a firmer stance. Within a week the boy's attitude had changed, and he was working satisfactorily in his arithmetic class.

In some instances the quality of a child's behavior and verbalizations may put a teacher off. She may fail to see the disruptive aspects of the behavior because she is focused on what appears to be florid psychopathology.

Example 2. A kindergarten teacher asked the consultant to come into her class to observe a little boy whom she described as severely disturbed because he was constantly talking about monsters. He did not seem to be fearful, but she felt that he enjoyed the monsters in some perverse fashion. He talked of little else, even indicating that the furniture in his house moved in threatening ways and that at night he could see and hear the walls moving and making noise. She said that he sometimes attacked other children in the class in an unprovoked fashion, but at this time she did not indicate the extent to which this little boy was following his own program in her classroom.

When the consultant came into the classroom to observe, he discovered that the child was almost completely on his own. He stayed in the back of the room, playing with whatever toys he desired, ignoring activities in the room except to walk up to some other child and take something away from him. The teacher hardly commented at all. At one point, for no reason whatsoever, the boy bounded past a little girl and smacked her in the face. On a second visit the consultant made an attempt to play with the child in the classroom. The child related easily, but it soon became clear that he was manipulative and would do things only on his own terms. He would test as far as he could and would act in a negativistic fashion, but when the consultant spoke sharply or held his hand firmly the boy would not go beyond the limit that was set.

On this basis, and following a conference with the mother who was told that the teacher might become somewhat more demanding of the child, the teacher agreed to set much firmer limits and to ignore his fearful fantasies as much as possible. The next day, as soon as the child came in, she took him aside and told him he either had to go in and join the group or he had to turn around and go home at once. Clearly in conflict, the boy stood looking unbelieving at the teacher, and then he began crying. The teacher stood her ground, repeating her ultimatum. Slowly and tearfully the child took off his coat, walked into the room and sat down at his place. That day and in subsequent days, the teacher continued to be quite firm with him. She found she could not give him an inch, but he was participating in class. His aggressive and destructive behavior stopped and the fantasies dropped out. Moreover, he was not tense or fearful in class. On subsequent visits the consultant was impressed with the child's calm and happy demeanor now that the teacher had established control.

Paradoxically, the "hands-off" phenomenon is sometimes initiated only after the school has made heroic efforts to establish a treatment situation for a family. Having effected a referral, and not hearing anything further from the treating agency, the school seems to assume it can help best by doing nothing.

Example 3. A family had two children in school, both of whom were showing the effects of marked neglect. They were coming to school late, sometimes dressed untidily in dirty clothes, and frequently they were not washed or even fed. Their work in school was poor, both children being unable to concentrate or to follow instructions consistently. The school social worker, the consultant, and the principal worked together to get the mother and father into the school. At that point it was discovered that the mother was an immature bohemian who would sometimes take off abruptly for several days at a time and that the father had withdrawn his attention from the family, locking himself in his room as soon as he came home at night. He felt he could neither force the mother to care for the children nor get her to accept a housekeeper. For the children's sake he was unable to consider a divorce seriously. At the urging of the three professionals, and on the grounds that the children were suffering, the mother and father agreed to accept a referral to a family service agency. Once the school had focused on the problem, the care of the children improved at once, and their work in school also improved to some extent.

At the beginning of the next school year the school received a brief message from the social agency through the school social worker, indicating that the family had terminated at the agency. The parents had decided to enter therapy with a private physician. The agency's message also indicated that the parents' relationship to each other was in delicate balance. There was some hint that the agency feared both father and mother were homicidal, suicidal, or both, and there was an implication that the school should keep out of the situation. For a number of months the school made no effort to reach the family. However, toward late winter, it became apparent that the children were being neglected again. Their work in school was clearly suffering, and in fact the third-grade boy was truant several days. At that point, despite the agency's injunction, the consultant got in touch with the family. He discovered that the parents were not in treatment and had not been for some time. They had started therapy, and then abruptly discontinued when the father decided he couldn't afford to pay the therapist's fees. The father had little or no idea of what had been happening in school, but, when informed, both he and the mother began paying more attention to the children. At the same time the principal began checking regularly on the children's attendance and on their care. She had them come to her office daily, and when she felt the parents were lax she so informed them. When the children began showing some of the effects of improved care, the principal also took the trouble to inform the parents that their efforts were showing good results. With concentrated attention, the truancy ceased and the children's work improved.

The existence of the "hands-off" phenomenon reflects a serious problem in contemporary child guidance and psychotherapeutic practice. For various reasons, one of which is the confidentiality of the relationship with the patient, clinics and private practitioners are reluctant to maintain continuous contact with a child's teacher, his principal, or sometimes even with professional services associated with the schools. Sometimes a clinic will send a social worker or a therapist for a one-shot visit to the school, but the professional person will rarely spend time in the classroom or take the time to become acquainted with the child's situation in school. Recommendations tend to be vague or so generalized they cannot be translated into specific programs for children in school. The clinic or the therapist rarely takes the trouble to get in touch with the school even when he can anticipate that the child may be entering a period of acting out related to his therapy. The school is left to handle the problem as best it can, and sometimes school personnel are actually handicapped in working with a child because of concern that school services will interfere with therapy. The feeling that anything done by the nonprofessional to the emotionally disturbed individual will inevitably be wrong and harmful can be quite debilitating. The "hands-off" phenomenon presents a potent argument for a closer relationship between mental-health professionals and the schools.

A teacher has a very understandable desire to avoid a scene or to avoid being seen as either incompetent or mean. It seems to be a law of nature that other adults inevitably assume that the adult in charge of a crying child is responsible for the child's state, either because the adult has treated the child cruelly or because the child's supervision has been incompetent in some respect. The adult who is responsible for the child who is crying inconsolably, whining, or in a temper inevitably feels uncomfortable in the situation.

Though there are surprisingly few aspects of a classroom that are public, loud shrieks and wails suddenly bursting forth from a usually quiet classroom cannot help becoming public knowledge in short order. The teacher is inclined to feel helpless in the situation and concerned that the child's crying will distress or excite all her other children. She is often perplexed about how to deal with the situation and feels the child will never stop. She is hesitant to take any firm action for fear the other children will think of her as a mean teacher. Some of the old hands, or teachers who are themselves experienced mothers, take the situation in stride, but for many the situation is extraordinarily difficult. And the situation is not helped when in disdainful and superior tones one teacher (usually teaching in the upper grade) lets the other teacher know that such disgraceful events never occur in *her* room. Some principals are understanding, but others are likely to berate the teacher for her inept and inadequate handling of children, sometimes stating the major fear: "What if a parent came in and heard this!"

In such a social context it is not surprising that many, but by no means all, teachers are prone to keep hands off a child who is likely to make a scene. The child is likely to be permitted to go his own way in the classroom with little interference, with poor consequences for the child's development, and with little satisfaction for the teacher, except for the knowledge that she has kept the peace.

Example 4. A seven-year-old white girl was in the first grade. She was both willful and negativistic and prone to burst into tears if anyone attempted to interfere with her. On more than one occasion she had been difficult to manage, and when the teacher attempted to insist she do something the child began to cry. In class she could be observed sitting alone at the rear of the room fitfully leafing through the pages of her book, occasionally running up to see what another child was doing, sometimes joining the group who were reading for a few brief moments. When she did complete some work and took it up to the teacher to show it off, she received a perfunctory, "good girl," but while she was sitting in her seat working the teacher paid no attention to her. If the child spoke loudly or really interfered with some other child, the teacher might intervene, but frequently she would ask the child who was the victim of aggression to give in to the little girl. In the hallway, when the group went to the basement, the little girl could be observed gaily darting in and out of the lavatory, nonchalantly pushing or pummeling some other child. The teacher stood by, and if the noise level was not too high or the damage excessive she did nothing.

When the consultant spoke to the teacher about the girl, the teacher stated that she didn't like the situation, but she felt she could do nothing about it. She found that whenever she insisted that the child do something the child was likely to be defiant, and she would be in the position of getting into a head-on conflict with her. Following a day when the child had a temper tantrum, the teacher reported she was badly upset and slept poorly that night. On another occasion, following a bad day with the child, the teacher spent almost an hour expressing her feelings of distress and talking about her dread of experiencing more such incidents with the child. When encouraged to try to structure a program for the child, the teacher adamantly refused. She indicated that she couldn't stand the strain and that another teacher had made remarks to the effect that the child's screams were disturbing her class. She felt the best thing she could do for all concerned was to let this child have her own way and not to fight with her. If she did fight with her, she felt the other children would perceive her as mean, and it would destroy her rapport with her class. The teacher felt that the only thing that would do any good would be to beat the child, but she couldn't because she had always been taught never to put her hands on a child.

Although she was angry and dissatisfied, she felt she could do nothing different and could only live with the child as best she could.

Other teachers do not find it necessary to be as timid in the situation and frequently such teachers will have far more success with given children.

Example 5. A second-grade teacher was working with a girl who had been diagnosed as a borderline schizophrenic by a child guidance clinic. The child would do fairly well in class, but from time to time she would insist on having something her own way. If the teacher refused, or if the teacher insisted she do her work properly, the child would sometimes scream loudly. The teacher, rather than being intimidated by the child's screams, took her out in the hallway and told her that she could scream all she liked but she would still have to complete her work. On another occasion the teacher headed off an incident by taking the child outside the room and challenging her either to do her work and control herself or to leave and go home. Once again the child backed down in the face of the teacher's obvious determination. She was controlled quite well during the year and progressed satisfactorily in her school work under this firm regime.

The first teacher's outlook was largely dictated by her fear of making a mistake, her fear of social censure in the situation, and by her underlying rage when she felt she could not handle the problem. In helping teachers to work effectively with such unmanageable children, we quickly became aware that part of the problem resided in attitudes in the school to the effect that teaching consists of the proper presentation of material to normal children who take in the material. To be sure, classroom management is part of the teaching job, but, in the view of many teachers, doing anything other than teaching in that traditional sense is baby sitting, demeaning, and not part of the teacher's job. The "hands-off" policy is not only consistent with the teacher's doubts about how to deal with the situation, but it is consistent with a tradition that says a teacher is not responsible for a child who is not normal.

The elementary-school teacher often is presented with frightening behaviors and situations about which she has little or no information and for which there are limited avenues and resources available that she can draw on to supply herself with the kinds of information she needs to take effective action. This is particularly true when the teacher is confronted with behavior that is as frightening and upsetting as an epileptic seizure. Because of the dramatic quality of such a seizure, as well as the limited experience and information available to the teacher, she often reacts to the situation by invoking the "hands-off" policy previously described.

When a teacher reacts in this way to a child's epileptic seizure, she is saying, in effect, that she feels ill-equipped to handle the situation and would prefer to leave it to the doctors. It is entirely understandable for a teacher to perceive the situation in this manner, and we would act no differently if we were not in the position of having additional information about the situation. However, when the teacher invokes a "hands-off" position with respect to the epileptic child, she is making certain assumptions about the child's condition and about the kinds of things she will or will not expect of the child in the future.[1] More often than not the teacher views the child as being extremely delicate and fragile and one who should not be pushed or pressured lest such pressure cause him to have another seizure. The teacher ceases to react to the child as if he were normal and frees him from whatever demands had been placed on him in the past. The teacher's concern for the child's health and welfare, coupled with her lack of information about the conditions surrounding the epileptic syndrome, cause her to perceive the child as imminently destructible and force her into the position of handling the child with kid gloves. Her motives are born only out of the best of intentions, but their implications and consequences for the child are often far worse than the epileptic condition itself. By keeping hands off the teacher may be accentuating needlessly the child's feeling of being different and may be insulating him from the social and formal learning situations that occur in the classroom setting. Unwittingly she may be placing the child in the position of not benefiting from the usual learning experiences that are available to all children.

The speed with which the "hands-off" policy is invoked is a reflection of the kind and quality of information available to the teacher. One of our functions in working with teachers has been, to provide them, wherever possible and appropriate, with the kind of information necessary to help them alter their perception of a situation. The child with epileptic seizures is a case in point.

Example 6. Mitchell was a six-year-old kindergartener whose teacher described him as "a little devil and spunky as all get-out." He was a somewhat hyperactive child with a limited attention span who reacted to the new school situation as if each day were filled with potentially bright and curious discoveries. He was generally all over the classroom, constantly sticking his nose into everyone's work, and making something of a nuisance of himself. Despite his difficulties in staying put for any length of time, his

[1] Some schools will not allow an epileptic child to remain in the school and will exclude him from normal participation or refer him elsewhere for his educational needs.

teacher felt that he was a boy of great promise and a boy who seemed to delight in much that the classroom situation had to offer him. Her main concern was with his overactivity, and it was decided very early in the semester that we both would try to evolve some coordinated approach to Mitchell and his sometimes disruptive exuberance.

Our goal in working with Mitchell was not to tame him of his eagerness nor to break him of his essentially spontaneous and creative approach to the learning situation; our goal was to provide him with a viable and understandable sense of structure, a structure that would enable him to utilize his talents in a manner more socially recognized and personally fulfilling. We felt that it was important for Mitchell to begin to understand that a certain amount of classroom structure and impulse control was important in the learning situation and that the rules and regulations governing a child's behavior in the classroom were not simply arbitrary laws, established without rhyme or reason, to thwart a child's enjoyment of school. We realized that in order to make this clear to Mitchell we would have to "sit" on him from time to time and apply sanctions appropriately and systematically whenever they were deemed necessary by the teacher. We also hoped that in the process of defining for him when and where certain behaviors were either appropriate or inappropriate we could utilize his obvious talents and creative energies in a more meaningful and relevant fashion.

Once we had defined our goals, we began to work with the teacher to implement them in the classroom setting. Mitchell's teacher—a mature, experienced, and sensitive woman—undertook her part of the project with a great deal of enthusiasm, and it was not very long before her efforts began to show concrete results. Although Mitchell was not particularly appreciative of the times his teacher would use physical restraint in order to impress on him the inappropriateness of some of his behavior, the fact that she systematically and repetitiously would explain to him exactly why she was doing what she was doing and how he could begin to exert some self-control over his own behavior soon began to bear fruit. Even though Mitchell periodically "forgot" when and under what conditions he could get up and run around the room or how he could get the teacher's attention appropriately, he slowly began to exhibit a greater amount of self-control and a more reasonable understanding of classroom procedures. After about three months, Mitchell, although by no means a little angel, was still vitally interested in school, was still working and learning in the classroom situation, and had begun to develop the kinds of behavioral controls that made his teacher's work a lot less taxing and certainly much more enjoyable.

One day in January, while we were observing another classroom in a different part of the building, we received an urgent message from Mitchell's teacher. A little girl from Mitchell's class came running into the room to tell us that her teacher had sent her to get us and take us immediately to the nurse's office. When we entered the nurse's office, we saw Mitchell apparently sleeping on one of the cots in the room. He had a small bruise on his forehead. The teacher was seated in a chair next to the cot. She was obviously upset, trembling as she sat watching over the sleeping boy in a concerned and apprehensive manner. When she saw us enter the room, she immediately got up from her chair, came over to us, and related what had occurred.

Mitchell had had an epileptic seizure. It had taken place a few minutes before we met the teacher in the nurse's office and it had occurred in the teacher's kindergarten class. The class was involved in an activity in which each child was learning how to use scissors and how to cut out a certain paper design which was to be pasted on a sheet of paper to form a mosaic. Mitchell was standing at his desk cutting out forms when he suddenly cried out in a loud and sharp manner. The teacher turned and saw Mitchell fall to the ground with his hands "almost pinned" to his sides. He rolled over and the teacher saw his eyes roll up into his head and his face become extremely pale; soon afterward Mitchell began to convulse, and then, almost as if exhausted, he appeared to fall asleep. The entire process lasted about one minute, but the teacher felt that it was "an eternity" before she could get Mitchell to the nurse's office.

It was only after the teacher had taken Mitchell to the nurse's office that she found that he had a history of epileptic seizures. We were both unaware of his condition until that time.

The teacher was extremely upset and shaken by the experience she had been through. Although she had heard about epilepsy and had taught school for many years, she had never before been directly confronted with a child's seizure. She trembled as she recounted the event and kept looking at the sleeping boy as she told us the story. Despite her understandably fearful and anxious reaction to what had happened, we sensed that she also felt somewhat guilty about the event, almost as though she had done something or was somehow responsible for Mitchell's epileptic seizure. We asked her about this and she quickly agreed, shaking her head and saying that the entire incident might have been avoided if she had known about the "child's condition." We asked her what she meant and she went on to tell us that she would not have put so much pressure on the boy and would not have pushed him so hard or tried to influence his behavior in the ways that she had. She vowed that in the future she would "go easy" with the boy, would keep her hands off him, and would try to make his stay in her classroom as free from the anxious and unpleasant burdens of discipline as possible. In short, she felt that the ways in which we had tried to discipline or influence the boy had in some way caused his attack. Despite the fact that we explored with the teacher the specific events that preceded the seizure and indicated to her how very little she had had to do with Mitchell during that period of time, she stood firm in her conviction that we had contributed in some mysterious manner to the onset of Mitchell's seizure in her class that day.

The teacher was tremendously upset, angry, and frightened; there appeared to be no point in trying to continue the discussion. Under the circumstances we felt that it would be much more appropriate to help the teacher calm down and collect herself so that she could return to her classroom and get through the rest of her day's work. Consequently, we merely remained with the teacher for a while and made arrangements for Mitchell's mother to come to school to take her son home, where he could rest more comfortably.

When we left the teacher, we went to talk with the principal of the school. He had long been aware of the kinds of things we were attempting to do with Mitchell in the classroom and had already heard about Mitchell's seizure that morning. Because he had been involved in much of the prior planning concerning Mitchell's classroom behavior, we felt it was important that we discuss with him whatever suggestions he might have about the situation and consult with him about some of the potential consequences of the teacher's current thinking. What concerned us most was the fact that the experience the teacher had been through appeared to be so traumatic that she was put in a position in which she was no longer willing to continue with the project that had been undertaken and that had shown such positive results in Mitchell's case. She appeared to be reacting to Mitchell's condition by withdrawing from the situation and by perceiving him as a child who easily could fall apart under the pressures that we had been exerting on him in the classroom setting. She was now perceiving Mitchell as an extremely delicate and fragile child who should be left alone and be made to feel as comfortable as possible. Although we realized that the teacher's new stance was partly a reaction to the frightening aspects of Mitchell's seizure and partly due to her lack of information about and experience with epileptic children, it seemed to be the kind of situation that could lead to future problems far greater in their implications than the epileptic syndrome itself. We also felt that the kinds of problems confronting Mitchell's teacher could easily be encountered by many of the other teachers in the school, were they suddenly to find themselves in her position.

One of the ways in which we felt we could begin to approach the problem would be to initiate a series of discussions with Mitchell's teacher, discussions in which we would try to provide her with the kind of information about epilepsy that was currently unavailable to her in the school setting. Although this seemed to be an adequate way of handling the situation, the conditions under which the crisis had arisen (i.e., the fact that we were intimately involved with Mitchell's teacher in the project and her subsequent reaction to the implications of what we had been doing with the boy), appeared to require a more impersonal and objective approach. We then considered the possibility of obtaining a film on the subject that could be shown to all teachers as a part of an in-service training program. Our emphasis here would be to provide them with a learning experience that might help them to understand the situation in such a way that, if the occasion occurred, they could deal with the problems from a point of maximal rather than minimal information.

The principal agreed that the latter approach appeared to be a wiser one. However, we were still concerned with the fact that in the general course of events it usually was a long time before a school actually could receive the visual-aid material it was requesting. In the present situation we felt that any and all delays in acquiring this film would make it more difficult for Mitchell's teacher to reorganize her already changing perceptions of the child and his condition. We conveyed this to the principal by telling him that we needed the film "five minutes ago." The principal agreed that the situation necessitated a minimum of delay. He immediately got on the phone and called the agency responsible for providing schools with visual-aid materials and supplies. He explained the situation to them in very specific terms and indicated his feelings that this was an emergency situation in which we could not afford the time to make out the usual written requests, forward them to the office, and wait until the agency could send the appropriate material. The agency understood the nature of the request and informed the principal that it would send over a film on epilepsy within the hour. The principal then dictated a memorandum to the teachers informing them that there would be a short meeting in the school auditorium after the children departed for the day.

That afternoon the elementary school's teachers gathered in the auditorium. After a brief introduction the film was shown. Since we had not had a chance to view the film before its presentation, we were somewhat hesitant and anxious about the way in which the film would present and describe the problem of epilepsy. As it turned out our fears were not substantiated by the film. It was a film expressly for teachers, and it presented the problem in a competent and relatively complete manner. It described in detail the differences between idiopathic and symptomatic seizures and presented a full delineation of the different types of convulsive seizures. In offering a picture of the phenotypic differences between grand mal, Jacksonian, petit mal, and psychomotor attacks, the film presented the teachers with a concrete set of examples in which emphasis was placed on the recognition of the type of seizure involved and the most appropriate way of handling it in the event that it occurred in the classroom. Although Mitchell's teacher seemed somewhat upset at the beginning of the film, she soon appeared to become much less upset and much more interested in the film itself. The film showed the different stages of the grand mal seizures and indicated how its particular characteristics (i.e., the clonic muscular spasms associated with the second stage of the seizure) differentiated it from the petit mal seizures in which the transient loss of consciousness was a predominant theme. Toward the end of the presentation the film made a particular point of emphasizing two variables which it indicated had to do with the relationship between a child's epileptic seizures and such factors as intelligence and functional psychopathology. The film made it very clear that psychotic symptoms and intellectual deficits occurred in only a small number of children who had epileptic syndromes and that most epileptic patients were mentally normal and competent. The second point made was that under suitable treatment (i.e., medication) there was no reason why the child could not be expected to participate normally in the classroom situation and therefore should be permitted to live as normal a school life as possible.

Following the conclusion of the film, a rather lively discussion ensued. The teachers, although initially somewhat irritated at having to stay after school, felt that the film was worthwhile and helpful in preparing them for the eventuality of having epileptic children in their classrooms. They also indicated their desire to develop a host of similar sessions devoted to some of the other areas in which they felt the need for some kind of ongoing training. In this context they mentioned such areas as mental retardation, the overactive child, etc. It was decided that we would continue these sessions in the future on a more regular basis.

As the teachers were leaving the auditorium, we had the chance to talk with Mitchell's teacher for a while. We discussed the film and she suggested with a slight smile on her face that she was aware that we had "cooked up the idea" because of what had happened earlier that day. We confessed and explained to her the reasons why we had decided to approach the problem in the way that we had. She understood our point of view and then began to discuss how and under what conditions we both could resume our "Project Mitchell." We discussed the situation and decided that it might be best to continue dealing with him in the ways that we already had developed and in the ways that had appeared to yield such positive results. The teacher felt that it would be wisest to continue in this vein, and indicated that she now had a different and more sufficient understanding of the situation, that she now knew of no reason to keep her from "putting my hands back on that little boy" and "sitting on him" whenever it seemed helpful and appropriate.

THE HYPOTHESIS OF MENTAL RETARDATION

As we already have indicated, certain potential dangers exist in the evolution, development, and utilization of any hypothesis. In the teaching situation these dangers can lead to behaviors whose consequences have serious implications for the child's ability and willingness to learn, for once the teacher has evolved a hypothesis about a child she will often limit herself to a smaller range of perceptual stimuli emanating from the child; consequently, she will be unavailable to perceive other stimuli that may be equally important. Similarly, the teacher may respond to the child solely in terms of whatever categories she has developed about the child. Under these conditions the teacher may be an unwitting participant in the self-fulfilling prophecy: she may respond to the child in ways that guarantee that the child eventually will behave in a manner consistent with the teacher's original hypothesis.

Nowhere are the implications of the process we have been describing more obvious than in the phenomenon we have come to call "the hypothesis of mental retardation." When a teacher decides on the basis of any number of variables (many of which may be incorrect) that a child is "slow," "backward," or "retarded," she will often begin to perceive and respond to that child in a manner very different from her characteristic way of responding to other children in her class. Not only will she behave differently with that child, but she will also reorganize her expectations for him and limit the kinds of experiences made available to him. When this process continues over a long enough period of time, both the teacher and the child begin to behave in ways that confirm and fulfill the limited expectations they have of one another. The child and the teacher become allies in an ongoing process of mutual exclusion. It is only by helping the teacher reorganize her perception of the child that this potentially vicious cycle can be broken.

Example 7. Cora was a seven-year-old girl who was repeating kindergarten. She had been retained in kindergarten because of the teacher's feeling that she had not mastered the kinds of skills that she would need in the first grade and had not done very well on the reading readiness tests she had taken. Moreover, Cora was an essentially nonverbal child who appeared to be morbidly afraid of the other children and she preferred to remain alone in the classroom situation.

During our first visit to Cora's class the child's kindergarten teacher had taken us aside and singled her out as a "slow little girl." We asked the teacher why she felt this way and were told that Cora's previous teacher had felt that way and that she (the current teacher) saw no reason to doubt her colleague's judgment in the situation. The teacher also informed us that she had seen no change in the child; Cora was still an essentially nonverbal girl and still exhibited no inclination to join in any activities with the other children in the class.

Over the next few months we were able to establish a particularly close and trusting relationship with the teacher, a relationship in which we both felt very free to discuss in an open and direct manner any and all of the children in the class. The teacher often allowed us to teach in her classroom and went out of her way to help us learn something about the kindergarten teaching situation from her point of view. It was always with an air of anticipation that we entered her room, never knowing exactly what she would ask us to do or whether we would be able to do it in a satisfactory way.

The longer we observed Cora, the more impressed we became with the child's emotional, as opposed to her possibly organic, problems and difficulties. She appeared to be a disturbed little girl, severely so, who was afraid of many things and who approached the learning situation in a markedly hesitant and anxious manner. We discussed these observations with the teacher. She agreed with us in the sense that she acknowledged the fact that Cora had many problems but it was her feeling that these problems were caused by Cora's "backward condition."

The teacher's approach to Cora could be described in two words: kindly and ignoring. The teacher often appeared to humor the child and went out of her way to be particularly kind and understanding in all of her interactions with the little girl. The teacher would also ignore many of the things Cora did, rarely stopping to ask the child why she was doing something and never bothering to try to involve her in any of the class activities. Because the child was no trouble, the teacher could spend most of her time dealing with the other children and leaving Cora alone to her own devices.

Despite the teacher's way of reacting to her, Cora began, almost imperceptibly, to move toward some of the other children in the class. Because this occurred over a period of some time, the teacher seemed to be unaware of what was happening. Gradually, however, we saw Cora begin to decrease the distance between herself and the other children. When the class was seated around the teacher at the front of the room, Cora was usually to be found at the other side of the room. Little by little she began to move closer; one week she would remain halfway across the room; the next week we saw her move a little closer; and the following week she was seated only a few feet away from the circle that had been formed around the teacher. All this occurred without the teacher's comment and apparently without her awareness.

One day we entered the classroom to find ourselves in the midst of a popcorn-making activity. The teacher had secured a popcorn-maker and was involved in showing the children how to make popcorn. The children were seated around the teacher and seemed to be enthralled by all that was going on. The teacher was using the activity as a way of showing children how to measure out the different quantities of materials (butter, corn, corn oil, salt, etc.). Much to our surprise we saw Cora sitting in the midst of all the other children. She was gazing at the teacher and seemed completely engrossed in the activity. While the teacher was measuring out the corn to be put in the popper, a few kernels fell on the floor and one of them rolled over to where Cora was seated. The teacher, seeing what had happened, cautioned Cora, who had picked up a kernel and was looking at it intently, not to put the corn in her mouth because it was "dirty and had been on the floor." Cora kept gazing at the kernel and then turned her attention back to the teacher. By this time, however, the teacher had looked away from the child and was going on with the activity. Because of the rapidity of the teacher's turning away, she had failed to see that Cora now was holding the kernel in her hand and was motioning in a way to suggest that perhaps the teacher might rinse the kernel in the sink and then put it back in the popper.

Because of the freedom we felt in this teacher's class, we interrupted the lesson and directed the teacher's attention back to the little girl. As soon as the teacher saw what Cora was doing, she smiled and nodded her head. Cora immediately rose and, with an air of great delight and satisfaction, went to the sink, rinsed off the kernel, and placed it in the popper. The teacher was completely taken by surprise but was obviously delighted by what the child was doing. When Cora had finished, the teacher commented to the class on how Cora had been able "to save a piece of popcorn for us" and how rinsing food that had been dropped on the floor was often a good way of not wasting food. Cora beamed and the lesson went on.

When the activity was over and the children were involved in free-play, we discussed what had happened with the teacher. We apologized for interrupting her lesson but indicated why we felt compelled to do so. The teacher, as we had expected, did not mind our interruption but was curious to know how she could have been so unaware of what Cora was trying to tell her. We then discussed the implications of hypothesizing that Cora was retarded or slow. In this context we were able to show the teacher how her perception of the child had made it unnecessary for her to think of the kernel situation in any other way except as a situation in which she had to warn the child not to eat the dirty kernel. Her perception of the child as retarded meant that she did not have to investigate the situation any further; that she did not have to linger on what the child was trying to do; that she could assume unquestioningly that the only thing the child was capable of doing was eating a kernel that had fallen on the floor. We then asked the teacher if she was aware of how, over the course of the preceding months, Cora had begun to come closer and closer to the rest of the class, how she had diminished the distance between herself and the other children and was now sitting together with them. Again the teacher appeared to be relatively unaware of what had been happening to Cora. The longer we discussed the situation, the more excited the teacher became about Cora and her relatively rapid rate of progress. She also became aware of the implications of the hypothesis of mental retardation and of the kinds of behavior that emanated from such a hypothesis. In this case the teacher, because of the nature of her perception of the child, was cutting the child off from her awareness and was not attending to the child in ways in which she usually attended to the other children.

From that point on the teacher began to respond to Cora in the same ways in which she responded to the rest of the class. She began to expect things from Cora and involved her in all of the class activities. Her perception of Cora and her problem had changed, and with that change came a similar change in the teacher's behavior.

THE CHILD COMES BY HIS PROBLEM HONESTLY

From the point of view of the teacher who is concerned about teaching a large group of children any child who presents special difficulties is a nuisance. As long as education is defined in terms of the preparation and presentation of material to children, the teacher's first inclination, when faced with a difficult child, is to experience the child as trouble. Finding her own efforts frustrated or finding that she must divide her attention in more ways than she feels capable of doing, the teacher frequently feels angered and resentful of a child who demands something different by virtue of his behavior. She may also feel anxious because her image of herself as a competent professional person is threatened. Although we are taught that human behavior stems from sufficient causes, in the classroom situation the teacher is not always able or prepared to seek causes. Understandably, from her viewpoint, the child is at fault for acting as he does, and it is her feeling that both she and the child would be better off if the child were away from her. Sometimes the consultant can serve an important function by helping the teacher to see that the problem has a background. When the teacher sees that a child does come by his problems honestly, so to speak, her tolerance for the problem and her willingness to make the effort to work with the child are sometimes increased.

Example 8. A teacher had been doing an admirable job with an aggressive, stubborn, unpredictable Negro girl of about eight. She found she could work with her only if she took a great deal of time to give her special attention and combined the attention with firm and at times even harsh disciplinary measures. The teacher felt constantly under strain, and because the child was given to prolonged temper tantrums she was inclined to avoid too many head-on clashes with her. From time to time the teacher would ask that the child be kept home, and for a while she was coming to school on half sessions. Once, after a particularly difficult day, the teacher felt sufficiently distressed by the child's behavior that she sent a telegram to the child's mother requesting the child be kept home the next day.

On the day the child was absent the consultant visited the classroom and inquired about the child. The teacher reported the experience of the previous day and wondered what could possibly have set the child off. Because a student teacher was present and could take over the class, the teacher and consultant decided to visit the home during the day to inquire about the child. On arriving at the house, about 10:30 A.M., we could hear loud rock and roll music. Inside the apartment three teenage boys and a teenage girl were together. They had either dropped out of school or were cutting that day. A half-dressed child of about four was wandering about the apartment, and the little girl in question was unkempt, her ill-fitting clothes in disarray. The mother was not at home.

Following this experience, the teacher could see why the child was so difficult to handle. Moreover, she was able to see that the child was clearly better off at school than at home and her resolve to handle the problem grew. That night the teacher called the mother on the telephone and in polite but candid and firm tones insisted that the child be in school every day, clean and reasonably well dressed. The teacher's call was followed by an immediate response by the mother who sent the child to school the next morning combed, washed, and in a clean, freshly ironed dress. The child's attitude reflected the visit and the care in that she was pleasant, cooperative, and motivated to work throughout the day.

Example 9. A kindergarten child in an inner-city school suddenly became negativistic, aggressive, attention-demanding and babyish, when earlier in the year he had not seemed to react in any exceptional manner. On two occasions the child had wandered out of the room, and when the teacher inquired about where he was going he indicated he wanted to go home and be a baby. Discussion with the teacher and a teacher's aid indicated that the child would respond if he could be held on someone's lap for a while, but neither the teacher nor the aid felt they could give him the time he seemed to need without stimulating a demand for such care in all the children in the room.

On the suggestion of the consultant, the child's mother was asked to come to school. When asked to help the teacher work with her child by offering some information about why the child seemed to regress, the mother said she had recently separated from the father. She had been at home with her children, but said that she had become so nervous and depressed by her situation that she had decided to go out to work to relieve her own feelings of distress. The five-year-old boy was now seen to be reacting to the loss of his father and also to the loss of his mother who left him with a baby sitter to go to work in the morning and who was not at home when he returned after school. When the mother returned home from work, she was faced with the physical care of four children and had little energy or time for affectionate play with the children.

The teacher, on hearing the story, felt an immediate sympathy for the child's situation. His need for special attention now seemed more understandable and, in consequence, it became less burdensome. The child's difficulties somehow became more manageable in the situation, and though he still showed difficulties from time to time somehow his problems seemed less distressing to the teacher who now felt she understood what was happening.

In the preceding example the teacher's tolerance for the problem increased when she could see how the problem grew out of a specific situation. In the next example the contact between teacher and mother led to an increase in the teacher's sympathy with and respect for the mother of the child and a concomitant increase in her sympathy for the child's problem.

Example 10. A Negro child was admitted to a first-grade classroom in midyear. His school record contained a psychological examination which indicated that he had been hyperactive and aggressive in kindergarten and was probably retarded. The teacher soon discovered that the child was indeed hyperactive and aggressive; in fact she could not turn her back on him without his attacking another child, often without any provocation at all. In talking with the consultant, she felt that a psychological re-examination and placement in a special class were indicated.

The consultant suggested a conference with the child's mother before conducting any further examinations or arriving at a disposition. The child's mother proved to be a highly articulate and proud woman. She related that she and her husband had recently been divorced and that she had made a second move out of her mother's home because of clashes there. Although she was eligible for welfare, she had stopped accepting welfare and had taken a full-time job. In full and complete terms she expressed her feeling that her entire sense of independence and self-respect were being crushed while on welfare, even though it was more difficult for her to manage when she was working full-time. She also informed the teacher the child was premature and that several of her children had had congenital cardiac or kidney difficulties. The mother was not complaining, but was simply relating the facts of her situation. She also indicated that she had been following her child's development closely through a pediatric clinic, and she requested that the teacher try to work with her child because she felt he could learn with sufficient encouragement.

In this instance the teacher was so impressed with the mother's strength of character and intelligence that she saw the child in a different light. Because the mother was a truly admirable person, and because she proved to be thoroughly cooperative, the teacher felt that her efforts with this child would not be wasted. She thereupon withdrew her referral for testing and agreed to observe and to work with the child through the remainder of the year, which she did.

Seeing the problem as an honest one is important in any situation, but it is particularly important in the inner-city school because of the stereotypes that abound about parents and children. Many, but by no means all, teachers are inclined to see Negro parents as neglectful, slothful, uninterested in their children's progress in school, and difficult to talk to as people. They are rarely inclined to see the parents as having a problem that might be influencing the child's behavior. Typically, we hear the phrases, "it's the home," or "I suppose they neglect him," but it is rare that a teacher seeks to discover any systematic understanding of the problem in the home. The problem is a bad one which is vaguely "out there," and it usually has no distinct substance for the teacher. To discover that the parent is struggling with very real problems in living, problems not very different from those the teacher understands, or might experience, is helpful in placing the child's problems in the realm of the familiar and the helpable. In those instances in which there truly is neglect, seeing the neglect vividly often creates a sympathetic appreciation for the child's situation. Seeing a ragged or dirty child in the classroom sometimes creates distaste for the child. Seeing a neglected home somehow places the child's problem in perspective, and makes it easier for the teacher to relate to it as an individual one. Seeing the child in a particular home or in relation to a particular parent somehow removes the problem from the vast and vague realm of a social problem "out there" and turns it into the concrete problem of this child in the here-and-now.

In this chapter we have tried to present the reader with a series of examples in which teachers' interactions with their children were a reflection of and determined by the nature of their perceptions and ideas about those children. In each case the teacher's behavior with respect to a given child was, to one degree or another, governed by whatever information or assumptions she had about that particular child. The fact that in many of the cases the information was incomplete or the assumptions inaccurate—or, indeed, that we were able to help the teacher reorganize his perceptions about the child—were not the primary reasons for this chapter. Our major concern has been to indicate to the reader that teachers, no less than psychologists or any other members of the mental-health profession, are both the beneficiaries and the victims of their own perceptual and cognitive processes. However, unlike their mental-health colleagues, teachers rarely have the opportunity of sharing their perceptions and hypotheses with fellow professionals. Rather, it appears as if teachers are all too often excluded from the kinds of experiences and training programs that could be of help to them in the quest for greater perceptual and theoretical clarity. Considering the conditions under which many of our teachers work it is surprising that they do as well as they do.

In all of the examples presented in this chapter the nature of the teacher's perception of a problem determined what that teacher felt she could or could not do with and for a child. In most of the examples presented here the way in which the teacher conceptualized the problem led her to withdraw from the situation or to interact with the child in a manner that confirmed her initial perceptions of that child and his difficulties. Our role in working with the teacher was one of helping her to understand the implications and consequences of her behavior and to recognize the existence of alternative hypotheses. We could not have functioned in this manner had we not developed a relationship of mutual trust and respect with the teacher.

Chapter 8

Authoritative Support

There are teachers who view their role with respect to the child—who view the discipline of education—as involving something more than those behaviors appropriate to the classroom situation. These are teachers who conceive of education and of their roles as teachers in terms of their involvement with, and commitment to, the needs and interests of the child both in the classroom setting and/or in other situations. For them education means an ongoing involvement with the child in whatever settings there are that may have consequences for the child's development and his ability to learn. These teachers view their classroom as only one of many arenas in which they can influence and affect the child's ability and willingness to learn.

Many variables account for the different ways in which teachers perceive the legitimate scope of their educational roles with respect to the child, and individual differences between teachers is not the least of these factors. It appears that some teachers almost naturally tend to become more involved with their students than others, and invariably relate to them in different ways and in different contexts. It is certainly true that a teacher's personal needs and interests, her own background and past experiences, play an important role in determining the nature and content of her involvement with the child. We know that teachers, like members of any other profession, choose to become teachers for a variety of reasons, some of which may be deeply personal and determined by a host of past experiences and feelings, and of which the individual may not be fully aware or understand completely. Similarly, once a person becomes a teacher things may occur that change or modify the experience of and the commitment to the teaching situation. For one reason or another teachers view their jobs differently, and these different perceptions have implications for the nature, content, and scope of the teacher's involvement with the child. Even the fact that a particular teacher may have a broader conception of her legitimate role with respect to a child than some other teacher does not inevitably mean she will act differently with the child than another teacher would. The feeling that the teacher would like to become more intimately involved with a child in settings or in ways that are not strictly defined by the teaching situation may often remain just that, a feeling, and may never become translated into those specific behaviors that actualize the intent. Many good reasons for this state of affairs stem from the legal, moral, and ethical implications of the situation. When a teacher wishes to broaden the scope of her involvement, or to intensify her over-all relationship with a child, she places herself in a personally vulnerable position with respect not only to the particular child but also to his parents, the other teachers, and the school's administrative personnel. She often becomes legally liable if she wishes to interact with the child in contexts that are removed from the school setting or if she wishes to assume the responsibility of caring for the child's welfare and safety in nonacademic situations. Her decision to intensify her relationship with a child may also place her in the position in which her actions and motives become the subject of her own and other people's scrutiny and questioning. She must often attempt to justify her extra interest and concern in a youngster both to herself and to her colleagues. The school's administration is often ambivalent in its feelings about a teacher who wishes to extend her relationship with a child; it may feel, on the one hand, that the additional involvement may facilitate the child's ability to learn but, on the other hand, that the increased involvement may jeopardize the teacher's relationships with the other children or that she may behave in ways that might embarrass the school. The teacher may, despite her nobility of purpose, similarly question the wisdom of her decision to intensify her relationship with a child. She may fear its effect on her ability to deal with the other children in her classroom or she may have serious questions concerning the relevance of her own training in preparing her to undertake a relationship with a child that extends beyond the school setting.

One additional factor often influences a teacher's decision whether or not to increase her involvement with a child: it is the factor of the aloneness that will engulf her once she departs from the structured environment of the school. It is an aloneness in the sense that the usual channels of communication, consultation, supervision and self-correction that are, however inadequately, available to the teacher in the school setting no longer remain viable parameters of behavior or fixed points of reference. When a teacher extends her relationship with a child beyond the confines of the school, she often loses much of the social and professional support that are available to her within the school setting. For many reasons—some good and some bad—her interactions with the child are no longer considered a school problem but fall into the realm of personal action and individual responsibility. The teacher is no longer perceived as acting as an agent of the school but is viewed as acting as an individual, independent of the school, and beyond its jurisdiction. Under these conditions the experience of aloneness is both physically and psychologically an immanent reality. The teacher who wishes to relate to a child in ways that extend beyond the school situation is a teacher who must accept the responsibilities of independent action for which there is little social support. Under these circumstances it is not too difficult to understand a teacher's reluctance to undertake a relationship in which she becomes increasingly involved with a child. We might say that the teacher who chooses to maintain and enhance her relationship with a particular child does so despite the contingencies of the situation and not because of them.

Once we become immersed in the culture of the school it is not very difficult to become painfully aware of the stresses and pressures a teacher experiences when she contemplates undertaking an "unorthodox" approach to a child. Her indecision, self-doubt, and personal anxiety become entirely understandable responses in terms of the vicissitudes and implications of the situation. At this point the consultants' function of "authoritative support" may be utilized to provide the teacher with the kind of support that may help her in making and carrying out her decision.

Authoritative support may be defined as the process by which teachers are given the "OK" to do the kinds of things they really want to do but are somewhat hesitant about doing alone or before consultation. It is the kind of ongoing support in which the consultant provides the teacher with someone who is willing to talk with her about the things she feels should be done in a particular situation involving her relationship with a child. More than that, it is the process whereby someone who is trusted and respected by the teacher is continually available to share her anxiety and doubt, her concern and involvement about a situation in which she experiences herself as acting in ways and in settings for which she has not been professionally trained. The most important aspect of authoritative support resides not so much in the "expert advice" that the consultant brings with him to the situation—for, in many cases, the teacher's need to perceive herself as the "amateur" in a situation is a myth that has been perpetuated by a history of status differentiation between the educational and psychological professions—but is to be found in its function of lifting that veil of aloneness that engulfs the teacher who wishes to strike out on her own or to act differently. The professional "OK" that the consultant gives the teacher is much more than a message of clinical approval: it is a clear communication that someone both agrees with and respects her ideas, and that someone is willing to share her burden of unorthodox and independent action.

Example 1. Philip was the oldest of four children whom the state had recently separated from their mother and placed in a temporary foster home. The children were removed from the mother's home because of the court's feeling that she was an inadequate mother and that her behavior was detrimental to the health and safety of the children. The court's action came after a series of incidents in which the mother came in contact with the police for offenses including drunken and promiscuous behavor, child neglect, and disturbing the peace. The mother's difficulties occurred during a one-year period in which she and her husband had separated. Philip and his siblings (two brothers, aged six and three, and a one-year-old sister) had been placed with a local family with the understanding that as soon as a more permanent placement became available they would be shifted, either individually or as a unit, to this new place of residence. Since the temporary placement was made before the beginning of the school year it was decided to allow Philip and his six-year-old brother to attend the local school until such time as they were to be relocated in another living situation.

When Philip entered his temporary elementary school he was almost nine years of age and was placed in the third grade. Because of the circumstances surrounding his placement in the community, Philip was a newcomer both to the community and the school. Unlike many of the other children in his class he knew no one and was unfamiliar with school as a social and/or educational setting. Besides the problems confronting any child in a new setting, Philip came into his third-grade class with many additional problems. The most important of these problems was his experience of himself as the oldest of a now transient and wind-blown group of brothers and sisters. Philip knew more about the situation than did his siblings; he had been told of the reasons for their temporary placement in the community and he understood that they would be moving on as soon as an appropriate placement could be found. Moreover, he also knew that there was a real possibility that he and his brothers and sister might be split up or placed in different settings without each other. In short, he was a little boy who was quite concerned with his role as big brother, as the oldest sibling who had to protect and guard his younger brothers and sister.

Philip's behavior in class made life very difficult for his teacher and the other students in the room. He would not accept instructions and behaved as if his one purpose in the classroom was to make sure that neither he or anyone else had a chance to profit from the learning situation. He would often jump out of his seat, run around the room, or exhibit other kinds of behaviors which made it increasingly difficult for the teacher to teach and for the other students to learn. He would act in ways to provoke or taunt the teacher, and he was often frightening and aggressive to the other children in the classroom. He refused to do his work and became enraged when he saw others trying to do theirs. Philip's behavior could most accurately be described as, at best, disruptive and, at worst, totally chaotic.

Philip's teacher was a woman with many years of experience as an elementary-school teacher. She was also the kind of person who took the position that troublesome children were also troubled children and that it was much more important to try to locate the problem than to attempt to alleviate the difficult classroom situation automatically by excluding the child or immediately referring him elsewhere for help. She was a teacher who accepted each problem child as a personal challenge and perceived her role in the context of a total learning experience for the child. Although a firm disciplinarian in the classroom, she was also quite gentle and sensitive to the needs of her children and particularly aware of the effects of environmental difficulties on their ability and willingness to learn in the classroom situation.

As soon as Philip began acting up in her class, the teacher called the administrative officials in the school and sought to familiarize herself with whatever information was available on the child. As it turned out, the school had the pertinent information on the situation involving Philip, his siblings, and their temporary placement in the community. Philip's teacher became both aware of and concerned about the kinds of pressures under which the youngster was functioning. She also became acquainted with Philip's "secret"—the fact that only he knew about the possibility that he and his siblings might be separated from each other once a more permanent placement became available.

The teacher now was able to approach Philip with information that was previously unavailable to her. She began spending more and more time with Philip and to use her knowledge of the situation as a basis for developing a closer relationship with him. Over a period of time Philip began to talk with her and started sharing his fear, anxiety, and loneliness with her. In a short while they had developed a close relationship, and Philip soon shared his "awful secret" with the teacher. During this time Philip's classroom behavior showed considerable improvement, and he began spending more and more of his time doing his work and devoting less time to behavior that was either aggressive or disruptive. At those times when he felt himself getting nervous or about to flare up he would approach his teacher and tell her about it. They would spend a little while talking about it and, after his teacher reassured him of her interest and understanding, he would return to his seat and attempt to continue his work. The longer Philip remained in the classroom, the more stable he became. His behavior and his work improved, and he began looking forward to coming to school.

In the process of getting to know Philip the teacher had several contacts with the people with whom he and his siblings were temporarily living. These were people who ran a state-licensed foster home and had done so for many years. Their home was utilized by the state for short-term or interim placements and they received a certain amount of money for each child placed with them. They were kind and gentle people who had learned over the years that for their own sake as well as for "the welfare of the children" it was best to provide as comfortable and secure an environment as possible without getting too involved with the youngsters placed in their charge. Consequently, they sought to offer the child a place of refuge but were concerned lest they establish the kind of intimate and involved relationship with a child that made their eventual separation a more painful and distressing event. The teacher understood their point of view and could empathize with their feelings. She felt, however, that part of the reason accounting for Philip's change in behavior could be traced to the fact that she had, indeed, been able to establish a more personal relationship with him. She also felt that there would be a great deal of upheaval surrounding the time when Philip and/or his siblings were to be relocated in their new home. More than anything else, she was concerned about how this transfer would occur, how it would be interpreted to the children, and how it would be handled.

Throughout the period of time in which Philip was acting up we had worked with the teacher in terms of helping her to deal with his outbursts in the classroom. We had come to know the teacher and were impressed with both her concern for the child and her ability to handle him in the classroom situation. Our relationship with the teacher has developed over a period of time in which we had been meeting continually, both in the classroom and elsewhere, to discuss Philip's behavior and problems. We had been able to observe the changes that occurred in Philip's behavior and had developed a great respect for the teacher's sensitivity, ability, and commitment to the youngster.

Despite the fact that Philip's behavior had undergone great changes— he was no longer a classroom problem and was doing quite well in the learning situation—his teacher appeared to be becoming more and more concerned about the situation with the passage of each day and each week. She seemed to be depressed and not a little anxious. We were somewhat puzzled by this turn of events and at one of our meetings asked her what was wrong. It was then that the teacher shared with us some of her fears, concerns, and ideas about the situation.

The teacher, although acknowledging the good that had taken place since she had been able to develop a closer relationship with Philip, was quite concerned about what would happen to Philip and/or his brothers and sister once they were removed from the community. She was particularly concerned with Philip and with the realistic problem of what would happen to him if he were separated from his siblings. She felt that there was no one, except herself, who was in a position to maintain a relationship with Philip or to handle the problem of his transfer from one home, community, and school situation to another. His foster parents, for reasons of their own, were unwilling to become increasingly involved with the child. The biological mother was unavailable and unable to assume the role of handling the transition. She, the teacher, wanted to assume that role but had serious doubts that it was appropriate for her to do so.

Philip's teacher had several reasons for questioning the wisdom of her desire to assume the role of his transitional mother. She did not know whether she was qualified to deal with the stresses and strains she felt would inevitably accompany the situation. She did not wish to usurp the foster parents' responsibilities or to place them in a difficult position with respect to the child. In listening to the teacher we were struck by the fact that by her behavior to the child up to the present time she had already answered these questions. She had already proved herself to be amply qualified to handle the situation, and the foster parents had already been approached by the teacher and appeared to be perfectly willing to allow her to assume some of the responsibilities they felt they did not want to assume. We shared these feelings of ours with the teacher and informed her of our belief that there was something else involved in her reluctance to become Philip's transitional mother. The teacher then told us what was really bothering her about the situation.

The teacher's major concern was not with her own ability or with the problem of usurping the foster parents' legal responsibility. She was really concerned with the question of her own motives in the situation. We told her that we did not fully understand what she was saying, and it was then then she explained her feelings to us.

Philip's teacher was a woman in her late fifties who had been teaching for almost 35 years. She was a tall, aristocratic-looking woman who carried herself with immense dignity and took great pride in her patience and self-control, but, when describing her doubts about her motives with respect to Philip and his problems, she became considerably less self-possessed and self-confident.

She told us that she had been married for 33 years and that her husband, a prominent physician in the community, had passed away two years before the beginning of the current school year. They were an extremely close couple and his death had left her alone and lost. Although she had three children, they were all married and lived with their families quite a distance away. Her visits with them and their visits with her were few and far between and usually coincided with the Christmas and Easter holidays. She had continued to teach, not out of financial need, but because it gave her something to do and kept her from constantly reflecting and thinking about her loneliness and the sudden emptiness that surrounded her life. She was essentially alone, and her teaching in school was all that she felt she could look forward to in an otherwise bleak and solitary existence.

It was for these reasons that the teacher questioned her motives with respect to her interest and involvement in Philip. She was concerned lest her own problems and needs be the reasons for her commitment to the child. She was unsure whether her desire to maintain and extend her relationship with Philip was determined by what she felt were his needs or her own.

Our feeling—and we shared this with the teacher—was that the teacher's ability and willingness to verbalize these doubts was concrete evidence of the fact that she was aware of the difficulties of the situation and that she was not acting selfishly or irrationally. We understood her feelings and could share her concern, but we also focused attention on the immense benefit Philip had derived from his relationship with the teacher. Moreover, we completely agreed with her estimate of the current situation and of the potential difficulties that would engulf Philip if there were no one whom he knew and trusted to handle his transition from one home, school, and community to another. Because of the teacher's feelings about herself and her own motives in the situation, we reaffirmed our willingness and desire to remain available to the teacher for consultation or a chat at any point she felt it would be helpful and that we would work with her in anything that she did. Most important, however, we told her that she was right in her analysis of the situation and that if she felt it would be helpful to Philip for her to maintain and enhance her relationship with him she should "do it, it's OK."

The teacher continued her relationship with Philip both in the classroom situation and in other settings. With the permission and approval of his foster parents, she began seeing him on weekends and taking him to different towns and functions in the state. She spent much time with him talking about his eventual transfer and his feelings about moving and being separated from his brothers and sister. Throughout this period Philip continued his progress in the classroom situation and was no longer a troublesome student. The teacher was amply able to maintain her individual relationship with Philip without letting it affect her responsiveness to, and involvement with, the rest of the children in her class. She used whatever nonacademic time she had available to continue her relationship with Philip and to prepare him for the inevitable transfer that would occur. Their relationship was a warm and comfortable one, one which Philip utilized to verbalize and explore his feelings with the teacher.

The time finally came when a new placement was found for Philip. As things turned out, it was a placement for him alone, which would not accommodate the rest of his siblings. Philip was quite unhappy about the situation, but was already somewhat prepared for it. The teacher handled the transfer and the period of transition. Not only did she accompany Philip to his new place of residence, she also served as a temporary liaison between Philip and his brothers and sister. She also prepared Philip's new school for his entrance and informed them of the situation and the kinds of things they should be on the lookout for in terms of Philip's behavior in the new setting. With the permission of the new parents, she continued to visit Philip during the period of time in which he was adjusting himself to the home and his new foster parents. When she felt that he had become somewhat acclimated to his new surroundings and had begun to develop a relationship with his foster parents, the teacher began to withdraw from the situation and decreased the frequency and duration of her visits. She finally established a letter-writing relationship with Philip and remained available to the foster parents as a source of information and advice.

Working in the public schools has demonstrated to us, time and time again, the fact that no teacher is equally effective in her ability to deal with every child in her classroom. This situation is neither surprising nor particularly unusual. The same statement could be made about anyone whose professional work involves a significant amount of interpersonal relations. In the field of clinical psychology we know that not every therapist is equally effective with each of his patients. Consequently, it is not surprising to find that teachers often work better with one type of youngster than another.

It is not invariably true that a teacher's ability to work effectively with a child is solely dependent on her liking the youngster, but such is often the case. The teaching situation is here, again, somewhat analogous to the psychotherapy situation. Although it is not always true that a therapist who dislikes his patient cannot treat him, it is often an important variable in the situation. It is for this very reason that the initial weeks of psychotherapy are often viewed as trial sessions in which both the therapist and the client have a chance to decide whether they feel that they can work together.

In our work in the schools we have often found it to be very difficult for a teacher to admit that she really dislikes a youngster, particularly when her dislike for the child is not based on classroom behavior or the like. In other words, it is difficult for a teacher to admit having negative feelings toward a child when that child is not demonstrably disruptive, troublesome, or antagonistic in the classroom situation. And yet teachers often dislike youngsters, and dislike them for reasons that have little or nothing to do with classroom behavior.

Perhaps the teacher would feel much better if only she could unerringly point to something, anything, in the child's behavior that could warrant or justify her negative feelings. If this were the case, she could then seek some sort of consensual validation for her feelings instead of having to deal with her anger alone and without benefit of any justifiable social support from her colleagues.

Regardless of the particular reason for which a teacher dislikes a child, as long as the teacher feels that there is no realistic basis on which to express her negative feelings about the youngster, we have the makings of a situation that is detrimental both to the teacher and the child. It is a situation in which two people are thrown together in a manner that limits the number of alternatives available either to the child or the teacher to escape from the other. The teacher will not often ask that the child be removed from her classroom and placed elsewhere when she has no demonstrable reason (e.g., disruptive behavior) to justify her request. The child, on the other hand, has no power or authority to influence the school's policy regarding pupil placement. We are therefore left with a situation in which two people are "stuck with each other for better or for worse," an unholy educational marriage involving two people who are poorly matched.

Many consequences result from the situation in which a teacher feels "stuck" with a child she dislikes, none of which is particularly helpful for either teacher or child. On a behavioral level the teacher's feelings may lead her to act in ways that hurt or humiliate the child. She may ignore the child, isolate him, or react to him in ways that impede his ability and willingness to learn. On a psychological level, the teacher may often feel tense, anxious, or uncomfortable in the classroom situation. Her day in school can become clouded by the internal pressures and stresses she experiences when reflecting on her feelings toward the youngster. Her ability to teach may suffer from the amount of energy she expends in thinking about the situation. For the child, school can become a frightening experience, in which there is little success or personal satisfaction. He, too, becomes tense and anxious and begins to react to the classroom situation in ways that make learning a more difficult and arduous task. In short, both teacher and student experience the classroom situation in a manner that impedes their modes of functioning and makes their participation in the learning situation uncomfortable and unsatisfying.

One of the functions of authoritative support is to provide a teacher with the opportunity to extricate herself and the pupil from this mutually unsatisfying relationship. We call it a function of authoritative support because the psychologist can allow or encourage the teacher to voice her hatred of the child without placing herself in the unenviable position of trying to justify her feelings. If the psychologist is not perceived as an agent of the administration and his relationship with the teacher is based on mutual trust and respect, the authoritative support he offers the teacher can enable her to verbalize her feelings without being bound by pride or by the necessity of assuming the burden of proof for her essentially untenable position with respect to the child. Unlike the administration or her fellow teachers, the psychologist need not be solely concerned with documented proof when a teacher wishes to divorce herself from a particular child. What we offer the teacher is a chance, free of the concerns of protocol and appropriateness, to express as fully as possible her feelings about a child. By so doing we can ally ourselves with the teacher (and the child) and offer her the kind of professional support that might enable her to undertake the kind of action she would not otherwise have attempted. Once she is finally able, without undue rationalization or false justification, to verbalize her feelings directly and openly—and to realize that her feelings need not be documented by proof in order to have important personal validity—she can then act to alleviate the situation. The function of authoritative support in this situation is to provide the teacher with someone whom she respects as a professional, who is eager and willing to listen to her feelings and to hear her out without demanding proof or passing judgment.

Example 2. From almost the first day we began sitting in on one particular second-grade classroom we became aware of some undefinable difficulty that seemed to exist between the teacher and one of the little girls in her class. The teacher, a young and pretty woman, who seemed to have great talent for teaching, often appeared noticeably short-tempered and unaccountably severe in her interactions with one specific little girl. Although the girl would constantly be raising her hand to answer a question, the teacher called on her only very rarely and would usually grimace if the child answered correctly or berate her loudly if her response were inaccurate. Instead of the teacher's behavior serving to decrease the girl's frequency of hand raising, it seemed to have no effect on her tendency to volunteer in class. The little girl appeared quite upset each time she was ignored, grimaced at, or scolded but would in a little while begin to volunteer all over again. This pattern of behavior on the part of both the teacher and the child was observable each time we sat in on that particular classroom.

A short time after we had become accepted as part of the furniture in the classroom and were no longer perceived as a stranger by the children or the second-grade teacher, the teacher approached us with the request that we "test Lucy to find out if she's retarded." Because it is not our policy to test children indiscriminately or without some understanding of the kinds of questions the teacher has about the child, we arranged to have a meeting with the teacher to discuss the situation.

The meeting took place over coffee and was scheduled at a time when we could have the teachers' room all to ourselves with no interruptions. At this time the teacher repeated her request for testing and specified her belief that the child was ill-equipped for regular second-grade work and might be better off in a slower class. We asked the teacher what made her feel the way she did and she seemed to have some difficulty in describing the variables which led her to question the child's intellectual capacities. The more she tried to spell out her reasons for doubting Lucy's potential, the more upset and tongue-tied she seemed to become. Noting that she was becoming more and more uncomfortable in the situation, we changed the subject and were soon talking about many of the other children in her class and about some of her experiences with children since becoming a teacher. As soon as the subject had been changed and steered away from Lucy, the teacher became buoyant and enthusiastic, describing her children and experiences in a lively and excited manner. She spoke of how much she enjoyed being a teacher and of how glad she was finally to finish school and get a chance at "real life" teaching. She went on to describe her goals in teaching and talked about the kinds of programs she would like to see instituted in elementary schools, particularly with respect to the second grade. Her speech and behavior were now markedly different from a few moments before. She no longer fumbled with her words or seemed at all uncomfortable. She spoke in a firm voice, appeared quite bright and animated, and exuded confidence. As our meeting came to a close we told the teacher that we would certainly consider testing Lucy, but that we would like to observe her over a period of time and that we would like the chance to meet her (the teacher) in the interim.

During the following weeks we did sit in on the classroom more often. Each time we found the situation to be essentially the same. The teacher seemed antagonistic and angry toward Lucy whenever she was placed in a situation of interacting with her. Lucy was becoming more and more bewildered and not a little angry herself. Although she appeared to try many different ways of pleasing and appeasing her teacher, none of them seemed to work, and the child was becoming more and more anxious and tense in the classroom situation. Both the teacher and the student were becoming active combatants who were using the classroom more as a battlefield than as a context for learning.

In our next meeting with the teacher she repeated her request for a psychological evaluation of Lucy. She felt sure that Lucy was not so bright as the other children in the class and that she was suffering from being in a situation that was too much for her limited potential. Rather than raise any other questions, we acceded to the teacher's demand to have the child evaluated but made as a condition for this evaluation the fact that we might meet to discuss the results of testing before the report was sent to the administrative office.

Lucy's testing was quite unspectacular. She performed within the normal limits of intellectual functioning and, although her behavior was somewhat erratic and anxious within the testing situation, little additional information resulted from the testing procedure. Lucy was a girl of at least average intellectual endowment who was performing within expected limits, albeit with a certain amount of anxiety. She was a rather unattractive girl who appeared to expend a great deal of energy to deal with what seemed to be a tendency toward shyness and withdrawal. She was a hesitant and somewhat self-conscious child whose almost driven outgoingness appeared to be a defense against her feelings of plainness of face and dress.

At our next meeting with the teacher we related to her the results of our testing. We showed her the testing protocol and discussed the testing procedure with her. We summarized the findings and indicated what we felt to be the important variables in the testing situation and how they might or might not have affected Lucy's performance. After we had completed our presentation the teacher appeared even more upset than before. She asked if we might not have made an error in our assessment procedure or if we had done anything to "make Lucy do better on the test." We assured her that such was not the case and reviewed some of the findings with her again. When we had finished, the teacher appeared somewhat depressed, almost despondent. We shared with her our observations of her behavior and she readily agreed that she was, to be sure, somewhat surprised and puzzled by the results of our testing. She maintained that somehow something was wrong with Lucy, something that might not have been picked up by the kinds of tests we had employed.

At this point we shared some of our classroom observations with the teacher. We told her how angry she had appeared to us whenever she was interacting with the little girl and how tense she appeared to become whenever she was put in the position of having to talk about or deal with Lucy. We then asked her if part of her request for testing might not have emanated from her desire to have some tangible evidence on which to request a transfer for the child? The teacher appeared a bit pained by our question but did not deny its implications. Instead she went on to describe how difficult the child was and how much better it might be "for her" if we changed her class. We agreed with the teacher that Lucy might be the kind of child who was difficult for her to deal with and that, on that basis, it might be a good idea for us to change her class. At this point the teacher protested, saying that she had no real basis on which to request a transfer for the child. She went on to add that if we had found Lucy to be somewhat retarded or backward then she would have some reasonable foundation for requesting a transfer. Since we had not found her to be deficient, the teacher felt that the others would think her "crazy or something" for wanting the child out of her class.

At this time we brought up the question of the teacher's real feelings toward Lucy. The teacher responded first by apologizing but then by going into a long monologue about just how much she disliked the girl. Without being able to specify the whys and wherefores of her animosity, the teacher spoke at length about the way she felt about the child, her physical appearance, her dress, and the way she just seemed to "get under my skin." The teacher realized that there was no rational reason for her feelings but could not help the way in which she felt about the girl. Try as she might, the teacher could not specify the origin or genesis of her feelings toward the girl, but she clearly conveyed to us the amount of time that she had spent since the beginning of the school term pondering and thinking about her feelings.

We could understand the teacher's feelings and could empathize with the amount of personal turmoil she had been through in thinking about the situation. We told her that it was often no different in the psychotherapy situation in which a therapist, for reasons of which he is unaware, feels that he just cannot work with a particular client. We went on to take the position that the most important feature of the situation was the teacher's awareness of her feelings toward the child and that the attempt to justify those feelings needed no concrete test or classroom behavior data. What was most important was the fact that the teacher, for one reason or another, found working with Lucy to be a difficult, anxiety-ridden, and unsatisfying activity.

The teacher seemed quite relieved, especially when she was told that psychologists have the same kinds of problems with some of their clients. She also felt better about finally being able to voice her feelings about a child without being afraid that the listener would think ill of her or feel that she was "crazy or neurotic."

We went on to make explicit our belief that it was a myth to think that every teacher should be able to work equally as effectively with every one of her students. Furthermore, we made it very plain that, just as the psychotherapist need not always justify his desire not to want to work with a particular patient, the teacher need not always feel pressured to catalog her reasons for not wanting to work with a particular student. The teacher responded by telling us of her desire to transfer Lucy to another teacher and to another classroom. She felt that it would be the best course of action both for the child and for herself. We agreed with her decision and told her that if she felt in need of any support in her attempt to effect this transfer with the administration we would be happy to be of whatever assistance we could.

During the next week the teacher approached the administration and arranged for the transfer. Her only justification was that she felt that someone else might be a more appropriate person for Lucy to be with. The administration accepted her reasons without asking her for any additional information or data. Shortly thereafter Lucy was placed in a different second-grade class and with a different teacher.

In this chapter we have focused attention on the ways we have functioned in order to help teachers to do the kinds of things they really wanted to do but were somewhat hesitant about doing alone or without consultation. In reality, the support we have given to teachers might be much less necessary if teachers did not feel so alone and so constricted in the teaching situation or if they felt more personally and professionally competent in the school setting. Be that as it may, we have found teachers able to function creatively and therapeutically both in and out of the classroom once they experienced a relationship in which they could discuss their feelings and ideas, and from which they could derive the kind of support they needed in order to broaden the definition of their responsibilities.

In the next chapter we shall explore several situations in which teachers must exercise their responsibilities under the most difficult of circumstances, under conditions in which they are confronted with the "unmanageable child." The problems surrounding the "unmanageable child" are often of a nature and degree that will test the efficacy of our modes of functioning in the classroom and our relationships with teachers.

Chapter 9

The Unmanageable Child

When he can neither be distracted nor dissuaded from his disruptive intents the defiant child presents an inescapable problem of classroom management to the teacher. The kindergarten child's tantrums in the face of frustration, the second grader's provocative toughness toward his peers, and the upper grader's smart-aleck horseplay not only contaminate the learning atmosphere of the classroom and tempt other children to rebel but also challenge the teacher's very authority. Indeed, these outbursts of unmanageable behavior threaten the maintenance of the child in the public school because school administrators usually exert the most intolerant pressure on the teacher to control the disruptive child and, if the teacher cannot do so, to exclude him from school. The conscientious teacher, realizing as she does the tendency of exclusion to aggravate the child's resentment of school, requires unusual measures to manage the extreme behavior of the child, measures for which her training does not prepare her.

At such times of clear crisis in the life of a class the beleaguered teacher has tended to turn to the clinic psychologist even if she has not seen fit to do so previously. She correctly perceives that, over and above the welfare of the individual child, her own role in the eyes of the other children is powerfully affected by her management of the crisis. From the sympathetic psychologist, however, the teacher receives no easy way out of the crisis but an immediate opportunity to scrutinize the nature and development of the outbursts so that she may quickly evolve influence techniques appropriate to the emergency. The teacher's urge to refer the child to the Clinic for treatment is resisted by the psychologist who explains how outbursts of extreme defiance are best handled in the classroom in which they are manifested. By his attentive interest and intimate first-hand knowledge of the crisis the psychologist makes himself readily available for close work with the teacher in understanding and managing the emergency. Though he may insist that the child's problem is best handled by the teacher in the classroom rather than by himself at the Clinic, the psychologist can offer the teacher assistance of various sorts apart from consulting with her. The psychologist may use his influence to secure from the principal a few more days of precious tolerance of the outbursts, and he may enlist the aid of other teachers or school personnel, as well as of the child's parents, in coordination with the teacher's efforts, to strengthen the total environmental impact on the child.

We may at this point anticipate the reader's reaction to the contents of this chapter by stating that we shall be describing aspects of our functioning that differ from those described in preceding chapters. We refer here to the fact that we shall at times be describing ourselves as much more active and directive than is usually the case and frequently being that way at a point in our relationship with a school when the consequences of failure can be disastrous *for us*. But crises are by their nature upsetting of routines of action, plans, and habits of thinking. Ordinarily we strive in the early weeks in a school to avoid getting involved in problems that clearly involve matters of school policy. In any event, whether in early weeks or later, problems are encountered that are of such intensity and fraught with such undesirable consequences for children or teachers that we are forced to take action about which we may be far from secure. Particularly in the inner-city schools, we find ourselves at times taking a degree of initiative because, rightly or wrongly, that is our perception of what we need to do. In a relationship to school personnel such as we have, we quickly learn to expect that with many problems time will not be on our side. We do not wish to convey to the reader the impression that our conception of our role is a surefire guide to or a cookbook for action. Our conception is essentially a series of generalizations about problems and approaches and not a spelled-out set of criteria by which specific problems may be identified and the approach of choice determined. Even if such criteria could be developed, crises often do not permit time to determine rationally and reflectively whether the criteria are being validly met.

Three sorts of disturbances seem to activate the outbursts of the unmanageable child: disturbances in his relationship to his teacher and/or school work, disturbances in his relationship to his peers in or out of school, and disturbances in his family. Before considering appropriate techniques for managing the child's outbursts, it has been our custom to "wonder out loud" along with the teacher about the particular disturbances that trigger the child. This initial process of seeking out a causal network for the outbursts is indispensable not only because the application of effective influence techniques requires some detailed knowledge of the child but also because it provides the teacher with a model for solving emotional problems posed by other children. In short, when a teacher participates with the psychologist in thinking causally and diagnostically about problem behavior she is more likely to see how a child comes by his problems honestly, if not pathetically, and the stalemate of mutual resentment and confusion between the teacher and child can be more easily softened.

In the inner-city elementary school the incidence of extreme behavioral outbursts is considerable. It is common for half the teachers in a school to have one or two unmanageable children in their rooms. From our experience with such children we have amassed numerous examples of the three types of disturbance that trigger such outbursts, and we discuss them before describing several cases more fully in order to give the reader an overview of the range of disturbances activating such behavior.

We turn first to disturbances in the child's relationship to his teacher and/or school work. These are the most common, although they are often associated with disturbances of the other two sorts. Basically, the teacher reacts to the child's learning and behavior difficulties with excessive fear and anger. The result is that she neglects or punishes the child, much to the detriment of her capacity to influence him. The teacher's impatient resentment comes through to the child, largely unaccompanied by the affection and willingness to help that children, no less than adults, require in order to think about their self-doubts. Thus outbursts of unmanageable behavior may be set off by a teacher's embarrassing, insulting, or threatening behavior toward a provocative child or, more subtly, by her angry isolation of a defiant child from the rest of the class without discussing the matter with him and leaving his resentment to fester for hours or days before returning him to his normal seat. Failure to identify and praise small but constructive efforts by a defiant child to improve his behavior may be profoundly disillusioning to him, especially when his confidence in his ability to change is hardly well developed. Besides failing to notice minimal constructive changes in the unmanageable child, the harried teacher may actually push the child away when he shows signs of becoming somewhat dependent on her. Some distraught teachers may even pursue an active though unconscious campaign of retribution against the unmanageable child, perhaps using him as a familiar scapegoat for the instigations of more subtly provocative children, perhaps allowing his victims to retaliate against him physically in the classroom. Behind such vindictiveness on a teacher's part is disillusionment with herself and the child. She communicates to the child that she has given up on him, indeed has come to expect and almost to depend on his disruptiveness, an expectation shared by the class, and thus further fixing the child in his antisocial role. If the teacher is disliked enough by the other children, the unmanageable child's outbursts may even be praised in a variety of ways in and out of school by his peers.

In all the examples outlined the teacher's behavior acts as a trigger to the child's unmanageable outbursts and not necessarily as the original cause; that is, the outburst is not produced solely by the teacher-child relationship, but it is made more likely. Indeed, the child's difficulties in getting along in school would try any teacher. It is, however, almost always the case that such difficulties lead to extreme antisocial outbursts when the teacher compounds the child's felony with her own misdeeds. Thus, when a teacher presses on with a lesson beyond the present capacity of a troubled child and denies him a more rewarding substitute activity, forcing him to sit through his ignorance as other children move ahead, she is inviting an outburst, no matter whether the child lacks basic perceptual-motor readiness in kindergarten or word-attack skills in third-grade reading. The frustration, confusion, and embarrassment that difficult material can induce in a child may go unnoticed by a teacher whose directions are not clear, evaluations of performance all too public, and insistence on attention either too slack or too ruthless. We have observed teachers with a reading group alternate between blandly ignoring mounting signs of noise and general excitement among the rest of the class and then suddenly turning around to berate the class, falsely singling out a supposed culprit and imposing arbitrary punishments that only inflame the class further. Such unfortunate situations are unintended invitations to the fostering of extreme outbursts for which the unmanageable child alone is then held responsible.

A second class of disturbances involves a child's relationships to peers in or out of school. Periodic outbursts of extreme behavior may reflect hidden feelings of loneliness. Interest in making friends may diminish with repeated failure and the child may react to his jealousy of other friendships by alienating himself from other children, with the unfortunate effect of reinforcing his unpopularity. What may appear to a teacher as silliness or excessive talkativeness may be for a child an anxious attempt to use his school hours to reach out to another child. Embarrassed or thwarted in these attempts in the classroom, a child may turn instead to more antisocial ways of establishing some relationship to his peers or teacher. Envy-arousing comparisons between his own and other classmates' abilities, especially when they are fostered by an unknowing teacher, may draw a child into various maneuvers designed to allay his sense of inadequacy and painful feelings of envy or in some cases into attempts by the child to exaggerate his inadequacies in a self-mocking parody. Even young children are usually conscious of their status in the classroom hierarchies of appearance, popularity, and ability. A child can be tormented by his knowledge of where he stands among his peers, and no small number of behavioral outbursts in the classroom stem from the pattern of peer relations holding in the school culture. The teacher who is unaware of this social network reduces her effectiveness in understanding and shaping children's behavior. The teacher who sees that classroom friendships need not serve delinquent ends, but may be the allies of learning, has discovered a potent asset in motivating and socializing her children.

The third type of disturbance is most often cited by educators: disturbances in the family life of the child. As some parents routinely blame the school for their children's classroom difficulties, some teachers routinely blame the home. It is safest for both parties to cast about in foreign territory for the reasons for failure. It is true, however, that inner-city parents sometimes send their children to school with far too few hours of sleep, no breakfast, or verbal and physical abuse that starts them off in school feeling tired, irritable, and withdrawn; in short, ripe for an outburst of extreme behavior. Such children can often be spotted by a sullen or hyperactive entrance into the classroom in the morning. Besides these family disturbances that children bring to school with them, the perceptive teacher can discern more serious upheavals in the home, both transitory and chronic, weighing on a child. The birth of a sibling, family jealousies, inconsistent or brutal methods of punishment, and outright rejection by a parent may underlie a child's unmanageability in school, as may frequent occurrences like the beating of a child's mother by his father or the summoning of police to restrain an irresponsibly alcoholic parent. Inner-city children carry such traumas with them to school, carefully shrouding them along with nearly overwhelming feelings of shame and counterhostility. A teacher's interest in family disturbances that trigger a child's extreme outbursts in school must be gauged by the psychologist to determine whether she focuses on family dynamics as a supplement to or as a substitute for a consideration of classroom dynamics. A teacher's understandable tendency to become skeptical of her ability to reverse or modify character traits sometimes assiduously cultivated in a child's home and peer culture must be brought to the surface and worked through with her. She must understand how a defeatist outlook toward a child readily becomes a self-fulfilling prophecy, which justifies less thought and effort on the part of school, family, and child. The teacher's pessimism in part reflects a widely prevailing view of psychological functioning that we have called "intrapsychic supremacy." Our alternative view, that a child's behavior in school is determined not only by intrapsychic factors but also by factors in the school situation as well as in the family and peer situations, must be translated into a compelling tactical program of classroom action if we are to enlist the teacher's enthusiastic aid.

Once the teacher and psychologist together have diagnosed the disturbances which have set off the child's outbursts, they discuss techniques of influence most appropriate to both child and teacher. The most important area of influence on the child is, of course, the teacher's attitude, which, if covertly hostile, can undermine the effectiveness of any positive actions she may superficially take. Thus in his consultations with the teacher the psychologist elicits the teacher's inevitable feelings of frustration, disillusionment, and anger toward the child. He frankly assures her that if he had had the unfortunate luck to have been the child's teacher he would probably have strangled him by now. The various ways in which the child has cleverly called forth the teacher's disgust are reviewed, as are the unfortunate effects of the child's success in angering the teacher. In this light the teacher's anger tends to abate, especially when she sees how she defeats herself by allowing the child to manipulate her feelings. The psychologist suggests that the teacher's frustration and anger be channeled into a plan of action to change the child's behavior. Two points are explored with the teacher. First, her natural sympathy for the child is cultivated, strengthened as it is in her conversations with the psychologist about how the child comes by his problems with distressful honesty and how his antisocial actions are, in part, calls for care, acceptance, reasonable limitations of his self-defeating disobedience, and special help in developing talents he fears he lacks. Once she sees this disguised, paradoxical plea from the child for what it is, the teacher is far more eager to help than to condemn. She is reminded of the superiority of acting reflectively in contrast to reacting excitedly. She is encouraged to follow the model set in her conversations with the psychologist: making careful observations, relating past and present observations, thinking causally and diagnostically about surface behavior, and responding to the child's needs and abilities rather than solely to the emotional effects he has on her. She is, for example, urged to distinguish misbehavior based on a child's upset or hurt feelings from that based on more calculated defiance and, in short, to become a calm engineer of school behavior.

Once the psychologist observes some positive changes in the teacher's attitude toward the child, he begins to consider with her two types of influence technique; relationship-building and defiance-suppression techniques. Because the child's disruptiveness has reached crisis proportions and the principal is often ready to suspend him from school, both influence techniques must be instituted simultaneously in the hopes of retaining the child in school. It is impossible for a teacher to build a relationship with a child whose defiance has resulted in his suspension from school.

The hundreds of every-day ways in which a teacher can effectively build a positive relationship with her children usually do not suffice with the unmanageable child. Special relationship-building techniques must be tailor-made for such a child. (1) The teacher must go out of her way throughout the school day, and even after school during brief meetings alone with the child, to make clear to the child her interest in helping him. She must express her understanding that he is unhappy both with school and with his disruptive reaction to being there. She must indicate her understanding of his difficulties and offer to help and be a friend to the child in his attempts to improve his behavior and settle down to learning. She is to utter such words several times a day, before and after any behavioral outbursts, when the child is relaxed or busy, when he is agitated or sullen. The words are to be said with feeling and reinforced by gently touching the child. She must continue to make the point without assuming that it has sunk in. She reinforces her new friendliness by praising the child for nondisruptive actions, by smiling at and touching him from time to time, by giving him odd jobs even if they have to be artificially created, by giving special rewards and opportunities regardless of how badly he behaved earlier in the day. Whispering to him to reduce his embarrassment at being singled out, she is to maintain a constant stream of communication with him, perhaps as often as every ten minutes, without appearing to compromise her professional dignity. The dialogue in which she tries to engage the child may not all be focused on his difficulties but on whatever he may be doing or even on trivial pleasantries. She should try even to share some humor with the child, possibly telling him a joke or listening to one of his. To herself the teacher can justify the extra effort as a first step in reversing the stalemate of mutual trust.

(2) The teacher must provide the child, wherever possible, with instructional materials appropriate to his interests and ability, even if this requires some individual lesson planning. She may even be able to devise a class lesson or unit on some interest of the child in which his special abilities may be highlighted, even if they should involve topics

like climbing heights, racing cars, or how fires start. For the child's specific educational lacks the teacher will give personal tutoring when she can find a few extra minutes during and after school, recognizing as she does the powerful relationship between a child's feelings of ignorance and his disruptiveness. Any signs of the child's awakening educational interest, aptitude, or progress must be praised lavishly, of course, and unnecessary educational frustrations must be eliminated.

(3) The teacher can make constructive use of other children as significant resources of her campaign. Any signs of friendship between the unmanageable child and another child are to be encouraged by allowing them to work together and even chat quietly. Children who inflame the unmanageable child are to be talked with privately and encouraged to help the teacher, any signs of their cooperation being praised by her. Interpersonal situations likely to overstimulate the unmanageable child must be carefully supervised or avoided altogether by the teacher, who also should try to keep the level of classroom excitement and noise to a minimum, taking care to relax the children. Periods of play and talk are regularly scheduled in the day, and the work-play discrimination is fostered by the teacher's reminders that there are times for each sort of activity in school. When they seem natural, class discussions on friendliness can be stimulated by the teacher who should concern herself as much with examples of friendliness as unfriendliness, an oversight by some teachers who only draw attention to undesirable behavior.

(4) The teacher must make every effort to observe and think about her children's behavior in a preventive manner. She must watch for the early-warning signs of social disagreement and educational difficulty and intervene casually before an explosion. At times distracting the children may be sufficient; at other times a discussion between the disputants before they come to blows may be advisable. Surprisingly few remarks by teachers to disputing children deal with the reasons for the dispute and how best to handle it; frequently teachers focus on the mere undesirability of disputing. The teacher thus can remain vigilantly aware of potential trouble before it starts, praising cooperative actions as much as inflammatory ones, working as swiftly and quietly as possible, but confronting the disputants discreetly when she feels it appropriate. At all times her goal is to be the cultivation of self-control by developing a child's concern with the consequences of his actions rather than by stimulating his fear of reprisal for stepping over the line.

The enormous effort and inventiveness required of a teacher in fostering good relationships both between herself and her children and among her children is sometimes defined as a distraction from her educational role by even the most kindly teachers. After all, she has a curriculum guide to cover and her children are evaluated against local or national achievement test norms. The psychologist can be of some help by pointing out how neglected emotional undercurrents festering in the class considerably reduce the teacher's educational effectiveness as much as they work against a child's developing his most human character traits. To neglect emotional factors in the classroom with an unmanageable child is to invite upheaval.

Relationship-building techniques for influencing the unmanageable child are indispensable to involving him constructively in the classroom, but they are usually insufficient to produce the dramatic suppression of hostile defiance that is necessary if he is to be allowed by the principal to remain in school. For the child's own welfare, therefore, it is necessary to work out with the teacher influence techniques that effectively suppress the child's defiant outbursts almost at once, unless teacher and psychologist feel that he would profit from a brief exclusion from school. The use of exclusion from school as an initial influence technique, however, is usually not nearly so effective with the defiant child as other measures. One of three techniques for suppressing defiant outbursts is implemented along with the relationship-building techniques in the case of each unmanageable child.

The most commonly recommended technique for suppressing defiant behavior is that of excluding the disobedient child from his classroom and placing him for half an hour in a classroom nearby. The success of exclusion depends on the preparation given by the psychologist to the teachers and school personnel involved, the support or toleration of the principal, and the precise manner in which the teacher prepares her class and implements the technique. Any such dramatic recommendation, of course, requires the approval and comprehension of the principal, whose begrudging acceptance of the plan could undermine teachers' use of it. The principal must also participate in selecting the relatively experienced teacher with whom the unmanageable child's teacher pairs. Teachers have an antipathy to imposing on each other: the excluding teacher usually feels embarrassed about depending on another teacher, and the receiving teacher is concerned about her class being unsettled by the visitor. These understandable concerns must be recognized and assurance given that the plan may be stopped if it creates more problems than it solves. The participating pair of teachers must be fully briefed on the rationale and dangers in the plan so that they experience as few surprises as possible in implementing it. From our experience with the exclusion plan we now routinely brief participating teachers on several points. When a child is received in another room, he is to be given a seat at the back and excluded from any form of participation or interaction in the class. Before making this clear to teachers we occasionally found the excluded child excitedly participating in the receiving teacher's classroom activities. We also now prepare the excluding teacher for the problem of a child refusing to leave the room. He is to be carried out by the pair of teachers if he is in kindergarten through second grade. Older children refusing to leave their rooms are to be informed that unless they do so their parents will be phoned immediately. Never has a child refused to respond to either pressure. Never has an excluded child posed the slightest problem in the receiving classroom. Never has a child greeted the exclusion with anything but distasteful embarrassment.

So far the exclusion plan has the ingredients of an effective technique for suppressing defiant outbursts: it immediately terminates the disobedient behavior without introducing complications in either the receiving or excluding classrooms. Its unpleasant quality for the child renders it an effective influence technique in shaping more compliant subsequent behavior. The most significant source of power adhering to the plan, however, is probably not its unpleasantness per se but its decisive ability to force on the consciousness of the child the limits beyond which he may no longer go; in short, to underline by dramatic action those rules that other children remember and obey through verbal injunctions alone. It also gives the teacher a measure of authority she had been lacking in verbal injunctions. If the plan is to maximize the child's chances of remembering and following classroom rules, it must be introduced to the whole class not as an angry punitive retaliation by a distraught teacher but as a way of helping children to remember to follow rules that allow them to enjoy learning. It should be explained to the children repeatedly that a child will be excluded not because he is unwanted or disliked but because he needs the brief opportunity in another classroom to reflect on the rules he has been disobeying. By introducing the procedure to the entire class in a group discussion it does not appear as though the defiant child is being singled out; the shock of implementing the technique is reduced to more manageable proportions; and its rationale is communicated during a period of relative calm in the classroom. In their actual implementation of the plan teachers are cautioned against excluding children when they are furious with them, waiting instead until they have regained their composure. At that point the child is to be given one private, unembarrassing warning which clearly states that if a specific behavior does not cease he will be excluded. If several children are acting up defiantly they are to be warned publicly, but in no case is a child excluded unless he has had one and only one private warning from the teacher to remind him clearly of the rule he is breaking and of impending exclusion if he does not stop disrupting the class. Contained in such private warnings must be the teacher's attempt to explain to the child how he is disrupting the class, together with whatever relationship-building techniques she feels appropriate and feasible. Should the child subsequently defy the warning intentionally, he is to be led out of the classroom by the teacher who explains to the entire class in the presence of the child why he is being excluded.

On returning to the classroom after delivering the child to the receiving teacher, the excluding teacher reviews the situation with her class, emphasizing the reasons behind the relevant rules and alternative ways in which the excluded child might have acted. Whenever possible her remarks are channeled into a group discussion that can be used to martial the support of the class in helping the excluded child. Once children have expressed their expected bitterness toward the defiant child in such discussions, the teacher can elicit more sympathetic interest from them in helping him, especially when she points out that she needs help from the class in teaching the excluded child to follow class rules. Such discussions, arising as they do after a genuine classroom crisis, form a meaningful basis for the teacher to develop with her children a causal and change-oriented view of surface misbehavior. If the excluded child is to derive from his exclusion the maximum incentive and minimum discouragement to changing his ways, the teacher must schedule a short after-school interview with the child on the day of his exclusion. Like the class discussion, the follow-up interview is an essential ingredient in effecting a rapid suppression of his defiant outbursts. During the interview the teacher can explain how she excluded the child to help him remember class rules rather than to embarrass him, how she hopes that in the future a warning will be sufficient to induce the child to control his behavior, how it is the child himself and not the teacher who decides whether he is to be excluded from the room. Finally, the teacher can use the interview to explore with the child whatever difficulties he is experiencing in the classroom, promising the child confidentiality if he wishes to reveal something personal. Throughout the interview the teacher makes clear her affection and respect for the child, indicating how his misbehavior is at least as discrepant with his own hopes for himself as it is with hers for him. The psychologist can be helpful in reducing the aversion some teachers express about "psychoanalyzing" their students. As long as they do not probe deeply and listen warmly and acceptingly to any problems the child discusses, their common sense and professional ethics, he tells them, are adequate guides. Most of the inner-city children who require psychotherapy will never receive it; thus the teacher's may be the only interest ever expressed in their emotional lives. Of course, the psychologist is always available to review with a teacher any material that baffles or disturbs her. We have never regretted encouraging teachers to conduct such therapy-like interviews, though we have played down the suggestion with some teachers more than others. One outcome of such interviews is that they establish an open line of communication between child and teacher by dramatizing the teacher's wish to help him by talking with him rather than by forcing him to change.

The exclusion plan has proved an effective defiance-suppression technique for influencing children through the fourth grade. Especially when applied as calmly and consistently as possible, in a program of relationship-building, the exclusion plan can greatly reduce mounting classroom tension in a relatively antiseptic way. We have not yet experimented with its use for unmanageable children above the fourth grade. Instead, for elementary school upper graders presenting problems of repeated disobedience we have found it desirable to involve the parents, the child's other teachers, and the child himself in a plan in which a parent is called to school to remove the defiant youngster immediately after an outburst and to confine him to his bedroom for the remainder of the day and the entire next day. He is then returned to school. This defiance-suppression technique, even more than the exclusion technique for younger children, is a last-resort measure, to be repeated several times in order to save the child from being suspended from school. Like all defiance-suppression techniques, it is not recommended until the psychologist has made detailed observations in the classroom, discussed matters with the teachers and school administrators involved, and reviewed the situation with the youngster in school. It is always recommended as a supplement to relationship-building techniques appropriate to the age and needs of the youngster, and its implementation is observed by the psychologist. Because the upper grader has several teachers, the plan must be even more actively coordinated by the principal than the exclusion technique. The principal along with the psychologist explains the plan to the teachers involved and emphasizes the same points as in the exclusion plan: the procedure is to be explained in a period of relative calm by all the teachers on the same day if possible, singling no one out in its explanation or implementation. Every effort should be made by the teachers to present it as a way of giving students a chance to think over school rules rather than as a clever triumph by the school over trouble-makers. In implementing it the teacher should give one and only one private warning to the youngster who has refused to comply with pub-licly uttered injunctions—the warning containing a clear statement of the rules that, if broken again, will result in the youngster's parent being called in. The teacher is also encouraged to appeal in a friendly as well as warning manner when she speaks privately to the defiant youngster. A teacher who uses this technique is advised to discuss the matter with the class after the defiant youngster has been sent to the principal's office and to solicit their assistance for the future. She is also advised to discuss the matter with the youngster when he returns to school, by emphasizing that it is the youngster who will determine whether there is a repetition of the procedure and encouraging the youngster to say how the teacher can help him to enjoy his class more fully.

The principal and psychologist, after meeting with the teacher, will invite the parents and youngster into the principal's office to join the discussion with the teacher and to outline the plan for them. Be-fore this meeting, however, either the principal or psychologist has pri-vately explained the plan to the youngster and his parents, making the meeting with the teacher a formalization of the plan. The principal explains that this is a last-resort measure to maintain the child in school rather than to push him out. Should he have to be sent home several times, he would be suspended from school, the exact duration of the suspension being left intentionally vague. The meeting is also used to allow the teacher to offer encouragement to the child and his parents and to stress their willingness to work with him. Such a meet-ing makes perfectly clear to the youngster the newly defined limits be-yond which he may no longer go with impunity, thus coordinating the approach of all his teachers and minimizing his chances of playing one teacher off against another. It has been our experience that teachers do not abuse the prerogative accorded them under this plan but rather feel more confident about their authority and are more giving to the youngster because they realize the power in their hands. From the youngster's point of view he usually realizes that the school at last means business and is concerned with his welfare. Such youngsters are often seen in brief psychotherapy at the Clinic by the psychologist be-fore implementing the plan, only secondarily to explore their underly-ing problems and primarily to help them to express their dissatisfac-tions in a more socialized manner. When specific needs or conflicts arise in psychotherapy with such youngsters, we have found it more

helpful to help them work their difficulties out with practical suggestions than to probe intensively. The focus of the Clinic meetings is on
their school adjustment and the potentialities that school offers them
for improving their present and future lot, emotionally and vocationally. The technique has proved effective with upper graders in suppressing their defiant outbursts when the parents' aid is skillfully
enlisted, and in cases in which hard feelings have existed between the
school and family the psychologist, as a kind of mediator unaligned
with the school administration, can sometimes be of inestimable value
in winning over the parents.

A third influence technique for suppressing otherwise uninfluenceable outbursts of defiance in kindergarten and (more rarely) reading-
readiness children is physical control. In their first year or so in school
some inner-city children heedlessly roam around the room, sometimes
running away from the teacher when summoned and screaming when
the teacher approaches them. They may cry for as long as an hour,
perhaps even turning over their desks, in a tantrum that is occasioned
by some academic or interpersonal frustration. Still other children may
systematically attempt to destroy property in the classroom, or, more
unusually, attack other children. Such displays can easily catch a
teacher off guard and leave her comforting or pleading with a child in
vain, as the rest of the class watches with some upset. The uproar created by such outbursts often brings in other teachers and the principal, who takes a dim view of the readiness of such children for school.
At such times the teacher often feels baffled and helpless in dealing
with the distraught child. The psychologist observing such children
usually finds that the teacher is fearful about following her instinct to
physically restrain or soothe the child on her lap. Such tactics are seen
by her as unprofessional and embarrassing. In discussing his observations with the teacher, the psychologist tactfully explores the inadequacy of exclusively verbal methods with young children who are
upset. The need for mothering and parent-like control methods is developed with the teacher, so that she can discuss her own feelings
about using such methods. Teachers often react to such a discussion
with considerable relief, confessing that they had wished all along to
establish more physical contact with the child. In some teachers it has
even unleashed feelings of tenderness toward their children, including
their favorites, which makes teaching a more satisfying experience for
them and the development of self-control more feasible for the more
naturally treated child. The mild repugnance of a few teachers to
physical methods of control, to restrain and soothe their children, can
usually be softened when they understand the needs of the young
child in school and the inadequacy of words alone for some children.

Once the child is seen as requiring various kinds of physical contact to aid him to relax and accept the limits set in the classroom, the teacher can more comfortably adapt different physical approaches to her usual verbal ones in a given situation. Thus she may forcibly but kindly sit a restless child down beside her or place a screaming child back in his seat or on her lap where she can soothe him gently. She may also intervene in the mounting spiral of frustration and rage of a child by sitting alongside him with her arm around him before he explodes into screaming. Such physical contact is often strikingly effective with young school children, especially when applied before an outburst. For such contact to have an impact the child need not be prepared as he must with the other two defiance-suppression techniques. The teacher must, however, intensify her relationship-building tactics with the unmanageable child, not assuming from his immaturity and vacant look that he is incapable of being reasoned with. Teachers often underestimate the capacity of young children to understand and discuss their own behavior and learning difficulties, which has the obvious effect of discouraging the child from talking out rather than acting out his difficulties. In our observations of teachers' use of physical-control techniques we have not found that it generates excessive dependency or resentment either in the unmanageable child or in his classmates. As long as the teacher keeps a keen eye alert to any jealousy or loneliness stimulated in other children by her attention to the unmanageable child, she can cope with these early signs in others. We have encouraged the teacher to explain to the class that when they are upset or have particular needs for her special care, they will receive similar attention. The children have seemed able to understand and accept this reality without manufacturing special needs. In all cases in which methods of physical control are used they form only a part of the teacher-psychologist influence techniques. Verbal methods are used, though in a more specialized manner. Whenever the child appears to be ready for more exclusively verbal methods of control and motivation, they are gradually instituted.

We shall now describe in some detail several cases of unmanageable defiance in elementary school children, selected because of the range in presenting symptomatology, triggering disturbances, and influence techniques applied.

RICHARD

Richard had never been referred to the consulting psychologist because the school and his family regarded him as hopelessly retarded, uncontrollably impulsive, and fantasy-dominated. He had learned little after four years in school and was so slow in a special class for the educable retarded that his teacher had recommended him for placement in a special class for trainable retardates. He had earlier been diagnosed at a child development clinic as mildly autistic with diffuse, mild brain damage caused by cerebral anoxia at birth.

The psychologist, during his classroom rounds in an inner-city elementary school, noticed Richard lost in fantasy at his desk, which was situated alone at the back of the room. The contrast between the boy's bizarre gesturing and self-absorbed fantasy and the intense interaction between the teacher and the rest of the children was gripping. Richard was literally in another world, spatially no less than emotionally. That his teacher and classmates fully ignored him was all the more remarkable, for the class was run on a child-oriented philosophy by the teacher, an attractive, acutely sensitive woman with several years of teaching experience and a certification in special education. The tenderly persuasive way in which the teacher guided her children and met their needs was truly a thing of beauty to observe. Not so with Richard. He was an outsider on each of the several visits the psychologist, with increasing fascination, paid to the classroom. Apart from about 20 minutes of daily instruction in small groups, Richard's only interaction with the teacher and children occurred when he would venture over to some child whom he would touch or occasionally hit as he pretended he was Superman or as he shuffled around the room in a self-mocking gait. Because he pestered the other children or broke them up with ridiculing laughter, the teacher explained that she had been forced to segregate him at the back of the room. If there was any doubt in Richard's mind that he was not welcome in his classroom, it must have been erased by his having been placed on a half-day schedule. He attended school only in the afternoon because during the period of seat work in the morning he would neither concentrate on his work nor leave the other children alone.

Richard in turn showed his contempt for school in a variety of ways. He struggled successfully enough to prevent his mother from dragging him to school on at least two afternoons a week. He defecated in his pants occasionally in school. Whatever simple work he undertook he did with maximum sloppiness. When he came out of his fantasy world to interact with the other children, he controlled them by making them laugh at him or by magically attacking them in the guise of Superman. Yet this pitiful lad could be sincerely described as "a lovely boy" by his teacher, who had never found him truly malicious and appreciated his occasional displays of sincere politeness and surprisingly mature conversation. On the psychologist's second visit to the classroom, for example, Richard asked him, "Are you a medical doctor?" listening attentively to the reply that the psychologist had come to the classroom to watch and see if he could help the teacher or any of the children. Richard then proceeded to describe his being knocked down several months before by a truck while he was riding his bicycle and revealed a scar on his leg.

The psychologist's guarded diagnostic impression was that Richard was playing crazy and was, moreover, a classic case of pseudo-retardation. Several rounds of teacher and family conferences and several phone conversations with the attending psychiatrist at the child development unit where Richard had been worked up, confirmed the psychologist in this impression. When at the age of seven Richard's intellectual ability had been carefully evaluated by a leading pediatric diagnostician, his IQ fell in the borderline range of functioning, considerably higher than his current educational performance would suggest. This estimate, moreover, was made against the usual background of emotional turmoil in Richard's life and may well have been an underestimate of his true intellectual potential. Richard's occasional moments of articulate lucidity and gracious warmth also pointed to undeveloped resources latent in the boy. The psychologist's observations of Richard's classroom behavior unearthed his lonely wish for friends, a starvation for affectionate contact that he did not know how to express appropriately. Neither his teacher nor his parents seemed aware of his loneliness at home and at school, and they reacted to him in ways that pushed him further into his fantasy retreat, which was at least peopled with imaginary playmates. The implication of these observations was that if Richard could be more naturally involved in the social life of the classroom, his rejection of work and normal behavior might decrease.

A final crucial element pointing to greater intellectual and emotional potential than had been suspected of Richard was his parents' inadequate understanding and handling of him at home. The boy's father presented himself as baffled and disillusioned with his son's impulsiveness and fantasy absorption. He tended to leave the boy's rearing solely to his wife who dearly loved and spoiled her son. She felt unable to impose effective bounds on the boy's irregular eating, sleeping, and bowel-control habits. Her conviction that her son was a member of some kind of rare species of atypical children could be discerned along with her powerful sense of guilt for having delivered the boy abnormally. All these parental difficulties had been noted by the psychiatrist who had handled Richard's developmental examinations at the local hospital. But the parents had shown little interest in participating in the standard pattern of psychiatric casework, and the child was not accepted for psychotherapy. The attending psychiatrist communicated to the psychologist strong doubts about the capacity of the parents to introspect and effect changes in their attitudes toward their son.

With the foregoing background of diagnostic impressions, the psychologist made his first intervention, characteristically in the classroom situation with the teacher, before recommending any changes in the home or seeing the boy individually at the Clinic. Richard's teacher was given every opportunity to discuss her more personal reactions to the boy, how he made her feel and what she really thought about him. When she believed the psychologist's assurances that no teacher could be equally effective with every child and that teaching Richard could, in the psychologist's opinion, easily generate unpleasant feelings in a person, the teacher was able to say how revolted she was by his occasional practice of soiling. She had recoiled from touching the boy since his first soiling and felt he was dirty. She also resented his inappropriate interruptions of a class she had worked so hard and successfully to motivate for work. The psychologist himself had to work to accept the teacher's difficulties in accepting a boy whose imperfect self-care disturbed her. It was tacitly understood by psychologist and teacher alike that this generally sympathetic and creative teacher had been taxed in a vulnerable place by the boy's behavior. Equally tacitly, teacher and psychologist seemed to agree that steps had to be taken to help the boy despite his objectionableness and no explicit plea had to be made to the teacher.

The over-all strategy of the psychologist was to help the teacher to reintroduce Richard into the life of the class in a way that would permit the teacher to protect herself from the distress the boy aroused in her. A gradual approach with two prongs was indicated: building a good relationship between Richard and his teacher and curtailing the boy's antisocial outbursts. No attempt was made at the outset to deal with Richard's soiling, especially since he had not soiled himself in two months. The psychologist also avoided confronting the teacher directly with the damaging effects of her rejection of the boy, for the rejection had been based on personality problems of the teacher that had to be respected if she was to cooperate in the treatment plan. As it was, the teacher showed herself incapable of proceeding any faster than what to the psychologist seemed like a snail's pace. Richard's unmanageable outbursts were to be dealt with, according to the treatment plan, in ways that would both effectively stop his outbursts and permit the teacher to keep the distance from the child she really needed to have. Thus, instead of segregating him permanently, the plan was to seat him with the other children and at the first sign of trouble warn him quietly that if he persisted he would be returned to the back of the room. He would be placed there, it was to be explained to him by the teacher, not because he was disliked but to give him a chance to think about the rule he had broken by misbehaving. After half an hour he would be returned to his regular desk, and the procedure would be repeated as many times as necessary. His regular desk among the other children would be called his good desk, the one at the back of the room his bad desk, and an appropriate label was pasted on each. This mild form of segregation gave the teacher the out she needed and at the same time made the rules he was breaking more salient for the boy. This defiance-suppression technique, moreover, was supplemented by various relationship-building techniques planned by the teacher and psychologist. The teacher was to maintain a continual personal dialogue with Richard, so that as often as every half hour she would chat with him quietly and briefly about how well he was behaving and working or use any pleasantry that occurred to her. She would, moreover, make plain to the boy her new interest in helping him and her liking for him, and she would highlight any positive changes, however slight, that occurred. In short, she would behave by design toward Richard just as she behaved toward the other children instinctually. For it was only with Richard that her sympathy and creativity had to be encouraged by the psychologist.

In his relationship with the teacher the psychologist was supportive of any technique the teacher reported in building a relationship with the boy. When the teacher proved able to follow the plan and to augment it in her own way, the psychologist began to speak more about the importance of involving him in friendships with other children and the value of keeping his mind on people or work rather than fantasy. The teacher came to interpret Richard's gesturing and fantasizing as signs that he required attention and involvement with people or work. When the boy began calming down and participating more in the class, the psychologist could suggest that he be segregated to a desk only a few feet away from his regular one if he misbehaved. Interestingly, the teacher implemented this suggestion by facing the boy's bad desk to the wall, revealing unconsciously her poor understanding of the relationship between his involvement in the class and his fantasy behavior. The psychologist explained this relationship to the teacher and the desk was turned around so that Richard could face the other children even when he was being segregated. By this time the teacher had developed a good relationship with the boy and was usually able to curtail his silliness by using a signal which only he and she understood—simply her saying "Rich." After three months of consulting with the teacher in this manner, Richard had become by the end of the school year considerably more cooperative in class and his attendance had improved. His educational handicaps, however, became glaringly apparent, for he could do little of the work to which he was now able to settle down. For this reason Richard was tutored three times a week during the summer at the Clinic by a college student carefully supervised by the psychologist. His attendance at school on a half-day basis with many absences had greatly limited any educational progress he might otherwise have made. His teacher's reluctance to put him on a full-day basis, lest he regress even after his behavior had improved, necessitated the summer tutorial work. The psychologist also hoped to use his continued contact with the boy during the summer as a lever in effecting certain changes in the parents' management of him at home, hoping to stabilize his home behavior sufficiently so that he would be more receptive to learning in the fall. Perhaps then his teacher would be able to accept him on a full-time basis.

The one-to-one relationship at the Clinic between Richard and the college student had three goals. First, to develop basic number and reading skills by using programmed-learning materials. Second, to improve Richard's attitude to school work, encouraging him to work for increasingly long periods of time. Third, to provide him with a warm human relationship in which he could feel accepted and learn how to get along without resorting to eccentric behaviors. Throughout their summer contact the college student drew analogies for Richard between his behavior at the Clinic and his behavior in school, thus continually focusing the boy's attention on the return to school in the fall. Before coming to the Clinic Richard had been repeatedly prepared by the psychologist, a frequent visitor to the classroom, so that he understood what he would be doing and why. The over-all goal, he understood, was to return him to school in the fall with more knowledge and a greater willingness to work hard. For the first few sessions Richard tried to transform the sessions at the Clinic into a playground in which he could act out his fantasies in concert with the college student. Play was initially limited to 10 minutes at the end of the session, and soon thereafter replaced by 10 minutes of conversation about anything the boy wished to discuss. His tendencies to become bored, fatigued, restless, careless, silly, seductive, or irrelevant during the programmed-learning tasks were all interpreted plainly to him as devices to avoid concentrating his attention on the work because he felt too stupid to do the work well. The college student's attitude was warmly accepting but firmly demanding of effort and attention on the boy's part, and Richard responded well enough to work the full 50 minutes after the first month. Richard read his first sentences. He mastered close to a year of phonics and basic number concepts up to addition by the end of the summer. He also was carefully guided when he became sloppy in his writing, and work samples of his old sloppy and new neat work were posted on the Clinic bulletin board. His active fantasy life was capitalized on by having him dictate stories to the college student who recorded them and had them typed up on a sheet of paper that Richard illustrated. The stories had diagnostic value in clarifying the boy's heavy use of grandiose themes, and Richard was helped to see how real strength comes from learning slowly rather than from performing magical actions. By the end of the summer Richard had developed a capacity for sustained attention and careful work. He had also learned how embarrassing and unfriendly some of his behavior was, although other aspects of his behavior were truly kind.

The psychologist involved Richard's 13-year-old sister in the summer tutoring by having her do half an hour of homework nightly with him, which he brought to the Clinic each time he came. Her assumption of responsibility made her more sympathetic than she had been to the boy and proved valuable in accelerating his educational gains. Two goals were established for the family during the summer, and the psychologist called several times on Richard's parents and sister to explain them. Follow-up telephone calls at the outset also helped get the plan started. First, Richard was to be in bed at 9:30 every night so that he could follow the pattern in the fall and not become tired in the afternoon when he eventually returned full-time to school. In the preceding year the boy's erratic bedtimes had produced fatigue that interacted with his hyperactivity in school to impair whatever learning efficiency he might otherwise have possessed. The enforcement of the constant bedtime, moreover, was the chief arena in which the psychologist planned to fight the battle of getting the parents to impose consistent limits on Richard's erratic eating and bowel-control habits as well as his generally immature and egocentric impulsiveness at home. When it became clear that it was toward his mother rather than his father or sister that Richard directed his uncontrolled impulsiveness, the mother was informed that unless she regained the upper hand she was condemning him to a life of retardation and uncontrol. The fear that this direct confrontation generated in the mother resulted in her forming a therapeutic alliance with the psychologist. Richard's mother showed herself willing to change her behavior, especially since she had seen some improvement in the boy toward the end of the school year. The follow-up phone conversations between mother and psychologist reinforced her emerging strictness with Richard, who seemed to be responding unusually well to her firm setting of bounds on his behavior. By the end of the summer the mother no longer felt she needed sedatives to control the boy at bedtime. All members of the family reported a calming down and greater reasonableness in the boy, whom they had taken with them on a family vacation without being embarrassed by him. Richard had taken to putting himself to bed alone on time, washing himself, tying his own shoe laces, and defecating in the right place. His relationships with all the members of his family had improved, and they enjoyed having him around.

A second goal set up for the family by the psychologist while Richard was attending the Clinic during the summer was the development in the boy of a sense of acceptance by others and by himself. The sister's kind but firm tutoring of him at home was closely supervised by the college student and psychologist to ensure that Richard's self-confidence was being bolstered. His sister understood that she was trying not only to teach him subject matter but also to show her love for him. Richard's father was encouraged to spend more time with the boy and to take him along on short trips in the neighborhood. The whole family was encouraged by the psychologist to trust Richard with a bicycle he had been pleading to use since he had been knocked off one by a truck the year before. The boy was to be allowed to ride the bicycle first in a park, then in other safe enclosures. When the parents felt that he had calmed down enough to be trusted with the bicycle on the street, they were to do so, but explaining all along to the boy the relationship between his privileges with the bicycle and his self-control in other areas. Finally, any positive changes noticed by the family were to be emphasized even more than misbehavior and the boy appropriately rewarded. The impression the psychologist tried to leave with the family was that they were to combine loving gentleness and trust on the one hand with consistent firmness on the other. Richard was to be actively involved in the family, as well as being controlled, and taught to grow up.

The payoff from the summer work with Richard and his family at the Clinic and at home was rewarding. On his return to school Richard was perceived by his family as "a new boy." Richard's teacher described him as "100% better." She found his attention span and capacity for completing independent work greatly increased, indeed, satisfactory. He could understand and follow directions and was able to amuse himself undisruptively after he completed his seat work. His knowledge of basic number and phonics concepts had moved forward astoundingly, the teacher reported. After a month of keeping him on a half-day basis, Richard's teacher placed him on a full schedule. She shared the psychologist's view that the most intensive educational effort was indicated for the boy in the coming year and seemed identified in her own mind with the challenge of accelerating his progress.

ALAN

Alan's crass rejection of learning and his unmanageably disruptive behavior constituted the number-one problem in a large inner-city elementary school. The most dedicated efforts of the school social worker, guidance counselor, and other key personnel had failed to reach the 10-year-old Negro boy or his embittered father who sorely resented the child's placement in a special class for the mentally retarded. The child's deteriorating school adjustment, as well as the vindictiveness of his college-educated father, the outspoken president of the local public housing residents' council, had doubtless contributed to the urgency of a request to the Clinic for its services both by the city supervisor of special education and the principal. Both the supervisor and the principal had been flooded by requests for help from Alan's teacher. The classroom was the scene of frequent bickering and fighting among the students, who disliked Alan as much as the boy and his family resented the class. The way in which the consulting psychologist handled the knotty problems posed by the case, his first in the school, illuminates not only the complicated relations within a disturbed classroom but also those between the classroom teacher and other school personnel and a problem family and the school. As with so many other school crises, lurking behind Alan's difficulties were critical issues about institutional arrangements and policy, especially with regard to special class placement and pupil discipline.

The normal procedure for a clinic psychologist beginning in a school is to spend his first month or so making the rounds of all the classrooms, quietly observing, and greeting individually the teachers he had addressed at the introductory faculty meeting. Not so in Alan's room, for the disorganization was so acute and the teacher's eagerness for help so insistent that the psychologist felt he could not defer involvement until he had familiarized himself with the school. Repeated observations in Alan's room, however, only demonstrated the boy's excellent self-control when a visitor was present. The other children's rejection of Alan was apparent, as was his sullenness, but none of the boy's provocative instigations could be discerned by the psychologist, who was struck with the short-tempered, uncooperative behavior of the children toward one another. The teacher seemed a bright, conscientious man with particular proficiency in using artistic and game-like materials and a sincere interest in the momentary needs of the children. In some ways he seemed a born psychologist, except when he discussed Alan at several luncheons with the consultant. Toward the boy his attitude was replete with cautiously expressed bitterness and hopelessness. He obviously felt that Alan had ruined his class with incessant teasing, quarreling, fighting, rudeness, and capriciousness about doing work. His referral of the boy for psychological help reflected his conviction that Alan was disturbed and disturbing, and he was delighted when the psychologist agreed to see the boy twice weekly at the Clinic. Rarely did the teacher show any inclination, after four discussions, to ascribe any role in the class disturbance to the other children or himself. The teacher seemed to treat the psychologist's understanding acceptance of his hostility to the boy as a kind of agreement with him in assigning exclusive blame to the child. Any attempts by the psychologist to shift discussion to a closer consideration of the other children or the teacher were defensively ignored or minimized. The teacher's model of the classroom crisis was that of a single disturbed and disturbing child who required emotional treatment in a clinic.

Because of his difficulties in communicating effectively with the teacher and the sparseness of his classroom observations, the psychologist's only option was to talk with Alan at the Clinic and to speak to his family, realizing that he would eventually have to enter into more meaningful confrontations with the teacher. Outside the class Alan was told of this twofold plan to help him and his permission to speak to his parents obtained. Before paying a home visit, the psychologist discussed with the school social worker her experiences with the family. She had found the father incensed about the school's special-class placement of his son and furious with the way they had "ruined the good boy I had sent to school." She sensed in him intense distrust of the white-run social agencies with which the family had dealt and even a conviction about the role of discriminatory practices in the school. It was with relief that she handed over to the psychologist the right to be the contact man for the school with this family whose other sons had also had considerable difficulty in school and in the community. The social worker and guidance counselor felt, moreover, that the father dominated the mother, who always sat nervously and silently during interviews.

The psychologist's home visit with Alan's father was the first of many and resulted in what proved to be a surprisingly good working relationship. There were several reasons for this. First, the psychologist presented himself as the representative neither of the school nor of a city agency, and expressed an interest in correcting, in his relationship with the family, past misunderstandings that existed between the family and such institutions. Second, the psychologist brought the color issue to the surface after a short while by making clear his personal commitment to civil rights and awareness of existing prejudice and discrimination in society. Third, the psychologist agreed with the father's assertion that the fault could not be all Alan's and ventured the opinion that if Alan's behavior improved he could work at regular class level. The psychologist in this connection assured the father that Alan's underachievement reflected the boy's attitudes rather than his basic capacity and gave him assurance that the boy was not mentally retarded in the sense of having already attained maximal utilization of his academic capacity. When the father agreed to work with the psychologist in any way suggested, the psychologist obtained the following commitments from him: the father would encourage Alan to talk freely and in confidence at the Clinic and would cease deriding the school or society in front of the boy, because such derision impaired the boy's ability to accept school discipline and work. When he grasped that the psychologist was also striving to promote his son to a regular class, the father became less insistent on blaming the school for his child's failures and more eager to help in restoring him to the path of learning. Because he saw that the psychologist had come not to judge or blame the family but to understand and help, the father felt free enough to admit how he had been insufficiently firm with Alan's homework and obedience at home, although he maintained that the boy was not much of a problem. The father also opened up about his own resentment as a boy toward his own father and explained how unhappy he was to have to stay at home without work and on welfare because of the pain from a spinal injury he had sustained.

For the next month Alan came willingly to the Clinic twice weekly, and occasional teacher-psychologist discussions were continued over lunch. Concerned with winning the rebellious youngster over, the psychologist devoted the first few sessions to exploring the use of a typewriter and tape recorder in helping Alan study for his spelling and arithmetic tests. When Alan's interest and achievement proved to be high, the psychologist asked for the boy's help in understanding the discrepancy between his Clinic and school performances. His initial response attributed responsibility for his school difficulties to others: the children teased him about being "mental" because he was in a special class. Alan's use of clay at the Clinic was truly creative, and he loved the praise he was receiving, often arriving half an hour before the appointed time. He volunteered to sing for the psychologist: praise was a new experience for him. Alan's delight in coming to the Clinic reached its high point after a month, and he deeply appreciated the Saturday morning art classes in which the psychologist had enrolled him in view of the boy's aptitude. Although the boy had acquired some insight into his school difficulties, primarily he had received massive doses of praise and acceptance. His school behavior and interest in work, according to his teacher, began to improve. The only serious discussions with the boy had concerned his preference for being a big fish in a little pond rather than a little fish in a big pond: Alan had stopped participating in swimming competitions when he lost a race at the boys' club and had said that he preferred the slower reading and arithmetic groups in special class to the more challenging ones. The way in which he held himself back was emphasized. In class he suddenly asked his teacher to be in the top groups and he worked hard enough to remain in them for a while. It appeared that Alan was improving.

After two weeks of this improvement Alan lapsed back into his old lazy ways, disrupting the class as much as ever, beginning now to skip Clinic appointments. Alan's father applied the necessary pressure on him to keep his appointments and the boy showed up, describing at length the unfairness of the children and teacher in school. The psychologist believed Alan and his father that no disturbance at home was triggering the boy's latest school outbursts. Alan's cooperation and motivation in his weekly art class were exemplary, said the teacher. All roads pointed to the psychologist's initial impression that Alan was one troubled child among other troubled children in a class that had been stigmatized by the school culture. More intensive discussion with the teacher was indicated.

When it became clear to Alan's teacher that the psychologist required far more detailed information about classroom happenings if some understanding of the crisis was to be achieved, he aired two grievances that threw a new light on the classroom difficulties. First, the school had been using the special classes as dumping grounds for other teachers' disciplinary and emotional difficulties rather than for more individualized instruction for slow learners. Placement in special class was for the "mental" children, as Alan's classmates had alleged. Besides the "mental" stigma, special-class placement carried with it the stigma of punishment and rejection for uncooperativeness, and Alan's teacher was clearly outraged with the misuse to which his class had been put by the school. He expressed to the administration his angry frustration by frequently sending disruptive children to the office, as if to remind them that the policing action they had forced on him prevented his proper use of the special class. More than any other child, Alan epitomized this stigmatic misuse of the special class. Alan had been placed in special class shortly after jumping out of his second-floor classroom window in ostentatious imitation of a demonstration the week before by the fire department. His regular fourth-grade teacher was ill when he disrupted the substitute teacher's class with the jumping incident as well as a host of defiant actions characteristic of him since kindergarten. That his disruptiveness more than his academic difficulties underlay the placement is proved by the fact that the Stanford-Binet intelligence test score that provided the justification for his being termed "retarded" had been recorded in the third grade. It was only in a fourth-grade regular class, after his jump, that the long-standing recommendation for special class placement was acted on, much to the detriment of the reputation of the special class. That Alan's academic underachievement reflected his uncooperative attitude rather than basic capacity is supported by his above-school-average scores on the reading-readiness test administered in the second grade.

A second legitimate grievance by Alan's teacher was the inconsistent handling of discipline by the school administrators. When the teacher angrily sent particularly defiant children to the office, the treatment they received there depended solely on the administrator who happened to see them first. In the hands of one person they might receive a tongue lashing or jostling about, from another a walk and even an ice cream soda, from another some schoolwork or an explanation of why they must behave. These inconsistencies played into Alan's hands, and he eventually came to seek out the right administrator when he was sent down to the office. These inconsistencies also strengthened Alan's charges to his father that he was being unfairly treated at school, and since the family and school were not on friendly terms matters deteriorated further as the father came to feel that the school did not know what it was doing. Throughout it all the teacher raged internally with the whole misunderstanding of the special-class program and inefficient discipline.

The teacher's two grievances were indispensable to the psychologist's understanding of the teacher's indignation and defensiveness, but more data were needed on the specific classroom situation. Here the psychologist found the teacher somewhat reserved and withholding as he subtly persisted in defining the psychologist's role as working with the child rather than the classroom situation plus the child. Moreover, the psychologist came to feel that any positive remarks he made about Alan were interpreted by the teacher as signs of softness or being hoodwinked by the boy, an interpretation partly justified by the fact that Alan's antics usually were manifested in the classroom among other children rather than in a one-to-one relationship. In addition to refusing to perceive Alan's problem as a manifestation of classroom difficulties in which even the teacher played a role, the teacher showed resistance to following through on any of the psychologist's concrete suggestions. When the psychologist suggested that the teacher talk individually and in small groups with the warring factions in the room, the teacher said he had tried that and "they only forgot after a few days." The suggestion that he keep reminding them was greeted with lukewarm ardor, as was the recommendation that he confront the children with the various feelings and motives behind their strife that the teacher understood full well. When encouraged to settle long-standing disputes between particular pupils, or even to get them to apologize after fighting, the teacher informed the psychologist that a better-known psychologist with whom he had once taken a course opposed apologizing. When the psychologist recommended that participants in a fight be placed for an hour in separate classrooms outside their home-room in order to reflect on their misbehavior, the teacher doubted the value of the suggestion. The teacher admitted the futility of deluging the office with naughty children, but persisted in doing so whenever the going got rough. The over-all impression garnered by the psychologist was that the teacher was essentially unworkable and probably contributing through petty acts of counterhostility and retaliation to the children's provocativeness. In short, there were sufficient seeds of truth in the boy's charges and sufficient disturbance in the classroom to justify the validity of a transfer of room, which would have to mean to a regular class.

Further investigation was felt to be necessary at the Clinic before any recommendation for re-evaluating Alan's placement. More direct pressure was put on the boy to describe and explain his classroom misbehavior. His heavy use of rationalizations and even lying was explored as self-defeating behavior. An attempt was made to develop his concern for the dangerous implications of his actions for his future, and this was related to his touchiness about an older brother who had been in jail. After several sessions the boy showed some signs of worry about his future and a realization of how he had damaged, though not destroyed, his chances for success in life. In dreams he recounted and in his transitory symptoms of nervous stomach Alan was beginning to evidence some small amount of anxiety about the consequences of his deeds. The Rorschach was administered along with the Wechsler Intelligence Scale for Children, and on both tests the boy revealed concern over the adequacy of his body and even a hint of feeling that he had some congenital defect, such as being "mental" or "stupid." He also spoke more about his rivalry with his older brother and his unhappiness over his father's not working. His IQ was in the normal range and confirmed the psychologist's view that the boy was neither retarded nor suitable for the particular special class in which he had been placed. His IQ score was probably an underestimate of his intellectual potential, for on difficult items he showed the same tendencies he showed in school: to become bored and inattentive or silly and expansively guessing. His unreflective approach to much of the intelligence testing was taken up with him as an example of his school problem, again with the reminder that he was seriously damaging his chances for doing well in school and therefore in the future job market. Because of his father's insistence, Alan continued to attend sessions despite a shift in tone at the Clinic from one of cultural stimulation and praise to one of serious exploration and interpretation. Some of his hardheaded uncooperativeness and provocativeness emerged at the Clinic, when he once playfully hid from the searching psychologist, but the boy was able to participate in the study of his behavior. His teacher reported some over-all improvement in his school attitudes, but the classroom continued to be an undesirable place for a boy with Alan's needs. He was neither working nor behaving so well as he might and needed to, and he remained a social outcast among the other children in the room.

The psychologist formed the judgment that in a very real sense Alan did not comprehend that school was not a playing field and that when frustrated by school rules he must not try to destroy the situation for others. The boy's disruptiveness seemed less motivated by seething anger than by a determination to get his own way, especially in competitive activities. A part of Alan was neither thinking nor talking during the sessions at the Clinic, and what the boy required was a teacher who was willing to follow through in patiently teaching him social skills while calmly but firmly setting limits backed up in the manner suggested by the psychologist. His present teacher had shown himself simply unwilling to work closely with the psychologist in shaping the boy's classroom behavior. Moreover, because Alan's IQ fell clearly outside the range for special-class placement, the psychologist began conferring with the principal about the possibility of transferring the boy to a regular class after being retested by the school psychological examiner.

In arguing his case the psychologist could lay before the principal Alan's new IQ score, the recently achieved cooperation of the father, and the opinion that the boy required a more stable classroom to achieve more self-control and academic progress. The principal agreed with the psychologist about the importance of involving Alan's present special class and prospective fifth-grade teachers in the decision. With some trepidation a fifth-grade teacher agreed to accept Alan, but the special-class teacher disapproved of the idea. He felt that Alan should not be rewarded for his bad behavior by a promotion in the middle of the school year. He also thought that the other children would kick up a fuss with which he would be left to deal, and he could see no suitable way of telling the children that Alan was being neither rewarded nor punished but shifted because it was best for him. The resentment the teacher had directed at the administration for dumping emotional problems in his room was now reversed into anger that they were considering removing one. The supervisor of special education was enlisted by the teacher to prevent the transfer, and a meeting was called among the supervisor, the guidance counselor, the consulting psychologist, and the principal. Despite the supervisor's genuine conviction that it was wisest for Alan to be placed in a regular class at the beginning of the next school year if his retest justified it, the principal decided to order the retesting at once. When Alan earned an IQ in the dull normal range, the principal arranged the transfer immediately. Pressures were brought to bear on his new teacher not to allow the boy to attend the World's Fair with his fifth-grade class, lest he misbehave, but she perceived that this would be starting him off in the room as a second-class citizen, undermining the goals of the transfer.

The psychologist also raised with the principal the inconsistent disciplinary handling of Alan, and a plan was worked out in which the assistant principal would be the sole administrator who would cooperate with the fifth-grade teacher. The plan called for Alan to be given several private warnings by the teacher if he persisted in disobeying, after which he would be sent down to the assistant principal, who would phone the boy's father to remove him from school and put him to bed for the remainder of the day and the next day, whereupon he could return to school. After the plan was cleared with the relevant school personnel, the father's cooperation was requested by the psychologist, and a meeting was called in the principal's office for all concerned, including Alan and his father. At the meeting the principal stressed the dire seriousness of this opportunity for Alan and the confidence the school had that he could settle down to good work if he tried. On the same day of the meeting in the principal's office Alan came to the Clinic, where the transfer and exclusion plan were thoroughly explained and discussed with him. The boy's delight in getting out of special class was tempered by his awareness that if he acted up in the regular class unpleasant consequences would follow for him. The game was up. For the remaining weeks of the school year Alan did not have to be sent home once and his behavior improved dramatically. His pestiness and unsocialized egocentricity remained in evidence, but not in unmanageably disruptive proportions. The success of the plan resulted in no small degree from the intensive follow-up work by the psychologist with the father, who came to see his own indispensability if the plan were to be taken seriously by the boy. Details of the plan were rehearsed with the father, who was periodically reminded to talk with his son about his attitudes and actions in school. Although the sessions at the Clinic helped to clarify certain distortions by the boy before they could explode and sabotage the plan, the bulk of the efficacy of the plan probably stemmed from the transfer of classrooms, united home-school front, and consistent treatment of the boy in school. Alan's new teacher displayed a willingness to cooperate with the psychologist and was effective both in enlisting other children in her class to help Alan and in watching for the earliest warning signs of trouble to which she responded warmly and firmly. Alan's father and the teacher kept in contact, and to this first-year teacher's courageous acceptance of the number-one school problem much of the success of the plan is due. The following fall Alan went into the departmental sixth grade, and the principal called a preventive meeting of all teachers concerned, Alan, his father, and the psychologist who by then had terminated his Clinic visits with the boy. His subsequent progress was in marked contrast to his earlier school career.

RAYMOND

The case of Raymond is interesting in two respects: the severity of the kindergarten child's unmanageable defiance and the way in which the teacher's and the psychologist's understanding of the child's difficulties dictated their choice of influence techniques. Raymond passed his first two months in school with quiet compliance. However, the advent of the Thanksgiving and Christmas holidays, as well as the return to school after these holidays, occasioned the most intense defiance from him. With a facial expression blank and taut, he stood at the back of the classroom destroying toys with systematic and deliberate calmness. He hardly seemed agitated, and, as he destroyed the toys or threw them around the room (though never at anyone), he carefully watched his teacher. If she tried to approach him he would cleverly maneuver himself around the desks so that she could not catch him.

When he was not disrupting the class, he would frequently go off in a corner to play with toys on his own, occasionally biting some of the toy bears' ears. The several days of defiance before and after Thanksgiving had been borne in desperation by the first-year teacher, but when the boy began to act provocatively two weeks before the beginning of the Christmas holiday, even more ferociously than before, the teacher asked the psychologist to try to stop in when the boy was acting up. Meanwhile, the principal's discovery of the destruction of property and the boy's upsetting effect on the other children had resulted in an ultimatum: if the teacher could not control him, he would be suspended for the year and readmitted to kindergarten the following fall.

During his classroom observations the psychologist did not intervene but remained impassively seated in a corner of the room, watching each of Raymond's outbursts, which sometimes occurred only feet from the psychologist. It was observed that three types of event triggered Raymond's disruptiveness or his walking away from the class to the back of the room: the daily calendar lesson or any reference to the Christmas holiday; any frustration connected with the distribution and collection of the milk containers; and any difficulties in drawing and writing or competing in a group game such as Simple Simon. It was further observed that the teacher's comments to and about Raymond intensified his provocativeness, for she would try to regain the attention of the class by remarks such as, "We won't look at Raymond," and, "Everyone pretend that you can't hear all the noise and watch me." Her understandable distress and worry, moreover, were communicated all too clearly in her facial gestures and posture and in thoroughly exasperated quality of voice.

Before discussing his observations with the teacher, the psychologist saw Raymond's mother several times. An attractive, well-spoken woman who conveyed the impression of withholding some information, she explained that she had never been able to control the boy at home and could not understand why he was so disobedient. She did not link the boy's difficulties in self-control with the fact that she held a job during the day and saw Raymond and his older sister, who were cared for by their grandmother, only a few hours each day. Nor did she link the boy's difficulties with the absence from the home of Raymond's incurably alcoholic father whom the children dearly missed. She spoke with convincing concern, though without insight, about his school difficulties, noting that he looked forward to coming to school. When told about Raymond's difficulties with the calendar, holidays, the school milk, and other difficulties she could contribute nothing. It was from Raymond himself that his teacher learned that the boy spent holidays with another grandparent, apart from both his parents. On a home visit the teacher had been introduced to an "uncle" who looked rather more like a boyfriend. It was from another child he was seeing at the Clinic that the psychologist learned about Raymond's propensities to set fires.

In pooling their observations, the teacher and psychologist agreed that Raymond had little respect for any female authority and felt more powerful than women as well as neglected and betrayed by them. His deliberate provocativeness toward women seemed to reflect his wish to punish them for depriving him both of the affectionate care he needed, as symbolized in his frustration with the school milk, and of the father who alone could set firm limits for him and provide a model of strong manliness. In short, the boy appeared to be rebelling against school and home for giving him neither a caring mother nor a strong father. The difficulties with the calendar and holidays seemed to reflect his anxious anger over being separated from his parents and teacher on holidays and being abandoned to the care of an elderly grandparent. Raymond's teacher and the psychologist agreed that the minimal interpretation they could give to his intolerance of making errors in his work or play was a strong tendency on the boy's part to deprecate himself, to regard himself as devoid of any competence. More deeply, his intolerance of his weaknesses might have signified his rejection of his own rather small body and his envy and jealousy of the abilities and friendship of other children in the classroom.

At first sight Raymond would seem an excellent candidate for intensive psychotherapy with an adult male. Yet the principal's pressing ultimatum and the acute nature of the classroom crisis suggested to the psychologist that there was insufficient time to prepare Raymond properly for psychotherapy in the manner we describe in Chapter 13. What was imperative was a plan to deliver massive assurance to the boy that he was wanted in school by the teacher. Since only a week remained before the Christmas vacation, it was felt that any defiance-suppression techniques should be deferred until after the holiday, lest unmanageable hostility be created in the boy. The psychologist received an extension of vague duration from the principal.

During the week before the Christmas holiday Raymond's teacher picked him up each morning at his home and had breakfast with him in a restaurant near the school.[1] The teacher's focus in the breakfast

---

[1] Particularly in the case of the new teachers with whom we have worked, we are no longer surprised at the degree of effort they will put out for a child away from school. Frequently the involvement has been at our suggestion and at other times it has been a spontaneous decision on the part of the teacher. It is our

conversations was on establishing a friendly relationship with him rather than on influencing him. In school the teacher kept Raymond on her lap during the calendar lesson and milk break whenever that was possible. The physical contact with his teacher clearly relaxed him, and the teacher followed up the physical contact with a great deal of special tutoring as she gave verbal instructions to the rest of the class. Whenever he showed positive social behavior the teacher redirected her remarks to highlight and include him, and during this period he smiled for the first time. Any extra jobs she could find for him, such as erasing the blackboards, she praised him for doing. The frequency and ferocity of his outbursts were halved in the week before the holiday. When he did start making noise or throwing things in the back of the room, the teacher stoically concealed her exasperation and explained to the rest of the class that she wished Raymond would join them, for they all liked his company. One morning Raymond disappeared into the bathroom for more than a few minutes, and when the teacher peeked in she found him silently holding his bleeding nose which he had apparently irritated through picking. The teacher wisely used the occasion to lavish the warmest concern on the boy, praising him for his braveness and saying how she wished he had told her about it earlier so that she could have comforted him. The boy seemed to be grasping the idea that he was important to his teacher in a way in which he had not done before.

Raymond returned from the Christmas holiday with the predictable hyperactivity and irritability. After he had been back several days his teacher explained to him at breakfast that from now on she was going to help him overcome his restlessness and disobedience. She told him that she was going to insist on his obeying her from now on, and how this would help him to feel more comfortable in school. For the entire week following this explanation the psychologist spent much of the morning in Raymond's class to observe and assist the teacher, if necessary, since a screaming struggle was to be anticipated. During this period the teacher was to avoid a showdown whenever possible by persisting in her relationship-building techniques, including placing the boy on her lap. When he ran away from her or misbehaved, however, she would catch him, with the psychologist's help if necessary, and return him to her lap or his seat. Providentially, during this period the

---

impression that these efforts and the satisfaction the teachers experience from such extra-school involvements stem in part from the relationship they have with the Clinic member, that is, it is done in the context of an interprofessional relationship in which the pursuit of understanding and the rendering of help are the primary values.

principal was absent because of illness and the spectacle of the teacher chasing and restraining the screaming child was confined to the classroom. The point of the physical restraint was to convince Raymond that he was not more powerful than the teacher who could gently but firmly supply external controls that no other woman had been able to do. During the screaming either the teacher or psychologist was to explain to the class what was happening and allow them to ask any questions about it. While Raymond was screaming he was to be uncompromisingly held until he stopped, then reassured gently that he was not going to be hurt in any way.

Once each morning for the following week Raymond was cornered by the teacher and psychologist when he ran away from the teacher and held by the psychologist until he stopped screaming. Each day he screamed less bitterly and for a shorter period of time, until the teacher was able to corner him and restrain him on her own, with the psychologist standing by. The teacher was advised how to restrain the child effectively, though by that time he had calmed down considerably and was far easier to control. It is a rare kindergarten child who would require the presence of the psychologist in the room to restrain him as Raymond did. In discussions with the teacher the psychologist emphasized the progress achieved by the physical-control techniques and the undesirability of the teacher's showing her understandable exasperation. After the initial week of struggle the teacher became more light-hearted about her recently acquired combat readiness and was heartened by the obviously decreasing intensity and durations of Raymond's struggles. By the third week of January Raymond had completely stopped screaming, running away, and destroying things, providentially again, just at the time of the principal's return to school. During this period of the teacher's establishing her control over him, Raymond became very dependent on his teacher, appearing almost exhausted by the struggle he had just lost. When he had stopped screaming and running away for two consecutive weeks the teacher gradually stopped asking him to breakfast, explaining that he could now understand how much she liked him without her eating breakfast with him, and he accepted her decision uneventfully. By February the boy showed evidence of a profound reorientation toward school: he participated willingly in group activities, began writing his name and tolerating mistakes, and interacted with the other children in a friendly way. Soon thereafter he even participated in the calendar lesson. He told the psychologist on his regular visits, "I've been a good boy" and his teacher proudly introduced him as "the new boy in our room."

In the middle of March Raymond had a temporary and mild relapse that cast considerable light on his earlier difficulties. In one week he became very jealous of attention, similar to that which he had once received, being lavished on another boy and began pushing and punching the children on the lines. It was learned that he also had set a fire in the neighborhood. In a phone conversation with Raymond's mother the psychologist was told that she had just remarried and that Raymond's behavior had improved tremendously at home. When the teacher elicited from Raymond that he was upset about his mother's remarriage, saying that she understood how angry that could make a youngster, he relaxed and no longer found it necessary to express his resentment. Without mentioning to Raymond that she knew about his fire-setting, the teacher scheduled a lesson on fire, inviting a fire marshal to talk to the children.

After Raymond's talk with his teacher about his mother's remarriage he returned to the path of forward progress that he had followed since mid-January and finished out the school year in similar fashion. His immeasurable gains in attitude and behavior at school seemed to have some carry-over at home, according to his mother. By the end of the school year this once fiercely unmanageable child was his teacher's favorite.

Perhaps no other child illustrates so well as the unmanageable one the principle that the manifestation of problem behavior in the classroom reflects among other things, something about the classroom. From an etiological standpoint the "causes" may be elsewhere, both in the past and present, but this in no way invalidates the point that sustained problem behavior is dependent on what goes on in the classroom. The attitudes and actions of the teacher, the ways in which she goes about understanding the child, the consistency and persistency with which she responds, the conflicts she may have about what she would like to do, the effects of the behavior of other children on the problem child—these are some of the factors that can heighten and sustain problem behavior. But the examples in this chapter also emphasize how crucial a role may be played by the principal and other teachers, not only because their attitudes and behavior can influence what a particular teacher thinks and does in her classroom but also because they can be crucial determinants of the range of possible remedial actions.

Labels like "unmanageable," "impossible," and "incorrigible" are ordinarily used by teachers to communicate two things: the severity of the problem facing the teacher and the diagnosis that the problem behavior is independent of what the teacher thinks, feels, and does.

There can be no question about the validity of the severity of the problem, but we cannot accept the validity of the diagnosis. In not accepting the validity of the diagnosis, we are far from intending a criticism of teachers who, like most of humanity, are not dispassionate thinkers and effective agents when confronted with crisis, emergency, or stress conditions.

Chapter 10

Translating Psychological Concepts
into Action

There is an enormous difference between understanding a phenomenon on a theoretical level and being able to utilize that understanding in a manner that makes relevant interventions possible. The general problem of translating understanding of a particular situation into actions appropriate to that situation is not confined to those in the mental-health professions.

It is in the clinical setting that a clinical psychologist accomplishes the transition between his understanding of the dynamics of a particular case and the type of intervention that appears to be appropriate. This translation of the clinician's conceptual understanding of a situation and the kinds of behaviors he judges to be important in terms of helping an individual deal with his problems usually occurs over a period of some time. Most often it occurs in the context of the psychotherapeutic situation and takes place only after the clinician and the client have had enough time to explore the situation to their mutual satisfaction. Because of the clinician's awareness of the importance of the gap between understanding and action, the question of timing assumes primary importance. The clinician must decide when and under what conditions a client is ready for a particular communication and he must time his intervention so that it becomes a constructive rather than a damaging experience for the client. One of the reasons for the care taken by the clinician in his interactions with the client involves the limited amount of time the therapist and his client spend together.

When the psychologist becomes intimately aware of and involved in the school culture (when the classroom, as it were, becomes his office) he is afforded the opportunity of being with his clients (the children) for a much greater amount of time than he would otherwise. He can observe the children, interact with them, and work with the

170

teacher for as long and as intently as he and the teacher feel necessary in terms of the dictates of the situation. By sharing and discussing their observations, the psychologist and the teacher can evolve a plan of action that can be implemented within the classroom and evaluated in a periodic and systematic fashion. The situation is one in which psychodynamic concepts can be translated into appropriate actions with a fair amount of control. Ideas and theories about a child, his problems, and his behavior can be tested in a setting that constitutes a significant portion of his daily life.

There have been many books written about "why Johnnie can't read," books that attempt to provide us with a framework by which we can understand more clearly the variables facilitating or impeding a child's ability to learn to read. It is seldom that any one particular variable assumes the potency of determining the direction in which a child's ability or inability to learn to read becomes channeled. More often than not a host of variables interacts to produce the conditions under which reading becomes a gratifying or upsetting experience for the child. Once in a while, however, it is possible to delineate the rather specific conditions that have resulted in a situation in which learning to read becomes an anxiety-evoking experience. In these cases a psychodynamic understanding of the situation appears to be parsimonious in terms of accounting for the data under consideration. The data appear to point irrevocably to a particular event in the child's young life, an event of such magnitude as to influence significantly the future course of the child's development. However, as we have indicated, an understanding of the psychodynamic importance of an event does not mean that the knowledge so gained can be translated effectively into appropriate remedial action. For this translation of theory to occur, particularly when dealing with sensitive and potentially disorganizing material, we must have more than a modicum of control over the situation. When the teacher and the psychologist work together in the classroom setting, this type of control becomes much more possible than it otherwise would.

Example 1. Johnny was a second grader whose teacher described him as "just about the nicest little boy you'd ever want to have in your class." He was a bright and outgoing child who was immensely popular with his classmates and his teacher. His smile was a warm and engaging one, and he often went out of his way to help another child who seemed to be in distress. He seemed particularly sensitive to the needs of others, and it was this sensitivity that appeared to draw so many of his classmates to him. He was one of the recognized leaders of his class, a little boy with whom the other children wanted to be.

The only area in which Johnny appeared to experience any difficulty was reading. Johnny could not read, and he seemed to become very upset whenever he was engaged in a lesson involving reading. Johnny's inability to read and his unwillingness to learn to read were a source of considerable puzzlement to his teacher and to us. He had been intellectually evaluated and was found to be of "superior intelligence." He did well in every other area of work and was outstanding in arithmetic. Because of the fact that he functioned so well in every other subject, Johnny was not retained in first grade even though he could not read. It was hoped that somehow "his reading would catch up to his proved ability in other areas." As the semester wore on, it became evident that these hopes would not be realized.

Each time we observed his classroom we became more and more impressed with the fact that there appeared to be two distinctly different Johnnys in the class. There was the Johnny who loved school and everything in it. This was the Johnny who helped other children, reveled in doing his mathematics, looked forward to playing games, and enjoyed drawing. During these times he was a little boy who appeared to be uniquely alive and exhilarated in the classroom. At these times learning seemed to be an exciting and wonderful situation to him. Then there was the "other" Johnny, the Johnny who seemed uneasy, restless, and anxious. This was the Johnny who appeared only when reading occupied the class. It was clear that he did not like reading and wanted to have nothing to do with it. Whenever the class would go to the library, this Johnny would ask to be left in the room and would become somewhat belligerent when told that he would have to go with the rest of the class. During those times that the children were to "read silently" at their seats Johnny's eyes would wander about the room and he would squirm restlessly in his seat. Whenever Johnny's reading group was called to the front of the class to meet with the teacher, he "suddenly" would develop a very short attention span and would become quite withdrawn.

We shared our observations with the teacher. Although originally she had believed that Johnny's problem was one of "paying attention," she soon became more and more convinced that there were other variables involved. Although we both tried to talk with Johnny, neither of us could gain any information we felt might be helpful in understanding the situation. Johnny simply told us that he did not like reading, that it was boring, and that he would rather do other things.

Because the situation was not getting any better with the passage of time, the teacher felt that it might be helpful if we met Johnny's mother. We arranged such a meeting and soon found ourselves face to face with a woman (Johnny's mother) who seemed frightened and anxious even before we could begin our discussion. She fidgeted with her clothes and seemed obviously ill at ease even though we had tried to prepare her for the meeting by minimizing the situation's "urgency." Before we could say a word Johnny's mother informed us that she knew the meeting had something to do with Johnny's inability to read. The mother told us that she knew of no reason that could account for her son's difficulty. She suggested that he might be "just lazy" and would do better if we put more pressure on him or punished him more severely whenever he would not "try to learn." As our meeting progressed, we got the distinct impression that Johnny's mother wanted to "get out" of the situation as quickly as possible. She obviously was nervous, seemed on the verge of tears, and appeared to be quite intimidated by the entire state of affairs. We therefore terminated the meeting as quickly as possible.

The teacher felt that very little had been accomplished by the meeting. She was most impressed, however, by the degree of anxiety and fear that the mother apparently brought with her to the situation. Although we had learned nothing about Johnny's reading problem, we did learn a great deal about his mother. We also learned that Johnny had an 18-year-old sister with whom he was quite close and that she went to the local high school. The mother had told us that she had become particularly close to him since the sudden death of their father three years before. The mother suggested that we ask the sister to come and talk with us.

A week later we met Johnny's sister. She was a great deal less frightened and anxious than the mother had been. Before we got started she apologized for her mother and told us that she had become extremely anxious and nervous ever since the family's loss of the father. Because of the mother's difficulties in accepting the situation, she (the older sister) had had to spend a good deal of her time taking care of Johnny. Because of the obvious effect that the death of her father had had on her mother, we asked her how and under what circumstances he had died. She then proceeded to tell us a story which provided us with a reasonably good idea why Johnny could not read.

Johnny's sister told us that their father died very suddenly of a heart attack on New Year's Eve three years before. Johnny was five years old at the time and was going to enter kindergarten the following September. The sister told us that her mother was in the bedroom getting ready to go out to a New Year's party and that their father—already dressed—was sitting in the living room with Johnny. The father suddenly groaned and his head dropped to his chest. Johnny looked at his father, shook him, and then ran to the mother and told her that "Daddy is acting funny." When the mother came into the living room, the father was dead. The sister then went on to tell us how very overcome her mother had been by the death of the father and how she had "not yet come out of it." The mother became, and still was, an extremely depressed woman. She rarely left the home and was frequently observed crying and wringing her hands and staring into space. The sister also told us that the mother did not want the children, especially Johnny, the youngest, to forget their father. Consequently, she often sat Johnny down and gave him one of the family albums to go through. She would make Johnny point out every picture in which his father appeared. We asked the sister what Johnny and his father were doing in the living room the night the father died. She answered us very simply: "Johnny was sitting on my father's lap and Dad was reading him a story from one of Johnny's children's books."

We discussed with the teacher the connection between the father's death and Johnny's inability to read. She was as impressed as we were with the dynamics of the situation. Our discussion was a full and complete one. We felt that the teacher had to be acutely aware of the state of affairs, not only because of the nature of the material involved but because the situation was one in which we would have to work together closely if we were going to attempt to intervene to any significant degree. We both felt that this was not the kind of situation with which to confront the mother. She appeared to be far too involved with her grief and much too anxious to be able to help. We felt that it would be important to work with her but that we could not count on her participation in helping Johnny with his reading problems. We then turned our attention toward the older sister. She seemed to be a relatively stable girl and was someone who had been able to develop a close relationship with Johnny. We agreed that she would be the most appropriate person to help Johnny outside the classroom. As far as the classroom setting itself was concerned, the teacher felt that she could now begin to work with Johnny in terms of exploring with him some of the variables that we knew were relevant. She could now begin by helping him deal with his feelings of guilt, anxiety, and fear with respect to reading.

We decided to consult Johnny's sister once more. At this meeting we discussed with her how she could be helpful to her brother, how his problems in reading might be related to his fearful memories of his father's death. Although we did not go into great detail, we did indicate to her how she could encourage Johnny to express his feelings about reading to her. We also arranged for the sister to keep in close contact with the teacher so that they could coordinate their efforts. We all agreed not to involve the mother unnecessarily in this project. The sister was extremely anxious to be helpful but somewhat hesitant about her ability to handle the situation. We therefore decided that the three of us would meet regularly to compare notes and discuss what Johnny was talking about, how he was reacting, and what changes were occurring in the situation.

When it is possible to observe a child over a long period of time, especially if during that time the opportunity arises of seeing the child in a variety of different settings, it becomes relatively easy to detect changes or slight alterations in the child's moods and behavior. This is particularly true in the classroom situation, in which, over a period of time, a basic profile or picture of a given child in terms of his general temperament, personality, and behavior is evolved. Consequently, if and when a child is perceived acting differently, this difference becomes a cue or a signal that something has occurred to alter his more or less characteristic way of relating to himself and/or to others.

Teachers often become quite sensitive to a child's nuances of behavior and often can spot potential areas of difficulty in this manner. We, too, have become sensitive to the fact that children often transmit their own danger signals, and we have learned to use them as the bases for preventive and remedial intervention. Once more, however, the problem becomes one of translating our psychodynamic understanding of a danger signal into actions that are appropriate to the child and the situation. Although our goal is always one of attempting to be helpful to the child who is experiencing difficulty, it is also our aim to use the individual case as an illustrative example of a problem that in one way or another may be experienced by many other children.

Example 2. Rhoda was a six-year-old child who attended one of the kindergarten classes we visited regularly. She was a small, plump, cherubic child who seemed to enjoy her days in kindergarten. Although somewhat mischievous at times, we always observed her to be an extremely engaging and outgoing little girl. Over the course of time in which we visited her classroom we had become accustomed to seeing her rushing around the room amiably "poking her nose into everyone's business." This was our picture of Rhoda.

One day during our regular visit to the classroom we were somewhat taken aback not to find Rhoda actively involved with any of the other children. She was seated quietly at her desk and was scribbling aimlessly at a piece of paper that lay before her. She appeared sad, almost forlorn. We were struck by the vast difference in her behavior but decided to observe her further to see whether or not this new attitude would persist over a period of time. Throughout the morning there was no change. Regardless of the activity— whether it involved circles games, listening to a story, or clay work—Rhoda remained a somewhat passive, withdrawn, and somber child. For want of a better word, we described her that morning as "extremely depressed."

After a while, when we finally were able to speak to the teacher, we asked her to give us her impression of Rhoda. As it turned out, the teacher had already noticed the change in Rhoda's behavior and had investigated the cause. The teacher told us that Rhoda's best friend, a little girl in one of the other kindergarten classes, had left the neighborhood during the week when her parents had moved to Florida. The two children had known each other for about two years and had become very close and good friends. Although Rhoda's friend had moved to Florida only temporarily (she was to return in six months), Rhoda was positive that she would never see her again. Consequently, she "went into mourning."

The teacher was quite concerned with Rhoda's behavior and, although she believed the child would "get over it in a few days," had noticed that she was not responding to whatever increased attention was given her. The teacher related to us how she had tried talking to Rhoda, had tried to reassure her that her friend would return, and had made her her "assistant teacher," but all in vain. Rhoda was not responding to the increased attention and had not reacted to the teacher's attempts to boost her ego.

In talking about the situation with the teacher, we had used the term "separation depression" to describe Rhoda's behavior. The teacher was quite interested in exactly what we meant by the term and we explained it to her. In this context we spoke about Rhoda's loss of a love object and of her subsequent depression and withdrawal. The teacher quickly thought of several other children who had formed quite close attachments for some of their classmates and, given the nature of today's rate of familial mobility, she was sure that in one way or another each of these children already had, or would in the near future, experience the loss of a friend or love object. Rhoda's problem, although currently unique in the classroom, might very well soon become the problem of several of the other children in the class. We agreed that what seemed to be needed in this case was a chance for Rhoda to express her feelings of depression in a manner not only appropriate to her needs, but also appropriate to the needs of the other child—appropriate in the sense that the children could share each other's experiences. It was also true that Rhoda's friend would be returning in six months, and it seemed important that Rhoda get a chance to experience this fact and be given the opportunity of maintaining whatever realistic relationship remained between herself and her departed friend.

After thinking about the situation the teacher came up with an idea that seemed to meet all of the requirements and needs. She would organize a formal learning experience around the subject of communicating with friends or members of the family who recently had left the neighborhood. She would have each of the children write a letter to someone who had moved away and someone whom he would like to retain as a pen pal. Because none of the children could actually write such a letter, the teacher would have each of them paint a card and would go around to each desk and ask the child to tell her what to write. The children were to bring with them to class the address of a friend or relative and the card would be sent away as soon as possible.

The teacher implemented her plan. Each child made a card and told the teacher what he wanted to say to his friend. When the teacher came to Rhoda's desk, Rhoda was eager to dictate her letter. In a very moving manner she had the teacher write how much she missed her friend, wished that she had never left, and wondered if she ever would "come back home again." The teacher faithfully wrote down everything that Rhoda had said. When the activity was over, the children sealed their letters, placed stamps on the envelopes, and sent them away.

Much to her surprise, Rhoda received a letter back from her friend in Florida. The letter, witten by her friend's mother, but also in her friend's words, was very similar to the one Rhoda had "written." Her friend really missed her and wished that Rhoda could have come to Florida with her. Florida was "very nice," but her friend was looking forward to their reunion when she returned to the neighborhood. Rhoda was overjoyed with her letter. She immediately went to the teacher and asked if she could "write another letter back." The teacher felt that it would be a good idea for Rhoda and her friend to correspond with each other for the duration of the time in which they were separated and volunteered to be "Rhoda's writer" for that period of time.

In a rather short time Rhoda came out of her depression. She soon became the "old Rhoda" we had known in the past.

Sibling rivalry is a common phenomenon among children, especially during the early years of their development. Jealousy and envy of each other's accomplishments and vying for parental affection and attention are characteristic behaviors among brothers and sisters in the same family. The classroom often serves the function of another setting in which a form of sibling rivalry can be detected among children as they strain and fight for the teacher's love and attention. The teacher becomes the parent substitute, and whatever unresolved sibling conflicts the child is experiencing are often worked through with this new substitute mother or father. Teachers become acutely aware of the way they are perceived as parental objects by their children and are often able to utilize the classroom setting as a way of dealing with these problems.

One of the most common variations of sibling rivalry—we might call it "presibling rivalry"—occurs when an only child is informed of the fact that he will soon have a little brother or sister. This becomes a particularly difficult situation for a child, especially when he is not prepared for the "blessed event" and when the parents themselves become anxious as they await the birth of their next child. If the child is unable to deal with the situation at home, he will often utilize the next-most-important setting in his life, the classroom, as the arena in which to act out his feelings. Under these circumstances, the teacher becomes a parental figure of a slightly different nature. The child is now competing with an unknown and unborn child for the love of his parents. He may also use the teacher in an effort to obtain the kind of information, reassurance, and clarification of the situation that he cannot obtain at home. The child may have many questions about the state of affairs, questions about himself, his prospective brother or sister, or questions about birth in general, that he now directs toward his teacher. The teacher's ability to understand and deal with the situation becomes an important variable in determining the nature of the child's current and future adjustment.

Example 3. Jody was a small, frail-looking, seven-year-old girl who was repeating kindergarten in one of the schools in which we worked. She was a quiet withdrawn little girl who was essentially uncommunicative in the classroom. She was repeating kindergarten because of the school's feeling that she was too immature for the first grade and had not mastered the skills she would need to function effectively in that setting. The school's hope was that the additional year in kindergarten would allow her to develop those verbal and nonverbal skills that would enhance her prospects of succeeding in the first grade.

After an initial period of difficulty, Jody appeared to be making a rather good adjustment to her new kindergarten class. She quickly developed a close relationship with her teacher, an extremely gentle woman who was experienced and competent. During her first two months in school Jody began to talk and seemed to be learning to interact with many of the other children in the class. She no longer remained isolated from the other children for prolonged periods of time and had begun to develop some friendships. Although she was not able to do her "formal" kindergarten work as well as had been hoped, she was beginning to act in ways that were much more socially and interpersonally appropriate to her age and to the classroom setting.

One day in the middle of November things changed abruptly. Jody came into the class and immediately withdrew into her shell. She wanted to have nothing to do with any of the other children and began behaving in a manner reminiscent of the previous year. She would not talk, participate in any of the classroom activities, or interact with any of the children. She became an isolate, sitting by herself and gazing out of the window. Despite the teacher's attempts to find out what was bothering her, the behavior persisted. The teacher tried talking with her on several occasions but the child ignored her. A short time later Jody began to display a host of aggressive and assaultive behaviors. She would often approach another child very directly and, with little or no observable provocation, hit the child and try to hurt him. This behavior continued and, over a period of time, the other children in the class began avoiding her and staying out of her way. Although Jody was now coming into contact with other children, her mode of relating with them was regressive rather than progressive in nature.

Because of our concern about the situation, the teacher felt it would be a good idea to meet Jody's parents and such a meeting was arranged. Because the father could not take the time from his work to attend the meeting, only Jody's mother was present.

Jody's mother told us that she had noticed a change in her behavior also. The mother was quite unhappy about the change, for she had thought that her daughter was "getting better." She went on to tell us that she was particularly concerned about her daughter's regressive behavior because it was occurring at a time when she (the mother) was least prepared to deal with it. The mother told us that she was now quite nervous and anxious herself, "what with being pregnant and all that." This was the first time we had learned that Jody's mother was expecting another child, and we asked why she was so nervous and anxious about the situation since she had already given birth to one child. The mother became quite overwrought at this point and informed us of all the trouble she had had carrying and delivering Jody. She also told us of her concern that the new child would "turn out like Jody." In pursuing the topic further, we found out that the mother and her husband had put off having another child because of their fear that the child would be born with all the problems and complications (forceps delivery, prolonged labor, etc.) that had accompanied Jody's birth. Because of their own anxiety, they had done little more than tell Jody that she was going to have a "little brother or sister." Their own fears and concerns over the pregnancy were quite evident, and it was clear that they were too involved in their own conflicts to be able to deal with their daughter's feelings, questions, and concerns about the situation.

After the meeting we discussed our impressions with the teacher, who felt that the parents were so overcome by the prospects they faced that they were unable to gauge the effects of their own anxieties on Jody. They were so involved with their own problems that they could not perceive the effects of their behavior (fear, nervousness, and anxiety) on Jody. We began to view Jody's classroom antics from the point of view that the child was acting out her own questions and feelings in a setting that might better tolerate this type of behavior. Jody's withdrawal and her attacks on the other children appeared to be her only way of letting people know that she had feelings and questions about her position with respect to other children. We felt that Jody had many questions about the impending event and that she had been poorly prepared for the birth of her sibling. We also believed that Jody's behavior was indicative of the fact that she was quite concerned about what would happen to her if and when her sibling arrived on the scene. More than anything else, we were impressed by how little we could count on the parents to be helpful in dealing with the problems of their daughter. They simply were not free enough to focus sufficient attention on their daughter's problems.

The teacher felt that under the circumstances it was imperative that she deal with Jody's questions in a manner in which the parents apparently were unable to do. She began by structuring a "share and tell" activity in terms of having each child tell or begin to talk about his own little brothers or sisters. Each child began to talk about what he liked and disliked about his younger siblings, about how it felt to be the older brother or sister, and the kinds of questions he had about them. The teacher also began to spend some time each day with Jody and, rather than wait for the child to bring up the subject, immediately confronted her with the problem. The teacher shared with Jody some of her own feelings about learning that she was going to have another brother or sister, and began talking about how she was able to help her mother take care of the new child. Jody gradually began to respond to what the teacher was doing. She began by sitting on the teacher's lap, patting the teacher's stomach, and asking if the teacher was going to have a baby. The teacher responded to this by beginning to explain to Jody, "how a baby lives in Mommy's belly," how it grows, and when it is born. Jody responded by asking more and more direct questions and finally inquired if the teacher's "Mommy still liked" her after her brother was born.

Throughout this period of time Jody's classroom behavior became less and less unpredictable. Although she did not renew her friendships with the other children, she did stop her assaultive behavior. She began drawing pictures of babies and immediately took them to the teacher, an act the teacher always responded to as an invitation from Jody that she wanted to talk a bit more. The teacher communicated with Jody's parents and told them of the things that Jody was concerned about and tried to make them aware of how they might be helpful. Without putting undue pressure on the parents, the teacher did make clear to them some of the questions and feelings Jody had. Throughout the remaining months of the mother's pregnancy the teacher continued her involvement with Jody, an involvement whose purpose was to allow the child to express her feelings and to offer her some answers to the many questions she had.

The time arrived for Jody's mother to give birth; as it turned out, the delivery was not a difficult one and there were no complications involved. The child was a healthy little boy. After the birth of their second child Jody's parents became markedly less anxious and fearful. Their fears had not been realized and they even began thinking about having another child in the near future. The more relaxed the parents became, the more relaxed Jody became. She had been prepared for the event by her teacher and her teacher had been able to offer the child the kind of support and information that the parents, because of the nature of their own involvement, had not been able to supply. Things became much calmer both in the home and in the classroom. Jody's regressive behavior vanished and she was able to continue the progress that had characterized her earlier months in kindergarten.

More often than not it is the troublesome rather than the troubled child who quickly comes to the teacher's attention. His behavior is usually of such a nature that it singles him out as a child with problems, as a child who requires immediate and constant attention. The troublesome child usually acts in ways that make teaching a difficult, if not impossible, job; he disrupts classes, frightens or annoys other children, and generally makes his presence known in direct and observable ways. Consequently, it is not surprising to find that teachers most often focus their attention on and ask assistance for the child whose behavior is strange, frightening, or interfering with respect to the learning situation.

The troubled child, on the other hand, is much less likely to be attended to or noticed so immediately or forcefully as the troublesome child. Although he may be a child with as great and disabling a problem as the troublesome child, his behavior is characteristically neither dramatic nor interfering. He generally does not act in ways that frighten the teacher, intimidate the other children, or significantly interfere with the normal classroom routines. More often than not his symptoms have a passive and quiet quality about them. He is usually withdrawn, unobtrusive, and silent.

Regardless of the behavioral differences in their symptomatology, both the troublesome and troubled child are, in their own ways, dealing with problems that are interfering with their abilities to learn in the classroom situation. Because of the nature of their symptoms, however, it is usually the troublesome child whose cry for help is acknowledged.

It is a sensitive and perceptive teacher who can step back from the immediate needs of the teaching situation (i.e., classroom order and discipline) to take note of those unobtrusive but troubled children in her class who need attention and help. It is no small feat for a teacher to be able to think and act in this manner. The pressures of teaching are often so great that most teachers can focus attention only on the child whose behavior is disturbing the classroom process. Once in a while, however, we encounter a teacher who is able to look beyond her own needs to maintain an orderly classroom and can become concerned with and focus attention on the child who is suffering in a quiet and unobtrusive manner. However, even when this occurs we are still confronted with the problem of translating our psychodynamic understanding of the child's problems into a plan of action that is both helpful to the child and appropriate to the classroom setting.

Example 4. Michael was a nine-year-old third grader whose class we had been observing for a long time. During that time we had never focused much attention on the boy or interacted with him to any significant degree. Part of the reason for this was that we, like the teacher, were most concerned with observing several of the other children in the class. The class itself was a problem class; that is to say, a class into which several of the difficult third graders had been funneled. That this was a class with many problem children in it was due to the fact that the administration felt that the teacher was an extremely capable, experienced, and competent woman who was willing and able to deal with children difficult for other teachers to handle. Our observations in the class convinced us that the administration had made a wise and thoughtful decision. She was, indeed, a superb teacher and a wonderful human being. She was in complete command of her class, and her strength, coupled with her creative and sensitive approach to her class and the learning situation, served to create an atmosphere in which learning became an exciting and wonderful adventure to many children whose previous school experiences had been uniformly unsatisfying. Another reason for our relative neglect of Michael was that he was one of the "good" boys in the class. His was not a behavior problem; he apparently did his work and never was involved in any of the periodic flare-ups that characterized the behavior of many of the other children.

During one of our regular coffee klatches with the teacher she asked us if we had spent any time observing Michael. We told her that we had not and asked her why she had Michael in mind. The teacher seemed a bit hesitant to continue but soon decided that "even though it sounds crazy and might be more a reflection of my own problems than Michael's" she would go on. She then told us that for some reason which she was not completely aware of there was something about the boy that bothered her. She admitted that he was not a behavior problem and was certainly no trouble in class, but that he was just "too, too polite—not at all like a nine-year-old boy usually is." She went on to talk about his excessive politeness and how his extreme deference made her a bit uneasy, almost as if his behavior was "too good to be true or even healthy." She then took out some of Michael's drawings and showed them to us. The drawings were about as polite as a rampaging gorilla. Each drawing, regardless of its particular content or theme, was replete with undercurrents of violence, blood, and murder. Even his "Christmas scene" was devoid of any cheerful or benign sentiments. The feelings and emotions that came through in his drawings were as unlike his polite and socially graceful classroom behavior as night is from day. Many of them showed a rather striking and morbid preoccupation with death, mutilation, and torture. In short, his drawings looked like the dire creations of a violently angry, sadistic, and hostile little boy.

After looking at Michael's drawings, we felt that the teacher's questions about the child were well-founded and not the reflection of any of her own problems. We told her this, and, after a short laugh about it, we asked her how she had come to focus her attention on Michael. She replied by telling us that she always made it a point not to get so overwhelmed or involved in her children with behavior problems that she had no time to think about the other children and their difficulties. We only could marvel at her sensitivity and clinical acuity. We told her that we would spend more of our time in her class observing Michael.

Our observations of Michael's classroom behavior soon began to yield a picture of the boy that was quite different from the polite and deferring youngster we had seen previously. His behavior, although never directly or openly aggressive, was covertly hostile, sadistic, and sneaky. When a little girl seated next to him dropped her pencil and bent down to pick it up Michael, ever so deftly and nonchalantly, moved his foot and kicked the pencil further from her grasp. When a boy was hurrying down the aisle to get to the front window Michael would look the other way and "accidentally" stick out his foot to trip the youngster. When the youngster fell, Michael smiled, apologized, and helped the boy get up from the floor. Over and over again we saw Michael do something or say something which invariably hurt another child. On each occasion his actions would be apparently accidental and without malice or forethought. It became clear, however, that his "accidents" were too numerous and regular to be unmotivated and we began thinking about him as a little boy under whose polite and sweet exterior there "burned volcanic fires fierce and wild."

We shared our observations with the teacher and together we began to think about and discuss the situation. The teacher, in a different context, had already had the opportunity to meet Michael's mother and had developed many feelings and impressions about her. Her primary impression was that she was an extremely rigid and proper person. The mother had spent some time telling the teacher how important she felt appearances and manners were and how the modern generation was not being brought up correctly to show appropriate respect for their elders and parents. She went on to relate how in her household Michael and his younger brothers were children who understood the uselessness of temper tantrums and obstinacy. Outbursts of anger and aggression were not tolerated in the home and unless the child could "quietly discuss his problems like a little adult" he was neither listened to nor recognized. The home, in short, was a quiet and dignified place, a place devoid of any displays of childish anger or temper.

The more we discussed the situation and the teacher's observations about the mother, the more we came to feel that Michael was learning to deal with his feelings by suppressing them and by masking them behind a rather fragile facade of civilized living. His more direct feelings of anger and aggression were clearly unacceptable at home and he was made to feel that these kinds of experiences were neither healthy nor normal for a little boy to have. It seemed, however, very difficult for Michael to disown these feelings completely; they did not dissipate with time; they did not slowly dissolve or suddenly vanish. Rather, it appeared that, unable to express them openly and directly, Michael was allowing his feelings to become known in more subtle, indirect, but nonetheless frightening ways.

With these kinds of observations and hypotheses in mind, we then began to think of ways in which we could use the classroom setting as the vehicle by which we could intervene in what we both felt was a process that was detrimental to Michael's development and growth. We felt that it was necessary for him to begin to experience his feelings of anger and hostility as neither unhealthy nor unacceptable, as feelings which need not always be hidden, denied, or suppressed. We felt it important that he begin to talk about and express his feelings more openly and directly and not continue to mask them behind a cloak of premature sophistication and respectability. More than anything else, we wanted Michael to be able to be a little boy who could get angry, have many questions and ideas about violence, and use the learning situation as a way of investigating and testing his fantasies.

The teacher began by having the children talk about their daydreams and nightmares or nightdreams in a series of "share and tell" sessions. Each child began by sharing with the other children some of his fantasies about what he liked and disliked, what he feared and hated, and what some of the things were that he wondered about a good deal of the time. During this activity many of the children began talking about their feelings and questions related to such themes as violence, murder, sadism, and anger. After each session the teacher would summarize what many of the children had talked about and then would indicate how most of the children seemed to have similar feelings and questions about the same kinds of things. They then discussed in very simple terms how and when each of these feelings were appropriate and the conditions under which they could be expressed more or less directly. Michael began taking part in these sessions and soon started talking about many of his own feelings and the things he would do "in secret." In this manner he related some of his fantasies about killing and death and some of the "terrible things" he did to small animals he caught or found. The children were intrigued with his deeds but soon began talking about similar things that they had done or thought. When Michael began talking about mutilating animals, the teacher artfully turned the discussion into a session in which she discussed anatomy and other related subjects. Day after day these "share and tell" sessions went on. Michael looked forward to each session and seemed anxious to be called on to talk about some of the other things he was thinking about and doing. The more he talked about his experiences, the less sneaky his behavior became. He appeared to loosen up and to drop some of his excessively deferential and reserved behavior. He began laughing a little more spontaneously and to become much more like a little boy than a "little adult."

With the passage of time, Michael became much more popular with his schoolmates. He began joining them in their ball games and spent less and less of his time alone or in isolation. His drawings were more benign in character and less obsessively concerned with gore. His over-all behavior was more openly aggressive but less ominous in its implications. He would get angry and sometimes fight, but he would not rely solely on indirect and potentially dangerous maneuvers by which to act out his feelings. In short, he became much more alive. The teacher, although acutely aware of the fact that she now might have to contend with Michael's newly exuberant and potentially disruptive behavior, was much happier in the knowledge that he was becoming much more the healthy little pest and much less the unhealthy little adult.

A common problem arising with children of all ages, but particularly with younger children, involves stealing in school. Stealing is a difficult and unpleasant subject to approach with children. Usually, the stealing is not serious. It involves small objects, for example, a pencil, a crayon, a puzzle, or more rarely, money. We are never sure that the first-grade or the kindergarten child understands the moral implications of stealing, and few teachers are inclined to punish a very young child for such an act. Nonetheless, repeated pilfering and sometimes even single acts of pilfering conjure up visions of future delinquents or worse. Stealing is most frequently approached as requiring action designed to show the child that stealing is wrong. Those oriented toward psychodynamic concepts tend to view stealing as an expression of some motivational force, frequently a wish to receive affection from someone in the environment who is denying such affection to the child. In consequence, stealing is taken as symptomatic of some disturbance and it is to be treated accordingly.

Example 5. A first-grade teacher approached the consultant about a little girl who had been taking things such as pencils, erasers, and crayons from the other children. On one occasion she had taken a small object from the teacher's desk drawer, and the teacher was in a quandary about how to handle the problem. Brief investigation indicated that the child's parents had been divorced a year or so before and that the mother was about to remarry. The information supported the inference that the child was anxious about losing the affection or attention of important people in her environment.

The consultant suggested that the teacher call the child aside and tell her that she was concerned about her taking things. The teacher was to accept the impulse to steal by saying she could see that the child would like to have the things she had taken. However, she was to explain it was not right to take anything without asking. She was told further that should she want anything at all she was to ask the teacher for it. The teacher might have to say "no" sometimes, but usually she would be able to give her what she needed. The teacher followed through, had the conference with the child, and reported that she did not say much but looked very serious. On subsequent occasions, the teacher was to call the child over and ask her whether she needed anything and to remind her that she should ask if she wanted anything. She later related an incident in which the child was alone in the room with the teacher's purse, which was open. The child went to get the teacher who was in the next room to tell her she had forgotten her purse. The teacher praised her effusively for her thoughtfulness and reinforced the idea that if the child wanted anything she was to ask the teacher. The teacher reported that she followed through on the suggestions, with the result that the child's stealing stopped entirely.

The potential of the classroom for dealing with children's disturbances in both a therapeutic and preventive fashion is very large. The classroom structure itself and the teaching medium may be used effectively and precisely to deal with anxieties children may have about life circumstances. In the following example a teacher dealt with a child's anxiety by teaching a lesson concerned with the problem with which the child was struggling. Open consideration of the problem in the classroom permitted the child to express and master a concern he was struggling with.

Example 6. A first-grade child had for some weeks been moody and relatively ineffective in class. One morning he asked to go out to the bathroom but was asked to wait. He asked again and was permitted to go. After a while, when the child did not return, the teacher became concerned. Just as she was about to send someone to look for him, the principal received a call from the child's mother to tell her that he had come home. When informed, the teacher discovered a small puddle under the boy's seat, evidence that he had wet his pants. The child was clearly distressed, both by what had happened and by other events, judging from the very unusual behavior he was exhibiting. The mother brought him back to school, and at that point revealed that she had recently returned from the hospital where she had undergone surgery. The child had been with a grandmother, and the mother indicated that it would probably be necessary for her to return to the hospital for a few days for further medical procedures. She said the last time she had gone the child had known about it, but she had never told him exactly when she would go. She entered the hospital one day while he was in school, and he returned home to find her absent. According to the mother's report, the child cried when he learned that she was in the hospital, but thereafter he was obedient and apparently happy. On her return he became very clinging and whiny, asking many questions about whether she would go again and about how she was. She was wearing a surgical dressing on her neck and was unable to carry out her normal duties around the house. She usually drove the boy to school regularly, but now that she was not well she was unable to do so. The child seemed to have a great deal of resentment that his mother was not doing things for him as she once had, and there was some suggestion that he was worried about whether she would still be at home when he got there.

On the basis of this information, the consultant advised the teacher to tell the child he was wrong to leave the building without permission but she could understand that he was very worried about his mother. The consultant and teacher then worked out a plan whereby the teacher would conduct a lesson on illness, surgery, and going to the hospital. The teacher, after a social studies lesson, began talking about hospitals. Several children were able to contribute experiences in which they had been in the hospital or in which relatives had gone to the hospital and had returned. The teacher also included some discussion about illnesses and the process of recovery, indicating that sometimes it took a long time for people who came out of the hospital to be completely well. The child apparently contributed some of his own experience and asked a number of questions about how people recovered. According to the teacher, he seemed much involved in the discussion, and at the end of it appeared to be rather calm and satisfied. From that time on, until the end of the term, the child's mood changed to one of normal exuberance, and his work became steadily good. He never again wet his pants in class and seemed perfectly at ease in school. It is instructive to learn from his mother that his clinging behavior persisted with her at home long after the disturbance disappeared in school.

Activities in the classroom may sometimes be adapted to meet a child's needs. It is necessary to know something of the possibilities in a situation in order to be able to find the circumstances in which a child's needs may be expressed. In the following example a hypothesis developed from projective tests was used as the basis for finding a satisfactory activity that would help to satisfy a psychological need in a constructive fashion.

Example 7. A first-grade child's test protocol supported a view of his aggressive behavior as partly reflecting his desire to identify with symbols of strength to be able to ward off threats of aggression directed against himself. The child would frequently attack other children, often without any obvious provocation. He was difficult to manage in class, his mother suggesting that he could be controlled only when his father threatened to beat him for misbehavior. The father was not available because the parents had recently separated. As part of a general effort to work with the child, the consultant and teacher discussed some of the test results. The consultant explained the child's fantasies around aggression and asked how the child could be given a feeling of being a physically strong person within that setting without having to fight other children. The teacher suggested she might give him the job of moving chairs following the reading group. He was to be given the job because he was strong, and she was to emphasize her pleasure at seeing him exercise his strength in this fashion.

This child's problems were quite marked, and no single effort such as giving him the job of carrying chairs would in itself make a significant difference. However, a good part of the child's disruptive behavior did disappear, and he eventually began doing some schoolwork. What is highly significant, however, is his mother's statement that the child was talking very favorably about his teacher and his school and was quite upset about the prospect of going to another school when his mother discussed moving away. Somehow, the child seemed to feel he had found something for himself in this school with this teacher.

Incomprehensible or "crazy" behavior is always distressing. Frequently, when a child's behavior is bizarre, it is difficult to appreciate that such behavior can also be a signal of some kind of situationally determined distress.

Example 8. A kindergarten teacher was working very effectively with a schizophrenic child. She was maintaining him in the classroom and found that he would follow along with the group for many activities. However, the child was unable to do any work if left alone. He would engage in various forms of self-stimulating behavior including biting his hand, rocking, and masturbating. The teacher was able to tolerate a good deal of his behavior, and she made a distinct effort to work with him in the class. Whenever the class was assigned a drawing, or some similar project involving handwork, she would always try to sit next to him for part of the time and help him do the work. She was content to give him the time and found he would attend fairly well when she was with him. At times when she was working with him, he would begin to make weird noises that would become progressively louder as she continued. In discussing the sounds with her, it appeared the child would make the noises when he was unable to handle the work she wanted him to do.

Discussion led to an interpretation of the noises as a distress signal that indicated his feeling of inability to handle the work. The consultant suggested that the teacher work with him until he began making the noises. She was then to tell him she understood that he felt he could not do the work, and therefore they were stopping. The teacher reported that she tried the tactic and felt considerably more comfortable in working with him. The teacher never again complained about the noises. She felt that she now had a method of handling this distressing habit and that it was comprehensible to her.

There are times when teachers have to handle difficult situations on the spot. In the following example the consultant happened to be available to help a teacher think his way through a difficult situation. The consultant had been working with the boy and his teacher for several weeks preceding the following incident:

Example 9. A fourth-grade boy told his teacher that he had found a hunting knife in the street. He voluntarily gave it to the teacher to hold for him until after school, exacting a promise he would get the knife back after school. Both consultant and teacher had considerable concern about the boy because he had been involved in a number of fights, and once had been accused of chasing a girl into her house with what he claimed was a toy hatchet. The teacher felt he was beginning to develop a good relationship with the boy, and he was worried about whether he would damage it if he did not return the knife to him. In discussion with the teacher the consultant suggested that the boy was in fact seeking protection against himself and that it would be serving the boy's interests to hold the knife. The teacher and consultant then worked out an approach to the problem. The boy was to be told that the teacher knew, of course, that it was illegal to carry a weapon and that the boy would be in great difficulty if he were found with the knife by the police. (Since the boy had already been picked up by juvenile authorities on several occasions, he could understand the reality of the statement.) Moreover, the teacher was to take the boy to the principal, who was to be given the knife to hold and was to commend the boy for his good sense in giving the knife to the teacher. The plan was implemented without a hitch. The incident did not mark any particular turning point in their relationship, but neither did it harm it. The boy accepted the teacher's decision and seemed at least as friendly after the incident as he did before it.

Sometimes academic and intellectual limitations are such that not much progress can be anticipated. When the school has already retained a child and provided him with remedial help and he has already been through a course of psychotherapy which ended with the recommendation that he be treated as nearly normally as possible, the school is left without recourse when he continues to have academic difficulties and to get into trouble. In this instance it seemed that the boy's behavior in school was in clear response to his feeling of inadequacy in dealing with his school situation.

Example 10. This fourth-grade boy presented a long-standing problem of underachievement. He had also been aggressive in the neighborhood, and many complaints about him came into school. His teachers reported that he had a short attention span and that he was hyperactive. He had been under psychiatric care, had been tutored summers, and had received additional remedial reading, all to little avail. Observations in class showed that he participated eagerly with those few things he knew but soon got lost in the material. He would then dawdle, daydream, or just sit over his work looking lost, disgusted, and hopeless. Following a series of conferences with his parents, it was decided to remove the pressure from him by taking away all extra services. His teacher agreed to program for him at his level in her room and to mark him much less strictly to avoid failure. He had already been retained in the grade, and because he had not shown much progress as a result of the retention, teacher and principal agreed to pass him along as much as possible. Once the pressure was removed, his teacher began reporting a changed attitude. He produced some modestly good papers, and as his work in school improved his mother indicated that he was doing his homework without argument. He seemed to feel more at ease in the classroom and discussed his feeling that somehow he was catching onto the work more easily. Observation in class at the end of the year confirmed that he was happier-appearing, attentive for longer periods of time, and much more receptive to criticism than he had been before. In terms of measured achievement, he did not improve that much, but his attitude and feeling about school certainly changed for the better.

Sometimes we not only translate the child's needs into some kind of program in the classroom but also help others to think about the dynamics of their interactions with the child. Sometimes the very act of considering what is going on makes the difference. In the following example the child's mother came to the school because she was having difficulties with her, because the child complained that she did not like school, and because she was beginning to feign illness to be kept out. The mother wanted the consultant to speak to the girl to straighten her out. The consultant listened to the mother attentively and promised to see the teacher before he did anything further.

Example 11. The teacher, herself Jewish, began the conversation by
saying, "She's my only Jewish child, and it's a shame the way she acts."
The child was resistant, negativistic, somewhat disrespectful at times, and
was turning in work the teacher felt was unworthy of her. The teacher was
initially critical of the child's mother, whom she felt spoiled the child, and
in consequence found herself either pushing the child hard or ignoring her.
In the course of the discussion with the consultant the teacher indicated that
she was worried about several problems at home in recent weeks and that
the problems had made her somewhat nervous. One of the personal problems
she discussed was the failure in school of a nephew toward whom she felt very
close. She had been working very hard to try to help her nephew continue
his education, and she felt he was not responding to her efforts. The
consultant made no effort to interpret the possible transfer of emotional
reactions from her family to this child but instead merely indicated that he
felt certain the teacher would be able to cope with this child, once her mind
was settled about the other issues.

Following the discussion with the consultant, the teacher began changing
her tactics with the child. She stopped pressing her about her work and
instead began giving her extra jobs around the room and praising her
profusely for her work. About two weeks after the interview with the
consultant the teacher reported that the child had attained the highest
score in her class on the annual academic achievement test. The teacher was
very pleased with her performance and made it a point to advertise her
achievement widely in the building. The child's mother, who was known in
the neighborhood, made it a point to tell the consultant about her daughter's
achievement, and then began to question whether she had been too hard
on the girl herself. From that point on, for the remainder of the school
year and through the following year, her performance in school was excellent,
and the attempts to avoid the school situation by feigning illness dropped
off completely. Her mother's complaints about her behavior at home ceased,
although in this case it is no indication that the problems there were
really settled.

The intervention in this case was really quite mild. The consultant
had a conference with the child's mother, called the problem to the
teacher's attention, and had a conference with the teacher. At that
conference the teacher brought in sufficient material to support the
hypothesis of a transference of her concerns about her own family to
her perception of this child's difficulties. The opportunity to talk out
loud helped the teacher to reconsider what she had been doing with
the child, and once she shifted her tactics the child's response changed
markedly. The consultant might have attempted some interpretation

of the displacement of her reaction from her own family to the child, but it seemed to be enough simply to support the teacher and to sympathize with the difficulty of staying with a demanding job when she was preoccupied with other issues. It can be a treacherous practice to attempt any kind of interpretation of the teacher's reaction. It is sometimes enough for the consultant to understand what is happening and for the teacher to receive support in doing what she is fully capable of doing.

A small but significant number of teacher requests for help from the consulting psychologist concern the nonextreme character problems of their students, problems that tend not to disrupt others in the classroom. A teacher may seek out the psychologist about a student's joyless perfectionism or friendlessness, compulsive chattering, or general nervousness. In discussing with the teacher his own observations and her judgments the psychologist may redefine the referral question in terms other than those presented by the teacher. Thus what the teacher perceives as prattle or nervousness may reflect the unexploited creative enthusiasm of a richly endowed child. The daydreaming and friendlessness of a youngster may be seen as more potentially serious deficits by the psychologist than the teacher. Once they have reached a working agreement about the possible meaning and gravity of a child's character problems, the psychologist often responds to the teacher's request for help by planning a set of diagnostic interventions she can carry out with the child to assess his understanding of the traits in question and his capacity to modify them without more direct involvement by the psychologist.

Example 12. A well-developed first-grade Negro boy periodically became sullen and stubborn in school. Every two or three weeks his moody uncooperativeness would manifest itself with no clear triggering incident. The teacher had learned to live with Orio's brief, periodic moodiness, partly because he rarely punched other children and partly because he was a good learner. In the last quarter of the school year, however, when the usual pattern showed no signs of softening, despite the good relationship between teacher and child, Orio's periodic negativism was discussed by the teacher with the psychologist. The psychologist was impressed with the teacher's lack of knowledge of the boy's feelings and conception about his moodiness. She had never discussed the matter with him lest she uncover more than she could handle. The teacher had kept hands off this aspect of the boy's character, but the psychologist in his observations was impressed with the accessibility of the child to discussion, indeed the likelihood that he would be willing to talk about the matter with his teacher. Taking reassurance in the psychologist's assessment of the situation and of his availability for overseeing the teacher if any deep-seated conflicts arose, the teacher waited for the next bout of moodiness and spoke with the boy about it after school. The psychologist had theorized out loud with the teacher about the possibility that Orio was very angry during these periods and did not know how to think about or use his angry feelings at such times. By backing off from his difficulties, the teacher was in effect reinforcing Orio's own neglect of his inner life at such times. With great excitement the teacher reported to the psychologist that she had followed the plan and talked with the boy some weeks later. Orio had talked about his parents' periodic quarrels, which came to blows regularly. He was able to tell the teacher that he did not know how to tell his parents how angry he was with them and took it out on others in school when he felt that way. The teacher was able to tell the boy that he also took out his anger on himself by becoming sullen. After several such talks Orio could speak about his anger instead of smothering himself in it, and his uncooperativeness diminished considerably during such periods.

The teacher's intervention may not have resolved the boy's home difficulties but it did strengthen his forbearance at considerably less cost to himself. Several features of the teacher's approach were underlined by the psychologist in his discussions with her. The teacher had not relied on a single contact with the child but had followed through on subsequent occasions. Teachers as well as psychologists sometimes make the mistake of assuming one-trial learning with a child, regarding a discussion as fruitless unless it has immediate payoff. The teacher, moreover, had not simply labeled the undesirable behavior and persuaded the child to alter it. She had instead explored its significance to the child, building on his understanding and vocabulary for the problem. Finally, by permitting the child to talk out his angry feelings the teacher was encouraging a model of emotional functioning for the boy that stressed insight and sharing instead of festering feeling, self-punishingly expressed. The child's grasp on such learning can be strengthened, while his shame is diminished, by participating in a lesson or group discussion on problems common to the daily life of her children. Thus teachers have been able to deal with their children's absent or drinking fathers, parental discipline, and questions of ethnic affiliation and skin color. In cases similar to Orio's in which the teacher was encouraged to explore with a child his emotional reactions, two factors are verified by the psychologist before he recommends the teacher's intervention. First, teacher and child must have a reasonably sound relationship which in itself has proved insufficient to alter the child's undesirable behavior. Second, the child's preoccupations, which have been interfering with his work and happiness, are explored with the aim of permitting the child to ventilate his concerns, rather than of encouraging the teacher to probe for and interpret unconscious meanings in the child's behavior. In short, the psychologist keeps track of the teacher's interventions to ensure that she is not taking a psychotherapeutic role for which she is not trained, a role that could easily produce more distress in the child and teacher than it eliminates.

The examples above indicate the range of possibilities for translating psychodynamic concepts into action in the classroom which would be of benefit to a child. It is not always possible to find some useful formulation, but the degree to which theoretical terms can be made operational in the classroom depends on intimate knowledge of the classroom situation. Intimate knowledge of the classroom situation depends on a psychologist being in the situation and available to those who have day-by-day responsibility for relating to the child.

THE TEST REPORT

If we were to evaluate recommendations in psychological test reports (or in reports of psychiatric evaluations) in terms of the degree to which they contain specific recommendations that can be translated into terms suitable to the classroom, it is our guess that few, if any, would pass. Recommendations for treatment at a child-guidance clinic that has a year's waiting list are of little direct help to the classroom teacher. Recommendations for "individual attention" say nothing and appear to the teacher as impractical burdens. Mental-health professionals are also singularly ignorant about the school situation and do not recognize the potential for constructive change. When we are in the situation it becomes possible to test the value of psychodynamic concepts by structuring situations so that the needs or anxieties thought to be present in the situation can be met. In the following examples some of the psychodynamic understanding came from test reports or brief interviews with the child, some came from inferences from classroom observation combined with information from the teacher, and some came from an application of theoretical principles to given acts. It seemed to us in each instance that the critical condition for success was a knowledge of the situation in which the behavior was manifested. Not every hypothesis, of course, was verified, sometimes because the execution of the recommendation was faulty, sometimes because the inferences were incorrect. Nonetheless, the possibility for arriving at a correct and workable formulation, translatable into terms suitable for the classroom situation, is enhanced to the degree that we are aware of the potential inherent in the school situation.

To the teacher, and probably to others in the culture at large, the sight of a psychologist without his test kit is sufficiently strange to cause considerable confusion about who the psychologist is and what he is to do. A teacher generally sees the school psychologist (many of whom function largely as psychometrists) only long enough to point out the child to be tested. Generally, she recognizes him only by the fact that he is carrying a testing kit; frequently a school psychologist will ask for a child after no social contact with the teacher other than a perfunctory greeting.[1] In part the school system itself makes for such minimal social contact because the psychologist is hesitant to interfere with the ongoing classroom activity. In part teachers refer children to the school psychologist in the vain hope that "something" will be done or with the implication that now that the referral for testing has been made the testing itself will somehow solve the problem. Depending on the school system, the pressure of referrals, the available personnel, the attitudes of the principal toward testing, and the personal relationship between the principal and the school psychologist, periods ranging from weeks to literally years may go by before a referral is answered.

The typical product of a psychological examination in the schools is a written psychological report. Early in our experience we were puzzled by the persistence with which a teacher would seek for a specific "yes" or "no" to the question whether the child was "emotionally

[1] School psychologists, social workers, reading specialists, speech therapists, subject-matter supervisors and assistant superintendents frequently treat the classroom teacher with a gross disregard for her professional competence and autonomy and, more surprisingly, with a gross disregard for common courtesies. In one instance a graduate student working under the consultant's supervision found it necessary to postpone two appointments she had made with teachers. The graduate student went to the school building well in advance of the appointed time and informed the two teachers she would not be able to keep the appointments. For the graduate student the act was a simple courtesy one human being automatically extends to another. Much to the consultant's surprise, both teachers independently made it a point to let him know what the student had done. Both seemed thoroughly impressed and, more surprising, both expressed an almost pathetic gratitude that the student had taken the time to cancel the appointment. When the consultant, surprised at the intensity of the affect, inquired about their reactions, both teachers related numerous instances in which appointments were made and broken without notice, in which supervisors were expected and never appeared, and in which visitors were announced and never came. In many instances, rearrangements of class schedules were made uselessly, or the teacher was left with the necessity of making some lame excuse to her class. That teachers tend to accept such treatment without protest speaks loudly about the image the teacher holds of herself as a professional person. It should be said that in our experience the above discourtesies occur with far greater frequency in our inner-city schools than in the typical middle-class or suburban school.

disturbed." In those few instances in which testing did confirm the suspicion that a child had a serious psychological disturbance, we were
surprised and puzzled about the teacher's response to the pronounce-
ment. Instead of expressing concern and anxiety about what was to
be done with the child, the teacher would frequently express a sense of
relief or even a sense of triumphant self-vindication: "I knew all along
something was wrong with that child!" We do not intend to minimize
or to derogate the teacher's concern for her children, but it seems that
tests are not valued so much for suggestions in classroom management
as they are for the emotional support the test procedure provides the
teacher. If a child in fact has a low IQ, the teacher is reassured that his
difficulty in learning is not her fault. If his IQ falls in the normal
range, the test report will sometimes allude to the child's anxiety, his
dependency, or to some other emotional problem in a fashion that
may place the blame for the problem within the child. The concrete
fact that the child has been tested is sufficient for some school personnel to categorize the child as either disturbed or dull. In either case
the teacher's responsibility for doing something about the child is
minimized. Clearly, if he is a dull child he cannot be expected to
learn. If he is emotionally disturbed, he does not fall within the teacher's jurisdiction and she need feel no guilt about either his lack of
progress or his lack of change in the course of a year.

It was not until we came to appreciate fully the degree to which a
teacher is left alone with a problem that we could also appreciate the
teacher's viewpoint without feeling she was a cruel, unconcerned,
heartless monster. In the absence of specific and concrete help, in the
absence of someone with whom to share a problem, and in the tradition that teaching consists primarily of the preparation and presentation of material for normal children, it is difficult to see how the
teacher would adopt other than the defensive posture exemplified in
the use of tests reports. The not-infrequent occasions on which a
teacher works with great dedication to help a difficult and troubled
child are tributes to the capacity of the human spirit to transcend adverse circumstances.

Although the Psycho-Educational Clinic fully intended to minimize the use of tests, situations arose in which it appeared that it
would be useful to test a child. In contrast to the typical situation in
the schools, the consultant never accepted a referral for testing until
he had first discussed the child with the teacher and observed the child
in the classroom.[2] This particular attempt to break through the lone-

[2] This is a statement about how we usually function or prefer to function.
As we indicated in Chapter 9, there are times to change the mode of function-

liness of the situation was not immediately successful. Although some teachers welcomed the opportunity to try something new with a child, others did not initially receive this variation in procedure with any great enthusiasm. In instances in which the teacher desired testing to determine whether a child should be placed in a special class, the consultant's refusal to test at once was seen as an unnecessary obfuscation or as questioning the teacher's judgment that the child needed help. It is only close and continued contact with the teacher that permits corrective discussion when misunderstandings arise.

Example 13. A teacher referred a first-grade child for testing because she wanted to know what would be a proper grade placement for her. When the consultant appeared to discuss the child, he discovered that she had recently entered the school and that she was almost completely unresponsive in class. The consultant observed the child in class and discovered that she was engaged in finger play suggesting that she was acting out some sort of fantasy. At this point the consultant suspected the child might be rather severely disturbed, and he suggested to the teacher that he would prefer to postpone any further examination until he could interview the child's parents. Although the consultant tried to explain his view that the child might be disturbed rather than slow and that her move into a new school in midyear might have been contributing to her disturbance, the teacher seemed rather distressed that the consultant did not begin testing at once. The consultant made a home visit only to discover that the mother and father had recently separated, that the father had been unreliable in meeting his commitments for support, that the mother was without funds, and that she was trying to qualify for the Aid to Dependent Children (ADC) program.

---

ing in a particular instance because it has been decided that the situation requires such a change. There are two related criteria by which such contemplated charges must be evaluated: the teacher or child is in need of help in a very pressing way and the change in functioning does not raise the possibility that the preferred way of functioning in the school will be seriously affected. For example, one of the Clinic members was observing in a classroom during the second week of his work in a school. The regular teacher was ill and there was a substitute who was a paradigm of incompetence. The principal was aware that the substitute was impossible, but no other was available for the two weeks the regular teacher would be absent. The Clinic member, not easily upset or bothered by difficult situations, was visibly bothered by what he had seen and raised the possibility of his taking the class for two weeks—a suggestion he was sure would be accepted by the principal. After much discussion, it was decided that such an action, coming as it would in the second week of work in the school and in the context of the knowledge that this was a problem school, was not advisable because it could contribute to a conception of how we function that would be so far from the mark that it would require months to undo. If this particular Clinic member had raised this type of problem three months later, the decision would have been otherwise.

The child's sleep had been disturbed recently and she had reverted to wetting her bed at night. The consultant returned to the school the next day, told the teacher what he had discovered, and repeated his previous suggestion that we wait with testing for a few weeks to give the child a chance to settle into the new situation. Some suggestions were offered for helping the child to adapt to the new situation.

Some weeks later a graduate student was assigned to test the child, and in keeping with Clinic practice he observed the child and tested her over a period of several weeks. When testing was completed, a conference was scheduled with the teacher and the findings were discussed. By this time the child had settled in fairly well, and the teacher no longer had any question about her intellectual abilities. She was responding perfectly well in class, and her peculiar mannerisms had decreased in intensity and in frequency. At the end of this conference, the consultant brought up the question of the teacher's reaction about putting off testing, and the teacher revealed her feeling that the consultant had questioned her judgment about the child. Once again the consultant explained his viewpoint that testing was not the answer to all problems, and this time he had the feeling that the message was received.

Even though a teacher requests help, and even though help in the form of testing is given, it is all too easy to underestimate the degree to which a teacher may misunderstand the nature of psychological tests. At best, many teachers have only a superficial familiarity with intelligence tests and no knowledge at all about projective tests. At times a teacher may even be threatened by the contents of a report, even though the issues are couched in the most careful language. The teacher may read criticism into a report where no criticism is intended. At times the consultant may need to provide a capsule course in psychological testing to explain his meaning.

Example 14. Because of a series of circumstances, several posttesting conference appointments had to be broken. Although the written report is the least important step in a referral, because of the delay in this instance the report was written, typed, and placed in the mail before the conference with the teacher was completed. The following week the teacher called the consultant about the report, obviously distressed about a sentence that said, "The child sees teachers as ogres constantly threatening to punish children at any misstep." She said that she had never threatened the child at all and in fact had made it a point to be exceptionally gentle with him, for in a previous conference the teacher and consultant had concluded that the child was highly anxious and required gentle encouragement rather than harsh or even firm treatment. The teacher was concerned lest the consultant and others who might read the report think that she had actually treated the child in a threatening fashion. The consultant hastened to reassure her that the report only meant to bring out the child's fantasy about teachers. When he showed the teacher the stories the child had written and the pictorial stimuli making up the test, she was considerably relieved.

At its best, the testing process we have evolved brings together the teacher, child, parent, and consultant as partners in an enterprise in which all have a mutual interest. In most instances testing is not carried out until the consultant has had an opportunity to discuss the referral thoroughly with the teacher and to observe the child in the classroom. At that point, if it appears that testing will be helpful or if the child seems particularly suitable as a candidate for testing for training purposes, the teacher and consultant will make an appointment to interview the parent. The interview is presented to the parent as a mutual problem-solving situation. The child's problem in school is described briefly by the teacher, and the parent is asked to contribute whatever information she can to help the teacher understand the child's behavior in school. The interview frequently brings out relevant information. At the end of the first interview the parent is requested to give permission for a psychological examination, with the understanding that no specific action will be taken until the results of testing are discussed with the parent and teacher.

The child is then assigned to an examiner who is instructed to tell him explicitly that his teacher is concerned about his performance in school, that she wants him to be able to do the best he can, and that the examiner wants to try to understand how he thinks and works so he can help his teacher work with him. After a few months the consultant becomes a very familiar person in the school building and the children all know him. Most go with him quite readily. If someone other than the consultant has to do the testing, as is sometimes the case, the consultant makes it a point to introduce the examiner to the child in the presence of his teacher. Every effort is made to minimize the unfamiliarity of the situation for the child. In almost all instances the children thoroughly enjoy the testing experience and look forward to spending further time with the examiner. The teacher experiences the repeated examinations as a form of working with the child, especially since the consultant makes it a point to make some kind of comment about each session and inquires about the child each time he sees the teacher.

When testing is completed, the consultant, the graduate student, if one has been involved, and the teacher arrange for a conference. The conference is structured as a sharing of ideas, and the teacher is encouraged to contribute her observations and comments as the test findings are reported. It is stressed that the teacher is not to let the consultant slide by with generalities or jargon she does not understand. She is encouraged to ask questions and to make the consultant be specific, concrete, and understandable. As the findings are discussed, the consultant makes it a point to ask the teacher about how particular ideas may be translated into action feasible in her classroom. In many instances the specific form of the recommendation for action comes from the teacher.

During the conference the consultant and teacher also discuss what the child may be told about the test findings, and a conference to interpret the test findings is scheduled for the consultant and the child. Such conferences are carried out with children as young as first graders. The consultant couches his findings in highly positive and reassuring language when discussing tests results with a child. The child is usually told that he did very well and that the examiner and teacher were pleased with his cooperation. No matter what his IQ, a child is always told that the tests showed that he is *not* dumb. He is told that the tests showed that he can learn but that sometimes it may be difficult for him to understand the work. When a child is intellectually more capable, he is informed of that, but again he is cautioned to expect that he may have difficulty in learning some things. In other instances some of a child's behavioral characteristics are interpreted, and the child is told how he may handle himself differently in a particular situation.

The child is also told that his mother will be asked to return for a conference and that in essence she will be told exactly what the consultant has told him. In most instances the child proves eager for his parent to come in, because the report is always couched in as favorable terms as possible without actually engaging in denial of clinical realities. Both teacher and consultant meet with the parent for the posttesting conference, and at this time various recommendations are discussed. By this time, sometimes three or four months after the referral, parent, teacher, and consultant are familiar with each other, and the conference comes as an expected climax to a series of activities rather than as a shock to the parent. Therefore, recommendations do not have to be considered in the context of meeting new and unfamiliar people.

It is important to note that the teacher is brought in as the consultant's colleague and partner at every step in the process. Even after recommendations are made, whenever possible the consultant attempts to remain in touch with both teacher and child in the implementation of recommendations.

Example 15. A Negro child who had been retained by her teacher was referred for examination to determine adequate placement. The teacher felt that the child should not have been retained for another year. As it happened, the consultant knew the child because he had met her a number of times in the hall and in the principal's office where she had been sent for disciplinary purposes. In class the year before the consultant had found the girl to be apathetic, disinterested, and disrespectful to her teacher, who felt she had to treat her rather sternly to live with her at all. The little girl related to the consultant in a seductive and flirtatious manner, and to some extent the consultant was able to use his relationship with the child to influence her behavior in the classroom. The consultant was undecided in his own mind about the child's mental capacity, and when the request for evaluation came in the context that the child should not have been retained he was sufficiently intrigued to test the child.

In keeping with the general plan the teacher and consultant met with the child's mother, and told her that they were puzzled by her performance in school. The mother agreed that the child was difficult to manage at times, and she attributed the problem to the child's father who adored her and who responded very positively to her seductiveness. Testing showed the child was at least of average intelligence, if not higher. Her failures revealed a lack of information and an unfamiliarity with aspects of language, typical of lower-class Negro children. In testing she was lively and alert, clearly motivated to do as well as she could.

In conference the teacher and consultant discussed the child's relatively good mental ability and both expressed concern that she be encouraged to use herself in a more positive fashion. An arrangement was made for the child to help a Negro teacher in the school, to give her some contact with someone who might be a model for her. It was arranged that she spend part of her day in another class which had more prestige among the children than her own. The child was informed of the testing results, and in particular she was told she could make something of herself. The child expressed a desire to become a teacher or a nurse. She was encouraged to discuss the problem of obtaining an education with the Negro teacher. On subsequent occasions, when the consultant met the child, he would remind her of what he had told her in testing, usually eliciting a big smile from her. The teacher and the consultant worked out the necessary arrangements with the other teachers and the principal. The teacher also continued to provide as much confirmation for the view the child was capable as she could.

Immediately after the conference with the child her mother was asked to return. The child was informed that her mother was to come in, and when she arrived at school the mother related how eager the girl had been for her to keep the appointment. Apparently the child had reminded her of it all week and could hardly contain herself that day. The teacher and consultant were able to inform the mother of a considerable improvement in the child since the previous year, and the consultant impressed on her his feeling that her daughter could easily complete high school and perhaps could do more for herself. The child's mother, in this conference, told of her plans to move because her present quarters were inadequate and because the child had to sleep in the same bedroom with the parents. The consultant cautioned her about moving in midyear, and requested that she at least permit the child to finish the year in the same school if at all possible. It is probably an indication of the effectiveness of the testing and consulting process that the family did not move during the school year. The child remained to complete the school year, did more than adequately scholastically, and her behavior problems diminished considerably, although they did not disappear entirely.

It is typical of the way schools operate that a child who is to be placed in special class is tested, and if he qualifies by having a sufficiently low IQ his parents are called in and informed of the decision by the principal. The usual expectation is that the parent will protest the placement and the principal will then have to sell the parent the idea. Once the parent agrees to the placement, the child is forthwith sent to the special class without any preparation. His previous teacher's experience with him is in no way utilized, and the special-class teacher is given a child with no other information than he has been failing in regular classes and has an IQ low enough to qualify him for the special class. Not every building has a special class, but even in buildings with special classes it is rare that the two teachers involved will make any effort to work together to expedite the child's placement in his new class. Wherever possible, the consultant has attempted to break into this situation by including the special-class and the regular classroom teacher in conference together to plan the child's entrance into the special class.

Example 16. Following the procedure outlined, the child was examined, and the mother informed of the recommendation that she be placed in a special class. By this time the mother was aware of the problem, and the recommendation did not come as a particular surprise. The mother, the teacher and the consultant were able to converse meaningfully about the child's difficulties in learning, and following the conference the mother was introduced to the special-class teacher and encouraged to see the pleasantly decorated room with its relatively few children. The consultant then arranged for a conference between the two teachers in which he asked the first to tell the second about some of the child's characteristics and her methods of dealing with her. The consultant contributed some of the findings from testing, and a plan was evolved to have the child come down to meet the new teacher shortly before lunch hour, so that the teacher might have a little time with her alone to introduce her to the room and her place in it and to become acquainted with her. The consultant then explained the recommendation to the child and took her down to meet the special-class teacher. The teacher met her, introduced her to two girls who had stayed a little later, and showed her around the room. One of the girls showed her the cloakroom where the children hung their coats, and she was given a place of her own. That afternoon she returned to her own class and told her teacher that when her mother asked her about changing classes she would say she wanted to change rooms.

Shortly after the child was transferred she responded to her new teacher's criticism of her work by crying loudly and unconsolably. The teacher related that she handled the situation by telling the child she could cry if she wished but that she still had to do her work correctly. The teacher indicated that she felt confident in responding to the situation because she had anticipated what she would do during the conference with the previous teacher and the consultant. The crying was something the child did characteristically in relation to relatively slight personal threats or failures. Knowing in advance that the response was to be expected of this child, the teacher was able to deal with it forthrightly and directly. Had she not had the information, the teacher might very well have been unable to deal with the child's tears. It is an instructive postscript to note that the child has adapted to the special class very well, that her behavior problems have been reduced substantially, that she looks happier, that she tries in school, and that her mother has stated explicitly that the special-class teacher is a good teacher. It is all the more important to note the child's improvement and the teacher's response to her because the teacher was in her first year and was having substantial difficulty with a number of other children in her class.

In this chapter we have attempted to indicate how psychological understanding or psychodynamic concepts can be translated into concrete actions in a classroom. More important than the issue of the quality or efficacy of how we went about handling the translation was our aim to demonstrate that the classroom situation—assuming that the consultant has the appropriate relationship with the teacher—is one in which the potentialities for bringing about change in children are enormous. The realization of these potentialities depends in large part on intimate knowledge of a particular child in a particular peer group with a particular teacher in a particular classroom. When attempting to change or influence a certain situation, it is necessary to know that situation as intimately as possible. The mental-health consultant who functions in the more traditional way (and does not intimately know the particular context in which the problem has arisen) encounters a number of difficulties. It is our contention that many of these difficulties are obviated and the degree of help markedly increased when the consultant's opinions and recommendations reflect the tempering influence of a detailed acquaintance with the situation in which some kind of change is being sought. Translating theory into practice requires knowledge of the arena of practice. This is not to say that such knowledge avoids errors or problems, but rather that it increases the likelihood of being in a better position to determine how to go about evaluating whether our efforts are in the realm of success or failure. Without knowledge of and access to the "data of practice," it is all too easy to avoid confronting our theories with the relevant realities.

In this chapter we have given examples illustrating, among other things, the importance of intimate acquaintance of the classroom in which a particular problem occurs. In the next chapter, which is concerned with the effects and potentialities of transfer of children from one classroom to another, we discuss the significance of knowing "from what and to what" we are changing a child.

Chapter 11

Transferring a Child
from One Classroom to Another

The usual concept of mental health makes the major assumption that mental health is a quality of the person. Given the intrapsychic wherewithal for mental health, the individual should be able to adapt or adjust to almost any situation except perhaps one in which he is exposed to prolonged stress. In the school situation such a concept is accompanied by an assumption that a child's difficulties in adapting to school are largely those caused by intrapsychic events that have a history in the child's earlier development. Even when the mental-health professional has a suspicion that a child's teacher is overly permissive, harsh, or neurotic in some respect, a failure of adjustment, reflected either in a learning disturbance, a behavior disturbance, or other distressing symptoms, is generally treated as a function of some intrapsychic weakness in the child.

Treatment of school problems is frequently carried out away from the school setting because of the same assumption that the important events to change are intrapsychic events. There is a second assumption that changes in such intrapsychic events occur only in the context of a therapeutic relationship that permits reliving and relearning of distressful experiences. Because of these two assumptions, changes that take place for other reasons or under other conditions are generally treated as less important and in fact tend to be derogated by labels such as "temporary" and "superficial." The position embodied in these two assumptions may be termed "intrapsychic supremacy."

If we take seriously the Lewinian concept that behavior is a function of person and environment $[B = f(P, E)]$, changes in B should come about if we make changes in either P or E. For a variety of reasons and until comparatively recently the mental-health professions have not taken the formulation seriously, and efforts to work therapeutically by changing *E* have been minimal. Occasionally, someone working with a child's parent will make some effort to have the parent change specific practices that seem to contribute to a child's difficulties, but even such changes are likely to be suggested primarily when the worker feels that he has some understanding of the psychodynamics involved in the practice. Occasionally, a child will be removed from a household and sent to an institution or a residential school, but such intervention usually takes place because of neglect or parental inadequacy in dealing with the problem. Removal of the child from a situation is rarely seen as a form of treatment in and of itself, because the basic problem is held to be within the child. Those who advocate family therapy have a concept of illness that involves the family as a unit. They conceive of individuals who may be adequate except as they are interacting with other members of the family group; that is, the problem is seen in the interaction of the needs and fantasies of the family members. Therapy is again directed toward changing the intrapsychic dynamics and the modes of relationship, but such shifts in relationship are not generally conceptualized as a shift in the environment.

If we take the formula $B = f(P, E)$ seriously, we may expect changes in *B* when *E* is changed. One of the far-reaching changes that may be introduced is a transfer of the child from one classroom to another. The teacher is different, the group of children is different, and the total atmosphere in two classrooms may be different. Tolerance for a particular behavior pattern can differ from one teacher to the next, and the academic demands of the situation can also vary. Some teachers conceive of teaching as a method of preparing and presenting information. Working with the behavioral or learning difficulties presented by individual children is seen as really outside the function of the teacher, and children who present special difficulties can be both frustrating and threatening to her. Others seem to pride themselves on working with difficult children. Even among these teachers, there are marked differences in their effectiveness with different children, as might be expected. One teacher may do very well with an openly defiant and aggressive child but cannot deal with a child who is negativistic or passively aggressive. Another deals effectively with a withdrawn and timid child but is at a loss to handle a child who is provocative. To some teachers academic achievement is of first importance, and a child who does not keep up with the group may find himself left out and looked down on by the others. In some classes a less competitive atmosphere is established, and a child who does poorly academically may not find himself subject to further social sanctions. In one classroom a teacher may already have two or three attention-demanding, aggressive, or otherwise difficult-to-handle children. The introduction of one more such child, or relief from one such child, can make a great difference in the way in which a teacher is able to respond to the rest of her group.

The point that classes differ markedly within the same school along a number of different dimensions is an obvious one. However, the differences are not generally used in any systematic fashion in managing learning or behavioral problems in school. Some principals feel no hesitation about changing children's teachers, for all or for part of the day, for a variety of reasons. Others seem never to conceive of such a possibility. Because of the feeling that each teacher should handle her own problems, any attempt to deal with a problem by arranging for transfer of a child from a class is viewed as an attempt to unload a problem on someone else. Under these circumstances, and we suspect such attitudes hold in most schools, arranging for a transfer is an extraordinarily delicate operation that necessarily will create, if not ill feeling, at least some anxiety and distress for all concerned during the period the transfer is being considered or accomplished.

The conditions under which to transfer a child and expect a good result also differ markedly. We must consider carefully the characteristics of the child, the characteristics of the teacher, and the nature of the group she already has in order to determine whether a transfer will be effective, for not all transfers are effective and not all are effective in the same way. Goals may be very different in different situations and the results must be assessed accordingly.

Why transfer a child from one classroom to another? The assumption that a teacher, with her personality and necessarily finite repertoire of techniques of teaching and relating to children, is equally effective with all children is clearly absurd when we consider that a classroom may be composed of 30 or more children of both sexes, of a number of different ethnic backgrounds, of several different religious persuasions, of a range of several years in age, and with a variety of personality patterns and learning styles. That mismatches occur is not surprising. That they occur relatively infrequently is a tribute to the adaptability of teachers and children.

Nonetheless, mismatches inevitably occur, and when they do a transfer is one possible solution to the difficulty. A teacher's distinct unwillingness to try to work with a particular child is one major reason for considering a transfer. Her feeling may be that the child does not belong in her group. Observation may confirm the teacher's view that she is not working adequately with the child; not only that they do not work well with each other but also do not communicate with each other and that it is not possible to help the teacher arrive at a different view of the child.

A transfer is also contemplated for positive reasons. Not only is it desirable to correct a gross mismatch but, if possible, to arrange for a match between the teacher's and the class's characteristics, on the one hand, and the child's, on the other hand. The degrees of freedom are limited in any one school. There are only so many first-grade teachers, and there is room for only so many difficult-to-handle children in any one group. The degrees of freedom would be increased if we could easily go beyond grade lines, but going beyond grade lines in either direction presents strong problems for both teacher and child, in terms of curriculum, social group in the classroom, and the need to maintain grade lines as a form of order and structure within the school system itself. Wherever possible, a child is placed with a teacher because the characteristics of her group and her methods of teaching and of relating to children will do something to control positively a child's less desirable characteristics and will permit him to develop positive modes of relating to the school.

A transfer may be accomplished without difficulty if it occurs cleanly within the set of unwritten school laws that place the burden for any educational difficulty on the child and the parent. Under conditions in which it is clearly understood that the problem is not within the teacher, or within the methods of teaching, a transfer can be readily accomplished. In the following example the reason for transfer was an "educational" one, and the child presented no special behavioral problem.

Example 1. A child had been promoted to an upper-grade level despite the fact that each preceding teacher had indicated she was not doing very well. The promotions had been made primarily at the insistence of her parents. Her present teacher was a clipped, no-nonsense person who tolerated little departure from her well-prepared arrangements for teaching her class. She tended to move along quickly and briskly, adopting a devil-take-the-hindmost approach to her class. A generally effective teacher with many children, she felt this child was not doing acceptable work at her grade level, could not do the work, and did not belong in her class. The child, who was passive and somewhat shy, frequently would not try to do the work at all, but even when she tried the teacher had little patience with her. She would quickly pass over her fumbling efforts and call on someone who could handle the work more adequately.

The principal, well aware of the characteristics of the teacher, on hearing from both parent and teacher that the child was failing eased her into a class at the next lower level taught by a relatively inexperienced teacher. The child, who was quite docile, accepted the placement. With the easier, more familiar work and the lesser degree of pressure for achievement exerted by the teacher (who was having her hands full with several more active boys), she settled into the new class without any difficulty. Her original teacher was satisfied that she was now placed correctly according to her level of academic achievement, and the new teacher was given a child who did not add to her burden of management. The expected parental complaint did not materialize, and the child remained in the class, happily doing modestly well for the remainder of the term.

In this example the transfer was initiated by the classroom teacher, the record supported her view of the child as slow, and the blame for the child's inadequate performance could be placed squarely on the parents who insisted on promotions and the child who could not cope with the work. The classroom teacher did not see it as her function to work with this obviously unprepared child and had no sense of responsibility or failure in this situation. Moreover, in this particular school the practice of having children transferred from one teacher to another was rather common. At no point did the transfer create any important stress for either of the teachers or for the child.

In most other instances the problem of arranging for a transfer is fraught with a potential for hurt and mutual recrimination comparable only to the situation in which one family member demands repayment of a loan from another or to some violation of ancient, primitive tribal custom. In most instances the potential for misfiring is so great that we have come to anticipate that the action in transferring a child will inevitably create difficulty, particularly if the child is active and aggressive and demands considerable effort in management. A teacher will feel that she has failed if the request for transfer is initiated by someone else; the teacher receiving the child will feel that she is being burdened with an unwanted problem and, moreover, is doing the job the previous teacher should have been handling.

In the following example a principal arranged for the transfer of a child from first grade to kindergarten. The child was a transfer student from another school who had come with a tentative promotion to first grade. The principal had placed him in a first-grade class with a teacher who tried working with him for a month with a permissive orientation, tolerating his puppyishness, which gave him a good deal of gratification, but making few demands on him. His behavior did not change. At the request of the first-grade teacher, the principal placed the child in the kindergarten.

Example 2. In the kindergarten the little boy immediately began acting in a disruptive fashion. He refused to follow any directions, refused to join in any group activities, and generally went his own way. When the consultant observed the child, it was clear that he seemed to be competing with the teacher for leadership in the class. He was noisy, boisterous, and attempted to attract the attention of other children by clowning. He would frequently make the children laugh at him while the teacher was attempting other activities with the group. He would station himself at the rear of the room, play with whatever toys he would select, and occasionally put a play hat on backward, bang some metal toys together, or knock down a pile of boxes, laughing gleefully.

Within a week the kindergarten teacher was completely distraught. She had been experiencing some personal difficulties and found the whole incident to be the straw that broke the camel's back. She felt she was in no condition to deal with the new child, and in fact her anger and tension were so great that she found it necessary to visit her physician and to take a heavy dose of tranquilizers.

The teacher was not only disturbed because she now had to contend with this active and noisy youngster but also angered because she felt the principal had treated her unfairly. She experienced the transfer as an example of favoritism and was angered because the other teacher had violated the code by not being willing to work with the child. The kindergarten teacher said that she did not give up on her problems, and she was resentful that the other teacher manipulated the situation so that she now had an additional, unwanted burden.

That one teacher is constantly on guard lest another dump her problems is demonstrated in the following incident in which the consultant attempted to arrange for a transfer for one child because it seemed indicated for her development. In this example the child had been doing very well, and the consultant and the original teacher agreed that she should be given an opportunity in a somewhat more advanced class, if not for the whole day, then for at least part of the day.

Example 3. The teacher and consultant had been working with a child who had a reputation as a discipline problem in the school. The child had been retained the year before, although her present teacher found her capable and thought she should have been promoted. On testing, the child had at least average intelligence. The consultant had counseled her on several occasions, emphasizing always that she had "good brains and could make something of herself." The child began responding quite well to the teacher's work with her, which consisted of equal doses of effusive approval and firm demand for her best productive effort. As she began responding to this treatment, both teacher and consultant felt that her efforts should be rewarded by a concrete indication that the school did not think she was dumb. It was decided to let her spend some part of the day in a better-rated class that had somewhat more prestige than the class she was in. The classroom was upstairs with the older children, and it was in keeping with this child's needs that something special for her would be meaningful.

After clearing with the principal, the teacher and consultant thought about how to approach the second teacher. The teacher felt she would be rebuffed if she herself approached the second teacher, and she suggested that the consultant deal with it. The consultant agreed because he believed he had a fairly good working relationship with the second teacher. He explained to her what was recommended and asked her if she would be interested in thinking about the child. Her immediate response was that the first teacher was attempting to put one over on her. The consultant indicated he was partly responsible for the request and asked if she and the first teacher would have lunch with him later that week to discuss the child and the recommendation, without any commitment on her part to take the child. She agreed, but she was clearly distressed, and that lunch hour she approached the first teacher without the consultant's knowledge. By chance he happened on the two women just after they had begun their discussion. It was clear that the second teacher was angry and indignant and the first teacher was defensive, but also somewhat angered that she had been attacked. The polite and formal terms of the discussion did not entirely conceal the heated emotions. After listening, the consultant intervened, indicating it was basically his responsibility that the transfer had been suggested at all. Both teachers then used the opportunity to get out of what had become a very sticky situation. Both blamed the consultant for not understanding the schools and children, indicating it was much too late in the year for a complete transfer. Within seconds both arrived at an agreement that the child would come to the second teacher's room for part of the afternoon and would stay with her own group for arithmetic and reading in the morning.

Although the consultant took the responsibility on himself for the suggestion and presented it only as a plan he would like to have the receiving teacher consider, she took it as an attempt to foist something on her, and she could not contain herself until the suggested conference date. Clearly, the question had touched off a strong emotional response.

Even when a child is difficult to manage and the teacher complains a great deal about the burden of having the child in her class, a transfer will not necessarily relieve her feelings. She may still feel that she has been inadequate in some fashion when a transfer is proposed. In the following example a child was transferred and then re-entered in the same class within two weeks. The teacher's response to both events is highly instructive.

Example 4. A child had been with a teacher about half the year and had been maintained about as well as anyone could manage with him. He tended to be loud, attention-seeking, somewhat aggressive, occasionally irrelevant, and his work was frequently failing. His parents were quite distressed at the reports from school, and they had been casting about seeking various solutions for his problem. They had been in frequent touch with the teacher and the principal, but with little satisfactory result. The teacher had complained often and loudly about being overburdened with the child and unappreciated by principal and parent for her efforts. At one point the teacher mentioned to the principal that she thought the boy played to the audience of other children whom he knew from other years. The principal accepted this diagnosis, and with little further ado transferred the child to another class where he would know fewer of the children.

The teacher responded to the transfer by expressing her hurt that the principal had acted without giving her a chance. She also felt that the principal thought she was not willing to work with a difficult child, whereas she asserted she was. Somewhat concerned that the other teacher would be able to manage the child, the teacher reacted by putting all the responsibility for the situation onto the principal. She denied that she felt bothered by the transfer, saying that if that's the way the principal wanted it, then she, only a teacher, had no responsibility for what the principal did. Her manner betrayed the hurt feelings her words were meant to deny.

Within a week the new placement proved inadequate. The group with whom he had been placed was rated a fast group, and he was unable to keep up academically. The second teacher found that she had to give him work completely different from that given to her slowest group, and the boy became progressively more unhappy. His behavioral difficulties were exacerbated, and he began complaining at home that he wanted to return to his former class. His parents informed the principal of the problem, as did the school teacher, and the boy was soon transferred back to his original class.

His teacher's reaction was highly instructive. Although before she had complained a great deal about the boy and about the difficulties he was creating for her, she now felt vindicated and even triumphant at the prospects of his returning to her class. She no longer spoke of the difficulties of managing him, but now commented rather proudly about the success of her methods of handling this very difficult boy. In fact, the event proved helpful to him because he seemed to appreciate his situation somewhat more and because the teacher was now even more motivated to work with him.

In attempting to arrange a transfer, it is absolutely essential that the consultant be fully aware of the teacher's position and her attitude toward him and toward her own work. A transfer—a ticklish business, even when originating within the school hierarchy itself—is even more difficult when an outsider attempts to arrange it, because he may not be fully aware of the teacher's position in the school or of the degree to which a teacher responds to the consultant's authority in an ingratiating or sycophantic manner. In the following example the consultant attempted to arrange a transfer for a child that involved lowering his grade level. The consultant was not thinking of the grade level particularly, but he had in mind a particular teacher who could handle the problem. He spoke to the principal and to the teacher separately, getting agreement from both for the transfer. As subsequent events showed, the consultant was not fully aware of the abilities and attitudes of the people involved.

Example 5. A boy had been in a class that had several substitute teachers when the regular teacher was out for surgery. He was a behavior problem, disruptive in class, and frequently would sneak out of his room and wander through the halls. The consultant spoke to a teacher who seemed to have very firm control in the classroom. Although she taught a grade lower than the boy's current placement, the consultant knew from his contacts with the child that he could not read at all and that the lower placement would be no loss academically. The teacher responded with apparent pleasure to the consultant's suggestion that he thought her capable of handling the child, and she agreed to try to work with him. The consultant then arranged a brief meeting with the teacher and the principal to discuss how the transfer might be effected. The meeting was to take place the following week on the day of the consultant's next regular visit.

At the meeting the principal left the teacher with the consultant to discuss the arrangement because he had indicated his willingness to go along. In approaching the issue with the teacher, the principal told her we were simply experimenting and that if it did not appear to be a workable experiment things could be changed again. The consultant and teacher had an amiable discussion about the problem the boy presented, but it should be stated that the consultant was doing most of the talking. The teacher appeared to be listening attentively and raised no question about the transfer. When the principal reappeared, the teacher raised the question about how the boy might feel about leaving his social group and being put back into a first grade. Just as we started to explore the question, the principal jumped in, stating his disagreement with the proposal, and suggesting that the boy be eased into the class by going in for an art period. He also spoke about it not being fair to the original teacher who had been out for at least six weeks, and he requested that she be given a chance to try with the boy. When the principal raised objections, the teacher excused herself from the conference and left.

In this instance, although the transfer was approached gingerly, the conference did not work out at all. Later reconsideration and gossip in the school suggested that the teacher who had been asked to take the child was somewhat frightened of the possibility of working with him and that she might have expressed her objection to the principal but not to the consultant. At the same time the principal was not eager to get into a difficult situation with his teachers and seemed to feel that his relationship with the consultant was the more expendable commodity. At issue also was the principal's concern that he would be replaced as leader in the school by the consultant. To some extent he seemed to be reacting to what he may have experienced as some usurpation of his functions.

The difficulties encountered in arranging a transfer are sometimes insurmountable. Nevertheless, there have been numerous instances in which the transfer could not be effected during the school year but could in all essentials be carried out at the time of promotion.

Example 6. Charles, a bright nine-year-old boy, seemed to have perfected a variety of ways of taunting, angering, and upsetting a wide variety of school personnel. He had come from another school and his reputation had preceded him. His adjustment to the new school was not helped by placing him with a third-grade teacher whose class was near bedlam throughout the year. Charles and his teacher represent about the worst mismatch we have seen to date. The teacher was a warm, dependent, overwhelmed woman whose response to a child's misbehavior was either to shout, do nothing, send the child to stand in the hall, or send him to the principal. Charles' needs for attention and for domination were sufficiently strong so that he ate up these responses to his misdeeds. The principal was aware of the teacher's inadequacy and the atmosphere in the classroom and, because he spent a fair part of his time lecturing Charles and calling in his parents for talks, he quickly referred the boy to the consultant in the hope that he had some magical influence technique he could apply to him. This referral was made two months after the school year had begun and the consultant had become familiar with the school.

Several talks with the boy and his parents and continued observation in the classroom convinced the consultant that the teacher was generally inadequate and could in no way be counted on to control herself or her children. Neither in the case of Charles nor several other boys did she have the personal resources to command their respect, to be consistently firm, and to channel their interests so that they derived satisfaction from learning.[1]

[1] The mismatch between Charles and his teacher was surpassed only by the mismatch between the teacher and this particularly difficult, inner-city school. Neither by background, personality, nor understanding was this woman appropriate for the setting. She was extremely dependent on the consultant, and after a time it was possible for him to raise with her the possibility of her requesting a transfer to a middle-class school in which her strength rather than weaknesses would come to the fore. After a number of discussions she requested the transfer, which was approved. Whatever the consultant could learn from independent sources about this teacher indicated she was doing a competent job in her new placement. From subsequent phone conversations with her it was clear that her feelings of competence and satisfaction were immeasurably stronger than in the previous year.

Charles was the most incorrigible and upsetting as well as the most bright and academically advanced of the problem boys.

The consultant came to the conclusion that the only approach that promised desired change—in terms of the boy's behavior, the other children in his classroom, the noise level on that floor, and the hostility aroused among other teachers—was to transfer him to a fourth-grade teacher who felt and was adequate to handle almost any kind of problem a child could present in a classroom. Initially, this teacher appeared to be a stern, punishing, no-nonsense kind of woman who would not hesitate a moment to put a child in his place, either verbally or physically. After spending time in her classroom we could see that our initial impression was correct and, in addition, that this teacher had a profound interest in, tenderness toward, and affection for "her children." She used these characteristics in an exquisitely sensitive manner.

The principal of the school did not agree with the idea of a transfer, reflecting many of the factors already discussed in this chapter and not in need of elaboration here. In June of that year Charles was promoted to the teacher to whom we initially wished to transfer him. During all of the next year Charles' behavior in class was in amazing contrast to that of the previous year. There were occasions when he needed to be reprimanded and punished, but this would in no way be noteworthy if we had been unaware of his previous school history. He always did his work, learned a good deal, and clearly liked and respected his teacher. One of the consequences of this change was that a vicious circle was broken into: misbehavior in school, stern notes sent to the home, heated discussions between parents and principal, sadistic punishment at home, misbehavior in school, etc.

In view of the gross difficulties involved in arranging for a transfer from one class to another, the reader may well ask, does it pay to try at all? Are the results worth the effort? In selected cases the answer is clearly "yes." In the following example we describe a highly successful transfer that demonstrates the interpersonal difficulties in arranging for a transfer, some of the conditions under which to arrange a transfer, and some of the transforming effects that may be observed.

Example 7. A boy of seven had come from another school with the recommendation that he repeat the first grade. He had received very low reading-readiness test scores, and the previous school questioned whether the child was retarded. His teacher was an experienced person but new to the particular school system. She referred the child to the consultant early in the term. She complained that the child was hyperactive, aggressive, spoke out freely, was overconcerned about making errors, and in general was a disruptive and disturbing influence in her class. She had put him out of the room on a number of occasions and had asked that he be placed on half-days.

The consultant observed the child and teacher on several occasions and indeed could observe some of the active, aggressive behavior of which the teacher complained. However, the boy did not seem to be acutely hyperactive. The teacher preferred to operate a classroom that provided more freedom of movement and of activity than did other teachers, even though she had several other difficult-to-manage children. It seemed to the consultant that her mode of working was not sufficiently structured or her disciplinary efforts sufficiently consistent to be effective with an active and aggressive youngster. Interviews with the child and with his mother convinced the consultant that the child had a great deal more ability than seemed apparent in school. In individual sessions he gave evidence of having more than a beginning grasp of reading, writing, and spelling, and his handwriting gave no evidence of the incoordination associated with a brain-damaged child. The child's mother indicated that he had been much indulged as a child because he had had a number of severe illnesses, but more recently she was trying to introduce more demands and more discipline. She noted that he was perfectly content if he could stay busy, and in fact he spent afternoons at home happily engaged in the schoolwork his teacher sent home.

The assumption was made that the boy was underchallenged by his first-grade placement. On a trial basis and after due consultation with all concerned, and with due assurances that one teacher was not permanently dumping a problem on another, the child was sent to a slow second-grade classroom for a reading lesson in the mornings. He was also to be given the additional responsibility of copying certain material from the blackboard and keeping a record of it as the class secretary. He was to be given the opportunity to read the brief notes daily in front of the class. The teacher started on the new program with him, and the consultant began seeing the mother on a regular basis, for at that point she seemed to be looking for help and it seemed that she herself required some assistance in maintaining a consistently firm attitude with the boy. The mother began reporting about the boy's feeling that he was picked on unfairly by the teacher. The consultant did not accept the mother's report at face value, but it was clear from her presentation that the child felt he was treated unfairly.

The boy responded to the suggested regime quite well for a while. He went to the new class for reading, feeling proud that he was selected for a special privilege and keeping track of the time himself. The teacher in the room to which he went for reading reported that he did fairly well academically but less well than the consultant had expected. However, he presented no behavioral problems in the second room at any time. After a while the child was put back on full-day sessions by the teacher herself because she noted some improvement.

Pressure of other affairs kept the consultant from checking closely with the teacher for a period of several weeks. However, at one point he saw the boy sitting tearfully in the principal's office, and once again the mother began talking about her feeling that the boy and teacher were not getting on together. Consultation with the teacher revealed that she had stopped the visits to the second classroom for reading and the assignment as class secretary. She felt that the child was not really getting anything different in reading from what she could provide, and she indicated her disappointment that the second teacher was not willing to take the boy permanently. Moreover, she found the boy's habit of speaking about his activities in the second classroom disruptive and undesirable. She had not discontinued the position as class secretary, but several other children had asked to do the same thing. When she agreed to let some other children engage in the same activity, it lost its value as a special task. Further discussion with the teacher revealed that her negative response to him was partly dictated by her perception of him as a "big shot" who liked to lord it over others. The consultant suggested reinstating the visits and the special activity precisely because the child needed to see himself as an important person.

Shortly thereafter the consultant found the child in the principal's office. The boy stated that he had not done anything wrong, but that another child had created the disturbance for which he was being punished. The consultant checked with the teacher who reported that he had done two things. The boy denied one of the offenses, but when faced with the teacher's reminder he concluded that he had indeed committed the second offense. He had stomped into the classroom rather loudly on returning late from lunch. It seemed that there might have been alternative methods for handling the particular incident, but the teacher had chosen the method of excluding the child from her room temporarily. On another occasion, at about that same time, the teacher indicated her feeling that the boy was not able to think abstractly because of difficulty he was having with material in the workbook. She asked the consultant to try the boy on the same material. Looking at the beginning first-grade workbook, the consultant found it took him almost a minute to understand the instructions and the concept involved in the exercise. In view of the lack of clarity to himself, the consultant assumed that the difficulty was considerably enhanced for the first-grade child. He thereupon offered some additional cues for the first exercise and found that the child grasped the material, completing the entire page of exercises quickly and correctly. The two incidents convinced the consultant that the teacher was probably not in touch with the child's needs, and he approached another first-grade teacher about her interest in working with the child.

The other teacher was approached for two reasons. One was her method of operating her class. She provided a great deal of precise ordering and structuring. Each lesson was planned in exquisite detail, and observation in her class suggested that it usually ran like clockwork. The discipline in the class was not accomplished through fear; the teacher infrequently raised her voice, but rather it seemed to come primarily from the order of the room that provided continuous activities to be accomplished in a consistent fashion day in and day out. The consultant felt that the boy would respond well to the procedures in the new classroom.

For example, in his original classroom, on entering in the morning, the children were permitted to circulate around the room talking to each other quietly and sharing whatever they wanted until the teacher was ready for the opening exercises. The teacher felt the children needed the opportunity to renew their acquaintance with each other and to say whatever they might want to say to her or to each other in this informal conversation period. In the second classroom work was on the blackboard waiting for the children. On entering, each one was to say good morning to the teacher and then go to the supply cabinet, obtain a piece of paper and immediately begin doing the work on the blackboard. The consultant felt that the boy would respond well to this prepared work.

A second reason for considering a transfer to the particular teacher was her remark some weeks before, made half seriously and half in jest, that she would gladly trade one of her problem children for this boy. The consultant was aware of some background of competitive feeling between the two teachers, but he took her comment as a communication that she would like to try to work with the child.

The consultant then approached both teachers immediately before his next visit with the child's mother and inquired about their willingness to accept the transfer. The new teacher agreed readily, whereas the original teacher was somewhat surprised but raised no objections to the move. The principal agreed to the transfer on learning that both teachers were in agreement, and at that point the consultant spoke to the mother, indicating that a place had become available in another teacher's room and that he would like to try to place the boy in the new room. The mother seemed delighted at the prospects of a change, but when she left the consultant she went to the teacher and expressed a great deal of anxiety about the move. She seemed particularly concerned about impressing the teacher that she did not initiate the request and that she had nothing against her. It is the consultant's impression that the mother was hostile toward the teacher, that she interpreted his comments about the teacher as hostile comments, and she was now concerned lest the teacher retaliate against her or her child. At any rate, the mother's display of affect was the focus for still another discussion with the teacher about the wisdom, the reasoning, and the timing of the move. At this point it seemed to the consultant that the teacher was experiencing somewhat ambivalent feelings. She was hurt at the implication that she could not handle the child, but she was relieved that she would no longer have to be in a struggle with him.

The transfer was accomplished immediately. The consultant explained to the child that he hoped he would get along better in a quieter room where the rules were somewhat different. The boy was obviously frightened, but he seemed to understand and he accompanied the consultant to the new room at the end of the school day. There he was introduced to the teacher who welcomed him and explained exactly what he was to do in the morning on entering. He was also told there was one important rule in the room he had to follow. He had to sit in his seat and not speak out, but if he wanted anything at all he was to raise his hand and the teacher would come over to him as quickly as she could to help him with whatever it was he required.

The transfer accomplished its purposes admirably. In subsequent months the child's aggressive behavior in school stopped completely, except for a single incident. Sometimes, when he seemed displeased with something, he made annoying noises resembling snorting, but the snorts decreased in frequency and intensity as they were ignored. His talking out continued, but it was partly treated as exuberance and was not seen as a disruptive element. On all subsequent visits to this classroom the consultant observed the child to be relaxed, busy, and fully participating in the activity in the classroom. To the consultant's knowledge he was never again removed from the classroom. The new teacher, of course, had a vested interest in reporting his progress, and so her comments must be accepted with some discount for whatever degree of competition existed between the two teachers. At first she indicated her impression that the child was not so bright as the consultant thought, but later in the term she stated repeatedly that the child had improved remarkably and was indeed doing very well. Appointments with his mother no longer seemed desirable, and these were stopped. The child was promoted at the end of the school year.

This example demonstrates a number of points.[2] First, it is probably impossible to arrange for a transfer of a child from one classroom to another without considerable emotional distress to some or all of the persons concerned, as was the case with the original teacher and the mother. Once the transfer was successful the boy's mother felt at ease, but the consultant had a certain amount of fence-mending to do with the first teacher in order to maintain a working relationship with her. Second, for a transfer to be successful it is essential that it be made for some distinct purpose, with the teacher and situation clearly and carefully understood. We have not yet had any examples of a transfer backfiring, but it is clear that not all children will benefit from them. The disruptive behavior pattern may repeat itself in the new room, as in Example 4.

Third, and perhaps most important, the rapid and dramatic change in this boy must raise important questions about a number of concepts and procedures in the mental-health field. In the second classroom both his behavioral and learning disturbances were minimal. In the first classroom they were exacerbated to the degree that a referral for outside professional help was strongly contemplated. In fact, the consultant did attempt to work with the child's mother until he became convinced that the best answer to his difficulty was a transfer. Under these circumstances can we think of a disturbed child or must we think instead of a child in a situation? It is also inadequate to think of the problem as stemming exclusively from a neurotic reaction

[2] Another example is the case of Billy in Chapter 12.

on the part of the teacher to a child. It is true that the teacher seemed to be overreacting to the boy, but it must be remembered that he had been considered a difficult child in still another situation. He was not so provocative a child that he would be seen as touching off anyone, but it seems clear that his undesirable characteristics were such that they could be elicited by situations that did not provide sufficient structure for him, independently of the teacher's emotional reaction to the child. The sudden, dramatic, and enduring change in the boy in the classroom situation leads us to raise questions about the general applicability of the conception of psychological disturbance we have earlier called "intrapsychic supremacy."

Another question we must raise concerns the tendency of the mental-health professional to treat any problem as having its origins in a situation removed from the one in which the problem manifests itself. When a child shows some failure to adjust or to learn in any particular situation, the mental-health professional is inclined to make the assumption that the child is revealing some failure of adaptation and to seek to treat the problem by treating the child. In the case of the boy in the last example the consultant's inclination was to work with the child's mother, particularly on learning the child's history, and referral to a psychotherapist was strongly contemplated, primarily because there seemed to be no immediate effectiveness to the environmental manipulations suggested by the consultant and carried out by the teacher. It became abundantly clear that the transfer succeeded in resolving the major problem quickly and effectively. The transfer basically represented treatment of the problem in its own terms in the situation in which it manifested itself.

Still another question has to do with the superficiality of the transfer as a method of treatment. It is true that the child would not have expressed any of his feelings toward the teacher, toward learning, or toward himself. He had not developed any new relationship with his parents or siblings. However, in place of school as a situation in which he received constant feedback of himself as failure and troublemaker, he was now receiving the positive gratification derived from learning. In place of constant lectures and squabbles with his mother, the child was now free of her complaints and her efforts to control his behavior in school. It was no longer necessary for her to admonish him constantly to be a good boy in school or to attempt to manipulate him by a series of external rewards and punishments. Both boy and parent were relieved of the anguish of contemplating a bleak future for him, and the child was free of the guilt and hostility that must inevitably accompany mother's plaintive pleas, "What am I going to do with you? What's going to become of you?" The one simple action of transfer reduced the occasions for difficult interactions between parent and child and between teacher and child and increased the possibilities for the child to receive satisfaction from his work in school. The new situation immediately suppressed one set of difficulties and permitted another pattern to be reinforced. It is difficult to believe that change based on any other form of treatment would have as rapid or as far-reaching consequences as the single act of transferring the child from one classroom to another.

This final example is presented not only because it describes a clear example of the positive consequences of transfer but also because it brings to the fore the role of one of the peripheral personnel in the school—the school nurse.[3]

Example 8. The elementary-school nurse was a married woman in her early forties who had lived for many years in the neighborhood served by the school. Her own children had attended the school in which she worked and had gone on to one of the city's high schools. Because of her long residence in the neighborhood, as well as her own involvement in the school, she was well known to many of the children and their parents.

In all our observations in the school we had been struck by the way this nurse perceived her job and the children with whom she came into contact. She was an extremely gentle and patient woman who appeared to have an almost intuitive knowledge and understanding of the frequent misperceptions and apprehensions that many children possess concerning the area of illness and medicine. Although meticulously clean, her office was decorated lavishly with the gaily colored pictures and cards that many of the school's children had made for her. She was a nurse who apparently took the "laying on of hands" maxim of medicine quite seriously, and she was often observed cuddling or soothing a child while ministering to his needs. More often than not she would spend a great deal of time listening to a child describe his symptoms, although they usually were observable. Generally, she would explain to a child what she was doing to him and always dealt with his feelings of pain or discomfort in a firm but understanding manner. If a child was sent home from school and was subsequently absent for more than a few days, she would call the parents and attempt to speak with the child to communicate her interest and concern about the situation.

---

[3] One of the reasons for selecting this example is to suggest that the role of school nurse has hardly been viewed as a mental-health resource in the school. When we consider that by training and selection the school nurse is neither equipped nor expected to be such a resource, it seems that discussion of the potentialities of the position is long overdue. Our own inquiries have not turned up one training program in psychiatric nursing that concerns itself with the school nurse as a mental-health resource.

In summary, her role as a nurse involved a commitment to herself, the children, and the community—a commitment that broadened the usual definition of school nursing. By perceiving her responsibilities in the widest possible perspective she acted in ways that were personally relevant and generally helpful to the child. Her tolerance, patience, and stability often resulted in the establishment of a relationship with a child that endured and grew long after the crisis situation involving the child had faded into the past. These personal and professional characteristics of the school nurse were to become the most important variables (variables that were to make a distinct difference) in the life of a troubled youngster named Tommy.

Tommy was a seven-year-old boy enrolled in the second grade. He was a well-developed, good-looking child of above-average intelligence who had entered the elementary school one year before when his family had moved into the area. Both academically and socially his performance and adjustment at that time were more than adequate and consistent with his abilities and talents. Although initially noted to be somewhat shy, he quickly made friends and was highly regarded by his first-grade teacher.

Tommy had had several of the usual childhood diseases (chicken pox and measles) and his last complete physical examination had been essentially negative. His teeth required attention, his vision was 20-20, and his hearing was normal. Thus, until the summer of 1964, Tommy was a relatively healthy, attractive, and bright seven-year-old whose developmental and medical history was essentially unremarkable. Although he experienced some minor difficulty when he entered the new school situation, his adjustment, both academically and socially, was completely satisfactory.

During the summer vacation Tommy, delivering newspapers, was viciously attacked and bitten by a dog. As he went up to one of the houses on his paper route the dog leaped on him, ripped his clothing, and bit him on the back and wrist. Tommy's screams eventually brought the dog's owner, who had to beat the dog repeatedly with a club in order to make him let go of the child.

Tommy was taken immediately to the office of a local doctor. His mother was notified and met Tommy there. His wounds were cauterized and injections administered for possible infection, and he was given sedatives.

Soon after this experience Tommy became very quiet and extremely withdrawn, not talking or playing with other children, and refusing to leave his home. About three weeks later he developed a cold and what was described as an "asthma attack" in which he was short of breath and had difficulty breathing. According to Tommy's mother it was during this time immediately following the incident with the dog that Tommy "woke up nights screaming and crying and at times running out of the house. He complained of a pounding in his head and imagined seeing things."

With the passage of time and the approach of the new school year Tommy's posttraumatic symptomatology appeared to become more involved and frightening. He began actively hallucinating and talking about "the ugly little man who's coming and putting bad feelings in my head." He became extremely frightened by loud sounds and constantly sought his mother's attention, reassurance, and protection. The only way in which she could calm him down would be to hold him and speak to him in a soft and quiet manner. After numerous consultations with the family doctor it was decided to put Tommy under the care of Dr. S., a "nerve specialist in town." Dr. S. placed Tommy on a regimen of medication (phenobarbital) to be taken three times a day after meals. It was his feeling that Tommy's condition was "an emotional reaction related to the strain stemming from his traumatic episode with a brutal dog." Tommy was told that the "pill he took to school would help him get rid of the spells."

It will be recalled that when Tommy initially entered the first grade he had experienced some minor difficulties in adjusting to his new living and school settings. It was during this period that he first came into contact with the school nurse. According to her he "often would come to me during the first few weeks of school complaining of a cold or stomach upset, but would be satisfied to just talk with me, have his temperature taken, and return to class." Following his successful adjustment in school he contented himself with visiting the nurse whenever the holidays were drawing near, at which time he would wish her a happy holiday, and would often give her a card that he had made for her.

On returning to school this year Tommy was assigned to a second-grade class. At this time he was extremely nervous and upset, often running away from the loud noises in the schoolyard, and frequently hallucinating. His single anchor of security in school appeared to be the faith he placed in "the pill that would help my spells."

Tommy's second-grade teacher was an essentially unresponsive and reserved person. Her approach to the teaching situation and to the children was all business. Her previous teaching experience had been confined to the parochial school setting and it was difficult for her to tolerate any interference with the academic standards and expectations she set for her students. Our observations in her classroom always revealed an academically competent teacher who was a stern and controlling disciplinarian and who utilized methods of shaming and rejecting to ensure the maintainance of an orderly, efficient classroom. Although never harsh or uncontrolled in her interpersonal dealings with the children, neither would she allow herself or them to minimize their personal distance in a physical or psychological manner. In short, however competent her preparation and however well-intentioned her philosophy of teaching, she was a teacher who was essentially unable or unwilling to deal with the particular and idiosyncratic needs of her children. She tended to perceive these needs as unwelcomed and unrelated interruptions in the processes and aims of second-grade education.

In terms of the teacher's relationship with Tommy, although upset and somewhat frightened by his behavior, she perceived his spells as essentially interfering; that is to say, as discrete behaviors that erected unwanted barriers for her in her attempts to present specific material to the rest of the class. As far as his pills were concerned, she viewed the responsibility for his taking them as a matter of concern for Tommy, his parents, and his doctor. It was not within the scope of her definition of her professional responsibilities to become involved in a problem that was distracting in nature and took time away from her teaching duties. This being the case, and because she was unable to materially reorganize her perception of the situation, she was content to allow Tommy to utilize the nurse and her office as the appropriate setting for such interactions. This removed Tommy from her classroom during his periods of stress, and at the same time enabled her to maintain her firm position regarding the limited and relevant areas of responsibility for a teacher.

From this point on Tommy began spending more and more of his time at the nurse's office, and it was here that we first met him. According to the nurse, whenever Tommy was in school—his absence rate for the months of September and October were extremely high—he would come to her office to take his pill or "whenever he felt a spell coming on." They would spend these periods of time talking and Tommy would describe vividly his feelings and tell her about the "things he saw." Often when his crying and trembling subsided she would call his mother, talk with her at length, and eventually have Tommy taken home. Although the nurse knew about the incident with the dog, Tommy himself soon brought it up during one of his particularly difficult days. They spoke about it at some length and the nurse, in the context of sharing and understanding his fear, related to him several other such incidents involving other children. It was during the next day that we met Tommy. On that occasion Tommy had come to the nurse's office and wanted to go home. He was sobbing uncontrollably and seemed extremely nervous when we came into her office. After he calmed down a bit we all sat around while Tommy told us about "the little man I saw in my class who was coming to put bad things in my head." Once more he spent a good deal of time talking about the past summer, but finally began speaking of the terrible difficulty he had whenever he felt a spell coming on and would have to ask his teacher about letting him go out of the class to take his pill. He ended by informing us of his desire not to come to school any more. After speaking with Tommy's mother and the teacher we decided eventually to change his class, and, for the interim, we put him on half days, both to minimize his anxiety-arousing contact with his teacher and to enable us to have the time to search for an appropriate second-grade teacher. During the time that he was attending school only in the afernoons he spent most of his time doing his school work in the nurse's office after his teacher had given him his assignment. We were, as yet, relatively new in the school. Although we felt the need to have Tommy's class changed, we wanted time to get a better idea of exactly which teacher would be most appropriate for him. Since neither Tommy's current teacher nor the school nurse minded him using the nurse's office as his interim "classroom," everyone agreed to this arrangement. This enabled the nurse and ourselves to utilize that period of time to search for, become acquainted with, and brief whoever was to become Tommy's new teacher.

The following week we were in the lunchroom during a time of the day when the school nurse usually is not in her office. Tommy entered the lunchroom looking obviously upset and a bit bewildered. He was grasping his bottle of pills tightly in his hand as he looked around for his teacher. Before we could reach him or he could see us he turned to another teacher and hesitatingly began asking her permission to take his pill. The teacher, noting his degree of upset and the air of panic pervading his speech, immediately took his hand and accompanied him out of the lunchroom. They proceeded down the hall to a fountain where she helped Tommy take his pill. Once this was accomplished the teacher took Tommy to her room where he calmed down in a relatively short period of time. With her arm draped gently around his shoulders she then took him back to the lunchroom where he sat at her class's table for the remainder of the period. In this very short time we knew that we had found Tommy's next second-grade teacher.

This teacher was a young and attractive woman who was relatively inexperienced in terms of the number of years she had been teaching. Her class was generally a bit more noisy than others but always jumping with activity. She was an extremely warm and accepting person who seemed most effective and efficient when she became intimately involved with and in the ongoing activities of her children. Although she never lost control of her class there was a pervading atmosphere of disjointedness in the sense that many activities might be going on at the same time. This looseness quickly subsided whenever she raised her voice a bit above the well-modulated tone in which she usually addressed individual students. Her lessons were not always totally prepared beforehand and sometimes were lost in organizing particular events. She was extremely patient with the children and utilized well both verbal and nonverbal cues to communicate her feelings to them. More than anything else she seemed to enjoy teaching and being with her children, and this enjoyment appeared to be reciprocal.

We immediately met with the nurse and the "new" teacher to consider the transfer of Tommy to her class. We discussed Tommy's difficulties and the reasons we felt she might be helpful. The teacher, in turn, communicated her desire to have him placed in her class and informed us that, indeed, she had a great affection for him and hoped she would be able to help him. It was decided that the school nurse would be the most appropriate person to handle the transition in the sense that she would both help to present the idea to Tommy and would remain the available resource whenever he felt the need to leave the classroom for any reason relating to his difficulties. It also was decided that the teacher would meet with us on a weekly basis to discuss Tommy's progress or lack of progress.

Tommy was transferred to his new class and immediately placed on a full-day schedule. During the first day the teacher spoke with Tommy about his difficulties and communicated to him how important it was to her that he get better and take his "spell pills." They established a procedure whereby he would not have to make any public statements in class prior to the granting of permission to leave the room to take his pill. Whenever Tommy was absent the teacher immediately called his home and spoke with him and his mother. Although Tommy was informed of the availability of the school nurse the teacher made it clear to him that his health, as well as his school work, was now also a joint venture between him and herself. To Tommy this meant that she very much wanted him to be able to talk with her about his feelings and his symptoms, and that her interest in him was as a "little boy" and not just as a "little student."

Tommy's progress after entering his new class was speedy and marked and was manifested in virtually all of the areas in which he had been experiencing profound difficulties. For purposes of clarity we describe these areas separately, although the reader should note that his behavior in each of these areas was influenced by, and interrelated with, his experiences in the others.

Tommy's absence rate from school decreased almost immediately after he was placed in his new class. In terms of academic performance, Tommy rose to be one of the top five students in his class. According to his grades as well as his teacher's observations, he was beginning to fulfill the above-average potential noted in the first grade. Although before his shift he was unable to concentrate, had difficulty maintaining attention, and was unwilling to work at anything but his reading material, he was now actively involved in the varied projects occurring in his classroom. In general his over-all academic performance, as well as his social adjustment, was at a higher level, occurred in a context relatively free of the debilitating effects of undue loss of attention or the inability to concentrate, and appeared to have become more inner-directed and self-satisfying than externally imposed.

Of greatest import were the changes that occurred in Tommy's symptomatology and schedule of medication. The week before his transfer was particularly difficult for him. His symptoms (fearfulness, phobic reactions to loud noises, periods of fitful crying, and apparent hallucinatory experiences) were quite pronounced, and the occasions necessitating his approaching his teacher to request attention for his "spell pills" seemed to exacerbate these symptoms. At that time he was on phenobarbital. During the time after his transfer to his new class he showed evidence of a steady and progressive reduction in the intensity and duration of his psychotic symptomatology. Soon after entering his new class the periods of fitful crying accompanying his pill-taking behavior subsided. He was gradually able to tolerate loud noises, although this aspect of his difficulty has been only recently eliminated. His hallucinatory experiences became less frequent and frightening, the more he spoke about them with his teacher. They, too, have not been reported for some time. In mid-December, approximately one month after his transfer, his medication was decreased to every other day, and by late January was further reduced. At present all medications have been discontinued. In a recent meeting of the school nurse, the teacher, and ourselves the teacher informed us that she had not noticed any changes since Tommy has been off medication. Tommy's mother reported similar progress at home and, except for the fact that "he occasionally has nightmares and wakes up crying," felt that "the worst is over." Our latest classroom observations and information would support this point of view.

As far as Tommy's relationship with the nurse was concerned, this, too, underwent a change. Although we made it clear to Tommy that the nurse was available to him whenever he felt he needed her, the frequency and duration of his visits to her decreased steadily after mid-November. Although he had been in her office virtually every day that he was in school and had remained there for significant periods of time, subsequent to his shifting of classes he began showing up less often and would remain for shorter periods. This change was a gradual process and occurred over a long span of time. By late December the nurse observed that Tommy "still comes to see me about little things and many times just to say 'Hello.' " Her most recent report indicated that, "Tommy has not visited my office in almost three weeks, except to look for a hat in the lost and found box!"

Tommy's example is one that may be understood on several levels. Perhaps the most obvious is the level on which we perceive change in a child as a function of the kind of teacher he interacts with. In this context we may view the case as an illustration of the different effects that the various personality characteristics of teachers have on the behavior and experiences of a child undergoing a severe post-traumatic psychotic episode. On another level, however—the level we are most concerned with here—Tommy's progress provides us with data concerning the variety of settings and individuals that emerge as relevant areas of inquiry concerning the learning experience of the child once we become truly immersed in the world of the school.

In this chapter we have shown how it is possible to think of the school as a whole in considering resources for helping children who are having difficulty. In transferring a child from one classroom to another, we are not only involved with the interaction of a teacher and a child but we necessarily become involved with the school as a whole. The unit of consideration necessarily expands, and as our view of the unit expands the actions that we can take and the resources available also expand.

Chapter 12

The Child at the Clinic

In Chapter 4 we described the way we presented our Clinic and its approach to all the teachers in a school with which we wished to establish a relationship. It will be recalled that we indicated earlier that the summary of our set speech to the faculty contained, with one exception, the major points we communicated to teachers. That exception was our offer to see at the Clinic selected children for whom something was required beyond what we could provide to the teacher. However, it was made explicit that this additional service would not be provided until after we had been in a school for several months, and that the reason for this was that our major focus was on how to help in the "here and now of the classroom" and not on "how many children we could take off the teachers' hands." If, we said, we started off by seeing individual children, we could in a few days fill up our available time and never get to the point of seeing how we could be helpful *in* the school. Consequently, although we recognized that there would be children who could benefit from treatment outside the school, we first had to devote ourselves to our major task: how to help within the confines of the school.

Despite these statements it was not unusual in the initial weeks of our work in a school to find some teachers, principals, and supervisors expecting that our chief (and immediate) service was one of accepting referrals for psychotherapy and psychological testing. Our practice of making classroom observations and working with the teacher was perceived by most people as ancillary to our presumed task of effecting change in the problem child or in his home conditions. It took some time to disabuse some school personnel of this narrow definition of our role as healers of the disturbed child, as rehabilitating him away from the school to return to the classroom to which he had been unable to adjust. In this chapter we are concerned with describing our work with the child at the Clinic, an activity that, though it represents a small

227

part of our work in the schools, well illustrates the principle that helping a person change in a particular setting requires us to know the setting intimately.

Our role of understanding and influencing here-and-now dynamics
in the classroom operates on the assumption that classroom conditions
may create or at least permit the maintenance of undesirable behavior.
From such a view, unless classroom dynamics are first thoroughly explored through observation and teacher conferences, seeing a child at
the Clinic is wasted manpower because in many cases the problem
children referred by the school have been misdiagnosed; in reality,
they are often children from problem classrooms. In such cases the consultant may suggest a redefinition of who the problem children are in
the room or a closer look at the teacher's contribution to the difficulty.

Our practice of carefully scrutinizing referrals for testing and psychotherapy does not stem primarily from manpower limitations. It is
based instead on our conviction that testing and traditional psychotherapy are not the methods of choice either for answering most school-
relevant diagnostic questions or for effecting change in disturbed classroom behavior. Much of the richly detailed knowledge of the child's
personality structure and case history, derived from sensitively interpreted tests and traditional psychotherapy sessions, simply has low payoff value to the psychologist advising a teacher in the day-to-day management of a problem child. It has been our experience that in order
to influence a child's school behavior the most productive and com-
municable understanding of a child can be obtained by focusing on
the here-and-now classroom and the role of the teacher. Teachers,
moreover, find little more than their curiosity satisfied by the typical
intrapsychic description of personality structure and details of case history; it is through their explorations of classroom dynamics with a consultant that most teachers sharpen the sensitivity of their own diagnostic and influence techniques in classroom situations.

Many of the problem children referred by the school, then, resolve
into cases of problem classrooms. A referral of the problem child to the
Clinic is *never* acted on in those cases where the teacher can effectively
improve her classroom through insights and advice gathered during
her conferences with the consultant. When, however, a classroom situation is basically sound, and despite her genuine efforts the teacher has
been unable to effect change in a problem child's behavior, the child is
then seen individually at the Clinic. Such cases constitute the first class
of children seen at the Clinic: persistently problem children. A second
class of cases are children from persistently problem classrooms. Such

children come from unstable classrooms to which they are prime con-
tributors. If no other suitable classroom is available, the child is seen
both for his own welfare and to assist the foundering teacher in controlling her children. Occasionally, persistently problem children or
children from persistently problem classrooms are seen at the Clinic
not primarily to change their behavior but to answer specific diagnostic questions raised by the consultant's observations. Thus children
may be seen at the Clinic for extended diagnostic evaluations of their
fantasy preoccupations, severity of psychopathology, or depth and extent of mental retardation. A special group includes children excluded
from school and placed on home-bound instruction for reasons as diverse as school phobia and unmanageable behavior disorder.

By the time teacher and psychologist have exhausted various classroom interventions and agreed that the child should be seen at the
Clinic, the psychologist is fairly well known to the child and his class.
In almost every case the child's relationship to the psychologist has
passed through three phases. First, after the original referral of the
child, or after the psychologist's own decision to study a particular
child, he may spend several hours in nonparticipant observation.
Whether or not the teacher introduces the psychologist to the class, she
is encouraged to try to ignore his presence, overtly if not covertly. The
psychologist's observations during this initial period provide important diagnostic data, enabling him to assess the adequacy of the teacher's perception of the problem and her response to it. During the second phase of his relationship to the class, the psychologist becomes a
casual participant observer, indirectly interviewing children in the
classroom about their perception of events both child and psychologist
have observed. Like an anthropologist in the field interviewing his in-
formants, the psychologist amasses knowledge of the classroom culture
without making the children feel they are betraying secrets. All this
talking is done casually, and one outcome is that the psychologist
achieves an easy-going acceptance by the class as a friendly, interested
observer. It is quite possible that some children incorporate the consultant into their image of "one of us," *because he is as subject to the
teacher's rules as they are while he is in the classroom.* During this
phase of his work, the consultant is no longer a dispassionate observer
and exerts quite an influence on his observational field, with children
often wishing to show him their work or to discuss some matter with
him in the back of the room. An outgrowth of all this pleasant interaction with the children is that talking to the psychologist becomes a
natural, high-status activity for the children, and when the problem

child or children are spoken to in the classroom they are spoken to not by a frightening stranger dealing with their discipline or learning problems but by a friend.

During the third phase of relationship between consultant and problem child the child is more directly confronted with his difficulties, usually outside the classroom in another room, and his response to the teacher's interventions queried. At this point many children can be helped, obviating a visit to the Clinic. Should the child's difficulty prove unmodifiable through the usual classroom interventions and individual conferences between child and psychologist outside the classroom, the psychologist lays the groundwork for a visit to the Clinic. The Clinic is introduced to the child as a place where consultant and child can further understand and help the child's difficulties and unhappiness *in school*. From the outset, then, the therapeutic focus is on the child's school behavior, its strengths and weaknesses. In addition to making crystal-clear the school focus of the Clinic visits, the psychologist describes the physical layout of the Clinic, the availability of toys and games, and the fact that milk and cookies are served. The child is told that he will be taken on a tour of the building during his first visit. It is explained that the psychologist will continue to observe in the classroom and discuss the child's behavior with the teacher, not to check up or spy on him but to increase his own understanding of the child's difficulties, and, finally, that the psychologist will contact his parents to get permission to take him to the Clinic. Frequently, the request for parental permission for taking the child to the Clinic has been preceded by several interviews with them and they too are encouraged to see the visits to the Clinic as a natural continuation of the now-familiar work carried out in the classroom by teacher and psychologist. The child is not portrayed as being disturbed, but as needing special understanding and help to which the parents can contribute by permitting and encouraging him to speak freely with the psychologist and by not using the child's visits to the Clinic as a weapon against him. Parents are advised to bring to the psychologist's attention any information or questions they may have, especially about the child's school behavior and attitudes. The school focus is also emphasized to the parents, and they are helped in conceiving new ways of showing their interest in the child's school life in its ups and downs, for example, by displaying his work, making enriching family outings, or reading to him. In general they are advised to seize every opportunity to heighten the child's intellectual curiosity and praise any positive school behavior, and to encourage the child to discuss with the psychologist any difficulties he is having at home or in school.

What emotional climate, then, has been cultivated by the psychologist before the child is taken to the Clinic for intensive individual work? First, unlike the usual procedure in a child-guidance clinic, children brought to our Clinic are self-referred in the sense that they discuss with the psychologist the wisdom of the referral before it is actually carried out. Indeed, the child knows about the planned visits to the Clinic before his parents, who are notified shortly after the child's and psychologist's decision. Because the discussion of the plan to visit the Clinic occurs between child and psychologist rather than child and parent, much of the parental shame and fear about psychotherapy is not communicated to the child or is communicated only after the psychologist has laid the groundwork. Second, a clear need for psychotherapy is established in the child's mind before he goes to the Clinic. Minimal and maximal goals of the Clinic interviews can be agreed on by child and psychologist. Despite his inevitable resistance to self-study, the child is less confused about the goals of therapy than he usually is before a visit to a child-guidance clinic. This clarity of focus on school difficulties facilitates, in a fair proportion of children, the early development of some positive motivation to understand and change themselves. Third, the psychologist, through his pre-Clinic school contacts with the child, establishes himself as a friendly, unmysterious visitor to the classroom who has been accepted by the children as one who knows the real score in the classroom, rather than as one labeled a "head-shrinker." A high level of at least manifest cooperation is almost always obtained from the parents because the child's school career, with its occupational and legal implications, is at stake. Unlike the more commanding psychotherapy referrals by juvenile courts, the psychologist's description of the Clinic visits minimizes the parents' sense of fear and coercion, for the Clinic is seen as offering cost-free additional help for their child's school problems. Many parents can thus see the therapeutic work as a kind of tutorial for their child's school difficulties instead of a mysterious probing into their child's sick psyche.

Children are characteristically seen for two one-hour sessions weekly at the Clinic, to which they are driven, in many cases, by the psychologist right after school. The unorthodox use of a child's psychotherapist as his chauffeur is a strict necessity, for few inner-city, lowerclass families have cars or a mother with few enough children and chores to escort her child to the Clinic; lack of adherence to scheduled appointments is frequently a problem in work with inner-city families. Regular attendance, so important in clinical work, can thus be assured. In those cases where it is felt desirable for a family to make its own arrangments for transporting the child, if such arrangements are in the realm of possibility the family is expected to do so.

From the time of the first drive to the Clinic, the child is period-ically asked to state his understanding of the reasons for which he is coming to the Clinic. In doing so his understanding is sharpened and distortions explored. Throughout the work with him the school focus must be kept clearly in his mind, even though his and the psychologist's quest for understanding school problems often leads them to issues seemingly far afield of school.

On his arrival at the Clinic the child is taken on a thorough tour of the building, allowed to try office equipment, shown the operation of the one-way mirrors, and introduced to the secretary and any staff members he meets. He is taken for milk and cookies in the kitchen. In the course of his tour certain Clinic rules and opportunities are ex-plained to him: any and all feelings and questions may be expressed at the Clinic, even those not usually talked about anywhere else; play material may be enjoyed but not destroyed; complete confidentiality is assured the child and he is told that the psychologist will consult him before any parent conferences are arranged. The fact that the psychol-ogist will maintain continual contact with the teacher is spelled out, for it is from his talks with the teacher that the psychologist learns more about how he can understand and help the child as he changes in school.

Individual sessions at the Clinic rarely follow the pattern of nondi-rective play therapy. For children with severe emotional or cultural blocks to learning the therapeutic hour is partly spent in doing school-work so that the child's work skills and attitudes can be examined. Tendencies to rush, guess, become bored or tired, not attend, or give up are identified as fearful attempts at avoiding a confrontation with school material that the child has come to regard as being hopelessly beyond his grasp. His self-defeating attitudes about learning from mis-takes and asking for help when he does not understand something are pointed out. His conviction of academic incompetence from repetitive failure experiences is explored. *Every attempt is made to compare the ways in which the child approaches work, play, and authority in the Clinic and in school, cross-referencing, as it were, as much as the ma-terial permits.* Direct discussion of the child's school behavior takes place and his understanding is checked against the psychologist's class-room and Clinic observations and teacher conferences. In addition to exploring with the child his self-defeating approach to the usual schoolwork, the psychologist encourages the child to dictate and illustrate his own stories, which he will be helped to read. The educationally retarded child comes alive at the idea of preparing his own book, his sight vocabulary increases, and he becomes more amenable to learning the mechanics of reading. The themes the child selects for his stories reflect his interests and conflicts that, when communicated with discretion to his teacher, permit her to build class lessons and projects around the faltering child's strengths and interests. In reflecting his conflicts and needs the stories can form a new basis for exploring his learning difficulties in the classroom. For some slow learners nonmotivational issues appear as perceptual-motor deficits requiring specific retraining procedures.

The child's approach to schoolwork as such is less central in cases of rebellious antisocial behavior. Consideration of such a child's grievances and distrust of people must come before or at least concurrent with any exploration of such a child's learning difficulties. Some of these children respond well to insight-oriented discussions dealing with their inner turmoil and social difficulties. Others appear much less conflicted and the therapeutic hours serve the diagnostic purpose of informing the psychologist that what is needed with such a child is a comprehensive home-school-Clinic plan for resocializing the child by a combination of positive and negative incentives consistently applied in all these settings. In such cases the Clinic sessions reinforce the new demands on the rebellious child by exploring the reasons for the rules, allowing the child a safe place in which to ventilate his rage, and emphasizing the futility of the child's continued attempts to defeat the newly forged union of home and school. The psychologist, with his intimate knowledge of classroom happenings, is well suited to confront the defiant child with less other-blaming interpretations of his provocative behavior than the child usually advances.

In the following pages we present four children who were seen individually at the Clinic. It must be emphasized that these cases are presented primarily to illustrate how our relationship to a child at the Clinic is explicitly organized around the problems of the child in school. From the standpoint of the child, teacher, and parent the visits to the Clinic stem from problems in school and therefore must be related in various ways to what is going on in school. It is to illustrate this approach, rather than the intricacies of psychodynamics and the complexities of the therapeutic relationship, that we present these cases. This is not to say that we believe psychodynamic considerations and formulations are of secondary significance in understanding and working with a child, but rather that we wished in this chapter to emphasize that we explicitly viewed our work with a child at the Clinic as an extension of our observations of and concerns and thoughts about him in school.

BILLY

Billy's first-grade teacher, a warm-hearted woman in her sixties with poor control over her classroom, had been unable to involve him in any constructive activities. He would move around the room at will, either absorbed in thought or punching other children. When Billy's defiance finally exasperated his teacher, she would chase him until she cornered him, whereupon Billy would emit a sound resembling a mixture of screaming and hilarious laughter as he rolled on the floor. His wildness had resulted in several expulsions from school by the principal, which had produced no discernible change in his behavior. In his classroom observations and talks with Billy the consulting psychologist became convinced of the severity of the boy's emotional disorganization. Billy seemed obsessed with a variety of sexual and destructive fantasies that he showed a strong tendency to act out indiscriminately. Many times Billy was so anxiously excited with some fantasy or need of his that his attention could not be gained for even a few seconds. In a few meetings with Billy's teacher her limited ability to understand and consistently react to him became clear. Because no other first-grade teacher in the school had shown particular strength in managing peculiar, antisocial behavior, the consultant's only possible recommendation to the principal, short of placing the boy on home-bound instruction, was that Billy be promoted at once to the second grade where there was an extremely competent teacher with interest and aptitude in managing disturbed children. After the principal's bewilderment at the recommendation had subsided long enough for her to label it "most irregular and unheard of," the psychologist discussed with her how placing Billy on home-bound instruction would guarantee his remaining a persistent nuisance to the school because he would by law have to be returned periodically for re-evaluation by the school, and home-bound instruction would not have provided him any opportunity for developing those controls necessary when learning alongside other children in a classroom.

For the benefit of the school and Billy the principal agreed to test the consultant's unusual transfer procedure. Billy was transferred to the second grade for an unspecified trial period while technically remaining in first grade. The change in Billy's behavior was dramatic. The skill of his new teacher in avoiding showdowns, detecting early signs of trouble and acting preventively, and coaxing him into some group activities stabilized Billy considerably. Billy, however, turned out to be a case of a persistently disturbed child even in a near-ideal classroom, and the psychologist decided to work with the boy at the Clinic. Although Billy's more peculiar antisocial actions had diminished to the point where the principal agreed that he should finish out the year in the second grade and remain with his new teacher for an additional year, Billy was not yet learning rapidly enough and showed more interest in his own fantasies than in anything else. The consultant's discussions with the boy in school, together with the transfer, had not gone far enough fast enough. In particular, Billy's daredevil climbing and occasional threats to jump from heights, his interest in fire, and impulsive embracing or punching other boys merited more intensive individual work. Of paramount importance was his failure to have learned to read and the ominous import of his not being enjoyably absorbed in school learning by the middle of the first grade. The longer Billy went through school without experiencing the success of learning, the more profound and persistent we expected his disturbance to become.

From the outset Billy understood that the reason for coming to the Clinic was to make clear to him why he had so much trouble and unhappiness in school so that he might begin to learn and enjoy it. "I come here to be taught to be good" was his version of our focus. Once at the Clinic Billy repeated his school restlessness and tendency to explore every aspect of any room in which he happened to find himself. Understanding that at the Clinic he could say or play out whatever he wished so long as he broke nothing, Billy took full advantage of the opportunity. At every turn his hyperactive behavior was connected by the psychologist to school and home happenings, even though he had grown far less wild in his new class. The boy came to see his daredevil climbing, getting into things, and provocative running away as having originated in attempts to "embarrass" his overprotective mother, whom he had maneuvered through his wild disobedience into restricting his movements. He learned how he had forced his first-grade teacher into a position similar to his mother's but had not been able to upset and control his second-grade teacher and the psychologist in that way. He saw how he was both actually freer to move and happier when he did not tantalize adults.

Billy understood that anything he said was confidential but that the psychologist would be continually in contact with his teacher and parents, the better to understand and help him. His parents were given the prerogative of seeing the psychologist at the Clinic whenever they wished or phoning him at home. In the early telephone contacts, initiated by the psychologist, Billy's mother was encouraged to grant him more freedom and responsibility at home, keeping him indoors as a punishment only when he ran away from her mealtime calls. As for the danger of his being injured while playing near home, she was advised to grin and bear it because her restrictive policy could only perpetuate his wild behavior. With much support, Billy's mother was able to submerge her anxieties sufficiently to give him more freedom coupled with the consistently firm punishment of remaining indoors when he ran away from her at mealtimes. Billy understood the agreement and how his freedom would be curtailed only if he disobeyed at mealtimes. He began to obey more, with occasional lapses, as he saw how certain definite consequences followed his wildness at particular times. Throughout the year-and-a-half that Billy was seen at the Clinic his mother and the psychologist spoke at least once a week on the phone, after Billy was asleep. Following usual Clinic practice, the child-focused parent-psychologist interviews were held not at regular intervals but when either parent or psychologist wished to discuss a particular issue.

The sessions at the Clinic suggested that there was more than an anxious restlessness or defiance in Billy's diffuse exploratory movements and need to manipulate objects. Genuine intellectual curiosity about the world, and specifically sexual curiosity, seemed to be contained in his hyperactivity. He showed above-average mechanical aptitude in learning how to operate the machines and gadgets he handled despite his excitability and shaky fine-muscle coordination. In manipulating objects Billy would try to take them apart to examine their insides, especially if they were animals or cartoon figures. From the blatantly sexual way in which he would play with the toy figures it was clear that his concern with their insides reflected questions about the anatomical differences between the sexes and the processes of sexual intercourse, conception, and birth. In his regular practice of clearing out the bottom shelf of the toy cabinet for use as his "bunk bed" Billy would crawl into the cabinet and close himself in for several minutes, again expressing through his play questions and anxieties centering around sleep, death, and possibly masturbation, as well as his wish to make a new home at the Clinic for himself and the psychologist. The way in which Billy's sexual wishes and curiosity, together with his sexual anxieties and confusions, motivated much of his hyperactive wildness, silliness, and defiance became clearest in his relationship to the psychologist. Whenever Billy's sexual interest was aroused at the Clinic it would be expressed not through words but through disorganized behavior. Much of Billy's wildness in school took on a new meaning and his difficulties in reading were hypothesized as stemming in part from his being overwhelmed by his own sexual associations to ordinarily nonsexual material.

The hypothesis that Billy sexualized reading material was put to a test by allowing him to select any three words each session that he had always wanted to learn to read. He would be responsible for illustrating pictorially and memorizing these words. He built up a sizable sight vocabulary in this way (his first success at reading a word and its illustration on a card), and he was tested each session on all earlier cards. His choice of words, however, such as gun, telescope, pickle, and a host of military and rapid-transit vehicles, unleashed diverse profanities and silliness which required the strongest influence by the psychologist to prevent their disrupting the lesson. As Billy began to use words more often to express himself, a process hastened by the introduction of a tape recorder, profanities were among his preferred verbalizations. When questioned about the meaning of his obscene language, Billy seriously maintained that he did not know and did not want to be told. The parallel between his rejection of school and sexual learning was pointed out to him, and when persuaded at last to discuss his understanding of the obscenities his ignorance and confusions were rank. In general he connected cruelty, insult, and filth with the anatomical differences between the sexes and reproduction. There were, moreover, many more homosexual than heterosexual preoccupations in his fantasy life and school behavior.

The psychologist felt that Billy's rejection of reading, and his defiance, could be most expeditiously approached through directly confronting him with his sexual conflicts and curiosity. Following usual Clinic procedure, the parents were first consulted for permission, explained the need, and prepared for the child's enlightenment at the Clinic. Such a procedure protects the therapeutic work from parental outrage when the child inevitably talks about his new discoveries at home, and gives parents their deserved right to determine when their children should be exposed to sexual information and by whom.

Operating on the well-supported hypothesis that Billy's sexual fantasies contributed significantly to his impairments in school learning and social behavior, the psychologist undertook in the sixth month of Billy's visits to the Clinic to confront him directly with the self-defeating effects of his sexual confusions, and enlighten him. Now in the second grade, Billy had continued to make progress in curtailing his hyperactivity but showed few signs of preferring classroom learning to his fantasy world. The psychologist's impunitive acceptance of

Billy's fantasies at the Clinic and interpretation of his strong resistance to verbalizing his sexual curiosity had failed to produce forward movement in the boy's learning difficulties. The psychologist reasoned that the direct analysis of Billy's sexual conflicts was the surest way of strengthening him for dealing with his rejection of learning. From the outset of his plan, the psychologist was perfectly sincere in explaining to Billy the rationale for insisting that he consider his sexual fantasies with the psychologist. Central to this rationale was the school focus of the sexual enlightenment.

After several sessions Billy was able to indicate in diverse ways that feelings and worries about his own body and sexuality might be upsetting his school learning and ability to get along with people. He understood that the goal of understanding his sexual attitudes was the facilitation of his school learning and social relationships. As his parents had been, so was his teacher alerted to expect more direct expression of sexual interest. The teacher was encouraged to introduce lessons about animal and human reproduction into the class if she felt Billy or any other child seemed to be showing concern about such issues directly or indirectly. Moreover, Billy's seat was changed by his teacher so that he would no longer be isolated from girls as he had been. The teacher felt this would help direct Billy's attentions to more appropriate persons, since she too had observed his homosexual playfulness. Finally, the importance of making a great push on Billy's resistance to learning was stressed to the teacher, whose expertise in managing Billy's behavior problems had had the unexpected effect of relaxing her awareness of his specifically academic learning difficulties. In this connection, she was encouraged to treat his exploratory handling of objects as a sign of curiosity on which she could build individual projects or class lessons.

A natural starting point for exploring Billy's understanding of sexuality was to have him define various common words of the street into the tape recorder, allowing him to add to his initial definitions while he was playing them back. The psychologist would then raise questions about the sources of the boy's understanding, his evidence, his degree of certainty, accuracies and errors in his account, and the overall feeling tone he attached to particular words. Stick drawings of the human male and female were completed by Billy on the blackboard in the therapy room, forming the basis for a more pictorial discussion of the anatomical differences between the sexes as well as of the processes of sexual intercourse, conception, and birth. When appropriate, the relevance of marriage and the family to sexuality was drawn into the discussions, which took place for varying portions of the hour over

many months. Weekly oral tests were administered to check his understanding and recall of the information presented. Central to these discussions were, of course, Billy's confusions and anxieties and the way
in which he dealt with them by acting silly or wild rather than by
thinking about his feelings and discussing questions he had with a
trusted adult. Reference was frequently made to the parallels between
Billy's anxious avoidance of sexual and school learning, yet how satisfying both sorts of learning were for him when he made himself stop
and think.

Two fairly clear-cut consequences ensued from these discussions. In
school Billy seemed calmer and responded favorably to his teacher's
renewed efforts to confront him with the necessity and joy of learning.
At the Clinic, however, he became more anxious, which he expressed
not through his customary silly wildness or defiance but rather
through verbalizing for the first time all sorts of personal concerns of
his. He spoke of sexual happenings he had witnessed between his parents and in the neighborhood. He spoke of his masturbatory acts and
other games he had played behind bathroom doors. Finally, he confessed indulging in sexual exploratory play with his younger sister,
which he wanted to tell his mother about "because it's right for her to
know." After the psychologist had prepared the mother, unknown to
Billy, the boy confessed to her all these guilty acts he had been carrying so anxiously around with him for years. With his new knowledge
and confessional relief Billy was able to give up almost overnight his
profanity and silly wildness and more of his restless hyperactivity. He
seemed to develop stronger heterosexual interests, or at least began
talking for the first time about girl friends, doing so in almost adolescent fashion though he was only eight. For two months he dictated to
the psychologist a letter or poem each session to mail his girl friend or
his female teacher, grandmother, or mother. Billy seemed to be finding
previously unexpressed love for all these women, as though in part to
repair the damage from his attacks on them. Toward his sister at home
and a disturbed, hyperactive girl in class (not unlike the old Billy) he
became blatantly protective and brotherly, comforting the disturbed
girl with surprising patience. Billy's teacher did all she could to foster
such behavior, often calling attention to the positive changes in his behavior, thereby reinforcing them.

Billy's sexual fantasies were only one element in his hyperactivity,
defiance, rejection of learning, and unusual social behavior. Over
many months at the Clinic Billy revealed a profound and unconscious
identification with his unstable father, who had deserted the family
when Billy was in the sixth month of treatment. An unemployed ex-

boxer with a criminal record for thefts during weekend drinking sprees, Billy's father, while drunk, would verbally and physically assault his wife in the children's presence. With some frequency he would break down the door in the early morning hours, yelling and throwing things around the house. In addition to providing Billy with a model for wildness and abuse of his mother, the father also represented the rejection of both literacy and employment. It took more than a year for Billy to discase his terror of his father's alcoholic rages, his own counter-rage, and finally his admiration and love for his father who at times could be warm and interested in him.

The therapeutic work on the boy's feelings about his father had two critical bearings on his school adjustment, which were worked through frequently with Billy. First, Billy was helped to see that he was imitating his father's dangerous behavior, which also had begun in his early school years, eventuating in his total illiteracy and criminality. Concurrent with confronting Billy with the negative features of his identification with his father was a campaign to alert Billy to the positive features he shared with his father: his physical strength, mechanical aptitude, rich imagination, and capacity for humor and charm. The difficulties of Billy's selecting only the healthy parts of his father's traits for imitation were explored with him in relation to his school behavior. Moreover, Billy's anxiety about surpassing his father in reading was brought to the surface. Second, Billy's teacher and the psychologist cooperated in a joint effort to foster his developing what might be called the vocabulary for assuming emotional responsibility for his behavior. Every situation was exploited for its capacity to induce guilt, concern, and the urge to repair damage produced by the boy's self-centeredness. Earlier, Billy's teacher had noted what she termed a lack of "emotional differentiation," or the way in which it was difficult to spot more subtle emotions than fear in Billy, such as jealousy or envy, regret or embarrassment, friendliness or affection. Even anger was most indirectly expressed by him. To aid in this development of emotional differentiation for Billy, he was taught how to apply the vocabulary for assuming emotional responsibility and how to label what he was feeling. By the middle of the second grade his teacher was able to exert effective pressure on him to say what and why he was feeling in situations of disobedience as well as of cooperativeness. In so doing she was joining with the psychologist in strengthening Billy's evolving tendencies to think about his feelings before acting them out impulsively and to use words rather than actions to express his feelings and needs. Late in treatment Billy spoke knowingly of his former nonverbal wildness in noting "When I used to act crazy no one could make me do anything." Much of Billy's new sanity lay in his wanting to help himself to enjoy the world of learning and friends.

By the time Billy entered the third grade with a new teacher he was capable of sustained periods of concentration on his work in class and had almost fully caught up with his classmates. His personal problems were real problems of growth, involving issues of shyness and fitting in with other children. His peculiar, antisocial behavior had all but disappeared in school, though he would still occasionally express upset through defiance of his mother, who was sincerely striving to achieve the right balance of understanding and firmness toward her son.

A youngster who brought to school overwhelming sexual and hostile impulses, Billy had been compelled to act out his fantasies with little experience in thinking and talking about them, and thus with minimal skill in tempering them. He turned away from learning and from people as he did from his disturbing confusions and anxieties. In developing the courage to be curious and open about himself and the world he became calmer, more reflective, more communicative, and more able to enjoy learning. Specific knowledge of his classroom behavior and a close working relationship with his teachers enabled the psychologist to help the boy to a useful understanding of himself and to more rewarding ways in which he could become more fully himself.

ERIC

Eric was referred to us, we might say, by the entire faculty of the inner-city school he had been too fearful to attend for 16 months. After the consulting psychologist's opening address to the faculty explaining the Clinic's services, he was told that if he really wished to be of service he would help Eric return to school. The vigorous assent by the rest of the faculty expressed their concern and frustration at this bright second-grader's chronic school phobia. In responding with a pledge to assist in this sincere call for help, the psychologist was not unmindful of the limiting, traditional definition of a consultant's role implied by such a referral. We accepted the referral for the sake of the boy and to establish a foothold in gaining the confidence of the school, although we knew that our future approach to referrals would entail first observing and working with classroom dynamics and the teacher-pupil relationship before we would see a child individually at the Clinic.[1] We considered the faculty referral in part resistive to our out-

---

[1] Here too, as we have indicated elsewhere, a decision was made that ran counter to our preferred mode of functioning, that is, we accepted a referral for

look since its implication was that the boy's school phobia was purely an "intrapsychic" problem, reflecting little or nothing about the school culture. As matters turned out, this implication was quite false.

Before calling on Eric's parents we held individual conferences with school personnel who had known him, and examined his records thoroughly. His reading-readiness teacher knew him as a shy boy with a severe speech impediment, any derision of which by other children she strictly forbade. For six months, she recalled, he repeated over and over again that he could walk to school on his own. His first-grade teacher emphasized his superior intellectual ability, acceptance by the other children, and tendency to show off the new toy he inevitably brought to school each day. In the first grade, then, Eric's academic adjustment was superior and social adjustment average, despite his speech difficulty. It was in the middle of the first grade that a slightly older boy punched Eric in the stomach, throwing him into an acute panic. No physical damage could be ascertained by the family doctor though Eric complained of pain in his stomach. After the punch he refused to walk to school and when forced by his parents to go, he would scream endlessly in school until his parents were phoned to take him home. For three weeks the school nurse, principal, assistant principal, and several teachers could not induce him to relax his screaming and participate in class. One particular teacher who had in the past successfully coaxed fearful children to calm down took it on her own to try a firm policy with the boy, at one point placing her hand over his mouth until he stopped screaming, at another point leaving him alone in an office until he stopped screaming. This teacher's placing her hand over his mouth and her leaving him in an office, in a "closet" as Eric perceived it, together with the older boy's punching him in the stomach, formed the principal conscious contents of Eric's school phobia. He also claimed that the deafening sound of the rattling fire bell made him nervous in school.

The school social worker had visited Eric's home and spoken with his parents. The father was described as living on a VA pension for psychiatric casualties sustained in combat. Presently an outpatient, he was diagnosed as a "chronic hypochrondriacal psychoneurotic" with hysterical throat closures and loss of breath under stress. On one occa-

---

individual treatment at the Clinic much earlier than we ordinarily do in the course of establishing a relationship with a school. The major reason for this decision was the strength with which so many of the faculty expressed their regret that Eric was not in school. It would perhaps be more correct to say that we sensed a degree of guilt feeling among the faculty that intrigued us to the point that we said we would look into the matter.

sion the social worker had found him too choked-up to talk about his son's difficulties, and she regarded him of little use in controlling the boy. The mother was described as a simple-minded woman with a compulsive interest in shopping. Eric's older sister presented no problem in school or at home. The family harbored the dream of moving out of its railroad flat closer to relatives in another city, but the social worker considered their wishes unrealistic in view of their limited income. The only psychological evaluation Eric had had was by the juvenile court psychiatrist who found him hypersensitive and low in his tolerance for frustration. The court referral was ordered when the family had been unable to persuade Eric to visit the school psychiatrist. Subsequently, the social worker was unable to enforce the recommendation of the psychiatrist that the parents make Eric begin treatment for his school phobia at the local child-guidance clinic.

Eric received each day an hour of home-bound instruction, provided by the city. His home-bound teacher described him to the psychologist as extremely conscientious and bright in his schoolwork, but most coldly detached in his relationship to her. In the year that she had been teaching him at home he had never greeted her or said good-bye, never smiled, and would only speak about his schoolwork. Her rare gentle attempts at reminding him how nice it might be if he returned to school were met by a stiffening of his muscles and upset silence.

Eric's parents were both invited to discuss with the consulting psychologist their son's difficulties, but only his mother arrived at school with the explanation that her husband had to remain with Eric because their daughter was not available to watch him. She presented the usual distraught picture of a frustrated parent whose child refuses to attend school or accept psychological help. Cooperative in detailing Eric's psychological development, she related how he used to refuse to defecate on the pot, only to soil his pants as soon as he was allowed off the pot. It was only the beginning of kindergarten that had induced him to use the pot. Eric's mother had insight into the way her son effectively used tantrums against his nervous father to get him to buy a new toy for him each day, realizing that his mother would stand by a refusal. The toys almost always had a monster theme, as did Eric's taste in films, television shows, reading, and drawing. Eric's mother viewed his nightmares, which occurred about once a month, as reflecting his horror of having been forced to stop crying in school and of having been beaten at home for refusing to go to school. In reporting that her son shared her bed while her husband slept in the parlor she failed to report how fearful Eric was of sleeping alone, explaining instead that the parlor was too cold for him in the winter. She wanted any help the psychologist could offer in returning him to school and getting him over his toy tantrums and monster obsession. She did not define his sleeping preference as a problem.

The suggestion that Eric be brought to the Clinic twice weekly at once to begin treatment produced uncertainty in her, concerned as she was about how her husband and the boy would react. Trusting her perception that both father and son would have all sorts of resistance to the idea, the psychologist offered then and there to drive her back to her apartment and wait for Eric and his father to return. Such a plan would undercut the parents' opportunity for communicating their own ambivalence and timidity to the already quite uncooperative boy. The psychologist spoke with Eric's parents while the boy waited attentively in the next room. Hiding his own anxiety about the father's propensity for hysterical attacks, the psychologist presented himself as a university person interested in helping children with school difficulties, and not a school- or court-appointed doctor for psychiatrically disturbed children. In the course of reviewing Eric's fear of school the psychologist sympathized with the abortive attempts of the parents to return him to school, making explicit how erroneous some people are in thinking that the parents of school-phobic children really want their children at home. The psychologist also did not disagree with the father's conviction that mismanagement at school had not helped Eric get over his fears once they had developed. In short, the psychologist strove to win Eric's father over, recognizing that without his support the boy himself could not possibly be prevailed on to come to the Clinic. Humor, combined with the reassurance and ingratiation described, enabled Eric's father to introduce the psychologist to his son in the other room as "a nice man; don't be afraid to talk to him." Motioning to both parents that he wished to be alone with Eric, the psychologist sat across the room from the boy.

A healthy-looking, handsome eight-year-old, Eric sat motionless, his eyes reflecting the dire seriousness he attached to the meeting. With gentle sincerity the psychologist acknowledged how fearful Eric had a right to be of a stranger who might force him back to school. Such a fear, however, was described as unnecessary, for a promise was made on the spot (with the psychologist's right hand raised) that Eric would never be forced to do anything against his wishes. All that was asked was that he come with his parents twice weekly to the Clinic where he and the psychologist would try to understand why Eric was so afraid of school, in order to make him strong enough to want to go back without being forced. The layout of the Clinic was described in detail, including the food and toys available there. Finally, the psychologist sat next to Eric while asking him to show how well he had learned to read. Eric got his reader and masterfully demonstrated his skill. He also agreed to show the psychologist the many stars in his workbook. Eric's first appointment was for the following morning, to minimize the time he would have to brood. In standing up to shake hands to say good-bye to Eric, the psychologist was met only with a minute automatic jerk of the arm as though the boy were supressing his urge to shake the psychologist's hand. As he left the psychologist suggested that Eric's mother take him to the Clinic the first time and the father leave the house to avoid being upset by any resistance his son might offer. Both parents agreed that the suggestion was a good one.

Less than 24 hours after the psychologist's initial conference with Eric's mother, the boy was at the Clinic on time with her. After a phone call he asked to make to his father to announce his arrival, Eric was shown around the Clinic. In the therapy room he told the psychologist he had only cried a little before coming because he was afraid that he might be hurt at the Clinic. Eric's behavior at the Clinic followed a clockwork pattern for the first six weeks. He would sit as long as he was required to, every ten minutes asking to see the psychologist's wristwatch, reading the time aloud and estimating the number of minutes left in the session. He would then ask to draw, always making monsters, after which he would read for about ten minutes. Finally, he would use blocks to build a highway with cars and a stop sign on it and a bridge over it. He calmly drove the cars across the bridge in his play, obeying the stop sign. Any suggested deviation from the routine was not welcomed.

In his extremely controlled and orderly activities and his compulsive time-telling Eric seemed to be expressing his fear of revealing or discussing his agitated inner world with the psychologist. He was attempting to keep the psychologist at a safe distance, like his homebound teacher, from a fear, as he put it, of being hurt or punished for expressing any manifest disagreement or anger with the psychologist. In sharp contrast to Eric's polite, orderly, overt behavior were the cruelly mutilating monsters, and assaultive children and adults in the inner world revealed by his projective test results. The Rorschach and Michigan Picture Tests were administered in parts for the first 20 minutes of the first four sessions both to begin unraveling his active fantasy life and to help him to define the Clinic as a place where irrational and unpleasant feelings could be expressed. Eric's test record showed him to be fascinated with rather than frightened by the power and cruelty of his monsters whose actions revealed them as symbols for cruel children, teachers, and parents forcing him back to school. Overtly phobic, Eric covertly seemed to be counter-phobic in his fascination with these terrifying fantasies. His responses also indicated strong concerns about his body being damaged from other people's assaults, which seemed to be a commentary about his embarrassing speech handicap as well as the abuse he had sustained at school and home. We could discern in his responses a deep striving to retaliate against his hostile environment, a striving he felt himself too weak to execute. When he did assert himself on the test, the imagined fear was that of being lost. Some test material indicated his loneliness from not attending school and his genuine wish to make friends.

Eric looked forward to coming to the Clinic and enjoyed being there despite the insistence of the psychologist that the first 20 minutes of the hour be the time they both try to understand why he was so afraid of school. From the outset the understanding of the school phobia and the return to school were the focal points of discussion and the boy understood clearly that these were his goals in coming to the Clinic. For the first month during these discussions Eric would stereotypically rehearse his school fears, achieving little emotional release from the discussion and anxiously awaiting the passage of 20 minutes so that he could draw, read, and play. His monster drawings, like his test fantasies, reflected his fascination with power and destruction, his play an avoidance of self-assertion, symbolized in the unfailing obedience of his cars to the stop sign. He showed interest, however, in whether his old friends and teachers at school had ever asked about him and whether there might be other children at the Clinic he could meet.

Initially Eric showed little insight into why he had been so upset by being punched and could only reiterate how unfairly he had been abused in school. The point he made over and over again was that school was a dangerous place for him. He shared the same concern as had been articulated to the psychologist by his father over his teeth which had been knocked out by a friend when he was much younger. When it was suggested to the boy that there was part of him he did not want to talk about and that it contained a wish to be strong and go back to school, he became agitated, grasped the sides of his chair, and asked for reassurance that he would not be forced back. The psychologist then interpreted that Eric might be less afraid of being hurt than of becoming so angry that he would badly hurt those who hurt him. This produced a disclosure by Eric of his fear that if he hit a child hard, and that child would tell his parents, a policeman might take him away. With repeated work on Eric's fear of his own destructive power, his drawings began to involve aggression among people, and one drawing depicted Eric swallowing the teacher who had put her hand over his mouth. The dreams he reported continued to involve monsters but they were threatening his own family now. The cars began to crash into each other and the police appeared as restraining influences in his play. At one point Eric was encouraged to practice punching the psychologist's hand as hard as he could and consciously to pretend that he was getting back at the boy who had punched him in the stomach. Eric and the psychologist role-played the difference between doubling up and screaming when punched, and bearing the pain and striking back. These activities were quite pleasurable to the boy and he derived obvious relief from engaging in them, becoming less constricted. As he showed real evidence of accepting the idea that retaliating in self-defense was fair, Eric was asked if he felt strong enough to go back to school. Adamantly, he said he did not and became upset at the prospect, demanding reassurance that he would not be forced.

After several sessions were spent chiefly on Eric's fear and hostility in relation to his peers, the psychologist drew attention to the fear and anger toward his family that Eric had never talked about. The boy responded at once with great pleasure in issuing forth with all the injustices to which he was subjected at home by his parents. The way they chased him with a broom under the bed and occasionally even bit him were rehearsed with the same regularity familiar in other spheres of his behavior. His father was singled out as being the most impatient with him, and he described an incident of several years past when his father pounded a spoon on a table which accidentally landed on the boy's head, resulting in several stitches in a hospital emergency room. Eric showed the psychologist several bruises he had sustained from his parents, and described the way they had once pulled his hair while dragging him to school. Eric's reaction to his parents' punitiveness was an angry one that he was able to talk about. He complained, however, that he was too small to hit them back and noted how his sister had protected him on occasion. He also described how his father would tease him cruelly by pretending he was going to keel over while holding his throat. Incidents in which his parents would try to trick him back to school by walking by a new route were described.

To clarify what was happening at home, the boy's sister was interviewed by the psychologist, with permission from Eric and his parents. A shy, over-controlled 12-year-old girl, she nonetheless had made a successful school adjustment. Cooperative and interested in her brother, she painted a very different picture from her brother's of the home.

She felt that her parents, especially her father, were insufficiently strict with him and too rarely stood by their refusal to buy him a new toy each day. She informed the psychologist that Eric slept with his mother because he was too afraid to sleep alone and too stubborn to try it. She felt Eric was not really afraid of his parents and doubted the psychologist's or anyone else's ability to get him over his stubbornness.

The psychologist's interview with Eric's sister confirmed his belief that the boy's phobic and somatic preoccupations were masking his own strongly hostile and controlling impulses that he too freely blamed others for directing at him. Besides identifying with his hypochrondriacal, immature father's rejection of work, he was succeeding in dominating the family by throwing up his screen of neurotic symptoms. Insofar as the father's feigned hysterical attacks and biting of the boy occurred with any frequency at all, they seemed to be reactive to the boy's stubborn greed and domineering provocativeness. In any case, it was the mother rather than the father toward whom Eric probably felt more anger than he was letting on, because she frustrated his greedy wishes far more effectively than his father.

The psychologist began to interpret Eric's provoking his parents' anger by his stubborn disobedience. Over a number of sessions, a list was made on the blackboard of Eric's fears in one column and his acts of provocative disobedience in the other column, focusing on his unreasonable demand for monster toys, his refusal to get to bed on time, his refusal to sleep alone, and his refusal to go to school. It was suggested that his fears and complaints about being abused by people reflected both his own controlling demandingness and anger at being required to toe the mark. The self-defeating price he paid for his limited success in getting his own way was spelled out, in speech and in diagrams on the blackboard. Eric listened with his usual attentiveness, and he understood and recalled the psychologist's interpretations. With Eric the psychologist evolved a program for helping the boy to accept legitimate rules. First, in a conference with Eric's parents the psychologist obtained their promise to exert no more direct or subtle pressure on returning him to school. Second, Eric's father would help his mother in enforcing the bedtime hour. Third, a bank account would be opened for Eric in which $2.00 weekly would be deposited; an additional $2.00 weekly would be given him for buying toys, and no amount of screaming would augment that allotment. If his father could not tolerate the boy's screaming, he would leave it to the mother to enforce the toy allowance. The family proved capable of maintaining the new rules, and Eric rapidly complied, with great pride in his own bank account and skill in budgeting his $2.00 toy allowance. At each session Eric and the psychologist used addition and subtraction to work out his bank balance and remaining weekly allowance for toys. The opportunity to calculate his financial assets and practice budgeting skill fascinated him, and he no longer screamed for toys, greatly reducing tension in the family. He also abided by the bedtime hour with only occasional exceptions, as his parents cooperated more fully in enforcing it.

With Eric's success in controlling his bedtime and toy-buying disobedience, the psychologist continued working on his school phobia. Eric was given the opportunity of walking to the local candy store with the psychologist for a drink. He fearfully refused to leave whichever parent was in the waiting room. He also cried bitterly one day when he discovered that his mother had left the Clinic to go to a store for a few minutes. When Eric's distress at being separated from his parents was related by the psychologist to his school and sleeping-alone phobias, he responded to the confrontation with his customary willingness to speak openly once given permission, as it were, by the psychologist. He claimed he had cried when his mother left the Clinic waiting room to go shopping because he thought she would forget about him or visit a relative in another city or even be hurt. He often worried about his parents' dying, abandoning or losing him, he explained. Eric's considerable separation anxiety was handled in two ways. First, his deep lack of trust in parents who had never really let him down was emphasized, and he was encouraged, whenever he felt panicky about being abandoned, to try to recall all the times in the past when his parents came back after leaving him briefly. As discussion about Eric's fears of being abused by people had resolved into discussion about his own controlling demandingness, so discussion about his separation worries resolved into discussion about his undeveloped ability to trust people. Second, in considering Eric's difficulties in trusting people, the psychologist drew attention to the boy's great rage with his parents for ever leaving him alone and the way in which his rage weakened his trust, in fact leading him to expect punishment for being angry. Thus Eric's own unreasonable demands were again seen as responsible for his distress. In considering Eric's rage at being separated from his parents, and the mistrust-punishment cycle occasioned by it, the psychologist recalled out loud how when he himself was a child he would sometimes feel so angry with his parents that he wished they would die and then would feel upset by his wishes. While playing with the cars, Eric remarked that he too had felt just that way and asked whether the psychologist's parents had died. The psychologist explained they had not and sketched in for Eric the distinction between thinking or feeling something and its actually happening or one's actually doing it. This seemed to bring the boy some relief. He talked about how he always crossed himself whenever he heard an ambulance siren in the street or when a fire truck raced by.

After two months of Eric's developing ego strength and insight into his greed, stubbornness, hostility, and mistrust, the psychologist felt that the time was ripe for systematically increasing pressure on the boy to relinquish his school and sleeping-alone phobias. On one occasion when the therapy room had run out of drawing paper, Eric was asked to get some from the secretary one flight below. He then said he had changed his mind and did not want any drawing paper. When it became clear that the psychologist expected him to carry out the request, Eric's eyes became watery. The calm but resolute firmness of the psychologist was communicated to Eric and he was able to force himself to separate himself from the psychologist and get the drawing paper. This incident was the first of several bringing to bear on him mounting pressure to tolerate separation experiences and then discuss them. Next came the psychologist's renewed insistence that Eric go for a drink with him to the local candy store. A similar clash of wills occurred, with Eric giving in. Finally, the psychologist announced that he thought Eric strong enough now to return to school, which had only two weeks left before the summer vacation. Anticipating Eric's refusal, the psychologist had ready a summer-school application which was presented to Eric as the alternative to his returning to school at once. Of course the boy chose summer school, which was seven weeks off, and he filled in and mailed the application.

During these showdowns with Eric the psychologist helped the boy to explore his feelings about clashing wills with the psychologist. The different ways in which his parents and the psychologist brought pressure on him were explored, and his different reactions to them as well. Yet Eric was given every opportunity to express his contempt for the psychologist, who had not only been patient with him but most insistent. When Eric finally admitted that he was angry with the psychologist, he began to draw angry pictures in which the psychologist, his father, and various school authorities were depicted as persecutors. Yet no retaliatory anger of Eric's appeared in the drawings. The psychologist pointed this out, and encouraged Eric to play more wildly and noisily with his blocks. Initially with great reluctance but then with pleasure, Eric began building block structures taller than himself, which represented buildings that were crashed to the ground by hurricanes, demolishing cars and people beneath, such as the psychologist. Soon his drawings began to show his own retaliatory aggression toward his father, though in symbolic terms. He also expressed his anger toward his father by betraying the family secret that his father bet on horses despite his living on a pension.

For the seven weeks before summer school began, Eric counted down the weeks remaining, each session writing the number of remaining weeks on the blackboard. With five weeks remaining he threatened to run away from home or throw things around his house if he was forced to go to school. Yet during this period his parents reported he was becoming less afraid of other children and no longer showed any fear of riding on trains. In response to his threats the psychologist expressed his understanding of Eric's anger but insisted that he return. No physical force would be used against Eric it was explained; it was simply expected that he would realize that he was strong enough to return. Moreover, the psychologist would be in the school throughout his first day and could be seen in minutes if Eric so desired. The importance of Eric's defending himself if attacked and his need to trust his parents' promise not to abandon him were worked through many times. Finally, the school's eagerness for his return was underlined by his being told that the fire bell had been softened especially for him, a change that the principal had accomplished after no small expenditure of effort.

In the remaining weeks before the beginning of summer school the psychologist concentrated on Eric's sleeping-alone phobia, on the hypothesis that if this could be relieved he would be further encouraged to return to school with greater confidence in his growing manhood and bravery. His fantasies about burglars breaking into his house while he was asleep were ventilated, as was his fear that a "bum might come in and punch me in the stomach while I'm sleeping." As with the earlier material on his peers and parents, his lack of trust in his parents' ability to protect him was explored, and the details of sleeping arrangements in his home were diagrammed on the blackboard and discussed. Eric conceded that if he slept in the room between his parents' and sister's rooms he would be securely surrounded and yet be able to feel braver. It was unnecessary to delve into his selfish disruption of his parents' intimacy, for one day, after several broken promises, Eric reported that he had been able to sleep in his own bed.

Eric remained anxiously resigned to his return to summer school in the month before its beginning. During this period the psychologist walked and then drove Eric to various stores to look around. He showed little anxiety about leaving his parents at the Clinic or their leaving him, and was obviously proud of his new-found confidence and strength. He said he wished to terminate his Clinic visits as soon as he began winter school, though he was unsure about whether he would return to winter school since his parents had been talking about moving. In a meeting with Eric's parents it was established that this was just talk on their part, and it was pointed out to them that unless they found a new apartment they should refrain from such speculations in front of their son because this made it harder for him to face up to having to return to winter school.

After 20 months of refusing to return to school, Eric began summer school uneventfully. His teacher had been thoroughly prepared for his arrival and made him feel comfortable, as did the new principal. In a few days Eric indicated he had decided to return to winter school, was already buying school supplies, and had suddenly lost interest in monsters because they were "too scary." No longer afraid of his friends and school, Eric became disenchanted with the scary monsters. When asked what he liked to read about instead of monsters, he said the World's Fair, as though to tell the psychologist that the real world was both less frightening and more intriguing to him. When asked how he managed not to be so fearful in bed at night he said, "I say to myself don't be afraid; everybody's here with you." On his entry into summer school, Eric agreed to visiting the Clinic once a week until winter school, when termination would occur. He asked if he might sometime ride his bike up to the Clinic and say hello. The psychologist happily said that he looked forward to that day.

After a week in summer school Eric told the psychologist that he had punched the boy who had originally hurt him in order to get back at him, and then they made friends. Unable to hide his delight, the psychologist agreed with Eric that from now on Eric should try to settle his disputes peacefully and strike someone only in self-defense. Though summer school was a total success for Eric, he greeted the return of winter school with some trepidation. In the first two weeks of school he developed a sore throat and then what looked suspiciously like a psychogenic fever. Sympathetic handling of him by the psychologist in school calmed him and he was not made to feel as though he had intentionally developed his physical symptoms, which were checked out by the family physician. A procedure was set up whereby Eric could go to the school nurse or guidance counselor whenever he felt ill or upset. Soon he began to express worry about the work being too hard, even though his warmly accepting teacher genuinely regarded him as the brightest boy in the class. The teacher followed the psychologist's suggestion that she continually remind Eric and the whole class about the importance of doing their best and not worrying after that. His sense of being stupid for not always completing his work abated.

Finally, he expressed his anxiety about being back in school by stubbornly refusing to wear gym shoes during gym period. He pretended to forget to bring his shoes in order to avoid wearing them, he explained to the psychologist, because he did not believe the gym teacher's promise that he would be permitted not to participate in gym even after he wore his gym shoes. The psychologist was able to interpret this noncooperation as another form of Eric's distrusting adults, and after the psychologist established a working relationship with Eric's gym teacher Eric was made by the psychologist to change into his gym shoes. When Eric resisted, he was gently but firmly guided by the psychologist, and a public scene was avoided. The occasional tendency at the outset of the school year for Eric to feign illness occurred only when his father brought him to school, and arrangements were made for the mother to bring him each morning, while the father walked him home. After several weeks of reinforcing in school many of the lessons from the Clinic, Eric willingly participated in every aspect of school activity and had a successful year in the third grade.

ROBERT

The case of Robert's angry rejection of the classroom exemplifies a special use of visits to the Clinic that we have found effective especially with younger children: a brief, intensive series of fewer than ten visits focusing on a particular school crisis, involving the most active collaboration of teacher and psychologist in managing the child's classroom behavior. In such cases exploring with the child his motivating fantasies and feelings is not systematically pursued; instead, particular adaptive actions are explained and encouraged, both at school and at the Clinic, with emphasis on the coordination and timing of the socialization pressures brought to bear on the child in both settings. Parental cooperation in specific areas is sometimes solicited. This approach has been most helpful with disturbed younger children who respond well to their teachers in mastering their difficulties yet require brief, additional direction from an outsider to hasten or deepen their classroom improvement.

Robert, a six-year-old Negro first-grader, was referred to the psychologist by the principal because his trance-like silences and rejection of work and people in the classroom were broken only by tantrums, crying, or attacks on the other children. Since his arrival from another school two months after the beginning of the school year, Robert's only constructive activity was to play with the same puzzle for hours, his tremulous hands, quivering lips, and tilted head reflecting his fearful loneliness. At the slightest provocation from the other children, to whom he did not speak, he would throw objects around the room, chase them with a window pole, scream, and climb under or tip over his desk, sobbing bitterly. After two weeks of his silent misery and hostility he was transferred to a reading-readiness room where the psychologist talked with him, as he played with his puzzle at his seat, for about 15 minutes several times a week. From these discussions the psychologist could only learn that part of Robert's angry depression was the suspicion that other children often laughed at him. The depth of the boy's tense, unresponsive depression concerned the psychologist, who after three weeks of observing and chatting with him paid a visit to his home.

The contrast between Robert at home and at school was unforgettable. Sullen and tremulous at school, Robert was happily outgoing and active at play with his younger and older sisters at home. His mother was genuinely surprised to learn of her son's difficulties, as his home and previous school behavior were cheerful and cooperative. Occasionally stubborn at home, he responded well to whippings and did not seem to resent his family. Of late, his mother observed, the boy would "stare off into space without speaking" a couple of times a week for no apparent reason, during which time he would neither play nor watch television. The family had learned to leave him alone in his bad moods, which his mother could only explain as sometimes occurring just before the onset of a cold. When the psychologist asked Robert to speak with him alone in another room, he happily came along and answered questions about his family and neighborhood. When, however, the subject of trying to help Robert with his school unhappiness was raised he became deflated, as it were, in seconds, retreating to his deeply sullen, silent mood, head down, body quivering. Sensing the boy's acute distress, the psychologist lifted him on his lap and for half an hour soothed him, saying how he understood the boy's upset, entreating him to relax and speak only when he felt he could. After listening to half an hour of soothing but school-relevant talk, Robert shed a tear, soon after beginning to sob bitterly. After playing a money-counting game, the psychologist concluded the home visit by proposing that Robert come to the Clinic once a week, explaining the purposes and procedures of the visits. Without replying directly, Robert seemed to be saying yes by asking for a present of a nickel from the psychologist, which he was given.

For a week before the home visit and for the week after it, before

Robert's first trip to the Clinic, his reading-readiness teacher and the consulting psychologist discussed tactics. The teacher was advised to note carefully the incidents intensifying his moodiness and tantrums, for no such information was available. She was frequently to make explicit her fondness for the boy, her delight that he was switched into her room, and her sympathy that he was feeling badly. When he was particularly moody or furious, she was to soothe him and empathize with his distress, while calmly trying to distract him from his hostile outbursts against the children or furniture. The teacher planned to offer him special opportunities for helping her and to lavish praise on him for any positive actions or restraint on his hostility. The first classroom goal was to encourage Robert to stop his tantrums and angry assaults on children.

The decision to take Robert to the Clinic grew out of the success in realizing this initial classroom goal, for he dramatically reduced his wildness within a week of the teacher's redoubled efforts. He was responding well to his teacher's interest and suggestions. Yet it became clear to the teacher that Robert flew into his wild states for any of the following frustrations: forgetting his milk money, and not receiving milk, not being called on for a desirable task, not receiving the teacher's attention when he demanded it, making a mistake in the most simple activity, or even not being able to find a crayon. Less depressed and angrily suspicious, he became more demanding and unsatisfiable. His reaching out to the teacher and willingness to join in some classroom activities had created truly unreasonable demands on the teacher's time, and she was becoming seriously upset about her inability to satisfy him while working with the rest of the class. As much for her mental health as for the boy's it was decided to see Robert at the Clinic to help meet some of his dependency needs and to clarify with him his difficulties in the classroom. The teacher was advised to do as much as she could for him, avoid angering him, and give more time to the rest of her class. Her sense of futility and of losing control, expressed in dreams she related to the psychologist, diminished as she grew able to talk about her frustrations and justify to herself, with the psychologist's support, spending less time with Robert.

In his talks with Robert at school the psychologist had joined the teacher in emphasizing the importance of Robert's controlling his angry wildness. Alternative responses to his wildness were suggested and backed up by the teacher. He was encouraged to go up to the teacher and tell her if he needed something or was feeling badly. He was also encouraged to correct his mistakes, erase them, or start anew, rather than fly into a rage. Robert understood that his visits to the

Clinic were to help him accelerate his developing self-control and interest in the classroom.

The first 20 minutes of the first three sessions at the Clinic were spent in giving Robert the Rorschach and Michigan Picture Tests. Results from the tests indicated that behind Robert's nonverbal, gloomy appearance was a youngster of above-average intelligence and imaginativeness, lacking any signs of serious psychopathology. His record, however, contained innumerable indicators of fairly strong anxiety, especially centering around the possession and destruction of food about which Robert showed an unusual amount of greedy interest. In fantasy his father seemed a neglectful, unsympathetic strong-arm man. There were hints that Robert was somewhat concerned about competing for his parents', especially his father's, attention with his older and younger sisters.

The remaining 40 minutes of the first few sessions were spent in free play during which Robert was encouraged to describe and interpret the behavior and feelings of the figures he maneuvered, with an eye toward stimulating his free verbalizing and interaction with the psychologist. During these first sessions, it was only in the therapist's car that any school-relevant comments were introduced by the psychologist, always focusing on the importance of Robert's curtailing his angry acting out and using words to communicate his needs and difficulties to his teacher. Robert's play during this period consisted of an unbroken cycle of sustained attack and counter-attack by the toy animals, soldiers, and cartoon figures. They bit, kicked, and rammed each other because they did not like each other or because one had taken some possession of another's. No forgiveness or reason or friendliness could be found in the gruesome scenes that Robert mechanically and joylessly enacted. His tremulousness was apparent throughout the play, though he did play with ferocious activity and was willing to talk about the toy figures.

The first major clue to Robert's difficulty was when the teacher noted how Robert became upset before lunch hour and three o'clock, times for going home. Monday morning also seemed especially unpleasant for him. Working with him on this at the Clinic revealed that he was terrified of whippings he received at home and feared that he would die from them. With the serious repetition of his fear of dying, his teacher sent home a note requesting that Robert no longer be beaten but just deprived of privileges. At the Clinic Robert's fear of dying was interpreted to him as his guilt over his misbehavior in school, and it was pointed out that as Robert exercised greater self-control he would be less guilty and less afraid of dying from a beating. An interview with his mother confirmed that the beatings were infrequent and that she had followed the teacher's advice, confirming the psychologist's hunch that Robert's fear were exaggerated. By focusing on the school-relevant components of Robert's irrational fear rather than the more intrapsychic components, it was hoped to bring them under the boy's control through good behavior in a situation over which the psychologist and teacher had considerable influence. In addition, action had been taken through the teacher's note and psychologist's conference with the mother to reduce the objective fear that he would be severely beaten at home.

Robert's difficulties in leaving and returning to school also seemed to reflect his anxiety over being separated from his teacher, on whom he had come to depend increasingly. His Monday-morning pouts in particular seemed to express his resentment about having had to leave her Friday afternoon. Confirmation for this interpretation became stronger when Robert began pleading to go home with his teacher for lunch and later to live with her. At first rejecting of his new school and upset at having had to move from three classrooms between the end of kindergarten and the beginning of his reading-readiness class, Robert clung now to his new teacher. This dependency was seen by teacher and psychologist as an inevitable outcome of the dependency-arousing management of the boy in the classroom. It was felt, however, that without forming such a close attachment, the incentive for Robert's relinquishing his rebelliousness would have been weak, and the change in his behavior too slow for him to be retained in school. His visits to the Clinic served the dual function of siphoning off some of his dependency needs from the teacher by providing him the extra security of a tie to the psychologist and of teaching him skills to enhance his independence. Two kinds of issues were worked through with the boy at the Clinic in this connection. First, he was encouraged to make friends in school, partly by helping other children in the classroom and partly by letting them help him when he needed something. This tended to reduce his clinging to the teacher, as she too encouraged his talking and playing with other children. Every sign of his interacting positively with other children, even when this interrupted his work, was fostered in school and praised at the Clinic. Second, to facilitate his making friends he was helped to see how sharing his toys was as important as not attacking other children. In short, the psychologist began to raise the question of Robert's egocentricity with him. His reaction to this first discussion of a criticism other than his acting wild was one of outrage. He threatened to leave the Clinic, and on one occasion started to do so, hid in the corner, and wept at the slightest hint that his selfishness or demandingness was to be discussed. Several sessions were spent on how intolerant he was of being criticized and how he would have to learn to think about and not just rage about his weaknesses. The distinction between selfish acts and his basic goodness was developed, as was the legitimacy of wanting to be selfish versus the acting out of his selfish wishes. Robert's regular practice of asking for money and later candy from the psychologist was taken up from the viewpoint of his greed. The psychologist explained that he used to give Robert candy when he saw him at school because he was upset and needed reassurance that he was liked. No longer, it was explained to him, was it necessary for the psychologist to prove his fondness by giving gifts. He said that friendship should be enough and Robert would have to curtail his demands. With initial resentment, Robert came to understand and then to accept the psychologist's decision to refrain from meeting his demands for candy at each contact in school. At the Clinic milk and cookies were available, but not at school, and Robert was helped to accept the distinction as a fact he could not alter with any amount of complaining.

The teacher's clever management of the other children's jealousy of the special attention lavished on Robert is interesting. She explained to them frankly that Robert needed her extra time in order to help him become more independent and that when any other children needed her extra time she would give it to them as well. The children truly seemed to understand the teacher's dilemma of wanting to share her time and having to give Robert more of it. Far from attacking the boy, they imitated their teacher in expressing concern and in helping him. On one occasion when Robert had begun screaming an immature Spanish-speaking boy started weeping bitterly in a corner of the classroom. Robert kept screaming until the teacher unvituperatively whispered to Robert that Jose was crying because he was frightened of Robert's screaming, whereupon he walked over to Jose and comforted him with his arm around his shoulders. That was the last time Robert screamed in class. An undesirable effect of the attention lavished on Robert was the tendency of one other boy to imitate Robert in the obvious hope of receiving the increased concern of the teacher and possibly of the consulting psychologist who visited the room twice a week. This same boy (Clifton) also imitated Robert's habit of tilting his head to one side long after Robert had ceased to do so. The teacher was encouraged to discuss with this boy his imitation of Robert and take remedial actions for him as well. Happily, by the time Clifton began manifesting his demandingness Robert had begun to involve himself much more with the other children, which freed the teacher for more time with Clifton.

With Robert's depressions, tantrums, and attacks diminished and his dependency softened, a new problem cropped up: Robert's clowning defiance of the teacher, aligning the children with him in his silliness. Once an alienated, brooding outcast, Robert became a witty, defiant leader by the Christmas vacation, some six weeks after he had been taken to the Clinic. Exasperated by Robert's ungrateful gift of defiance for all her extra effort, the teacher was once again despairing over the boy. At this time teacher and psychologist worked out a new plan for Robert and for another child who had shown increased rebelliousness as the year had worn on. When a child was not defiant because of a real wound or upset, he was warned once about his defiance and if it persisted excluded from the classroom for half an hour, being made to sit out the time in an adjoining room. The teacher of this room had agreed to the arrangement and to helping Robert's teacher bodily remove any child who resisted. The exclusion was to be used only after explanation, distraction, or other management techniques had failed, and was to be carried out not in anger, which would allow the child to feel he had upset the teacher, but with resolute calmness. The children were not to be threatened with exclusion; it was simply to be used, after one warning, when less drastic measures had failed. The exclusion policy was an immediate success for this new teacher of the inner-city child. It reduced rising tension in her by giving her an effective escape hatch for the unmanageable child, and it made the necessary point with the children, who loved and respected their teacher, but who at times became too excited with the permissive, active atmosphere of the classroom. Reading-readiness children, it must be remembered, are kindergarten children not prepared for first-grade reading, usually because of poorly developed-visual-motor co-ordination and insufficient socialization at home.

The exclusion policy was explained at great length to Robert in his final sessions at the Clinic as not being a punishment angrily meted out but as a way of helping him to notice and recall certain rules he had trouble in following. He was helped to see how he and not the teacher was responsible for whether or not he was excluded from the classroom. For the first month after the exclusion policy was introduced, Robert had to be removed five times, and only rarely after that. The hurt feelings of a child and his resentment about having to be excluded always served the basis for a useful chat between teacher and child after he was re-admitted to the room, considerably calmer and more receptive than when he had left.

After 10 sessions with Robert, he was seen once every two weeks for a month and finally terminated. It was made clear to him that his growth and success in school, rather than some subtle punishment, lay behind the termination. The invitation, moreover, was extended to him to return to the Clinic whenever he felt he had something to talk about with the psychologist whom he very quickly could contact in school or through his teacher. Robert was proud not to have to come to the Clinic any more and remained a friend to the psychologist when he visited the classroom weekly. By the end of reading-readiness Robert was in the top reading group and showed only minimal and occasional signs of his earlier sullenness and defiance.

TOM

While observing Jack, a zealously rebellious third grader referred by his teacher, the consulting psychologist noticed how frequently another boy, Tom, was the target of hostile attacks in this very poorly controlled classroom. An enormously obese, white nine-year-old, Tom could be regularly observed seething with hurt feelings and rage, only too ready to be drawn into verbal and physical battles with the group of Negro children who ran the "blackboard jungle" room. As an emergency measure to relieve some of the pressure on the teacher, who was quite incompetent at controlling the inner-city child, the psychologist saw Jack twice weekly at the Clinic. The excitable, occasionally provocative behavior of the scapegoat Tom was noted by the psychologist, who was eager to observe the boy's adjustment in the fourth grade. (The teacher came to realize in the course of her discussion with the psychologist that her professional skills could best be used in a more stable, middle-class school and she applied for a transfer at the end of the school year.)

Although no referral had been made for Tom, the psychologist became concerned about him when in the fourth grade his emotional excitability and touchy temper manifested themselves again despite the benevolent but strict classroom atmosphere. Observations and teacher conferences disclosed that the boy was absent from school half the time and falling rapidly below grade level in all spheres of his work. The teacher, a highly capable, experienced older woman was sympathetic to the boy but shockingly accepting of his plight. At length it became clear that the principal had directed the teacher to tolerate Tom's personality difficulties and academic slowness because his mother had informed the school of the boy's near-fatal case of measles encephalitis two years before. Tom was regarded by his teacher and principal as suffering from the after-effects of brain injury and they were afraid to place any upsetting demands on his scholastic or social behavior. The school had timidly followed Tom's mother's advice that her son not be pushed, although no one in the school, including the visiting nurse, had any such recommendation on the forms supplied by the family pediatrician who had attended Tom during his illness.

What the consulting psychologist had uncovered during his inquiries about Tom was an attitude, foisted on the school by the mother and willingly embraced without medical evidence by school personnel, which was maintaining and strengthening the boy's self-defeating behavior. In addition to his chronic absenteeism and academic laziness, Tom's provocative touchiness and even his obesity were being tolerated and subtly nurtured by the school's hands-off, low-pressure attitude.

From classroom observations and casual discussions with children in the fourth grade the psychologist learned how Tom's stubbornness and touchiness provoked other children, alienating him from them. From four chats with Tom outside the classroom the psychologist learned how upset and worried the boy perpetually was. Tom talked all too freely about concerns for his own and his parents' health, reeling off episode after episode of sicknesses and accidents, actual and potential. Besides his obsessional health concerns, Tom disclosed his worry about falling behind the other children academically. When asked about his obesity, he said he felt that he looked like "a fat pig," describing how he would stuff himself with food and take very little exercise. He also depicted the family atmosphere as one of constant bickering between himself and his mother on one side against his senile paternal grandmother, of his bossing around and swearing at anyone who did not give him his way, and of his often wanting to act like and be cared for like a baby. According to his 18-year-old brother, Tom's behavior could be described only as spitefully infantile. In short, Tom knew that he was acting childishly but could do little to help himself.

The psychologist had an extended telephone conversation with the family pediatrician before consulting Tom's parents. The pediatrician reported that he was aware of the boy's absenteeism and infantile demandingness but that his advice and firmness toward the parents had proved wholly ineffective. Exhaustive tests indicated that Tom had sustained no brain damage from his serious illness and that the family was falsely ascribing personality change to nonexistent residual brain damage. Thoroughly disgusted with the overprotective, overpermissive handling of Tom at home the pediatrician advised the psychologist not to waste his time with the well-intentioned but inept parents. He also explained that Tom stayed away from school so often because he persuaded his mother that he had headaches or throat pain in the morning.

With Tom's permission, his parents were seen at the Clinic for several interviews that were explained to the parents as required because of the rapidly deteriorating school performance of their child. The matter was frankly put to them as a crisis affecting not only his promotion to the fifth grade but his future academic and vocational achievement as well as his personality formation. It was pointed out to the parents that unless understanding of the boy's problems could be developed and appropriate action be taken immediately in school and at home he would be severely limited academically, vocationally, and emotionally for the rest of his life. Their interest in his health, it was stated, was misplaced and sidetracking them from the real issues in his life. This alarming confrontation of the parents was decided on for several reasons. First, it was true that Tom was developing personality patterns highly likely to defeat his growth. Second, only five months were left in the school year before the promotion decision, and the parents were told this. Finally, it was felt that the only hope of mobilizing and changing family attitudes within the limited professional time available for spending with the parents was through a crash, anxiety-arousing approach coupled with highly specific suggestions and guidelines for the parents to follow. They were told that the pediatrician had been consulted and that unless the psychologist was given more cooperation than he had been given, their son's academic, vocational, and emotional development was in serious doubt.

The decision to involve Tom's parents more actively than most parents are involved in treatment was based on the psychologist's assessment that Tom's symptoms were being reinforced at home where, by the boy's own admission, he had been ruling the roost. The decision to follow a get-tough, alarming approach with the parents was based on their history of poor cooperation with the pediatrician and the real consideration of limited time before the promotion decision.[2]

[2] It would be unfortunate if the reader concluded that this type of direct, blunt confrontation was (or ever is) taken lightly by us, that we were unaware of the responsibility we were assuming for whatever consequences might ensue. Whenever we have resorted to this approach, it has reflected two overriding considerations. First, *time was not on our side* and if some kind of change was not quickly introduced there was every reason to believe that the situation would become less amenable to change. In Tom's case we were aware that not only was a promotion decision only a few months away but that if he were promoted he would go to another inner-city school, the characteristics of which were more unsavory than his present school. The consequences of retaining him an additional year in the fourth grade would in our opinion have reinforced present problems

The parents' account of the family also indicated a directive approach with them. They had refused to accept the pediatrician's word that the boy had no residual brain damage or personality change from such brain damage, and usually withdrew from depriving or limiting him in any way from fear of upsetting him. However it was pointed out that in their overprotection they were stimulating unmeetable, and therefore frustrating, infantile needs that interfered with his school performance. Tom's father admitted spending little time with the boy, with whom he was fed up because he would switch off his father's television programs to turn to his own preferred channel, as well as because mother and son shared the same bed while the father slept alone in the parlor. Both mother and father talked at length about their own health problems as well as their son's during the interviews and spoke with contempt for nonwhites and their lower-class neighborhood, thus showing how they reinforced the boy's health and interpersonal difficulties. Tom's mother obviously infantilized her son and presented herself as afraid of his temper tantrums. Finally, the need for a directive approach with specific advice for the parents to help them out of their tangled problems was indicated by the way in which the obese mother identified with and used her son to punish her mother-in-law whose presence at home she resented. She would sympathize with the boy's intolerance of the meddling, forgetful old woman, and this added to the unstable atmosphere in the family.

A specific program of advice was outlined for the parents to follow. First, whenever the boy complained of illness in the morning, his temperature was to be taken and the pediatrician phoned; the pediatrician, who concurred with the plan, was henceforth to make the medical decisions about whether Tom could remain at home away from school. If Tom refused to abide by the pediatrician's decision that he go to school, he was to be forced to, with a strap if necessary. Absenteeism without the pediatrician's consent would have to stop at

---

and created some additional serious ones. A second consideration in this approach to parents is "the diagnosis" that we are dealing with parents whose response to the confrontation will be movement towards and not away from the desired change. In short, approaching parents in this way is never done cavalierly. In the numerous instances we have had to use this approach there has never been anything resembling an unfortunate consequence. We have used this approach *only* with inner-city parents, primarily because the attitude of school personnel toward middle-class parents tends to be so cautious and even fearful that they have not viewed our suggestion, in those instances where we thought it appropriate, with favor even though they themselves viewed the instances in the same way as we did. In general, and for very different reasons, school personnel in the inner-city and suburban schools prefer not to confront parents.

once. Second, Tom was to sleep in his own bed after being gently told that henceforth his parents desired the privacy of their own room. He was not to be made to feel as though he were being kicked out or as though the decision had been the psychologist's rather than the parents'. Third, any rudeness or disobedience at home was to be promptly stopped, first by reasoning with him and, if that failed, by strapping him, with both parents supporting each other in front of the boy. Fourth, the parents were to confine all their talk about health concerns to the privacy of their own bedroom, as this was disturbing the boy, and to play down any of his interest in bodily health. Fifth, the parents were to cease undermining the boy's ability to accept the neighborhood or nonwhites and emphasize the importance of getting along with all people and getting outside the house after school to play more with other children. Compliance with any of these new patterns was to be praised lavishly and rewarded tangibly. Tom's father was encouraged to take an active hand in all these programs, disciplining the boy more as well as playing with him more.

Each of these points was carefully explained and rehearsed with the parents for several interviews, and adoption of them demanded by the psychologist. The parents, moreover, were given some insight into the importance of Tom's involving himself more in boyish activities as he disentangled himself from his mother's overindulgence. The parents were not spared the implication that if he remained so close to his mother and estranged from boyish involvements his sexual identity might be impaired. During these blunt interviews the parents were handled gently and warmly, and they perceived the psychologist as a friend to whom they could turn whenever they wished. But they also perceived the psychologist as insistent on immediate and complete cooperation. As things turned out, the parents proved generally capable of the tasks laid down for them.

After the fourth parental interview Tom was seen at the Clinic once a week for eight sessions. He understood that the over-all purpose of the Clinic discussions was to help him enjoy and achieve more in school, academically and socially. He also understood from the outset that he and the psychologist would be talking about his behavior at home since it was contributing to his school difficulties. While Tom was being seen at the Clinic the psychologist held brief conferences with his teacher who was apprised of the program worked out with the parents and the pediatrician's recommendation that far more pressure be exerted upon the boy at school as well as at home. The teacher was encouraged to give Tom a half-hour of individualized homework nightly, which she was to insist on having handed in the following morning. The first time the boy failed to hand in his homework his parents were to be called to school for a conference. In addition, Tom was to be placed in a remedial-reading group with the reading specialist three half-hours a week during school. With the reading specialist and teacher a plan was worked out whereby Tom would be drilled by a bright fourth grader of his own choice for the first 15 minutes of each morning on work assigned by the reading specialist. The teacher, in general, was to increase her academic demands on him, taking great care to give him work suitable to his ability level and as much aid and praise as she could manage. She was, moreover, to make plain to the boy the intent behind the renewed efforts with him: to catch up to grade level and facilitate his enjoying learning. No longer was he to be regarded as too disturbed or ill for academic work. With respect to his excitable touchiness and provocativeness with other children, the teacher was to begin to discipline him as sternly as she would any other child, and point out to him privately after each of the two or three flare-ups a week the inflammatory role his own stubbornness and spite played in the incident. Here again specific advice and reasoning was to be administered, along with as much praise as possible; but when necessary Tom's provocativeness was to be stopped by fiat. The teacher was encouraged, moreover, to keep alert for any prejudice emanating from him and to deal with it privately or in formal lessons.

For the first three sessions Tom's liking for the psychologist carried him along and he seemed to be accepting the new absenteeism policy, sleeping alone, strict management at home, and intensified school demands for increased work output and social self-control. He even followed the psychologist's advice that he overcome his squeamishness about swimming with his class, and in discussing his social anxieties about displaying his obese body agreed to weigh in once a week with the school nurse who would be meeting with his mother to plan a diet. Tom also reported with obvious delight a calmer, more interested treatment of him at home despite the strictness, and more involvement with his father and brother. In school he volunteered for board work for the first time.

Tom missed his fourth session at the Clinic and came late to school several days in a row. He also failed to bring his homework to school. In a phone conversation with his father the psychologist learned that Tom had begun to dig in his heels and oppose his parents' new-found strictness. An emergency appointment was arranged at once for his parents to whom the notion of resistance and the importance of their holding the line was thoroughly explained. Tom was to be forced to come to school and Clinic, if need be, and be shown that his testing of his parents' determination had not weakened them. The parents were to express their understanding of his anger and stubbornness and say that they knew he could not change overnight, but they were to insist that he comply with the program worked out among pediatrician, parents, school, and Clinic. If they had to apply the strap in order to control him, they were to do so without screaming or threatening him and with as calm resolve as they could muster. If they were too upset to compose themselves, they were to wait before they strapped him. Moreover, they were to make sure that Tom arrived on time for future school and Clinic days.

Although Tom had been friendly and apologetic toward the psychologist in class after he had refused to come to the fourth session, he repeated his refusal and had to be dragged to the Clinic the following week by his mother, this time successfully. In the therapy room he refused to speak for 15 minutes, bitterly avoiding the psychologist's gaze. Tom finally began to talk when it was suggested that he felt hurt and neglected by having to attend school when he felt ill in the morning. He proceeded to insult his pediatrician and imply general disgust with all adults involved in managing his life, including the psychologist. This material allowed the psychologist to reiterate and deepen certain information about the boy's health. It was explained to Tom that while he had been nearly fatally ill, as he himself knew only too well, he had incurred no brain damage that forced him to act differently from other children. What he needed to do was to trust his pediatrician's medical skill more, as he had saved his life. Yet the psychologist sympathized with Tom's perception of his being made to go to school: it appeared cruelly indifferent to his feelings. In this connection two points were made. First, the way we feel is not always the best indicator of how ill we are. Second, it was not the pediatrician or anyone else who would decide whether Tom should attend school, but his objective temperature: when that went up to 100 degrees he should stay home; otherwise he must obey the law and attend school. Thus the decision-making policy about staying home from school was depersonalized to facilitate its acceptance as a fact rather than an insult. The pediatrician was to be consulted only when symptoms other than fever were present, and surely he, rather than Tom, was the best judge of their significance. This simple explanation, together with the psychologist's empathy for Tom's injured feelings, greatly calmed him. Never again did the boy refuse to follow the attendance policy set up with the pediatrician.

The work at the Clinic with Tom did not take the form of exploring his fantasies or the meanings he attached to various life events. Instead, the goals of seeing him were to decrease his obsessional concern with his and others' health and to encourage him to restrict his greedy and provocative demandingness, toward the end of relaxing him enough for greater involvement, facilitated by stepped-up environmental pressure, in his schoolwork and friendships. By the tenth session Tom had almost talked himself out about his own and others' illnesses and accidents. A "scary feeling" that would obviously come over him before going to school had diminished, as had certain violent dreams he had been having. He showed more pride in his schoolwork and began spending much more time outdoors with friends after school, a tendency reinforced by his parents. He lost several pounds in the following five months, which, coupled with his growth, streamlined him somewhat. His motivation to work in school improved considerably and he began making up some of the considerable ground he had lost in the last two years. His teacher found him more relaxed and friendly in school, and rarely absent. Despite Tom's limited intelligence he had covered a fair amount of ground during the big push and he was promoted to the fifth grade. At the psychologist's suggestion, Tom spent two successful weeks in camp during the summer before the fifth grade, his first period away from home.

In this unreferred case the consulting psychologist surfaced and dismantled a false ideology successfully foisted on the school by the disturbed parents of a disturbed child. By tying his assault on the family's misconceptions of Tom's health to the boy's prospects for promotion, as well as his future educational and vocational success, the psychologist created a climate of alarm and cooperation producing more forward movement than the family pediatrician had been able to achieve. With the hands-off attitude of the school altered and specific pressures exerted on the boy at home and at school, his flight from learning was reversed. His social and emotional adjustment was also facilitated by the program of specific tactics laid down for family and school to follow. The work with Tom at the Clinic was brief and focused on persuading him to adopt certain courses of action rather than on exploring his inner dynamics.

As we have pointed out the dropout or attrition rate of children from contact with a child-guidance clinic is generally very high. We have had, however, only one case that did not continue clinic contact; it, in fact, involved failure to come to the first visit. Our results are based largely on work with inner-city children, and there is no doubt that our policy of picking up a child at school or home, in those instances where it is necessary because of parental inability or unwillingness, accounts for the high rate of continuation of contact. It is the inner-city children who are underrepresented in our child-guidance clinics because they cannot, for one or another reason, adapt to the procedures of the clinic. Chauffeuring a child is viewed by us as a way we must on occasion adapt to the characteristics of the family in order to achieve our goals. It is also worthy of note that in none of the four inner-city schools in which we work has there been a child who, in the past recallable by teachers and principals, has been seen in any child-guidance clinic for diagnostic and therapeutic purposes. In the middle-class or suburban schools with which we are affiliated there were, by contrast, a number of children being seen in these clinics—we did not have to make inquiry we were spontaneously told so. We do not need exact figures to conclude that inner-city children are underrepresented in child-guidance clinics.

The important thing, of course, is whether our approach achieves the goal of maintaining the child in school, facilitating the degree and enjoyment of learning, and giving him more of a chance of becoming a productive person. The cases we have presented are representative of the population of problems with which we have worked as they are of the results achieved.

Chapter 13

The Inner-City School and the
Convergence of Resources

It has been rightly said of clinical settings that two staffs would be helpful; one to do the work and one to go to the meetings. The issues are complicated enough in the closed society represented by the child-guidance clinic or the mental hospital, but the problem assumes gigantic proportions when we begin dealing with the variety of agencies in the community that have some degree of responsibility for children and their parents. The first purpose of this chapter is to serve fair warning to any mental-health professional that if he truly becomes involved with the community, he will also become involved, sometimes it seems inextricably, with all the agencies and all their regulations and attendant bureaucratic structure. The professional should be prepared to spend long, wearying, frustrating, and only occasionally fruitful hours in telephone conversations, individual meetings, and group meetings in order to get some action in a given case. He must decide early in his career whether the game is worth the candle; at least one such involvement is recommended for everyone's education.

The second reason for writing this chapter is to outline some of the problems in present-day practices, even though we fully recognize that present practices are limited by restrictions in the statutes that regulate the agencies, and in the by-laws that have grown up around these regulations. It is our belief that the concept of the whole person is violated by the legal division of responsibility for the care of people into pieces that follow arbitrary lines laid down by accidents of history, by a legal rather than a human view of the way people live, and by the exigencies of the political climate that permit one program but not another. However they grew, current practices in many instances do not serve human needs, and urgently require re-evaluation from the point of view of human needs.

The third reason, however, is the most important for the purposes of this book; the chapter views an old problem from the vantage point of teachers and those like ourselves who are in a helping role in the inner-city schools. From such a vantage point several things may become clear to the reader: (1) A fantastic number of people and agencies can become involved in a single case. (2) In most instances the problem, be it child or family or both, is discerned in school with varying degrees of clarity and urgency in the early elementary school grades. (3) As in the case of all other agencies the school deliberately delimits its area of action and responsibility—a delimitation that, though understandable in terms of traditions, contributes to the child's school difficulties. (4) Most disheartening, in everyday work it is easy to develop the paranoid attitude that the major concern of community agencies is to keep teachers and other school personnel as uninformed as possible about problems and actions that affect the teacher as well as the child in school. (5) The problem of morale among inner-city school personnel is not something solely dependent on within-school factors and actions.

The multiproblem family is a well-known phenomenon in the inner city. Such a family is known to every social agency in the city because of the multiplicity of its problems. A substantial proportion of the work load of every community social-service agency is comprised of relatively few families called the "hard core." Not only do such families keep all of the agencies busy, but they are probably in the business of producing the next generation's welfare cases, the next generation's special-class population, the next generation's delinquents, and on and on.

Example 1. One consultant had had contact with such a family over a two-year period. He had met the family because two of the children were presenting severe behavior problems in the school, and remained in contact throughout the school year, even when the family moved to another neighborhood and the children were attending another school. About a year after the consultant stopped this contact, he was invited to attend a joint case conference with representatives of various agencies that currently had some responsibility for the family.

The conference was called by the Visiting Nurses Association, the most recent group to deal with the family. The visiting nurses had contact with the family because the mother was in need of surgery and had some suspicion about the recommendation for surgery. The stated purpose of the conference was "to develop a plan for providing some assistance to Mrs. M. and her large family."

Present at this conference were the VNA staff nurse and her immediate supervisor, the school nurse and her supervisor, the principal of the school, the school social worker, a social worker from the Aid to Dependent Children Program (ADC) (her supervisor was not present), and the consulting psychologist. Not present, but involved, was a representative of the municipal housing agency, which was their landlord. The family was renting in a building, slated for razing when that area of the city was to be renewed, owned by the relocation agency. Represented at the meeting by written reports were two school psychologists and the pediatrics and obstetrical departments of the local hospital.

At that time one child was out of the home, whereabouts unknown, and another was at a home for delinquent girls. The oldest boy at home, then about 13, was involved in a sexually tinged incident with a girl in junior high school that could have involved this family in legal action. The next two girls were adjusting fairly well in school, but one had been quite difficult to manage in the past. Although the girls presented little difficulty in school, their attendance was poor because they were frequently kept home to help with the younger children. The next-oldest boy had been an extremely difficult problem in school but seemed to have calmed down somewhat. The next two boys were both problems in school. The older of the two had an arm withered by polio and was in difficulty in first grade. The boy in the pre-kindergarten hit, bit, and scratched other children but did not want to go home. There were also two younger children in the home, one an infant about whom little was known.

The school social worker and the school psychologist were involved with the family for obvious reasons. The school nurse had become involved because of various health problems manifested by the children, and because the children's aggressiveness in school had from time to time resulted in injuries requiring bandaging, and the mother had been concerned about getting adequate explanations about what had happened.

The ADC social worker, who was relatively new to the agency, had seen this family only once in the previous six months. However, she had a thick file with detailed reports from a number of other workers who had had contact with the family over the years. The agency had a view of the woman as uncooperative because she had become excited when the agency insisted that she help them find the various fathers of her children so the agency could bring legal action to have the men contribute to the support of the children, and because she had voluntarily failed to report a rent decrease that had occurred after their apartment building was taken over by the relocation agency. In the course of the conference the consultant raised the question about the privileged nature of information that might be revealed at this conference. The ADC social worker indicated that it would be her legal obligation to pursue any indication that there was any violation of ADC regulations. Thus as a result of his contact with the family, if the consultant were aware of any adult males in the family picture, or if he were aware of any work Mrs. M. might have been doing, he would not feel free to reveal such information in the conference.

The discussion continued around the problem of helping this family to get a refrigerator and a washing machine. According to the visiting nurse the refrigerator was so small and in such uncertain condition that Mrs. M. was restricted to buying food a day at a time, and thus to spend some part of each day shopping. Her washing machine was broken and she therefore spent part of each day in the laundromat doing the wash for the family. The ADC worker indicated the problems in helping Mrs. M. to replace these items. First, any item costing more than $50.00 had to be approved at some supervisory level. Although it was clear this family needed a washing machine and a refrigerator, the ADC worker indicated that she could not authorize the purchase. Second, the ADC allowance for appliances is so low that clients are forced to buy used appliances that tend to wear out shortly after the 30-day guarantee is up. Third, ADC regulations are such that the client must obtain three written estimates on the items and submit these to the ADC worker. Clients report that not all stores, or not all salesmen in the stores, are willing to give these estimates, even though the ADC worker has sent the client. We can imagine the courteous treatment an ADC recipient receives in a used-appliance store when seeking a written estimate of price! One purpose of obtaining the written estimate is to be sure the client actually receives the item she has selected. However, clients are not given help, or information about how to shop for used or new appliances.

It was the visiting nurse's impression that the woman was spending a large proportion of her allowance on laundry. The nurse's impression was substantiated by the school nurse and the principal, who agreed that the children were generally dressed reasonably neatly and cleanly. The ADC social worker indicated she was not aware of the situation, but she would agree to increasing the family's laundry allowance. However, she could not act until after the close of business for the next check because any change put in too near the time a check was due to be sent out would cause it to be held up.

Finally, in view of the visiting nurse's report on the state of the woman's health, it was suggested she be considered for the homemaker-aid service. The ADC worker indicated that a physician's recommendation might be necessary for the homemaker to be approved. There was some question raised about the possibility of finding a homemaker even if funds were granted, because ADC regulations limited the amount that could be paid for a homemaker to $1.25 per hour. Where could trained, reliable help be found to work at that rate?

We have described the process in some detail because it shows how limited each agency's function comes to be. The school social worker can deal only with the family's relationship to the school, even though it is perfectly clear that the mother's state of health and energy are relevant to the children's response to school. The ADC worker seemed to limit her function to the details of the client's finances, as the guardian of the purse strings. She was in no way free to work with this family around any other consideration that arose. The school nurse had responsibility for various aspects of the children's health, but could not deal with the family's health, while the visiting nurse could deal with some of the children's health problems, but could not relate to the family's problems in school, nor could she arrange to have the home-making service introduced because her agency could not pay for the service. Each professional group had thick folders with overlapping and duplicated information.

We may well ask what a psychologist was doing at a meeting concerned with getting homemaking service for a sick woman with eight children who needed a refrigerator and a washing machine. None of this seems the concern of the psychologist, who normally has a defined responsibility for a patient who comes to his office. From the viewpoint that he provides a traditional service, we can clearly answer that none of this is the psychologist's business, except as it helps him to understand his patient's world. However, as soon as he enters into the community, and particularly as soon as he begins to deal with residents of the inner city, he inevitably encounters the multiplicity of service agencies, each of which has some partial responsibility for the family. It is impossible to avoid dealing with more than one agency, if only to obtain information about what is happening in the child's life.

Example 2. Early in our experience in the schools a consultant came across a child who struck him as the most ragged and bedraggled child in the kindergarten classroom. The child was first seen crying in a corner of his classroom because he had not received milk that morning. Milk is provided for children only if the parents send money for it each week. This child had not had milk money before, finally had brought it, but still did not receive milk because it was Friday, and money brought in on Friday purchased milk for the following week. Subsequently, it was learned that the child was repeating kindergarten, that he was a pleasant child but hardly ever participated verbally in the classroom. Through the course of the year there were several incidents in which the child took things from the kindergarten classroom. These incidents were handled in an understanding but firm fashion by the classroom teacher.

Toward the end of the year the child was given a reading-readiness test on which he scored just about zero. An individual psychological examination revealed an IQ of about 85. At that point the consultant, the graduate student who tested the child, and the teacher had a conference with the boy's mother, in which the tests were interpreted to her. The conference seemed to be a pleasant one and the mother seemed to understand the findings indicating that the boy was probably of normal intelligence. She was told we were concerned about the possibility that his relative lack of communication would interfere with his performance in first grade. The graduate student agreed to make time available to see the boy through the summer, at no cost to the mother, to work with the child to help prepare him for first-grade work in the fall. On the surface the mother seemed to express her pleasure that the boy would have the opportunity, and she agreed to bring him to the Clinic, located within a ten-minute walk of her home.

She never kept the initial appointment and through the early part of the summer at least six letters and telephone calls setting up further appointments were made. At that time we had not yet adopted the policy of picking up and delivering such children to the Clinic, and after a number of broken appointments the mother was sent a letter indicating she could contact the Clinic if she wished to pursue the matter. She never did.

In first grade the child was placed in an experimental tutoring program. As part of the program the consultant and the boy's tutor visited the home to invite the parents to a meeting at the school to describe the program to them. On this visit the consultant and tutor observed enough in the home to leave a strong suspicion the woman was a prostitute and that the child's home was a brothel. Although the mother gave her approval for the child's participation in the program, she did not appear in school, which was across the street from her apartment.

The child worked effectively in the program but at one point was out for a period of a month or more because he had ringworm. After a period of time the school nurse went to investigate and discovered the ringworm was not being treated. It was not until she followed up and threatened to reveal the neglect to the ADC social worker that the mother made any effort to seek treatment for the child. On another occasion the child was found crying softly to himself in the classroom. Investigation revealed a chipped tooth that was paining him. Again treatment followed firm insistence by the school nurse that the mother correct the condition.

At the age of seven this child was involved with juvenile police from the youth bureau. He and another child were suspected of stealing money from the cash register of a local store. The juvenile authorities took him out of the classroom and questioned him in the school building for more than an hour. There is nothing to indicate the child's mother was ever notified of the incident. A casual interview on the street with the mother's "boyfriend" indicated he was aware of the trouble but neither he nor the mother had been informed that the police had questioned her child.

Not long after this incident the consultant received a call from the school indicating that the mother had been arrested on a charge of "lascivious carriage." (According to one attorney, it is a law applied almost exclusively to the Negro lower class, and characterized by him as one of the most unconstitutional laws on the books.) She was given five months in jail because she was already on probation, having previously been found guilty of breach of the peace. Five younger children had been placed with relatives. The two older children remained with a neighbor whose husband was a cousin of the children's mother. At this point the consultant called the ADC social worker and asked about the possibility of a permanent foster-home or institutional placement for these children. The ADC social worker's surprised response to the consultant's question provided a most revealing insight into the welfare program's problems. Her immediate and spontaneous reply to the request that the agency seek permanent foster-home placement for these children was, "Oh, we only do that in case of an emergency!"

As it happened the placement with the neighbor seemed to be beneficial for the child. The woman seemed to be a lively, warm individual with a good understanding of children, and willing to look out for the child in meaningful ways. Her husband, who had a police record of minor offenses, also seemed interested in the boy and told about how they were spending time with him. The family was receiving an allowance from ADC to care for the children, but the boy's response in school showed he was receiving more than minimal care. He was coming to school regularly and was working effectively in school. He seemed to be neatly dressed and clean most of the time. For the first two months of the placement the child apparently did not say anything at all about his mother, and repeatedly told the woman who was caring for him that he preferred to stay with her. None of the children knew what had happened to their mother. They had been told she had to go away "down south" to take care of a sick relative.

On the Monday following Mother's Day, both children were acting disturbed in school. The boy seemed somewhat bedraggled on the next two days. The consultant made several efforts to reach the boy's guardian by telephone. He visited the household and spoke to the man, who was very evasive about the boy. A telephone call in the evening finally reached the woman, who said that the boy had heard his mother was coming back for him and this was the reason he was upset. The consultant called the ADC social worker to ask what she knew of the situation and discovered she not only knew nothing about it but didn't even have a current telephone number for the family taking care of the children. Apparently no plans were being made for the mother's return.

After the consultant's telephone call, the ADC social worker called the probation department and discovered that the only probation officer who dealt with women prisoners was unaware of the date of her release. Further telephone calls revealed that there was no predischarge planning at the women's prison. The ADC social worker could not obtain authorization to visit the mother in prison. The probation worker would see her when she had time *after* she received notification of the woman's release. The ADC social worker also indicated they had no control over the woman's decisions about how she was to live until she reapplied for aid for children living in her home. When she left prison, without any planning that anyone was aware of, the mother would pick up the children, find her own place to live, and then come to the ADC office to apply for her welfare payments. At that point ADC would have some grounds to talk to her about her plans for her children and herself. The only alternative available to ADC, at least according to the way the social worker presented it to the consultant, was to institute a neglect charge against the mother and to make the children wards of the state. Because there were seven children involved, the worker felt she would have to institute a neglect petition for all the children and she was extremely pessimistic about receiving approval for such an action from her supervisory level, or about the possibility of finding a suitable home for the children.

That ADC regulations might permit more leeway for action is not the issue. From the point of view of the worker, an apparently intelligent, sincere, and interested woman who was going to leave the agency sometime before the mother was to be released from prison, the situation left little room for constructive action.

What has all this to do with a child in school? In this case the child had contact with the youth bureau, the school nurse, and the ADC social worker, while his mother would have contact with the probation officer. In no instance do we see any of these agencies taking on responsibility for working with the school. Each agency controls only a small part of what is happening, and liaison or exchange of information occurs only fortuitously. In this case it was only the consultant's persistence that provided any information to the school. The consultant's efforts were not sufficient to encourage any of the agencies to gain a relationship with the family or with the school except as he provided the liaison in his own person. The ADC social worker made no effort to inform the school that the children's mother was arrested and that the children were to be farmed out to a neighbor. It seems such information is relevant to the teacher's understanding of the child and to her working with the child. That the information should first come to the classroom teacher by way of gossip from children is scandalous.

When the child was questioned by youth bureau workers in the school, members of the school staff were present, but these were strangers to the child. Aside from the fact that we can challenge the necessity for questioning a seven-year-old child in the school building, as far as is known the youth bureau made no effort to contact the child's mother and there was never any kind of follow-up. The ADC social worker was not notified of the situation by the youth bureau, although with the information provided by the classroom teacher that the child also pilfered in school, some kind of intervention seems to have been indicated.

The classroom teacher was excluded from the situation entirely. An excerpt from her description of the situation follows:

We were preparing to have our milk at 10:05 this morning. The principal asked to see the child, and said that he would return the child in a few minutes. When he failed to return by 10:25, I inquired and was told that he and two other boys were being questioned about a theft by three men from the youth bureau. [The teacher goes on to describe her efforts to check on what happened to the boy. She saw him being questioned, sitting with his head down, not answering at all. At no time was she invited into the room or told what was happening.] The child returned to the room at 11:30, crying. His shirt was wet from sweat and his handkerchief was wet.

It was the classroom teacher's responsibility to deal with that child the rest of the day and on subsequent days.

The present structure of helping agencies is such that each agency is concerned with a little piece of the person. The classroom teacher is responsible for teaching the child to read and write. That he may be hungry, ashamed of his poor clothing, concerned about what happened to his mother, and angry or depressed because he feels that no one cares about him is relevant to her problem in teaching him, but corrective measures are beyond the resources of the school. The youth bureau seemed concerned with catching the criminal and had nothing to do with the child's parents or with any other agency concerned with him. That there were important implications for the child's attitudes toward school in their questioning of him in the school building did not seem to occur to the youth bureau authorities. When the mother comes out of prison and takes the children again, neither the probation officer nor the ADC worker will notify the school to indicate the drastic change occurring in the family situation. Experience with this child's mother indicates that she will not approach the school herself, and, in fact, she has failed to respond to repeated and persistent overtures to take advantage of available help for the child.

The prediction that the child will not be prepared to function adequately in society seems easy to make. That future problems are in the making requires no particular genius to foresee. That many agencies are aware of the issues is also perfectly clear, and the helplessness of the variety of agencies to deal effectively with the problems is disheartening. In part the problem arises because each agency takes a limited view of its responsibilities. The school seems to have the best position with respect to the child, but as long as the school's responsibility is limited to education defined as reading, writing, and arithmetic, it will not be able to make use of its strategic position to intervene preventively in a definitive fashion. Cases such as this can be repeated over and over again and force us to reconsider the nature of the school as an institution.

Example 3. A fifth-grade boy entered his new school in October. This was the sixth school for him since the beginning of his school career. Within weeks he was in continuous difficulty with several teachers. He talked back to his teachers, refused to do the work, sneaked out of class, acted like a clown, got into fights with other children in the lavatory, and in general was thoroughly disruptive. The principal received almost daily complaints that this child had been in fights outside the school building, that he had threatened other children and extorted money from them. A number of parents had complained most vigorously about the boy's activities. He spent much of his time in the principal's office doing nothing, although at times the principal or a teacher would keep him busy in some fashion. His school record indicated failures in academic work since the earliest grades, and they also indicated that he had been a behavior problem since first grade.

At one point the boy was involved in a sexual incident with a first-grade child. He had pulled the other child's pants down in the toilet. The principal then decided he could refer the case to juvenile authorities, and he referred the child for examination as part of the school's referral procedure, which includes a psychological examination and a report by the school social worker. Because it was desirable to complete the testing as quickly as possible, the consultant wrote a letter to the boy's father explaining the difficulty and asking that he be brought to the Clinic for an evaluation. The boy's father was not entirely surprised by the request, as he had had previous conversations with the school principal. On the appointed day neither father nor boy appeared. The consultant then drove to the boy's home, finding the apartment with some difficulty. When he was admitted to the apartment, he found the boy was still asleep. The father was defensive and evasive about failing to keep the appointment. After a brief discussion that seemed friendly enough, the boy's father promised to have him at the Clinic in an hour. After an hour and a half the consultant returned to the apartment and found the boy awake, dressed, and eating a sandwich. The consultant then took the boy to the Clinic himself, the father expressing some relief that he did not have to participate and could go about his own business. Testing was completed that afternoon.

In the following week the consultant spoke to the school social worker, the ADC social worker, and the probation officer. The school social worker indicated that her responsibility ended once she completed her report. Her job was to gather information to be forwarded to her superior, who would collate all the material and send it on to the juvenile court. The ADC worker indicated that her responsibility was limited to a child who was in the home of the mother, who was on the ADC roles. Because he was living with his father, an informal arrangement worked out by the probation officer, ADC was not technically responsible for the child's welfare.

The probation officer had never notified the school of his previous contacts with the boy. The boy was on informal probation, and the probation worker hesitated to inform the school because he felt the school might then act in a prejudiced manner toward the boy. However, the lack of communication resulted in an extended delay in processing the referral to the juvenile court. Had the principal been aware of the probation worker's relationship to the boy, he might have contacted him directly about the new problem that arose. There was a second consequence of the lack of communication. At one point later on the probation worker complained that he had not known that the boy was not doing well in school. He said that it was his impression the boy's problems manifested themselves outside of school only. The discussion with the probation worker gave some awareness of the problem involved in initiating any action. First, the case would have to be placed on the court docket, an action taking at least two weeks. Second, unless it was possible to insure some form of financial support for this eleven-year-old child, he could not be placed in any facility other than a reform school. It was not clear how financial support would be arranged. It was possible ADC might accept responsibility. However, if the ADC worker said she could not, then the probation officer would have to take the matter to his supervisor, who would then take the problem to the ADC worker's supervisor for further action. The probation worker indicated that the court did not like to initiate neglect proceedings against a child's family, in order to protect the reputation of the court. It was the worker's impression that the court preferred some other agency to initiate the complaint.

One week later the probation worker had determined that ADC was not responsible for the boy, but he felt that the Child Welfare Department would assume responsibility. Three weeks more passed. The boy had been in additional difficulty in school and out and had been held in the Children's Building for a few days on at least one occasion. At this point the probation officer had discovered openings existing at two residential facilities. Although the psychiatrist serving the court had seen the child and recommended placement in one of the two centers, the Department of Child Welfare felt it could not pay the charges at that institution even though the state's own residential treatment center had no room for the boy at all. This contact was the first time it was revealed that a court psychiatrist had seen the boy. At no time was his report or his advice made available to the school directly or through the school psychiatrist.

At this point the principal asked about providing homebound instruction for the boy. If he could be excluded from school, the school system would provide instruction at home, for one hour a day, for an indefinite period. The way the child spent the rest of his time would be his parent's concern. Homebound instruction could be obtained on recommendation of the school psychiatrist, who would have to certify that the boy needed to be excluded from school on medical grounds. The psychiatrist indicated his willingness to accept the consulting psychologist's report in lieu of his own examination, but he also asked if the court psychiatrist's report could be made available to him as additional support.

Three weeks more passed. The boy had been cutting school regularly and when in school had been spending the bulk of his time in the principal's office. Because there was no further action, several telephone calls revealed that the consultant's report had gone to the school psychiatrist; the court psychiatrist's report had gone to the office of the Director of Pupil Services; and both reports eventually would have had to go to still another office to the individual in charge of homebound instruction. The school social worker, who helped track down the various reports, received the impression that homebound instruction was difficult to obtain because of a shortage of teachers. However, when the consultant called the office for homebound instruction, he learned from the secretary assignment would take only a day or so because the situation was not very tight for elementary school children.

One week later the boy was finally seen by the juvenile court judge, clearly an able, concerned individual. The judge interviewed the boy and his parents and informed them of his decision that the boy was to be placed in a residential center as soon as a facility was available. The boy was apparently frightened by the proceedings, but his fear lasted only a day or two before he was again in difficulty in school. He had been placed in his regular classroom again, but his teacher had received no information at all from anyone about what was happening. The teacher was both resentful and fearful of the boy, suspicious that nothing would happen and that she would be stuck with him for the remainder of the year.

Even though the boy was in frequent trouble outside the school as well as inside the school, there did not seem to be any effective way to set and to enforce any limits. The probation officer found the boy's father as evasive and as passively noncooperative as the consultant had. Moreover, the probation officer did not feel he could keep the boy in the children's building as a form of detention because it was already overcrowded and not meant to be used for such a purpose. It was his feeling that all he could do was wait until the residential placement had been cleared.

Two weeks later the probation officer was informed that one of the private residential centers had refused to accept the boy for placement. They had had fourteen applications for three openings at their last intake and they decided to accept other children. The probation officer now reviewed the application to the first center recommended by the court psychiatrist, and he said he would begin to make inquiries about other centers as well. Through the next two months the boy continued to be in difficulty in the community and in school, when he was there. The boy was in the Children's Building several times but he seemed oblivious to the fact that the incarceration was meant as a deterrent. His father quoted the boy as saying that he didn't have to worry about getting into trouble because the judge wasn't going to do anything anyway. In the meantime he had joined forces with another eleven-year-old boy and both set out on a campaign of petty thefts, petty extortion, truancy, and one incident of fire-setting.

A further telephone call to the probation officer brought the information that the neglect petition would be heard six weeks from the date the consultant called, fully six months after the original referral to the juvenile court through the school. It seems that Child Welfare was obligated by law to conduct its own investigation, an investigation that would include material from the schools and the court but would also involve a search of previous agency records and new interviews with the boy's parents. A call to the court clerk indicated that the earliest possible date for a hearing was six weeks away, and the date could not be moved up because of the need to have the Welfare Department's investigation in the hands of the court two days before the case was to be heard. A call to the Department of Child Welfare revealed that a worker would be assigned to the case in time to complete the investigation for the court but since the date was six weeks away "there was no hurry." At that time no worker was available to make the investigation. It appeared that the court and Child Welfare cooperated in setting a date administratively convenient to both agencies.

In view of the fact that the boy had been involved in one fire-setting incident and had started to carry a knife, the consultant urged the probation worker to attempt to find a more rapid means of setting limits for this child before something really serious happened. The alternative of reform school still existed, but in lieu of this alternative no other placement or means of control was readily available.

Two additional possibilities were investigated. If the boy returned to his mother and was placed on the ADC roles, ADC might assume financial responsibility as a medical expense, provided its state office approved the request. The boy actually had to establish physical residence in his mother's apartment for him to be considered eligible, even though there was no legal separation or divorce and no binding agreement of any kind that placed the boy in his father's custody. Inquiry at the ADC office revealed some reluctance on their part to put the boy on the ADC roles solely for purposes of expediting his placement, and indicated that the various investigatory and supervisory channels would require almost as much time as waiting for the court date.

A second possibility was considered. The City Welfare Department might agree to pay the bill until the neglect petition was heard, and the Child Welfare Department would take over responsibility. Discussion of this alternative led to a situation that can best be described as "Catch 22." It was the thinking of the probation officer and his supervisor that City Welfare would not consider the request unless the boy's father would agree to pay some proportion of the expenses. The probation officer felt it would be necessary to ask the father for $200 if he was to have any success at all with City Welfare. When we looked back on the difficulty the probation officer and the consultant had in obtaining the father's cooperation in the first place the requirement immediately looked hopeless of fulfillment. The boy was to be placed because of neglect, but the father was expected not to neglect the boy! The probation officer made one or two unsuccessful attempts to see the father and then resigned himself to wait until the court date.

The court date finally arrived. In the meantime the boy had been involved in innumerable difficulties in school and in the community. He was made a ward of the state and placed in a private residential treatment center. A final irony was revealed in the Child Welfare Department's report. On the paternal side, the boy's family was known to social agencies in an unbroken line since 1904.

Throughout this whole process, the primary liaison between the agencies and the school was the consultant. Had the consultant not been present in the situation it is likely that little or no information would have come to the school. The school social worker was limited to half a day a week in the particular school, and may or may not have followed through. The principal, the classroom teacher, and the other teachers in the building who observed this boy sitting in the principal's office, or who received complaints about him from parents, saw only the slow-moving, unconcerned, faceless, and ineffective bureaucracy—"They were doing nothing." That such experiences have important and undesirable consequences for teacher morale needs no further elaboration. That teachers and principals may sometimes feel there is no use in doing anything becomes perfectly understandable. In view of the situation, that principals and teachers remain as concerned as they are for the welfare of their children is a distinct tribute to their humanity.[1]

CONCLUSIONS

The tragedy in each of the cases we have presented lies in the fact that all of the professional workers seemed to be sincere, concerned, intelligent individuals who were trying to do their jobs in the best way they could. At no point did we encounter stupid, brutal, or officious people; far from it. If anything, the professional workers felt themselves to be the victims and the captives of their own agency limitations. In some instances those wise in the ways of agencies might have been able to move the structures with greater facility to obtain given ends; however, in all three cases cited the worker involved either had been with the agency less than a year, or left the agency in the course of the year. The workers themselves were young, eager to do a good job, and frustrated. After receiving an explanation of one set of complicated agency regulations, a consultant began to express a cautious comment about the regulations when he was interrupted by the agency worker who said, "Yeah, they are a lot of crap!"

Over the years the passive resistance of agency clients to intrusion by the agency and the limitation of agency resources to cope with the problems of their clients do lead to a sort of cold war between workers and their clients. Some of the workers seem to have resigned themselves to the situation and act defensively to avoid blame and criticism for themselves. Sometimes we detect a note of hostility toward the clients and an attempt to voice the view that the clients are "bad."

The real issues lie not so much in the people but in the piecemeal development of institutions, each designed to deal with one function only. Because of the laws regulating public agencies and the bylaws and administrative rules that have developed around these laws, each agency is inclined to define its functions in the narrowest terms. Financial limitations are an important cause of the narrowing of the

---

[1] The verbatim transcripts of our teacher discussion groups in the appendix of this book contain some poignant instances of aspects of the problems raised in this chapter.

definition of function, but money is not the only factor. The true culprit is the conception that a person is a set of essentially unrelated needs and characteristics that may be treated or manipulated independently of each other.

In large part the multiplicity of agencies and their overlapping and separate aims were derived naturally from a set of historical accidents establishing services to deal with given problems as the public conscience became aware of the problems. An agency was established and funded for a particular purpose. In the course of time the problems changed but the conceptions and the laws regulating the agencies have changed much more slowly. As May (1964) has pointed out so well, the ADC program was never meant to provide full and complete social and psychological services to the urban poor. Its original purpose was to provide financial assistance to the genteel poor. The ADC program is by no means geared to act in a remedial or even a preventive fashion insofar as the social and personal problems of the children and adults are concerned.

Similarly, the juvenile court (and its youth bureau), though it is meant to be a remedial agency, is basically part of the law-enforcement structure. For the most part it has been our impression that the youth bureau detectives, who are not policemen, tend to see themselves as policemen and to limit their function to finding a culprit. Insofar as we have observed the operation, therapeutic or preventive functions are limited to giving the youngster a sharp warning. Probation officers often try to develop closer relationships with the children they service, but their functions sometimes seem to be limited to supervising the child and seeing that he follows whatever restrictions seem advisable. A fuller and more complete service is beyond the resources of the court as it is presently constituted. Probably the most telling indication of the law-enforcement characteristic of the juvenile court is the fact that the court must resort to the petition of neglect in order to arrange for anything other than an adjudication of delinquency and incarceration in a training school or a reform school. The court is authorized to purchase psychological and psychiatric consulting services, but apparently does not have its own funds or its own therapeutic resources, particularly for younger children. We are not being critical of the court, nor are we arguing that an expansion of traditional clinical services to the court would be the answer. Clearly, the Cambridge-Somerville (Powers & Witmer, 1951) and other studies (Meyer, Borgatta, & Jones, 1965) have shown that traditional counseling and psychotherapeutic services are of limited value in preventing delinquency. What our experience suggests is that the juvenile court has tended to have a narrowly defined function that makes it necessary for the court to deal with a variety of helping agencies, and makes for delay in action. The unfortunate partitioning of the person into a number of separate functions, each to be handled independently by another person or another agency, might be relieved by a broader definition of the responsibility of the court, implemented with the funds and personnel to provide a service meant to be preventive and relating the work of the court to the work of the school.

Most problems are first discerned in the school. A sizable proportion of the behavioral problems seen in older adolescents or in young adults reflects the inability of the school to deal with the problems as they are manifested in the school. The youngster who was finally sent to a residential treatment center had been a behavior problem in school since the first grade. The youngster whose mother went to jail, and who had been questioned by the police for stealing in the first grade, represents a problem in the making. We have already referred to the impotence of the school and other agencies in this case. If 25 per cent or more of an elementary school's population is on welfare, why not somehow combine some of the functions of the school social worker and ADC worker in one person located in the school building? If a child is absent from school because he has no shoes, or because of his clothes, the ADC worker may deal with the problem directly. In those instances where children are not being given the full care necessary for adequate functioning in school, the ADC worker who exercises financial control may be in direct contact with the problem, and interminable delays related to interagency exchanges may be avoided. A similar liaison between court and school is also possible. Why not combine some proportion of the work of a school social worker with that of a probation officer? The problem of coordinating services comes about because we view a child as a delinquent as far as the court is concerned, as a reading problem where the school is concerned, and a neglected child where a child-welfare worker is concerned. In fact, it is one child, responding differently in different situations.

But the major purpose of this chapter was not to present solutions (which we do not have) or to describe problems that are, in fact, longstanding, but rather to indicate how the handling of these problems defeats the aims of teachers, shatters a sense of professional accomplishment, and contributes to attitudes in and experiences of children that make school learning of small significance in their lives. In Part II we describe our involvement in certain aspects of the "War on Poverty" programs. It is in no sense a derogation of these programs to state here that they have not directed themselves to the issues raised in this chapter. In fact, what we have attempted to describe and discuss in this chapter leads to the conclusion that what we see in our inner-city elementary schools is a kind of guarantee that these new programs—directed mainly to problems of employment, training, retraining, and drop-outs—will never suffer from a shortage of candidates.

The problem is not one of more money for more personnel for more agencies. In part the problem lies in the fact that the school is a social agency dealing, willingly or unwillingly, with a full range of social, personal, and educational problems. It seems the school needs to begin to define its functions more broadly if it is truly to do the job circumstances force upon it. But when we put the problem this way we clearly run up against the weight of tradition and the problem of how to introduce change in ongoing social systems, a problem that does not lend itself to the easy answer of "more money to train more people to do more of what is currently being done." In the absence of new ideas and an intimate working knowledge of the problem, money is a necessary but far-from-sufficient condition for change.

Chapter 14

Accomplishments, Failures, and Limitations

In the previous chapters we endeavored to describe the types of problems with which we became involved in the school setting and the ways in which we dealt with them. We now attempt to view our experiences from the standpoint of our stated clinical purposes and over-all research goal (See Chapters 3 and 4). The first half of this chapter gives our view of what we think we accomplished; the second half considers the sources of failure in our work and the limitations imposed by the setting on what we might expect to accomplish.

ACCOMPLISHMENTS

At the very least, the material we have presented indicates that we were able to become part of the school setting in such a way that what we said and did made a difference in the behavior of children and teachers. This, of course, does not necessarily mean that whatever difference we made was "good." The significance of the statement should be viewed in terms of the two major goals that gave rise to our Clinic, one of which was to develop a way of functioning so that we could be helpful within the confines of the school in relation to whatever the school considered a problem, regardless of the contribution of other factors (e.g., family) to the etiology of the problem. Helping school personnel in relation to what *they* considered problems was only one aspect; as important was another aspect that involved change in relation to what *we* considered problems but were not brought to us for diverse reasons. To get to the point where these aspects could be dealt with candidly and with minimal possibility that relationships would become unduly strained or even severed presupposes that we had accomplished an earlier objective, to become part of the school setting in such a way that what we said or did had positive significance for the school personnel. Accomplishing this objective was no different from what frequently confronts us in research, where the initial problem is whether or not we have a workable procedure or experimental manipulation, regardless of the relation of the ultimate findings to the initial hypotheses. From this standpoint we think our material demonstrates that it is feasible for outsiders to become part of a school so that they are confronted with problems, situations, or issues that, *whether dealt with or not,* will influence the lives of children and adults. It is important to emphasize that most of our work involved situations in which some process of change, however puzzling, was already proceeding in a direction considered maladaptive for the child, be it in terms of the learning process, peer relationships, or child-teacher interactions. This was equally true for those instances in which teacher behavior was the focus of our attention. In both types of instances the question was not whether the situation required change or intervention but rather what kind and degree of change was possible.

Although we are aware that helping to bring about change is not synonymous with whatever might be considered "good," we do conclude from the representative sample of material in the previous chapters that in numerous instances change was effected that allowed children and teachers to do their assigned tasks more effectively. In certain types of instances, such as in arranging transfers of children from one teacher to another, the change in learning and social adaptation may often be dramatic, quick, and obvious. In other situations, such as the new teacher whose class is disorganized to the point of bedlam, the change in teacher and children can also be dramatic—to the point where children are involved in learning and the teacher feels that both she and the children are even enjoying the process. The most frequent type of situation we encountered involved two types of changes: first, helping the teacher understand that a child's behavior can be understood other than in the way she perceives it, and, second, that if she were to change her understanding or interpretation, it would have consequences in her response to the child. For example, if a teacher assumed a child's behavior in school to be solely or in large part a function of a bad home situation, her way of handling the child would be different than if she assumed that something about the classroom contributed to, or reinforced, or even exacerbated the behavior causing concern. A variant of this is the frequent instance in which the teacher interprets behavior as etiologically a direct function of IQ, oblivious to the fact that not all children with that IQ have the same style of behaving and learning. It is not particularly difficult to get a teacher to change her perception, at least on a verbal level. It is far more difficult to help her change her overt behavior in the direction of consistency with the new interpretation. Although we shall say more about this in connection with the problem of failures, there have been an encouraging number of instances in which teachers' overt behavior changed with a corresponding change in children frequently accompanied by verbalized surprise that "it worked."

In presenting and discussing our case material, we endeavored wherever appropriate to describe the situation in a before-and-after manner so that others could judge several things: the range and complexity of problems, our way of coping with them, and the degree of face validity to be attributed to the consequences we described. In several important respects, however, our emphasis on instances or individual children probably underestimates what we accomplished. For example, it will be recalled that in Chapter 4 we stated it was our aim (or hope) that a consequence of working with a particular teacher about a particular child would be that she would transfer, to some degree, whatever understanding she gained to her interactions with other children. We were unable to assess the results of this aim in any formal or systematic way. However, there were several things that suggested it was at least partially achieved:

1. In two schools, both in the inner city, one of the more drastic ways with which they dealt with extremely disturbing children was to exclude them from school for varying lengths of time. When we began work in these schools it was not surprising that these children were brought to our attention to see what we could do. We had some success with many of these children, in that they returned to school and further exclusion was not necessary. Toward the end of the first year we became aware that the number of exclusions had dropped to nearly zero. What apparently happened, particularly in the case of teachers who had been previously involved in exclusions, was that they brought children to our attention before resorting to exclusion, in the hope that whatever worked to bring excluded children back to school was applicable to children for whom exclusion was now being considered. In other words, it seemed as if their previous experiences in working with us influenced their actions and decisions in relation to other children. It may be that what they had learned was that we could be helpful with difficult children. It was our impression that these referrals reflected, in addition, an awareness that the teacher was in some way contributing to the difficulty, a principle that had come up explicitly in working with excluded children.[1]

[1] After this book was completed we were able to obtain data on the number

2. There is wide variation among teachers in how they respond to children who engage in behavior disturbing either to the teacher or the class. Many teachers publicly reprimand, or warn, or punish the child, and infrequently is there any subsequent private discussion with the child. Although the spontaneous public response of the teacher is understandable, and frequently necessary, the teacher is often aware that her response is ineffective. In fact it is the child who is incorrigible to public reprimand who elicits in the teacher a variety of reactions that often reinforce the behavior the teacher wishes to stop. In working with teachers in relation to such children we tended to emphasize two things: the teacher's public response was ineffective and this had to be faced, and what needed to be tried was a private discussion centering not on punishment but on the teacher's desire to understand the behavior and to help the child in regard to it. In short the teacher had to recognize and communicate to the child that at the same time that she could not ignore misbehavior, she wanted to understand its occurrence and work with the child to change it.[2] Since the suggestion for private discussion usually meant that the teacher would have to make time for it either before or after school, and at both times she had other things to do in relation to her work, the suggestion initially was not always viewed with enthusiasm. The decisive factor enabling the teacher to try such an approach (which could not be a

---

of children in the New Haven schools who had been placed on homebound instruction because of emotional disturbance. Such exclusion follows a series of procedures, one of which is a psychiatric evaluation. One of the findings from these data is that from the time we began working in four inner-city schools only one child was excluded, a rate significantly lower than in the period before we began our work, and, in addition, significantly lower than the average rate of exclusion in ten inner-city schools with which we are not affiliated.

[2] As we shall see later, the most serious obstacle the teacher has to overcome is the implicit belief that overt change occurs quickly, that by talking to a child *today* his behavior will be different *tomorrow*. The idea that change could only be expected as a consequence of consistency and persistency of approach was almost always a focus of our work with teachers. "We cannot expect to see any change tomorrow, the day after that, or even next week. Children do not unlearn old behavior and learn new behavior that quickly. What we can hope for is that at some point—usually at the point where you are discouraged, your patience is at an end, and you are understandably entertaining some homicidal thoughts about the child—you may begin to see a hint of change. It isn't easy, but then again neither is the present situation we are trying to change." It also should be noted that when we fell into the trap of assuming that because we said something once or twice to a teacher we could expect her to change, our efforts were frequently ineffective. What holds for the approach of the teacher to the child is equally true for our approach to the teacher.

one-shot affair) was the explicit recognition that what the teacher was doing with the child during the course of the day was ineffective and a source of distress to the teacher—and we were as concerned with the teacher's feeling of distress as we were with the behavior of the child. In any event, we became aware that a number of teachers adopted this approach with children other than those whom they had referred or discussed with us. It was our definite impression in some instances that this transfer occurred not only because the approach worked (certainly not with all children) but because the teacher found it enjoyable and rewarding to be with a child in a role in which personal feelings could be given more direct expression.

3. The most frequent indication that teachers tended to transfer principles from one situation to another was in their own verbal reports to us. Although these reports were unsolicited, they nevertheless cannot be regarded as compelling because of the possibility that the teachers perceived that such reports would be pleasing to us. This is not to say that these reports can be disregarded but rather that we do not regard them as having the same significance as events we observed. In this connection it should be noted that, without our knowledge, the superintendent of schools in one of the systems in which we worked held a meeting of substantial length with each of the faculties of two schools to determine what we were doing, its value, and whether our services should be continued. We were soon informed about the meetings by the superintendent and the teachers, both of whom agreed that these meetings were in the nature of a searching interrogation by the superintendent as to the specifics of our approach and its value to the teachers. That the evaluation was favorable and was the basis for the request that we try to include more schools was somewhat surprising to us because the meetings were held several months after we began in the schools and we were then far from secure, as we later were, about our personal relationships and effectiveness in these schools.[3]

---

[3] In point of fact these meetings turned out to have a number of consequences for our Clinic. News spreads in a number of directions, although not always in as fortunate ways as in our case. For one thing, the nature of our work in these schools (both inner-city ones) quickly reached the local community action agency (Community Progress, Inc.) with which we had just begun to explore a possible role for our Clinic and, as a result, facilitated a relationship that turned out to be enormously significant for us. In addition the superintendent of schools informed the president of our university about our work and, needless to say, his communication to us was not unwelcome. Although positive feedbacks must be carefully evaluated, there are times when we need to accept them for what they appear to be.

The development of the Psycho-Educational Clinic represented, as we tried to make clear in our early chapters, a variety of factors: historical, professional, social, and research. From the very outset we tried to keep clearly in mind—more because of our conception of the realities as we viewed them and less as a defense against the possibilities of immoderate failure—that the value of our efforts would probably lie in what we learned about the outlines of future preventive programs and not in what we could accomplish on the clinical level. Although this is still our viewpoint, we nevertheless feel that we have been able to demonstrate a clinical effectiveness well beyond our initial expectations. We were able in most instances to become quickly and solidly a part of the school, to establish relationships of mutual trust necessary to changing perceptions and actions, to play a role in bringing about significant changes in the classroom learning and adaptation of a number of children, to help a number of teachers review and reorient their thinking in a way productive of a change in atmosphere that seemed to involve most, if not all, of the children in the class—these were among the things we accomplished in most schools on a twice-a-week basis over a two-year span. Unlike the initial weeks in each school when we were uneasy about our focus, uncertain about our potential effectiveness, and anxious about our tenure, at the end of two years we were richer by the friendships formed and the knowledge gained, and more convinced than when we began that the elementary school was a physical and psychological setting *in* which the mental-health worker could function more productively than his present training allows him to realize. In this connection, it is our opinion that the large measure of success with children seen in the Clinic reflects in large part the fact that treatment simultaneously involved the child, teacher, and psychologist *in* the school; that is, the Clinic was an extension of the school rather than, as is usually the case, a setting unrelated to and not in meaningful communication with the school.

One of the important consequences of our activities was the strengthened conviction given to several views we held before beginning our formal work in the schools (Sarason, Davidson, and Blatt, 1962):

1. In the course of teaching a teacher is an applied psychologist who is constantly diagnosing and treating, that is, she is engaged in a decision-making process on the basis of which she acts, or chooses not to act, in order to influence the behavior of children.

2. The training of teachers ill prepares them for this role, a lack of which they are acutely aware and in many instances gives rise to a personal morale problem that further handicaps them in their work with

children. An additional factor contributing to this unhealthy situation is that a teacher, despite the fact that she is surrounded by people, is essentially *alone* in grappling with her problems. It may very well be that our most important accomplishment in the schools, and the basis for whatever effectiveness we had, was that teachers no longer felt alone in handling their problems.

3. The mental-health professions have an extremely important role to play in training programs for teachers, and their continued failure to engage in such activities can only be regarded as unfortunate in the extreme.

In connection with the last point we should emphasize that we are suggesting that the mental-health worker become involved with teachers in their training years, that period in which they should be learning and applying psychological principles necessary for understanding and managing their own behavior in relation to that of children. We emphasize the training period because so much of our work with teachers in the schools involved issues, problems, practices, and information which, if more adequately dealt with in the course of training, would have enabled the teachers to feel more competent and to do a more effective job.

When we first started working in the schools, we were asked in several instances in the early weeks not to go into several classrooms *because* the teachers were new. At that point we did not, of course, challenge this view even though we quickly learned that some of the new teachers were having a rough time and had sought the help of older teachers, particularly in relation to management problems. It is no exaggeration to say that later in that first year several of us spent a fair amount of time undoing what had been done earlier in these classrooms. By the second year of our work we were able to help these principals understand that it was precisely *because* teachers were new that our presence was necessary.

Our experience with new teachers led us to suggest the formation of what we termed "teacher discussion" groups. All new elementary teachers in one school system were asked if they wished to participate in such groups to be held at our Clinic once a week for ten weeks. Each group was to consist of no more than ten teachers and was to be led by one Clinic staff member and graduate intern in clinical psychology. Participation was strictly voluntary and it was further emphasized that the contents of the discussion were to be determined by the teachers and there were to be "no lectures or sermons." Three groups were formed and each continued for ten weeks, although attendance varied considerably. A stenotypist was present at each meeting and the transcripts were later available to the teachers and Clinic personnel. In the Appendix we present the transcripts of four meetings, two from one group and one from each of the remaining groups. Each of the groups was led by a different Clinic member and clinical intern.

The transcripts in the Appendix are presented in full for several reasons: (1) They may convey to the reader unfamiliar with schools something about how teachers think and talk about some of their daily problems. (2) Many of the problems discussed in these transcripts are identical, in form and content, to those presented to us in our work in the schools. (3) They may serve to illustrate the problem of the relation between teacher-training programs and the realities of the job as these teachers saw them. (4) They do convey aspects of the culture of the school, particularly in relation to the urban setting.[4] (5) They do support, if further support is necessary, the conviction that the school is a natural focus for any community mental-health program concerned with early detection and prevention of problems. (6) These transcripts indicate that in these discussion groups—held away from and outside of the power structure of the school—teachers manifested a degree of initiative and spoke with a degree of candor and involvement ordinarily missing in whatever meetings they participate in at their own schools.

As we have indicated, one of the major reasons for organizing teacher-discussion groups was that we could gain an additional vantage point from which we could begin to view the over-all research problems in which we were most interested: how to understand and describe the culture of the school, and the conditions and processes that facilitate or interfere with the introduction of change into an ongoing social system such as the school. It is our opinion that our experiences confirm the wisdom of the decision that our understanding of the school would be incomparably broader and deeper if we were in some sort of helping relation to the school than if we studied the problems in less personal ways with more traditional methodologies such as

[4] It is perhaps necessary to remind the reader that one of the several purposes in starting the Psycho-Educational Clinic was to have a vehicle for approaching the problem of conceptualizing, describing, and understanding the school culture. As we pointed out earlier, we have not directly discussed this problem because of our awareness of its complexity and the dangers of premature conceptualizations. The school culture is and will remain for us a primary object of study and will be discussed in future publications (Sarason, 1966).

questionnaires, formal interviews, surveys. We do not intend derogation of these traditional methodologies, but rather wish to emphasize
that they did not seem appropriate to the problems as beginning steps.
We felt a kinship to the anthropologist who goes to a foreign culture
armed primarily with the knowledge that his understanding is limited,
his personality and behavior of prime but unclear significance, and
that the passage of time will be occasionally marked by insights that
give meaning to the unmarked intervals and a more secure anticipation of the future course of events.

We have deliberately avoided systematically discussing or conceptualizing the culture of the school. We did not think it appropriate
to our focus here (i.e., to describe the activities of our Clinic in several
settings, of which the school is only one) to present our views about the
culture of the schools and processes of change. In addition, and more
important, we did not feel our experiences to be that extensive or our
understanding acceptably complete to attempt at this time conceptualization of the culture of the school and processes of change. We consider these problems to be of such theoretical and practical importance
that caution and reflection should be far more heavily weighted than
a sense of timeliness that can result in premature and mischievous
speculations of which education has a surfeit.

FAILURES AND LIMITATIONS

Although we believe our material indicates that our work in the
schools was effective and productive in terms of the help given to children and teachers as well as the knowledge gained by us about the
school setting, it is equally true that we have come to certain conclusions about sources of failure in this type of work and about limitations in the scope of what we may expect to accomplish. We clearly do
not wish to convey the impression that our work in the schools did not
meet with problems, difficulties, failures, and disappointments. Our
task in this chapter is to try to understand the obvious fact that life
does not always proceed according to our hopes.

THE PSYCHOLOGIST

From time to time we have stated that it was extremely unfair to
expect that a teacher should be equally effective with all children in
her class. Similarly, we should not expect the psychologist to be
equally effective with the variety of personalities he encounters in a
school. In any one school teachers vary considerably in age, background, manner, competence, self-confidence, and a host of other

factors, and it is unrealistic to expect that a single psychologist would be capable of responding with equal effectiveness to all of them. This is another way of saying that some teachers evoke feelings and attitudes in the psychologist that interfere with the relationship, his perceptions, and the help he can be to particular children. This situation can occur not only because of negative feelings aroused in the psychologist, but because of strong positive feelings as well.

Example 1. In one instance, representative of several we have encountered, the psychologist had developed a strong liking and respect for a teacher who indeed was an insightful, resourceful individual with a deserved reputation for getting children to develop academic skills. In fact, his regard for the teacher was such that when she initially referred a child because the child was creating problems in the classroom, he tended automatically to assume that the child must be a serious problem if he could not get along with this teacher. In other words, the psychologist had adopted an attitude that made him oblivious to the principle that there must be something about the classroom that plays into the difficulties of the misbehaving child. The psychologist observed the child rather briefly in the classroom, the brief observation confirming his quick judgment that the child was a difficult managment problem. A series of discussions were held with the teacher as to how to understand the child's behavior and what steps might be taken to bring about a change. In the midst of this, and in connection with another project, a member of the Clinic started a series of observations in this classroom and it became clear from his reports that this teacher obviously disliked the child, blamed him for things he did not do, and even openly ridiculed him in front of the children—teacher behavior that surprised the psychologist. Another observer was put in the room and his observations were in line with those of the previous one. Subsequent extensive observations in this classroom led us to conclude that this teacher, who was effective with and understanding of most children in her classroom, took a dislike to the few children who showed a very slow rate of academic progress. Because these few children tended to manifest other problems as well as academic ones, it facilitated her seizing on these other problems as reflections of willful opposition or "bad character," resulting in a type of teacher-child interaction that exacerbated the disturbing behavior.

On the basis of our experiences we have concluded that it is precisely with teachers for whom we have strong positive regard and respect—who are cooperative and welcoming, who we have reason to believe are psychologically sophisticated or at least have a verbal facility with psychological concepts, or who make us feel we are towers of wisdom—that we have to be on guard against the danger of selective perception and uncritical thinking. That we fall prey to these dangers is less important than how it may affect children.

When the psychologist has strong positive feeling and respect for a teacher he may overgeneralize her competence and straight-thinking to all children and all problems, and this can be a source of failure. The major corrective available against this type of failure is prolonged, systematic observation in the classroom.

As we might expect, it is not too difficult to identify failures due to our negative feelings about a teacher. The most clear form of this is when we simply avoid contact with the teacher either because we are intimidated by her or because her incompetence is such that we do not want to take on what seems to be the impossible task of effecting change in her. In at least two instances the psychologist found himself so upset sitting in classrooms the teachers could not control that it was with great difficulty that he controlled his wish to inform the appropriate authorities about the situation. Flight and very superficial visits were his modes of defense, despite the very real problems of children and teachers. Why we consider the psychologist to have failed in these two instances may become clear from what follows below:

Example 2. For administrative reasons it was necessary for the Clinic member in this school to be replaced by another staff member whose manner of approach to teachers was much more direct, that is, he had less hesitation or difficulty in confronting a teacher with the truth as he saw it. As important as this was the fact that he could be open and direct in a manner to which it was hard to take offense—a combination of characteristics admittedly rare. After his initial weeks in the school he decided that he could not avoid confronting the two teachers with the impossible situation in the classrooms. This he did and with remarkable results. As it turned out, both teachers were agonizingly aware of their difficulties and covertly had been hoping that someone could help them, although they did not know how and from whom help could be obtained. A series of meetings were held with each teacher, the Clinic member's detailed observations of the classroom examined step by step, and the contribution of the teacher to the difficulties discussed. Within two weeks the change in these classrooms was a source of comment on the part of other teachers who had been aware of the problem and to some of whom the two teachers had come for help. It must also be said that one of the problems of these two teachers was the critical, nonhelping attitude of the principal, who had made clear that some of their classroom practices were to be discontinued. One of the achievements of the Clinic member was to encourage the teacher to take a stand with the principal on issues of classroom organization and child management. The teachers were able successfully to do this, ultimately with the result that they felt that their classrooms reflected their own conceptions and ways of doing things.[5]

[5] These two teachers had never taught before, except for some weeks of practice teaching.

Thus we see that the psychologist, like teachers, can seize on aspects of reality to justify inaction or to excuse failure. He may unjustifiably blame teachers in much the same way teachers sometimes blame children. But there is another lesson that can be drawn from these instances, and this concerns the fact that not all psychologists are equally appropriate for work in the school as we have conceptualized the role. By appropriateness we refer to characteristics and attitudes that make it possible for an individual to become part of the school, to be viewed by it as a source of help, to be able to point to situations where there is clear reason to believe that a desired change has occurred, and to be able to be aware of those situations that bring out his limitations. To make this point more clear we present below those characteristics that should ideally be possessed by the psychologist in the schools, the absence of any one of which may seriously interfere with part or all of his work (in which case the relationship with the school is terminated).

1. He must have a profound respect for the problems and responsibilities of school personnel that can withstand whatever negative feelings are aroused by inadequacy of personnel, psychological obtuseness, and rigidity of practices. The psychologist is there because he wants to understand and help, and not to give expression to his presumed superiority or critical faculties.

2. He must be one who can control his own impatience and tolerate the setting of limited goals. The frequent discrepancy between what can be done and what should be done can neither be a source of discouragement nor of inaction. The psychologist who is wedded to a way of thinking and practicing in which the goal is to help the individual achieve marked personality change is not likely to view work within the school setting as his cup of tea, an attitude that sets into motion the dynamics of the self-fulfilling prophecy.

3. It is not in conflict with what has just been said to state that he must be one who does not underestimate the capacity for change in teachers. We have been aware from our own experience that those staff members who have been most effective in helping teachers change, and sometimes very dramatically, are those who, having brought about a situation of mutual trust, can express their ideas and feelings to teachers in a forthright, unambiguous, and complete manner. It is as if, given the context of mutual trust, they operate on the assumption that straight talk, however unpleasant, will produce results, and it frequently does, to the surprise of those of us for whom confrontations are not easy.

4. He should be someone who, because of personality and/or

theoretical persuasion, can accept a situation in which he basically has no policy-making function or administrative authority. There is much that happens in a school that can cause a psychologist to want to take over in order to correct injustices, cut through paralyzing red tape, and bring about the good life. To the extent that he wittingly, or unwittingly becomes part of the power structure and struggle in a school he runs the risks of becoming a different kind of person and of being differently viewed by the teachers. In our conceptualization the psychologist is one who should become an extremely influential person in a school but not a powerful one in an administrative sense.

Earlier we stated that in approaching and working in the schools we felt a kinship to the anthropologist who is going into a foreign culture knowing that the quantity and quality of information he will obtain will in part be a function of his personality and tactics. An extremely interesting and instructive book could undoubtedly be written about "the failures of the anthropologist." The aim of what we have said in the previous pages of this chapter is to indicate that we must face squarely—indeed that it is in the nature of things—that the psychologist can be a contributing factor to limited effectiveness or outright failure.

THE TEACHER

In our experiences we have found that we have been able to work productively and harmoniously with most teachers. There are some teachers, however, with whom our efforts have met with little or no success. It is not easy to make a single generalization to account for those teacher characteristics contributing to what we would consider failure or too severe limitations in what we wanted to accomplish—or rather, what needed to be accomplished—in the classroom, but in the following paragraphs we attempt to indicate the most important and troublesome characteristics that we encountered.

There were a few teachers, usually no more than one in a school, whose level of insecurity was so strong that they could never feel comfortable having a stranger in their rooms. We would expect such a person to have inordinate difficulty in asking for help, particularly if this meant that someone would then come in to observe what was going on. Such an attitude was by no means infrequent when we first started to work in a school, but it dissipated with time. What we are describing here is the teacher in whom this attitude was of such strength as to successfully defeat us in our efforts to develop a relationship of mutual trust. There is a tendency for this type of teacher to be older than the average, although we do not regard age as an explanation; for every older teacher with whom we had an unproductive relationship there were several teachers of equal age with whom our relationship was a productive one.

We encountered some teachers whose level of psychological sophistication or "psychological-mindedness" in regard to children was so simple as to make a meaningful discussion between us an exercise in futility. When a teacher sincerely believes in and argues the position that "children are born that way," or "when you give children an inch they will take a foot because that's the way they are," or "you must never let children get too close to you"—when this type of statement *characterizes* a teacher's way of thinking, it is not surprising that our work with this teacher is not very fruitful. The fact that we encountered few of this type of teacher is less encouraging than it would seem, because it is this type of teacher who tends to ignore, exacerbate, or produce problems in her classroom.

In many instances we were able to get teachers to understand how unrealistic the expectation was that any new approach to a problem child would meet with quick success, but there were a number of situations in which, despite verbal understanding, the teacher could not follow through in a persistent and consistent manner. There were a number of different reasons for this inability. First, teachers (like everybody else) vary in their capacity to act in a manner consistent with their ideas, and they also vary in their awareness of the discrepancy between intent and action. The teacher who was unaware of the discrepancy tended to be one who became easily discouraged.[6] Second, there were some teachers whose internal resistance to change was sufficiently strong that they never got to the point of trying the new approach, despite verbal acceptance of the need to change. Third, particularly in instances of children who were seriously disturbing in the classroom, the teacher's dislike for and anger toward the child were of such proportions as to make unfeasible a consistent and persistent approach. Although we do not view future training programs as pan-

[6] What we have sometimes found helpful in our work with teachers is discussion of the perspective that teachers have in working with a child who has a reading problem, a child with whom all teachers have had some experience. With such children teachers are quite aware that changing the child's attitudes and habits in relation to reading will require time, patience, and consistency. What, we ask, justifies taking any other perspective with a child whose classroom behavior we are trying to change? Although this may enable the teacher to see the general principle, it does not, of course, ensure that it will be appropriately implemented, and it is here that training programs are deficient.

aceas, or view present ones as convenient scapegoats for current problems, we feel very strongly that the obstacle we are here discussing would be less troublesome if the teachers had a more profound grasp of the problems and principles of behavior change; a grasp that is not obtainable by reading books or listening to lectures (Sarason, Davidson, & Blatt, 1962).

These characteristics hold for a small number of teachers. A more general problem, of greater import for mental-health programs in the school, concerns the relative absence among teachers of a point of view that facilitates the development of a preventive approach to problems, be it of the primary or secondary type of prevention. Although we stressed the point that we were as interested in preventing as in ameliorating problems, teachers rarely referred children either at the point where they were uncertain about the existence of a problem or where they had some reason to believe that a problem might develop. It was part of our standard verbal approach to state that it was likely that we could be of most help to teachers and children at that point when the teacher *first* found herself thinking and puzzled about a particular child, the point at which her overt action or lack of action can be extremely significant for the child's subsequent behavior. Once we were truly part of the school and familiar with the children we could spot behavioral changes in a child that portended difficulty, and we could take up the matter with the teacher (who frequently had also noted the change). However, being in a school no more than two days a week, and finding that insufficient to follow through on the problem children already referred, we could not focus on a preventive approach to a significant degree. It may well be in a number of our schools that the teachers were aware of the limitations in our available time and referred those cases most troublesome to them. However, in a few schools, particularly suburban ones, where pressure from disturbing children was not so great and where our time was not so filled, there was no greater tendency to refer children about whom there was a question whether there was indeed a problem deserving of attention. Thinking and acting preventively are not skills much used either in or out of the school setting. That they are in short supply in the school setting must be a matter of serious concern for any comprehensive mental-health program that seriously attempts to involve the schools. Here too we have been driven to the conclusion that the skills of thinking and acting preventively, reflecting as they do a point of view about the nature, course, and significances of child behavior, must receive their foundations in the preparation of teachers to a far greater extent than is now the case. The problem is not only the teacher-in-the-school but the teacher-in-training.

We have tried to describe the difficulties we encountered in order to emphasize two points. First, we want to make clear that our work in the schools was not always easy and successful. Second, some of these difficulties could be avoided, to an undetermined extent, if the training of teachers were more appropriate to the types of problems they actually face and must deal with in their role as teacher.

THE PRINCIPAL

We anticipated that one of the more serious obstacles to our work in a school would be the principal. This anticipation was based on three considerations: our functions could be viewed by the principal as similar to some of hers; by training the principal is not prepared adequately to handle the many difficult problems that come her way; and, as a result of the first two considerations, we might expect that the principal would feel threatened by our presence because it would highlight any inadequacy, particularly if we established effective relations with teachers and children. In two schools the strength of the principals' resistance was such as to force us to decide to terminate the relationship. Interestingly enough, in both instances the principal said explicitly and heatedly, "You are doing what I am supposed to be doing." We decided to withdraw in each case when it became apparent that the principal could not tolerate our role, was extremely bothered by her lack of "formal" authority over us, and made it difficult for teachers to talk with us. Although the reactions of the principals in these two schools were unmistakable, it was our feeling that some of the principals in the other schools shared similar reactions in the early weeks of our work but did not (or could not) bring them out into the open in an unduly interfering way. In any event we were able in these other schools successfully to overcome the initial resistance of the principals and to perform our work in the way we wished. This is not to say that the course of our relationships with principals was smooth and uneventful. This was not and could not be in the nature of things because with a number of children and teachers we had worked out a course of action that required not only the approval of the principal but, in addition, a change in her policy. For example, in one school it was the policy of the principal to suspend the "unmanageable child" for several days after he had acted up in the classroom. When together with the teachers we worked out an approach that might temporarily increase rather than decrease the noise level in the classroom—and it was the noise level that bothered the principal—it was not surprising that the principal did not view our proposed efforts with enthusiasm. It was to her credit that she went along with our plan, however reluctantly or however much expecting us to fall on our faces. Fortunately we did not fall on our faces. The point is that the principal is the most important person in a school and to a significant extent can facilitate or block what we try to do. In those schools in which the principal was completely supportive there was hardly a limitation to what we could do. In other schools where this degree of support was not present—less because of oppositional tendencies and more because of a highly practiced tendency to avoid change and to fear repercussions from higher echelons—there were definite limitations to what we might think of doing in certain kinds of cases. Even here, however, we have found that as time goes on the scope of these limitations discernibly decreases.

At this point we should make clear that what we have said about principals (and about teachers as well) holds for the eight schools in which we began our work. What has to be kept clearly in mind is that our entrance into these schools was not accomplished because of a request from a principal, but rather because of an arrangement initially made with superintendents of schools. In subsequent years, as our work became known in the area, we began to receive requests from principals to have their schools affiliated with our Clinic. In the four schools we were later able to take on, the port-of-entry problem was far less vexing and difficult than in the schools in which we originally began, even though the staff members assigned to these schools had never worked in a school before. We attribute this primarily to the fact that the principals spontaneously requested our help, knew of our program, and were prepared to support it even though they knew it might require changes in practice.

THE INNER-CITY AND SUBURBAN SCHOOLS

There is not the faintest doubt in our minds that the effectiveness and scope of our work in inner-city schools were greater than in the suburban, middle-class schools. That there are more obvious problems in the inner-city schools goes without saying. Race, family disorganization, mobility, attitudes toward school, teacher morale, inadequate school facilities are only some of the major factors on which inner-city and suburban schools differ to a degree that has to be experienced in order to be appreciated.[7] On the days we were in the suburban schools we could plan what classrooms we were going to visit, when we would

[7] Part III concerns our work with a community agency devoted solely to the problems and people of the inner city. It was this agency, in fact, that made it possible for us to enter the inner-city schools. A careful reading of Part III will give the reader some appreciation of the nature of the inner-city schools as this may be gleaned from the case material of youth who were once in these schools.

have teacher conferences, or when we would be meeting with the principal or other supervisory personnel. In the inner-city schools such planning was sometimes wasteful because crisis and catastrophe could be expected to involve us in all sorts of unplanned activities. A child hitting a teacher, fights among children, destruction of property, visits by police because of suspected out-of-school transgressions on the part of some children, violent temper tantrums, stormy visits by parents who were sometimes drunk and threatening to teachers were some of the unplanned events and their consequences with which we might be greeted. This is not to say that these events were daily occurrences (although there were periods when this seemed to be the case), but rather that they happened with a frequency sufficient to extinguish in us any surprise reaction. After a time we came to view ourselves as a kind of fireman who puts out psychological fires and then tries to determine their origins.

Although we were much more needed in the inner-city than in the suburban school, and our impact on the former much greater than in the latter, it would be incorrect to conclude that the two types of schools are most concerned with basically different kinds of problems. *In both types of schools, that which causes the greatest concern to school personnel is the overtly disturbing child.* That such a child is found in great numbers in the inner-city schools should not obscure the fact that in the suburban schools it is precisely such a child who causes the greatest upset in school personnel and who receives the most attention. Although personnel in both types of schools are aware that many other children have difficulties intruding on their school performance, it is the overtly disturbing child—the child who interferes with the teacher's plans, taxes her patience and understanding, and arouses strong anger—with whom the teacher becomes personally involved to an extent not ordinarily experienced by her with less disturbing types, who may be equally disturbed. It is the disturbing child who galvanizes school personnel to think and act with a remedial intent. However understandable such a reaction may be (and it is far more understandable in the inner-city than in the suburban school), it results in or facilitates such a constricted view of problem behavior as to unduly affect the kind and amount of attention teachers and others (like ourselves) can give to the disturbed but not disturbing child. From the standpoint of the disturbed child we may say that, in terms of being helped, it pays to be disturbing.

It can be seen from the above that the greater need for our services in the inner-city schools stemmed primarily from the comparatively larger number of children who were management problems. *In terms of children whose level, rate, and efficiency of school performance seemed to be reflecting some kind of personal problem, it is our impression that the inner-city and suburban schools do not differ nearly as much as they do in frequency of management problems.* In this connection it is relevant to present data from two large suburban-type junior high schools. These data were collected in the course of a longitudinal study of the relation between anxiety and indices of intellectual and academic performance (Sarason, Hill, & Zimbardo, 1964; Hill & Sarason, in press). Relevant here are the data bearing on the following questions: during the course of the first year of junior high how many children come to the attention of school personnel for reasons of personal difficulty, overtly disturbing behavior, or inadequate school performance? Through the cooperation of these schools we were able to obtain the data presented in Table 3. It will be seen in

TABLE 3

STUDENTS WITH PROBLEMS IN JUNIOR HIGH SCHOOL:
DATA ARE BASED ON SAMPLES FROM TWO SUCCESSIVE YEARS

7th-Grade Boys (1963–4; 1964–5)

	Number in Study	% with Problems	% Interim Problems	% Guidance Problems	% Discipline Problems
School *A*	250	61	54	22	16
School *B*	312	51	44	31	7
Both	562	55	49	27	11

7th-Grade Girls (1963–4; 1964–5)

	Number in Study	% with Problems	% Interim Problems	% Guidance Problems	% Discipline Problems
School *A*	246	53	46	21	2
School *B*	301	29	22	16	0
Both	547	39	33	18	1

that table that the most frequent problem was the child who received an "interim"; that is, his school performance was considered inadequate in one or more subjects to a degree that merited a warning note to the parents. It should be noted that the average IQ in both schools was 111; there is a small Negro population; and the community has nothing resembling slums. It may, therefore, come as a surprise that out of a study population of 1109 children, 47% had come to the special attention of school personnel.[8] In the great majority of instances

[8] Presentation of these data to personnel in other junior high schools in similar communities did not occasion great surprise. There undoubtedly is variation among suburban communities as a function of practices, standards, and complete-

the problem involved a discrepancy between potential and actual performance (which usually meant failure or near-failure in courses).

We were only mildly surprised by the above findings because over the years of the longitudinal study our involvement in the elementary schools in this community left us with the strong impression that the suburban or middle-class school, however quiet and smooth in operation, contained many children whose difficulties in school learning and adjustment were not of the sort to force teachers to attend to them.

It was our opinion that the suburban schools had as much need for our services as the inner-city schools. The tendency of school personnel in inner-city and suburban schools to be less concerned or less aware of the inefficiently functioning but not disturbing child clearly served as a limitation on the range of problems brought to our attention. Although this limitation was somewhat countered as we became more and more a part of a school, we are of the strong conviction that the most effective and productive approach to the problem would be one involving changes in teacher-training programs to encourage a more discerning comprehension of what constitute danger signals in the behavior of children in school. Our experience encourages us in the belief that as teachers gain such a comprehension their effectiveness to cope independently with problems will likewise increase. This belief and hope reflects not only our experience but the knowledge that, since the number of mental health personnel will not in the foreseeable future increase in proportion to the numbers needed, the only practical approach would be one that focuses on training teachers.

A FINAL POINT

We have been, and will continue to be, involved in evaluating our work in the schools. It is our opinion, however, that in the long run the most important contribution we can hope to make is in illuminating the kinds of problems encountered in schools and the potential for help, change, and prevention that exists in that setting. We consider it unfortunate in the extreme if the reader, in disagreement with our orientation and the specifics of what we do, has failed to see the scope and seriousness of the psychological problems confronting us in the schools—a failure that can only help to maintain the gulf between the schools on the one hand and the mental-health professions on the

---

ness of records. In any event, there is little reason to doubt that the number of children whose level of academic performance is markedly below their potential (as inferred from test scores and parental background) is uncomfortably high.

other hand. How to bridge this gulf, how to maximize the utilization of processes of help and prevention, should take second place to no other problem confronting the mental-health fields, particularly in these days when these fields are emerging hesitatingly from the isolation of the clinic, hospital, and private office into a wider arena of thinking and practice. We can only hope that the weight of tradition will not unduly constrict the range of innovation and experimentation or transform the new problems and opportunities into old and familiar frameworks that, while adequate for some problems, are inadequate for the new ones.

PART III

COMMUNITY PROGRESS
INCORPORATED

Chapter 15

Community Progress Incorporated (CPI) and the Neighborhood Employment Center

The psychiatric clinic, the social-work agency, and the mental hospital are the major public facilities for dealing with those problems in living we term "mental or emotional illness." We describe here a new and different kind of facility for the amelioration of human misery and for helping people to achieve their fullest potential. This new facility is unique in that it not only offers a service to individuals who have personal and social difficulties, but it also makes an active attempt to change the social conditions that help to create the human waste.

In the chapters to follow we describe some of the programs of New Haven's Community Progress Incorporated (CPI) in an effort to show how those programs relate to the over-all mental-health problem, and to describe how staff members of the Psycho-Educational Clinic functioned as consultants to various programs within CPI. Because CPI is so new and so unfamiliar we describe some of the programs in great detail. In the present chapter a brief overview of CPI is presented so that the reader may have something of a feel for the proportions of this unparalleled effort at social engineering. We then describe the Neighborhood Employment Center (NEC), an operation basic to what CPI does. The NEC staff, its functions, and its methods of working are discussed at some length because the NEC represents a powerful alternative for servicing people who will not or cannot use traditional mental hygiene clinics or social-work agencies. In addition it has the potential to be a powerful aid for those who are receiving care in traditional settings. We discuss our consulting role in some detail because the Psycho-Educational Clinic functions through its consulting relationships in a variety of settings. We feel that a description of our experience may provide others in the mental-health professions with useful ideas about how to relate to the similar programs rapidly mush-rooming all over the country. The work crew, a key technique in helping both youth and adults, will be presented in detail for similar reasons.

Although an important aim in our presentation of this material is to indicate how we functioned in these settings, it is equally important in our minds that readers gain the kind of understanding that will allow them to recognize that it is possible—in fact, it will be necessary—to meet and deal with mental-health problems in settings quite different from those to which mental-health workers have heretofore been exposed. In the long run our particular ways of functioning in these new settings are less important than the recognition by the mental-health fields that they must look to new settings and orientations if they are to serve other than a restricted portion of a community.

CPI

On Labor Day in 1961, Mayor Richard C. Lee of New Haven, Connecticut, urged his city to launch a concerted attack on the problem of unemployment and its attendant personal misery and human waste.[1] A Mayor's Committee on Manpower Resources and Employment was appointed to develop programs in business, industry, and government designed to retrain those who needed newer skills and to open new opportunity to those who had previously been denied it. At about this same time the Ford Foundation provided a substantial grant to New Haven to establish Community Progress Incorporated (CPI). CPI, created through the combined efforts of the community council, the redevelopment agency, the board of education, and the mayor, was designed to develop and coordinate a program in human renewal on a scale equal to the physical renewal programs of the previous decade.

What is this agency like? In the words of its executive director, Mitchell Sviridoff:

CPI was designed (1) to coordinate a massive attack on the conditions which lead to and grow out of poverty; (2) to assure the comprehensiveness of

[1] Much has been written on the nature and consequence of poverty. Two recent collections of papers would give the reader a fairly comprehensive picture of different aspects of the problem. One of these is *Daedalus* (Journal of the American Academy of Arts and Sciences, 1965, which is devoted to "The Negro American." The other is "Poverty in America," a book of readings edited by Ferman, Kornbluh, and Haber (1965). The reader would also find rewarding the thoughtful and critical articles by Cahn and Cahn (1964) and Glazer (1966), both articles pointing to problems and strategies in the war on poverty.

that attack by working cooperatively with all the major institutions of the community; and (3) to raise the resources necessary to fund such an attack.

It is an agency designed to stimulate other agencies, to coordinate their efforts, and to create new programs whenever it seems necessary. It is incorporated as a nonprofit organization with a nine-man board of directors, three of whom are appointed by the mayor and one each by the community council, the United Fund, the board of education, the redevelopment agency, the Citizen's Action Commission, and Yale University. In 1965 additions were made to the Board in order to represent "the poor" directly, in keeping with the provisions of the Economic Opportunity Act of 1964.

CPI's funds come from a variety of sources, public and private. A large proportion of the funds comes from the Ford Foundation, with the remaining money coming from the Federal government under the Juvenile Delinquency Control Act, the Manpower Development and Training Act, the Housing Act, the welfare amendments to the Social Security Act, and the Economic Opportunity Act of 1964. The money is spent in two ways: CPI routes funds to other agencies to enable them to initiate programs, and funds its own programs. The arrangement for expending funds involves sprawling, interconnected relationships among CPI and other state and city agencies. Unless one is intimately associated with the program, it is difficult to keep up with the tangled threads of programs, liaisons, and relationships. Volumes of memos record inter- and intra-agency meetings to develop programs, to review programs, and to discuss and settle problems that arise. It is clear the over-all program is massive.

CPI sponsors basic programs in education, but these are established and administered by the superintendent of schools and his staff. A pre-kindergarten program, remedial reading, in-service training, after-school tutoring, summer school, Higher Horizons for curriculum enrichment, and an in-school work-study program have been supported or sponsored by CPI. An adult literacy program and a community school program involving sports, crafts, discussion groups, little theater, and other recreational programs have been developed. A CPI Neighborhood Services Office and staff are located within each of the seven community schools, and these serve as liaison among the schools, the community, and other CPI services.

The Neighborhood Services staff actively recruits residents of the neighborhoods for the various CPI programs and for the opportunities available in the employment centers, in training, and in the community school programs. The staff serves as a link and referral source to other health and welfare agencies as needed. The neighborhood staff has also encouraged the development of independent neighborhood groups and organizations to develop programs and obtain services that will benefit that neighborhood.

The origin of the Manpower program, the NECs, and the functioning of the work crews will be described in detail. In addition to the Neighborhood Employment Centers, which reflect the joint effort of CPI and the Connecticut State Employment Service, the Manpower division is responsible with the State Employment Service and the board of education for the development of training opportunities: the on-the-job training program in which jobs are solicited and employers paid a subsidy to train inner-city applicants; the work-crew program; the intermediate work-crew program in which youth are assigned individually rather than in crews and can work and be paid for 32 hours a week; and the Skill Center where remedial education and vocational training are conducted. The Manpower program is responsible for the development of jobs as necessary, for liaison with the appropriate training agencies, and for liaison with labor unions to be sure that programs developed are consistent with union policies and not in conflict with private industry. A labor consultant, in close touch with the various unions and councils of unions, is retained.

A Concerted-Services Program, located in a low-income housing project and designed to provide comprehensive medical, social, and rehabilitative services has been developed. Independently funded, the program is closely tied in with CPI employment programs. A new Unified Social-Services Program has been developed to provide more professional counseling and better liasion with other agencies. The program operates closely with the Neighborhood Services and Employment staffs and, in fact, is housed with them.

Another major CPI program, just beginning at this writing, is a training institute. Developed at the request of those concerned with antipoverty programs in Washington, the training institute will serve to prepare workers from the New England area to operate in CPI-like programs. Actually, CPI has been serving for some time such a training function in that visitors from all over constantly come to see CPI programs in operation.

This brief overview of programs may give something of the feeling for the activity, the buzzing, the growth, the influence, and the impact of CPI. When we consider that CPI was first chartered in April, 1962, its development is indeed staggering.

THE NEIGHBORHOOD EMPLOYMENT CENTER

The Neighborhood Employment Center (NEC) grew out of one of the early CPI programs. Using additional funds available through the Manpower Defense Training Act (MDTA), CPI joined the Mayor's Committee on Manpower Resources and Employment to create an important training opportunity. The Connecticut State Employment Service, in partnership with the Mayor's Committee and CPI, had been referring candidates for the new training programs. However, it quickly became evident that a large number of the people who would be eligible for training simply did not visit or view the State Employment Service as a place where significant opportunities might be found. Many thought of the State Employment Service office as the "unemployment office," where they went to receive a check or to obtain day work. CPI's Neighborhood Service Centers found it necessary actively to recruit candidates for the programs. The recruited candidates were strongly motivated to enter the training programs and they did well as a group, but attitudes and traditions were such that many people from inner-city neighborhoods would not use the facilities of the State Employment Service. Recognizing the problem, the State Employment Service cooperated with CPI in establishing three Neighborhood Employment Centers (NEC) in three separate inner-city neighborhoods when funds for a youth-employment program became available through the Office of Manpower and Training (OMAT) and the Federal Juvenile Delinquency Control Act. Three such centers were established by October, 1963, to serve the needs of youth from 16 to 21. Shortly after, the centers were also ready to work with adults.

WHY AN EMPLOYMENT CENTER?

On a national level the over-all unemployment rate for out-of-school youngsters between the ages of 16 and 24 has been between 11–12% since 1959. A sample taken in 1963 indicated that one-third of all high-school dropouts between 16 and 21 had left school by the age of 16. Within this group unemployment among nonwhites was 25.8%, for whites, 18.6%. Although the teenage unemployment rate is the highest of any age group in the labor force, unemployment is particularly high among those with less than a high-school education. These youngsters have an unemployment rate close to double that of high-school graduates (Freedman, 1965).

The underlying reasons for the high rate of unemployment among young people are generally viewed in the context of supply and demand factors that characterize the vocational setting. These teenagers, for example, are often new entrants to the labor force and, therefore, particularly vulnerable to layoffs due to their lack of seniority, inexperience, and unfamiliarity with the ways of the job market. Similarly, since most of them work in lower-skilled occupations, their earning potential and job security are unstable. So much for unemployment on a national scale. What should be kept in mind is the fact that the national statistics are averages based on regional differences and a pooling of youngsters whose parents belong to both the upper and lower socioeconomic classes.

When we turn to the unemployment statistics concerning youngsters from the inner-city families of New Haven the picture becomes even more frightening, in terms of the percentages involved as well as the long-range implications of the rates of unemployment. The latest report (Community Progress, Inc., 1964) on the rate of unemployment among inner-city youngsters between the ages of 16 and 21 comes to the following conclusion:

> Of those out of school and seeking employment or training, the unemployment rate is about 41%. Considering the fact that those who could not be contacted were all of poorer economic, educational, and social status, the unemployment rate could be as high as 55%. Considering only those employed and unemployed, the unemployment rate as measured is 53%, but could be as high as 65%.

Although the variables accounting for this staggering rate of unemployment are many and varied, one fact remains clear: by being essentially unemployable these youths have begun their own generation's participation in that seemingly endless cycle of poverty that characterizes so many inner-city families. These youngsters, because they are both unemployed and no longer within the school setting, are in a position to become known to, and the responsibility of, various city and state welfare agencies, law enforcement institutions, and private organizations, and to become the concern of these agencies on what has historically come to be a relatively long-term basis. It is in this manner that poverty tends to be handed down as a sort of pitiful legacy from parents to children, from generation to generation.

The unemployed adolescent remains unemployed for sufficient reasons. He usually has no skills to sell. The adolescent who has no job is likely to be deficient in formal education. He reads poorly, he writes with great difficulty, and he can handle only rudimentary arithmetic.

He may have little or no idea of how to fill out an application form or how to conduct himself in an interview. Standard paper-and-pencil ability tests may bar him at once from consideration. He has a long history of doing poorly with such tests in school. Frequently his aspirations for position or for money far outweigh his present worth on the job market.

His personal appearance and his manner may lead an employer to think of him as a "hood" whether or not he has had run-ins with the law. He may have an unrealistic appreciation of what to expect from a job or what an employer expects from him. Even if he can find a job, he may not hold it because of his attitudes about working. He may see a boss as another authority figure, ready to push him around. He may not really comprehend the demands that he should come to work every day on time, that he should work all day, and that he should demonstrate interest and willingness to work and to learn. He may be too shy to ask for criticism himself and the employer may be reluctant to offer constructive criticism. It is frequently easier for an employer to let an employee go than to risk unpleasantness by cautioning or criticizing a new employee, particularly if the new employee is of a different racial or ethnic background from the employer.

Sometimes a more capable individual will not reach out to fulfill personal potential. A view of himself as inferior or incapable, or a sense of hopelessness about the future, is an effective internal restriction against reaching for something more. An applicant may be short-sighted and ask for any job at all, right now, rather than look ahead. That the job is unsuitable or that it would not prepare him for anything else is frequently not considered.

From his previous experience with schools he may have deep misgivings about his ability to learn. He may have learned to expect hostility and rejection from teachers and employers. Given his personal expectation of failure, and his feeling that teachers and bosses will cause him further pain, an initial lack of enthusiasm for any further formal training is understandable.

In many poverty-stricken families there are repeated living crises. The father may not be present or he may be in and out of the house. The father may be unemployed himself, and in many instances may provide a poor model for the son. Crowded, inadequate living quarters may dampen spirits while exposing the child to open displays of sex, aggression, and drunkenness. Frequent moves may prevent any sense of belonging to the neighborhood, and ties to other people may be weakened. Experience with welfare workers and chronic dependence on relief may make for a loss of personal dignity and difficulty in relating to the helping agencies of the community. The sense of resentment, frustration, helplessness, and hopelessness may combine into a distinct feeling of alienation from the larger world, and a restriction of movement and thought to narrow but familiar pathways.

In view of the problems and attitudes of many of the potential applicants, it was not enough to open an office and expect that applicants seeking opportunity would walk in. CPI had to be ready to go out and recruit applicants as necessary. Workers knew they had to go out into the streets and into people's homes to bring them into the office. Once in the office the necessary steps of application, evaluation, referral, placement, and follow-up had to be handled in such a fashion that applicants developed trust in the NEC. Inner-city applicants tend to view any official body as a set of frustrating rules, administered by impersonal, bored, officious drones who force them to wait interminably for no good reason. It was necessary to make the screening and evaluation steps as simple and as understandable as possible. Given the impatience and shaky self-esteem of many of the applicants, the process of evaluation had to be presented in such a fashion that applicants understood it to be in their own interest. Staff had to deal sensitively with sensitive issues. Criminal records, personal and family problems, legal entanglements, complicated relationships with welfare agencies, and intimate medical histories are not discussed easily with strangers who may be seen as representatives of hostile or indifferent authority. Condescending attitudes, a lack of sympathetic appreciation of the applicant's position, or rigid adherence to red tape could easily drive applicants away. Even after an applicant completed the evaluation, methods had to be developed to help applicants enter and stay in the various programs.

The handling of the total application process was clearly critical for the success of the whole operation. If NEC was to develop a reputation as a place to receive real help, the staff had to be able to relate to applicants with difficult problems humanely and effectively. It is clear that the demands on the human relations skills of the NEC have been indeed great. The remainder of this chapter deals with some of those demands, and attempts to describe the ways in which members of the NEC function in relation to the demands of the situation.

STAFF AND ORGANIZATION OF THE NEC

The NEC staff has none of the professional personnel found in mental-health or family-service agencies. There are no psychiatrists, clinical psychologists, or trained case workers. The decision to staff

NEC with nonclinical personnel was in part deliberate and in part forced on CPI. Attempts were made to hire professional workers to participate in the NEC. However, clinically trained personnel were not readily available. There certainly was no pool of interested professionals in the immediate area. Although CPI executives extended the search for people and interviewed numerous candidates at professional meetings, it was difficult to interest mental-health professionals in an unorthodox and possibly temporary setting. Because it was clear even at that time that many of the inner-city population would have minimal personal assets of the kind that would make them "good cases for therapy," mental-health professionals were leery of the situation. They tended to view the job as impossible because the problems of poor people are chronic, and the poor are known to be relatively nonverbal and unmotivated to change. Even those mental-health professionals who expressed an interest seemed concerned with instituting a familiar form of practice. Although trained case workers were interviewed for the job of coordinator, they were not hired because CPI executives felt that they were too insistent on imposing a case-work agency mold on the NEC. Case workers, for example, expressed considerable concern that the NEC would not have a proper supervisory structure.

CPI executives felt it was necessary to resist professionalization, with its emphasis on method, technique, and formal training, if they were to strike out in new directions. The evidence suggested that traditional methods were not adequate to handling the problems of the inner city, and there was no reason to believe that traditional methods would be effective in this new setting. They anticipated the distinct danger that the professional would attempt to turn the new into the familiar, subverting the spirit of the new. Yet there was need for people trained in vocational areas who were effective in interpersonal relationships.

The staff for each NEC now consists of a coordinator, two vocational counselors, two placement interviewers, and three neighborhood workers. The three NEC's are under the general direction of the CPI director of manpower. The coordinator (who also has responsibility for a CPI Neighborhood Service Center located in a community school building in that geographic area) is the over-all supervisor for the NEC. Each office also has an administrative head, either the vocational counselor or the placement interviewer, who is responsible for the day-by-day operation of the office. Though the coordinators and neighborhood workers are CPI employees, they are assigned to the Neighborhood Services Division. The counselors belong to the Manpower

Division. The placement interviewers are actually employees of the Connecticut State Employment Service assigned full-time to the NEC's. The Employment Service personnel were placed in the NEC offices to provide liaison with the State Employment Service and to learn the operation of the NEC for the time when the State Employment Service would assume full responsibility for such centers.

In each center, in a relatively brief period of time, these individuals with diverse backgrounds and loyalties and diverse administrative lines came to identify with the NEC as a unit and were welded into a working team. That such a team developed is a tribute to the organizational skills of the CPI executives, to the interpersonal and leadership skills of the coordinators, and to the flexibility and spirit of the people themselves.

THE COORDINATOR

The coordinator is the most highly trained member of the NEC team. Two of the coordinators were experienced, professionally trained social workers with backgrounds in community organization and settlement-house work. A third had background as a recreation and group worker. The coordinators were to lead, advise, consult, supervise, and help select and train personnel for the centers. They were not to have direct contact with clients. The coordinators originally represented the centers in communication and negotiation with CPI central headquarters and with other community facilities such as clinics, hospitals, schools, and social agencies. Later other staff members took over these functions. The coordinators generally provided the direct leadership in the day-to-day operation of the NEC in its early stages.[2]

THE VOCATIONAL COUNSELOR

At the beginning of the NEC, the hope was to use vocational counselors trained in testing, interviewing, and guidance. Some of the vocational counselors who were hired actually did have appropriate educational backgrounds, including the M.A. degree in counseling or guidance. However, the backgrounds of other counselors varied. One

[2] In subsequent pages it will become clear that the NEC deals with as full a range of psychopathological phenomena as can be found in any psychiatric clinic, or in any case-work oriented social agency. In light of this fact, it is instructive to note that none of the coordinators, vocational counselors, or neighborhood workers would have qualified to work in such clinics or agencies to handle clinical problems.

was a former school teacher working toward the M.A. in guidance. Another was a college graduate with varied employment experience who had been a social worker with the Welfare Department and a probation worker with the Department of Corrections. Another was a college graduate with a psychology major who had some background in personnel work. Still another had served as a counselor with a YMCA program. Few had any degree of specific and supervised training in working with people with personal problems.

The vocational counselor participates in the process by evaluating an applicant's experience and interest in light of his background. He arranges for aptitude testing and interprets the results of tests to the applicant. He also makes recommendations to the staff for training or placement. The counselor offers continued interviews, as necessary, to promote job or training adjustment or to advise applicants about further opportunities or employment upgrading.

The counselor deals with a variety of client problems and helps his client arrive at some vital decisions about his life. An employment problem may involve highly sensitive areas, and a high degree of interviewing skill and tact is necessary to maintain a good working relationship with the client.

Example 1. A client who was born with an additional, rudimentary finger came for services. The client appeared somewhat uneasy about her hand, tending to hide it. She was referred to the Bureau of Vocational Rehabilitation (BVR) for evaluation. The Bureau found she was without serious handicap and that the condition was not readily correctible by surgery. The NEC staff as a whole had been inclined to place the girl in a relatively isolated position where she would not have to interact with other people and be embarrassed. However, the counselor scheduled an additional interview with the client, and discussed the client's feelings about her hand with her. The counselor had the basis in the BVR report for offering the client considerable reassurance that she was not handicapped. In further discussion the client revealed she felt somewhat uneasy about her hand but not so much that she was unwilling to work closely with others. Having discussed the issue with the client, the counselor was able to recommend a clerical position in a public library.

Example 2. A client coming for a job revealed she was rather depressed, agitated, and had suicidal thoughts. She was quite ambivalent about referral to a mental-hygiene clinic, but came to see the counselor for a number of interviews in which she ventilated her feelings and used the counselor as a source of support. The counselor was finally able to persuade her to seek clinic attention, although it was clear he had been an important source of help to her over a period of several weeks.

Example 3. A client had been in and out of the office over a period of months seeking a job. He was sent out for a number of positions but either did not keep the position or did not even go to get it. A neighborhood worker had maintained contact with him through the whole time and had continued to try to help him although the client failed each time. The client was finally sent for an interview with the counselor. The counselor used the interview to confront the client with his self-defeating behavior and was able to help him plan for a more permanent training position. The confrontation with the client centered around the client's apathetic attitude, aimless seeking, and poor personal appearance.

Example 4. A client with a history of several arrests for homosexual activity was seeking placement. He had marked effeminate mannerisms and was a suspected transvestite, but one of his important liabilities was his sloppy personal appearance. He appeared in the office unkempt, clothes unpressed, and shirt open. The counselor's job began by discussing his personal appearance, stressing that his effeminate manner was not so much a handicap in obtaining employment as his personal sloppiness. Further interviews revealed that the man did not appear for job interviews dressed as he did for his NEC appointments. However, he did reveal he was reluctant about revealing his arrests to employers. He denied any arrests when filling out application forms, even though some employers might have had means of checking his records. As he talked he revealed a great deal of his life and fantasies as a transvestite. The counselor's task was one of keeping himself and the client focused on his assets and liabilities as an employee while not expressing criticism or disapproval of the client as a human being. The counselor attempted to advise him about his manner of taking an interview and of the risks he ran in falsifying applications, while at the same time he explored vocational interests and training possibilities with him.

The examples make it clear that vocational counselors in an employment setting are frequently called on to help people with problems of deep personal and emotional significance. The problems are not very different from those that might be seen in an outpatient psychiatric clinic or in a family-service agency, except that most of these clients would not seek (and had not sought) help in another setting. In each instance, because of his strategic location, the counselor had the opportunity to intervene in some significant aspect of the client's life. The NEC counselor is required to use himself to promote changes in behavior and in attitude, much as he would in a therapeutic or a casework relationship. The involvement of counselor with client and the client with the Center and the process of obtaining employment, provides a situation in which significant personal problems are highlighted.

THE PLACEMENT INTERVIEWER

The placement interviewer is an employee of the State Employment Service assigned to the NEC. It is the function of the employment interviewer to review the client's work experience, to ascertain the specific skills and training he has had, to decide on the specific position to which an applicant is to be referred, and to handle the details of placement. Placement interviewers are required to have a minimum of two years of college training and some background in business or industry. They must know the labor market, the requirements for specific jobs, and personnel practices, as well as employers and working conditions in various industries.

In addition the placement interviewers were selected for the project on the basis of their personal reputation for being able to work with inner-city applicants. They also provide the concrete evidence of liaison and partnership between the State Employment Service and CPI. If the State Employment Service should decide to continue to expand the NEC concept, trained employees would be available to start additional offices.

The placement interviewer shares in dealing with the problems the clients bring in seeking employment. He must have sufficiently skilled interviewing techniques to determine work experience exactly. He must discover relevant information about an applicant, including personal habits and information about criminal records when necessary, but he may not conduct an inquisition. In arranging for details of placement he may offer advice about personal appearance, or about the impression the applicant makes when he is being interviewed. Occasionally the placement interviewer or the counselor will use a role-playing technique to prepare a client for the employment interview. If a client is rejected for a job he may return to the placement interviewer for information as to why he did not get the job. The interviewer must select a position for the client, but must tread a fine line between underestimating a client because of his particular work history and overestimating him because of the desire to fill an attractive position with a client who does not have the usual background for the job.

In many respects the placement interviewer is in a critical position in the NEC. He is the staff member who finally matches the applicant with the appropriate job opening. By his attitudes toward his clients, and by his approach to the employer, the placement interviewer can make or break any placement. If he reads the employer's job specifications too literally or too rigidly he will demand a great deal before he suggests a given job for an applicant. Similarly, he may look too literally at an applicant's credentials in terms of job history or test scores and fail to see potential in the applicant. He may have had long-standing contacts with particular employers or with personnel people. Over the years employers may have come to respect the placement interviewer's judgment about applicants, and the interviewer may be able to convince an employer to take an employee who does not meet the specific requirements the employer has stated in the job description. The placement interviewer, if sold on an applicant, may attempt to get employers to relax some job specifications that do not seem critical for a position. By his enthusiasm and aggressive imagination he may help to break down barriers to employment and at the same time convey a sense of support to the applicant. If he should act in opposite fashion, emphasizing an applicant's liabilities and the difficulty in getting a job for someone without skills, the placement interviewer may inadvertently contribute to the applicant's sense of hostility or defeat.

Example 5. A client who had fairly good credentials kept insisting on a job that paid somewhat more than he could reasonably expect to receive. The placement interviewer sent him out for several jobs, but each time he did not get the position. Feedback from the personnel offices and reports from the client indicated that he was handling the interviews in a way calculated to antagonize the personnel people who saw him. The placement interviewer then confronted the client with the information about how he was handling interviews and insisted that he would not be sent out for any further positions until he had discussed his difficulty with the counselor.

Example 6. A client who had a history of arrests for drug addiction was desperately seeking a job. He was living alone, had no money, and seemed suspicious and distant. The placement interviewer knew of his history, but it was not clear that the client knew this information was available. The interviewer felt unable to send a man with a record out on a job without letting the employer know of his history; on the other hand, the client seemed desperate and needed concrete help at once. The placement interviewer felt he would not return if his record was brought up or if he was pressed for a psychiatric referral. The interviewer's uncertainty may have been conveyed to the applicant, because he did not return. Follow-up interview by a neighborhood worker revealed that the client was working part-time, and that he was rather isolated and could not work closely with others. The applicant revealed his feeling that the NEC was against him, and it became the placement interviewer's job to deal with these feelings when the applicant was called in to see the interviewer a few days later. The placement interviewer needed considerable courage and sensitivity to explain that the applicant could not be sent out on a job without revealing his record to an employer.

Clearly the position of placement interviewer involves far more than simply arranging for placement in a suitable position. The interviewer must work with and around the applicant's personal idiosyncrasies as much as any other staff member.

A most interesting position, partly because it is so different, is that of the neighborhood worker. The neighborhood worker is an untrained person who comes from the neighborhood he serves or who has been brought up in similar areas. It is the neighborhood worker's job to gain rapport with the applicant and to tell him about the various opportunities available through the NEC. The process of gaining rapport may take the worker out into the street, into the applicant's home, or into the local pool hall in order to make a contact. To some extent then, the neighborhood worker recruits applicants. He takes a complete history and arranges for the applicant to take aptitude and ability tests. It is his job to explain the meaning and the importance of the tests, but not to interpret the results. He arranges for further appointments and contacts the school or the home for further information as needed. He records whatever impressions he has of the applicant as part of the record. It is also his job to follow up the applicant to see that he keeps future appointments. If the applicant fails to keep appointments, the neighborhood worker contacts him to find out why and to urge him to come in again. The neighborhood worker is present to introduce the applicant to other members of the staff and when necessary he accompanies the applicant to interviews with employers. Even after an applicant has been placed, the neighborhood worker may be assigned to follow him up, to maintain contact and interest. He also presents cases to the staff disposition conference and participates in the decisions arrived at in conference.

The position clearly has a great deal of responsibility for which we traditionally demand intensive training. None of the neighborhood workers has any specialized training for the position, and formal in-service training is minimal. Coordinators provide supervision, but whatever effectiveness the neighborhood worker possesses comes from his personal style in relating to others.

In the absence of training it is clear that the selection of the neighborhood worker is a crucial factor. Generalizations are difficult to draw. According to one coordinator who has been successful in selecting workers: "It's either right or wrong. There never is any question about neighborhood workers when you meet the person. There is nothing you can go on at all." Most of the workers are attractive, likable people. The women tend to be lively and vivacious. The men are generally outgoing, warm, and friendly, but their styles vary. The older men are quiet, solid, independent, and sensible. The younger men tend to be more active and lively. Almost all give an impression of stability. All seem to be earthy people, free of any obvious prudery or noticeable inhibition of aggressiveness. Most are surprisingly articulate and sensitive. As a group they seem to have a great deal of "psychological-mindedness." There is recognition of behavior that does not make sense, and an eagerness to have rational explanations for what is observed.

Example 7. An adult, female Negro with a rather stable background had refused to accept a fairly well-paying and prestigeful position, and instead took a sales position that paid substantially less. She turned down the job because she felt the position or the company could not be any good if they would hire her. The neighborhood worker presenting the case was genuinely puzzled by her action. He asked the consultant in a conference, "Now what would make a woman do something like that?"

The neighborhood worker and others in the office knew the family. Some questions brought out the fact that the woman's older sister was a very well-paid, well-known professional, and that the younger sister had always been overshadowed by the other. Given this information, the consultant suggested that the woman may have been responding to her lifelong experience of being second to her sister, and felt she was inadequate. It was pointed out that her feelings about herself were limiting her ability to make the most of herself. The concept was illustrated by Groucho Marx's well-known line, "I wouldn't belong to any club that would have me as a member." After this discussion, the group was willing to recommend that the woman consider referral for continued counseling even though their view of her was as a stable, effective person.

The neighborhood workers come from a variety of backgrounds. One was known in his neighborhood as a respected civic leader. One had had experience in politics and had been a committeeman. A woman had originally been hired as a secretary. Still another was a man known to the coordinator through business contacts the man had had with the coordinator's wife. Another was related to a well-known business family in that area. At least two of the younger people had actually come to the NEC looking for jobs for themselves. Several of the workers have had a rather variegated work history. One had been "knocking around from job to job" and had come in "cold and hungry" looking for anything at all. Another had worked at all sorts of odd jobs from age nine onward. Still another had spent two years in the service and had various sales positions. Another man had had a rather checkered career, but most recently had held a civil service position. One man was a well-known local athlete who had received a tryout with a major professional team.

Formal educational backgrounds also vary widely. A few have had less than a high-school education. Several more have completed high school, and others have had some further study. Several workers are attending college at night to work toward a degree. The necessity for preparing written reports is one limiting factor in selecting neighborhood workers, and the workers themselves sometimes express some concern about the adequacy of their written work. However, the atmosphere in many of the offices is such that the workers feel free to call on those members of the staff with more formal education for help as necessary.

The neighborhood workers have experienced the problems the applicants face in their own lives. The following material is taken from a tape-recorded discussion with the staff of one of the NEC's. The first excerpt is from a young man of Italian background, while the next two excerpts are from two Negroes. Not all of the employees have come from the same backgrounds, or have had the same experiences, but it is clear that most can tell similar stories. These particular workers are highly articulate. In the first quotation, the neighborhood worker offers us his recollection of "street-corner society" and his knowledge and experiences with the way of life of the adolescent "tough guy." He describes his experiences in a matter-of-fact way, without apology, and perhaps even with a little wistfulness. He does not seem far away from his life as an adolescent.

I graduated from high school, went to college for a year and came in the office again as an applicant around last April or so; bouncing around from one job to another, hanging in and out of school, sort of, you know, broke and hungry. And I came in the office and met Al. He interviewed me in the car on the way down. He was taking an applicant downtown for his work-crew job, and he interviewed me and I came back and went through the process.

I remember you told me once you were brought up right in the immediate area.

Well, actually I lived in the H. area. But I was familiar with G. Avenue. This was an enemy section when I was a kid. And it was attacked every other night or so, in between their attacks on us.

You had a schedule?

Ya, we used to give each other a break. Just so we wouldn't pass each other in the car on the way out and to give us something to do. When I was hanging around the corners you didn't go into the G. Avenue section unless you had someone from your section there. In other words, there was sort of an imaginary boundary line that separated the two sections. Oh, then there was D. Avenue too, which wasn't too prominent at the time when I hung around the corner. It was sort of quiet and they were sort of afraid of us, but the two main groups were G. Avenue and the H. section, which was the Guinea-green. You wouldn't think of going to G. Avenue by yourself. You wouldn't go in with under six guys. When I was hanging around C. Avenue and around there, you didn't know too much about G. Avenue. I wouldn't know the streets I do now and there was no association. You might go in on a Friday night to a dance in that section.

You knew the big streets?

Right, this was it, you never knew the small streets and where to find them. You just had no association whatsoever—you were cut off. And usually your section was designated as a block, and you called it the block, and you stayed on the block. And there were small groups where you hung around, in the section of the city where you hung around, like you were from C. Avenue or you were from D. Avenue or Five Corners and there were hundreds of different groups, but the thing was all these groups in the H. Section would band together if there was ever any trouble at G. Avenue. It was the same way on R. Street, K. Street, or J. Street. They were all separate gangs that would all band together against a common enemy. And the whole city was sort of broken up this way. The funny thing is a lot of the friends I've made or hang around with say in the past three or four years have all been guys from other sections. In other words, this is what I mean by the groups being gone and everyone sort of associates with everybody else now; and there's sort of that feeling that when I was a kid and hung around the corners I hated you, and might have broken this guy's head. But now that you're all friends, all go out together . . . that's because it's all broken up and there's no more gangs now.

In the next excerpt a young Negro neighborhood worker describes his early life, his experience in the armed services, and his previous work experience. He speaks in a highly articulate way about his life, with feeling and with just a touch of bitter humor in describing his service experiences. His previous work history and his work with CPI demonstrate his high degree of competence.

Oh, boy, I really don't know where to start. I should start when I first moved into town. I moved from upstate when I was about four years old and we moved down to the corner of E. Street and G. Street. There used to be a house across the street from the Town Building that was so rat- and roach-infested we couldn't stand it anymore. Then we moved from E. Street to P. Street. It was a very poor type of housing; cold-water railroad-type flat. There were four rooms, eight of us to occupy the four rooms. Six kids sleep in one room and Mom and Dad occupied the other. And of course we had a living room and the kitchen which we were seldom in. We lived on the fourth floor and our play yard was the street or the nearest corner we could find. And we carried bananas for extra money. This was in the banana kingdom. I carried bananas for extra money. I started carrying bananas when I was about nine years old.

When you talk about bananas, you're talking about real bananas?

Real bananas I'm talking about. . . . We carried the bananas with the live tarantulas and the green snakes with the brown stripes down their backs. They weighed 75 to 80 pounds per bunch and you got about a penny per bunch for carrying them. We used to unload trailer truck after trailer truck from say about 3:30 in the afternoon to about 10 or 11 o'clock at night just to have money to go back and forth to the movies or to buy a pair of clothes that my mother and father couldn't afford out of regular house money.[3] The type house that we had to live in and the amount we had to pay for it was really phenomenal. We had to pay, I think it was $115.00 a month for this four-room apartment, on the third floor, cold water flat, with bathroom facilities that were really atrocious. We had a private bathroom that had just a commode. That was it. As far as taking a bath, I didn't know anything about taking a bath until I went to the Boy's Club on J. Street. We always had to stand up at the kitchen sink with perhaps a 15-gallon, not 15-gallon, five-gallon porcelanized tub and wash off in that. This was our bathtub. I didn't know what a shower was until perhaps I was about 12 years old. I became a member of the . . . what's the name . . . the G. Boy's Club.

I've done everything from selling newspapers to working with a tinsmith, to shining shoes, to washing windows, from working on cars to even stealing, when I was a little boy, to get along. I've done a little bit of everything.

We had to carry oil from the gas station that was perhaps three blocks from where we lived. We used to have to carry a five-gallon can of oil each and every day. If my brother didn't do it, it was then always forced on me, because maybe he had to go to work to help support the family bills and what not. And I'll never forget the thing I hated. . . .

What was this oil for?

This oil was for heating the house. The thing I hated most was going to school the next day after carrying this oil home. See, perhaps five gallons of oil would last about a day and a half and then that night coming from school you had to get more oil. What I hated most was going to school with oil smell on my clothes. And this is something, kerosene, I don't care how much you wash your clothes and wash your clothes, you don't get the smell off. I've never been afraid of any hard work and doing anything whether it was carrying bananas or helping the fellow who occupied the first floor in his tinsmith shop. As far as doing any sheetmetal work, when I was seven years old I used to go down to A. & Son, who was the fellow that owned this establishment. And I

---

[3] It puts this material into sobering perspective when we realize these events took place in the 1950s.

used to help him make leaders and gutters for roof leaks and stuff. And then when his help didn't show up on Saturday morning after perhaps going out on a binge the night before, I used to go out on the roofs and perhaps help him anchor the leaders and hand him up the gutters. I used to make between $10.00 to $25.00 a week with my paper route and shoe-shine and carrying bananas and this sort of thing. So as far as work background, I've really had it. I can remember my father's first car was a 1937 Ford, four-door sedan. Somebody poured sugar in the gas tank and we had to rip it apart and put it back together again. That's where I got my interest in cars. And as far as schooling is concerned I attended C. School, and I went to B. School which no longer exists. And I went to H. Junior High School. And then from junior high I went to the high school for about six months or so. Then we moved to one of the suburban areas. This was a little bit better housing. We had three rooms on the first floor and the attic had one continuous room. Actually it was a three-room house with a converted attic. All the kids slept in the attic with partitions made out of unpainted wallboard. At the time my two older sisters were in the process of getting married. And this meant, glory hallelujah, more room and all this sort of stuff. So we shipped them out. Then my brother decided that he wanted to move out and get his own apartment, and at the time my mother took sick and she had some sort of kidney ailment. My brother didn't really get a chance to get into his own apartment. He had to stay there and I was in my junior year of high school and it was either one of two things: it was either stay in school, forget about my mother, and you know, let my father continue working or else let him stay home and be the nurse that he couldn't afford to pay for, and quit school and get a job to pay the $113.00 a month for rent and buy the coke that supplied the heat. This was carried on for a period of eight months or so by my brother and myself. Then after my mother passed away we moved again about three-fourths of a mile away. My father had decided that he had had it. He brought up his kids and everyone was old enough to care for themselves. I was 20 years old at the time. I wanted to get married, but I decided that I wanted to go into the service, this is what happened.

You dropped out of high school?

Ya, I dropped out of high school and I was working for about eight or nine months or so, then I decided I was going to go into the service. And I did. I stayed for the great length of about three months or so. I took my high school equivalence test, and shipped out to an air force base. And I was there about two or three weeks or so and I got mixed up with a group from Georgia. There were only two Negroes in the complete crowd. I had been in the Civil Air Patrol when I was a kid and of course with a stripe. Actually as far as my training was concerned the stripe didn't mean anything, but after I got out that meant instead of being an airman third class I was made airman second. I don't know whether the fellows took this as a slap in the face because I was Negro, I was black; I don't know exactly what it was. But they put me in charge of the barracks, I was barracks chief over seven or eight guys. I knew this other fellow from New York. We had buddied around while we were in the service. I figured this is a pretty hard to beat guy and I figured this is the guy to back me up if I needed some assistance. So I made him my assistant barracks chief and we earned honorary flight for two weeks in a row. Honorary flight gets a three-day pass instead of just a 12-hour pass which means that we can go into town, we could just about do anything we wanted. So when I was trying to get these fellows squared away for their pass they would paperclip my uniform, you know they had the gig system at the time. They would paper-clip my uniforms, they would turn my foot-locker upside down. You know, just things that really break it off. So the next thing I knew I was seeing a head shrinker, this is what they called him at the base, you know. So anyway, I went to see the head shrinker and he, you know, he examined me, and he asked me what kind of problems I was having. As far as I knew I wasn't having any problems. The night I got back from this head shrinker the guys really started breaking it off, we were going to have a GI party and they really behaved very hostile. They started calling me, you know, "you black bastard, who gives you the authority to tell me what to do." It got so bad, the only way to defend my-self against these guys was to make a swagger stick out of a piece of ½" steel, and challenge any and everybody in the barracks. Me, I'm a small guy. I don't make trouble with anybody and I took this bar, this fellow that was my assist-ant took pictures in case anything came up you know to serve as evidence as to what was going on. I had to sleep with this thing beside me every night, this little piece of cold steel. At night my light would still be burning. Of course, I would be dead scared to turn this light off for fear someone would come in with either a razor blade or a switchblade and whatever they could get and shove it in your gills. So I would sleep for six hours and my buddy would come in and sleep for six hours. We kept continuous guard. We never had a barracks guard. We were the barracks guard so that they could sleep and not have to worry about having to pull guard duty. We always pulled the guard duty because we knew if we both went to sleep at the time it would mean one of us wouldn't wake up the next morning. So then they gave me an honorable dis-charge on the condition I wasn't able to adjust to the military way of life. After four years I could appeal this, and so I said forget it, I won't appeal it.

After I got out of the service I got married. I moved to S. Avenue where I stayed for about a year. I had the apartment set up and this fellow that owned the house said I'm sorry but you have to move because I'm going to make a restaurant out of it. I had to put all my furniture in storage, and move in with my mother-in-law. During this time I had been working on cars. I started out as a car-wash boy. I worked from car-wash boy into grease monkey, from grease monkey to mechanic's helper, from mechanic's helper into a full mechanic, from a full mechanic to a unit repairman, from a unit repairman into a new-car make-ready foreman, and from a new-car make-ready foreman I moved into the used-car service department and a mechanic again. Then I moved to the used-car service manager. I left to go to a subsidiary of the company where I was a service manager for a period of about four months. They decided they were going to close up the shop so I moved back in the capacity I had before I left. I tried to play hero and lift up a Volkswagen engine into a car by myself where I pulled a blood vessel from my kidney, and then there was a happy day with CPI.

How did you get over to CPI?

Well I lived next door to P.B., who is a work-crew foreman. He said if I was looking for a job perhaps you could go for some job training and get into another field. They have an office that might be of help to you. They spoke to me and told me some things that were going on and told me the sort of things that they were looking for in a neighborhood worker. The different qualities that they were looking for in a neighborhood worker. Someone who perhaps lived in this area, someone that knew the problems of the people in this area. A general all-round man or woman. Someone that had a little compassion for people. Someone that had a little feeling for people, someone who would be able to say, "Well look, this is the way I grew up too. I know some of the things you're going through. Let's work together. If we work together maybe we can help you out. You know, I've made it, here's your chance to make it too. Perhaps with a little more schooling or a little more training . . ." And here I am now.

The next man, a Negro of about 40, is not a neighborhood worker but a vocational counselor. He had a college degree, but had no specialized training in either vocational counseling or in personal counseling. Before he came to CPI he worked as a social worker and did receive some in-service training in the welfare and the probation departments. In reading his job history, it should be remembered that this man was a veteran, an athlete, holder of a scholarship to college, and that he is talking about the prosperous period immediately following the Second World War. He is not talking about the depression of the 1930's. The transcript unfortunately does not give the full flavor of his narrative. On tape his story comes through with a dry humor and superb timing. His experiences with racial discrimination are emphasized by his tone of voice and by what he does not say. The manner in which he was employed by CPI is not atypical, and reflects the pattern of rapid, convulsive growth that occurs when a new grant or government contract is finally approved.

When I got out of college, the problem was trying to find a job and just before I left school my dean told me he knew this fellow who worked in the personnel department in a big company. He said him and Ed had been to a couple of teachers' conferences in the South and he would write a letter to Ed telling him about me. Well, I knew Ed and I knew that he worked in the personnel department at this big company. He was a Negro. After I got home I hacked around for a couple of months and I finally decided maybe I better go up and check this thing. I went up there and he told me sure enough he

had the letter. He said, you know Ed was a very nice man, he had been working at this company for a number of years. He talked to me very frankly. He
said, "you know this is a big outfit. You know what I'd like to do is get you in
here on the ground floor and have you, say, work three months in one department, three months in another department, and make the rounds of the whole
organization. In that way you'd be better prepared to move up. "But you
know," he said, "I don't know if I can do this, because you know I'm here and
the only reason why I'm here is because they don't know what to do with me.
I've trained white boys who come in. I've trained them and they've moved on
and they've got terrific jobs."

To make a long story short, he couldn't work this deal that he had proposed
but he did get me in. I was working as a machine operator which was track A
and was considered a pretty good job. I was making fairly good money; and I
don't know what happened I can't remember exactly. I know it was my foreman. I got on the job, I learned the job so well, this was an incentive job, and
I learned the job in three or four days. The bad thing the foreman found out
was that I was a college graduate and he started to give me a hard time. One
thing led to another and finally he complained to his foreman that I put out
bad work. We had a long talk, the three of us, and his foreman gave him hell
because I told his foreman that when he trained me for the job, I think he
showed me in about an hour's time. I caught on and he left and that was it.
So his foreman gave him hell and told him that anytime you hire a man you
stay with him until you're sure that he knows the job and don't go by what he
says. Anyway I worked there for about eight or nine months, ten months. I
didn't like it, because I felt I could do better so I had a thought to go down to
New York. I had a lot of friends in New York and I roomed with one of my
buddies that I went to school with. I had no luck in New York for some time,
you know, going from employment agency to employment agency and going
to the State Employment Service, etc. Finally I got a phone call about 2:00 in
the morning. My buddy called and said my uncle wants you to go to work for
him. His uncle owned a cab company. He said, "can you come down?" I said
"I'm sleeping," but I drove up to this place. His uncle has a fleet of cabs. He
has about 100 cabs and I sat down with his uncle in his office upstairs over the
garage. He has this plush office. He's a Negro and he was telling me how he
would like me to come to work for him as a dispatcher. Then he says 50
dollars a week, but you know it worked out all right for a while. I took the
job and it was a pretty nice job. I made $50 a week and I was just passing these
other fellows who were cab drivers out and whenever they would come in, or
I'd catch them when they'd come in. I was working from about 8:00 to 4:30
or 5:00. Most of the guys started out say 2:00 in the morning. They'd get in
10 or 11:00 in the morning. If they had a good night, they'd always give the
dispatchers a dollar, two dollars, and so forth. Thirty or forty or fifty guys who
had a pretty good night, you know, you can make a good enough salary.

I stayed there for about six or seven months and then I left, I can't remember why. Then I ran into another buddy of mine. This guy was much older
than I was, and he was an old-time waiter. He used to live in my home town

and he knew me when I was a young guy. I was living at the "Y" and I went downstairs to eat. It was on a Sunday, a very lonesome kind of day when you're away from home, and he was down there eating. He recognized me and I recognized him and we almost kissed each other. So he told me he worked across the street in the Club. I don't know if you know what the Club is, but it's a Negro supper club in Harlem. He said, "You know there's a waiter over there just got fired," and he asked me what I was doing. I said I wasn't doing much of anything. So he said, "Would you like to wait tables?" He said, "We don't serve any meals. All you have to do is serve liquor. We work in the cabaret part you know. On Sundays they have two dances. They have a dance in the afternoon and they have a dance at night. You start out about 2:00 in the afternoon and work till 5:00. That's one dance. Then you clean up and at 7:00 another group comes in and they do a dance." The pay is nothing. I think they were paying something like 75 or 80¢ an hour, but the tips were out of this world. So he said, "As a matter of fact one guy got fired last night because he got too chummy with one of the guests. Why don't you come over and I'll have you talk to the owner of the place." He took me over to talk to the guy, told him I was from his home town and the owner said I was hired. It worked out real good. First I started out working just on Sundays. Then I worked Saturdays and Sundays. I was doing all right. It was a rough life because the bar didn't close until 3:00 or 4:00 in the morning and by the time you cleaned up it was 5:00. Then you went to an after-hours joint and you didn't get home till 7:00 in the morning. It was pretty rough.

Then I went to Macy's and got a little job working as a shoe salesman. It was a real nice job. We worked on a commission basis. Working in the shoe department, if you sold a pair of shoes you got a commission. It you sold shoe polish with a pair of shoes you got a commission. They had certain shoes that had been there that they couldn't get rid of. If you sold those shoes you would have gotten still a higher commission. So it was a nice job. I lasted there a couple of months and then I had to quit.

I came back home 'cause I still didn't get the kind of job I wanted. I started writing letters at home and having personal interviews. I went to D&B too. I went to all kinds of insurance companies everywhere. I couldn't get hired. I even wrote to the mayor. You know, veteran, native of the city, etc. I want a job. I even got an appointment with him. As a matter of fact they gave an exam one time. I forgot what the job was for, some local job. I took the exam, two exams for a job in the city and came out highest on one exam and second highest on the other exam. This was in the paper. I didn't even know it. People were calling my house, telling me. "I see you made out very well." You know, they read this in the paper. *I still couldn't get a job!!*

My father had been working down at one of the fraternity houses at the university. He's been working around the university for many, many years. I was a grown guy. But he feels here's a poor guy so he said, "Look they need a waiter in one of the fraternity houses." So I said, yeah sure. So he said, "Well they need a waiter and they need a bartender. Why don't you go down and see this guy?" The steward was across the hall so I went down and talked to him and he asked if I had any experience at all and I said oh, yeah. So he said, "We serve breakfast and we serve dinner." He said, "You got yourself a job that pays fifty bucks a week," and he said it goes till June.

So I took the job and it was lousy. I worked and I worked and I finally said this was not enough for me. I had a girlfriend and we had been going together for about seven years, so we decided maybe we ought to get married, or at least she decided. So I said, "Gee if we get married, I'll have to get more money." She had been working as a nurse in a sanatorium. I said that I would have to get another job. So I went to the AR Company and filed an application. They found me a lousy job which bugged me because with experience, education, college graduate, you know, terrible. I got the job, working from 11:00 at night to 7:00 in the morning and from there I would go to the fraternity house where I would serve breakfast and then go home and sleep from 1:00 to about 5:00. Then go back down and serve dinner and then go home for a couple of hours and sleep and then go to the AR Company. I did this for about four months and I saved about $750 and we got married. So after that I still kept the job. After I got married I left AR. I kept the job as a waiter, and went back to W. and got a job in the rolling mill. They work around the clock, 7:00 to 3:00; 3:00 to 11:00; 11:00 to 7:00, and the inspectors have to go over the rolls of metal for all these different companies. I stayed there for a while.

I was making pretty good money, but I still wasn't satisfied. So finally I got laid off and said well, I've got to do something. The exam for a social worker came up and I decided I'd better take this exam. I took the exam and I passed and I got a call from the welfare department. I went down and I was interviewed by a lady. We talked for about an hour. She was head of child welfare. She asked me a lot of questions, experience, etc. I didn't have any experience, but I passed the exam and that was the criteria. Well, anyway she says that right at the moment they didn't have any vacancies, but there was a possibility that they might have an opening in public assistance. So I left and about two weeks later I got a call from the public assistance division. The lady wanted to know how I felt about women who had babies out of wedlock.

I stayed there seven years and it was a very nice job. I loved it. I rose up to the point where I could be supervisor, took the exam and came out, out of about 35 people, I came out fifth in the state for a supervisor's job. Well, I moved up the scale in working with the welfare people. Every year you get these little increments and after 15 or 20 years you sort of get to where you're making a fairly decent income.

All the time I was working as a social worker I was taking exams, as a matter of fact any exam that came up. I think the second year that I was working in one of the departments as a social worker I took the parole officer's exam and about two years later they called me. They wanted me to work out of town and I didn't want it. Then in November they called me again because they had a vacancy in the local office. I went up to see him. They got the increment and they got the increase in pay and it was worth my while to make the move, so I moved over to the probation department. I worked there for two years and I liked the work very much, very nice, very nice people.

While I was at the probation department I belonged to a club. We used to have people come and give talks. One night one of the CPI people came to our club meeting. He talked, this was 1962, and he said that if we knew anybody who had any kinds of skills or any kind of experience and so forth and so on, they'd be happy to talk to them because CPI was going to expand and so forth. So we asked questions and after his talk and I talked to him and told him I was working as a probation officer and I had worked as a social worker. He said, "Gee, why don't you put in an application." Two days later I got the application from CPI. So I filled it out and sent it in. Two days later I got a phone call and I was asked to come down and see H.C. So I went down and met H.C. We sat down and talked. I think this was even before they started to hire any people. He mentioned the fact that they wanted to hire three counselors. He said, "You know we looked at your application." Actually I wasn't filing the application for CPI, I was filing the application because the man said we get all kinds of different companies calling us looking for people with qualifications like the telephone company, gas company, for Negroes. So he said, "You know we were looking over your application and we marked you for us." But he said, "we're waiting to hear about the money. If we hear about it we'll get in touch with you."

I waited and I waited and waited and I didn't hear. About a month and a half later I called him and set up an appointment. I went in to see him and he told me, "Well, I'll tell you what happened," he said, "we needed three counselors and we hired them and these three people had just a little more education than you had. But don't forget about it. The door's still open." I think he said the first three counselors were hired as counselors for youths. He said eventually an adult program will be started and we will be needing more counselors. I wasn't pressing because I had a job.

I guess it was around July, I had just come back from vacation and I got a call, "Can you start working Monday? Your name is on the list here and some-one was supposed to call you, but you're supposed to start work on Monday." So I said, "Well gee, I don't know." So he said, "The boss is away on vacation and he was supposed to have had this letter written to you advising you that you would start working with us." So I said, "Well look, I haven't seen H.C. in months. We haven't even discussed salary, or anything." So he said, "Well gee, H. will be back in a couple of days," he said, "but kind of stand by because I think you are supposed to be working for CPI."

It was so fast, people were coming up to me and congratulating me. My wife is doing some research work, she's working with the university this past summer. She came home and said, "Hey, you work for CPI." So I said, "I do, eh." So she said, "I saw your name on a memo." People were calling. I walked down the street people were congratulating me, "How do you like your job?"

Anyway, finally I said I better try and get this thing straightened out. I called and I made an appointment and I went in and I saw H.C. He said, "Yeah we want you to work. I don't know what happened, but we'd like you to come to work as a vocational counselor." He said, "How soon can you come?" and I said, "Gee, as for the people I work for, I'd need at least a month." So he said, "Fine, take a month and come work for us. We don't want them to feel we are taking you away, but we'd like to have you." So I sent them my resignation and came to CPI.

As a result of having experienced some of the same problems, the neighborhood workers seem to have a sympathy and tolerance for the situations their clients find themselves in. Although terms such as "bum," "slut," "real stupid kid," "no good," "lazy," or "crazy Dominic" are used to describe applicants, the terms really seem to have a descriptive and not an evaluative quality. There is little sense of righteousness, or punitiveness, or any feeling that help should not be offered because the client is morally questionable. Clients with a criminal record, with a homosexual problem, or with illegitimate children are treated with an attitude of tolerance and acceptance. In conferences some of the more blatant sexual escapades of clients are presented with some raucous humor, but as far as can be seen most applicants are treated with respect. The neighborhood worker prides himself on his feeling for people. He approaches his clients with an attitude of "I made it. You can make it too."

The neighborhood worker may sometimes share the outlook of his applicants too closely. He may be too ready to settle for any job for his applicant. Part of his eagerness to place his client arises from the employment goal of the NEC.[4] Sometimes the worker's own attitudes may be blocks in encouraging his applicant to look ahead. A worker who unconsciously shares the assumption that his client is indeed a less worthwhile human being will be inclined to be pessimistic about the possibilities of change.

Example 8. An 18-year-old Negro boy, a high-school dropout, who had spent some time on a work crew and who proved to be responsible and stable in that situation, was placed on several jobs that required no skill and were dirty and low-paid. He worked at these jobs for short periods before he was either fired or he quit. He was now looking for another job because his mother was threatening to put him out of the house. When he turned 18, she had

---

[4] Many applicants do not have jobs because they are not ready for jobs. This fact frequently is not recognized by the applicant, and the lack of readiness in the applicant is a source of frustration for the neighborhood worker and for other staff members as well. The ultimate aim, of course, is to help an applicant accept a job. However, at times the worst possible solution for some applicants is a job. Not being ready, the applicant will either be fired or he will quit. If he is fired, his sense of defeat and hopelessness is increased. If he quits, he builds a history of short-term stays on a variety of jobs, which makes it difficult for an employer to view him as a steady person. At conferences the consultant frequently will argue that it is not in the applicant's interest to get him started on just *any* job without adequate support and preparation.

stopped receiving welfare support for him. He now needed a job urgently, but beyond his immediate need he seemed directionless.

The placement interviewer, responding to the urgency in the neighborhood worker's presentation, suggested another stop-gap position as a floor boy in a small machine shop. Since there was no formal apprenticeship program at the shop, the probability of advancement for a young Negro was quite low. At this point, the consultant raised the problem of whether NEC was really doing him a favor by finding him a stop-gap position. The likelihood was that he would work a short time, loose his incentive to continue, and then quit. He would be building a record of short-term employment that would make it difficult for him when he applied for further jobs, and the pattern of working at dead-end jobs would be reinforced. It was agreed his situation was urgent, but in this instance it required looking beyond the immediate need and beyond accepting what was happening as an inevitable part of a way of life. Further discussion led to a plan to stay in touch with him while a specific training opportunity was sought for the boy. If a stop-gap job was necessary, then it should be offered to him only with the understanding that he stay in touch with the NEC until he could enter some training situation.

The neighborhood worker sees every client and therefore has to deal with every difficult situation that arises. He is the person who maintains continued contact with the clients, and he is the one who may have to bring unwelcome news. If no job is available, or if the applicant does not qualify, it is the worker who must explain. A large percentage of all applicant contacts are handled by neighborhood workers.

THE PROCESS

When an applicant appears at an NEC office, a secretary obtains minimal information about him and arranges for an appointment with the neighborhood worker.[5] The appointment is made as quickly as possible, preferably on that day. The neighborhood worker then interprets the program and the intake process, describing the various resources available. An application form is completed. An appointment is made with the vocational counselor who interviews the applicant about his aspirations and tries to determine his strengths and weaknesses. The counselor also arranges an appointment for the applicant

[5] Although not directly involved with applicants, the secretary is a "gatekeeper." Her attitudes and approach to applicants in the office and on the telephone can make an important difference in whether or not applicants return, and in how they respond to being asked to wait. Sometimes a young and attractive secretary will bring adolescents into the office, but the conditions of their coming may be a mixed blessing. A secretary may also be a model for young girls who come in. As applicants become familiar with the office, she may become a friendly figure with whom applicants enjoy conversing.

to take a series of routine aptitude tests. Both neighborhood worker and counselor attempt to prepare and to reassure the applicant about the tests. Many applicants are leery of testing because they know they have done poorly in the past. If placement seems possible, the applicant is referred to the placement interviewer who attempts to place the applicant in a suitable position.

For any decision other than direct placement, the case is brought up at a weekly disposition conference attended by the staff, the coordinator, the psychological consultant, and a representative of the on-the-job training program.[6] On appropriate occasions other interested persons—welfare worker, school teacher, representatives from other CPI programs, and work-crew leaders and supervisors—are also present.

The supervisor of the NEC office presides over the disposition conference. The conference permits a pooling of staff information about an applicant in arriving at a plan of action. However, staff members frequently hold disparate viewpoints about an applicant, and the process of resolution of such differences in viewpoint encourages thoughtful and sometimes lively and heated discussions about an applicant. The conference is an institutional safeguard against subjectively based, overidealistic, or overly pessimistic views of applicants. The decision reached at a conference is usually supported by all members of the staff. In practice the implementation of decisions is supported by all staff members, helping to maintain the cohesiveness of the office. Responsibility for following through on recommendations is assigned at the conference.

Shortly after the disposition conference the applicant is seen by the neighborhood worker or the counselor, who interprets the staff's recommendations. The neighborhood worker then follows through, providing whatever support and encouragement is necessary until the applicant is safely started on a job or in a training program. Support may be as little as calling an applicant to remind him of an appointment, or as drastic as picking him up at 5:30 A.M. to deliver him to a work site his first morning.

The process from application to placement may take as little as a day or it may stretch out to weeks, depending on the applicant and the

[6] Originally every case was to be presented at a weekly conference. However, the case load has grown to the point that such a course is unwise and unfeasible. Some of the centers have daily staff conferences, and in others routine cases are settled quickly between the office supervisor and the appropriate staff member. Staff members have started to save difficult or puzzling cases for presentation at the weekly conference attended by the psychological consultant and others. A verbatim transcript of one disposition conference constitutes the bulk of the next chapter.

available resources. For many applicants another interview is scheduled with the counselor to have test results interpreted during the waiting period. With others the neighborhood worker may phone from time to time to let the applicant know NEC is working to help him. Still others are encouraged to stop in at the office and to check regularly for new opportunities.

A number of different resources are available. The disposition is not an automatic process, but requires careful thought to match an applicant with the best available opportunity for him. An applicant may be recommended for direct placement if he seems ready for a position. The placement interviewer has a list of openings that come to CPI directly, and he has access to positions listed with the Connecticut State Employment Service. CPI has a staff of job developers who actually canvass employers in the community to encourage them to list jobs with CPI. On occasion the job developer attempts to convince an employer to create a position suitable for a particular applicant.[7]

CPI also has an On-the-Job Training (OJT) Program in which it encourages employers to hire young or untrained workers by offering a subsidy of $30 a week up to 26 weeks, to make the training worthwhile to employers. The employer must hire the applicant at something over the minimum wage, and must give assurance there is a permanent job at the end of the training period, if he qualifies. CPI job developers and OJT supervisors seek out such opportunities and make the positions available to the NEC staff.

For adolescents placement in the work crew is possible.[8] There is also an intermediate work-crew experience in which an adolescent is placed in a work setting for training, receives $1.25 an hour for up to 32 hours of work per week. Another eight hours are spent in classes conducted by CPI as part of the program.

A variety of other training programs is available for adults. Applicants who are heads of households may receive a stipend while attending a training course sponsored under the Manpower and Defense

[7] CPI sometimes uses the work crew or some other training opportunity as a means of "holding" an applicant. Sometimes applicants are in distinct need, in an economic and in a psychological sense. The placement is made as a means of providing immediate help and enabling CPI staff to evaluate the applicant. It is desirable to refer work-crew members and others in training programs to better jobs or to better training opportunities as the applicants seem ready. Having had experience with him in a training situation, the staff feels comfortable in recommending an applicant who otherwise would look like a poor risk. For the applicant CPI provides the equivalent of a set of references to an employer. Disposition conferences frequently are held around an applicant who is already placed.

[8] The work-crew program is described in Chapters 17 and 18.

Training Act. Applicants who are functionally illiterate may enter the Basic Education Program and receive a stipend while learning reading, writing, arithmetic, and the use of hand tools and simple machines.

CPI has been serving as the Job Corps screening agent for males, and when openings are available applicants are recommended for the Job Corps. Finally, the staff may decide that a referral to some other agency such as the Bureau of Vocational Rehabilitation, or a psychiatric clinic, or a family service agency is indicated. Such referrals are made, but experience suggests they are very often unsuccessful, either because the applicant does not follow through on the referral or because the helping source has too long a waiting list.

AN ILLUSTRATIVE CASE

NEC works as a team in handling its clients. The separate functions of the neighborhood worker, counselor, and placement interviewer are maintained, but the group works together to help a client.

Example 9. A girl of about 17 came to the NEC because she had dropped out of school. She had previously been in an academic high school, but she was more or less asked to leave. She went into a vocational school and behavior problems soon reasserted themselves. It was not too long before she was in difficulty at the new school. Her family had taken her to a psychiatrist. He recommended that her mother enter treatment and that she enter group therapy. Her father refused to accept treatment and the recommendations were not followed.

At the time she came to the NEC she was described as scrawny with hair flying. She wore glasses and she was homely. She impressed the neighborhood team as "a real stupid kid." However, her General Aptitude Test Battery scores were quite good, causing the team to look at her in a different light.[9] The counselor interpreted her test scores to her in an attempt to interest her in returning to school. She refused, indicating she was disinterested in her program at school and was going to a vocational school only because she had been asked to leave the academic high school, to which she had no intention of returning. The counselor referred her to the placement interviewer who sent her out on a routine job only after she agreed to improve her grooming. She worked at the job three weeks, but she said she got bored. However, she was sufficiently related to the NEC that she called to ask permission to quit the job.

During the time she worked she had made it a practice to call the NEC or drop in regularly. She seemed to take a liking to one of the young male

[9] Much as we try to guard against it, it is clear that the staff feels more comfortable and more enthusiastic about working with the high-IQ, high-verbal person than with someone who scores poorly on psychological tests.

neighborhood workers and she would call him frequently. She would talk about her boy-friend problems with him, would discuss bowling, or bring up her plans to buy a car. She would also talk about needing money and feeling pressed to get a job. The neighborhood worker would listen to her and occasionally offer concrete advice. When he felt he did not want to handle the issues she brought up or when he got bored with her, he would ask her to see either the placement interviewer or the counselor. The placement interviewer would talk to her about the necessity for developing some definite goals, and both placement interviewer and counselor would talk with her about her grooming and manner of speech. Many of these interviews were brief and informal.

She was sent out for another job, but this time she was also encouraged to enroll in a typing course. She did so, but after a few weeks her attitudes led to conflict with school authorities and she dropped out of the typing school. About three weeks after she had been on the second job, she called the counselor in a panicky state. Her employer, she said, had made sexual advances to her. The counselor advised her to quit at once and told her to return to the office.

When she returned to the office, she was given a typing test and it was found that she had picked up a great deal in the few weeks before she had left typing school. She was advised to get additional help in typing from her father who had been a typing teacher when in service. The placement interviewer also arranged for her to come in weekly to take a typing test. If she were to obtain a position as a typist, she would have to pass a typing test. This support was vital because the girl said she was quite frightened of taking any kind of test. An opportunity for a civil service examination came up but she continued to be quite anxious. She feared taking the examination, and she was worried she would not be accepted even if she did pass the examination. The placement interviewer and counselor were outspokenly encouraging and supportive and with their assistance she took the examination, passed it, and was placed.

She has continued contacts with the office, but she has been working steadily. She initially began to improve her grooming and speech at the insistence of the staff, but her apparent crush on the neighborhood worker may have also helped. Whatever the reason, she is now well-groomed whenever she is seen in public, her negative attitudes and behavior problems have disappeared, and she is working steadily.

This girl had been referred for psychiatric treatment but her family refused to follow through. The NEC was an acceptable resource to her and to her family. A number of people worked with her (and no one worked with her family) in contrast to typical clinic or social agency practice. No one attempted to help her work through her anxiety about taking tests, her crush on the neighborhood worker, her earlier attempts to hide her attractiveness, or her dependence on the

NEC. Her dependence was accepted, and her anxiety was met with support and reassurance rather than probing and interpretation. In each instance there was a direct attack on the surface aspects of the presenting problem with insistence she behave in a certain way, with direct advice, or with very direct support and encouragement. One can argue she is not "cured" when that term is used in some ideal sense, but who would be willing to argue that in the same amount of time any form of clinic treatment would have been more effective or more efficient in helping this girl?

THE INVOLVEMENT OF STAFF WITH THE APPLICANT

From the discussion and the illustration above, it is clear there are many problems in the NEC that parallel those to be found in the psychiatric clinic or in a social agency.[10] The goals and methods of the NEC may differ from those of the clinic or agency, but the problems in human relationships are not essentially different. Applicants come when they are in need of help with vital problems in living. Applicants who present themselves as desperately in need, or those who are apathetic, or chronically dependent, or hostile, or aggressively demanding stir all kinds of feelings in the staff members who relate to them. Moreover, staff members have a need to see themselves as competent and as fulfilling an important mission. It is important to the staff to feel that their efforts are successful in helping others. Where powerful feelings and desires are stirred, it is clear that judgment may be affected in various ways.

Clinical training, supervision, and institutional practice are valuable in minimizing the kind of subjective involvements with clients that may be detrimental both to the client and to the worker. In clinical situations and in the NEC the soil is fertile for the development of rescue fantasies, dependent relationships that retard the client's progress, or mutually hostile and rejecting relationships that prevent both client and worker from making the best use of available resources.

In clinical situations we speak of counter-transference that requires the worker to be as sensitive to his own needs in the situation as he is

[10] Throughout we shall be making comparisons between the NEC and a more traditional mental-health service. We do not intend to disparage the traditional service, but we draw comparisons to highlight the similarities and differences between the Clinic and the NEC. The effectiveness of traditional services for inner-city applicants has been called into question, and the NEC presents a different model that demands, at this stage in its development, open-minded if not sympathetic reception.

to his client's. It is clear that NEC staff members do things differently in many respects than professional mental-health workers, but how we are to view their actions is not clear. We can speak of rescue fantasies, and of sentimental, unrealistic, inmature enthusiasm, but often enough the worker's unbounded enthusiasm is helpful and meaningful.

Example 10. A Negro boy of about 17 lived directly across the street from one of the centers. He was often seen around his home doing nothing and wearing torn, dirty clothes. Several contacts had failed to bring the boy into the office. When he finally was encouraged to come in, information from school records indicated he had been classified as trainable retarded and had been in special classes for the trainable throughout his school career. His IQ varied around 45. Undaunted, the NEC staff went ahead and arranged for him to start as a member of a work crew. His body odor created the first problem. His home had no bath facilities, his body odor was quite strong, and the boys on the crew and the foremen found him hard to take in the car going to the work-crew site. The neighborhood worker and the work-crew foreman arranged for him to have access to the showers at the community school gymnasium. They also worked very carefully with him to help him to buy some new clothes. One achievement that made the staff feel proud was the boy's independent purchase of a new pair of shoes. These efforts at getting him to improve his personal hygiene continued throughout the contacts with him.

On the work crew the boy proved to be friendly and steady in the sense that he was fairly reliable in working at a job in one place once the foreman told him what to do. He made a favorable impression on the work-crew foreman throughout his stay. His teacher in the educational component of the work-crew program, an untrained but intelligent and psychologically sensitive young man, was very pleased with his response to efforts made to help him to recognize some simple street signs.

Because of the favorable experience with him over a period of three months, the NEC staff sought employment for him. He had expressed an interest in working with horses, so the staff located a position as a stable boy and took him out for an interview. The horses were highly trained polo ponies, and the boy seeing lively horses was frightened at first. Later he attempted to feed the horses by hand. However, it was felt the demands of the job for flexibility would be too great for him and the project was dropped.

A second attempt was made to find him a job shoveling fertilizer. The discussion with the boy's father took on a comic aspect when the father was inclined to turn the job down because the rate of pay (minimum legal wage) was too low. He seemed to be negotiating for more money even though there seemed to be little chance the boy would ever be able to find a position on his own. Finally the father agreed to let the boy take the position. The plant was located a considerable distance from his house. His father actually worked near the plant but his hours and the boy's did not overlap closely. Public transportation was available, but the trip was long and required changing buses. The boy tried once, found the trip too complicated, missed a bus and never arrived at work. He made it one other day, but for unknown reasons did not work steadily on the job. He came late another day, and by the end of the week both he and the employer were ready to call it quits. The boy returned to the work crew.

A few months later another attempt was made to place him on a job. A position as a worker on a refuse truck was obtained. For some unknown reason the best time for the applicant to meet the employer was 5:30 A.M., when public transportation was not available. If the employer felt the boy would work out, he was prepared to arrange for transportation for him. A neighborhood worker met the boy at 5:00 A.M. and transported him to the work site. The boy worked one or two days and then quit because he could not stand the odor of the refuse and he felt the work was beneath him. His reason for quitting seems ironic in light of the previous refusal of other work-crew youths to ride in the same car with him because his own personal hygiene left much to be desired. When the boy was again returned to a work crew, the staff arranged for him to swim and shower at a community pool with them. The staff continues to make strenuous efforts to see that he bathes, takes haircuts, and washes his clothes.

We can raise serious question about the expenditure of staff time and effort in trying to help a boy with severe mental deficiency who comes from a multiple-problem family known to every agency in the city. The work-crew experience is not meant to be the equivalent of a sheltered workshop to be continued indefinitely. The staff now sees this boy and his family as a challenge to do what the traditional agencies have failed to do; it is not clear to what extent the efforts to help stem from such a competitive feeling and to what extent they represent the humane motivation of staff to help. Thus far the friendliness, interest, and enthusiasm of the staff have been reciprocated in the boy's efforts to keep himself clean, to buy some of his own clothes, and to respond to the work crew and the educational situation. However, it is questionable whether the staff is realistically appraising the limitations of this boy, and whether it would not have been wiser to refer the boy to an agency geared to deal with the mentally defective.

At times the concept of help may go considerably beyond what the professional mental-health worker would consider appropriate. The professional mental-health worker usually limits his contact to the office and defines the helping relationship in terms of discussion and thinking about personal problems. The heroic efforts many NEC workers make on behalf of their clients are considered to deviate from the prescribed course and frequently to be unwarranted manifestations of the worker's "neurotic" need "to give." Every clinician can probably think of instances in which the giving of a cigarette to a patient was considered a deviation from accepted practice, as it well might be in the context of a given case. However, applicants at the NEC are often in need of food, money, and shelter, as well as other concrete forms of support. Help from a friend may be defined in considerably different terms than help from a professional worker.[11] When the professional sees help that goes beyond what he is prepared to do himself, he may find it difficult to *interpret what he sees*. The following example is rather extreme, but in lesser ways similar occurrences arise in the relationship of worker to applicant.

Example 11. A neighborhood worker met a man slightly older than himself whom he had known when both were considerably younger. The older man had a history of trouble with the police and at present was down on his luck. He indicated he wanted to make a break with his old way of life, but couldn't do it because of all the temptations the street and his acquaintances offered him. The neighborhood worker then offered to share his own apartment with the acquaintance and he tried to get NEC to locate a position for the man. He was too old to qualify for any of the youth training programs, but a position was made for him as assistant to one of the supervisors of a CPI program. The NEC staff went along with the worker's recommendation, largely out of an idealistic motive to help, but partly because the neighborhood worker had committed himself and the staff was trying to support him. He worked on the position for a while and seemingly was doing well, but one day he got into a fist fight with one of the older adolescents on a work crew. He probably had been provoked by the teenager, but it was felt he should not have acted as he did. The position was terminated.

Discussion with the man revealed he felt that the NEC was genuinely interested in him and he clearly trusted the staff. He was concerned about losing his temper and "lousing himself up," and expressed a great deal of concern about having hurt his family in the past. He was ready to accept referral for psychotherapy, and he actually made some efforts to restore his relationship with his wife and child. NEC continued to try and find a position for him elsewhere.

The case came to the attention of the consultant after the man was already living with the worker and plans to put him in a job were in progress. In a clinic or social agency a worker who went to such lengths to help his client or his patient would be seen as acting out some personal motive. In this instance when the case came up in conference there did not seem to be much point in exploring the situation from

---

[11] A young woman, a first-year psychology trainee in a mental hospital, was the subject of a conference because she gave a chronic schizophrenic patient (not her case) a box of candy for his birthday. The significance and the propriety of this act was the subject of considerable debate.

the point of view of motives. Instead the worker's willingness to inconvenience himself in order to help in concrete ways was approved. He was then cautioned about any further involvement with the man beyond being a friend to him. In particular he was cautioned about getting himself involved in anything which seemed even to smell of being illegal, in order to protect himself and the reputation of the NEC in the community. Responsibility for following the case was turned over to one of the counselors who had had experience as a probation worker, and the worker was cautioned to keep the roles of friend and professional helper separate as far as this individual was concerned.

The NEC staff members frequently develop and maintain relationships with many of their clients that go beyond the confines of help given in relation to the specific task of employment. Being in the neighborhood, workers see former applicants frequently. They do not hesitate to say hello and to inquire about their activities. Similarly, former clients call the neighborhood workers for help with other problems. For example one woman called a neighborhood worker to ask him to help get her husband out of jail. Workers sometimes exchange Christmas cards with applicants. On occasion a worker brings in a friend or relative in the hopes he may land a lucrative position. On occasion he treats the pool of jobs almost as a private patronage supply, and attempts to use his position either to promote his own status in the neighborhood or to stimulate a view of himself as a big shot. A young worker has occasionally joined a group of boys out on the town on a Friday night. In some instances staff members have loaned money to applicants or have paid carfare. They have helped applicants buy clothes, and in a couple of instances have encouraged applicants to use various public bath facilities.

The concept of help is thus extended considerably beyond the definition typically accepted by professional mental-health agencies. Whether such an extended form of help is more or less helpful is not at issue. "Nonprofessional" efforts to help do not seem to be destructive, in the sense that no instance of harm to a client has come to our attention as a result of such efforts at friendship. Lacking the restrictions of clinic tradition, it is clear that NEC staff can develop a broad variety of relationships with applicants. Which types are effective and which are destructive remains to be determined.

It has been indicated that many of the workers seem to have "psychological-mindedness" and an intuitive feel for the problems presented by their clients. Many of the staff have the same kind of insightful appreciation for their own emotional responses to many applicants, to the anxiety-provoking aspects of their job, and to themselves as stimulus objects. We rarely hear a sophisticated discussion of emotional reactions of staff to clients, yet staff members are frequently aware of their personal involvements and can discuss them openly, sometimes seriously and sometimes through the medium of jokes and kidding.

The following quotations are taken from a tape-recorded discussion with the staff of the NECs about their jobs and about the consultant's relationship to the staff. At no point was the subject of the worker's own feelings introduced directly as a topic for discussion. The quotations were elicited as part of a discussion of various aspects of the job.

The job really gives me a chance to put into practice what I thought I knew all along—for years—talking with people—I think that I know how to talk to people and I like to see just how many I can get in here. *It's a little selfish motive too.*

In this example, the worker makes no attempt to disguise the narcissistic elements of his motivation on the job. He asserts his feelings in straightforward fashion.

In the next example the worker clearly indicates his awareness of the other person's position and his anxiety about being harmed physically. He is also keenly aware of his stimulus value as a light-skinned Negro. Because of his appearance he may expect a form of distance and resistance he might not get otherwise. He is discussing his feelings about walking into a strange apartment:

There are a lot of things that go through your mind on how you're going to . . . you don't just walk into people's houses and say, "Here I am. I'm going to give you some advice," especially when you've got four, five guys around. Frankly, myself, I had this feeling today looking for another client in the poolroom. Well, I'm not too well known. I do go in the bars, but there is sometimes a little mistaken identity. Well, let's face it, we can talk about numbers racket, drinking, anything; of course, I've been familiar with these things all my life, but most places I go and places like that, they walk away. Either they think I'm a cop, to begin with—I think everybody wanted to run out of the poolroom because of these recent arrests, and surprising, I find that being light-skinned raises a doubt in the minds of most people I meet—they don't know I hear it, "There's a white man to see you." You know these are the things you think about. They do happen. Who is this guy? Is he from special services or what? They don't know me. Am I a Negro? This is the thing I think about when I went into the house yesterday and saw these guys sitting around (four or five Negro adolescents), but you just go on in, "Hi, how's the party going. Glasses all around, where's mine?" You know. The fellow was sitting there. I walked over to him and said, "Can I talk to you a minute. Let's go in the bedroom." We went in to talk. I told him exactly what I was there for.

The next several quotations indicate staff members' awareness of their own involvement with applicants.

We have our subjective feelings and we get involved. There's no question about it. If we didn't we don't belong where we are.

As we work with the individuals you can only be so objective. There is some subjectivity involved. As a result, I think sometimes in working with a client we start pushing the things that we feel is what we want him to do.

A neighborhood worker discusses his view of the consultant's role with the NEC, clearly indicating his awareness of his emotional involvement with his client:

You can perhaps take a lot less of a stand for an individual that you don't know—you can be an unbiased person. Like when we have our disposition conferences, you come in with an unbiased opinion. Perhaps where maybe a neighborhood worker is really excited by an applicant and feels this is the one thing that has to be done for this applicant, this is the only possible avenue— you would break this down and say realistically is this the only possible avenue this guy can go on and go to success?

In the next quotation, the worker expresses his awareness of sexual temptation and the seductiveness of some female applicants.

I've met some doozies. Let's face it. Some of the female applicants you know, they're looking for jobs, but there's just a way you handle them, you can say "no" in a nice way to a lot of things without being insulting or trying to embarrass anybody. They all have feelings.

In the following quotation, a worker is discussing his experience in calling on a woman who had asked for help with a personal problem. She was in emotional distress, and it was his job to tell her about possible resources for help. In his comment he openly expresses his feeling of uneasiness in trying to help the woman.

I had these alternatives I was going to bring to the woman, but you know, what was I going to do, throw them on the table and run out the door? The only thing I could say when I walked in the door was "hello" and that was it; and I wouldn't know what to say from there.

We have noted that the staff tends to be outspoken and uninhibited about expressing aggressive feelings. In the following quotation, discussing his response to the consultant, the neighborhood worker is direct in expressing his viewpoint.

Most of the staff like you and respect you and respect the opinion you give us, and are willing to carry it out. I think if it was any other way I'd just say the hell with what you think, I'm going to do it my own way.

NEC workers are no more immune to affectively misdirected judgment than any other clinical staff. However, staff members also seem to have a good level of insight into the possibilities of such effective involvements. Perhaps the best conclusion is that psychological and personal insight is not the exclusive possession of the trained mental-health worker.

PROFESSIONAL ETHICS

The problem of ethics and confidentiality enter into the work of the NEC staff. If anything the problems are more difficult to resolve because there are no guidelines. Employers are entitled to know the applicant, but how much should be revealed? In individual instances the workers have to concern themselves with maintaining a relationship with other community agencies while protecting the reputation of the NEC in the neighborhood. If the centers developed the reputation of being "spies" for the welfare department, or if it was felt they were too close to the police or probation workers, the effectiveness of the NEC would be materially affected. There is also the problem of communication of information among agencies. A professional agency is reluctant to send out professional reports, even when the client agrees, to a source it fears may violate confidences. A professional clinic is also reluctant to risk misinterpretation of reports by lesser-trained people. By and large the various agencies have been cooperative, but issues arise every bit as much as they do in clinic or social-agency practice.

Example 12. A neighborhood worker had been effective in helping a young man with a long history of juvenile offenses get placed on a job. He had maintained contact with the applicant, and on this occasion received a telephone call from the client informing him he had quit his job, had gone away for a few days, and had gotten married. He was not broke but was without any job or any place to live. The neighborhood worker agreed to meet him at a local restaurant. At that meeting the neighborhood worker was introduced to the client's "wife" who told him a fantastic story about herself. He became suspicious and on intensive and prolonged questioning both his client and the girl admitted she had run away from a residential treatment center for adolescents. He then informed his client he was breaking the law and urged him to help the girl return to the institution.

The next day the police called the neighborhood worker wanting to know the whereabouts of the client and the girl. The neighborhood worker was informed that the police wanted the client for questioning, but indicated he was not yet charged with any crime. The neighborhood worker felt himself to be in a dilemma. He wanted to protect his client but he also felt it necessary to cooperate with the police. He admitted having seen the girl and the young man together, and indicated that as far as he knew she was to take a bus back to the institution. He was now concerned about what further duty he had toward the client and whether he should inform the police if the client contacted him. He was advised by both consultant and coordinator that he would be fulfilling his responsibility to his client if he insisted that the client contact the police before NEC would take any further steps to help him, but he did not need to feel he had to inform the police of the client's whereabouts.

Example 13. A relative of a 17-year-old dropout called the NEC to determine if the girl was being serviced through the NEC. The neighborhood worker indicated that the girl had been an applicant at the agency but that it was difficult to find an adequate placement for her because she lacked saleable skills. He indicated the center's continuing interest in working with the girl. The relative passed the information on to the girl's mother and by the time it reached the applicant, she was informed that the center thought she was worthless and no good. She was berated over and over again for dropping out of school and for being no good as far as providing support for the family was concerned. The neighborhood worker discovered the problem when he followed up sometime later in an effort to discover why the client had not kept further appointments which had been scheduled for her.

There is a distinct problem in conceptualizing, developing, and maintaining professional attitudes in relation to the client. There are really no guidelines. Employers are entitled to accurate references, but the NEC staff members also want to protect their clients. It is necessary to maintain confidential records in order to maintain the client's trust, but what kind of information should be released, and to whom, are difficult questions. It is not clear that the ethical standards of the clinic apply to the NEC. The staff members sometimes obtain knowledge of violation of the law. They may know when a condition of probation has been broken. They may also be aware of violations of Welfare Department rules. Do their responsibilities as citizens take precedence over their responsibilities to their clients? Thus far the NEC staff has tended to learn toward adopting the ethic of the clinic. However, it remains to be seen whether legal sources would recognize in any degree the confidentiality of the client's relationship to NEC. It is certainly necessary for clients to have trust in the NEC and to be willing to speak freely to staff members, but the conditions of the helping contract are not at all clear and the issues require careful thought.

THE PSYCHOLOGIST AS CONSULTANT IN THE NEC

A consultant normally enters a situation because there is a problem that might be helped by special knowledge and skills not available in the setting that has the problem. Even if people with similar training and skills are available, a consultant is sometimes helpful because he is an outsider. Consultants are used in different ways. In one setting a consultant may examine a patient and make recommendations for treatment or disposition; in another setting he may be strictly a teacher. He may conduct a seminar in diagnostic testing, or in psychotherapy, or in research problems. In still another setting he may examine the functioning of the total organization and make recommendations for increasing its effectiveness. Typically, a consultant enters a situation with a defined purpose in mind and his activity is usually sharply limited to that single defined purpose.

A sharply defined consulting role is, however, not the only one professional mental-health workers may fulfill. A consultant may also become part of the setting by becoming thoroughly familiar with the day-by-day operation of the setting, with the problems as they are manifested in the setting, and with the values, goals, folkways, and mores of the setting. It is this type of role that characterizes our activity in the NEC and has forced us to keep constantly in mind the purposes for which this helping agency was developed.

The major goals of the NEC are to help applicants prepare for employment at the highest level each can attain. The NEC is not a social agency and it is not a mental-hygiene clinic. It is a helping agency with its own methods of helping. Help is obtained in the process of seeking employment. An applicant's personal difficulties may be discussed with a staff member, but the staff member is less interested in helping the applicant to achieve a verbalized insight than he is in seeing him settle into a program. For the applicant, help comes in the process of mastering the demands of an employment or a training situation, and in learning directly that his own personal characteristics interfere with his effectiveness. He receives help in a personal sense from the sympathetic attention, interest, and support of the people working with him, but such support is not an end in itself. Progress is seen in the applicant's change in the direction of becoming a good employee and other psychological changes are considered secondary. The major goal is employment, and the consultant functions to help staff help applicants move in the direction of *that* goal.

In our work with the NEC no specific mission was stated. The consultant was to make himself helpful in whatever ways he could. Because there was no clear-cut mission, a role evolved as the consultant became related to the NEC. In this process the port-of-entry problem was less acute than in other situations. First, the NEC was not under criticism from any source at that time. It was a new operation, one of the first of its kind, and the staff had no cause to fear criticism. Second, there was no sense of competition of staff with the consultant. The areas of competence were quite different. The consultant was not there to show the counselors how to do vocational counseling; neighborhood workers were not involved with questions of interview technique, and certainly did not see themselves as "treating" personnel. Third, the job is a difficult one and produces many anxious moments for the staff. The consultant, with his doctoral degree and institutional affiliation, was seen as a high-status person available to help the staff. Once the initial strangeness wore off staff and consultant quickly accepted each other.

The role of consultant in this continuing sense is a somewhat strange one. The consultant has no position in the table of organization of the NEC or of the Manpower Division of CPI. He has no specific authority to direct anyone to do anything. If he is to be effective, he can do so only because he can command the liking and respect of those who use his services. He has a continuous problem not to usurp the authority of supervisors, while at the same time he exercises some supervisory functions. Staff members consult him about aspects of their jobs, but his suggestions must be congruent with the aims of the agency supervisors.

The identification of the consultant within the agency represents another problem. The consultant is hired by the administration but he is to relate to the interests and needs of the NEC staff. The consultant will be totally ineffective if he is seen as a tool of management or if he is seen as management's spy. On numerous occasions the consultants have been used by staff members to discuss personnel problems or problems in their relationships with other employees, to ventilate concerns about their relationships to their own supervisors, and to consider tactics for approaching issues within the organization. The consultants have made it a practice to avoid discussing such issues with anyone else without the specific knowledge and permission of the people involved. If anything, the consultant maintains a position of independence. He maintains his position as an outsider by maintaining a task orientation at all times. His job has come to be one of being helpful in thinking through ways of solving problems and not in judging the adequacy with which people perform their jobs.

Nonetheless the consultant has the task of becoming part of the center, and it is necessary for others to feel he is part of the center. The consultant tends to identify closely with the goals of the setting, supporting the staff when events prove frustrating, as they often do. Although the consultant may come from a different discipline with a different orientation toward problems, it is not his job to impress others with the superiority of his method of working and the secondary status of the methods of those who call upon his supposedly superior skills and knowledge.[12] It is his job to try to understand the applications of the methods of the agency using his services, and to help to sharpen the instrument so it may be used to its fullest power. He may do this in various ways including suggestions for variations in technique and approach.

In becoming part of the center the consultant has adopted the practice of the center to be called by his first name. However, some of the staff are somewhat uncomfortable and insist on using the consultant's title. Where appropriate the consultant has discussed his personal business and shared stories about children, cars, and boats. He has traded off-color stories with some of the men, and when asked has offered suggestions about problems with children, about careers, and about readings for term papers. He has loaned and borrowed books, and has attended office parties and other social affairs with the staff. All this does not indicate that the consultant has become "buddy-buddy" with the staff. He maintains his role, but in the process of becoming part of the center has accepted some of the ways of those with whom he works. It is our belief such a relationship can be established without losing appropriate distance and without loss of respect for the position.

The consultant has used his position, personal influence, and pro-

[12] Many of the problems in the consulting role are discussed by Howe (Bellak, 1964). She writes,

The point is simply that the people of the community do not feel that they need the psychiatrist's help; instead he needs theirs. He is no longer in a position to be "accepting" in his attitude toward them; instead, he must tactfully seek their acceptance, patiently court their favor, and humbly wait until they see fit to bestow (or perhaps not to bestow) on him the honor of a rightful place among them. Their decisions are the ones he must accept and it is to their judgment that he must defer. How then can the psychiatrist consider that he is responsible for the development and utilization of a community resource for psychiatric patients? The answer is simple: he is not. The responsibility belongs to the community (to the town or city and its agencies, to the county, the state and the nation) and is not his except in so far as the community, through those empowered to speak for it, freely decides to entrust that responsibility to him. For this to occur, he must first have demonstrated he is worthy of their trust. (p. 30)

fessional contacts to help in the work of the center, just as he would if he were a member of the staff:

Example 14. It was necessary to try to arrange a no-fee or a low-fee referral for psychotherapy on a fairly quick basis. It appeared the client needed help quickly and it did not seem advisable to wait for an opening at an outpatient clinic. The consultant made the contact with a private practitioner and asked him to accept the referral.

Example 15. A young Negro who was very impressive personally had just dropped out of high school. The reasons for his dropping out were not clear, but he wanted a specific kind of job, and no other. When an opportunity became available the consultant's office arranged for the young man to be used as a part-time research assistant until a more permanent job could be developed.

While the organization was growing, and before it developed a feeling for its own worth and its own potency, it was difficult for the NEC staff to speak directly to the higher-status professional community. The NEC staff did not speak the same language, and did not know what to expect from the professional community. Although the coordinators are usually the spokesmen to other agencies, sometimes the consultant assisted in this function.

Example 16. At one point representatives of the NEC staff met with members of the psychiatric and social-work staffs of an outpatient mental-hygiene clinic. The purpose of the meeting was ostensibly one of exploring how the two agencies could work together. The mental-hygiene clinic staff made it clear they accepted patients for psychotherapy only when the patients met the criteria for treatment established by the clinic. They had had a poor experience with unmotivated clients and were unwilling to commit any resources, or modify intake procedures in any fashion at all, even on an experimental basis. There was a clear refusal even to consider any other course. The meeting was rapidly getting nowhere because there did not seem to be any basis for discussion. The consultant was able to use his knowledge of the operation of outpatient clinics to elucidate the clinic's intake policy and procedures. This was accomplished through a series of questions to the psychiatric and social-work staffs which encouraged them to describe the details of their clinic. Once some level of communication had been re-established, the consultant also assisted the NEC staff in describing the operation of the NEC, and to indicate how its facilities might be of some use to the staff of the mental-hygiene clinic. Though little had been accomplished to arrange for treatment for NEC clients through the mental-hygiene clinic, *the clinic began to refer some of its patients to NEC for service.* Hopefully, a continuing relationship between clinic and NEC may eventuate in a more fully cooperative relationship.

The consultant's position as a high-status person associated with and identified with the goals of CPI provided another kind of support for the staff. CPI's very existence is a concrete and telling criticism of the failure of the schools, the welfare department, and various social agencies. That the traditional agencies were trying to deal with enormously difficult problems with inadequate resources, and with programs oriented toward another era and another set of problems, does not take the sting out of the criticism. Moreover, in many instances people in the traditional agencies were neither consulted nor informed of the new developments. Such bypassing was motivated in part by a conviction that consultation with traditional agencies would merely bring requests for more funds to do the same job that had already been found to be lacking in effectiveness. It is understandable that employees and officials of traditional agencies should feel suspicion and hostility toward the new agency. However, the NEC staff and other CPI workers identify closely with CPI as an agency and when an attack occurs the workers feel hurt and threatened because their jobs have such personal significance for them. There is little awareness of the worker's own role in stimulating some of the hostility, or in understanding attacks when the worker perceives himself as performing a worthwhile human service in circumstances where others have failed. Sometimes the worker expects appreciation and is hurt and puzzled when his efforts are met with deprecation and hostility. It then becomes the consultant's function to place the attack in perspective and to support the worth of the work of NEC despite external criticism.

For some time our consultants had been aware that the NEC staff members had a critical attitude toward the schools. Staff spoke of "push-outs" rather than dropouts and at first workers were inclined to be uncritically accepting of the statements offered by some applicants to the effect that they had been badly abused and misused by the schools. Later experience corrected some of the initial misimpressions, but sometimes the staff attitudes were communicated in their contacts with school people. A supervisor in the school system reported incidents in which NEC personnel were viewed as "demanding" school records. In another instance, an NEC staff person was attempting to obtain information about re-entering into school a girl who had had an illegitimate child. The school supervisor was trying to explain the school's rules governing re-entry, but he felt that the staff member impatiently accused him of being prejudiced against the girl.

Incidents such as these, magnified many times over by feelings of resentment and hurt, feelings elicited by the very existence of CPI, provide the background for the following occurrence at a disposition conference:

Example 17. NEC staff had been working with a modicum of success with a young man who had been classified as special-class material by the public schools. The public school had known him for years before he became of age and left school. School officials had not been contacted immediately, but as specific job plans were being developed for him the NEC staff invited the boy's teacher and a principal to the meeting.

The NEC staff was enthusiastic and eager in presenting their work with this boy. Much effort had gone into working with him, and the staff felt he was responding. When the boy left school he was almost entirely illiterate and he had been described as negativistic and unwilling to learn. Now, under the tutelage of one of the neighborhood workers, he was beginning to pick up some words in reading and, more importantly, was showing considerable motivation to learn to read street signs, store names, and other simple but practically useful words.

As the NEC's experience with this boy was related, the school principal became more critical of the efforts and he was, not too subtly, deprecating the efforts of the neighborhood worker to teach the boy any academic skills. While the meeting was conducted on a polite and restrained level, after the disposition conference was completed and the school personnel had left, it was clear the NEC staff were puzzled and angered. They had been trying to do a good job, had succeeded to some small degree, had invited the school people in to help, and now found themselves under attack as inexperienced, starry-eyed, and insufficiently concerned with the dangers of working with someone who needed exceedingly close supervision.

In the post-mortem discussion, the consultant was able to elicit expressions of anger and puzzlement about the attitudes of the school people. It was then possible to interpret the principal's reaction as a *counter-attack* upon CPI. Where the NEC staff saw themselves as fulfilling a specific function, the very existence of an operation such as CPI implies a failure of the traditional institutions to handle the job. There was some discussion of how missionary zeal is often maintained by assuming an incompetent and evil-intentioned "enemy." It was pointed out that in order to work hard to help an applicant it was not necessary to assume that the school people were intentionally doing a poor job. The discussion may have contributed to a somewhat softer attitude of NEC staff toward school officials. The consultant's function at this meeting was to put the frustration into some perspective so that what was happening could be seen to make sense. At the same time, he used his prestige to support NEC against the attack.

Many other frustrating events arise and whenever possible the consultant responds to the discouraged tone, or to the sense of helplessness or defeat, by using his professional authority or the weight of his word as a person of status to help overcome the morale problem. On occasion the staff has put in a lot of work and time helping a client only to discover he quit his job, began drinking again, or somehow did not fulfill the requirements of the job and was laid off. When the failure seems to lie in an applicant's intellectual or characterological deficiencies, some have a tendency to use the case as confirmation of the hopelessness of the inner-city population. When such cases arise, the consultant emphasizes the fact that frustration was to be expected and that the NEC would not exist in its present form if the job was an easy one.

On other occasions the staff finds itself frustrated by the rules and regulations of other agencies, or by interpretations of the law. For example, part of the difficulty in placing youth under 18 are child-labor and workmen's-compensation acts that restrict hazardous occupations to those over 18. Welfare regulations, now in process of changing, are such that an applicant who takes a job may very well lose out financially because he does not qualify for welfare funds if he is working. He cannot make as much working (because of his limited skills) as he can by accepting welfare. Adolescents paid through the work-crew program find their family's welfare checks decreased by the amount the adolescents receive as work-crew members. NEC staff either cannot place people in what seem to be appropriate positions because of such regulations, or the applicants themselves are disinclined to seek jobs because they literally cannot afford to work. In other instances applicants do not accept certain positions because they are holding out for a higher rate of pay. Apparently, some inner-city workers are more farsighted than they are usually credited with being. Expecting that he will be the first to be laid off, and knowing his unemployment-compensation check will be partly based on his last hourly rate, the urban worker is thinking ahead in a practical sense when he tries to push as hard as he can for a higher rate of pay, irrespective of what anyone tells him of the job's future prospects.

When such social realities frustrate the staff, the consultant sees it as his function to encourage others to take up the problems with the CPI executive level in the hopes that the regulation can be changed. Many of the staff see laws and bureaucratic regulation as unbending and unchanging. The consultant holds out the prospect that such regulations may be open to reconsideration or reinterpretation. In other instances the consultant tries to bring historical and social perspective to the immediate situation to prevent laws and regulations from being seen as blocks deliberately introduced to frustrate the staff's purposes. It is sometimes important to cite the historical conditions that led to the child-labor laws, or the purpose of welfare regulations, at least as they were originally promulgated and interpreted. The concept of "problem creation through problem solution" has been used as an interpretive principle in helping the NEC staff to see its own functions in social and historical perspective.

Though the disposition conference is the main medium through which the consultant relates to the NEC group, there is another monthly conference of the staff with the director of the manpower division. At this meeting the NEC staff and the executive body, located in a downtown central office, have an opportunity to exchange information, to air gripes, to note problems and to suggest solutions. The meetings were originally suggested by our Clinic staff because of a morale problem noted in the offices. The consultants from our Clinic attend these monthly meetings and are active in helping the NEC staff express their viewpoint to the executive level. Such support was necessary because staff members felt ill at ease in bringing up issues that might be considered criticisms of the executive level. At other times the consultant has taken it upon himself to voice what he thought was the viewpoint of the NEC staff when new proposals were brought up at the monthly meetings. The support the consultant has lent to the NEC staff has been important in helping to establish a working relationship with the staff and, surprisingly, it has resulted in only occasional friction with the executives.[13]

The consultant is also available for individual conferences with workers and supervisors about personnel problems. Such conferences may take place after the disposition conferences, but the consultant has made himself available at any time. The consultant has also seen it as his function to try to prevent workers from thinking of professional clinics or social agencies as the final answer to any difficult problem. There are certainly situations in which referral to a psychiatric clinic, to a psychotherapist, or to a family-service agency is appropriate and necessary. However, such referrals are difficult to effect, and even when

[13] A distinct problem can arise when supervisory level personnel or the executive level feel the consultant is usurping policy-making or supervisory functions. At times the consultant's suggestions or comments may seem to have the force of law in an office, or the consultant may encourage others to take actions the executive level later disapprove. The problem was anticipated in discussions with the executive level and with supervisors. When differences of opinion did arise, the consultant and others concerned had sufficient trust and confidence in each other that they could discuss their differences and settle them.

the applicant follows through on the referral there is no guarantee the troublesome problem will disappear immediately. An adolescent who is on a work crew will still appear every day, and an adult who is placed on a job still has to meet his employer's requirements. It is clear that referral to a professional agency will not result in the immediate dissolution of whatever undesirable characteristic the applicant has.

Referral of a problem to another agency is made with the hopes that the second agency may be able to handle a problem the first agency cannot. In one sense the referral is made for the client's benefit but in another it is a worker's method of relieving his frustration with the client. When the consultant makes the point that referral will not solve the problem for the client, he removes a method of relieving frustration. However, the consultant's statement that another agency may not be able to handle the problem as effectively as NEC is highly flattering to the NEC staff. It is NEC's job to work around the psychological problems presented by the applicant, and to influence the psychopathological features through helping the applicant master steps in preparing himself for employment. The consultant's resistance of the temptation to teach concepts of psychopathology, his attempts to keep the staff focused on the issues the client presents to them, and his confidence in the ability of the staff to deal with the problems are highly supportive of the work of the staff. His support helps to relieve some of the sense of frustration, while he discourages the tendency to "dump" a problem through referral.

What skills and knowledge does the consultant require in his work? Because psychological tests are used, and because Negroes and lower-class clients do not score well on tests, the consultant frequently provides technical information about tests, their uses, and limitations. Those not familiar with test-validation procedures are inclined to see the test as an absolute predictor of occupational success. Moreover, test manuals assert there are occupational families for given patterns of scores. Sometimes counselors or placement workers are inclined to take the norms and suggestions as absolutes, although most maintain a flexible attitude.

On numerous occasions the consultant has presented the argument that the tests are not absolute perfect predictors of job success. He has discussed the concept of test validation and has argued that in an operation like NEC, it is the staff's job to find the test's predictive failures. Case histories such as the one presented by Sarason (1959) of a girl with an IQ in the 70's who functioned very ably as a laboratory technician have been cited. Evidence that some people are mentally deficient only by test standards has been presented and discussed.

Clark and Plotkin's (1963) findings are cited to indicate that high-school IQ tests or scholastic-aptitude test scores predict neither college grades nor completion of college for Negro youth attending integrated colleges. The consultant has also made an effort to have NEC staff consider very closely motivational aspects of test-taking. For example, many Negro applicants will sacrifice speed for accuracy. The applicant may obtain a very low test score, but be correct on nearly every item he has attempted. In effect the psychologist has used his technical knowledge to try to prevent any overestimation of the significance of test scores.

The consultant clearly requires knowledge of psychopathology and personality dynamics, but he also needs some background in techniques for managing problems in a life setting. Experience in institutions in ward management, camp directing, public-school teaching, residential treatment center, or a similar institutional setting where the goal is one of adaptation to a group-living situation can be helpful. There are circumstances in which it seems necessary and desirable to make specific suggestions to handle difficult situations. Frequently the problems have to do with acting-out adolescents, but at other times issues of psychopathology come up and it is necessary to understand and respond to the psychopathology.

Example 18. A work-crew supervisor, an unusually capable, calm, and personable young woman, originally a secretary, had an adolescent girl with a history of hospitalization for an undefined mental disturbance. The girl was working in an office, and from time to time she would act in bizarre and distressing fashion, becoming quite demanding of special, unrealistic considerations. She swallowed a number of aspirin tablets, letting the supervisor know she had done so. The supervisor found that the girl would become more demanding if her demands were met, but she frequently would calm down if the supervisor firmly insisted she get back to her work. The supervisor was concerned about whether she should continue working with the girl. Her manner in presenting the case suggested a liking for the girl and a sense of confidence in her ability to work with her, but she was concerned because the girl's behavior seemed so crazy. The girl also was threatening to quit if she did not get some additional concession, but the supervisor's description of her actions suggested that the girl was attempting to test and to manipulate the situation.

Her records indicated she was supposed to have maintained contact with a psychiatric clinic on an outpatient basis, but she had refused to keep her appointments. In view of her history of hospitalization and the apparently histrionic suicidal gesture, it was felt advisable that she be under regular psychiatric care. The consultant had not interviewed the girl, but on the basis of what he learned from the supervisor he suggested the supervisor be quite firm in insisting that the duties of the position were to be carried out properly, and that she confront the girl with the alternative that she could not continue working on the work crew unless she did follow through with outpatient care.

Following the conference with the consultant, the supervisor confronted the girl with the alternatives and was relieved to find the girl accepted her demands rathers docilely. The supervisor's consistent, firm attitudes have also succeeded in minimizing instances of behavior which were formerly distressing.

Example 19. As part of a follow-up study of applicants who had been to the office, a summertime neighborhood worker ran across a woman who was outspokenly bitter about her previous experience with the NEC, and indeed a check of the record did find some small degree of justification for her feeling that she had been maltreated at the NEC. She had demanded a position so she could earn enough money to buy uniforms to enroll in a practical-nursing course. She was on welfare, and had been on welfare for some time past. She was sent out for a job but on arriving was told the job paid the minimum wage and not more as she had been led to expect. Even though she wanted a position only temporarily, she angrily refused to accept the position and did not return to the NEC. Discussion of the case with other members of the staff suggested that she was a troublesome person in the neighborhood, in constant conflict with school and political authorities about a wide variety of issues. Although she was constantly flailing about, there was never any record of constructive protest or follow-through on any of her complaints. One of the staff had seen her in action at a public meeting and was shocked by her intemperate and incoherent style of voicing her opinions.

Usually clients are followed up until there is clear indication that they are not interested or until there is some other resolution of the case. The summer neighborhood worker, an idealistic college student out to show up the pretentious phonies who would not work with a difficult case, brought her up at a disposition conference, challenging the regular NEC staff to work with her. The consultant intervened at the disposition conference suggesting there was good reason to leave well enough alone here. There was a good possibility she was an injustice seeker and the next thing to a litigious paranoid. He was able to discuss some of the general characteristics of such people, pointing out that faultfinding and argumentation were probably deeply ingrained parts of her character structure. There was no clear evidence she was motivated to do anything else except seek situations she could complain about. She was probably more expert at faultfinding than any of us would be in convincing her otherwise and, on these grounds, it was suggested that the initiative for her returning to the NEC be left with her. It was agreed to send her a routine but polite post card inviting her in again, but no more intensive follow-up was to be undertaken.

The consultant tries to help the staff to arrive at a decision that comes out of the staff's deliberations. In this situation a combination of psychotherapeutic and teaching techniques seems to be required. As the expert at the conference, the consultant, like the therapist, tries to create and maintain an atmosphere in which everyone feels free to participate and to communicate. The coordinators and supervisors have worked to create such an atmosphere in their own offices, so the consultant's job is really one of maintaining an atmosphere already present to a large extent. Staff members recognize the necessity for expressing their opinions freely in order to help the client and also to help maintain relationships in the office. Issues argued out at the conference table prevent festering bad feeling among the staff members.

The consultant serves as a mediator among the various workers, trying to bring out the opinions and feelings about a client held by various people who have had contact with him. The workers sometimes identify closely with applicants. Sometimes opinions are formed rapidly and a worker commits himself to a recommendation that does not seem appropriate for an applicant. Others at the conference may disagree vigorously and it is the consultant's function to get the viewpoints stated and to attempt to restructure and to restate the issues. He needs to be sensitive to the feelings of the workers and to see the merits in any particular position. He can then reorient the discussion. Just as the timing of therapeutic interpretations is important, so is the timing of interventions in the conference important.

Example 20. A neighborhood worker was discussing a boy of about sixteen who had numerous juvenile offenses. In her efforts to sell the client to the group, she was minimizing and excusing much of what the boy had done. He was arrested once for brandishing a knife during a fight with another boy. The worker insisted he was not really at fault because he was only defending a friend against an attack. One of the work-crew foremen picked up the tone of denial and was sarcastically attacking both the worker and the boy. The meeting threatened to get out of hand and the focus of discussion, disposition for the boy, was becoming lost. The argument began to polarize around the issue of whether society was too soft on the hoods or whether the police were brutally unjust to poor innocent boys. The consultant intervened by helping the foreman bring out the enormous difficulties in dealing with a hostile and aggressive adolescent, because this information was relevant to placement for the boy. The consultant helped the worker to see that the boy was trying to put his best foot forward for her because he wanted something from her. The focus shifted to the difference in behavior the boy showed in two different situations, and the workers were able to learn something from the interchange.

The consultant did not deal directly with the worker's denial of the boy's problems or her overidentification with him as a personal deficiency that needed correction. He dealt with the issue by pointing out that it was absolutely necessary for the worker to believe in her client if she were to be effective with him, but that sometimes this necessary belief led to a blindness to the client's difficulties that might result in an unfortunate placement for him. The consultant did not interpret or reflect the feelings of anger that were clearly apparent in both worker and work-crew foreman. His tactic was to restate the issue so that both work-crew foreman and neighborhood worker made a positive contribution to the disposition conference.

The following quotations from a tape-recorded discussion of how the NEC staff perceive the consultant's activities highlight the effectiveness of psychotherapeutic skills in the disposition conference.

We become opinionated. We want to win our point. If we don't win our point it hurts us. Each of us has an idea. Each of us has his own point and we drift. You come in with one or two words and you break the stalemate. You come in almost at the right time. One or two words and we're on the right track. You cause us to think differently. We reflect back. Maybe the other guy is right too.

The neighborhood workers have a lot of things inside themselves, but they can't articulate them very well. You help the workers get it out, through the kinds of ways you use yourself. . . . You appear to have the ability to help a person get out some of his feelings about something. You seem to sense the general direction in which one wants to go, and you have the ability to help him get it out of himself, spoken. You may have to use words in doing it, but this helps stimulate a person to say it. You help workers to think out loud and to talk out loud.

A neighborhood worker says:

You have this knack or this gift of making people feel at ease so they can talk. A lot of times I can freeze up, but you can come from one level to the next level. This is a gift a lot of professional people don't have, being able to talk to people at different levels, and this is, I think, something that you have. I feel at ease talking with you, and I feel I could talk with you anywhere at any time on any subject and I wouldn't be made to feel below, you know this sort of thing.

The comment of the last worker seems particularly important. Just as the professional sometimes may have trouble communicating with the lower-class patient, he may have difficulty in communicating with a staff worker of that background. A graduate student, observing one of the consultants working with NEC, raised the question of why a psychologist was necessary for the position. It seemed to him the consultant was relating to the group just as any intelligent, articulate, sensitive human being might. He could not see that the consultant's activities were purposeful because they were couched in common language and expressed in conversational tones rather than in the stilted, couchside manner adopted by some psychotherapists. An analogous remark was made in the schools by a teacher who said, "You know it's funny, you don't seem like a professor somehow."

The consultant, like the therapist, tries to provide support to others who have to deal with anxiety-arousing issues through his own manner in dealing with staff and issues presented. He must be sensitive to the anxieties that are aroused, and flexible in his methods of dealing with the anxiety.

Example 21. When patients began to be referred to the NEC from the state hospital, the staff of NEC felt a great deal of anxiety. The anxiety was clearly apparent in the discussion of whether or not NEC should accept such referrals, whether the workers could be of help to the patients, and whether anyone would hire a former mental patient. The issue came up around a patient who came with a diagnosis of simple schizophrenia. At the disposition conference the consultant interpreted the general feeling of anxiety by talking about how the image of the mental patient was one of a raving maniac who was dangerous and would kill or rape someone. In discussing the issue he deliberately overdrew the issue, attempting to interject some humor into the situation. At no point did he ask any of the staff to openly express their own feelings of fear and uncertainty. The consultant then pointed out that no one was crazy in all ways and at all times, and that there are jobs where it pays to be crazy. The consultant pointed out that there were many routine jobs conducted in relative isolation, in which mental patients functioned effectively even though they were objectively quite disturbed.

The focus shifted from the problem in dealing with the person's mental instability to trying to understand his specific characteristics and then tailor a job to take advantage of his assets and minimize his liabilities. In the case of the schizophrenic the consultant was able to interpret the hospital report to show the man's strengths: he seemed to go into the hospital every few years for a few months to recover from some stressful situation, and in the past he had worked fairly steadily at routine, isolated, menial tasks. There seemed to be no reason why he could not be helped to find a similar position, and it was emphasized that it was not the job of the NEC to cure his mental illness. Once the issue had been refocused for this case, it eased acceptance of other referrals from mental-hygiene clinics and State hospitals.

One worker commented about the consultant's role in helping them with their own anxiety:

It's the way you attack a problem. Everybody is all heated up, anxious. You sit back, calmly think about it for a second or two and say, you know, in such a tone of voice . . . it's like a driver in a motor boat who is doing 110 miles an hour and who knows really how to handle it, and perhaps the young guy is getting in the motor boat for the first or second time and really thinks he can drive it but he's really not too sure of himself. You can sit back, you've got the confidence in yourself. Your speaking voice is another asset. The tone of voice you talk in. How can I put it? You can calm down a situation just by muttering a few words. Hold tight. Let's take a look at things. Let's evaluate the situation. Let's pick it apart and look at it face value.

Another one of the staff expressed her feelings about the consultant's presence by saying, "People aren't alone with the problem." [14] Her sentiments were echoed by another worker who said with great feeling, "You know it!"

The consultant has stated that he is available at any time for a discussion of problems around individual cases. Staff members know they may call the consultant and he will try to answer telephone calls as soon as he is free. Individual conferences have been scheduled as necessary. Occasionally conferences were scheduled in early morning hours, in the evening, at lunch, or on Saturdays. The staff has been very reasonable about the opportunity to call the consultant. The opportunity to call is a form of support and reassurance, but it does not seem to have created an overdependence.

As part of his function, the consultant may suggest specific techniques or tactics to approach problems presented by given clients. The suggestion may involve a modification of the usual modes of working with clients, in keeping with the concept that the consultant attempts to improve the usefulness of the NEC as an instrument.

Example 22. A neighborhood worker had had a number of interviews with a 16-year-old dropout. The worker had been concentrating on trying to find a job for the boy and had been unsuccessful in locating anything. However, the boy kept coming in and the worker felt at a loss to know what to do with him. The consultant suggested he talk to the boy over coffee about his thoughts about his future. It was pointed out that the boy was not yet 17 and that he would be looking for work for a long time. The worker met with the boy and found that he was interested in getting into the navy when he turned 17. The consultant suggested the neighborhood worker help him to purchase a book of past navy tests. Clearly, the boy could not join if he could not pass the test, and he could not get a good position or good training if he did not get

---

[14] The reactions of NEC staff are strikingly similar to those of teachers to our consultants. It is our impression that teachers and NEC staff appreciate most the fact that we involve ourselves rather intimately in their problems in *their* settings, a degree of involvement they have not previously encountered and to which they initially respond with caution, suspicion, and hope.

a good mark on the test. With the neighborhood worker's assistance, the boy bought a book and the two of them went over some of the tests. When the boy ran into difficulty with the tests, he was quite receptive to a suggestion that he go to night school to brush up on math and English. The neighborhood worker tutored him for a few sessions, and then helped him to register in school.

The NEC concept of service is one of providing active help and the staff have a great reluctance to give up on an applicant. A favorite phrase in one of the centers is: "Let's pick him up, dust him off, and try again." It is policy that NEC attempt to work with anyone who comes in and not to say "no" arbitrarily to any request for service. However, there are times when it seems desirable to refuse a request for service because the service does not seem in the interests of the applicant.

Example 23. A boy had been on and off work crews several times and was a constant problem to the community (he had numerous difficulties with the law), his family, and the NEC. It seems he would appear for service shortly after he got into trouble in the community. The juvenile court judge, happy to see he was being rehabilitated, would either suspend his sentence or extend his probation, despite the fact that he had broken probation on several occasions. It also appeared that his father would plead his case both at NEC and at the court. His father felt he was a wild boy who would settle down, and he was concerned lest the entire family be shamed by his being sent away to reform school. The boy's father was a respected person who could present a most pathetic, heartrending picture of his and the boy's plight. He constantly succeeded in winning everyone's sympathy and in gaining another chance for his boy.

At one point the boy had been seen by a psychiatrist who felt he was very anxious and desirous of help for himself. The boy, however, felt he could not enter treatment because his father would then see him as crazy. Shortly afterwards the boy got into legal difficulties again. Again his father pleaded with NEC to help him. Although he had failed to adapt to the work crew on several occasions, and it was apparent he was continually being protected by his father, the psychiatrist repeated his opinion that the boy could be helped if he would enter treatment. However, the psychiatrist felt he would be breaking a confidence if he expressed such an opinion to the court without the boy's consent, and the boy was not about to consent. The consultant suggested that NEC indicate to the father that the boy would not be acceptable to NEC unless some form of psychotherapeutic help was forthcoming. The father vigorously opposed the idea and succeeded in shaking the neighborhood worker's resolve. The worker agreed to see if the boy would get a job so that he could go before the court penitent and employed. The morning the boy was to come in for an interview for a job he slept late and missed his appointment. At this point the psychological consultant repeated the restriction that nothing be done for the boy at all unless he agreed to enter treatment. When it was clear that NEC was holding firm, the father agreed that such a recommendation be made to the court along with the stipulation that the boy's continued attendance in treatment and at the work crew be made a condition of his probation. The court was to be notified at once if he broke his appointments or stopped attending the work-crew sessions.

As this case turned out, the boy did enter treatment but he did not keep his appointments regularly and his attendance at the work crew was irregular. The boy quickly got into trouble again and, once again, his father attempted to manipulate the situation to protect the boy. By this time the father's efforts to use NEC for his purposes were clear, and staff had little problem in refusing to assist further. The idea that conditions could be established under which service would be forthcoming, or the idea that it was possible to serve by refusing service, were concepts that led to a modified view of what constitutes help.

THE PANEL INTERVIEW

The NEC is really a representative of the social order and, as such, it is potentially a powerful force not only in changing individual work patterns but also in changing attitudes and self-images. The existence of the NEC itself is a sign that the larger society is saying, "We have confidence in you. We think you can make it. We want you to make it." If it is true that attitudes toward the self are shaped by what society tells people society thinks of them, the existence of an institution that says, "We think well of you" should be of great value in modifying the feelings of self-hatred that some believe members of minority groups feel toward themselves. The concept that the self-image is formed partly as a function of feedback from the larger society was put to use in fashioning a counseling technique that has had some limited application. The technique, devised by the consultant, uses the staff of the neighborhood center as the authoritative source of feedback. The following case exemplifies the technique.

Example 24. A 19-year-old Negro male who was a high-school graduate came in to the NEC seeking a job. He was placed as a shop assistant to a custom lamp manufacturer. The young man was very well liked and did a good job. He even wrote some promotional material on lamps, but since the company was very small there was no place for him except in the shop. He worked there for several months, but then lost interest and resigned. When the counselor pursued the issue he found that the young man just felt the job was not for him. He really had a desire to write, and wanted to go to college, but he felt helpless and hopeless about his situation. He had made some scattered efforts to obtain information about scholarships but had not pursued anything with any vigor. At the present time he was living alone in a room. He came from a broken family and did not feel he could live with his mother in her apartment. He lived close to an aunt, but really had no one to encourage him in his ambitions. He had no thought about what he wanted to do, except that he wanted to write, and was not satisfied with a menial position. His case was brought up at a disposition conference after he had quit the job in the lamp shop.

The young man had made a very favorable impression on both the counselor and the neighborhood worker. However, his ambition to write was viewed with some serious question. He had not done much writing, and even now when he was not working he was not actually producing very much. His General Aptitude Test Battery scores indicated only average verbal ability, and his high-school record was spotty but generally poor. The group at the conference had a lot of questions about him. Although he had had a job with a boss who liked him, he had not kept it. His college ambitions did not seem to be very strong, and there was some question about why he had not pursued a college course in high school. Despite the questions, both neighborhood worker and counselor felt the young man had much to offer, although they too wondered about why he had not followed through. The group did not feel satisfied that they had had enough contact with the young man to feel they knew him. Someone suggested it would be helpful if all present met him and, at that point, a counseling technique was devised.

The consultant proposed that the boy present his own cause to the group who then would decide whether they would support him in his ambitions. Actually the group had agreed to support the applicant's request if it seemed at all reasonable following the interviews. The counselor, who had had most contact with him, was to call him and tell him to prepare a written statement to be presented in person to the staff of the NEC. He was to include some of his wishes for the future, and he was to expose himself to questions from the group. He was told further that if he convinced the staff he was capable, the staff would support him by finding another job for him and would assist him as necessary in making applications for college.

On the appointed afternoon a group of eight people met with the applicant. The applicant was seated at the end of a long conference table. The counselor, who was to act in the role of his advocate for this meeting, sat at his left. Half the group were Negro and half were white. The applicant appeared in jacket, shirt, and tie, and all the staff had also been encouraged to wear jackets in a formal manner. When the applicant was introduced to the staff, appropriate titles were employed. The effort was made to make the situation formal and formidable to ,a certain extent.

The counselor had been instructed to be the applicant's advocate. He introduced the applicant, stated his feeling that the applicant was indeed a worthy prospect, and he encouraged the applicant in his presentation. When the applicant faltered slightly, or when the presentation seemed to lag, it was the counselor's duty to introduce further material which would help the applicant in presenting his case. After the applicant presented himself, the staff questioned him about his presentation and about his plans. The counselor did not participate in the questioning. When the applicant was having difficulty with a question, or had not answered a question as fully as he might, the counselor would interject a comment or would remind the applicant of other relevant information.

The applicant's presentation, including the recitation of a poem he had written recently, was very effective, lasting about 15 minutes. The staff spent another 20 minutes questioning the young man. The staff had been instructed to ask whatever questions seemed pertinent, but not to conduct a hostile cross examination. The meeting went unusually well. The applicant was personable and presented himself ably. He was clearly nervous, but it would be remarkable if he were completely at ease in the situation. He answered all questions with apparent sincerity. He attributed his poor grades in school to a lack of hope to do anything more, and indicated that his interest in writing stemmed from the interest an English teacher took in his work. Despite attempts by various members of the staff to discourage his desire for college, and offer to place him in a good job immediately, he defended his ambition strongly. He wanted to write and he saw college as a vehicle toward his ambition.

At the end of the questioning period, the applicant was asked to leave the room. The staff then discussed his presentation and evolved a plan to present to him. The staff would plan to obtain a position for him. The counselor would follow up with him by helping him to make applications at colleges, and by helping him to get started in night school to brush up on mathematics. He was to put some small part of his salary into a bank account each week to save for clothes and other incidental expenses. The staff were in wholehearted agreement with the plan.

The applicant was called back into the conference room and was given the staff's decision that his presentation had been effective and that the staff had sufficient confidence in him to support his ambitions. The plan was outlined to him and the group congratulated him. The applicant was clearly impressed by the procedure. He was not demonstrably joyous, but rather he seemed almost stunned. There seemed little question that he would follow through, and the staff were well pleased with the afternoon's work.

The applicant did return and within a month he was placed in a job. He returned to the office again for further interviews with the counselor. He wrote for scholarship information and actually made out a budget setting aside a small amount for savings. However, shortly afterward, the follow-through began faltering. First, night-school registration was already closed, and he could not be admitted to any courses. Secondly, the boy's high-school counselor said she did not feel she could support his college ambitions because of his indifferent record. The applicant was not aware of the high-school counselor's opinion but it may have subtly affected the NEC counselor's optimism. Thirdly, the NEC counselor became ill and missed an early appointment with the applicant. Although the applicant was informed of the counselor's illness, the applicant apparently missed the following appointment and then for a period of two weeks did not respond to efforts to reach him. When he was finally contacted and came in for an appointment, he related that he stayed on his new job three weeks and then inexplicably found himself dispirited, moody, and somewhat depressed. He simply stopped going to work, describing himself as "lazy." He felt rather chagrined and concerned that he had let other people down. When he came for the interview, his appearance had also changed. He was no longer the clean-cut young man with jacket and tie, but his hair was now "processed," and he was identifying with a group of hip friends who did not share his other ambitions. The experience seems to have mobilized an identity crisis for him and may have pushed him toward a choice.

The NEC counselor was somewhat discouraged, but not ready to give up on the applicant. He was discouraged because the applicant had started out so optimistically and then, unaccountably, had given up. The counselor scheduled further appointments with the applicant and at this writing continues to see the applicant. The case indicates the necessity for close, continuing follow-up, particularly when an attempt is being made to break with long-standing social attitudes and expectations. Clearly, the struggle is with the entire neighborhood, and heroic measures are necessary. The panel interview seemed to have stimulated hope and positive effort for a period of five to six weeks, but apparently much more support and action were necessary before the boy could follow through on a course of action oriented to goals set in the future and far removed from the actions of his friends.

The panel interview has been used in other instances with selected clients. It may be useful when it is desirable to support an applicant's ambitions, or to try to provide a large dose of reassurance and support for an applicant. The following excerpts indicate some of the feelings and ambitions applicants are able to express through this medium. In this interview the applicant is a 17-year-old Negro male who had recently dropped out of high school.

Q. When did you first start hating school?
A. The first time I remember hating school was about the fifth grade. I didn't hate the teacher or the school itself, it was just that I always got restless and then I would get up and walk around. I had no interest in schoolwork. The only time I was happy was at recess and at play period.

Q. Why did you decide to quit at this time and how did you come about doing it?
A. Now at high school it was the same and I wanted to quit, so I stayed, thinking that it would be different. I knew that I needed a good excuse for quitting. This was when I really started to be a troublemaker. I tried everything. Finally, I told my uncle that I didn't want to stay in school. This is when I came to see Mrs. P. and she made the necessary arrangements.

Q. Where do you really desire to live? Why?

A. I desire to live here where I'm happy. First of all, my uncle has a way with boys and having a son the same age that I am we get along very well. We get our heads busted when we need it and we have our fun also. He has trained us on odd jobs and corrected our mistakes by showing us how to do it correctly. My aunt I can talk to with ease and a feeling of being free, as I would my own mother. Having someone around being my own age helps too.

Q. Do you think that you will return to school?

A. No, I am sincere about my feelings about school and the only school that I'll attend is apprentice training on the kind of work that I want.

The technique of the panel interview was adopted as part of the initial Job Corps screening process. When the first group of boys were to be selected for the Job Corps, the last step in the application process (when it was clear the boys qualified in every other way) was a panel interview. A group of eight to ten people met with the applicant at the downtown headquarters of CPI. The Job Corps applicant was accompanied either by a work-crew foreman or by a counselor who knew him. As in the previous situation, the boy had the task of presenting his reasons for wanting to join the Job Corps. The counselor or the foreman was there to assist him as necessary.

The panel interviews were typically short and there was no opportunity to provide immediate feedback to the applicants. The modification in technique was necessary because there were large numbers of interviews to be carried out and quotas for the Job Corps were not known at that time. The atmosphere of the panels was friendly and supportive, a factor that was probably important in determining the relative ease with which most of the boys handled themselves in what was ostensibly a stressful situation. Although a few of the boys had difficulty in expressing themselves in more than a few simple words, many more were surprisingly articulate. Observers who had little or no previous contact with work-crew boys and NEC applicants were very favorably impressed. The boys were described as likable, good humored, reflective, insightful, and eager for opportunity.

The favorable impression many of the boys were able to make indicates their ability to meet the stress of the situation. At the very least we can say the panel interview, conducted as described, is not overly stressful to the vast majority of inner-city youth. It is not clear the success experience in handling the panel interview has any lasting effect, but it is clear that many of the boys took the opportunity to express something of what they felt and experienced in a way they had not done previously, and certainly not to an audience of receptive authority figures.

PROBLEMS AND LIMITATIONS OF THE CONSULTING ROLE

The consultant has a number of problems in maintaining his usefulness. First, he is in a position in which he is tempted to set himself up as an indisputable authority. It is distinctly necessary for him to recognize the developing competencies of others, and not to present himself and his views in such fashion that it is impossible for others to dispute him. If there is no possibility for disagreeing with the consultant, it does not mean that others agree. It simply means that disagreement will not be expressed and an attitude of covert resistance to his influence will be encouraged. There is a distinct danger that he may respond to the deference extended to him by talking too much. He is then in danger of getting himself into the position of being the outsider telling others how to do their jobs.

A second problem has to do with the importation of professional pessimism into the agency. The experienced professional tends to view applicants by the standards treating agencies use to evaluate the good therapeutic risk. The professional is frequently inclined to say "nothing can be done here," that is, to approach the problem of helping the other person with a minimum of enthusiasm, and eventually prove he was right in the first place. There is the tendency to judge an applicant by clinic standards, and to argue that if this applicant was not a good risk for psychotherapy he will not respond to any effort to help him. The consultant is often tempted to say, "Forget about this person. You can't help him." However, he has curbed this tendency sharply. As one of the neighborhood workers expressed it, "There is a danger that you would tell us the job couldn't be done. However, you don't tell us it's impossible so we continue to try and succeed in helping an applicant."

A third problem faces the consultant when the workers do begin developing independent competencies. At an early stage in the development of a new service organization, the anxiety level is fairly high. Methods have not been developed and tested, and the need for the help and support of the consultant, from the point of view of the worker's morale, is great. However, with organizational growth, and with continued experience in the setting, the initial uncertainty and the hope for magical solutions give way to the realities the staff encounters. The number of practical alternatives becomes clear in the course of time. When the staff's anxiety level decreases, the emotional need for the consultant decreases, and in fact he may be in gross danger of becoming, from the new point of view of the staff, an overpaid fifth wheel. Just as it is necessary for the psychotherapist to recognize the time for termination of a therapeutic relationship, it may be necessary for the consultant to recognize when his major usefulness has come to an end, or when it is necessary for him to fulfill a different function. From his point of view, it may be difficult to give up the position of the respected opinion-giver, but it may be a reality he must anticipate.

A final problem arises when the consultant begins to relate to the agency in ways that are convenient for him. Though it is useful for him to stay close to developments in the agency, as time goes on he may not have the same closeness he once did. As a personnel change, so do the relationships the consultant has developed. The older staff members are like familiar friends, while newer members are strangers. The feeling tone of an agency may change in subtle ways, and because the consultant tends after a period of time to relate only to some partial aspect of the whole operation, he may not be fully aware of the changes.

CPI, as a rapidly growing service organization, has a policy of promoting from within. Workers move up rapidly to better-paying and more prestigeful supervisory positions. Whereas early in the operation the motive to serve was predominant, desires for personal advancement come into play once the possibilities for advancement become clear. The consultant may misread some of the motivational forces if he does not maintain a closeness to the whole organization. He may then finds his efforts to maintain continued interest in what *he* feels is important are frustrated because he no longer finds the enthusiastic spirit of service that comes from newness and hope. The consultant has the continuing problem of recognizing the changing feeling tone of the agency, and recognizing the shifting relationships within the agency so that he remains truly of help and does not become an outside critic unrealistically carping at an inevitable change.

A CRUCIAL FACTOR?

We do not pretend to know all the factors that made it relatively easy for us to become closely related to the NEC and to gain the feeling that the relationship was beneficial to us, the staff, and the clients. In discussing this matter among ourselves it occurred to us that there was a selective factor that might well have been the necessary, albeit not sufficient, ingredient in the relationship which was developed. This factor was that those clinic members who worked in CPI settings (we include here the work crews and the NEC) were people who were (a) relatively unimpressed with their professional labels and academic titles, (b) attracted to new settings for rendering help, and (c) convinced that education does not guarantee wisdom and that professional training is by no means a guarantee of interpersonal effectiveness, flexibility in technical approach, and openness to change. There may be doubt about the *degree* to which clinic members had these characteristics, but *there can be doubt that these characteristics or attitudes were possessed by the NEC staff in high degree.* In short, it is our belief that the NEC and clinic staffs very quickly recognized an identity in attitude that made the port-of-entry problem no particular problem. Whereas in the schools the port-of-entry problem could sometimes be characterized as a battle, in the NEC it would be an exaggeration to characterize it as a skirmish.

In the following chapter, we shall present a verbatim transcript of a disposition conference. The reader may obtain from this a clearer picture of the operation of the NEC and of the way in which the consultant relates to the total operation.

Chapter 16

The Disposition Conference

The disposition conference is the equivalent of an intake conference in a clinic or a hospital. It was originally introduced into the process as a method for implementing a CPI policy to the effect that *all* staff members share in the responsibility for decisions. As we have already indicated, the NEC staff members differed widely from each other in background. They held varying attitudes toward lines of communication, some being prone to check every move with someone else, others leaning toward a "do-it-yourself" philosophy. Complications would arise when a neighborhood worker would skip all of the steps in the evaluation process and send an applicant out on a position, or when with all good intentions the worker would promise the applicant a training course or a job, and then discover the applicant could not qualify. On the other hand, it sometimes occurred that NEC's desire to have complete records, and to have an applicant complete the process would outweigh need, and an applicant would get into the treadmill of "come back next week for another appointment." The requirement that all cases be staffed through a disposition conference represented an assurance that the CPI policy of shared responsibility would be carried out, and it represented a form of control to ensure that an applicant "touched bases" before being referred to a job or to a training opportunity. It also represented an institutionalized form of control in relation to the affective involvement of applicants and staff. Because several people had seen the applicant, and the group pooled their impressions, any highly idiosyncratic opinion received a hearing and could be checked against the reality of information and impressions gained by others.

Psycho-Educational Clinic consultants attended disposition conferences weekly, in addition to having individual conferences with staff members on call. The disposition conference proved to be an excellent vantage point in that the problems of the applicants and limitations in the program quickly became apparent. When an applicant came in and the conference could not come up with what seemed to be a satisfactory disposition, when follow-ups to staff dispositions revealed that applicants were incapable of carrying through, or when cases came up repeatedly, gaps in service or the problems the applicants presented became abundantly clear. We have already provided some indication of how the consultants functioned in relation to the disposition conference. In the material to follow, a verbatim transcript of one disposition conference, the reader may see the operation of the conference, the staff, and the consultant, although the bare words cannot fully convey the spirit of the meeting.

. . . verbatim proceedings of a disposition conference, held at a Neighborhood Employment Center, at which time the following were present:

v.c. Vocational counselor

p.i. Placement interviewer, Connecticut State Employment Service

n.w. I. Neighborhood worker

n.w. II. Neighborhood worker

s.i. Student intern (special undergraduate summer replacement)

c. Coordinator

dr. p.e.c. Psycho-Educational Clinic consultant

DORIS SMITH

n.w. I: Doris Smith. She is 19 years old. She is single, and she lives with her stepmother and father. She is Negro, and she has had difficulty with the law.

v.c.: What type of difficulty?

n.w. I: Just truancy.

v.c.: That's all?

n.w. I: In the school.

dr. p.e.c.: If a kid is truant from school, how does she get to the police?

n.w. I: Shall I read the report or what?

v.c.: Why don't you go ahead and read the report, where she has been, what transpired to have her sent where she went.

n.w. I: I called Mrs. D. She is a social worker on B. Street. She gave me this information. Doris Smith was expelled in February, 1961 for beating a teacher. She was a constant behavior problem in school. Her home environment was very poor.

It was decided that she be sent to The School for Girls. Her mother died when she was six years old, and her father was constantly drunk, plus he was living with a woman who he later married.

She took an aptitude test while at The School for Girls and scored 93. She was subject to periodic outbursts of violent temper and aggressive, destructive impulses. The only person she seemed drawn to is an older married sister. She is now living with her father and stepmother.

Mrs. D. visited the home and said that the stepmother has the most unusual, adverse personality she ever saw. She is working with Mrs. C. of The School for Girls on the possibility of Doris moving in with her sister. She has an application for state aid, but Mrs. D. feels, along with Doris, that she is probably motivated toward securing a job.

I called Mrs. C. too. She called my home last night.[1]

v.c.: What is her occupation at The School for Girls? Is she a social worker?

n.w. I: She is a social worker at The School for Girls, Mrs. C. She called my house and gave me a report on Doris. She was committed in February 1961 due to troubles in school. While at the Girls' School she was a problem, violent temper outburst. She left in October, 1962 and moved back home, but was brought back the following month, November, 1962, due to conflict with her father, who suspected that she was, you know, doing things, that she claims she wasn't.

Mrs. C. talked with Doris yesterday about living with her sister who is married, and Mrs. C. thinks that Doris and her sister had trouble with the stepmother before, before they were married. She hopes that the Humane Society will look into the situation at home there.

Doris is very interested in being a nurse's aide which, you know, CPI is going to look into for her. Mrs. C. feels that Doris is a capable girl. The social worker doesn't want this case to be an ADC situation. She had made arrangements to have somebody take care of her baby. She has a baby 10 months old.

dr. p.e.c.: Doris?

n.w. I: Yes, and Mrs. C. has made arrangements for somebody to take care of the child when she is working, or when she secures a job.

v.c.: Who is going to take care of the child?

s.i.: Her stepmother is taking care of her now.

n.w. I: I spoke to the high school guidance counselor. I called her this morning. She came to the high school from the junior high in September, 1960. She left February, 1961 and went to the Girls' School. She had no passing grades for tenth grade, due to the short time there. In the ninth grade she passed every one of her subjects but one major and one minor, and they wouldn't tell me what. They said she was a constant behavior problem at school.

dr. p.e.c.: Who is the father of the child?

n.w. I: I don't know.

s.i.: D. R. is the name.

dr. p.e.c.: But her having the child was not a reason for her going to The School for Girls? I am not clear as to why she went.

[1] It is characteristic of the NEC staff that applicant business is not restricted to office hours. It is not at all unusual for NEC staff or work-crew foremen to receive calls, or visits from applicants at any time, day or night, or on weekends and holidays.

N.W. II: I am trying to find out where the child came in.

N.W. I: She told me that the reason she went to The School for Girls is because of the difficulties that she had at school. Both the social workers told me this. I don't know when this child came.

N.W. II: Could it have been the time she was out, and her father put her back?

N.W. I: Evidently she must have been pregnant at the same time. I will tell you what happened. Mrs. C. wouldn't tell me anything about her having the baby, because she didn't want to tell me anything. She said she didn't feel it was important, you know.

V.C.: I have got it. I interviewed her. Let me break in here. She left high school after this fight with the teacher. She maintained the teacher scratched her, and she reacted and hit the teacher. She was transferred. The school educational people got together at her high school and decided that she needed a new environment, so she was sent to another high school. She was truant again. At this time she became pregnant. This was in 1962.

N.W. II: But V.C., that doesn't match, 1962 and 1964—and the baby is only 10 months old.

N.W. I: She will be a year old in August.

DR. P.E.C.: Nine months pregnancy and 10 months living. All right. She got out of The School for Girls when?

N.W. I: October, 1962, and went back November, 1962.

DR. P.E.C.: When did she get out of The School for Girls? What I am getting at is . . .

N.W. I: How long she has been out?

DR. P.E.C.: Yes.

N.W. I: I think I missed that.

DR. P.E.C.: How did she get here?

N.W. I: I will read that for you.

DR. P.E.C.: Go ahead.

N.W. I: She came in on her own, and she was looking for full-time employment or a training program. She left school—it has down here—because of pregnancy, and that was the second high school, 1961. The subject she liked best in school was English, and the subject she liked least was math. She came out of the Girls' School October 26, 1962. She has no work record.

V.C.: Evidently she had the baby after she left The School for Girls.

N.W. I: Right.

DR. P.E.C.: All right.

V.C.: In October of 1962 she had the baby. She was up there at School for Girls while she was pregnant. She wants to be a seamstress or a salesgirl. She told me she was going on state welfare, but that is not true. She has an application for state welfare. Mrs. D. and Mrs. C. don't want to put her on the state because she is capable.[2] She told me on the phone last night

---

[2] "Going on the state" is the term frequently used when a woman applies for state welfare under the Aid to Dependent Children (ADC) program.

that the girl is very much interested in becoming a nurse's aide. She is looking forward to it, and they want to help her.

P.I.: What did the girl say?

N.W. I: In fact, Mrs. C. was down in New Haven at her house yesterday. I tried to get in touch with her, you know. I called Doris' house, trying to get in touch with Mrs. C. to have her stop in and see the vocational counselor, but I couldn't make contact. And she told me it was Doris' idea that she wanted to be a nurse's aide, and she is interested in it. Both of these counselors, you know, are helping her.

V.C.: What can she picture herself as doing 10 years from now, according to the application?

N.W. I: You know, it's a funny thing, she has down here "seamstress." "Name three kinds of jobs you would like to get if you could get them: 'seamstress and salesgirl.' If you could have any job you wanted, regardless of the location or the amount of extra training or experience required, what job would you choose? 'Hairdressing.' Why do you want to be a hairdresser? 'Because I enjoy hairdressing, and it is something I have been doing' "—I can't read the rest of it—" 'the best I could do.' "

"Considering your future very realistically, what job or occupation do you expect to go into as your life work? 'Seamstress. Work on sewing is something I really like to do.' What can you picture yourself doing ten years from now? 'Seamstress.' "

DR. P.E.C.: Can you tell me what you thought about her. What is your reaction to her? We have gotten a lot of facts about her. How did you react to her as a woman?

N.W. I: Well, you know, I interviewed her, and I was very much surprised when I read this. In fact, I had her write this myself, just this. I wanted to see if she could write. She has a terrific handwriting.

V.C.: She never mentioned in her initial interview anything about School for Girls.

N.W. I: Nothing.

V.C.: But when she came in and talked to me—

N.W. I: You would never guess it.

V.C.: —she started to open up, and mentioned casually that she had been in The School for Girls for around eight months. I notified the neighborhood worker and got him to check the Girls' School as to the record, and then all these facts came to light after we found out about it.

But my initial impression was that she was just a high-school dropout, had a pleasant personality.

N.W. I: Me too.

V.C.: She looked perfectly stable to me. But then after all this came out, we know she had these latent problems, emotional problems. I might as well go into my interview with her. She lives with her sister, does she not?

S.I.: She lives with her father and stepmother. I don't know whether the sister lives there too.

v.c.: She may be moving.[3] She told me she may be moving to 628 Senate Street in a little while, in that she has difficulty at home. So I jotted down her sister's name and address, phone number, for future reference, in case we can't locate her at home.

n.w. I: What is her sister's name?

v.c.: I do not know. I didn't find that out.

n.w. I: Do you know it?

n.w. II: I am trying to think. I might.

v.c.: I have all this information. She had a fight with a teacher at the high school. The teacher scratched her, and she in turn hit the teacher. The child is still staying at the father's home with the stepmother. She left the first high school because of the fight, was transferred to the second one, and was truant there. She went to court also on the basis of this truancy, and the court decided that she should go to The School for Girls—the juvenile court. This is one area we didn't cover. Maybe we should have, but it wasn't done.[4] Maybe we can do that later.

p.i.: How old is she?

n.w. II: Nineteen.

v.c.: We should follow that up possibly to get more information from the court, to find out what went on in the case, to give us a little clearer picture. At The School for Girls she was trained in sewing, homemaking. She worked in the infirmary. I asked her about the different types of tasks she did—greenhouse work, waitress work. I asked her which one she preferred, and she said that she liked to work in the infirmary, and sewing. So the infirmary is related to the type of work that she could do on one of our work crews, nurse's-aide work crew up at the convalescent home.

So my recommendation, what ran through my mind right then and there, was that this would be an ideal situation for her temporarily, the girls' work crew, to give her a closely supervised situation under a work-crew forelady, and also bring her up in remedial skills. Part of the educational component of the program would do this for her.

So my recommendation would be the girls' work crew, if there is a vacancy available. She has had all these problems, and has to get squared away in the world of work, stabilize her personality. She wanted to go to hairdressing school, but she didn't have the money. Whether she has this ability or not, I don't know. Maybe we will have to place her in a work crew as a proving ground, until such time as we find out what she really wants to do. She likes being around people.

[3] Residential changes occur often and abruptly in the inner-city population. The small nuclear family seems to be less important than the extended family and workers often make contact with relatives other than parents.

[4] NEC is oriented toward action, and as a matter of policy extensive histories are not obtained. Most of the time detailed information is irrelevant but sometimes the action orientation does result in a paucity of relevant material.

Also at The School for Girls she ran away a couple of times. I got this at the end of my conversation with her. So she didn't like the School one iota, and resents authority, At the School she had a fight with a girl. The girl called her black. She was a white girl. She is very sensitive, this girl, a very, very sensitive girl. To me it seems that she needs very close supervision.

My recommendation would be the girls' work crew, notification to the forelady of this girl's past history, and that she needs sensitive supervision in a crew of girls working in an infirmary or convalescent home.

She was tested here. I will go into the scores right now. First of all, DR. P.E.C., you had a question.

DR. P.E.C.: Well, the question I had was: How unstable is the girl? [5] The fact that she is sensitive on the color issue is certainly not an indication of instability. The fact that she got pregnant also would not necessarily be an indication of instability. That she didn't like school and she didn't like the Girls' School—.

P.I.: For a girl of that age to be pregnant, wouldn't there be a connotation that there is something wrong in her life, in order to conduct herself that way? If she were an older girl, it might be one thing. But a younger girl, I would think that usually there is some trouble, some instability in some area, maybe not necessarily with her—

C.: But it might not relate at all to the world of work.

P.I.: I am not concerned with the world of work. We are talking about her as a personality.

DR. P.E.C.: The reason that I am raising this question now is that when V.C. says—and rightly so—that she is going to need or probably requires some very sensitive kind of supervision, the question is, "Well, what should be the nature and the orientation of that supervision?"

Joan E. is the one who will be the work-crew leader. Joan, therefore, becomes very important as to how she relates to the girl, and what her objectives are going to be insofar as Doris is concerned.

P.I.: Do we really know what her objectives are at this time, other than she wants to be a seamstress or a hairdresser?

DR. P.E.C.: I am talking in terms of Joan E. What are her objectives with this girl?

P.I.: Has Joan met this girl?

V.C.: She will.

DR. P.E.C.: Coming back to the question that you were asking, P.I., coming back to this kind of family background, the mother died at an early age, and we can just assume without knowing anything further that life was far from happy.

P.I.: Right.

DR. P.E.C.: She didn't get along with the stepmother. The fact that she gets

---

[5] The consultant frequently will try to limit discussion about psychopathology in order to prevent the staff from being frightened off from working with a person labeled as disturbed.

closeness via sexual relationships is not in itself an indication of pathology or instability.

P.I.: I don't mean pathology, no. I meant that there was an unstable situation, and probably that might have been a reaction to it. That is merely hypothetical.

DR. P.E.C.: What was your reaction to this girl, V.C.?

V.C.: My reaction was that she was a very neat girl. She needs understanding more than anything else. I think she has to get in with a group of girls who have had problems common to hers, under a work leader who understands the situation, Joan E., so that she can create maybe new friendships, and the work crew acting as a launching pad, a proving ground for her to reroute her life and overcome a lot of these problems she has had.

My impression of her is that I think, through good supervision and understanding, she has good possibilities. She has got a lot of good characteristics. She is neat. She talks very well. She is a good writer.[6] We let her fill out the application blank.

P.I.: She writes well—handwriting.

V.C.: Yes.

N.W. I: If we didn't know that she had been to School for Girls, I think she would have escaped us. I just pulled it from her now.

DR. P.E.C.: She would have what?

N.W. I: I don't think I could tell. I wouldn't be able to tell unless she told me.

DR. P.E.C.: I think you are prejudiced.[7]

N.W. I: How?

DR. P.E.C.: Just because this gal got pregnant . . .

N.W. II: He means, if she hadn't said she had been to School for Girls, you would have never known it.

DR. P.E.C.: But he was somewhat surprised when he found out.

P.I.: Maybe he is trying to point out something else. Maybe the handwriting is one thing. Maybe his initial impression, her presentation was that of probably being a girl more meek in nature.

N.W. I: No. I just thought she was . . .

DR. P.E.C.: A good girl?

V.C.: I thought she was very personable.

P.I.: This is the impression.

C.: He has never been to The School for Girls so he doesn't really know what the characteristics are.

V.C.: Any applicant can create a good first impression. She withheld the School for Girls. She wants to cover that up.

N.W. II: Naturally.

[6] Such traits are highly prized because they are the ones that get an applicant through a personnel office and onto a job.

[7] The consultant's intervention serves a training function. He wants to point up the danger in making assumptions about an applicant.

DR. P.E.C.: But it is in her favor that she didn't, the fact that on her own she told it to you, and then she unburdened some more.

V.C.: There may be other things that she did not tell me that might come to light through close relationship with Joan E. She might open up more in the vocational aspect with Joan E. rather than with me. She might feel I am too much of an authority figure. She might tell me I am too much of an authority figure. So a person working more closely with her might uncover more of her personality. At first she was reluctant to tell us anything. The next day she came to see me, she told us a little bit more.

DR. PEC.: Sure.

V.C.: In the long run, with Joan E., maybe . . .

N.W. I: She is basically honest.

P.I.: She might be belligerent anyway.

N.W. I: I think it is due to her home.

DR. P.E.C.: I think the reason I said what I did to N.W. I is that we can look at this girl in a way so that she has got two and three-quarters strikes against her. Now, this is a girl who comes from a background, who has already had a life which has not been a good one. There is no reason to believe that she is in any conscious sense an evil girl. I think one of the most important things that we can do for the people that come in here is to say, "Okay, that's in the past. Our job is to do the very best we can for people, and to create the breaks for them." [8]

P.I.: I suppose the work crew with Joan E. would be a first step.

DR. P.E.C.: I think there is a prior step here maybe, and that is maybe for V.C.—maybe this ought to be kind of routine and perhaps it is, I don't know— but I think that V.C. maybe ought to see her one more time, not only to prepare her for the work crew, not only to make her feel that we're all behind her insofar as the future is concerned, but just to reinforce in this girl's mind that when she walked in here, she was walking into an agency that is committed to do whatever it can for her, and that there is a two-way obligation, what she needs to do, and what we need to do.

V.C.: I think you are right. This will be done. I sent S.I. out this morning to check on the home situation, what type of home atmosphere she lives in, the environment she lives in.[9] S.I., will you relate that?

S.I.: Doris was not home. I spoke to her stepmother. She was taking care of the baby. Apparently Doris doesn't tell her parents what she is doing. She doesn't know what she is doing, and I guess that is understandable, given some of the situation. Her stepmother told me an awful lot in about five minutes. She was very willing to speak about her stepdaughter. And she mentioned the fact that Doris was resentful to her. She was taking care of the baby, and it was about 110°, and she really looked under the weather.

[8] The consultant often has to repeat the basic purpose of the service to prevent workers from developing a pessimistic attitude toward applicants.

[9] The NEC does not insist applicants and their families come to the NEC. Home visits are made frequently.

P.I.: This is the stepmother?

S.I.: Yes. She said she would be willing to keep on taking care of the baby, or else with her sister, if Doris did work. I mean, they do want her to work. But she is stuck with the baby, and Doris is out, you know, walking around.

She seemed to be quite a nervous, tense person. But I wouldn't say that what that woman said who claimed she had an adverse personality. I don't know. She seems to be very tense and nervous. I am sure she has problems of her own. But as far as adverse, I don't know if I would go as far as that. She told me all this in about five minutes.

V.C.: Doris was tested. She scored 83 IQ in the verbal, which is a little below average. This is just a reflection of lack of schooling actually. She only went through tenth grade, so her score is understandable. But the nonverbal score, 77, is low. An IQ of 77 in the nonverbal, which is supposed to measure people regardless of any academic achievement or grades.[10]

C.: I think, v.c., for some people, if they have developed this verbal potential, the verbal is a better indication if it is higher than the nonverbal. So that if you took a nonverbal, you would score low. So maybe because she went to tenth grade, maybe she is fairly verbal, maybe somewhere up near her possible potential.

V.C.: Arithmetic, minus 16. She didn't even register on the scale. For the work crew, if she is placed in a work crew, the remedial component would benefit her. Inspection test, 50th percentile, which is a low score. Minnesota Clerical, number comparison, 19 per cent, and name comparison, 9 per cent, both low scores, mechanical aptitude test, 75th percentile in mechanical knowledge. I don't regard this a a good index. I think she guessed and happened to hit it lucky.

C.: Why do you say that, v.c.? [11]

V.C.: I say this, c., because it deals with tools and equipment that I know she never ran across in her life.

C.: We don't know that. I don't think we should ever say that. I think we should take the score, especially if it is a high one, and say, "This gives us some indication that there is potential here." This upsets me. Once in a while we fall into that.

N.W. II: I don't see where you can guess on those things.

P.I.: Maybe she used these in a school, like the infirmary, or hairdressing.

V.C.: This test is more geared for boys than it is for girls. Even if the test did mean anything, what occupations are there for girls with high mechanical ability?

[10] It happens frequently that a staff member will discuss tests and their interpretations in a way that is either wrong, incomplete, or misleading. The above is an example of a statement the consultant could have challenged. It was his decision that to have challenged this statement would not have been productive at that particular time.

[11] Staff members are encouraged to challenge each other and to participate freely in the deliberations.

c.: Sewing-machine operator.

N.W. II: They can run machines in factories.

V.C.: Coordination is a score which would be more apt for a sewing-machine operator. Spatial perception score, 21st percentile, which is below average. In the shop-arithmetic score, the tester put an asterisk here, "She showed lack of motivation to complete the last section of the battery, answered at most only a few questions, and then just stared at the test booklet. No reason was given for her lack of interest."

c.: I think in a case like this one of the values of the testing as we give it here is that someone would have interceded here and tried to prod and see if the girl would continue. This doesn't seem to have been done in this case. Because of it, we don't have any true indication of this kid's shop-arithmetic ability. I think we ought to try to communicate to the examiners that we are more interested in their potential, even if they have to urge them on to finish. Unless somebody does this, we are not going to get the true potential. We are going to get something related to motivation.

DR. P.E.C.: Do we know how they are preparing these kids for the testing? Is it a matter that you show up at a particular time and you are given the test?

P.I.: Yes.

DR. P.E.C.: They are not told why these tests are being given?

N.W. II: V.C. does that.

DR. P.E.C.: I know he does but apparently some of the people coming through here will be seen elsewhere for testing.

N.W. II: They get it here.

V.C.: The tester comes here. It is the same setting.

c.: Some we send to the State Employment Service for tests.[12]

P.I.: I refer them, but I tell them what the test is about, why they are taking it.

DR. P.E.C.: It is important that they do their best, but they should know that it is by no means the sole basis for any decision we would make or any help that we can render.

c.: I think it is important, if somebody sits there looking at a booklet, someone should—

P.I.: On that mechanical thing, you said that was guesswork; and yet on another element of the test she didn't even bother at all. There is a little inconsistency, why she applied herself to one and not the other.

V.C.: The shop-arithmetic is the last part of the mechanical-aptitude test. The mechanical-knowledge is 10 minutes, spatial-relations is 10 minutes. The shop-arithmetic is 15 minutes, and it is given all at one time. She undoubtedly got frustrated by the whole thing at the end. She just said, "The heck with it all."

---

[12] Cutting scores had been established for entry into Manpower and Defense Training Act courses. The State Employment Service was largely responsible for those courses. NEC works closely with the State Employment Service. The placement interviewer (PI) is paid by the State and assigned full time to the NEC.

DR. P.E.C.: You know, this is a good example of a problem that we have been talking about from time to time. She is going to go on the work crew. All right, v.c., you will see her and you will be talking with Joan E. I think it is so important that this kid understands that when she goes on the work crew, we are still interested in her, and that there really be a way whereby a month from now or six weeks from now we can sit down with Joan E. and say, "What's going on? Should v.c. see her again? What should we be planning?" [13]

This is in the form of a question. Seamstress—who trains seamstresses? Is there any place that trains seamstresses? And is there a demand for seamstresses?

P.I.: There is a demand for seamstresses, but it is difficult to train them, because a seamstress works on an expensive item; usually they are expensive items. There isn't any extra material where they can, say, take a trainee and put her on this until she becomes trained for that work.

N.W. II: There is a lot of handwork too, isn't there?

P.I.: Most of it is handwork.

DR. P.E.C.: In other words, this is a dying profession, so to speak?

P.I.: The garment or the bridal shops, say, get their seamstresses from the garment industry, people who no longer want to work in the garment factories, and they will go to a formal shop of some kind, and they become the seamstress. But it is difficult—in fact, we have got an OJT for a seamstress, and we have been having difficulty with it because we are sending girls who have an interest in seamstress and who might have made their own clothing, but that isn't enough.[14] Like I say, the man said to me that the garments are expensive, and they have to take the garment apart, take a whole creation apart and fix it so it will fit the person.

DR. P.E.C.: It seems to me that there ought to be some kind of a training program. You have got a public vocational school for boys apparently. Do you have anything for girls?

V.C.: By the way, I invited the voc-ed man at CPI here today. He didn't appear.

N.W. II: They have dressmaking at the vocational high school, I think.

P.I.: They do dressmaking, right, but that is in a regular place. In other words, girls attend the vocational high school on a regular class basis.

C.: It would seem to me that if someone at CPI in the manpower section could make an assessment of the needs in the future along these lines, that some sort of institutional training, either at the vocational high or in the new Skill Center could be worked out, with financing from the federal government to do this, even if it meant buying some materials to use there, so they wouldn't have to work on expensive materials.[15]

[13] The consultant tries to think preventively and wants NEC staff to plan for future contingencies.

[14] OJT is On-the-Job Training. An employer can receive a subsidy for a period of up to six months to induce him to accept an applicant for training.

[15] Problems and issues arising in the disposition conferences are fed back to the executive level in memos, or at the monthly staff meeting with the executives. New

DR. P.E.C.: Places like Macy's will open up, and they are going to have need for seamstresses. Where does Macy's get them from? Why don't we make sure that we bring this up at the next monthly meeting downtown, next Monday.

C.: Very good.

N.W. I: I don't know if you remember, but we brought this up about alterations. All this goes along with seamstress. When we were getting the leads on setting up the programs for school, night school, a lot of people expressed a concern in doing alteration work, especially people with large families, that could cut down on the cost of clothes or something like that. This is a class that we have needed for a long time. I don't know why they just keep having sewing materials. You have to work on new materials. A lot of people can't afford to work on new materials. They have stuff at home that they can cut down for the kids, or themselves, or what have you. That is where a lot of seamstress work could come in.

C.: So then, V.C., you will be having the counseling session with this girl?

V.C.: Right.

C.: And investigating whether or not she is willing to go into the work crew, explaining to her the whys and wherefores of the work crew, and what we are trying to learn from it, how it will help us begin planning with her for a meaningful career.

V.C.: Okay.

DR. P.E.C.: Let me say just one thing. Let's not discuss it and go on to the next case. Let's come back to the discussion that P.I. and I were having before. The chances are that about sixteen years from now her little child, who is now ten months old, is probably going to be discussed in a meeting like this. This is a kid who is already beginning life with all the breaks against it.

V.C.: She has two and seven-eighths strikes.

DR. P.E.C.: Two and seven-eighths strikes against it to begin with.

FLORA LEE

N.W. I: Flora Lee, 19 years old, born in South Carolina. She came in on her own looking for full-time employment or a training program. She is single, living with her mother and father. She has one sister and three brothers. She lived in New Haven for two years. She didn't work at all last year. She doesn't know what her family income is. She is Negro. She doesn't drive; no trouble with the law.

She made an excellent appearance when she came in; high-school graduate. Did she have a diploma?

N.W. II: Yes.

---

programs or modifications in existing programs frequently originate at these conferences. The Skill Center is a CPI-operated vocational and educational training center, equipped with classroom and shop facilities. It was not yet open at the time of this meeting.

DR. P.E.C.: Here or down south?

N.W. II: Down south.

N.W. I: Down south, J. S. Wilson High School in South Carolina. She took a business course. The subject she liked best in school was accounting. The subject she liked the least was history. She wants more education.[16]

V.C.: I would like to add one thing. This girl, N.W. I.—you didn't take this down, I found out in my interview—she graduated from a junior college.

N.W. I: It is in here. She completed junior college, A.B. degree.

V.C.: It was an A.A. degree, Associate in Arts degree.

N.W. I: She wants to go to a college or university now. She states that her high-school marks were average. As far as her work history, she works now at the Sea Club in East Haven. She works at the snack bar. She ended working there last year. But when I called out there, she is working there now.

S.I.: That would be just in the summer.

DR. P.E.C.: It is a beach club.

N.W. II: She just started back.

C.: Where does she work there?

N.W. I: She works behind the snack bar. She worked there from July to September.

N.W. II: It must be a summer job.

N.W. I: It must be summer. She is there now, 40 hours a week. She makes $35 a week. When she started, she was making $35 a week, and now she receives $40. She secured this job on her own. She likes it. She left it last year to go back to school.

C.: Do you know anything about minimum wages, as far as private clubs, restaurants?

P.I.: Sometimes when they tell you how much they make, they might tell you their take-home salary, so you can't always tell what they are making.

N.W. I: I always ask them if it is before taxes or after taxes, and I made a note. If it is after taxes, I put "A.T."

P.I.: Clubs, restaurants, don't have to pay the minimum in the federal law.

N.W. I: They can pay $1.15.

DR. P.E.C.: But she gets even less. She started at $35 a week.

N.W. II: There is a possibility she might be making tips.

N.W. I: Her other job was at a record shop, a record store. She typed and sold records. This was in June, 1962, and she ended in September, 1962. She claimed she worked 40 hours a week there, and she was making $15 a week.

C.: Is this in the south?

N.W. I: Here. That is $15.

N.W. II: She told me it was a friend of hers, or something, that she worked for.

N.W. I: She liked it; and she left that job to go back to school.

[16] The worker has been reading from the application form completed at the initial contact. This case reveals the problems of the southern Negro who is competing in a northern urban environment.

DR. P.E.C.: When you say "go back to school," you mean to this junior college?

V.C.: Yes. She came up here for the summers, and returned to South Carolina for school.

DR. P.E.C.: I get it.

N.W. I: She is currently unemployed. She is getting parental support.

P.I.: She is working at the Sea Club now, isn't she?

N.W. I: Evidently she is not making too much, because when they asked her why she came in here, she said she was looking for full-time employment or a training program.

P.I.: She can't be working 40 hours.

DR. P.E.C.: Or else she knows that what she has at the Sea Club is just for the summer.

N.W. I: The three jobs she would like to get, or what she thought was a good job, was accounting, secretary, and typist. She would like to be trained in accounting, because she studied this in college. And considering her future very realistically, as far as her life work is concerned, she hopes to become a C.P.A. She thinks it is an excellent-standing job; and ten years from now, she would like to be a C.P.A.

P.I.: I interviewed her briefly. She filled out this application. She asked questions about it. Under subjects she had a whole bunch here: Typing, shorthand, accounting, introduction to business, and secretarial practice. Her favorite subjects are accounting and typing. She liked history least.

In shorthand she says she can take 80 words per minute, and in typing she said she can take 45 words per minute with five errors. She says she knows how to operate a mimeograph machine. I have the same work record; and also that she would like to be an accountant. I think what she had in mind at this time was to get a job as a typist, and that is what we are concentrating on now. That is what I expect to look for for this applicant.

Tentatively, I am thinking of the econometrist at an insurance company. Incidentally, her extracurricular activities were in the college choir and the newspaper staff. Her hobbies were basketball, dancing, and swimming, and there is a little bit of photography in there too.

She could take shorthand, and her typing isn't too bad. Also, an econometrist, there is some bookkeeping involved in that job, and she might be able to handle it. I am a little concerned about her spelling. I notice some words that she has misspelled. I could go over that. I would see her again before I made a referral for her. Maybe we could straighten that out.

She looked like a nice girl, neatly dressed. When I did speak to her, she expressed herself well. She did have a mature attitude about herself.

V.C.: I was impressed initially with her sincerity and very calm nature, good verbal ability. I also got the same information P.I. did. It corresponds, that she can type 45 words per minute with five errors; 80 words per minute in shorthand. I went into detail about the junior college. The name of this college is Helping Hand Junior College in Craggy Hill, South Carolina, a two-year college, business major. She only took, however, one course in accounting in junior college. She had a B in this. The course was Introduction to Accounting. She also took shorthand and typing at college, secretarial practice, introduction to business, biology, history, English.

She had a B average in English. She did not have a straight office machine course, although she has knowledge of the mimeograph machine.

While at college she had a six-weeks on-the-job training program whereby some of the girls do clerical work for instructors or teachers in the college, mimeograph work for the instructor, and typing. I talked to her about C.P.A., and told her that to become a C.P.A. she would need quite a few courses in accounting and business. She does not want to go back to school in the fall because of monetary difficulties primarily. She hasn't even applied to any college as of the present time.

She stated that her sister is going to college this year, and her mother is now interested in providing financial backing for her sister, and can't afford to send two girls.

What ran through my mind at the time is on-the-job training that CPI might have in banking or related fields, secretarial- or clerical-type field, which would lead to accounting.

c.: Maybe bookkeeping or payroll, something like that.

v.c.: Bookkeeping, payroll, right. I went ahead and wrote a letter to D.D. and D.A. and the people involved in OJT, stressing this girl's qualifications, which she has, and the potential that she has in this banking or accounting or bookkeeping field.

She was tested, again. Verbal IQ of 84; nonverbal IQ of 99, which is in the average range; arithmetic percentile of 32. This is a little below average. However, on the test she had 41 right and 1 wrong, so that she is very accurate with figures.[17] Inspection, 17, which is below average.

c.: I would like to go back to this arithmetic. I am just wondering if somewhere along the way we may not be missing the boat in preparing the people for tests. Time after time—these are people from the lower-class population who are used to living at a slow pace, working at a slow pace. Not having developed study habits, they are expected to do maybe 80 examples, and they do 40. Sometimes they do all 40 right. Are we getting a true picture? Is there some way maybe we should be encouraging them to work a little faster? I don't know.

v.c.: In this particular case, I don't think so. I think the girl has gone to college. In the case of the typical applicant, I think maybe you are right, but this girl—

c.: She came from a southern Negro family, she went to a school in the south.

n.w. I: That junior college is probably a good high school.

---

[17] This test pattern in which speed is sacrificed for accuracy seems to characterize many inner-city applicants. The discussion that follows provides an excellent view of the problem of interpreting the test scores and the educational background of many southern Negroes.

c.: The pace is quite different probably from up here in the north. I am thinking that in encouraging them to work faster, we might be doing them a disservice.

N.W. II: I agree with you. Do you know what I am doing right now? I am tutoring a fellow to take a test. You know, if I took an examination in trigonometry right now, I probably wouldn't pass it. You know why? It is not because I don't have the ability. It is because my proficiency is not good, due to the fact that I haven't, you know, done it. Now, here is a fellow who comes in here and he wants to be a cook. I know he is interested in being a cook. For instance, if he takes a test to go to the Kitchen Arts Institute—v.c. is going to give him a test. He is going to read the paper and he says, "Well, here is mathematics. I won't pass."

Well, look, when you are in the eighth grade, you take fractions. When you leave the eighth grade, it is very rarely that you use fractions. You don't expect a fellow to sit down and divide fractions, and let's say add them, and mixed numbers and what not, very proficiently, particularly in a time test. And you read the test score, not that they only got a low score, but that they are incapable.

v.c.: However, let me just throw this one thing out. The test battery that we administer is not going to deprive them of any job. This test is merely to screen. Should we, on something like arithmetic, where there is three points off for each error, should we stress speed or should we stress accuracy? I am going on this premise. When a kid gets a job, it seems like the employer would prefer that a guy be accurate at the outset, and then progress in speed, which will come naturally, maybe. But accuracy, to me, is far more important than speed, in this world at least.

N.W. I: But this is a fast world now, v.c.

v.c.: But you have got to start off with one or the other.

N.W. I: Otherwise you will miss the boat. They want both.

c.: Would you have been more impressed if this girl had done 80 and had two wrong? Would you have considered this a better score than 41 and one wrong?

DR. P.E.C.: I think you are both right, and I am not sure that you are touching on the central question. Let's look at it this way. N.W. I says that that junior college was probably a good high school. What N.W. I is saying there is that we don't know how to evaluate what it means to get these grades in this junior college. I think what c. is saying is that when a kid gets 40 right and one wrong, we don't know what it means. If, for example, they were to work faster, would they have gotten a higher score? Let's assume they worked slow at the time. They are given a certain amount of time, aren't they, for this thing?

v.c.: Yes.

DR. P.E.C.: Let's say when the time is up, you say to them, "Okay, keep on going." You want to get some idea of what is the ceiling here. Are we dealing with a functioning ceiling? Is this the way they usually function, or is it that they could do more? Now we are in a bind. Unless the testing is being done by people who are sensitive to these kinds of things, and provides us with this kind of information, then we have to raise the kinds of questions that c. is raising.[18] I agree completely. Accuracy is very important. But we may be selling a lot of these people short, because to them, they are going to do it, each one; and so time goes by and they haven't done as much as they might do.

I feel very envious of N.W. II. He says that if he took a trignometry test, he would probably fail. I would flunk it quicker than you could shake a stick at it.

N.W. I: You said something about stopping them when the time is up, and then going on. I wonder if we could try this for an experiment. Where they stop on the time element that you give them, just draw a line, this is where they stopped on the time element, and see just what they would do from there on.

V.C.: Proportionately, yes. We could do that.

N.W. I: For an experiment.

P.I.: It doesn't prove much, because you are just going to—

N.W. I: It will give you a little idea.

P.I.: This is a criterion. If you go past the time—

N.W. I: After the time you draw a line. This is what they did up to the time they were allotted.

V.C.: It all boils down to the results of the tests as a tool in measuring human potential.

DR. P.E.C.: I want to go on record right here and now as saying that I think that the way the testing is being done, or probably will be done as numbers get greater and the like, is likely to work against getting a true picture of a lot of these people. Now, the bind, of course, is that it takes a lot of time to do the testing in a way that allows you to observe what is happening, so that they are prepared for it, and where you can experiment in a way that N.W. I indicates.

C.: I would think this would have implications certainly for the research division of CPI, to maybe take some people in an experimental session, to coach them if they have to, give them practice at adding, not exactly what they are going to be doing on the test but something similar, and then give them the test, before and after, and find out really what the differences are, and if anything can be drawn from this in the whole testing program.

DR. P.E.C.: Is this the test that they use in arithmetic where you add horizontally, whereas in school, as somebody said, "I was taught to add up and down?"

V.C.: I have been against this test battery from the very outset.

C.: I would think some middle-class guy who took a lot of algebra that went horizontally designed this test for kids who never saw it.

DR. P.E.C.: All right, let's come back—

V.C.: We could make this recommendation to the research department.

C.: At least think about this, and maybe try a couple of experiments that might give us more valid testing procedures.

V.C.: For this type of applicant.

DR. P.E.C.: I think we ought to bring that up.

[18] Testing is conducted in small groups by people who are not *clinically* trained.

P.I.: If she were to be referred to a bank, the chances are they would test her first there too.

N.W. I: Yes.

V.C.: And what do they go on?

P.I.: At the insurance company they are tested. A good many cases where bookkeeping is involved—

DR. P.E.C.: There would have to be an intermediary between CPI and wherever she is referred. Can we take that up? What should we do?

N.W. I: Mrs. D. at the insurance company doesn't give you any in-between.

DR. P.E.C.: Who is she?

N.W. I: She is out at the insurance company. She doesn't give you any in-between.[19]

V.C.: I didn't go through all these scores.

DR. P.E.C.: Well, don't say controversial things, so we don't get off on these tangents.

V.C.: 39th percentile in mechanical knowledge; first percentile in spatial perception; sixth percentile in shop arithmetic. Minnesota Clerical, 19th percentile in numbers, and sixth percentile in names.

However, I am going to once again go on the accuracy angle, even though it is controversial. She had 101 right in the numbers and none wrong; and 78 right in the names, with one wrong. So there again, it corresponds to the arithmetic accuracy.

DR. P.E.C.: These tests were probably standardized on a bunch of kids coming out of high school from northern schools.

V.C.: Northern schools, with speed and accuracy.

DR. P.E.C.: I think there are some things we really have to ascertain. In fact, can she take dictation, and how well? Also, can she type and how well, This, it seems to me becomes crucial. Because if, in fact, she can take dictation as she states, and if her typing is okay, then that suggests one line of jobs. If in fact she may be rusty on this—I don't know.

P.I.: We do have typing tests. You know that.

DR. P.E.C.: We have got to understand, when we give a girl like this a typing test, that this is a very anxiety-arousing situation for her.

C.: It would seem to me that with the opening of the Skill Center that not only should these kids have the opportunity to be tested, but we should be able to send them there for a couple of days so that they can practice on some things and then be tested. If we then ascertain that they are not working fast enough, or they need improvement in skill, we can plan the next step.

DR. P.E.C.: The worst thing that can happen to this girl is that we send her to a job on the assumption that she is in fact as good as she is telling us. They will judge her by white-girl standards, and she gets hit over the head and it is a defeat.

It is like that girl who took the course for the telephone switchboard.

---

[19] The NEC staff, particularly the placement interviewers, develop relationships with personnel officers of many local companies.

She shows up at the telephone company and they won't have anything to do with her. This girl is going around, she thinks she is a college graduate, and yet she is going to get knocked to hell when she fails, when she fails in tasks that a college graduate would be capable of doing.

N.W. I: Why don't you call Jack and see if he has got a typewriter that she can work with while she is in the office, and then she can take a typing test.[20]

C.: Do you think it would be better to do this immediately, and continue our contact with her while she has the job at the Sea Club, with the hopes that the Skill Center will be ready by September?

N.W. I: If she is working part-time at the Sea Club, I don't see why, if they have got a typewriter down there, she can't be practicing.

DR. P.E.C.: This puts a lot of responsibility on her at the wrong time of the year.

V.C.: The Skill Center won't be developed, C., until maybe September at maybe the earliest, more likely December.

C.: That is why I am posing this question. Do we now just try to place this kid without knowing much about her potential, or do we try to have some sort of a holding operation.[21]

DR. P.E.C.: My feeling would be to see if there is some secretary at CPI with the appropriate skill and personality who could work with her for a morning, or for an hour, and give us an idea as to what, you know, she can do and what she can't do. This should be as low anxiety-arousing a situation for this kid as could be set up down there.

C.: We could probably do it here where we would be in close contact with her.

DR. P.E.C.: I think we just ought to tell her again that this is to determine where she is at this point, because we are going to be developing facilities whereby her proficiencies in these areas can be increased. I would do it that way.

C.: If something does comes up in OJT, this practice is going to help her, rather than if she walks in cold.

DR. P.E.C.: This is like the business of training people to take tests. It is the same with these people, going out for a job. If you give them some preparation and practice—.[22]

N.W. II: They do that in the post office. When you apply for a job in the post office, they send you a sample copy of a test. That is to increase their efficiency. They give them time to practice writing numbers.

[20] CPI will frequently use its own facilities to help an applicant prepare for a job. The applicant may not have access to a typewriter to practice for a test.

[21] CPI will try to use its various programs to hold applicants until something more suitable can be developed. In this way an applicant in need is not put on a waiting list and does not feel he is getting a brush-off.

[22] Again, the preventive orientation.

c.: Also, if the typical middle-class housewife who hasn't typed in a while is going out for a job, she either has a typewriter or knows someone who has one, and borrows it and practices; and these people don't have this advantage. Somehow, we have to structure our program so that they get this.

v.c.: I wonder if there is any possibility of a closely supervised girls' work crew in clerical. We don't have girls' work crews in clerical.[23]

DR. P.E.C.: For this girl, I think the Skill Center is a natural.

c.: I don't think the kid should be under the pressure of having to produce for some agency up to what they would normally expect for what they pay. I think this should be in a situation where they are learning, and they are not having to turn out work at such and such a rate, with such and such a proficiency.

P.I.: Suppose in turn that she needs a job soon, rather than in September?

c.: What we have to do is the same thing we are saying, try to get her in here and see if Alice can meet with her, give her some things to type. Say to her, "We don't even want to look at what you do the first two mornings. After that we will take a look to see how well you do, and send you to the State Employment Service to be tested, and we will find out."

v.c.: 45 words per minute with five errors isn't too good. I know I was doing better than that in the army. For a girl who is trained—

DR. P.E.C.: I think here we have to tell her what is being planned in terms of the Skill Center, on-the-job training; but the most important thing that we can do for her now is to determine what her actual level of proficiency is, and we can build from there.

P.I.: We might be off base. We are talking in terms of typing, at least for a short while. We run off numbers. She has had four semesters of typing. With four semesters of typing that isn't very good, only 45 words a minute with five errors. I think if we could avoid typing for this girl it would be better. If we could get her into something like bookkeeping, or something related, that would be better.

c.: We could set up her experience here, so that she might do some statistics and recording for us, which would also give us an indication of how well she could do this. She could help Alice with her monthly report.

v.c.: There is a job available.

P.I.: You are talking about an econometrist. Even that requires typing. It requires typing.

v.c.: Are there any jobs that you have related only to bookkeeping?

P.I.: I don't know what I have. What I have open is at least three weeks old.

DR. P.E.C.: I am a little fearful of placing her a job now, because this could be a very humiliating experience. We don't know what they are expecting, and we are not sure what her level is. Incidentally, one thought I had at the beginning—

[23] Such a program has since developed.

v.c.: I was thinking of this, that if there was a job which required only this amount of talent, you know, if we did have a job—

DR. P.E.C.: If we did.

v.c.: —if it would meet her goals and qualifications and characteristics.

DR. P.E.C.: If there is a job available where we know something about its demands, and we have reason to believe that even if she isn't as good as she is telling us, she is still going to be good enough, then I would say okay. One thought I had earlier was, what about this duplicating machine thing for her, which brings her into office work.[24]

c.: The course is started already.

v.c.: By the way, we have six at least from our center, six out of the 15 in that. Last week J.B. that we discussed did get into this.

N.W. I: What about this United Fund one?

v.c.: That has been filled.

DR. P.E.C.: I think we ought to try to get her in and just tell her what we have been thinking and what we are planning and what things will develop.

P.I.: I think it would be a good idea.

DR. P.E.C.: On a day like this it's better to go to the Sea Club.

N.W. I: We forgot that s.i. made a home visit.

s.i.: Her brother took the message. He was very polite. The home seemed clean, neat and well-furnished.

VIRGIL SMITH

N.W. I: Virgil Smith. He was born in Michigan. He came in on his own looking for full-time employment or training program. He lives with his aunt and uncle. His mother and father are in Ohio. He has been in New Haven a month. He has no physical limitation, and he is not yet classified in the draft. He is only 17. He is a Negro and he hasn't been involved with the law.

Good appearance. He went to tenth grade in high school. I must say right now, I think this fellow is going back to school. I think he is going to high school.

DR. P.E.C.: Why did he come to New Haven?

N.W. I: He told me that. He is very vague on that. He told me he got into a little difficulty in school.

v.c.: He told me that he came east for a vacation, and had problems with his family in Michigan, family problems.

N.W. I: He told me he had difficulty . . .

v.c.: He said he plans to stay here for more than one year.

N.W. I: He told me that—he is very undecided what he is going to do. Frankly speaking, I think all he wants is a part-time job. He was a football

[24] A Manpower and Defense Training Act program (MDTA).

player at school. He played basketball, football, belonged to the Red Satans Pep Club; hobby, reading. The high school coach has contacted him. He has been over there, you know, fooling around.

Every time he comes to see me, he is very undecided about what he is going to do. I think that you are wasting your time with him. I think you will find him in high school this year.[25]

c.: What direction are you moving with him?

N.W. I: He never gave me any indication that he really quit school. From the outset, when I first saw him, he asked me for a part-time job. I said, "Well, we don't have any part-time jobs. We don't have any summer jobs." So he changed his story.

I'll be honest with you. I am pretty sure this fellow is going to go to high school, and I am willing to bet my money that you will see him at high school. He told me he got in difficulty in his home town, and the difficulty has something to do with school. That is what he told me the first day I met him.

I don't know him. He came here. I can talk with his friends. He wandered in here one day and I interviewed him. He was telling me how he is a top-flight athlete, how he got in difficulty in school with the teachers or something, and his father and mother decided to send him here.

One day he came in and told me he was getting ready to buy a 1964 Ford for $900, to take over the payments from a buddy of his, and he was writing home to a buddy of his to take the money out of the bank.[26] I said, "You know, Virgil, you don't know what you are going to do." He said, "I think you are right. But I am going back to school." I will tell you what is really on his mind. He wants a part-time job while he goes to school. He knows that we don't have any part-time jobs, so I think he is really faking. He writes here, he stated his marks were average. He dropped out of school, he had to go to work. That is not true. He never dropped out of school. He came here when the school year was over, he came to New Haven.

c.: I think this does bring up something that we are not presently geared to, serving in-school youth, either part-time jobs or summer employment. I do think, if we are going to get at the roots of the whole poverty program, somewhere along the line CPI or someone like CPI is going to have to develop programs for in-school youth, for summer part-time work that might help keep them in school, for some summer jobs. If the kids don't have them, they are going to be dropping out to get jobs. They are going to be getting in trouble to get money, and they are going to end up here anyhow, only a heck of a lot worse off.

So I hope by next summer something will have been structured. I hope

[25] At the time of this conference CPI did not have programs for summer work, i.e., for youth who wanted part-time or temporary employment. Such programs were subsequently developed.

[26] Once an applicant gets started, he will drop into the office to chat about all sorts of problems with the staff.

somebody will be asking for funds to do something. I think it would naturally be tied in with these neighborhood employment offices, although the State Employment Office does have some sort of a program for youths.

Once again, the State Employment Center is not near where these kids are. It doesn't have the resources, I don't think, to really do the job, I think somewhere along the line, work crews for in-school youth have got to be considered. We are on two demonstration ones at one school but it is not under CPI. It is under Community Schools.[27]

N.W. I: That is a very good idea. I went to visit some of these boys' homes. I was going to tell you about that. I think that is the best idea I have heard in a long time. Many of these youths, I know, would stay in school. You know what their mothers told me at their house? One fellow said, "Gee I was ashamed to go to school," and his mother, she said, "Yes, he has clothes in the closet, but he has outgrown them." She said, "My son have got into trouble." She said, "If my son could find a part-time job, he would never have dropped out of school."

Another thing about CPI, I think they made a very bad mistake this year, this summer. I know it is a new organization, but I think they made a very bad mistake in not providing some type of summer jobs for the kid who is going back to school, because many of these kids would like to have summer jobs to buy pants, shirts, so they can go back to school.

Really, you are encouraging, in many instances, kids to drop out of school. This Virgil is a typical case. When you tell kids, "I'm sorry, we don't have summer jobs, or places are geared for high-school dropouts or high-school graduates," if they are on the ball, you know, if they **are on the** ball . . .

N.W. I: You are pushing them to drop **out.**

N.W. II: We are doing it.

N.W. I: Yes.

N.W. II: I know another young fellow who has come here, you know, looking for a job. He told me the same thing. I know the fellow is going back to high school. I found out in my class.[28] He is going to play football next year for the high school. I had to do some serious thinking. I said, "I'm going to see v.c. and talk about this."

V.C.: I think the recommendation has been made about summer work crews.

N.W. I: A kid said, "I want to get on a work crew for the summer."

V.C.: Oh, sure, this is something c. and I discussed last March.

C.: I think we have got to keep after it, v.c. We have enough time between now and next summer to bring this up at our meetings.

[27] A CPI originated and supported program operated by the New Haven School System.

[28] This neighborhood worker has a class at a recreation center in the neighborhood. The worker's involvement in the neighborhood brings him much valuable information about applicants.

D.R. P.E.C.: Let's bring that up at our monthly meeting on Monday.[29]

N.W. I: When the people read the papers this year that they were going to get the kids off the streets, you know, the kids really thought they meant it. "They are really going to give us summer jobs." I wasn't working here then. I thought they were going to get the kids off the streets. But the only kids who can get part-time jobs are kids who have graduated or dropped out.

V.C.: He seems like a sincere boy to me. He stated he might want to go to evening school, he had no intention of going full time. It conflicts with what N.W. I says. I think N.W. I is right, however. I think you are right and I was wrong. He does seem kind of flip, a kid who would shade the truth a little bit in order to latch onto a full-time job just for the summer. He realizes school is vital. He wants to become a lab technician.

He will have to complete high school to get a job of this nature. We also talked about the reason for his coming east. I mentioned that he had trouble with his family. He stated that his real father was killed, and his stepfather brought him up. Virgil stated that his stepfather never took him anywhere, never did anything for him.[30] He got along real well with his mother. Within the family, he has six sisters. He is the sole brother.

N.W. II: Oh, boy.

V.C.: So you can understand that is another reason for him coming east. I don't blame him. I have one, but that's enough.

N.W. I: He told me none, no sisters or brothers.

V.C.: I went into this in more detail. A lot of these kids change. I get more information when they come back a second time. They figure it might do them a little more good, or something. I don't know. His stepfather, however, had huge bills in the family, and this was the reason for his dropping out of school in the first place, the financial problem. He liked chemical lab in school, he liked working with formulas. He likes to read, fiction stories mainly. He likes auto mechanics. He mentioned that as one of his goals.

I asked him what he has done. He changed brake shoes, windshield wipers, and he has taken motors out of cars. I don't know whether he has got them back. I know I got my rifle apart, but I couldn't put it back together.

My impression is that he would shade the truth in order to get a job.

P.I.: He seems well-mannered, neatly dressed, and while he doesn't have a clear idea of what his vocational goal should be, he appears to have given it some thought. He expressed an interest in lab technician, but does not have much of an idea what it is about. He also mentioned auto mechanic. He has worked on cars, but not much. I believe the applicant would be receptive to vocational guidance. I said I would make my recommendation after the test, to see if he had any mechanical aptitude, by the test.

The test thing. Verbal IQ, 74; nonverbal IQ, 99; arithmetic, 50th percentile; in the arithmetic, 49 right and no errors.

---

[29] This is the meeting with CPI executives. The NEC staff has an opportunity to discuss issues with the executives directly.

[30] The absence or inadequacy of the father is very common in this population.

Inspection, which related to auto mechanics, 32nd percentile; coordination, 17th, which is below average. Mechanical, 16th percentile; spatial perception, however, 75th percentile. That, related with inspection, might show that he does have mechanical ability, even though he doesn't have the knowledge right now. Taking the spatial perception and the inspection together, and the arithmetic, it points to the fact that he may have aptitudes in this area, although he may have aptitudes in several other areas.

P.I.: Drafting might be one, but I think his high school . . .

DR. P.E.C.: What year high school would he go into?

N.W. I: Eleventh grade.

N.W. II: Third year high school.

C.: I certainly think, if you have a feeling that this boy not only can be pushed back to school, but almost wants to go, and is hiding it, then this calls for a meeting with him, with the two of you sitting down and laying your cards on the table and talking with him about high school, and how important it is, and exploring the possibility of maybe pulling in the high-school coach, or somebody, bring them together formally around planning his interest in the school, getting his records in here from Michigan, what have you, and see if we can get him back to school.

V.C.: This boy is a dropout, is he not? When did he leave, in the middle of the year?

N.W. I: He said he finished school, the school year, and he came here to New Haven. The first thing we told him when he came in the door, we didn't have any part-time jobs or summer jobs, and he changed his story. He sat down and he talked to me and he told me how—.

V.C.: Could we get the boy into a work crew?

N.W. I: He is very impatient.

DR. P.E.C.: Have we thought in terms of talking to the aunt and uncle?

V.C.: Did you go to this home?

S.I.: I went, but nobody was home with Virgil.

V.C.: We attempted to go this morning.

DR. P.E.C.: How did he strike you?

S.I.: Nice boy.

N.W. II: He was making a home visit to see the home.

N.W. I: He is a nice fellow, very impatient.

DR. P.E.C.: I think, along the lines that C. was talking, it would be very important that he does go back to school in September. Now, did he in fact finish the second year out in Michigan? Is the football coach interested in him?

N.W. I: I doubt it.

C.: Well, do you know?

N.W. I: Well, I doubt it.

C.: You ought to find out whether he played first club in Michigan.

N.W. I: I saw him on the basketball court myself. You know, I have played sports. You know the test. I think the test that V.C. gave him is an accurate picture of him. What did you say his finger dexterity was?

V.C.: 77th percentile, a little above average.

N.W. I: You know, you are not a halfback in football if you are clumsy. I know something about sports. I am not saying he is not a good athlete, but I really think—I can find out in a day.

C.: Whether or not he is, I think we ought to work with a guidance person or somebody in the school administration.

DR. P.E.C.: When you take everything that you have said, what it adds up to is that this kid needs a good series of counseling sessions.

N.W. I: That is true. That is what I am saying.

DR. P.E.C.: Somebody has got to plan the future for him, and what he has got to do, and what the significance of school is.

V.C.: That is what I am saying.

DR. P.E.C.: Again, I don't hold it too much against the kid that he shades the truth in order to get a job, because that is what society is forcing him to do, in a way. I am just a little bothered by all the questions we have about him. I think that our focus ought to be: Can he really get into high school in September? Now he has got to know that the high school is going to write to Michigan and get his record, and he should go back to school. I have a feeling from all the questions here that I don't know what the score is. I don't know what the problem is.

P.I.: Something happened in Michigan—is that what you mean—to promote this situation.

DR. P.E.C.: If he has been here a month, that means he arrived early in June. The chances are school didn't end there that early in June.

N.W. II: Out west and down south, it may.

C.: Anyhow, you have got to face him up to the situation. He can't just say he dropped out because of difficulties in school. What are the difficulties? Have him explain them, and what have you. I think the idea is to push as hard as we can to see if we can get him into the high school, whether it means going to a guidance counselor or a principal, or a football coach if he happens to have football skill.

V.C.: Who is available at the high school?

C.: The principals are around. There must be some staff during the summer. If you can't contact them, you can go to Dr. Y., Director of Pupil Services. If he can't get in, maybe we have to think about employment, or work crew or something else. But if we can get him back to school, that is something else.

DR. P.E.C.: He has to be told that in terms of some of the things he would like to do, he seems to have the ability to do it, and for what he wants to do, schooling is the most important thing.

C.: And I think if N.W. I could visit the aunt and uncle and find out what their thinking is, they might be interested in his going to school, or they might want some income.

N.W. I: I can find out why he is really here.

V.C.: All right. If you can do that we will certainly appreciate it.

BILL MORRIS

N.W. I: Bill Morris, 17, born in Georgia. He has been here one week.[31] He came in on his own looking for full-time employment or a training program; single.

He lives with his sister here. His mother and father—or his mother is in Georgia. He didn't work at all last year, Negro, he doesn't drive; he hasn't had any brushes with the law.

He made a good appearance. He is a high-school graduate from Northport, Northpost, or something.

N.W. II: Northpost.

N.W. I: He has a general course. The subject he liked best in school was government. The subject he liked least was geometry. He doesn't want any more education.

D.R. P.E.C.: May I ask a question? He is 17 and has already graduated high school?

N.W. I: That's right. He will be 18 in January. He states his marks in school were average. He played basketball and baseball. As far as comments, he stated that although he is interested in salesman, he knows he wouldn't make a good one, due to his shyness.

He would like a job as a stock clerk until he reaches 21 years of age. He will try to become a policeman.

The only work history he had was at a chain restaurant, dishwashing, in the summer of 1963. He worked eight hours a day, and made $1.15 an hour, and he got it through his brother-in-law.

He said the job was okay. He left it because he went back to Georgia. I didn't even check, because there are so many chain restaurants, and I didn't know which one he worked at. Currently unemployed, and is getting support from his sister.

There are three kinds of jobs he would like if he could get them—or what three jobs he would think are good jobs—engineer, insurance salesman, and policeman. And he would like to be trained as a policeman. He would like to be a policeman because he likes dealing with people, and he is interested in law enforcement. As his life work, he wants to be a policeman. He thinks this is an excellent-standing job. Ten years from now he wants to be a policeman.

N.W. II: He was very positive on that. I tried to check him, but I couldn't. I just wanted to make sure that that is what he really wanted to do. I said, "Are you sure?"

N.W. I: Maybe he likes a uniform.

N.W. II: I wanted to find out, "Really, do you want to be a policeman?"

DR. P.E.C.: Did you see him, v.c.?

---

[31] That applicants headed for CPI immediately upon arrival in the city is an indication of the impact CPI has had in the inner city.

v.c.: Yes, He liked American government in school, the civics and these types of courses related to the political system, and authority. No preference as to outdoor- or indoor-type work. He never took the initiative in the conversation. He is a quiet, withdrawn southerner. He has only been here a short while.[32]

N.W. I: He said a week here.

v.c.: So he is getting familiar with our type of society up here. There was no work in Georgia, so he came here. He thought he would conquer new worlds. I think, instead of going west, they are coming north. He doesn't believe he would be a good salesman. I agreed with him 100 per cent—at the present time at least. He is not an extrovert. He is an introvert.

I didn't have too much of a conversation with him. He just wouldn't open up. I tried all sorts of counseling approaches. It was either yes or no or maybe.

N.W. I: With all that is going on down there, the poor guy is scared out of his pants, as it is.

N.W. II: He told me it was pretty hot down there.

N.W. I: After all, he is coming up here, he met you, he was probably more at ease with you.[33]

N.W. II: The reason why I had to ask him, "Are you sure you want to be a policeman?" was because if he was sure, I wanted to see whether there was some area where CPI could help him. That is the only reason why I was really trying to find out. But he was positive. "I want to be a policeman." In other words, what he was telling me, "I'll take any job until I reach 21 years of age, and then I am going to try to join the police force."

I said, "Well, if you want to go on the police force, you have got to know the right people, to get recommended."

P.I.: He would have reference, he would have to live here a while.

N.W. II: I said, "What are you going to do until you are 21?"

v.c.: He was tested, and he scored very low in all tests. Verbal IQ, 63. He wasn't tested in the nonverbal. Arithmetic, 2nd percentile; inspection, 2nd percentile; coordination, 17th; mechanical knowledge, 2nd percentile; spatial perception, 1½ percentile. I don't think the scores are a good index at all of his aptitude. I throw the tests out as meaningless. I don't know what the situation was. I don't know how he felt during the test. S.B. gave the tests.

DR. P.E.C.: Was he tested in this office?

v.c.: Yes.

DR. P.E.C.: Does S.B. travel around and do this?

v.c.: He goes to the different offices to do the testing.

DR. P.E.C.: Does he do it in small groups?

v.c.: Small groups.

[32] Many southern Negroes find it difficult to relate to a white interviewer and are exceedingly reserved in the situation. The problem may be even greater in the testing situation, as the discussion below indicates.

[33] N.W. I and II are both Negro. v.c. is white.

N.W. I: With v.c. they are at ease because he has counseled them and he tests them.

v.c.: The thing is, I have so many other duties, I can't be on hand for every test situation.

DR. P.E.C.: What do you do nights? The answer is, we have got to face this kind of thing. Granted, you can't do all of it. What is involved in giving these tests? There is no great shakes in the giving of it. Where the skill comes in is how you prepare a client for it, putting him at ease, and making him feel that if he has any questions or any anxiety, he can talk to you about it. Here is a kid who comes up, one week out of the south—

c.: One thing we might be able to work out here, v.c., that wouldn't tie you up for this whole testing period, would be if you could do some of the initial explanation, and be in there until they started these. Then if one or two of the neighborhood workers might stay in through the testing procedure and watch how things go in each test, we could get them aside and talk to them about something.

v.c.: You know more about this than I do, DR. P.E.C. Can you divorce effectively pretest orientation and administration? Can you cut it up and can you still obtain the same results?

DR. P.E.C.: I think this is what we have been talking about, that we are dealing with people who were not part of the group on whom these tests were standardized. We are not dealing with the usual run of clients, so to speak.

We have discussed four cases today. Three of them have come up from the south; two of them came up very, very recently. We have no reason to believe that they know what they were walking into. You put them into a situation which is playing to their weaknesses rather than to their strengths.

You certainly need explanation, why you are giving them tests, what role tests will play.

v.c.: Well, I do that. I don't think the orientation is duplicated. When I have given the test, I have duplicated the orientation. I have told them once, and then at the test site, which is here, I have said it again.

DR. P.E.C.: The other thing is, when somebody gets a minus score, or gets practically zero percentile score, one of the things you do is to sit down with somebody and say, "Look, I want to try to understand why you are having this difficulty."

There are failures and there are failures. There are near misses and gross misses.

It seems to me very wasteful—this is what you are saying, v.c., and I agree—when we sit here and we discuss a case and we say, "We are not going to pay any attention to the test score."

P.I.: Our problem is this, especially in view of the fact that some of these people are recent arrivals from the south, that if we don't have a test as a criterion, what are we going to use as a criterion?

DR. P.E.C.: I am saying to use the test. We have to use the test, but we want to use them so that they are informative to the maximum, and helpful to the client. This means we cannot be satisfied with merely listening to numbers.

c.: I feel strongly that someone who knows the applicant, who has some relationship to him, whether it is a neighborhood worker or what, should at least be in attendance throughout the whole test, because this will give them a feeling of some support. Also, they know you are trying to help them.

s.i.: If they have a question.

c.: Instead of putting the pencil down, they might look at you and start writing.

dr. p.e.c.: The question that we are facing so frequently is, let's say, that somebody has a percentile of two per cent. Is it that he misunderstood the directions? Why two per cent? Is he that low really?

p.i.: Now, in view of the fact—say this guy had two per cent. I can understand what a tester could go through too. One man, if he doesn't understand what is going on, you can explain to him for 15 or 20 minutes and he might become even more frustrated because even at the end of 20 minutes he still doesn't know what's going on.

d.r. p.e.c.: Well, you don't pursue it that much.

p.i.: The administrator has to proceed with the test.

n.w. I: You have to ask, "Is there any part you don't understand?"

p.i.: Now, we find out he has a low score. Now we can go and investigate his low scores.

dr. p.e.c.: That is what I am saying. Once you give the test—

p.i.: But I thought perhaps maybe we are trying to correct the test administration at the application level.

dr. p.e.c.: No. I am glad you brought that up. We are not going to coach them. We are not going to give them more time. It is a time kind of thing. But having prepared them, having given the test to them, let's find out what kinds of failures they are making here. You know, it makes a difference if you ask a kid—routinely when I give a school achievement test to a kid I will score it and find out he is in, say, the eighth month of the third grade. But I sit down with him and I go over the ones that he did wrong. And I say, "Well, let's look at this. Why did you answer it in this way?" I want to find out how the kid thinks about it.

Sometimes, as I said before, they are near misses; sometimes they are gross misses. Sometimes you are going to find out the guy just doesn't understand the instructions.

c.: I think we have some evidence here on one of the cases we discussed this afternoon that someone put down his pencil and stared at the test. Somebody should be in the room trying to encourage the person to continue, if he has to pick up the pencil and stick it in their hands, if it is going to be a meaningful test to us.

dr. p.e.c.: v.c. brought this up a couple of months ago, about a couple of kids that you saw in the office.

c.: One of the outstanding examples here is in the early days of CPI when we gave our first battery of tests for X-ray technician at the public school in the evening. One guy quit right in the beginning of the test. I happened to be there. I knew the guy. I just went over and sat down and I looked at him. I picked up the pencil and I handed it to him. He continued. He passed the test. He got into the training program, he passed, and he is now working. He is not a failure. These human factors have to be also considered in testing.

v.c.: Absolutely. There is a twilight zone between being a good administrator and being a good human being in the test situation. You have got to differentiate as to when you have to apply the human aspect and when you have to still retain the administrative power over the kids.

c.: Except that our service is supposed to be humanized, in comparison with most traditional services. We have to always think of it from that point of view.

p.i.: I think perhaps we ought to get back at the failures on the tests through counseling.

c.: I think that is an excellent suggestion too. I believe in prevention, if possible, first.

p.i.: The trouble with the prevention part is that it is time-consuming and you are trying to solve—like in the case you brought out, it sounds more exceptional than anything else. With these fellows, when they are taking a test, they really don't know what is coming off, a lot of them, and you have to explain. You could spend a long time explaining while the test is being administered. It is not the proper time.

c.: How much time are we spending today in discussing these test results. Maybe some more time should have been spent then, and we could whip right through, if we thought the test scores were valid.

If it takes an hour to discuss the tests, maybe another 10 minutes spent at the tests might pay off.

p.i.: An attempt should be made at it. I don't mean to say that because a person puts down their pen, they don't know. I think an attempt should be made to get at what the cause of that is, and if it could be eliminated right there and then—I am saying "if."

When you can't reach the applicant, then the tester has to stop and administer the test and at a future date, like perhaps further counseling, to find out what the real trouble was.

n.w. II: When v.c. counsels these people, and says, "Come in and take a test on Wednesday," the young people wait to take the test and they see this other man walk through the door, all authoritative, you know, with the briefcase.[34] I want to tell you what happens. I think c. is right. I was in the hospital one time, and we knew a fellow they called Jim, the bartender. He had one of his kidneys taken out and the doctor was trying to prepare him for another operation, a minor operation. He went and talked to him psycho-

---

[34] The workload was such that it was necessary to have one person in charge of testing for all the offices. This person was necessarily a stranger to the applicant.

logically. But when he found out that this doctor wasn't going to operate on him, he went into cardiac arrest. We think he went into cardiac arrest due to the fact that he was aware that his doctor wasn't going to operate on him.

I think this follows through here. Now, I am confidential with v.c. I walk in and I find out he is not going to give me the test, and this man walks through the door. It's true.

v.c.: I know, I know this is true.

c.: I think part of v.c.'s role might be in preparing him. One of the vital things that a tester must have is a sense of humor. If you see a group of kids that are awfully nervous, and you can inject something to loosen them up . . .

DR. P.E.C.: What can we do about this?

c.: The first thing is to begin maybe preparing the kids that you want to give the test to. Maybe a guy with a tie and a briefcase is going to give it, but it is still right here. I think we ought to try to have someone in there, whether it is a neighborhood worker in here, throughout the test, and give the kids a little support.

P.I.: But if you are going to have somebody in here, it has to be somebody who has seen these people. It will be one neighborhood worker, maybe one neighborhood worker who has seen half the people there.

c.: We might set it up so that they have seen the kids before.

DR. P.E.C.: We will have to do something. I think c. and v.c. ought to take the initiative in figuring out what should be done.

P.I.: This will be eliminated when you have a Skill Center, because we won't use testing primarily as a criterion in the Skill Center.

v.c.: They will be tested right there in the Skill Center.

DR. P.E.C.: That will raise other kinds of questions.

c.: Let's not get into that yet. There is another possibility, as we get a second counselor, that maybe v.c. could spend more time in there.

DR. P.E.C.: Part of it is the selection of the person. You have to get the right one.

v.c.: All I can say is that the first thing you have got to do in testing is to put these kids completely at ease.

DR. P.E.C.: Well, let's go on with our friend.

v.c.: He wants to become a policeman.

DR. P.E.C.: You were giving us the scores.

c.: What is his size, physically?

v.c.: Minnesota Clerical, which is the last test given, number comparison, 45; name comparison, 25. Those were his two highest scores. I can't use the test as a measure. It is impossible.

c.: Is there some way we might get some sample tests for policemen, that we might be able to somehow give this kid some practice, and get an idea of whether even four years from now this is a real possible thing? And if so, what preparation can we make, what kind of employment do we try to get him, what kind of night school do we try to get him to take?

v.c.: I am familiar with all the people that work in the youth division. I could call the lieutenant and have him talk to him. I will tell him about the type of boy we have, and maybe make an appointment with the lieutenant to talk about policemen's work.

N.W. I: He is only 17.

V.C.: That's okay. At least he will get more knowledge of a policeman's type work in the future.[35]

N.W. I: I think he has a pretty good idea that he wants to be a policeman.

DR. P.E.C.: Let me ask this question: Is there any job that could be developed for him or made available for him which has to do with the police department or some form like that?

N.W. I: There was a job in the police department for a work-crew kid.[36] Did that go by the wayside?

V.C.: That was electrical work crew, working in the police department, but on wiring.

C.: We might investigate the possibilities of a work-crew placement with, say, the traffic division of the police department, where they paint the lines, but they are all cops that are doing this. This might be some way of at least introducing him a little bit. But I think we have to think about some meaningful employment between now and the time he reaches 21.

P.I.: If he is only 17, the only thing I can think of right now is a work crew. He is not old enough to get most jobs.[37]

C.: Did he say anything about the service? It seems to me, if he is going to have to go eventually, it is somewhat in line with police work. At 17 he could get in the army and get the service requirement over with.

DR. P.E.C.: If he ever got into the military police in the army, and he had the ability and had the good record, this would certainly be in his favor. I assume it would be in his favor.

C.: He can go into the service now if his parents sign for him.

V.C.: Whether this test is valid or not, I don't know. But say it is valid. He will not get into the army. They will screen him out. That is what they are doing with many, many people these days. They are being more selective.[38]

N.W. I: Here is another thing. This is what they have been talking about too, about these kids that have been turned down for the army. They are supposed to be setting up something.

C.: That is the poverty program.[39]

[35] NEC staff tend to take an applicant's stated ambitions seriously, even though staff members are aware of the difficulties confronting the applicants in achieving their ambitions.

[36] CPI's close tie with a variety of municipal agencies is revealed in this comment.

[37] Workmen's-compensation laws and other regulations bar applicants from many positions because of their age.

[38] Again, the psychological test is a bar to opportunity, despite the fact that the validity of test scores for many positions is either poor or unknown.

[39] CPI was operating in full swing well before the passage of the Economic Opportunity Act.

N.W. I: Here is a high-school graduate with scores like this. Something is wrong somewhere.[40]

P.I.: That is a southern high school.

DR. P.E.C.: But he graduated.

P.I.: We have an applicant of a northern high school who graduated in a special class. He had very low norms.

DR. P.E.C.: But he graduated even before the normal age, you see. Ordinarily, if you came through the special class, you would have graduated at a later age.

S.I.: Are you sure he graduated.

N.W. I: We can only take his word.

C.: We had a candidate who had two years of college, not junior college, but college in the south, whom we tested, and from the test scores he was recommended to attend a literacy program. This guy blew up. Then somebody didn't believe him, and he wrote and got his transcript, and he had something like a B minus average in a southern college.

DR. P.E.C.: May I make this suggestion? Has he thought of the army? If he really has this deep motivation to become a policeman, the one thing he could do in this respect before 21 is to see if he can get in the army, and then ultimately into the military police, if this is what he wants to do.

N.W. II: I told him that.

DR. P.E.C.: What did he think about it?

N.W. II: He said he is going to think about it. I said, "The best way for you to do is to join the air force, and get in the air force police, or the army."

DR. P.E.C.: I think this ought to be discussed further with him. The second thing is that since he has been up here such a short period of time, in order for him to be able to make an adjustment and for us to get an idea of how he works and what he can do, why don't we temporarily think in terms of some kind of work crew for him? This will give him an idea, give him time to think through whether he wants to go into the army. If he decides he wants to go into the army, then I think somebody ought to take the initiative of contacting the recruiting service, and maybe at that time we ought to raise the question of giving him an individual intelligence test.[41]

V.C.: A Wechsler.

DR. P.E.C.: A Wechsler or something like that.

N.W. I: He is 17. His parents will have to sign for him, and they might not go for it.

DR. P.E.C.: He will be 18 in January.

C.: I think the basic "ed" part of the work crew will give us a better indication over a period of time what his potential is.[42]

[40] The rate of unemployment is as great among Negro youth who are high-school graduates as it is among those who are dropouts! (Dentler, 1964).

[41] NEC staff are willing to be quite protective of applicants and support them in many ways that in another setting would be called "overprotective."

[42] As part of the work-crew experience, the boys spend two afternoons a week in class (Chapter 17).

DR. P.E.C.: This will give him time to think, and it may be that something will turn up that will be more appropriate for him.

P.I.: I have got a question about basic "ed." Do we have any idea what the boys are doing in basic "ed?"

C.: I think in the beginning they are learning about these kids. They give them an inventory. Most of the kids, many are interested mainly in money. So they started off and they are learning about checks and income tax. They are really trying to feel the kids out, and find out what level they are functioning in. So we couldn't get too much.

N.W. I: I see in some of the folders, R.C.'s work crew, he has written a question about asking them what they are getting out of the basic "ed" program. I have seen two of them. They really enjoy it, and they think they are getting a lot of help out of it, and that is going to do them good. I saw S.R.'s comments, and I saw R.B.'s comments.

V.C.: It gives us an indication of their writing ability too.

N.W. I: Their spelling is terrible.

DR. P.E.C.: Ordinarily, one shouldn't think of the army as a dumping ground. Here is a kid who is interested in this. He wants to be a policeman that badly, and it just seems to me that this is something that he ought to think about, and that we ought to be discussing with him. The work crew will give us some indication.

P.I.: But the service, we don't know their criteria.

C.: We have to investigate that and try to prepare him.

P.I.: Is he big enough, mature enough?

V.C.: I don't know what the criteria are in the army for any position they place a kid in. I have seen guys in the motor pools that should have been barbers.

C.: Even if he didn't get into the military police, you know, the uniform and guard duty, it's about the closest thing you find to police work.

N.W. I: At least he will get more schooling in the service now. That is one thing.

DR. P.E.C.: I think you ought to be discussing this with him. He should know that the work crew is going to be a temporary kind of training which will give him the time to adjust to the area, to give us an idea how he works.

C.: I think one thing we should try is to find out if he attempted to join any service in the south. You see, in Georgia it would be a lot easier for him to join, because the competition wouldn't be as great.

DR. P.E.C.: May I also suggest that if this kid wants to get into the service, and the parents or guardian would be willing to sign, that we invite the recruiting officer here to a special meeting to discuss it. We would then become informed as to what are the procedures, what are the levels. If we invite him here, the chances are that he will put out to do whatever he can.[43]

V.C.: I know the recruiting officer down there. His name is V.B. He is a very good guy.

---

[43] CPI wants to have close working relationships with all potential resources, and interested persons will frequently be invited to meetings.

DR. P.E.C.: I think we ought to be informed on this.

P.I.: Perhaps have him address everybody in the work crew.

C.: We ought to have this knowledge.

DR. P.E.C.: I think it is important that we have this knowledge.

V.C.: This is another part of the work-crew educational program, as I see it, a knowledge that they have a military obligation, and that it may affect their lives if they do not choose the right program in the army. There is a two-year draft program, and there is a three-year enlistment program.

DR. P.E.C.: I would love to find out what the score is, and also about these kids on the work program from the reform school. Does this automatically rule them out insofar as the army is concerned? We would find out what training programs are in fact available in the army.

V.C.: I think maybe we could do this on our own. I am planning to call meetings concerning work crews and maybe every two weeks or so have a person come in that may have a bearing upon the boy's life in the future.

DR. P.E.C.: Very good.

The meeting was adjourned at 4:15 P.M.

The above transcript is representative of disposition conferences as they were held at one NEC, approximately nine months after the program began. A Clinic consultant attending another NEC was surprised and pleased at the remarkable similarity in level and tone of case discussions at this meeting to those held at the other three centers at the same time. It must be emphasized that the particular transcript is representative of the range of problems coming to the NEC *at that particular time;* shortly before and after that period much more severely disturbed individuals began to come to the NEC with increasing frequency, a tendency reflecting the important role of the NEC in the area it serves. Although the bulk of cases continued to be similar to those discussed in the transcripts, there were a sizable number of cases with current or past history of blatant psychopathology. As a check in this impression we categorized 34 consecutive cases brought up at the disposition conferences of one NEC, approximately 16 months after the above transcript was obtained. In the following statement of results an individual is entered in only one "category."

1. In nine of the 34 cases the individual had been an inpatient in a psychiatric setting in the recent past. Four cases came from a state hospital, three from a private psychiatric hospital, and two from special psychiatric settings for disturbed adolescent boys.

2. In four of the 34 cases the individual had recently been in a correctional institution or (in one case) under the jurisdiction of the juvenile court.

3. In five of the 34 cases there were blatant psychological deficits which raised questions about the individual's trainability or employability, for

example, adolescent alcoholism, "recluse" behavior, repetitive displays of hostility and aggression, and unusual immaturity.

4. In 16 of the 34 cases we found what we can only term as the "usual" amount and severity of problems one expects in inner-city people. This group is formed primarily "by exclusion" and in no sense reflects a judgment that they are without serious problems.

The above data are presented for illustrative purposes and are not intended as any precise statement of what the actual state of affairs would be if all cases over longer periods of time were scrutinized. Although it is our belief that the actual state of affairs would not be appreciably different, we do not feel that the statement that people coming to the NEC run the gamut of psychopathology requires special documentation.

In the following chapters the reader will obtain a highly detailed view of the work-crew program, one of the major innovations CPI has developed as a means of working with adolescents. The work crew is not the only possible disposition, but it is a major resource for work with adolescents. The reader should keep in mind that he is obtaining a picture of only one part of the CPI program.

Chapter 17

The Work Crews

The work-crew program began in the summer of 1963 as a pilot project supported by funds made available by the New Haven Foundation. At that time it was organized to provide 21 youths (out of work and school) from two inner-city neighborhood settlement houses with a summer of work experience under the close supervision of a foreman. With only about five boys in each crew, four work crews were established, each one provided with a specific work assignment and work site. Despite certain difficulties and problems, the initial program appeared to make a real difference in the lives of many of these youngsters, and several of them, even after this relatively short but intensive group work experience, either returned to school or were able to secure permanent jobs.

Though the need was recognized for a more involved program in terms of the necessity for a remedial-education component as well as for more varied and meaningful work experiences, the pilot project indicated that significant changes could occur in the lives of youngsters when the vocational setting was utilized as a therapeutic tool. Similarly, it indicated that this setting provided a meaningful vehicle for the involvement of appropriate inner-city personnel as the key individuals who could help and train troubled youngsters. The fact that these foremen could get to the youngsters in a way and to a degree in which other, more professional, individuals could not is a phenomenon of no small importance at this point, and one to which we shall return. Suffice it to say here that, as with so many other aspects of CPI's program, the work crews were initially conceived of, organized by, and implemented with essentially nonprofessional personnel. That is to say, with the exception of the work-crew coordinator, those most directly involved with the program—the work-crew foremen and their supervisors—were people with no formal training or academic background in those areas (psychology, sociology, social work) usually felt to be of primary importance in doing remedial work with adolescents.

Since the summer pilot project of 1963 the work-crew concept has grown in terms both of programming and the number of youths serviced. Financial support for the program has come from local, state, and national sources. From September of 1963 to June of 1964 the work crews, funded through the Department of Health, Education, and Welfare (HEW), the Office of Manpower and Training (OMAT), and the City of New Haven, serviced 131 youngsters in 15 work crews. During the summer of 1964 the program involved 166 youths in 20 work crews, and was supported by OMAT and funds administered through CPI. From September 1964, through February 1965, funds provided by OMAT and CPI were utilized to provide services for 100 youngsters on 18 work crews. Due to the overlapping nature of funding and the resulting carry-over of youths from one program to the next a total number of 305 youths have been serviced to date. At the present time there are 100 youths in the program and a total of 18 work crews (15 male and 3 female crews). The disproportionate number of male crews is to some extent intentional, but it is also because of realistic factors in the community. It is intentional to the extent that in our familial structure the male is viewed as the individual most responsible for providing the major source of income for the family. In this context his ability to hold down a job has direct effects (a steady source of income uninterrupted by periods of childbearing and early child-rearing activities) as well as indirect consequences (problems of masculine identity, self-esteem, and self-image related to his position as the head of a household). In terms of community realities there are more potential work areas available to male work crews than there are to female work crews. In any event, without denying the importance of training females for productive careers, the inner-city male remains the primary concern of the work-crew program.

GENERAL DESCRIPTION

The work-crew program involves a prevocational training and remedial education experience for inner-city youths between the ages of 16 and 21. In the following pages we attempt to describe the general structure and content of the program.

A work crew is made up of between five and seven youngsters and one foreman. Each youngster is paid $20 per week for his participation in the program. The program itself consists of 20 hours of work plus 4½ hours of remedial education each week. The small number of youngsters in each work crew is itself an important variable in the program, and is based on both theoretical and practical considerations.

On the one hand, because the work-crew experience is an intensive and complex one, the limited number of youngsters in each crew makes close supervision and individual guidance more feasible for the foreman. He can spend more time with each youngster and can get to know him more intimately than would be the case if he had 15 or 20 individuals on his crew. On the other hand, since the foreman transports his crew to and from its work site, a larger group of youngsters would result in acute problems of automobile transportation.

Each work crew operates out of its own particular home base, that Neighborhood Employment Center (NEC) serving the inner-city neighborhood from which its youngsters are drawn. Every weekday morning the crew (youngsters and foreman) meet at its NEC and depart as a group for its work site. At the end of each work day the crew returns to the NEC. Since there are 18 work crews, each of the three NECs serve as the home base for several crews.

In addition to its home base each work crew has a specific location, its work site, where it is expected to perform certain jobs and tasks for a variety of public agencies. The selection of appropriate work sites for the work crews was itself a formidable task, and depended both on matching sites with the skills of foremen already in the program and on selling the work-crew concept to potential agency participants. A final consideration in the selection of sites was the need to provide meaningful work settings for the youngsters, settings in which the training received could prepare them for work opportunities on the job market. Since this latter requirement could not always be met in a realistic fashion, the work sites could most accurately be described as prevocational settings where the development of appropriate work attitudes and habits are the primary goals. The work sites, therefore, represent a wide range of settings in which these work attitudes and habits can be developed in terms of the varying interests, skills, and levels of readiness of the youngsters. This being the case, the content of the work done on the work sites varies from more general skills (painting, raking, etc.) to more particular training (carpentry, nurses-aide, and machine repair). The assignment of a youngster to a particular work crew is thus dependent on his needs, aptitudes, interests, and level of readiness. At the present time the program work sites include a VA Hospital (grounds maintenance, painting, and machinery), a convalescent hospital (nurses-aide training), the public golf course (grounds maintenance), a greenhouse (plant care), the New Haven Boys Club (carpentry), a garage (mechanics), the Park Department and Department of Public Works (painting and maintenance work), the public library (librarian and clerical training) and several other settings with similar functions.

From its inception the work crews sought to include in the program a remedial-education component designed to provide the youngsters with some educational experiences they either missed or failed to master while in the public schools. By linking the educational component to the work crews themselves the attempt was made to help each work-crew member further his own educational background so that he might better qualify for a worthwhile job or job-training opportunity. The curriculum includes basic reading, arithmetic and language skills, job-training experiences (the filling out of applications, the learning of job relations and ethics), occupational information skills (social-security practices, labor laws, taxes, medical insurance), and personal health education (grooming, appearance, etc.). The long-term objective of the education program is to provide each individual with learning experiences commensurate with his capacities, needs, interests, and goals. As with the work crews themselves, the attempt was made to maximize individual instruction by keeping class size as small as possible. The classes themselves were graded in order to provide remedial education to youngsters of comparable ability and past academic experience. Because many of the instructors in the program are teachers, and because it was realized that most of the work-crew youngsters have had poor educational experiences, special precautions were taken to make the remedial-education component of the program as dissimilar from public school as possible. This was done in several ways: first, by utilizing a community house as the setting for the remedial-education component of the program, and, second, by limiting the program to four and one-half hours a week (one and a half hours a day, three days a week). It was made clear, however, that participation in the work-crew program included mandatory attendance in the remedial-education classes.

Although later we discuss in some detail the content of one boy's day on his work crew, let us now turn to what may be considered a general description of the work-day schedule.

8:00 A.M.: The work-crew members and their foreman meet at the NEC that serves as their home base.

8:00–8:15 A.M.: The crew travels to its designated work site in the foreman's car.

8:15–8:30 A.M.: The work goals for that day are discussed and individual assignments are handed out.

8:30–12:00 NOON: The work-crew members do the work assigned for that particular day. The foreman supervises the work and utilizes the time for individual instruction.

12:00–1:15 P.M.: The entire crew has its lunch with the foreman in the area of the work site. After lunch a period of time is set aside for group discussion. At this time any problems relating to the day's work or to the group's interpersonal relations are brought up for discussion by the foreman and/or the other work-crew members. The day's work is reviewed and general goals for the next day are set.

1:15–1:30 P.M.: The work crew leaves its work site and travels to the Jewish Community Center, the setting for the remedial-education program.

1:30–3:00 P.M.: At the Jewish Community Center the work-crew members break up and go to their assigned classrooms. The foreman visits these classrooms during the time the youngsters are being instructed.

3:00 P.M.: Following the completion of the day's remedial-education program the work crew is driven back to its home base by the foreman and the work day ends.

Variations in this schedule occur on those days when there is no remedial-education component and on the last day of each work week. When no remedial-education is scheduled the work crew spends the additional hour and a half on activities related to the work site. On the last day of each week the hours from 2:00–4:00 P.M. are set aside for recreation. At this time the crew goes to a local community school where the gymnasium and pool have been reserved for ball playing and swimming activities.

THE PROCESS

The procedure by which a youngster becomes known to the NEC, is evaluated, and is placed on a work crew is known as "the process." It is a procedure often involving the entire NEC staff (neighborhood worker, vocational counselor, diagnostic tester, neighborhood co-ordinator), but one in which the youngster is rarely lost through a myriad of unrealistic referrals, undue waiting periods, and prolonged periods of separation from the agency. Although this mobilization of the NEC's resources has been described, the reader may find it helpful to see how a particular youngster was brought into the work-crew program.

JOHN

John is a 17½-year old Negro youngster who was recently released from the Meriden School for Boys. He returned to his local neighborhood (one of the inner-city areas) after having spent one year at Meriden for car theft. This was his second conviction for stealing a car, the first one occurring approximately three years ago after an escapade of drinking and smoking marijuana cigarettes.

John had completed the sophomore year in high school. A review of his record, however, indicated that John had been the recipient of several social promotions and was actually almost two years behind his current class in academic performance.

John was observed hanging around one of the street corners by a neighborhood worker and the first contact was made at that point. Since the neighborhood worker had known him for some time—and knew about John's having been at Meriden—their talk centered around John's experiences at Meriden as well as his current and future plans. John told the worker of his intention to re-enter school in the fall (it was now early spring), and to just "kind of hang around" until then. Later, over a cup of coffee, John spoke at some length about his mother's recent death (a fact the neighborhood worker was already aware of) and his reluctance to remain at home with his stepfather, a man with whom John had a particularly poor relationship. As far as his future was concerned, John spoke of a gratifying experience he had had while working in the hospital at the Meriden School for Boys and indicated his desire to explore job opportunities in which he could be of help to ailing people. As far as school was concerned, John indicated his expectation that due to his age he would probably be put in the "graduating class next September."

The neighborhood worker, impressed by the depressive tone in John's voice and his seemingly unrealistic educational expectations, spoke to him about coming down to the CPI employment center and brought up the possibility of John's using the intervening months until September to earn some money and, through the remedial-education component of the work-crew program, prepare himself for his re-entry into school. John thought the plan sounded reasonable and accompanied the neighborhood worker to the NEC.

At the NEC the neighborhood worker introduced John to some of the other people in the office. One of these people was the vocational counselor. John looked a bit bewildered, so the neighborhood worker helped him fill out an application and remained with him while he was interviewed by the vocational counselor. Because vocational placement was not John's primary reason for coming to the NEC, and because the vocational counselor, like the neighborhood worker, was somewhat disturbed by John's obvious state of depression, general aptitude testing was put off. Instead the two workers spent the rest of their time with John explaining the work-crew program and talking about John's interest in working around a hospital setting. John brightened up a bit but remained essentially depressed and withdrawn. He left the office with the neighborhood worker who promised to keep in touch with him during the next few days and until the work-crew possibly could be fully explored. The promise was kept.

John was staffed a few days later at the weekly disposition conference held   the NEC. Both the neighborhood worker and the vocational counselor, along with the NEC coordinator and other staff members and consultants, were present.

John's case was reviewed both in terms of his past history and the impressions obtained by the staff people who had spent time with him. Several factors were elaborated on and explored:

1. John's record indicated that on both of the occasions on which he had been picked up for stealing a car he was not, so to speak, in the driver's seat but was actually the accomplice. In neither instance did he try to escape, but actually seemed to welcome capture.

2. It was clear that before each offense John had been particularly depressed. The first offense coincided with his real father's departure from the home; the second occurred two days after his mother had been admitted to the hospital for a serious operation.

3. John's current depressive state (related both to the death of his mother and his inability to get along with his stepfather) was clearly a danger signal and appeared to involve a degree of alienation from himself and others that could easily place him in his characteristic state of being susceptible to suggestions involving antisocial behavior.

4. It appeared that John had an unrealistic view of his future as far as his placement in school was concerned. As he was fully two years behind in his work, it was felt that he was merely readying himself for another letdown by anticipating high-school graduation in one year.

5. Most important, it was felt that the interim period between now and the beginning of school (between March and September) might be utilized to (a) offer John a chance to pursue his interest in working around a hospital, (b) provide John with a group experience in which his feelings and attitudes would not inevitably have to lead to social withdrawal and alienation, (c) give John a chance to appraise more realistically his educational goals without initially placing him in an academic situation laden with potential difficulty and personal failure.

It was the feeling of those present that in this instance a work-crew experience was not only important and potentially helpful, but should be implemented as quickly as possible. It was felt that he should be placed on a work crew that functioned in a hospital setting.

Immediately after the disposition meeting the neighborhood worker went out to see John. He told John of his assignment to the work crews and arranged to have John meet his new foreman. Finally, the neighborhood worker accompanied John to the NEC for John's first day of work.

In our description of the process utilized to involve a youngster in the work-crew program one point stands out above all others, that is, the degree to which contact is maintained with an individual from the moment of initial encounter to the time of final placement in the work-crew program. In many ways it is a prototype of the kind and degree of involvement that characterizes many of the activities of the work crews.

THE YOUNGSTERS AND THE WORK-CREW PROGRAM

The reader will recall that we described the work-crew program as a *prevocational* training and remedial-education experience. The term "prevocational" is not a fortuitous one, for the primary objective of the work-crew program is *not* to train the youngsters for specific jobs or to help them find jobs, and it would be fallacious and misleading to think that it was. Indeed, were the vocational messiah suddenly to appear on the horizon, and in one swift sweep of his hand guarantee and place each work-crew youngster in a well-paying, secure, and long-term job, there would be no appreciable change in the problems for which the work-crew program was conceived and developed. The goal of finding employment for youth is not an irrelevant aspect of the program, but a sudden plethora of available jobs would not solve the kinds of problems for which the work crews were formed. The genesis of the problem is not to be found solely in the world of work; it also resides in the private and public worlds of the youngsters themselves.

When a youngster comes into the work-crew program he is not only unemployed, he is also—at least at that time—essentially unemployable. He is not out of work solely because he possesses no salable or marketable skills. Were this his only problem he could be directly placed—or already would have placed himself—in a situation in which he could acquire those skills necessary for employment in a particular vocational setting. He is unemployed because his feelings and attitudes, his work habits and interpersonal relations, have combined to produce a youngster who is socially and psychologically unprepared to enter into, become part of, and succeed in, the world of work. His unemployability is both the product and the symptom of a pattern of life that has left him ill-equipped to cope with the responsibilities and obligations of the existing social order. His feelings about himself and others are the feelings of a youngster who has become alienated from a world he does not understand, a world with which he cannot cope in any meaningful and self-satisfying manner. In essence then, the work-crew experience is not for the unemployed, it is for the unemployable; it is not for the boy who is looking for a job, it is for the boy who cannot look for a job; it is not for the youngster who is out of work, it is for the youngster who is out of touch with himself and the society in which he lives.

Because the major problems confronting the work-crew youngsters are not jobs but are "problems in living," the primary focus of the work-crew experience is remedial in nature. The most appropriate description of the work-crew program is that it utilizes the vocational setting as a therapeutic tool in order to stabilize, influence, and redirect the lives of its youngsters, both now and in the future. As this is the case, its primary function is to create a work-oriented therapeutic milieu in which it becomes both possible and feasible to deal with those personal and interpersonal problems that characterize so many of the lives of its youngsters. By focusing its attention on work habits and attitudes the work-crew program is actually involved in making available to its youngsters an ongoing therapeutic experience that might not be possible in many other settings. In the daily context of working with others, each work-crew youngster is placed in the position where he must, sooner or later, begin to examine his own attitudes and feelings in terms of how they affect him and others in the work-crew situation. His own "working behavior" becomes of legitimate concern to himself, his foreman and the other youngsters on the crew. The personal and interpersonal problems and attitudes a youngster brings with him to the work-crew situation are the kinds of problems and attitudes that affect his and other people's functioning, and are therefore fair game for discussion and intervention in that setting. The role of the foreman is crucial in this context, for he becomes the focal point and catalytic agent in many of the therapeutic interventions involving the youngsters.

The term "work habits and attitudes" covers a wide range of behaviors that are dealt with in a remedial fashion on the work crews. For some youngsters this initially may involve the learning of appropriate job-oriented habits such as promptness, perseverance, and vocational responsibility. For most, however, the work-crew experience has a more generally remedial and therapeutic focus. This focus is the use of the work setting as an arena for the kinds of personality and attitudinal changes that have individual implications extending far beyond the occupational setting.

It is clear that the youngsters in the work-crew program are in need of much more than a preparatory work experience. In our present discussion we have attempted to focus attention on the fact that their needs and problems are of such a nature as to require intensive and often extensive remedial interventions, the kinds of interventions usually associated with the more traditional clinical therapeutic process. Were we to attempt to assign clinical diagnoses to the youngsters, these diagnoses would likely run the entire gamut of emotional and psychological pathology. We would then be describing these work-crew youngsters—and quite appropriately so—as schizoid personalities, psychopathic personalities, organic pathologies, psychoneurotic problems, character disorders, and as characters in any other diagnostic category currently utilized in labeling patients. Their histories, symptoms, and behaviors are essentially no different from those of many of the patients who are currently being treated in clinics or by private practitioners.

It would be a legitimate question to ask why these youngsters are not being seen or treated by clinics and private therapists. The answers are many and varied, and are not entirely accounted for by the lack of financial resources or the unavailability of clinical facilities. They appear to be more firmly embedded in the sociological and cultural variables that separate these youngsters from the institutions and clinical facilities available—and often not so readily available in a psychological sense—to them in the community. Part of the answer may also be sought in our traditional definitions and conceptions of what the requirements and conditions for appropriate clinical interactions are, and in the nature of what constitutes clinical functioning. Be this as it may, we are still faced with the realistic situation that these youngsters are not being seen in the clinics, and in all probability never will be.

Of the approximately 100 youngsters in the 18 work crews currently participating in the program, about 64 per cent are Negro, 33 per cent are white, and 3 per cent are of Puerto Rican and American Indian parentage. All are between the ages of 16 and 21, and all are out of work and out of school. All are single; approximately 83 per cent are males (Community Progress Inc., 1964).

At least half of the boys and girls in the program were born in New Haven. The next largest group, approximately 33 per cent, were born in the southern states. In descending order, the remaining youngsters were born abroad, in other states in the Northeast, in other parts of Connecticut, or in the Midwest. About 48 per cent of all the youths have lived in the New Haven area all their lives. Only 12 per cent have lived in New Haven five years or less. Although the work-crew program was organized to serve youngsters between the ages of 16 and 21, the median age is 16, and well over 90 per cent are between the ages of 16 and 18.

In terms of the household status of the youngsters in the program, 52 per cent are living with both parents. The next largest group, approximately 27 per cent, are living with their mothers only. The remaining youths live with other relatives, with friends, or alone. The median number of persons in the households where the boys and girls live is five, but at least 77 per cent of the youngsters live in households of five members or more.

With respect to formal education, well below ten per cent of the youngsters in the program have completed high school. At least 84 per cent are behind in their formal education, either because they dropped out of school or were left back. (The statistics concerning formal education are unavailable for some of the youngsters because they either could not recall or would not relate the status of their earlier educational experiences.) Several of the youngsters can neither read nor write; some cannot sign their names and do not know the alphabet.

At least 37 per cent of the youths have had some contact with the law for offenses more serious than loitering. (Again, these statistics are based on their own reports of trouble with the law.) Several are on parole, and many have been confined in various correctional institutions before joining the work crews. Most of those who have had contact with the law have been arrested for offenses involving petty theft, auto theft, breaking and entering, burglary, and assault.

Statistics are a convenient and necessary way of summarizing and organizing data. They are helpful in providing the reader with a structured and concise overview of the general characteristics that depict a particular population. This is as true for the statistics concerning the youngsters in the work-crew program as it is for the statistics applied to any other set of individuals. All statistics must, of necessity, sacrifice some degree of individual complexity and description in the quest for categorical clarity and preciseness. Consequently, any statistical summation of the boys and girls in the work-crew program must be viewed as a shorthand and composite description of a group of individual and unique youngsters.

A statistical overview is much more meaningful if it can be balanced by a more detailed description of individual cases. The fact that 37 per cent of the youngsters in the program have had some contact with law enforcement agencies does not tell us much about why and how these events came to pass; nor do the statistics provide much in the way of helping us understand the circumstances, motivations, and experiences of the youngsters in that group. The same can be said of almost any other statistical description involving the work-crew boys and girls. There may be a variety of reasons for dropping out of school and a host of different feelings associated with being a dropout. In each instance there is a tale to be told and no two tales need be the same.

Our goal in the following pages is to provide the reader with a somewhat more comprehensive and differentiated picture of some of the boys and girls in the program. In each case we attempt to go a bit beyond the information provided by the statistical overview of the program. Each individual described is currently on a work crew and has been for a varying amount of time. We have observed and interacted with these youngsters in a variety of work-crew settings including the work site, the remedial-education component of the program, and recreational activities. In each capsule portrait we attempt to supplement whatever information is known about the youngster with the impressions we have gotten of him in the different phases of the program.

HENRY S.

Henry is a 17-year-old white boy who has been on the work crews for about three months. He came into the program as a result of his state welfare worker's urging and has quit the program once for a period of five days during the three months. Although he was out of school and unemployed for a long period of time before his entrance into the program, he did not come onto the work crew until a few weeks after the death of his father. After his father passed away Henry went to live in the home of his older brother and sister-in-law, and the state paid them a certain amount of money to keep him. Henry was unhappy in that setting and was eventually transferred to the home of his older sister and brother-in-law. His sister and the welfare worker quickly became extremely concerned about Henry's behavior. He would sit in the home for long periods of time and stare out of the window at passing cars, saying nothing and occasionally humming to himself. He did not seem to take an interest in anything or anybody and often spent his entire day roaming around the house in his pajamas. After numerous talks with his welfare worker Henry agreed to go down to the NEC and talk with the neighborhood worker and vocational counselor about the work crews. Shortly thereafter Henry was placed on one of the CPI work crews.

Henry is a tall, gaunt boy who looks younger than his stated age. He is not particularly good-looking; he has hair that always looks tousled—as though he has just awakened from a long nap—and a complexion scarred by the effects of a lingering acne condition. His eyes appear tired and dull and he often stares at things as though each object holds some mysterious secret that is always eluding his gaze. He moves in an unsure and erratic manner, and we often get the impression that he cannot decide whether or not he should begin to run. Even when his attention appears to be focused on something he finds particularly interesting Henry retains his restless, preparing-to-move behavior.

Henry's behavior on the work site varies from day to day and from activity to activity. At times he suddenly becomes extremely interested in almost everything going on about him. He approaches people and things as if they suddenly had become extremely important and interesting. At these times he literally will bombard the foreman and the other crew members with endless questions, often repetitious in nature, about what they are doing and why they are doing it. The world is suddenly transformed into a host of totally new and fascinating things, all of which must be investigated lest they suddenly disappear. At other times Henry appears to be totally preoccupied with thoughts and feelings that have little or nothing to do with what is going on about him. At these times his restlessness becomes a way of getting away from anything or anyone whose presence might interfere with what he is thinking. He moves away from people and isolates himself from any stimuli that might impinge on his privacy.

Henry was born in another state. He has two siblings, a brother 31 years of age and a sister 19 years of age. His father was a seaman and away from the home for long periods of time. Henry's mother died when he was eight years of age, and he was placed in an orphanage for a year. After spending one year there he was sent to a country hospital for reasons that are still unclear to him:

"I always wanted to be alone and they said I was sick."

After being released from the hospital Henry went to stay with his father in Florida. From that point on life became a continuous series of residential changes. In the six years they were together, Henry and his father moved a total of eighteen times and their movement took them through Florida, California, Arizona, Tennessee, Mississippi, and North Carolina.

"I think my father knew he was dying, and we were always on the go."

They finally settled in Connecticut (near Henry's married siblings) when the boy was 16 years of age.

Henry's formal education was sporadic at best. Because he was constantly moving from state to state, up until the time he and his father settled in New Haven he never was able to attend any one school for a prolonged period. In each school he felt himself to be a continual outcast and knew that sooner or later he would move on again. Henry did not like school, both in terms of the formal learning situation and the almost inevitable difficulties that he had with the other youngsters:

"Kids were always pushing me around and I was too skinny and scared to fight back. They didn't like my looks and always beat me up. One time they kicked me off the school bus and almost killed me."

He quit school after completing the first half of the ninth grade in New Haven.

Henry's one lingering interest concerns cars and almost anything related to automobiles. When he speaks of the go-cart he once owned, his eyes light up and he talks about it in a manner that suggests a good deal of Henry was tied up in that vehicle. Each time he recapitulates the problems he had in building, maintaining, and racing his go-cart, we get the impression that the go-cart was an extension of Henry, that he tended its needs as though they were his own. Although his go-cart was destroyed some time ago, Henry's hobbies still include building model cars, working on go-carts, and stock-car racing. He wants to be an automobile mechanic.

We already have indicated what appear to be the two very different ways in which Henry behaves on the crew and at home. Henry is somewhat aware of these differences and has been trying to talk about them. As he puts it:

"Sometimes I like to just go off in a corner and stay alone. Some time I even try to talk to myself about my mistakes and all. But other times I just kind of like to go away and make believe we're all together again. Me and my mother and father are sitting around the supper table, and just kind of talking about what happened that day. We talk and we talk and sometimes it almost seems all real again."

SELVYN W.

Selvyn is a 16-year-old Negro boy whose lawyer got him into the CPI work-crew program as part of a court-approved probationary plan. Unlike most of the youngsters in the program, Selvyn's participation on the work crew is mandatory, and any long absences must be reported to his probation officer. If, for any reason, Selvyn quits or is ousted from the program he is likely to be placed in a correctional institution. Selvyn has been with CPI for seven months.

Selvyn's entrance into the work-crew program was preceded by several run-ins with the law. In July, 1964, Selvyn and several other boys stole a car and went joy-riding in the downtown area of New Haven. Because of the commotion they were making a policeman stopped and questioned them. He then arrested them, and Selvyn was put in jail. Because he was under age he was transferred to the juvenile court, reprimanded, and let go. In August he was picked up by the police on a breaking-and-entering charge. He was again referred to the juvenile court authorities and again released after a lengthly talk with officials of the court. In September Selvyn stole a car and drove it toward New York. He got sleepy and pulled off the road to take a nap, was apprehended, and was returned again to New Haven. At that time Selvyn's mother arranged to have him bailed out. The bondsman warned Selvyn that it would be the last time he would come to his aid. In October Selvyn again stole a car, was caught, and spent the better part of a week in the New Haven jail. Once more he was released after a final reprimand and warning from the court officials. In November Selvyn stole a rifle from the back of a parked car. As he walked away with the rifle he was caught, but broke free and ran away from the police. They ran after him and cornered him in an alley. When he would not surrender himself they shot their guns a few times in the air, and the boy came out and gave himself up. Following this incident Selvyn was put in jail and then was brought to court. It was at this hearing that Selvyn's lawyer arranged for Selvyn to be placed on a CPI work crew as part of his two-year probationary period.

Selvyn is the oldest of six children. He has three brothers (ages 7, 6, and 1) and two sisters (ages 8 and 5). He was born in New Haven and has lived there all his life. Selvyn's father died when the youngster was nine years old. Selvyn lives with his mother, stepfather, and siblings. The family is partially supported by the department of welfare.

There appears to be some connection between the time at which Selvyn dropped out of school and the time that he started getting into difficulty with the law. When Selvyn left school in the ninth grade he left it feeling angry and defeated. According to the youngster:

"I was going to quit even if they didn't kick me out. They took me out of a Division B class and put me in a Division D class. Everyone knows that Division D class is the class for dummies and that they don't do anything. I wasn't going to be in any Division D class and be called a dope."

Whatever the basis for shifting Selvyn from one division to another, the result was one angry, disappointed youngster. His involvement with the law followed closely on his exit from the school system. Even more interesting is the observation that Selvyn appeared to handle each unlawful incident in a manner that almost assured he would be caught. It is difficult to joy-ride a stolen car in the middle of town without drawing notice. It is hard not to be caught in a stolen car if you park it on the shoulder of the Connecticut Turnpike and take a nap. It is relatively rare that the theft of a gun from a parked car in broad daylight is not noticed or caught. In each instance it seems as though the boy was going out of his way to make sure he would be caught, going out of his way to fulfill the image of the "dummy" who has been thrown out of school.

Both on and off the work crew Selvyn is a hardy, good-natured youngster who is slow to anger and quick to smile. He is a short and somewhat stocky boy who accepts ribbing about his weight in an easygoing fashion. His attention span is relatively short when he is confronted with things in which he is not terribly interested. Once he becomes involved in a task that he likes he can remain with it for a long period of time and endure a great deal of frustration. Regardless of how involved he gets, however, we get the feeling that Selvyn sees the world and other people as relatively humorous, as something best not taken too seriously. Selvyn spins in and out of settings as if they were created for his own casual enjoyment. People and things are fun as long as you and he accept the fact that nothing of a permanent nature is implied in the association. Selvyn is the observer and recorder of human foibles, seeing much, taking it all with a grain of salt, and almost inwardly laughing at the incomprehensibility of the people and processes going on about him.

Selvyn thinks that he would like to seek a career in the armed forces. As he puts it:

"Why not? The eats and clothes are OK, you might learn something, and you might get around and see a lot. The girls like army men and the whole thing could be fun."

RICHARD L.

Richard is a 16-year-old white youngster who has been on the work crews for a short time. He came into the program a month ago at the request of one of his friends who was already on a work crew. His friend suggested that he go down and speak with one of the neighborhood workers about the work-crew program and about the chances of his eligibility to become a member. Richard saw this as a way for him to begin to "set myself on a straight line." At that time Richard was awaiting a court hearing on a charge of breaking-and-entering. Although he had worked "now and then" on a laundry truck, Richard was willing to take a cut in pay in the hope that he would be able to be in a situation that offered the prospect of a daily schedule. Richard spoke with the neighborhood worker and was placed on one of the work crews.

Richard is a short, skinny, good-looking boy who walks with a somewhat exaggerated spring in his step and wears elevator shoes. Because he is slightly built and wears tight continental pants, his elevator shoes only seem to accentuate his shortness.

Richard speaks as if every word he says ought to be taken as a direct challenge. When speaking with someone he rarely looks that person in the eyes, but almost invariably focuses on the other person's Adam's apple or chin. He speaks in short, clipped phrases that, no matter how quietly he is talking, sound as if they had been shot from a muted revolver. Even when engaged in a conversation, Richard often turns his back on that person and quickly surveys the situation to check on who, if anyone, is listening or who is in the immediate area. It seems quite important that he be fully aware of any and all movements that take place about him, almost as if these movements have a direct and determining effect on what his next move will be. His behavior is like that of a person who constantly finds himself placed in a new and potentially dangerous situation: he must be acutely aware of the placement and behavior of those who might attack and he must be ever-vigilant and ready to respond to any ominous or unpredictable movements that take place around him.

Once Richard becomes convinced that an individual's movements do not signal the beginning of an assault he can begin to relax and allow that person to enter his space of free movement. When this happens, a metamorphosis occurs, and a shy, somewhat self-conscious 16-year-old boy emerges. He can begin to smile and laugh ever so gently about the fiction of Richard as a "hard man." He can talk about how difficult it can be constantly to feel vulnerable, small, and frightened. At these times, once Richard is sure that his "confession" has not fallen on the wrong ears, he can speak about his love of the soil, the things that grow, and the wonder of a stone that "lives on and on." As Richard puts it:

"You keep seeing this grass every year and you wonder where it goes and where it ends. If you put a rock in the bushes, a heavy rock, you know it's going to be there for ever and ever, no matter what happens to you."

Richard was born on the outskirts of New Haven. He lives with his mother, stepfather, and one of his older brothers. Richard has five brothers and one sister. Three of his brothers (ages 25, 23, and 20) are married, one (age 18) lives in the home, and one (age 14) is living in a foster home. His only sister (age 19) is married and lives in the Midwest. His mother was divorced in 1959, and when she remarried a year later the family moved into the city. His real father is currently living in New Haven. Richard's mother is employed periodically as an assembly worker in a local industry and his stepfather drives a truck.

Richard has "no use" for almost all the members of his family. According to him:

"Well, my real father was a wino. Him and my mother would always fight and I'm glad he's gone. Me, I always fight with my 23-year-old brother. He's an ass-hole, a brown-noser, and always taking over. I argue a lot with my mother. She always nags me about staying out of trouble. She's probably right but she never stops nagging me."

Richard also feels that he has very little status in the home and very little say as to what should or should not happen at home:

"I can't do nothing in the house. I can't play my records or watch what I wanna watch on T.V. I gotta do what everyone else wants to do. I'm the youngest now and they never let you forget it."

Richard left school in the ninth grade for reasons that are somewhat similar to the reasons and feelings he has concerning himself and the ways in which the other members of his family react to him. He did not like having to stay in classrooms for extended periods of time. He felt "penned in and cornered." He always felt imposed on by teachers and experienced his entire stay in school as a place where people were always trying to make him do things without consulting him. Richard got into constant arguments with his teachers because of their desire that he "do something" and his desire to be "let alone."

Richard's first contact with the law occurred in August, 1964. He and a group of his friends were caught in a stolen car. Richard says he was unaware that the car had been stolen. At that time he was taken to juvenile court, given a talking to, and told, "keep your nose clean from here on."

In November Richard stole a car and took it out of town to race. As he was racing down a road he lost control of the car and it cracked into a telephone pole. Richard is not sure exactly why he took the car, but says:

"I was just walking around with a friend. I was feeling pretty disgusted. I don't know exactly why I did it. Maybe it was because I had nothing to do, or maybe it was because I had a beef with my girl."

The police arrived on the scene and Richard was taken to the hospital where he remained for one week. He was then taken to juvenile court but was released after being warned not to get into any more trouble.

From December, 1964 to March, 1965, Richard committed a series of crimes in which he broke into various restaurants in the New Haven area and stole a total of $600. In this case Richard feels that he "had to" steal the money:

"My mother was out of work and she was getting ready for an operation. All I heard at home was bills, bills, bills. I figured I had to finally help out and get the money to pay off the bills. After I got the $600 all the bills were paid."

Once all the outstanding bills were paid off Richard became somewhat frightened at the ease with which he had been able to obtain the money. He had broken into seventeen establishments and had never been caught. He began to think that "things were getting out of hand." Richard then got in touch with a friend of his who was on the police force and arranged to meet him in a pool hall. He told his friend about the thefts he had committed and asked him for advice on how to go about extricating himself from the situation. The police officer suggested that Richard accompany him to the police station and make a complete confession. Richard agreed to do this and was told that he would receive some consideration because of the manner in which he had gone about "turning himself in." Richard was then allowed to go free on bail and is now awaiting a hearing.

Richard thinks that he would like to be a lawyer some day. He puts it this way:

"I like the lawyer's racket. I know what it feels like to be in trouble. Someday I want to be a lawyer for kids."

KENNY D.

Kenny is a 17-year-old Negro youngster who has been in the work-crew program for almost a year. He came onto the crew shortly after having been expelled from high school. His expulsion was preceded by a series of suspensions, all of which emanated from his "incorrigible" behavior in the school setting. This behavior has variously been called "provocative," "aggressive," and "disturbed." He came into the program as a self-referral and presented himself one day at the NEC serving his neighborhood.

Kenny is a tall, extremely handsome, and well-built youngster who is probably the best-dressed boy in the program. He dresses in neat, conservative, Ivy-League attire and usually is meticulously groomed.

Kenny prides himself on being the "coolest cat" in the program. Nothing, supposedly, ever fazes him. He acts as if his entire being were an impenetrable shield, an impervious armor whose coat of arms is an I-don't-give-a-damn smile. Kenny is bright and perceptive, quick to size people up and detect their particular sensitivities and weaknesses. He exploits these weaknesses in a taunting and offhand manner as if to suggest he has seized on some long-hidden secret and understands it fully. However, his attacks, no matter how direct and painful, are made with the ease and precision of a deft surgeon. His assaults and cuts are made neatly and quickly, and he immediately retreats as if he were a graceful ballet dancer exiting from a suddenly darkened stage. Before any retaliation can come, Kenny is gone or he is smiling warmly in a completely disarming manner. No matter how infuriating or provocative his behavior, Kenny remains an engaging youngster who is well liked by the foreman and the other boys in the program. Kenny is liked almost in spite of himself and he never ceases to be both amused and satisfied with this state of affairs. As he puts it:

"I'll cut you down and you'll come up thanking me. But that's life, baby; that's life."

Kenny was born in New Haven and has lived in the city his entire life. He lives with his mother, stepfather, younger brother, and sister. His mother's first husband, Ken's father, lives in Washington, but Kenny gets to see him periodically.

For all his apparent "coolness" Kenny is a boy with problems and his problems are easily recognized by many people. Kenny drinks and his drinking has gotten him into difficulties both in the school setting and on the work crews. Although he has often been referred—and has gone for varying amounts of time—for psychiatric treatment he prides himself on the fact that few doctors have "gotten anything out of" him:

"It's a panic. I'd go to the shrink and snow the man so fast it wasn't funny. He'd try and ask me all kinds of questions and I'd cool it so bad he'd like to wind up with some head doctor himself. Nobody ever got anything out of me."

Kenny isn't very sure of his future and, knowing Kenny, his position is almost predictable. Kenny will not, at least at the present time, allow any-one to feel as if he has truly committed himself to anything. For them to think this would be an insult to Kenny. All his energy appears to be wrapped up in creating the impression that no one thing in the world is more salient or warrants any more personal commitment than any other thing. The world is an equivocal series of events, and Kenny acts as if his role in life is to dispel anyone's illusions that this is not so. For Kenny disengage-ment has become a way of life and he has a stake in maintaining his stance as the work crew's herald of the "cool world."

ALBERTA F.

Alberta is a 19-year-old white girl who came into the work-crew program approximately six months after she graduated from one of the New Haven high schools. During the time after her graduation and before she joined the work crews Alberta tried to work at a variety of jobs. She worked as a waitress, a counter-girl, and a salesgirl. Each time she was either fired or laid off after only a brief period of employment. Alberta and her employers had totally different impressions about why she was discharged. The employers felt that Alberta was not doing a satisfactory job, that she was often late, given to daydreaming, or irresponsible. From Alberta's point of view the reasons behind her being discharged had something to do with "bosses always making passes" at her, the other women employees not liking her, or the sudden "slackening off" of business. In any event, Alberta came to her NEC looking for a job. After an interview and testing by the vocational counselor it was felt that Alberta was not ready for full-time employment and that a period of time on the work crews might be helpful. She was placed on a female work crew that used one of the public libraries as its work site.

Alberta is a pretty girl who looks somewhat younger than her stated age. She wears clothes that appear a little too young for her but she is neat and spends much time on her hair, make-up and "just primping" each morning before coming to work.

In many ways Alberta does not want to grow up and she spends much of her time in an endless battle against advancing time, age, and responsibility. For her there is nothing fascinating or exciting about adulthood or maturity, and adolescence is a period of time that must, at all costs, be perpetuated and carried on and on. She is a little girl whom time must forget, or at least overlook.

Alberta is the oldest of eight siblings, all girls. She was born in New Haven and has spent her whole life in the city. She is currently living at home with her mother, stepfather and sisters. Two of her sisters are the children of her mother's first husband. Her father died when she was eight and her mother remarried the following year. Her other five sisters are the children of this second marriage.

Many of Alberta's feelings and fears of adulthood appear to be rooted in her experiences at home. She feels her parents are pushing her to get married, leave the home and set up her own household. Often she wonders about the reasons for this pressure. She is not sure if they really want her to be happy or whether they just want her out of the house to make more room for everyone else. Alberta is Italian, a fact that causes her much difficulty when she contemplates her fate:

"I hate Guineas, especially boy Guineas. All they think a girl is for is to get married and have babies and babies. I can't stand the idea of babies. You get fat and sloppy and your figure is ruined and you can't wear pretty dresses or go bowling. You stay at home and there's screaming and crying and no fun at all. I'll never get married even if I leave home. I don't want babies, ever."

Alberta's most pleasant memories are those of her days in high school. She was an average student and was able to keep up with her work. High school for her was much more than a place of learning; it was the center of her social life and a setting in which she was able to get the kind of attention that was not forthcoming at home. She loved the dances and the football games, the hustling between classes and the clamor of boys and girls meeting outside the school. To this day she can recall school events with a great deal of clarity, precision and excitement, almost as if she were reliving them over and over again:

"Annie came over to me and told me about her new boyfriend. He was a hunk. Even though we were sophomores I knew that Annie would marry him. We used to stand and watch him at football practice and then wait for him after it was all over. Annie wanted me to wait with her so it wouldn't look like she was chasing him or easy to get. He would come out wearing this big, furry sweater and tight pants. Annie almost fainted every time he looked at her. Me too. I'd look at him and wonder if he knew my heart stopped every time he walked past us. Boy, *is* he a hunk."

This lapse or confusion of tenses is typical of Alberta. For her the past is much more alive than the present; even in recollection it promises a greater fulfillment, a greater job, than does the future.

Alberta knows that she is no longer a 16-year-old high-school student. She is well aware that the clock cannot be turned back at will. But Alberta also dreads what may lie ahead. At these times she begins to daydream and to erect a fictional future, a future filled with all the hopes and dreams reserved for the very young. As she puts it:

"I know it's silly and all that. But sometimes I daydream that my knight will ride up on his shining white charger and whisk me away to our personal castle in the woods. I guess that these days his white charger will really be a new, sleek, white Impala but the rest of the story may be the same. We'll live happily ever after in a land of friendly animals and big, puffy clouds."

Perhaps the simplest and most truthful thing that can be said about the work-crew youngsters is that, despite the grouping that inevitably results from a purely statistical treatment of the data, they are distinct and different, each with a life style and a view of the world unique to himself. What they as a group have in common—their conflicts and needs, their hopes and fears—are the things that all adolescents, regardless of their socioeconomic status, share to one degree or another. The work-crew boys and girls are not a group of people whose problems place them in a category apart from the rest of the world their age. What they are experiencing and feeling and the problems they are dealing with are not unique to the inner-city youngster. The search for a meaningful identity and the need to comprehend a world that is perplexing and often frightening are not quests that belong to any one group of adolescents more than any other.

In general each work-crew youngster has a problem in living. The specific nature of the problem may vary from youngster to youngster but all, in one way or another, have developed coping behaviors that are either maladaptive or unsuccessful in dealing with the problems with which they are confronted. It is for these reasons that the work-crew program is not primarily a job-seeking process but a remedial group experience for youngsters whose problems would not dissolve if they merely were given jobs. What these youngsters need—and what the work-crew program attempts to furnish—is an experience in living, growing, and maturing.

A DAY IN THE WORK-CREW LIFE OF WILLIE P.

We have attempted to give the reader some idea of the content and structure of the work-crew program. In this context we have described the nature and origin of the program and have offered some descriptive background on the youngsters who make up the work crews. In providing the reader with the chronicle of one youngster's day on his work crew we hope to describe in greater detail both the nature of the program and its effect on one of the boys who is currently participating in it.

As an observational record the following chronicle has as its focus anything and everything the youngster does during one particular day on the work crew. It follows him from the time he meets his foreman in the morning to the time he is dismissed in the afternoon. For purposes of presenting as full a commentary as possible we have adopted an observational technique not dissimilar from the one utilized by Barker in *One boy's day* (1951). One youngster was selected as the subject for the observation. We followed him for one complete day and recorded, as completely as possible, everything he did and said. Our focus invariably shifted from microscopic to macroscopic levels of description depending on the nature of the activity taking place and the amount of time available to describe the youngster's reactions and behavior. We allowed ourselves a degree of inferential freedom with respect to the youngster's motives, emotions, and experiences at any point in the observation. We felt it was important and appropriate that we record in as direct a manner as possible our immediate perceptions of what the youngster was feeling and experiencing at any particular time. We also felt it necessary to describe things in everyday language and try not to resort to the utilization of theoretical jargon that went beyond the descriptive data. What we are most interested in is providing the reader with a full and rich account of the events and settings comprising one day in the life of a work-crew youngster.

WILLIE P.

Willie is a 17-year-old Negro youngster who has been in the work-crew program for about six months. He became a member of the work crews shortly after dropping out of school in the tenth grade. The neighborhood worker in Willie's area makes it a practice to check periodically with the high schools to find out which youngsters recently have dropped out. Once he gets that information he visits the youngsters' homes to find out if they have jobs, or what the situation is. He made such a visit to Willie's home, spoke with the boy, and got him to come down to the NEC for an interview and evaluation. Willie was subsequently placed on a work crew.

Willie was born in New Haven and currently lives with his mother, stepfather and six siblings. He has two brothers (ages 20 and 8) and four sisters (ages 16, 14, 12, and 3). Willie's real father died when the boy was three or four years old, and four of his siblings are the children of his mother's second marriage.

Willie's family is on welfare and he feels that poverty was one of the primary reasons for his dropping out of school:

I was ashamed to go to school. I didn't have any clothes or money, and I kept hearing how poor we were from my stepfather. So I decided to quit and get a job.

Willie hopes to return to school and attend evening classes in order to get his diploma. He wants to be a mechanic or an electrician and he is currently in the mechanics work crew.

Willie dislikes living at home and does not get along with his stepfather. He feels that he is always being picked on and resents what he believes to be the differential treatment accorded the children:

I hate my stepfather and always have. He works off and on as a construction man and is always getting on me. He only likes his kids and not my real father's kids. Even though I turn over $10 a week he's never satisfied. And my own mother is always sticking up for him all the time.

Willie is a tall, slender, good-looking youngster with a pixie-like face that crinkles and glows when he smiles. He wears his hair in a high "process" and is extremely concerned about his looks.

When Willie is having a good day he is an utterly delightful and captivating kid, but when he is having one of his bad days he can behave in unpredictable and frightening ways. His moods fluctuate rapidly and he can be both frightening and ingratiating within a short span of time. When angered he may either lash out or become extremely quiet and withdrawn. At such times he becomes like a seething cauldron and people go out of their way not to cross him. Yet he can display a sense of humor almost unmatched in the work crews. He can take everyday events and present them in ways that make the ordinary look exciting, and the mundane refreshingly new.

Did you guys ever think that this old lawn mower might have cut the grass that was the great, great, great, great, great, great-grandson grass of the grass George Washington walked on?

Much of Willie's anger stems from the fact that he perceives himself as a person who is continually being put upon, whose gracious, self-sacrificing behavior is never reciprocated. He feels he is always being taken in or taken advantage of and that people and luck are always against him. As he puts it:

I always have bad luck. When I have a little money I lose it, get rid of it, or have it stolen. Everybody's against me. I go home when I get paid and I give them money. But when I need it they won't give it to me.

Like my brother. I always gave him money when I had it. He won't give me a quarter for nothing.

Like my sister. She goes with this boy. He comes to the house and I give him money to take her out on a date. When I need it he won't give it to me.

And my mother. She'll give my sister's boyfriend money, but not me.

Willie has had relatively minor run-ins with the law. In 1961 he and a group of his young friends were caught trespassing on Yale property and, after a talking-to, were released. In 1962 he was taken to the police station for breaking a fence in the housing project in which he lived. Again he was released after a brief "chat." Later that year he was taken to juvenile court for beating up a boy in school who, Willie maintains, had drawn a knife on him while he (Willie) was only defending himself. Willie was spoken to by juvenile officials and again was released after a brief period of detention.

Perhaps the most important thing about Willie is the way he perceives himself in relation to the world. For Willie the world is composed of a series of traps that have been laid to ensnare and hurt him. People cannot be trusted because they take advantage of him and then reject him. The Fates have formed a secret alliance against Willie, and Willie—because of his essential goodness and unwillingness to learn from past experiences—is the constant victim of their schemes.

WILLIE'S DAY

Willie is a member of the mechanics work crew. He has been on the crew since it was started in January. The mechanics crew has as its work site a garage utilized by the Park Department. The work crew has the job of maintaining and repairing some of the lawn mowers used by the Park Department personnel in cutting grass at various public greens. Willie's foreman is a mechanic who has had extensive experience in caring for and fixing both light- and heavy-duty machinery. He is 32 years old and left a better-paying job in another part of the country to come to work as a foreman at CPI.

8:00–8:15 A.M.

It is a hot, sticky day in New Haven. Grey clouds hang over the city like a sagging, faded awning.

Four kids wait at the NEC as the foreman pulls up in his car. One of them leans against the door, apparently unaware of the foreman's arrival. A tall, slender youth, he is wearing tan corduroy pants and a collegiate-looking long-sleeved sweater drawn over a short-sleeved shirt—this is Willie.

The foreman, dressed in work pants and a dark blue flannel shirt, emerges from the car. A short, stout, smiling man, he walks in a plodding but distinctively lively manner toward the boys in the work crew.

Willie turns his head quickly and faces his approaching foreman. He stares at the man and smoothly glides away from the building to block the foreman's path. Willie and his foreman confront each other as if both had set foot on a bridge too narrow to accommodate both of them at the same time. As they stand looking at each other, the other boys watch Willie's face as if to determine what kind of mood he's in.

WILLIE: "Morning, Leo." He scowls as he greets his foreman and the greeting sounds partly like a challenge. His eyes dart from the foreman to the onlooking boys.

FOREMAN: "Morning, Mr. P." He greets Willie with mock formality and a slight smile begins to spread across his face. Willie looks as if he, too, is about to smile, but he quickly scowls again and, with his hands on his hips, he bumps stomachs with the foreman. The foreman does not budge. Willie is about to bump him again but instead his features break into a warm, welcoming smile.

WILLIE: "Oh, hell. I guess I didn't have breakfast again." The foreman laughs and throws an arm around Willie's shoulder as Willie leaves and goes to stand against the wall of the NEC once more.

The supervisor of foremen sticks his head out of the NEC office and informs the foreman that Vinnie's (another member of the crew) mother has just called to let them know that he will be late. A couple of the other boys groan. One laughs and says: " Yippee."

Willie seems to become a little restless. He looks around and ambles over to the foreman. Without saying a word he begins to kid around and wrestle with the foreman, trying very hard to pin him up against a car. The other boys watch as Willie and the foreman scuffle, and the foreman suddenly grabs Willie's hands and pins them to the boy's sides. Willie glares and one of the other boys calls: "Hey, don't tire him out Willie. He'll be too tired to work." The foreman laughs and pulls away.

At this point Willie spots two girls walking on the opposite side of the street. He strains his neck to look over the car at them and then calls to them.

WILLIE: "Hey, stuck-up." The girls continue on their way without paying any attention to him.

WILLIE: "I said, hey, stuck-up." One of the girls now turns and looks at him briefly.

WILLIE: "That's more like it." He quickly turns away from the girl before she can resume her original course. He smiles as he turns his head.

8:15–8:30 A.M.

It is beginning to rain, and it seems as though a heavy mist has settled over the city. Two of the boys immediately jump into the foreman's car. Willie remains with the foreman.

Vinnie finally arrives and saunters over to the foreman.

VINNIE: "I'm late, baby."

FOREMAN: "I know. Your mother called. We're gonna have to put Willie to sleep under your bed so he can get your ass up on time." As he says this the foreman glances over at Willie. Vinnie laughs and Willie smiles.

The crew's departure is further delayed as one of the other foremen has trouble starting his car. Willie and a few of the other boys run over to the stalled car, push it into the street, and get it running fast enough for the driver to get it started. They then wave and run back to their foreman and jump into his car, where he joins them.

The crew is ready to take off. Five boys and the foreman are in the station wagon. Three are white boys (ages 16, 16, and 17) and two are Negro (ages 17 and 16). The foreman hesitates for a moment as though waiting to see whether any more boys will show up.

Willie sits in the front seat next to the foreman. He stares at his watch, and finally asks one of the other boys what time it is. On being told he stares down at his own watch and adjusts it in an almost delicate manner. Leaning back, he places his right hand on the back of the front seat and gazes out the window. Although the other boys are talking among themselves in the back seats Willie continues to stare away from them.

8:30–8:45 A.M.

As the foreman starts the car Willie takes his arm off the back of the seat and seems to push himself deeper into his seat. The car is a beat-up 1957 Ford station wagon.

After they have started the foreman looks through the car mirror and speaks to the boys.

FOREMAN: "Hey, do we have enough cakes for everyone?"

A BOY: "I don't know; ask Willie, he's treasurer."

WILLIE: "You'll see." He looks a bit angry, and his answer comes out almost like an explosion. It appears as if he interpreted the question as a personal assault.

This crew has a unique system for providing its members with refreshments. Because the boys seldom bring their lunches they all chip in 75¢ at the beginning of each week. The money is given to the treasurer of the crew (Willie) and it is his responsibility to see to it that the money is used to provide the crew with an ample supply of cakes, pastries, donuts, tea, and coffee. These are kept at the garage where the crew works and are available to the boys any time they feel hungry.

A few moments later Willie turns to the foreman.

WILLIE: "Leo. Stop at the A&P. I gotta get more cakes." The foreman nods and continues on his way. As they are driving some of the other boys begin to comment about passing cars and although their comments are loud and animated Willie remains silent, looking straight ahead. The foreman finally pulls into a supermarket and Willie gets out and sprints for the door. A few moments later, his arms full of packages containing donuts and cakes, Willie scrambles back to the car calling to the other boys, "Here comes Santa Claus." The other boys laugh as Willie, grinning, gets back into the car.

8:45–9:00 A.M.

As the foreman and the boys start off again, the car begins to buck and some of the boys in the back seat lean forward to look at the gas gauge. Willie does not. Instead he takes out a new pack of cigarettes, carefully rips the cellophane off, and calmly takes out a cigarette. He seems almost oblivious of the bucking car and the concern of the others. He carefully lights up his cigarette and throws the match out the window. The car suddenly stalls.

FOREMAN: "Damn, I think I'm out of gas."

WILLIE: "Looks that way, don't it?" The foreman starts the car up again and gets it rolling. In a moment it stalls. Some of the boys are getting excited and begin good-natured muttering and joking about the prospect of having to push the car to the work site. The foreman gets the car started again, and with everyone in the car helping with body-English, they make it into a nearby garage. The foreman gets out to talk with the gasoline attendant and the boys begin an animated conversation about the automobiles in the used-car lot next to the garage.

A BOY: "Man, look at that mean-looking Chevy."

WILLIE: "It don't look so mean with its fender smashed in."

The foreman gets back into the car and they take off again. Traffic is pretty heavy now. Willie sits with his right elbow and arm on the window ledge next to him. It has stopped raining and a fine, grey mist has enveloped the damp, bleak city.

The foreman stops for a light and turns around to the crew members in the car.

FOREMAN: "Hey, you guys. Did we ever make this light yet?"

WILLIE: "No."

TWO OTHER BOYS: "Yes." Willie turns around and looks at the two boys who disagreed with him. He shakes his head and grimaces.

The car winds its way through some of the outskirts of the city over an undulating and hilly road. Some of the kids in the car (but not Willie) emit gleeful shouts and cries of "whee" as the car goes over hills and bumps. After winding around a small mountain the car heads down to an avenue and, after a few minutes, pulls into the garage, the crew's work site.

9:00–9:15 A.M.

The garage is set into the basement of a large, stone-faced house. On the grounds are big, sprawling areas covered with grass and trees; the garage itself has big red doors opening onto a concrete driveway that runs down into one of the major avenues in New Haven.

The area inside the garage is studded with a conglomeration of work benches, old and new lawn mowers, and a few small engines. A blackboard on which several diagrams have been drawn has been propped up with musty wooden crates in front of one of the long work benches. A lawn mower has been mounted on one side of the work bench, and a big red tool chest sits on the other.

Even before taking over this crew the foreman felt it was important for each boy in the mechanics crew to have his own tools, which would bear his own name and for which he would be completely responsible. He knew that the feeling of possession was an important part of the program and felt that each youngster ought to have the opportunity to experience himself as a "real mechanic," complete with the tools and responsibilities of his trade. Consequently each youngster was given his own set of tools and a big tool chest was obtained to hold all the material.

Because he has been on the crew the longest period of time, Willie is in charge of the key to the crew's tool container. He goes straight to the tool chest and opens it and the other boys amble over and take out their sets of tools. One of the boys goes over to a lawn mower mounted on one side of the work bench and begins to study it, as the foreman has told him to "check it out."

Willie takes out his own tools, places them on the table, and saunters to the back of the garage; he emerges pushing a lawn mower. He carefully bends over it, winds, and pulls the starter. He listens intently to the sound of the motor for a few moments; it begins to sputter, stall, and finally dies.

9:15–9:30 A.M.

The foreman looks around the room and asks one of the boys to start the coffee. The boys in the crew had chipped in with the foreman and bought an old water heater from the Salvation Army. It is a samovar-like heater standing atop an old and rusty oil drum. The pot, shined and scraped, stands gleaming in an otherwise dark and dusty room. The boy in charge of the water heater rapidly fills and plugs it in.

Meanwhile Willie is leaning over his stalled lawn mower with a concerned and questioning look on his face. He looks at the foreman out of the corner of his eye as if debating whether to ask him for advice. The foreman, not seeing this but aware that the machine has stalled, walks over to him.

FOREMAN: "Sounds like too rich a mixture of fuel."

WILLIE: "Fuel? I don't even remember putting fuel in this thing." As he talks Willie twirls and flips a screw-driver he is holding in his hand. He avoids looking at the foreman while speaking with him.

FOREMAN: "Maybe you don't remember putting gas in because you were out yesterday."

WILLIE: "Maybe so." He finally looks at his foreman and begins to smile weakly.

WILLIE: "I'll adjust the fuel mixture and put some more gas in."

FOREMAN: "O.K., I guess you don't want to talk about why you were out yesterday. Check with me later." Willie bends over the machine and begins to work on it for a few moments. However, after a short time he begins to get restless, frustrated; he fidgets and compresses his lips as he paces around the mower with hands on hips and eyes shifting from one part of the machine to another. A concerned grimace appears on his face.

9:30–9:45 A.M.

Willie grabs the handles of the lawn mower and pushes it back into the garage. He pushes it angrily and impatiently as a mother might drag a naughty child whose all-day tantrums and stubbornness have worn out her patience. After getting the mower halfway into the garage he stops and looks in the foreman's direction but not specifically at him.

WILLIE: "Hey Leo, this damn thing won't work." The foreman trudges over to him and they lean over and try to start the mower. The foreman adjusts the fuel input and Willie begins to clean the top gear. After a while the foreman looks at Willie and smiles.

FOREMAN: "Willie, go get the carburetor specs. We're not getting anywhere without the specs for this machine." Willie grumbles a bit but soon gets up and disappears in the direction of the work bench. The foreman remains on the floor poring over the mower's carburetor. When Willie does not return after a few minutes the foreman gets up and goes after him.

Willie is seated near the samovar at the left side of the long work bench, eating a donut and drinking a cup of coffee. Spread out in front of him is the appropriate lawn-mower manual. As he drinks he is poring over that section dealing with the carburetor.

Before going over to Willie the foreman stops to deal with three of the other boys who are trying to take apart one of the lawn-mower engines. He spends a few moments with them and pats one of them on the back as he turns to join Willie. Willie has been watching out of the corner of his eye and appears a bit angry, almost jealous.

9:45–10:00 A.M.

The foreman finally trudges over to Willie and asks him whether he has found the carburetor yet. Willie nods silently and turns the page slowly, pointing to an outline and illustration of the carburetor frame. He says nothing as the foreman leans over the table to get a better view of the manual. Willie stares at the manual without looking up.

WILLIE: "What did you say it needs?" Before the foreman has a chance to answer Willie's question he suddenly is called away by one of the Park Department employees who has just wheeled in a troublesome lawn mower. Before leaving he looks at Willie with a "what can you do?" expression.

FOREMAN: "I'll be right back. Just keep studying that carburetor." As he departs Willie mumbles something under his breath. The foreman does not hear it, but Willie ends with . . .

WILLIE: "See you tomorrow, Mr. Busy."

10:00–10:15 A.M.

Willie remains sitting quietly, slowing sipping his coffee. He closes the manual abruptly and begins to look around the room. The other boys are crowded around an engine cleaning the spark plugs, and adjusting the timer. Willie looks at them like a little boy who is excluded from a game he wants very much to play. He looks angry, moody. The sullen pout becomes a grimace as he compresses his lips.

Turning away, he leans back and takes another piece of cake from the big box of refreshments. The foreman does not return and Willie stares straight ahead. He slowly gets up and pours himself another cup of coffee. After carefully measuring two and one-half spoonfuls of sugar he sits down and begins to sip the brew slowly. His back to the boys grouped around the lawn mower engine, he faces the doorway through which the foreman has recently gone. He impatiently glances toward the entrance of the garage.

10:15–10:30 A.M.

Willie reluctantly opens the manual and leafs through the pages, once more finding the section marked "Walbro Carburetor—Frame 86." He stares down at the pages for a moment and again glances toward the entrance to the garage, sadly, and he sighs unconsciously. Glancing around the room once again his eyes finally, ever so hesitantly, look at the pages lying open in front of him, which he slowly begins to read out loud:

"Initial adjustment to this carburetor is made by adjusting power and idle adjustment screws 1 and 3 in (clockwise) finger-tight (using a screwdriver and forcing these adjusting screws too tightly closed will ruin needle and seat). Back out both power screw 1 and idle-adjusting screw 3 one and a half turns (counter-clockwise for initial adjustment).

Power screw adjustment is made with the panel control knob set on 'Run' and the engine warmed up to operating temperature, and preferably with the engine mounted to the mower. At this point, turn screw in or out for adjustment and smoothest engine functioning favoring a slightly rich adjustment to compensate for load conditions. Next, turn Panel Control to 'Idle.' Back out idle speed regulating screw 4 several turns (counter-clockwise) and then adjust idle mixture screw 3 back and forth for smoothest operation at minimum speed engine will operate. Readjust 4 idle speed regulating screw for 1800 rpm using a tachometer. Top governed speed is adjusted by self-tapping screw 2 at base of panel control shaft. Turn this screw in to increase governed speed, out to decrease speed. The threads of this screw are usually centered in the fitting at 3200 rpm"

10:30–10:45 A.M.

Willie reads slowly and somewhat laboriously, stopping often to re-read previous words or sentences. He does this several times and then begins to trace the diagram of the carburetor with his finger. He often looks away with an expression of anger mixed with frustration. At these times when he looks agitatedly toward the door he seems to will or at least expect the foreman's return.

Sooner or later he glances back to the manual in front of him and begins to reread the entire section. Each time he reads a little further before looking away again, but each time he looks away with a pained and somewhat defeated expression on his face. He appears to be suffer-ing as he looks toward the doorway for deliverance. None is forthcom-ing and Willie continues to endure until the foreman's return.

10:45–11:00 A.M.

As Willie is bent over the manual the foreman finally returns. Willie does not see him approach and is intently tracing the carbu-retor pattern with his finger. The foreman smiles as he sees Willie working and approaches him quickly.

The foreman sits down beside Willie and silently begins to read the manual. Willie appears almost startled as the foreman sits down, but does not glance in his direction. Instead he remains bent over the manual and shoves it over about six inches toward the foreman. They both remain silent for a long time, equally engrossed in reading the material about the carburetor. After some time the foreman speaks.

FOREMAN: "Gee, I wish they'd write these manuals so that folks could understand it better. You finding it tough Mr. P.?"

WILLIE: "You know I am Leo."

FOREMAN: "Yeah, I guess I do. What say you and I forget all the fine detail and try to trace this thing together? You read each sentence out loud and I'll trace it with my finger."

WILLIE: "O.K., so long as you got the time."

FOREMAN: "They had some trouble with a mower. It wasn't one of ours but they thought it was. I had to set them straight and adjust the thing in front of their own eyes."

WILLIE: "Yeah, I know." He says this in a manner suggesting that he questions the foreman's explanation. The foreman does not react, although he seems to sense Willie's suspicion.

Willie and his foreman pore over the manual and slowly get through the section concerning the lawn mower's carburetor. They close the book and review what they have gone through. Willie nods his head as if he understands what he has to do. He gets up and walks over to his lawn mower.

11:00–11:15 A.M.

Willie grabs the handles of the mower and wheels it out to the driveway in front of the garage. Energetically he puts his tools down beside the mower and unscrews the top of the carburetor. Once he removes the carburetor he begins to trace the pathways that were outlined in the manual, the ones he and the foreman studied. He begins confidently and his movements are sure and direct. However, in a little while a pucker appears between his eyebrows, concern becomes apparent on his face, and unsureness shows in his gestures. His movements become almost aimless as his fingers wander idly and he tugs, pulls, and taps different parts of the mechanism absent-mindedly. He glances away with a lost and detached expression on his face, looks down at the carburetor, and then at his hands.

Willie looks disgusted, almost despairing. He glances out at the trees and follows the line of flight of a bird that suddenly has bolted from the roof of the garage. The bird disappears over the trees and Willie looks back down at the lawn mower, in much the same manner as he might regard an entrenched and immovable enemy. Suddenly he picks up the screw from the top of the carburetor and hurls it as far as he can. He straightens up and watches as it disappears into the bushes behind a clump of trees.

He looks down at the lawn mower and back into the garage. He stoops down to rummage through his tool kit, picks out another screw, and begins to replace the top of the carburetor. With his screwdriver he begins screwing in the new screw to bolt down the upper part of the carburetor. It's tough going; the screw doesn't fit the hole on top of the machine. Willie labors over it; the strain is apparent on his face as he uses both hands to get the new screw into place. He slowly pulls it out and looks at it. Something is wrong with it; it is sheared off, the once-symmetrical grooves now almost perfectly smooth.

11:15–11:30 A.M.

Willie takes the screw and slowly walks back into the garage. He does not look at the screw any more but goes directly to the foreman and gives it to him as if it were a booby-prize, a joking gift. The foreman looks at the screw and then at Willie with disbelief and mounting anger.

FOREMAN: "What happened, Willie?"

WILLIE: "I stripped it, right?"

FOREMAN: "What happened, Willie?"

WILLIE: "I don't know. I was trying to put the top of the carburetor back on and it happened."

FOREMAN: "O.K., Willie, let's take a little walk over to your mower."

The foreman walks briskly past Willie out of the garage and onto the driveway. Willie follows in a somewhat reluctant but obligatory manner. He emerges from the garage to find the foreman stooped over his lawn mower examining it closely.

FOREMAN: "Willie, you know damn well that this isn't the right-sized screw for this mower. What happened to the other one, the real one?" His words come out with a mixture of irritation and disgust. Willie looks at him with his eyes narrowed and his face suddenly hardened into an almost frightening glare. He takes a step closer to the foreman but suddenly turns and races away. The foreman stands watching Willie run down the driveway and throw himself on the grass at the foot of a hill. He opens his mouth as if to call, but quickly snaps it shut. He looks down at the screw in his hand, tosses it into the bushes. He bends over the mower, studying the top of the carburetor, and sees the gaping hole made by a screw much too big for the opening. He looks toward Willie again and then slowly walks back into the garage. Willie remains seated on the grass.

11:30–11:45 A.M.

Willie is still sitting on the damp grass, his arms locked about his knees. He stares straight ahead, lost in thought, possibly regret. Now and then he shifts his position and digs his right toe into the grass in front of him.

The foreman ambles out of the garage and walks slowly down the driveway, cutting across to Willie. He sits down and looks at the boy. Willie does not acknowledge his presence and the foreman finally throws his big arm around Willie's shoulders. Willie is much calmer than when he left.

FOREMAN: "Willie, you mad at me?"

WILLIE: "No, I'm mad at myself for walking out on you."

FOREMAN: "Maybe it's better to walk away and cool off instead of throwing a lot of loose words around that you'd have to apologize for later."

WILLIE: "I don't know, I just couldn't get anything right today."

FOREMAN: "Is that why you tried to force the wrong screw into the hole?"

WILLIE: "Yeah, that's right. I just got all mad and hot inside. I just couldn't trace the carburetor once I got outside the garage. I don't even know why I brought the stripped screw back in with me."

FOREMAN: "Neither do I. What say you and me take that whole carburetor apart piece by piece first thing in the morning?"

WILLIE: "That's good with me, so long as you don't take off every five minutes."

FOREMAN: "You got a deal Mr. P." Willie looks up at his foreman with a slightly quizzical smile on his face.

FOREMAN: "Look Willie, it's time to clean up. Get the guys to clean up the place while I go make a call."

WILLIE: "OK Leo. We'll be ready to go at noon."

Willie and the foreman get up and Willie starts back for the garage as the foreman goes toward the office. Willie continues up the driveway and into the garage.

11:45–12:00 NOON

Willie walks into the garage with a slight spring to his step. Because all the other boys were in the garage when Willie ran away no one saw the incident. He moves briskly among them.

WILLIE: "Leo told me to take over till he gets back. It's clean-up time. I want two guys on brooms. Vinnie take care of the coffee pot. Rick, you're in charge of stacking up the mowers. Henry, here're the keys to the tool chest. Get all the tools put away."

There is a little grumbling as Willie gives out clean-up assignments with sergeant-like authority, but the boys quickly get about their work. Willie goes to a radio that stands plugged in against a wall on the other side of the garage and turns it on. When it has warmed up he flips the dial to a station playing rock-and-roll music, listens for a moment, and turns up the volume. The radio blares, filling the garage with the grinding sound of a nervously jumping melody.

The rest of the boys begin humming or singing along with the record. They break into a few short dance steps as they go about their assignments. Willie looks on, smiles, and shakes his head slowly. He walks out to his lawn mower, glances down at it for a moment, and immediately grabs the handles and wheels it back into the garage. He pushes it over to where Rick is lining up the other lawn mowers and places it at the end of the row.

The boys work rapidly. In a matter of a few minutes the shop is put in order: the floors have been swept, the tools put away, the coffee-maker emptied, rinsed, and placed underneath the long work bench, and the lawn mowers stacked up. Willie surveys the room with a smile suggestive of pride.

The boys look at Willie, he nods his head approvingly, and they file out of the garage. Willie looks around the room once again and goes over to shut off the radio and pull the light switches. The garage is once more a dark, musty, quiet place, and Willie walks quietly out the door, closing it behind him.

12:00–12:15 P.M.

The foreman is waiting in the car outside the garage. A few of the boys squint a bit as they reach him and he laughs. They also laugh and poke their heads inside his window.

FOREMAN: "O.K., it's a little early to be starting back. What-say you guys loosen up and cross-country race for a few minutes. No wrestling though. I don't want anyone slipping and breaking an arm on my time." Four of the boys race off. Willie and Rick remain behind and climb into the car. Willie sits in the front seat again; the other boy hops into the back. The three sit in silence. Willie leans his arm against the ledge of the window and strains his neck to watch the four other boys as they race around the garage and up a hill behind it. He has a slight smile on his face as he watches them.

At about 12:15 the foreman looks at his watch. It's time to go. He motions to Rick to go round up the boys and Rick takes off. Willie and the foreman sit quietly.

12:15–12:30 P.M.

The other boys race back to the car with Rick in the lead. They are breathless and somewhat excited as they jump into the car, occupying the same seats as before. The foreman looks around, silently checking heads.

FOREMAN: "Guess nobody got killed out there. Let's get going." He starts the car and they take off. In a few minutes it begins to rain, a pounding, steady downpour. As the foreman turns on his windshield wipers the kids, including Willie, begin to laugh. The wipers jerk and squeak sporadically across the expanse of glass and soon the foreman joins in the laughter. However, he turns the laughter into a discussion of why wipers work better under certain conditions than under others.

FOREMAN: "Willie, remember what we talked about the last time we got caught in a rain? Why do the wipers work better when the gas pedal isn't pushed down all the way?"

WILLIE: "Because of the vacuum in the car that makes the wipers go faster or slower."

FOREMAN: "Right. A car works best and most economical when there are about 21 inches of vacuum." Willie steals a quick glance around the car as though to assure himself that the other kids heard the foreman say "Right." They did, and he turns his head forward once again with a sideways glance at the foreman.

FOREMAN: "When you push the gas pedal down you decrease the amount of vacuum in the car. And when you decrease this vacuum you decrease the power that the windshield wipers have to work with." He demonstrates this by pushing his foot down on the accelerator and having the boys watch the action of the windshield wipers. He does this several times until the boys look convinced. The car moves on and for a time the only sound is the sound of the windshield wipers straining and slamming against the sides of the windows.

12:30–12:45 P.M.

One of the boys brings up the subject of a car he has heard about that is able to go from a standing start to 80 miles per hour in only two seconds. The other boys listen to his story and fill the air with hoots of good-natured but derisive laughter. They think they are being put on and aren't buying any part of the story. The other boy holds his ground and describes the car. He tells them that it is the "Green Monster," housed in the Daytona Speedcar Museum. He goes on to describe it more fully, relating that one of the reasons it can achieve such speeds is that it has rear tires 4½ feet high. Again the other boys act as if they do not believe him, and he vows to bring in an article the next day to prove he is not lying.

Throughout this exchange Willie remains quiet, but it is clear that he is listening to every word that is being said. He often turns his head to face the boy who is talking and acts as if he too has doubts concerning the veracity of the tale. He purses his lips as though to suppress a laugh and often looks as if he is about to join in the conversation. He does not, however, and remains silent but attentive.

The car is moving through the streets of New Haven again. The rain has let up and a shroud of fine mist hangs over the car. It is early afternoon, yet the streets appear strangely deserted and devoid of the usual hustle and bustle of this time of day.

12:45–1:00 P.M.

At last the car arrives at the Jewish Community Center, the setting used by the CPI work crews as the place for the remedial-education component of the program. It is a large center, set near the middle of town. It is comparatively new and modern in design, with large windows and what appears to be an extremely functionally oriented structure.

The foreman maneuvers the car into position beside a parking meter. The boys get out as he puts a coin in the meter; they have already started across the street to the Center by the time he catches up with them.

Willie seems to shorten his stride a bit to let the foreman catch up with him, and they walk up the stairs into the Center together. They walk silently side by side through the door, past the lobby, and up the stairs to the second floor.

The second floor has a series of classrooms along a corridor that runs the length of the building. Each room is used for Sunday school or other religious instruction when it is not used by CPI. There is a large assembly room on the floor, where all the work-crew boys congregate before reporting to their assigned classrooms.

Willie and his foreman enter the assembly room. Many other boys and their foremen are already there, and there is some laughter and loud talking going on. Several boys are singing popular songs toward one side of the room. Others are seated or standing around, smoking and talking with each other or with the various foremen.

Willie tries to look casual as he enters the room and glances around. His eyes dart toward the front of the room and then toward the back, looking for a place to sit. He seems unsure where to position himself. The foreman also looks about the room, spots one of the other work-crew leaders, and goes over to the window to talk with him. Willie walks slowly to the far left-hand side of the room and sits down on a chair that is somewhat removed from a group of boys who are sitting together. He looks down at his hands, then scans the room once more in a furtive manner. He leans back in his chair, stretches out his legs in front of him and folds his arms. He closes his eyes for a moment but quickly opens them and scans the room once more. Willie seems suddenly relaxed, more so than at any other point during the day.

The assembly room is almost full.

1:00–1:15 P.M.

The supervisor of the remedial-education program sits behind a desk situated in front of the boys. He looks around the room straining his neck to see all the boys. After a while he stands up and comes around to the front of the desk, asking the group to quiet down. Then, glancing down a list he is holding in his hand, he calls out several names. These youngsters are to be tested that day to determine what class they should be placed in for their remedial education. This is a standard procedure. They are new boys and before they are placed in any particular class they must be evaluated with respect to their educational level. These boys are told to remain in the room after the rest have been sent to their classes. The next announcement is a reminder to the boys to put out their cigarettes before leaving the room, as smoking is not permitted in any other part of the building. Some of the boys groan and hiss as he says this, but the supervisor only smiles and repeats his instructions.

Throughout this period Willie sits quietly, almost oblivious to what is going on about him and in front of the room. Never looking at the supervisor, he keeps his eyes glued on the toes of his shoes, which are extended in front of him. Periodically he squirms in his seat and taps his left shoulder. He seems less comfortable now than he was a few moments ago.

The supervisor of the remedial-education program dismisses the boys: "OK gentlemen, you may now go to your classes."

All the boys begin to move slowly toward the door of the assembly room. Some are still talking among themselves and all have already put out their cigarettes in ashtrays provided for that purpose. Some are still humming as they saunter out the door.

Willie gets out of his seat slowly, almost as if he were straining to make the move. He walks quietly, eyes straight ahead, toward the door. He places his right hand in his back pocket and his left hand dangles loosely at his side. He leaves the room with an expressionless face.

He walks slowly down the hall toward his room, the second from the stairway. He goes into the room, briefly looks around, and almost shuffles into his seat at the extreme left-hand side of the last row. He sits down abruptly, stretching his feet out in front of him in much the same manner as he had in the assembly room. He gazes for a long time at the wall.

1:15–1:30 P.M.

There are seven other boys in Willie's class and they have taken seats in positions scattered all over the room. No two boys are very near each other although they can, and do periodically speak with each other without having to raise their voices.

Willie's teacher comes into the classroom; he is tall, conservatively dressed, and appears to be about 30 years old. Striding into the room with a portfolio and a sheaf of papers under his arm, he walks directly behind the desk at the front of the room and surveys the boys. He smiles, places his papers on the desk, and comes around to the front of the desk, to a point much closer to the boys. He stands looking at the boys for a moment or so. Willie looks at him and then away to the window on the far side of the room. He turns to the wall once more and studies it closely, as if it had some dark secret written all over it. He does not look back at the teacher for a long time, and only then when the teacher begins to speak.

TEACHER: "Good afternoon, gentlemen, I hope your morning's work has not tired you out too much." A few of the boys briefly snicker at this but soon fall silent. Willie looks at the teacher with an empty and slightly annoyed expression on his face, quickly turning his face toward the wall again.

TEACHER: "Today I thought it might be interesting if, before turning to our grammar exercises, I had a chance to begin to discuss with you language in general. By this I mean that I think you would find it helpful to know where our language came from, where it got started, and where its roots lie." The teacher goes on to discuss some of the history of the English language. He talks about the Latin influence on our language and grammar and gives a few examples in Latin. He talks in a slow but methodical manner and enunciates each word with a great deal of effort. After each sentence he pauses as though making sure that what he has just said has had sufficient time to settle and be absorbed. At times he places his right hand on the edge of the desk and taps the papers he has placed there. At other times he walks slowly or sways to and fro in front of the class.

Only one of the boys seems at all interested in what he is saying. The others either recline or sway in their seats. The boy who appears interested is hunched forward in his chair. He does not shift his gaze from the teacher's face, whereas the others seem to be looking around the room in an almost mechanical manner, making sure that their glance falls on every aspect of the floor and ceiling.

Willie, too, appears highly uninterested in what the teacher is saying. He lounges in his chair and fixes his gaze on a point above the entrance to the room. He stares at the point as if there is some hypnotic attraction there that has him under its spell and power. He does not blink his eyes for a long time. I wonder. Maybe he is hypnotized.

1:30–1:45 P.M.

Willie suddenly turns his gaze from the doorway directly toward the teacher. A look of almost sublime indifference covers his face. He looks directly at the teacher and grimaces. He then returns his gaze to a mythical point above the doorway.

The teacher continues his lesson on the history of the English language. He appears to have noticed the boy who seems interested in his lesson and he directs all his words to that boy. Occasionally he glances around at the other boys but quickly comes back and focuses his attention on the interested listener.

Willie now shifts in his seat and stretches. He extends his arms in front of him and raises them over his head, reaching and clawing. He then opens his mouth and emits a long, entirely audible yawn. He does not cover his mouth with his hand, but instead lets the yawn break loose and engulf the entire classroom. The teacher stops in the middle of a sentence and some of the other boys in the class turn in Willie's direction. It is quiet for a moment until the teacher speaks.

TEACHER: "It's too bad you're tired, Willie, but you're not helping by distracting the entire class. Maybe you should have stayed at home today instead of coming to work."

WILLIE: "Maybe." He says this with a look of mock fatigue and a certain amount of scorn. He looks away from the teacher, stretches again, turns to gaze at the wall until the teacher resumes his lecture, then looks straight ahead once again.

Several of the other boys seem to be getting quite restless and they sit and squirm in their chairs. Another boy yawns, not as loudly as Willie, but enough to cause the teacher to stop once more and look at him caustically. The boys snicker at this, and Willie smiles broadly. One of the boys lets his head begin to droop and he looks almost ready to doze off. The teacher notices him and calls out his name. The boy quickly jerks his back to an upright position, smiles, and tells the teacher that he was "only faking." The teacher runs his hand over his head and continues with the lesson. He seems quite annoyed with the behavior in the class but says nothing. Instead he begins talking in a somewhat louder tone and stops paying most of his attention to the one boy who is interested in what he is saying. Instead he scans the room as he speaks.

1:45–2:00 P.M.

The teacher appears to be coming to the end of his lecture. Willie now looks at him directly and smiles whenever the teacher's gaze falls on him. Willie's smile is a cross between sarcasm, challenge, and anger. He now throws his right foot across the writing area of his seat and grabs the back of his neck with his left hand.

TEACHER: "Sit straight in your seat. Get your hands on the desk in front of you."

WILLIE: "Shove it."

TEACHER: "Come on now, Willie, let's not try to show off in front of all your friends. Just put your foot where it belongs and your hands on the desk."

WILLIE: "No." The other boys are now smiling. Even the boy who seemed interested in what the teacher had to say is beaming. They all start laughing and leaning forward in their seats watching the teacher and Willie. Their laughter is almost taunting in nature, but they are taunting Willie and the teacher in the same way. One boy claps his hands and another begins "egging on" both Willie and the teacher. The teacher looks around the room and then back at Willie. Willie returns the teacher's stare. Now there is no smile on Willie's face. He looks angry, menacing, and not a little scared. Suddenly the teacher looks away from Willie and addresses the rest of the class.

TEACHER: "OK, take your break now. I'll expect everyone back in ten minutes." The teacher then looks back at Willie.

TEACHER: "Willie, you go to the assembly room." Some of the other boys seem disappointed by this turn of events. They groan and moan in a taunting manner.

Willie leaps up from his chair and stalks out of the class. The teacher follows, close on his heels, as Willie walks down the hallway, pauses briefly at the door to the men's room, and continues to the assembly room. When he enters the room he goes directly to the window, shoves his hands into his pockets, and stands gazing out at the parking lot adjoining the Center. Slowly he draws a cigarette out and lights it up. He begins to smoke it but continues looking out the window.

Willie's foreman is in the room, and the teacher goes directly to him. They talk for a while and the foreman, while listening to the teacher, often looks over toward where Willie is standing. Willie has not turned around. He stands with his back to the foreman and the teacher on the other side of the room. The teacher continues speaking quietly to the foreman. He no longer looks angry. The foreman nods his head a few times, and the teacher finally turns and leaves the room. By this time the other boys from Willie's class have entered the assembly room. They smoke and talk among themselves, but no one goes over to Willie. They act much the same as they did before class.

The foreman gets up and goes over to Willie. They stand together in silence for a while before anyone speaks.

FOREMAN: "Teacher tells me you gave him a hard time today."

WILLIE: "Yeah."

FOREMAN: "What happened?"

WILLIE: "I don't know. I got bored."

FOREMAN: "OK so you got bored, but the teacher tells me you really mouthed off at him."

WILLIE: "I did not. You can't do nothing in that class. He talks and talks and don't say nothin'. He's an ass-hole."

FOREMAN: "You used to think I was an ass-hole until you finally started listening to what I had to say."

WILLIE: "That's different."

FOREMAN: "How?"

WILLIE: "I don't know. It's just different that's all."

FOREMAN: "The teacher asked me to come and sit with you in class. I told him I'd do it and I'm going to. Now come on. I'm not asking you to do any work in that class today but the teacher doesn't want you giving him a hard time. Now let's go."

Willie and the foreman get up and go across the room to the door. Willie walks a few paces ahead of the foreman and does not turn around. The foreman follows him out of the door and down the hall into the classroom.

2:00–2:15 P.M.

Willie enters the classroom and goes directly to his seat next to the wall in the back of the room. The foreman sits next to him. Willie stretches his feet out. Suddenly he yanks himself up out of the seat and looks down at his foreman.

WILLIE: "I'm going to the bathroom. You wanna follow me there too?" The statement is made with a great deal of sarcasm. The foreman smiles.

FOREMAN: "No, Willie, I think you know what to do in the bathroom by now." The foreman smiles again. Across Willie's face a slight smile begins to flicker, but he immediately suppresses it. He shrugs his shoulders and leaves the room.

A moment later the teacher comes back into the classroom. He looks at the foreman questioningly but says nothing.

FOREMAN: "Willie will be right back."

The other boys saunter back into the room. A few of them nod to the foreman as they resume their seats. He nods back at them. It is a bit tense in the room as the teacher comes to stand in front of the desk once more.

Willie enters the room again and, without looking at the teacher, he immediately walks back to his seat. Once again he stretches his legs out in front of him and links his hands behind his head. The teacher sees this but says nothing.

The class lesson is resumed. The teacher begins to review grammar with the boys. He is trying to teach the boys to identify a particular word: "Is it a noun, verb, adjective, or adverb?" Picking up a piece of chalk he writes a sentence on the blackboard: "Jane is running quickly into the big house." Looking around the room he calls on various boys to identify the parts of speech of words "running," "quickly," "big," and "house." He calls on the boys individually but carefully avoids calling on Willie. Some of the boys know the answers to the questions asked of them. Some do not. No one appears very interested in the lesson, whether or not he knows the answer.

2:15–2:30 P.M.

Willie and the foreman sit quietly. Neither looks at the other. Willie occasionally glances toward the front of the room in the direction of the teacher but never directly at him. Instead he lets his eyes wander along the outer edges of the blackboard in a manner reminiscent of a periscope that has been poked from under the water and is scanning the horizon.

The teacher goes on with the lesson. There is not much enthusiasm manifested in the voices of the students but they appear to be trying to answer the questions correctly, even though some slouch in their chairs and others play with the pencils they hold in their hands.

The foreman sits placidly and watches the teacher. He seems somewhat more interested in the lesson than the students. A few times he moves his lips as if anticipating the answer to one of the questions being asked by the teacher.

Willie glances over at the foreman and scowls. He immediately turns his face away to the wall next to him. He takes his arms from behind his head and lets them dangle at his sides. He lets them sway slowly and come to rest as if they had decided on their own to stop swinging. He looks around the room with a disinterested but somewhat calmer expression.

At approximately 2:30 P.M. the teacher dismisses the class. As they begin to get up from their seats he shuffles the papers that are lying on the desk behind him.

Several of the students almost bolt for the door. Others saunter out much more slowly.

Willie and his foreman get up to leave. Not a word is said or a glance exchanged between them as they begin to head for the door. The teacher does not look up from his shuffling of papers as they go by him and out of the classroom. Willie walks a step or two in front of the foreman on their way back to the assembly room. In the assembly room Willie leaves the foreman and again goes to stand by the window. Again he lights up a cigarette and stares out the window as he smokes it.

2:30–2:45 P.M.

The foreman looks around the room and begins to get the boys in his crew together. They all come over to where he is standing except Willie who joins the rest when called. The foreman looks around for a moment, waves to one of the other foremen, and says, "OK, let's go."

Almost as though the foreman's words were a signal for action, Willie bounds ahead of the rest of the group and leads the way down the hall to the stairway. He walks with a slight spring to his step, an almost joyful lilt to his walk. He pushes past one of the youngsters from another crew and bounds down the stairs, taking them two or three at a time. He walks briskly out of the Center and down the steps to the street. Once on the sidewalk he looks around the street and waits for the other boys and the foreman to catch up with him.

All the boys come out of the Center and cross the street to the foreman's car. It is not locked, and they all jump in, again taking the same seats they have had. Willie again sits in the front seat, his elbow perched on the top of the window ledge.

The foreman climbs in, sighing as he starts the car. He suddenly looks tired and a bit drained of energy.

It is not raining. Even the heavy mist that engulfed the car on its way down from the garage seems to have lifted and dispersed into a lighter and brighter haze.

The car takes off. It is a bit quiet now as the boys all seem more concerned with their own thoughts than with starting any kind of conversation. The foreman appears to feel the same way as he concentrates in a preoccupied manner on the car a few lengths in front of him.

Willie is also silent. He gazes out of the window and occasionally turns his head to look at someone they have just passed on the street. He lets his hand drop off the window ledge and fall gently to his knee.

The car stops for a red light and the foreman turns around and looks at the boys in his crew.

FOREMAN: "Tomorrow we're going to take Selvyn's mower apart from beginning to end. OK?" A few of the boys nod their heads and Selvyn says, "Sure thing."

The light changes and the foreman eases the car forward. An almost thankful silence once again reigns. The foremen, the boys, and Willie seem worn out.

2:45–3:00 P.M.

The foreman finally pulls the car up in front of the NEC. The boys remain in the car for a moment or so after it has come to a stop. Then, almost as if suddenly rejuvenated, they jump out of the car. Willie gets out of the car a little slower than the rest and stands leaning against the right front fender.

FOREMAN: "OK you guys, see you tomorrow. Vinnie, get here on time. We got a big day ahead of us with Selvyn's mower." As he speaks the foreman moves over and stands near Willie.

The other boys wave or say goodby and take off. A few sprint away, but most walk, some more quickly than others. Willie seems about to walk away also when the foreman puts a huge arm across his shoulders. Willie looks up at him but does not move away.

FOREMAN: "Tough day, Willie. I'm tired, maybe getting a little old."

WILLIE: "Yeah, tough day."

FOREMAN: "What happened at the Center?"

WILLIE: "I told you already."

FOREMAN: "Guess you don't want to talk about it, huh?"

WILLIE: "Guess not. I'm cuttin' out Leo. Maybe tomorrow. OK?"

FOREMAN: "OK, Willie, tomorrow. Don't be late."

WILLIE: "Yeah, I know, we gotta take Selvyn's machine apart."

FOREMAN: "Right."

Willie and the foreman look at each other for a moment almost as if each is waiting for the other to say something. Finally Willie begins to walk away and the foreman lets his arm fall off Willie's shoulder and come to rest at his side.

WILLIE: "So long, Leo."

FOREMAN: "So long, Mr. P."

Willie begins to walk slowly up the street to the corner. The foreman remains standing against his car, watching him. As Willie gets nearer to the corner he breaks into a run, crosses the street, and disappears quickly around the corner. The foreman stands for a moment and then walks slowly through the door and into the NEC.

The chronicle of Willie P.'s day on the work crew was not obtained secretly. We simply accompanied Willie, his foreman, and his crew from the time they met in the morning until the time they broke up in the afternoon. Both Willie and his foreman knew we would accompany the work crew that day, and they knew why. It is important, for a variety of reasons, that the reader be acutely aware of the conditions under which the observational record was obtained.

Our presence on the work crew was not an unexpected or novel event. We had been with the work crew and its youngsters many times before the day on which the observational data were recorded. We knew the boys and they knew us, for we had participated together in other settings and in other ways, and we discuss the significance of this state of affairs later in this section. At this time, however, the reader should understand that our being on the work crew and accompanying and participating with its members in the different settings comprising the work-crew program, was neither a new or unexpected event. Our ability to obtain the naturalistic observational record of Willie's day on the work crew grew out of and was a function of our relationship with the work-crew program, its youngsters, and its foremen.

We have included this detailed description of "one boy's day" for a variety of reasons, the most important of which is to provide the reader with as complete and as concrete an example as possible of the content and process of the work-crew program. Willie is not an atypical work-crew youngster and his day, with all its triumphs and tragedies, was not terribly different from the days of many of the other boys and girls in the program. Willie is not a special case hand-picked for illustrative purposes; he was one among any number of youngsters who could have been chosen as the subject for this observational record. Willie's problems are the kind of problems that, although never exactly duplicated, occur in varying forms and to varying degrees in many of the other boys and girls on the work crews, as, indeed, they occur in many non-work-crew adolescents.

Clearly, Willie's problems and difficulties are not solely the result of unemployment. Were we to be able to provide Willie with an interesting, well-paid job with a future—and to provide him with this job tomorrow morning—Willie's problems would not vanish. His unemployment is only one symptom of much greater problems; Willie's problem with people, himself, and the world he lives in. It would therefore be a mistake to think of Willie only as a "vocational problem." It is more accurate to think of him as unemployed—or rather, unemployable—because of his many problems. The day Willie gets a job, keeps it, and begins to view the world at large as a place where he rightfully belongs will not occur when the world presents Willie with an available job. It will occur when Willie presents the world with an available Willie.

Willie is his own generation's contribution to the "prophecy of poverty." Whatever gifts and talents he possesses are currently hidden within the complex fabric of a young man who behaves as if he experiences himself as someone who is alienated, excluded, and disenfranchised from the world in which he lives. For Willie, and all the Willies on the work crews, the work-crew program is not simply a "holding process" to accommodate youngsters until a job becomes available. It is a program whose primary focus is to provide Willie and youngsters like him with a remedial and therapeutic experience in living.

The length of time spent on a work crew varies from youngster to youngster. Some of the crews are, indeed, only a holding operation, a program to involve the youngster until some vocational placement becomes available or is developed in the community. For others the work crews become a relatively long-term setting, a prevocational, remedial, and therapeutic situation. The decision concerning whether or not a particular youngster is ready to "graduate" from the work-crew program depends on the evaluation of his foreman and the observations and impressions of those people (neighborhood worker, vocational counselor, work-crew supervisor) who have had contact with him through the processes and programs emanating from the NEC.

It is important to CPI that the work-crew youngsters *do* "graduate," for it is one of the few concrete ways in which the organization can evaluate the effectiveness of its social interventions and rehabilitative programs. Since the explicit focus (even if it is not the explicit reality) of the work-crew program is to help youngsters find and hold jobs, CPI is extremely concerned that the work crews do not become dead ends in the sense that they become identified as such by the youngsters and do not lead to other, presumably more advanced and better-paying, training and/or vocational opportunities.

Because of CPI's concern that the work crew not become a permanent fixture in a youngster's life it has been conceived of as a stepping stone to other vocational and educational settings. As this is the case, several alternatives or "next steps," some of which are described here, have been developed in the hope that the work-crew program may serve as a means of evaluating and preparing the youngsters for a variety of programs beyond the work-crew setting.

1. *Direct placement.* Direct placement involves referring a work-crew youngster for full-time employment to some agency, industry, or concern that has advertised or listed a job with CPI or the Connecticut State Employment Service. Sometimes, however, a youngster is referred for a job CPI has either "developed" in the community or "gotten wind of" through the private information of its personnel or direct contact with the prospective employer. Because some of the work crews offer more specific training than others, some work-crew youngsters have received the kind of prevocational experience that qualifies them for full-time employment. Before a youngster is referred for this, or any other kind of placement, a disposition conference is held in the attempt to evaluate his progress on the work crews. Similarly, the youngster is consulted in terms of whether or not he feels the potential placement involves the kind of work and experience he wants or is willing to undertake.

2. *On-the-job training (OJT).* On-the-Job training is a referral in which the potential employer and CPI agree to share the expense of training a work-crew graduate for an existing job at the employer's place of business. The youngster is involved in a job-training program for which he receives full-time pay and works a regular work day. The employer and CPI communicate on a regular basis with respect to the trainee's on-the-job performance and development. At the conclusion of the agreed-on period of job training (or at any point in between) the employer must decide whether or not to hire the youngster for the position for which he has been in training. If the employer decides to hire the trainee he must then assume the full financial responsibility for the youngster's salary, benefits, etc.

3. *Job Corps.* Since becoming a functional reality, the Job Corps has been utilized by CPI as another alternative available to a work-crew graduate. At present the Job Corps is only available to the boys in the program, but the expansion of the Job Corps seems to indicate that it will soon be ready to accommodate girls also. The Job Corps is an away-from-home training and educational program designed to prepare youngsters for jobs in either a rural or urban setting, depending on the youngster's abilities, aptitudes, and interests. The training received at the Job Corps camps is utilized there and in other areas. Each Job Corpsman receives a monthly stipend in addition to room, board, and clothes.

4. *Back to school.* CPI attempts to support, in a variety of ways,

those graduates who elect to return to the public schools to finish their high-school educations. Because most of the youngsters in the program have either dropped out or been excluded from the public schools, for those youngsters who wish to return to school CPI informs the schools of the youngsters' progress and attempts to prepare the way or handle the problem of transition in a manner helpful both to the school and the youngster. If the youngster has a particularly difficult financial problem, CPI will try, in conjunction with the school, to develop work-study programs in which the boy or girl is able to work part-time while attending school either during the daytime or at night.

5. *Intermediate work-training program.* The intermediate work-training program is the newest of the alternatives available to a work-crew graduate. It involves the training of 100 males and 100 females in individual placements. The intermediate program is for those youngsters who are interested in public service and who are felt to be capable or prepared to work with other people under conditions of reduced supervision. The boys and girls in this work-crew follow-up program are placed in various public-service positions and agencies and receive more specific training than would be possible in the regular work-crew settings. Enrollees work 28 to 32 hours per week, at $1.25 per hour, from which Social Security (FICA) and withholding taxes are deducted. In addition to the work, each intermediate work-crew member is required to participate in an eight-hour education and skill-training period housed in a newly constructed Skill Center.

Our focus in this chapter has been primarily on the work-crew youngsters, their backgrounds, personalities, problems, and attitudes. We have also attempted to describe the rationale and content of the work-crew program. The reader undoubtedly has become aware of the importance of the work-crew foreman, a title that does not adequately convey his role, goals, and problems. The next chapter, therefore, is devoted to a description and discussion of his activities.

Chapter 18

The Work-Crew Foremen

The term "foreman" does very little to help define the kinds of activities and the nature of the responsibilities involved in being the leader of a CPI work crew. The term, taken from the factory setting, usually is understood to depict an on-the-job relationship between a supervisor and his workers, and generally is confined to a description of the vocational responsibilities and obligations comprising that role. Only in a most limited fashion does this definition offer an accurate job description of the CPI foreman. It is descriptive to the extent that the occupational setting is initially utilized as the basis for individual and group interactions whose remedial focus is the development of those work habits and attitudes important in securing and holding down a job. However, these interactions and relationships do not remain confined to the work setting, and the work-crew leader is often experienced by the youngsters in ways far more complex and diverse than we would expect from the term "foreman." Although his focus must remain on the vocational setting, the work-crew foreman is often thrust into roles more aptly described by the terms "therapist," "father," "mother," "counselor," "teacher," "big brother," and "friend." In this chapter we discuss many of these roles and indicate how the term "foreman" is a short-hand way of summarizing functions as extensive or as limited as the dictates of the particular situation. Before we do so, however, it is important that we understand who the foremen and foreladies are, where they come from, how they are selected, and what it is as human beings that they bring with them to the work-crew situation.

FOREMEN: BACKGROUND CHARACTERISTICS

As we have pointed out, CPI's functioning in the inner-city setting was predicated on the use of existing community facilities and person-

462

nel. By and large the work-crew foremen and foreladies are people who properly could be called indigenous to the inner-city community; and in those cases where they are not indigenous by birth they are certainly "indigenous" in terms of past experience, length of residence, or socioeconomic identification. Of the current 18 work-crew foremen and foreladies, 13 were born in New Haven, and, except for tours of duty in the armed forces, have spent all of their lives in the city. Ten of the foremen are white, eight are Negro; 14 are male, four are female; 11 are married, seven are single, one has been married and divorced. Perhaps the best index to indicate the degree to which these people are part of the local scene is the notation that their average age as a group is approximately 34 years, and they have spent 27.4 of those years in continual residence in New Haven.

In terms of educational training and past work histories the work-crew foremen and foreladies are essentially nonprofessional personnel. They have had neither the formal training nor the academic background in those areas (psychology, sociology, social work) generally acknowledged to be of importance in preparing people to deal effectively with troubled adolescents. For the work-crew leaders the situation is reversed; of the 18, only one is a college graduate and only two others have had some college experience. Of the remaining 15, 12 are high-school graduates and three never completed high school. Similarly, their vocational backgrounds offer little to suggest that they have had the kinds of experiences that would be helpful in working with youngsters. Their occupational backgrounds cover a gamut of experiences ranging from being self-employed to being the recipient of welfare checks. The continuum extends from highly skilled workers to semi-skilled and unskilled laborers. Briefly, some of these previous positions include mechanic, machinist, policeman, carpenter, gun assembler, X-ray technician, press operator, bartender, salesman, secretary, and stock boy. Clearly, the ease and effectiveness with which the foremen deal with the work-crew youngsters must be based on variables other than academic preparation and previous vocational experience. All we know at this point is that the foremen and foreladies know the inner-city setting and know it intimately and, further, that their own backgrounds are not too dissimilar from those of the work-crew youngsters.

One of the variables to be considered might be the manner in which the foremen originally came to CPI, including the bases on which they were evaluated and hired for the job. In the behavioral sciences we are well aware of the difficulties inherent in the selection processes of personnel, (whether or not the procedures utilized for selection and evaluation involve tests, profile analyses, interviews, etc.), and of the variable predictive efficiency that these selection processes possess.

Most of the foremen originally came to CPI either because of a dissatisfaction with their previous jobs or because they had been laid off on account of automation or the economic vicissitudes of the industry in which they had been employed. The formal qualifications for the foreman's job—at least as printed in *The work-crew handbook*—offer little help in understanding the bases on which the 18 were hired, whereas others were rejected, particularly because the applicants were not tested or evaluated with the aid of any standardized tests, measures, or questionnaires. The job specification was for someone who was over 21, had a driver's license, was more mature than the work-crew members, was able to accept responsibility and maintain control, was in good physical health, and was the possessor of some basic skills that could be passed on to others. In point of fact, an applicant was hired or rejected on the basis of two variables, one relatively objective— the stability of the applicant's previous work history; the other relatively subjective—the interviewer's perception of the applicant's degree of commitment to the inner-city population and his willingness to work with them. In no case did the interviewer, (the work-crew coordinator) try to sell the job to an applicant. In fact, he did just the opposite; he painted a rather dismal picture of the nature of the work, the hours, the pay, and the responsibilities. The underlying assumption in this maneuver was that those who persisted and could not be frightened away were the kinds of people who perceived the foreman's role as something more than a "job."

The importance of describing just what kinds of people these foremen are lies in the fact that clearly there was the feeling from the very beginning that not every individual could do the kinds of work involved. To be able to function effectively in the diverse settings and contexts comprising the foreman's areas of responsibility necessitates an individual operating under the aegis of a particular implicit or explicit set of assumptions about himself and others. In this sense a majority of the foremen are "naturals," for their assumptions reflect a particular philosophy of action that makes being helpful an almost natural consequence of this specific value system. As this is the case, and for purposes of specificity, we try to describe some of these characteristics and to illustrate the ways in which they enable the foreman to function in the work-crew setting.

COMMITMENT

Perhaps the most outstanding characteristic of the foreman is his deeply personal and ongoing commitment to the youngsters in the program. Unlike the disinterested observer who attempts to be helpful by long-range design and plan, the foreman's involvement with the youngsters is immediate, tangible, and concrete. It is the involvement of one human being, not standing on prescribed ceremony or procedure, reaching out to another in a consistent and mutually understandable manner. What this means to the youngsters is difficult to put into words. Basically, however, it connotes to them an ongoing interest that is new and often frightening. Eventually it comes to mean an involvement and availability that the youngster can depend on, and one that often becomes stable and mutual. In this context let us not underestimate the element of hope that is communicated to the teenager. It is hope in the sense that a stable and relevant yardstick of adulthood, the foreman, becomes the therapeutic fulcrum in a relationship.

What we have called the foreman's commitment to a youngster clearly involves his availability to that youngster on both a psychological and a behavioral level, and it takes the form of acting in specific ways both in and away from the work-crew setting. These acts, most often concrete and anticipatory in nature, occur in the context of the development of a relationship and provide the youngster with the feeling that adults indeed can be depended on and are not always mercurial or inconsistent.

From the foreman's point of view the matter of a boy's daily attendance is of great concern. Absence from the work crew is often a good indication that something is wrong and that something is bothering a boy.

Example 1. After his first week on the crew one of the boys did not show up for work on a Monday morning. Because each crew leaves the NEC promptly at 8:15 A.M. the crew left without him. During that day's lunch break the foreman called the boy's home to find out why he had not made it to work. In a tone the foreman experienced as somewhat distant and seemingly unconcerned, the boy told him that he had overslept but would try to make it the next day. He did show up the next day, but was absent again the following morning. This time the foreman did not call. Instead, he showed up at the boy's house the next morning at 8:00 A.M.

When the door finally was opened, the foreman encountered an initially bleary-eyed but soon astonished work-crew youngster. After a short period of silence, a time in which the foreman felt the boy was trying to regain his composure and air of nonchalance, the foreman had the boy get dressed and took him to the NEC where the crew was waiting.

During that day's lunch break the foreman sat down with the boy to talk about why, after a week's time in which the boy had shown up on time each morning, he suddenly had missed two days of work. The youngster maintained that he had overslept and that no one had awakened him on time. Instead of arguing with the boy or going any deeper into the youngster's apparent need to appear unconcerned, the foreman told him of his feelings about the importance to both of them that the boy not miss work unless it was completely unavoidable.

Without waiting for the boy to respond, the foreman told him that for the remainder of the week he would call at 7:30 A.M. to wake him and would pick him up at 8:00. However, the foreman felt that there was some realistic basis to the youngster's contention that it was difficult for him to wake up on time and that nobody in the home was up at that hour. Consequently, they worked out a plan whereby the foreman would lend the boy enough money to buy an alarm clock, and he would be repaid in weekly installments of 50 cents until the purchase price ($4.50) was made up. In the meantime, he would pick the boy up each morning.

The plan was put into effect with results more far-reaching than mere insurance of better attendance. The boy soon dropped his air of almost studied nonchalance and disinterest and became much more involved with the other work-crew members and the foreman. In a relatively short time he became less withdrawn and less isolated and began participating in aspects of the program that he had previously shunned.

Although nothing more was said of the incident for a long time, the boy eventually spoke to the foreman about it in a manner strikingly different from his previous manner. He began to talk about his earlier feelings: that nobody really cared whether or not he showed up, how he himself had found it necessary to show others that he, in turn, did not care either.

In short, the incident became the basis for the development of a relationship in which a boy, after a period of "testing behavior," could begin to talk with an adult about questions and concerns that he long had had about himself and about others. Part of the reason he was able to do this was that his foreman had acted in a specific way that indicated his interest and concern in the youngster, and that disconfirmed some of the boy's views about the content and structure of interpersonal relationships involving the adult world.

Although a boy may in time come to feel that a foreman's interest in him and commitment to him are sincere, it is not always easy for him to act on these feelings in ways that are helpful to him. Often a youngster, unable to put these new feelings of trust into words, waits until some personal emergency creates the conditions under which he is forced to turn to the foreman in a dramatic and unexpected way. The manner in which the foreman handles the situation has consequences that are both immediate and long-range and often involve him with people other than the youngster.

Example 2. Phil's history on the work crew was essentially unremarkable. After an initial period of suspicion and aloofness he soon became quite involved with the work crew as a whole. In the five months that he was on the crew his attendance was good; his work (painting) improved, and his general attitude toward working with his peers and an adult appeared quite satisfactory. He took part in all the activities of the work crew (discussions, recreation, etc.) and, although not overly enamored with the remedial-education component of the program, he attended classes regularly.

The foreman noticed, however, that periodically Phil would show up on the work crew puffy-eyed, and it appeared as if he had had little or no sleep the night before. On those occasions (perhaps once every week or every 10 days) Phil would be irritable and hostile to everyone on the crew, including his foreman.

When this occurred the foreman would leave Phil alone during the morning but would use the later-morning coffee break as an opportunity to sit and talk with him. By this time Phil would generally have calmed down quite a bit and the foreman would ask him what had happened to "set him off." The foreman noted that Phil often seemed on the verge of opening up but that, at the last moment, he would grow silent. More often than not they would wind up joking about things, and Phil would relax and become his old self again.

One Monday Phil was absent but returned to work the next day. He was anxious, disheveled, and distraught. This time, without waiting to be asked what was wrong, Phil grabbed the foreman and, before he was able to say anything, broke down and wept uncontrollably for a long time. The foreman took Phil away to a quiet spot and remained with him until he had regained sufficient composure to talk. It was only after some time, and after intermittent periods of crying, that Phil was able to tell his foreman the entire story.

Phil felt that from the very first day he entered the work crew, he had been subjected to merciless and almost constant harassment at home. This harassment, in the form of insults, threats, and degradations from his father, had increased in intensity and duration throughout the period of time that he had been on the crew. Phil did not know why his father did this or what he hoped to accomplish by it. All he knew was that he could not stand it and that it made him furious with and anxious about himself and everyone else.

Phil went on to tell the foreman that the previous Sunday evening, after a particularly violent scene with his father, he had run out of his house in a rage, raced downtown, and smashed a parking meter, only to be immediately apprehended by the police. He was taken to the station, booked, jailed, and finally was bailed out by his mother and an uncle. A court hearing had been set for two weeks from then and Phil was sure he was going to be "sent up."

The foreman, not asking why Phil smashed the parking meter, wanted to know exactly what Phil's father had said to him. Phil told him his father was constantly calling him "stupid" for working for $20 a week and for being "conned" by CPI into doing slave labor that only "jerks" and "punks" were capable of doing. Phil went on about how he would often run out of the house and walk around until he was sure his father was asleep before going home again. The foreman then asked if those were the evenings that preceded Phil's "tough" days on the crew, and Phil nodded affirmatively. Phil ended by informing the foreman of how he had really wanted to talk with him about it but how he "choked" whenever he had previously tried to bring it up. The foreman understood Phil's feelings and suggested that between them they might try to work things out.

Before the day of the court hearing the foreman did two things. First, by working with the personnel at the NEC and Phil's lawyer, they were able to put together an impressive but realistic file on Phil's behavior and progress since coming onto the CPI work crew. It was hoped this might provide the judge with the kind of data that would make probation, rather than incarceration, a more appropriate course of action. Second, the foreman went to visit Phil's father. Phil's family had been on relief for several years and the foreman quickly perceived a relationship between the father's chronic unemployment and his attacks on Phil since the latter's entry into the work-crew program. In talking with the father the foreman got the feeling that he was angry, jealous, and envious over Phil's new position— meager though it was—as breadwinner for the household. To a man who has been unemployed for a long time, the sight of his son consistently involved in a work-oriented program is not always a thrilling situation.

After repeated visits in which the foreman became friendly with the father and had a chance to spell out the content of CPI's program for adults as well as teenagers, he got the father to come to the employment center.

Phil's day in court went as was hoped. The decision of the court was to place him on probation with the proviso that he stay in the CPI work-crew program. Phil remained in the community and on the work crew and his father began his own involvement in a CPI retraining program.

In this example the foreman's sense of commitment to a youngster led to his involvement with people not originally in his area of responsibility. He felt that unless he worked directly with the parents, particularly the father, he would be unable to alter a potentially disastrous situation. It is not unusual for the foreman and foreladies to act in this manner, for in their attempts to work with a youngster they must often deal with an entire family. Clearly, their commitment to a youngster leads them into areas that extend beyond the work-crew setting.

One of the factors in the concept of commitment is the idea that a relationship does not end when the participants in that relationship are physically separated. For many of the youngsters the problem of separation is the ultimate test of both their hope of being able to function independently, as well as their fear of being abandoned once they have left the work-crew setting. The hope for self-sufficiency as well as the fear of loneliness and isolation are understandable emotions, particularly in youngsters who have rarely experienced a reciprocal relationship with an adult. For the foreman this poses the problem of behaving in such a way as to convey the lasting nature of his commitment to the boy without unduly undermining the boy's striving for independence and adulthood.

Example 3. Frank was a 17-year-old boy for whom it took a long time to be able to feel secure and unthreatened on the work crew. Characteristically he would handle his own insecurity and feelings of worthlessness by assuming an air of bravado and by behaving in ways that were both provocative and aggressive. The longer he was on the crew, and the more he interacted with his foreman, the clearer it became to him that no one was challenging him on the crew and that his own manhood did not necessarily involve the total absence of feelings of weakness.

Once Frank felt he could trust and confide in his foreman, they became very close. In their private discussions Frank would raise all kinds of questions involving Frank's concerns about his goals (to be an IBM programmer) and the manner in which his academic failures appeared to have undermined his chances of achieving them; he had questions about girls, sex, independence, and a host of areas related to his conception of manhood. The longer they were together the more Frank appeared to mature and grow. After about nine months on the crew both Frank and his foreman felt that he was ready to try a situation in which he could get the training and schooling that would prepare him for IBM-type work.

At about this time the screenings for the first contingent of Job Corps candidates were taking place. This first group of youngsters were to go to a Job Corps camp in Maryland where it was understood they could, among other things, receive the initial training and education necessary for eventual work in a computer-programming center. It appeared to be an ideal post-work-crew setting for Frank, and he readily applied, was screened, and accepted into the Job Corps. Frank left New Haven amid the fanfare that usually coincides with the inauguration of a new, exciting, and promising program.

Frank and his foreman communicated by mail. Frank's early letters were filled with enthusiasm and talk of "good eats and lots of nice guys from all over." After a time, however, Frank's letters became less enthusiastic and assumed the same belligerent and hostile tone that had characterized his early behavior on the work crew. At the end of one of these letters Frank was able to write that he missed "the guys and New Haven."

The foreman was concerned with the change in Frank's attitude about the camp, particularly because Frank never really specified the content of his disenchantment. He was, however, aware that Frank finally had been able to hint that he might be feeling lonely and homesick. Four other foremen had boys at the camp and, like himself, wanted to see the boys and get more first-hand knowledge of the camp, so it was arranged to have the foremen go to the camp for a weekend. The following Friday, directly after work, the foremen drove a CPI car to the Job Corps camp in Maryland.

As expected, the boys were delighted to see their foremen. Most of them, to one degree or another, had ambivalent feelings about the camp but they all seemed to share a certain amount of homesickness and a longing for their own familiar urban setting.

Frank and his foreman had a chance to talk in a way similar to their discussions on the work crew. They initially spoke of the Job Corps program and its possibilities and difficulties, but they soon began to talk about Frank's mixed emotions about being in a new and often frightening situation. The foreman impressed on Frank the fact that the physical distance between them was the necessary result of Frank's own development and growth as a man, but that it certainly need not lead to their permanent estrangement. In this content the foreman shared with Frank some of his own experiences of being separated from friends. Finally they arranged to meet in New Haven whenever Frank got his first leave to go home.

In the foregoing example we have attempted to make the point that the foreman's relationship with a youngster does not automatically cease once that boy graduates from the work crew. What makes this a problem of commitment is the fact that the boys often need to experience a good deal of personal continuity in their over-all relationship with CPI, and the foreman must bear, and usually does bear, the primary responsibility for the maintenance of this continuity. We should add, however, that from the foreman's point of view this responsibility is not experienced as a demand, but rather as a natural consequence of his ongoing interest in the youngster.

MATURITY

By maturity we refer to the quality communicated by the foreman to the youngster that implies responsibility as well as levels of expectation. Most of the foremen and foreladies are themselves pragmatic individuals to whom feelings of responsibility and levels of expectations are not personally experienced as necessarily antithetical to the demands of the society in which they live. By being able to relate to the youngsters in specific and concrete ways they are able to transmit to them notions of meaningful and mature behavior in an imperfect society. Thus when the foreman becomes a sort of an ego-ideal to his youngsters it does not carry with it the condescension and empty "moralizing from above" that these boys and girls have often experienced in the context of their participation in other institutions such as the schools or public agencies. In short the foreman's system of values is not perceived as a sell-out to what has been experienced as a basically oppressive and unresponsive society. By and large the foremen are responsible, down-to-earth people whose standards for others in the work-crew setting are not materially different from their expectations of themselves, and whose human aspirations for the youngsters are essentially no different from their own human aspirations. When they offer themselves to the youngsters as relevant figures for identification or as behavioral role models they are not presenting them with images that are difficult to introject. They are, day in and day out, confronting the teenagers with an adult role model whose roots are embedded in the same soil from which the youngsters grew up.

One of the primary ways in which a youngster is faced with the reality that people not only have obligations to him but also have expectations of him is in the area of discipline. Since the work crews are job-oriented settings, many of the foreman's interactions with the youngsters occur in the context of their developing a meaningful and relevant working relationship. Each member of the work crew is expected to do a day's work for a day's pay, and the foreman must decide how to deal with deviations from that pattern. The problem of maturity enters the picture in terms of how a foreman disciplines a boy and the lessons implicit in the ways in which he discharges his authority. One of the more extreme disciplinary measures available to the foreman is his power to dock a boy a day's pay when the foreman feels a particular youngster has not performed the work to his satisfaction.

Example 4. One warm spring day James, a 17-year-old boy who had been on the work crew for about three months, showed up for work and immediately made known his feeling that everyone should take a day off. His suggestion was initially met with humor and joking agreement by the other boys and the foreman. In the foreman's car on the way to the work site, James spoke of what he would do with his mythical day off, and was joined in this by several of the other work-crew members.

Once on the work site the foreman gave the boys their individual assignments for the day. This particular crew was involved in the care and maintenance of the grounds surrounding a large VA hospital. The activities for that day included mowing, raking, and clearing out the debris from an area adjacent to one of the driveways.

James accepted his assignment in an offhand manner and made a parting comment, albeit in a somewhat humorous fashion, to the effect that the foreman had to be a communist because he had not been willing to be democratic and to take a vote for a day off.

It soon became clear to the foreman that, for all his good-natured kidding around, James was not in a mood to work that day. He observed him leaning on his rake and looking at the sky for long periods of time. He went over to James and spoke with him about the assignment he had given him and told him that it would be impossible for him to finish it if he kept "goofing off." He added that he understood James' desire for a day off, especially with the weather as beautiful as it was, but that they had a responsibility to the hospital to fulfill the task for which they had been contracted. James listened and when the foreman finished, said in a loud and sarcastic voice: "OK, big boss, I got the word."

For the next half-hour James did his work in a grudging and inefficient manner, which necessitated the foreman warning James that if he continued his present behavior he would be forced to dock him the day's pay.

After the lunch break when all the other boys had returned to their jobs, James remained lying on the grass. He told the foreman that he was tired and that he thought he would rest awhile. By this time all the other youngsters were craning their necks in anxious anticipation of the expected showdown. Instead, the foreman took James away from the group to an embankment some distance away where they sat down to talk.

They rehashed the events of that day and, since James could add no extenuating circumstances to account for his behavior, the foreman indicated his decision to take some disciplinary action. James immediately asked if he was going to be thrown off the crew. The foreman told him that this was not his intent but that he did feel it necessary and warranted that he dock James' pay. The foreman went on to ask what gave James the notion that he would be kicked out of the work-crew program. James responded, "Because I goofed off and put you down." The foreman again explained to James how and why he was being punished and indicated to him the fact that self-discipline was an essential part of the working situation. He ended by specifying his intent to discipline James in such a way that "the punishment fit the crime." When they had finished talking the foreman sent James home with the understanding that when James came to work the next day the incident would be considered a thing of the past, unless James wanted to talk about it further.

James returned the next day and did want to talk some more about the incident. This conversation led to questions involving boredom, the ability to maintain motivation once the content of a job had been mastered, and other problems concerned with the vocational setting. The conversation eventually led to a series of group discussions in which the rest of the boys on the work crew participated.

In the process of docking this youngster the foreman was able to make the boy aware of several issues, many related to the area of work but some having implications in other areas of life. In exercising his authority the foreman clearly indicated that he had expectations of his boys in much the same way they had expectations of him. More importantly, he showed them that authority was not a blind, irrational, unforgiving force in adults, but that it had a purpose and was open to inquiry. The punishment itself was based on reason and was within reason, and both factors were explained to the youngster immediately and not at some point in time when the event was no longer a clear and relevant issue. Finally, the boy was made aware that an error or a mistake need not have irrevocable consequences in his relationship with the foreman.

Because many of the youngsters for various reasons have been excluded or have excluded themselves from significant areas of community life, they often have a profound fear and distrust of institutions that others take for granted. Part of this fear and distrust is based on insufficient information, but much is founded on the youngster's inability to perceive himself as the kind of person who has a legitimate right to "want in" on various aspects of community life. In many cases the foreman must assume the role of the agent who interprets the society to the youngster. He can assume this role only because the boy, in identifying with him, has identified with an adult who by word and deed has assumed the responsibility of undoing the fear and distrust the youngster has of society's institutions. The youngster often feels that if the foreman has dealings with certain institutions in the society then they may be safe for him too. A case in point is one youngster's adventures with the local savings bank.

Example 5. Henry, an extremely suspicious and volatile 15-year-old boy, was on the work crew for a long time before his foreman felt secure enough to leave him alone even for the shortest period of time. His career on the crew had been marked by frequent outbursts of temper followed by brief periods of remorse and relative calm. In time—and after innumerable instances that exasperated and frustrated those people trying to work with him—Henry began to change. Although he was not by any stretch of the imagination healthy, he did appear to gain a measure of control over himself and some ability to tolerate moderate frustration without exploding and treating those around him to a public exhibition of his almost total command of the language of profanity. He remained suspicious, and though he no longer distrusted his foreman he retained a distinct contempt for almost everything and everyone else. Before Henry could trust people they had to pass his own personal baptism of fire.

One day after he received his weekly pay check, Henry and his foreman got into a discussion about money. The foreman asked him what he was going to do with his money and Henry told him of his plans to save up enough money to buy a bicycle. The foreman inquired whether Henry had a savings account and Henry responded by blowing up and saying that he had no use "for any f——— savings bank." The foreman, used to the fact that Henry often reacted to novel and unfamiliar ideas in this manner, let him finish his tirade. The foreman then asked Henry if he knew what a savings bank was and if he had ever been in one. Henry responded by shaking his head and the foreman continued by explaining to Henry what a bank was, how it functioned and why it might be a good place for him to save his money. The foreman ended by showing Henry his own bank book and indicating to him where, when, and how he had accrued interest.

Henry seemed both interested and dubious at the prospect of getting "free money" at a bank. Moreover, the foreman felt that Henry's never having been in a bank reflected something about his over-all estrangement from so many areas of community life. The foreman suggested that Henry accompany him to the bank so that they could look it over and get a better idea of just what went on there. Henry was a bit resistant to the idea but felt that with the foreman there with him the chances of being conned were somewhat reduced.

They went downtown to the bank. The foreman introduced Henry to one of the bank's officials, explained why they were there, and accompanied Henry while he was shown around the bank. The "guide" tried to use the tour to explain the rudiments of a savings account to Henry. Both Henry and his foreman were treated with the courtesy and respect usually shown prospective new-customer accounts. Henry was impressed by the interest shown in him and somewhat awed by all the things that went on in the bank.

Henry decided to open an account that very day but informed the people of his intention to check on his money very often. During the next few days Henry did indeed check up on his money and was treated with the same respect each time he appeared.

Besides the obvious suspiciousness that characterized much of Henry's general behavior, it appeared to the foreman that some of his initial hostility and fear concerning the bank was because of a feeling that the bank was no place for Henry to be. Consequently, by bringing the bank into Henry's immediate experience, the foreman was creating a process wherein societal images built on years of exclusion were being undermined and undone. Not "just anyone" could have done this. It had to be done by a person with whom Henry had had extensive experience and someone whom Henry could not identify with the ruling hierarchy.

One of the characteristics of the mature person is his ability to acknowledge his own fallibility without experiencing each of his mistakes as a general indictment of his worth as an individual. Many of the work-crew youngsters live in a subjective world populated by polarities. One is either black or white, good or bad, with little room left for the subtle shadings of grey that permeate most people's lives. Many of the boys and girls experience their participation in the work-crew program itself as an index of their own worthlessness and inadequacy. For some this feeling is often replaced by other more positive feelings the longer they remain on the crew. For others, particularly those who err while on the crews, the work crews are perceived as a final verification of what so many people have told them in the past, namely, that they were born bad. The foreman's own maturity, especially his capacity to function in the role of an adult who is trusted by a youngster, must often fill in those shades of grey that the youngster's negative self-evaluations omit. By so doing he helps the youngster to further differentiate the world and himself in a more realistic and helpful manner.

Example 6. Claire was a 16-year-old girl who had dropped out of school some months before joining the work-crew program. She had left school with the feelings that she was stupid and that she would never get a job. Indeed, before coming to CPI she always had been turned down whenever she applied for a job.

Claire's behavior on the crew was characterized by her "I-can't-do-it" response whenever she was asked to do something or learn something new. Her forelady, not willing to accept this statement as fact, worked with her very closely and would not let her go until Claire had mastered a task well enough to teach it to others. After a fairly short period of time a gradual change was noticed in Claire's behavior. She became a bit more self-confident, needed less prolonged individual attention, and became somewhat more assertive on the crew.

One day all this changed. Claire showed up for work looking as beaten and miserable as any girl could look. She was both agitated and depressed and her eyes appeared puffed up from crying. Claire told her forelady that she was pregnant, that she did not know who the father was, and that even if she did, "Who would marry me anyway?" The more they talked the more self-condemning Claire became. She painted a picture of herself as a failure in all areas of life including her looks, her education, her abilities, and her future. Claire ended by adding that "they all said I was no damn good and they're right."

Claire's forelady understood the extreme unhappiness that she felt and could sympathize with the girl's despair. She felt, however, that Claire was all too characteristically generalizing from a mistake to a way of life. She spoke with her about the importance of not confusing an error with an unwarranted indictment of herself as a person. "We all make mistakes," she told her, "but that doesn't automatically make us bad people." She then recapitulated Claire's own history on the work crew and how she was often "putting herself down" before even trying to do something.

Claire's forelady went on to share some of her own mistakes in life with the youngster. Claire was somewhat taken aback by this but began to understand the point that her forelady was making. She began to realize that if her forelady, someone whom she had perceived as perfect, was capable of making serious mistakes without being contaminated for life, then perhaps she was too.

In the example above the forelady was confronted with a girl who saw no distinction between a mistake and an almost predetermined way of life. Beyond this was the girl's confusion between maturity and infallibility. By feeling comfortable enough to share with this girl some of her own experiences of failure, the forelady was able to dispel some of the useless polarities with which the youngster viewed herself and others, as well as to offer her a more realistic picture of adulthood and maturity. In both cases the results were obtained with the absence of those moralizing and condescending attitudes with which this girl had been confronted in the past.

TRUST AND RESPECT

The variables of trust and respect, though implicit in the characteristics described previously, are qualities in and of themselves that provide the foundation for the emergence of a relationship out of which many activities can follow. Here the foreman brings with him an unspoken concern and faith in the youngster's present and future potential to function in a reliable and self-enhancing manner. Lest we underestimate the implications of this trust and respect with which the foreman perceives the youngster, it would be well briefly to review the perceptions that have characterized many of the interactions these youngsters have had with other agencies and service-oriented programs. Most public agencies, for one reason or another, cannot avoid the problem of implicitly or explicitly "labeling" the clients with whom they have ongoing relationships. These labels, subtle though they may be, have consequences in terms of how the agency perceives the client, how the client perceives the agency, and how the client perceives himself. It has been our experience that rarely, if ever, have a majority of the work-crew youngsters had contacts with agencies or individuals in which they were not implicitly judged and reacted to as derelict, incompetent, or irresponsible people. From the agency's points of view it becomes difficult to do things *for* and *to* people over a long period of time without communicating to them a feeling of despair and pessimism about them. Similarly, it is difficult for an individual constantly to be on the receiving end of state or federal aid without experiencing himself as worthless and his position as static and irrevocable. From this point of view much of the work-crew youngsters' previous behavior may be understood as a self-fulfilling prophecy in which negative self-images become the basic parameters for subsequent sets. What seems important in enabling these young sters to trust and respect themselves is the fact that the foreman trusts and respects them. He places trust in kids who have rarely experienced themselves to be trustworthy and he respects youngsters who have never had much self-respect. This, coupled with the fact that the fore-man does things *with* and not *to* a youngster, creates the conditions under which mutual trust and self-respect can develop.

The foremen and foreladies always find it interesting to see what happens to a youngster when he or she is suddenly put in a position of responsibility. They see this not only as a way of assessing progress in a youngster but also as a therapeutic tool in and of itself. What this means to a youngster is difficult to describe, but one thing seems certain; the youngster is confronted with the fact that someone whom he respects and admires views him in a manner in which the youngster may not view himself, namely, as a responsible and competent person. What we may call the "other-fulfilling prophecy" often begins to operate and the kid begins to perceive himself in ways that had been beyond the scope of his experience.

Example 7. Cecil's past history was not too different from those of several other youngsters on his work crew. He was a 17-year-old boy from a family long known to public assistance agencies. He was a high-school dropout whom the teachers had called "incorrigible" and who had already had a few run-ins with the law for offenses involving fighting and petty theft.

After coming to CPI, Cecil was placed on a work crew that took care of the greens at a local public golf course. During the two months that he was on the crew his work was adequate but not the least outstanding. During that time, however, he had developed a relationship with his foreman that, though not so close as the foreman would have liked, was warm and friendly. Cecil was essentially a loner and the foreman, after initial attempts at getting close to him, respected his need for privacy. What bothered the foreman, however, was his feeling that Cecil was capable of doing a much better job than he was doing and that he had leadership qualities he was not utilizing. He spoke with Cecil about these feelings of his but Cecil would respond by saying, "I do my job. What else d'you want?" When the foreman told him of his belief in Cecil's leadership potential Cecil just laughed and told him that he had "the wrong boy."

One day some time later the crew had just gotten to the work site when the foreman was called away to the main office. Without hesitating for a moment he handed Cecil the work assignments for that day and told him to take over until he could get back to the crew. Before Cecil could manage a reply the foreman turned and took off for the office.

When the foreman returned to his crew he found everyone doing the work in much the same way as they would if he were present. Cecil, on the other hand, seemed to be working harder than the foreman had ever seen him work. Periodically Cecil would stop, survey the other guys, and immediately return to his own job. When he asked Cecil how things had gone in his absence Cecil responded in a somewhat embarrassed but obviously proud manner, "Fine, just fine." Not another word was said about the entire incident.

From that time on Cecil became the foreman's unofficial assistant. Whenever the foreman was unexpectedly called away he would leave Cecil in charge of the crew. He also began giving him additional duties that called for a greater degree of responsibility and trust. Cecil responded by working harder, interacting with the other boys to a degree he had not before, and, in general, becoming much more involved with the work-crew program as a whole.

In Cecil's case the foreman initially acted in such a way as to leave the youngster with no alternative but to accept, albeit momentarily, a position of responsibility, the capability for which he had previously denied. Although they were not particularly close, Cecil respected the foreman and was, in turn, respected by the foreman. By placing Cecil in a position of unavoidable responsibility he was also confronting him with the realization that the foreman was acting in terms of his own perception of the youngster's capabilities and had not bought Cecil's self-depreciating line. Cecil's subsequent behavior was not only a fulfillment of the foreman's prophecy, but it became the vehicle by which Cecil's own feelings about himself could change.

We have already mentioned the difference between doing things *for* or *to* someone and doing things *with* someone. It is a crucial distinction to make in terms of how the recipient of the aid experiences himself and others in the situation. Often the most important variable in the process is how the "helping situation" is interpreted to the recipient of that service and the degree to which his perceptions are explored and taken into account before a judgment is made about his receptiveness to help and his potential for self-help. What exasperates many agencies is their feeling that the recipient of their aid neither trusts nor respects the very agency that is trying to help him, and that he acts in ways (e.g., fails to keep appointments, does not take prescribed medications) that nullify the benefits of the services offered. What often is not understood is that besides the general implications of being dependent and "on the dole," a person has many feelings and ideas—often invalid and irrational notions based on insufficient information—about the content and consequence of a service that has been offered to him. The fact that he fails to keep an appointment is almost invariably attributed to the client's untrustworthiness and lack of responsibility, whereas in reality it may have been due to his fear and anxiety about the appointment itself, fear and anxiety that are based on a paucity of relevant information and the feelings of aloneness and dread that accompany those circumstances. A case in point is the scheduling of a medical appointment for a work-crew youngster.

Example 8. Chuck was an 18-year-old boy who had been on the work crews for about two months. Because of a series of perceptible tics he had, involving apparently uncontrollable gross facial and head movements, he was the object and butt of many jokes by the other members of the crew. Chuck was an affable boy and seemed to be used to this type of kidding. Although he did not like being called "Goofball" he had apparently adjusted to the fact that he would usually be referred to in this or some similar fashion. Since he took the ribbing in a good-natured way and since he was, indeed, a likeable and popular boy, the ribbing itself diminished with the passage of time. During the early days of Chuck's presence on the crew, when the ribbing was at its peak, the foreman decided not to make an issue over it. He felt that to do so would exacerbate the situation and draw further attention to Chuck. He told this to Chuck and the youngster agreed with the foreman's point of view.

When the ribbing had subsided and when the foreman felt that he and Chuck were close enough to talk about it, he began to speak with Chuck about the tic. Chuck readily spoke about the problem and, for all his denials, the foreman felt that the boy did, in fact, have some concern about it. Chuck maintained, however, that it was "just nerves or something."

Some time later the foreman was informed that Chuck had not kept any of the appointments that had been set up for him with a local neurologist. These appointments were for a complete neurological work-up, including X-rays and an EEG. Those who made the arrangements for Chuck were somewhat angered by his seeming irresponsibility and lack of interest in things being done "for his own good."

The foreman approached Chuck about the matter and Chuck shrugged off the entire affair by saying that he was all right and didn't need to have his head "opened up." The more they talked about it the more convinced the foreman became that Chuck was extremely frightened and apprehensive about visiting the neurologist, and that he was particularly afraid of the EEG. Although Chuck knew what X-rays were, he knew nothing about the EEG, what it was for, how it was done, and what it meant. Chuck asked the foreman if he knew what it was. The foreman did not know and told this to Chuck. He also indicated to Chuck that maybe the two of them, together, could find out.

The foreman promised to go with Chuck to the doctor whenever the next appointment was set up. Chuck seemed somewhat relieved but still rather anxious. During the period of time before the next appointment was to take place the foreman and Chuck spoke a great deal about their feelings about doctors and the things they did.

The day of the appointment the foreman picked Chuck up and drove him to the doctor. He remained with Chuck in the waiting room and accompanied him into the office when the doctor was ready to see him. Before the doctor had a chance to do anything the foreman explained to him his and Chuck's interest in knowing as much about what the doctor was doing as possible. The doctor was surprised but quickly understood the situation and began explaining in as concrete and reassuring a way as possible what he was going to do, why he was doing it, and how he was going to do it. The foreman remained in the room with Chuck and the three of them had a running conversation for a good deal of the time they were in the office and while the doctor was examining Chuck. When they finally left, Chuck was much less anxious and even a bit interested in some of the things that he and the foreman had learned. Another appointment was set up for the following week.

When the day arrived for the second in the series of appointments the foreman again accompanied Chuck to the doctor's office. This time he remained in the waiting room while Chuck went in to see the doctor. When Chuck was finished, he took him home again and listened while Chuck told him of things that the doctor did.

When the time for the third appointment rolled around Chuck told his foreman that he thought he might "go it alone" that day. The foreman understood what Chuck was really saying, that he was no longer afraid and wanted to handle it on his own, and gratefully bowed out. Chuck had no more trouble keeping that or any subsequent appointments.

From the agency's point of view Chuck was perceived as someone who did not appreciate the fact that people were trying to do things "for his own good." From the foreman's point of view appreciation was the least important factor to be considered in understanding Chuck's inability to keep his medical appointments. He saw Chuck as feeling frightened and alone and he respected both the basis and relevance of these feelings. The things that were being done for and to Chuck could never have been accomplished until someone perceived him in a way in which doing those things with him became the predominant focus in the helping relationship. The agency could not do this because their past experience had placed them in a position where they had neither the trust in, nor the respect for, the feelings of the very client they were trying to help. The foreman had no such dilemma.

There are several consequences resulting from the judgment that someone is untrustworthy; the most obvious is that the individual is removed or kept away from situations in which trust is a primary requirement of the behavior of the individual in that setting. The individual is told that until he proves himself trustworthy he will not be allowed to enter a situation in which his honesty is put to the test. The difficulty of this position is that the individual cannot easily prove his trustworthiness as long as he is excluded from those situations relevant to his proving himself. This paradox results in behaviors that are often self-defeating both from the point of view of the society that has made the judgment and from the point of view of the individual who has been judged. The work-crew youngster who has committed a crime often has been, since that time, under the scrutiny and suspicion of many agencies and institutions in the city. However, though he may not have been in any subsequent trouble, he has similarly not been allowed to enter those situations where he can once more find himself in a position of trust and responsibility. To be able to keep out of trouble does not mean that a youngster ceases to have questions about himself and his own capacity to be trusted and respected. The longer he is kept out of situations in which he can prove himself, the greater his self-doubt becomes, and the more likely he is to act in terms of how others have come to view him. The fact that the foreman can entertain the luxury of trusting a youngster means that he will make available to that youngster situations in which the boy can come to trust himself.

Example 9. Tommy, a 19-year-old boy, came onto the work crew while still on probation after a conviction on a charge of breaking and entering. Unlike some of the other youngsters who had been in trouble with the law, Tommy wore his conviction like a badge of dubious honor. He was extremely arrogant and pompous, and he never seemed to tire of telling the other boys on the crew of his encounters with the law. In a tone apparently calculated to gain a mixture of fear and respect he would often caution the other members of the crew not to leave any money or valuables in sight when "old Tommy's around."

From the foreman's point of view there was an empty ring to much of Tommy's boasting. The longer the foreman knew Tommy and the more involved they got with each other, the greater this feeling became. Tommy, however, seemed to have a great need to impress people with his badness; and the more involved he became with the foreman the more impelled he felt to warn the foreman against trusting "Crazy Tom." Although Tommy was a good worker it was very hard for him to accept a compliment on his work and he would always shrug it off by reminding the foreman that he was just "doing my time."

The foreman invited Tommy to come to his home to help him sand down a bar and a hi-fi cabinet that he was making. After some reluctance

Tommy accepted because he "had nothing better to do." They went to the foreman's home and, after working for a while on the furniture, the foreman decided to go out and get them some sodas to drink. Tommy asked the foreman whether he intended to leave him alone in the house and the foreman responded by telling him he saw no good reason why two men should have to go to the store for a couple of bottles of soda. Tommy warned the foreman against this, saying, "If I were you I'd never leave old Tommy alone in a house. You might come back and find it all but gone." The foreman laughed, told him that he would have to take his chances, and immediately left. When he returned they had their sodas, finished their work, and the foreman took Tommy home. The foreman did not mention anything about the fact that when he had returned with the sodas nothing was missing. Because Tommy enjoyed helping the foreman with the furniture he came over to the apartment several more times and each time the foreman left him alone for a period of time.

At one of the meetings of the crew one of the boys made the suggestion that because all of the boys liked to drink coffee in the morning, it might be cheaper in the long run to buy a coffee-maker and brew their own coffee at the work site. The rest of the boys thought this was a good idea and decided to try it. After the initial investment all the boys were to chip in fifty cents a week for coffee, Coffeemate, and sugar. The plan would save them money and increase the number of cups of coffee each boy would be able to consume during a week.

The plan required that someone be appointed to take care of collecting the money at the beginning of every week. In addition to collecting the money, this person would be responsible for using any leftover money to buy "treats" on Friday. Before the meeting broke up the foreman appointed Tommy to take care of the money. Tommy appeared visibly shaken by this unexpected move and quickly cautioned the crew in his characteristic fashion. The foreman, instead of letting Tommy go on and on, as was usually the case, quickly dismissed his "bull" and adjourned the meeting.

The next week Tommy began his functions as treasurer and, after his customary introductory remarks, did an excellent job. The longer he was treasurer the less frequently he felt impelled to remind everyone of his untrustworthiness. In addition the foreman noted a change in Tommy's over-all attitude on the crew. He gradually became less boastful in a self-depreciating way and considerably less arrogant. His relationships with the other boys seemed to improve as his need to instill fear in them diminished. Tommy now began to take pride in his accomplishments and was able to accept recognition for a job well done.

In dealing with Tommy the foreman was much less impressed with Tommy's delinquent past than was the boy himself. What did impress the foreman was Tommy's need to view himself and to have others view him as an unreliable, frightening, and untrustworthy individual. The fact that he did not share Tommy's perceptions of himself enabled him to act as others were unable to act. As this was the case he could place Tommy in situations that allowed him to act in ways leading him to changes in his own perceptions of himself. Tommy was eventually faced with the reality that there was some validity in the implicit judgment the foreman had made about him, a judgment in direct opposition to the one others held about him—and the one he had come to hold about himself.

MUTUAL CONCERNS AND COMMON EXPERIENCES

Many of the foremen and foreladies either grew up and/or subsequently settled in some of the inner-city neighborhoods serviced by CPI. The others, generally, have come from backgrounds and environments that are similar to those of the majority of the work-crew boys and girls. It is partly this communality of similar backgrounds and experiences the foreman is able to share with his youngsters that accounts for much of the ease and rapidity with which he can establish meaningful relationships with them. Similarly, "mutual concerns" —questions and problems the youngsters have that have evolved in a context well-understood and even personally experienced by the foreman—facilitate the formation of this bond between the foreman and his kids. Some of these concerns involve questions of race, school experiences, and a host of other variables that often are approached most comfortably and spoken about when the participants in that interaction have similar and agreed-on points of departure or frames of reference. The fact that many of the foremen and foreladies are themselves members of minority groups, that some of them have not completed high school, and that they are not perceived by the youngsters as members of the ruling hierarchy—and yet *are* experienced as mature adults—are immeasurable strengths and attractions in the eyes of the work-crew youngsters. In short, the foreman and his kids speak the same language. However, there is one other point to make in this context. We should not overlook or underestimate the fact that by virtue of their own particular past experiences as well as their own familiarity with the conditions surrounding youngsters in the inner-city area the foremen are in the unique position of possessing a usable framework of knowledge that may well be unavailable to other individuals. The possession of this body of knowledge and the ability to use it in appropriate ways are often the variables that facilitate the formation of ongoing relationships in which the foreman's help is not perceived as condescension. It is perceived as help coming from someone who "knows the score" and has been "over the course" himself.

One of the specific areas in which most of the work-crew youngsters have experienced extreme difficulty is the classroom setting. The fact that almost all of them are, for one reason or another, high-school dropouts is indication enough that they were unable to handle the academic situation as it was presented to them in the New Haven school system. For some the difficulty supposedly was because of intellectual deficits; for others it involved behavior problems; but for all it was a combination and interaction of both variables. Disregarding for a moment the specific nature of a youngster's school difficulties, there is one thing about which we can be relatively certain; the high-school dropout leaves school with a multitude of feelings about himself and the academic situation. In many cases some of these feelings are centered around the teacher and the way the youngster felt when confronted with the teacher in the classroom setting. The images and ideas youngsters have about teachers and the learning situation do not cease to exist once they have left the formal academic setting. These images and the behaviors they lead to are important variables to be considered if the youngster ever is to return to an academic or academic-like setting, as is the case when a work-crew youngster participates in the work-crew remedial-education program. His feelings about the learning situation, particularly his attitudes about the teacher and what he feels are the teacher's attitudes toward him, are important considerations in determining the degree to which a youngster will benefit from a remedial-education program. The foreman is often the person who is in the best position, because of his own past experiences, to understand and deal with the youngster's feelings about school and his ability or willingness to learn in the classroom setting.

Example 10. Charlie, a 17-year-old boy, came onto the work crew after he dropped out of school and was unable to get a job. Although he had lasted until his sophomore year in high school, he had been the recipient of several social promotions and his reading level was somewhere below the fourth grade. Although he knew that his participation in the work-crew program included his attendance at remedial-education classes three times a week, he willingly joined the work-crew program.

It soon became clear that there were two Charlies instead of one in the program. There was the Charlie who quickly became an integral and productive member of his crew while the crew was on its work site, and there was the Charlie who was a constant behavior problem in the classroom of the remedial-education component of the program. On the work site

(Charlie was in the mechanics crew) Charlie was cooperative, attentive, and completely involved in learning about the repair and maintenance of motors used in lawn-mowing equipment. He often worked overtime and frequently amazed his foreman with the nature and complexity of the questions he asked related to the work he was doing. The foreman saw him as a boy who was extremely motivated and had good potential in the area of mechanics. In the classroom Charlie was a terror and virtually unmanageable. The longer he was in the classroom the more unruly he became. He was not willing to take direction from his teacher nor was he able to control his behavior. Often, for the sake of the other youngsters whom he was upsetting with his antics as well as to "free the teacher to teach rather than spend all his time disciplining the boy," Charlie would be excluded from the classroom and would be sent to stay with his foreman.

The foreman, himself a high-school dropout, tried to talk with Charlie about the latter's problem in the classroom. Charlie maintained that he did not like the classroom and that the teacher thought "he was a dope." In reality, as the foreman found out by speaking with the teacher, this was not exactly the case. Although the teacher was angry at having to spend so much time controlling the boy, he felt that Charlie was not stupid but "just incorrigible behavior-wise." The foreman, knowing that Charlie was a dropout, felt that the difference in Charlie's behavior on and off the work site was too great to be attributed to general incorrigibility. Furthermore, aware of how he himself had been anxious and nervous in the classroom setting and how he too had seen little connection between what was being taught in the classroom and what his vocational interests were, the foreman felt that Charlie had come to resent both the content and nature of the formal learning situation. He knew that Charlie had a hard time dealing with the verbal world and felt that he was responding to the teacher as being "way up there," isolated and removed from him, his interests, and his ways of expressing himself.

The foreman began sitting in Charlie's class, ostensibly to help maintain discipline, but actually to observe the boy and see if he could help him. In the class the boys were being taught fractions and the foreman quickly saw several difficulties inherent in the classroom situation. First, the fractions were being presented in a rote fashion, in a manner that made it difficult to see their applicability to the working or real-life situation. Second, it was being presented in such a way that it was not too difficult to understand Charlie's feeling of being talked down to by someone "way up there." The teacher, a man of good intentions whose heart was in the right place, did not seem to be able to communicate in such a way as to reduce the distance that existed between himself and his students. The learning situation was being experienced in much the same fashion as when the boys were in the public schools. It was characterized by the teacher's personal remoteness, by the students' experience of the irrelevance of the content matter, and by the attendant anxiety, fear, and hostility resulting from feelings of personal inadequacy and inferiority.

Because the teacher was all too happy to have someone relieve him of the burden of having to worry constantly about Charlie, he left the foreman to his own devices in the classroom. The foreman began by sharing with Charlie some of his own feelings about school and the things that bothered and upset him about the classroom situation. He then began to try to explain to him the particular reasons why it was important to understand fractions in order to work with machinery. In order to illustrate this, the foreman brought into the classroom a micrometer and used that as a basis for understanding numbers, their multiplication and division. He spoke with Charlie in the same ways in which they had spoken countless times on the work site, stressing the application of what he was doing to the vocational setting. Charlie began to work with the foreman in the classroom. Even more importantly, he began to use the work site as a classroom, showing some of the other boys the ways in which to use numbers on the job.

In this example the foreman, operating in terms of how he himself had experienced the classroom situation, was able to deal with those feelings in a youngster that adversely affected his ability and willingness to learn in the classroom setting. Moreover, he was able to broaden significantly the boy's perception of the relevance of the learning situation so that school and work were no longer experienced as totally dissimilar and mutually exclusive situations. The foreman's knowledge and understanding of the gulf that existed between the teacher and the work-crew youngster—a gulf predicated on different perceptions, attitudes, and values—was derived from his own experiences in the formal academic setting. By being able to translate his own experiences and the information derived from them in a relevant and appropriate way he was in a better position to view the learning situation from the point of view of the work-crew youngster and to deal with it so as to reduce some of the anxiety and fear that was interfering with the boy's ability to learn.

One of the problems involved in developing an educational curriculum is in deciding on the different methods and processes that may be utilized in teaching specific material. More often than not the educational institution must make decisions concerning the appropriateness of certain needs and interests the students may have, in terms of their applicability to the learning situation. Because of the importance placed on the continuity and uniformity of educational practices there is often little room left to change a program once it has been organized and implemented. Those areas of interest not perceived as relevant to the formal learning situation are relegated to the status of extracurricular activities and scheduled at times when they do not compete or interfere with the school's regular program. Rarely, if ever, are the youngsters' extracurricular interests used as the foundation on which more formal learning experiences are organized. The decision to change the focus of the learning situation or to alter the structure in which the learning situation is presented to youngsters must often be based on information presented to the school indicating that such a change might be helpful in facilitating the learning process. At CPI the foreman, because of the nature of his ongoing contact with the youngsters, is in a position to offer such information and to take part in its implementation.

Example 11. One of the CPI work crews has been placed in a local greenhouse setting. Their job on this work site is to help in the care and maintenance of the plants and shrubs that are grown there. This involves learning about soil, transplanting, potting, clipping, etc. The work is done outdoors or indoors, depending on the weather.

The foreman of this crew was a man who had some experience as a professional entertainer. For a period of time he sang with a group that achieved some degree of fame through its recordings and appearances on the entertainment circuit. The boys in his crew knew about him and, because they, too, enjoyed singing popular songs, group singing and harmonizing became one of the activities of the group at times when they were working where their singing would not interfere with the work being done by other people. Where he felt it appropriate the foreman allowed the boys to sing and often joined in with them.

Most of the boys in this crew, as in other crews, had no great liking for the remedial-education component of the program. Needless to say, their progress in the classroom was not comparable to their performance on the work site. They almost always were restless in the classroom setting and constantly were looking forward to the break between classes and for the educational program for that day to be over and done with. During the break they would often congregate in the halls and sing together. It was decided that this behavior was disruptive, and they were told not to sing in the halls. This being the case they often spent their breaks singing in the boys' lavatory.

The foreman, noting, as others did, the boys' apparent interest in singing and music, wondered why this was not perceived of as either a relevant classroom activity or as a vehicle by which the learning situation could be made more interesting or appealing to the youngsters. When he and others talked about this the focus quickly became an exploration of how the boys' interests in singing could be utilized to facilitate their learning of the three R's.

Through conferences with the teacher, who was not aware of the degree of ongoing interest the boys had in music, a plan was drawn up that would utilize this interest as a background for the presentation of educational materials. This involved changing both the focus and content of the classroom situation. Thus, for example, instead of reading "John and Jane Take a Trip to a Grocery Store," they would attempt to get materials related to popular music or the biographies of prominent people in the field of jazz music. Similarly, it was thought that mathematics might be taught in the context of the writing and reading of music, its different rhythms and beats (e.g., a whole note, a half note, a quarter note). In short, the attempt would be made, with the foreman now functioning in the classroom as another teacher, to utilize a particular area of interest as the vehicle for presenting and teaching remedial educational material.

In the case presented above the ability and willingness of his boys to learn was perceived by the foreman as involving a restructuring of the classroom situation. The school's initial emphasis was on maintaining continuity and uniformity in the processes of teaching, but the foreman's major concern centered on maintaining continuity and uniformity in the youngsters' perception of their interests and the different settings in which they could be developed. He did not perceive his own interest in singing as necessarily antithetical to the goals of the remedial-education program, but rather as a level that could be utilized in making the learning situation more concrete and relevant. By being able to communicate this feeling to the youngsters on his crew as well as to the teacher in the remedial-education program, he was able to have a plan adopted that had a greater probability of success than the one previously in use.

Because all the work crews include both Negro and white youngsters, problems of race relations and being able to get along with others have already been placed in the context of an ongoing group process. For some of the boys and girls, however, the situation is one in which they are forced to examine their feelings in very concrete and specific ways. The youngsters are often faced with situations in which their past experiences, attitudes, and self-images markedly affect their ability and willingness to function in the work-crew setting. The foremen and foreladies are well aware that for some of the youngsters this involves a self-confrontation with implications extending far beyond the work-crew situation. Their awareness stems from the fact that they themselves, as members of minority groups, have had to deal with the same kinds of problems in their working experiences. By utilizing the work site as a practical learning experience, and their own relationships with the youngsters as the basis for communication, the work-crew foremen are in a position to deal with questions of race relations in a concrete and day-to-day fashion. The lessons in living they teach to the youngsters are not perceived as emanating from an alien and unknown quantity, but as coming from someone who has been, is, and always will be a person who, by virtue of his birth and experience, cannot help being concerned with the same kinds of problems that confront the youngsters.

Example 12. Dolores was a 17-year-old Negro girl who had recently moved to New Haven after spending all of her previous life in a southern community. Although she had graduated from a Negro high school she had been unable to find the kind of work she wanted to do. Because Dolores wanted to explore the possibilities of becoming a practical nurse, she was placed on a work crew receiving nurse's aide training at a local convalescent home for the aged. The work at the convalescent home involved helping nurses care for the needs of elderly, chronically hospitalized people who were, for the most part, bed-ridden and unable to care for themselves.

For a long time after joining the crew—a crew composed of both Negro and white girls whose forelady was a Negro woman born in the South, who had come to the New Haven area in her late teens—Dolores was a different worker, but a girl who consistently kept to herself and was extremely quiet and rather remote. After a while, however, she seemed to begin to feel more comfortable on the crew and began to interact with some of the other girls and the forelady. Her increased interactions were largely confined to the other Negro girls and Dolores maintained her silence and isolation whenever the crew met as a whole to discuss problems that had arisen on the work site.

Some time later, having gotten to know the forelady better, Dolores began questioning her about the work crew. What seemed to amaze Dolores most of all was the fact that a Negro woman was in charge of a crew composed of both Negro and white girls. The more they discussed this and other related problems, the more the forelady began to understand the nature of Dolores' behavior around white people and some of the attitudes she held about herself. Dolores did not seem to be able to talk about these feelings directly but made them fairly explicit in terms of her behavior. Her quiet hostility toward the white girls inevitably led to her being excluded from their conversations and girl-talk, conversations in which the other Negro girls participated. Dolores, in turn, would always react to this exclusion by interpreting it as a rejection of her because she was Negro, rather than because she had made it amply clear that she was uninterested in joining the group. It appeared as though Dolores, because of her past experiences, approached each situation with antennae primed to perceive any and all stimuli that would lead her to believe people were reacting to her unfavorably because she was Negro. By so approaching each situation, she was actually creating the conditions under which her being rejected became an event with a very high probability of occurrence. It was an unhappy but self-fulfilling prophecy. The forelady understood this because it was an attitude and a behavior pattern with which she had all too often come in contact. In a matter-of-fact manner she discussed this with Dolores and ended by telling her that 'The white kids aren't keeping you out because you're

a Negro; they're keeping you out because you're acting like a creep."
Dolores thought about this, rejected the idea, and stormed away.

A few days later Dolores got into some difficulty while working at the
convalescent home. She was asked to give one of the bed-ridden patients
a massage. The patient was an old Italian woman who was well-known for
her temper and the choice of words she used when angry and upset. Dolores
reluctantly accepted her assignment and went into the patient's room. A
little while later all those present in the corridor were treated to a great
deal of shouting, much of it involving a healthy dose of the language used
by the old woman when she was particularly enraged. As everyone hurried
to the room Dolores emerged and ran down the hall. She was fuming. The
forelady went after her and caught up with her near the end of the
corridor. She now was crying and was extremely overwrought. She related
to the forelady how she had gone into the room and had started giving the
patient a massage when the woman suddenly started cursing her and
screaming at her. When the forelady inquired why Dolores felt the woman
had gotten upset, Dolores shrugged her shoulders and said, "Because she
doesn't like us Negroes and hates me." Dolores was put on another assignment and everything soon calmed down. The forelady then went in to see
the patient. The old woman was still angry and upset, but able to speak
to the forelady. She told the forelady how "this girl came in the room and
began rubbing me like I was a piece of wood. No young bitch is going to
do that to me and I don't care who knows about it." The forelady left and
sent a different girl in to finish the patient's massage.

After the day's work the forelady called a meeting of the crew to discuss
the day's events. The discussion centered around Dolores' run-in with the
old woman. Because of the way in which these meetings were handled,
Dolores had to tell the crew her view of what had transpired and she told
them very much the same story that she previously told the forelady. The
forelady then related what the old woman had told her immediately after
the flare-up. Many of the girls began laughing when they heard what the
patient had told the forelady and the manner in which she had told
her. They each, in turn, began to relate their own personal experiences with
the old woman. They all agreed the woman was a "tough patient" who was
very easy to anger, had a whiplash tongue, and was cranky, irritating, but
"a fun old lady." Dolores felt that everyone was siding with the old woman
against her. At that point one of the other Negro girls began talking about
Dolores' view that the old woman "had it in for her" because Dolores was
Negro. She indicated that the patient "had it in for everyone because she's
just that way about everybody." The others agreed and went on to
illustrate the ways in which they tolerated and humored the old woman.
Eventually the girls got around to asking Dolores if she really had man-
handled the patient. Dolores finally began talking about her feelings
concerning her taking care of white people and her feelings about the white
girls in the group. The forelady let the discussion go on, knowing that
Dolores finally was beginning to talk about some of the things that had

been bothering her for a long, long time. This was to be the first of many group discussions concerning problems of race and the feelings the girls had about each other and themselves.

The example described above is not unique on the work crews. It occurs in varying forms and in differing degrees. What sets this example apart from those that might arise in other contexts is the willingness—indeed, almost the need—of the foremen and foreladies to deal with some of the problems of human life that are usually either avoided or dealt with in a manner that does not facilitate interpersonal communication and understanding. The foreman's concern with these issues is not of recent origin and the youngsters know this. His feelings and attitudes cannot be dismissed easily as coming from an outsider who has never really experienced the difficulties of minority-group membership.

In many of the cases we have described—cases that depict the characteristic ways in which the foremen and foreladies function on the work crews—the reader may be aware of the often "nonpsychological" orientation utilized by the work-crew leaders in their interactions with the youngsters. It is clearly nonpsychological only in terms of the terminology utilized (or not utilized) in conceptualizing a problem and in the actions often taken to cope with the problem.

But by "nonpsychological orientation" we might also refer to that spontaneous response characteristic, essentially unsullied by formal psychological training, that is so much a part of the arsenal of weapons the foreman uses in his day-to-day encounters with the youngsters. It seems to be an important characteristic in the sense that it frees the foremen from the often-inhibiting effect that excessive metatheoretical speculation has on the ability to intervene directly and actively in the life of another. This is not to say that the foreman acts impetuously or that he does not reflect on the bases and consequences of his acts. However, by using the work setting as his "therapeutic level," the foreman is able to act and react in what appears to the youngster to be a more specific and concrete manner, a manner more readily understood on an immediate basis. From an exclusively theoretical perspective the foreman may consequently commit discrete acts, which we may term "invalid" or "wrong," but this does not inevitably mean that they are not helpful in the broader sense of the term. Most important is the fact that his acts take place in the context of a relationship that is constantly developing and essentially helpful. It therefore becomes a matter of pragmatic concern for us carefully to differentiate between what we mean by "valid" or "true" and what we mean by "helpful" and "useful." From this point of view the foreman's behavior with a work-crew youngster and what a therapist might do with a client in the more traditional psychotherapeutic setting are much more alike than they are dissimilar.

In describing the foremen and foreladies as "naturals" we have made reference to the fact that not every individual could function in the different ways and different settings in which the foreman is able to function. It takes a particular kind of person, with a particular view of himself and others, to be able to be helpful to youngsters on whom most other people have given up. We could point to the foreman's lack of formal training and supervised preparation as one of the variables accounting for his willingness to engage those whom others have variously termed "incorrigible," "irredeemable," or "lost." This is not to suggest that the more formal kind of psychological training inevitably leads to a reluctance to work with the kinds of problems manifested by inner-city youths. However, the training received may prepare the professional to deal with these problems in a setting which, although he may feel most comfortable, may not be the most appropriate for him to be of maximum help. The foreman's ability to be helpful appears, to a degree, to be dependent on his intimate awareness and knowledge of the inner-city setting and the inner-city youngster. Much of this knowledge is predicated on years of involvement and experience with the inner city.

Chapter 19

The Consultant

In much the same manner as the term "foreman" was only a shorthand way to describe the diverse functions of the work-crew leader, the term "consultant" does little to define the nature and content of our interactions with the work-crew leaders. The term may be most useful if we employ it as a means of describing to the reader some of the differences and similarities between our view of clinical functioning and the more traditional conceptions of clinical practice in use today. The ultimate importance of such a distinction resides in the implications that each of these points of view has for the development, maintenance, and effectiveness of the helping relationship.

Generally speaking, an agency's decision to seek the help of a consultant and their conception of the content of the help that they will accept are based on several conditions. One of these conditions is the agency's awareness that it is confronted with a problem it feels it cannot deal effectively with in terms of its existing personnel. Because this is the case, the agency, already having determined the general area of concern, seeks out the individual or individuals whose knowledge it deems will be helpful in solving the problem. What the agency expects—and rightfully so—is that the expert who is selected will be able to offer the kind of advice and help that is appropriate to the particular case. The decision to employ this consultant in the future is then predicated on the agency's view of the nature and degree of help it has received. From the consultant's point of view the situation is perceived in very much the same way. His advice and counsel in respect to a particular case has been requested, and he will do the best he can to utilize his knowledge, training, and professional experience in a manner that will be helpful to both the client and the agency. Both the consultant and the agency perceive the consultant's role in terms of the specific and discrete needs of a particular case and the matching of these needs with the professional competence of an expert.

493

The relationship between the consultant and the agency is a formal, circumscribed one, and is characterized by definitions of each other's areas of responsibility and competence that have been mutually agreed on. Both the consultant and the agency agree that the consultant is a visitor to the agency and that he will deal with a particular problem the agency has brought to him. The decision to accept or reject the consultant's suggestions is ultimately a matter of agency concern and policy. The consultant is not perceived by the agency, nor by himself, as an integral part of the agency; and it is expected that he will confine himself solely to those problems that have been brought to him.

Our concern with the role of the consultant as described above involves the degree to which it facilitates or impedes the clinician's ability to be of maximum help once the community (schools, public and private agencies) becomes the major focus of his work. Under those conditions it would appear to be extremely important that he know both the community and the nature of the agency. It is important that he be perceived as an integral part of the organization and not as a periodic visitor or invited guest. In short his ability to be helpful to clients and his effectiveness within the organization depend to a large extent on his willingness to perceive himself and others in ways that he had not previously, and to function in settings that previously had been foreign soil to the traditionally oriented consultant.

We have viewed the question of our working relationship with the CPI work-crew foremen and foreladies as another instance of the more general phenomenon referred to previously as the port-of-entry problem. In this context it is essentially the same question we were confronted with when we began our involvements with the public schools, the Neighborhood Employment Centers, and the New Haven Regional Center. In each case we were concerned with the general problem of how we, members of the discipline of clinical psychology, could enter into and become effective, accepted, and trusted coworkers with members of other disciplines, occupations, and organizations. In each setting our desire to be helpful had to be predicated on a more than casual awareness of the personnel, structure, and traditions of the organization or institution. In each case our effectiveness depended largely on the degree of mutual respect, trust, and cooperation that developed as a function of the nature and content of our ongoing involvement with the agency.

The decision that made it possible for us to begin to work with the foremen was an administrative one and was arrived at by those individuals who were in policy-making positions at CPI. This in itself was an important phenomenon in the sense that it reflected an attitude taken by CPI which was in great part influenced by the nature of earlier experience with other members of our Clinic staff. Before our involvement with the work-crew foremen, other members of the Clinic staff had been functioning for some time in the NECs that had been set up in various inner-city neighborhoods of New Haven. Their mode of functioning at the NEC disposition meetings served to create the climate whereby the Psycho-Educational Clinic could be perceived by CPI in ways in which other professional, academic, and service-oriented institutions could not be perceived. We were trusted and respected as an agency that no longer could be viewed as an invited guest but, instead, as an integral part of the organization. This perception of the role of the Clinic in CPI affairs now made it possible for the administration to seriously consider ideas and suggestions concerning other areas of its functioning that it might not have entertained as long as those suggestions were perceived as coming from outsiders. The administrative decision to have us begin to work with the foremen clearly was made possible by CPI's altered view of the role of the Clinic in its operation, and it was a response to the suggestions and observations made by Clinic members already working in the NEC settings.

The conditions under which we began our work with the foremen and foreladies were atypical in many other respects, and it is important that we describe these conditions so the reader may have a better understanding of the background that played such an important part in determining the nature and content of our involvement with the work-crew program. In the first place the work-crew program was not floundering and we were not asked to become involved with it in the hope that we would bail it out. Nothing could be further from the truth. In point of fact the work-crew program was considered to be one of the most successful and helpful projects in CPI's domain. It already had been functioning for some time and had proved itself to be an exciting and dynamic program with tangible results from the points of view of CPI and the community at large. Clearly, these are not the usual conditions under which a consultant is brought into a program.

From our point of view the assumptions underlying our initial involvement in the work-crew program were founded on the position that the preventive aspects of clinical functioning were as important as its remedial aspects. As this was the case, the fact that the program was, for the most part, doing well was not accepted as the only criterion determining whether or not it was important for us to become involved with it. The focus of a preventive orientation is the anticipation of potential problem areas; and it necessitates the kind of action whose goal is to create the conditions under which to reduce the probability that future work of a remedial nature will be necessary. It was clear to those members of the Clinic already involved in the NEC that the work-crew program very well might run into problems in the near future. This feeling was based on observations concerning the rapid growth and proliferation of the work-crew program and the implications this development had for communication and the sharing of experiences among the foremen and between the foremen and their supervisors or other administrative personnel.

Lastly, it is important that it be understood that our decision to become involved in the work-crew program was not a decision made in response to a request for assistance on the part of the foremen and foreladies. Like the teachers in the schools, the foremen did not ask for our services, whether or not they felt individually the need for some kind of aid. The request was administrative, and the work-crew foremen were not consulted. Their lack of choice in the matter, coupled with the factors previously described, was an important consideration in determining how we were able to perceive, define, and carry out our role as consultant to the work-crew program. Perhaps the most important consequence of this understanding of the atypical conditions under which we became involved in the program was that it enabled us to become acutely aware of and sensitive to the attitudes with which we would initially be greeted by the work-crew foremen.

Our entry into the foremen's world was met initially by attitudes best described as "suspicious and deferential." Both attitudes were understandable and clearly related to the history of the work crews and the views held by the foremen toward personnel coming from the professional or academic community. In both instances the attitudes had a basis in reality and had to be dealt with before we could be perceived as the kinds of individuals who could be trusted and worked with in an ongoing and mutually beneficial manner.

The suspicion with which we were greeted was determined in part by the history of the growth of CPI in New Haven and by an awareness of the fact that, by and large, this growth had taken place in the absence of any significant participation by the academic and professional communities. The difference between "town and gown" was clear, and was evidenced by the general reluctance on the part of the academic and professional communities to become intimately involved in the initial growth and subsequent development of a community-action program. Although this point of view was not clearly applicable to the Psycho-Educational Clinic, we still were perceived within the context of an academic community that had failed to respond to the

previous calls for assistance made to them by the fledgling organization. Therefore it was not too difficult to understand the initial suspicion with which we were viewed when we first came onto the work
crews. Here were psychologists from an academic setting—the same
setting that initially had refused to commit itself to the CPI program
—coming to help what most of the foremen believed was an already
successful program.

However, as we have indicated, the foremen had no choice as to
whether or not we would be consultants to their program; thus a second attitude—that of an uncomfortable deference—soon manifested
itself. It became clear that if we were to be there, we would be there
solely as experts to whom troublesome youngsters would be referred.
In this sense we were viewed and responded to in essentially the same
ways that agencies relate to someone who has been invited into a setting to offer his expert advice and professional counsel to help them
deal with a particular problem. We have termed this an uncomfortable deference because the attitude served not only to limit and restrict
the definition of consultant, but also because it had as its goal the
maintenance of distance between ourselves and the foremen, and the
work-crew program as a whole. From our point of view the function of
this attitude was to accentuate the process whereby the foremen could
utilize the consultant or expert stereotype of the psychologist as a convenient vehicle to thwart or make more difficult the development of a
close working relationship. The essential variable in this process was to
be the systematic objectification of the intruder by limiting all interactions with him to those comprising his assumed area of competence.
Thus we found the foremen and foreladies isolating us from their
world by relating to us as the expert to whom troublesome youngsters
were to be referred for evaluation and/or treatment.

It was our feeling that as long as either of these attitudes existed it
would be impossible for us to function in the setting in the ways in
which we had hoped to be able to function and in the ways in which
the philosophy of our Clinic dictated we would have to function if we
were to be of maximum help both to the program and to ourselves.
Before we could be accepted and perceived as an integral part of the
program we had to convey our point of view to the foremen, by both
word and deed, and disconfirm many of the perceptions and expectations they harbored about us and about the professional community as
a whole.

We began, quite simply, by sharing this dilemma and our feelings
about it directly with the foremen and foreladies. We indicated what
we felt might be some of their attitudes and feelings toward us on

their learning of our inclusion in the program as consultants. By placing ourselves in their shoes, so to speak, we traced what we believed to be some of the bases for their feelings and attitudes towards us and utilized these feelings as the vehicle by which we could begin to talk about our ideas and expectations of each other. Because many of these feelings were so close to the surface, in a comparatively short time we were able to deal with many of the areas that had initially separated us. In this context we were able to start talking about many of the things which typified the "town and gown" difficulties as well as some of the problems the foremen felt they were confronted with when placed in the position of having to relate to a clinical psychologist.

In subsequent meetings with the foremen and foreladies we attempted to detail some of the ways in which we perceived ourselves and the role we hoped to play in the work-crew program. We told them of our desire to be of help to them in their work but also clearly informed them that we felt we had much to learn from them. As was the case in our work with the schools, we felt that we could be most helpful only if the helping relationship involved us in the ongoing learning process of becoming familiar with and intimately understanding the work-crew setting. We told them frankly that we were not sure of how helpful we could be to them and that we certainly were not there to tell them what to do or how to do it. Our basic concern was in getting to know the setting, the youngsters, and the foremen; whatever help we could be we hoped might be predicated on our becoming an integral part of the work-crew process. More than anything else we told them of our hope to be able to work *with the foremen* and not be perceived as people whose allegiance was to the organization or any of its administrative personnel.

Although we have summarized much of the content of our initial contacts with the foremen, the reader should be aware that these introductory meetings were spread over several weeks. During that period of time the amount of information-gathering that took place on both sides was extensive, to say the least. The foremen and foreladies were acutely interested in our backgrounds, with particular emphasis on the degree to which our knowledge and information came out of books as opposed to the experience of life. They were deeply concerned about the sources of our alleged expertise and this concern mirrored their own feelings of conflict and difficulty in relating to professional and academic people. These feelings were discussed freely and much of our time was spent in exploring the sources of our perceptions about each other.

Throughout this process several things became clear. The most important fact was our mutual experience of the possibility that we could, indeed, talk with each other, and that we did speak the same language. The longer we met and the more involved our discussions became, the more open and relaxed we felt with each other and the less time we spent discussing the differences and similarities between our backgrounds, experiences, and points of view. More and more time began to be spent discussing a second fact that soon emerged: that we were all deeply concerned and committed to the process of helping the youngsters in the work-crew program. The realization that we shared a common goal and that the path toward this goal was one that could involve a mutual learning experience was of primary importance in facilitating the development of a relationship characterized by mutual trust and respect.

In the context of our meetings, and in the hope that we might begin to become familiar with the work-crew setting, we began accompanying the foremen and their crews out to the work sites. This in itself proved to be important in the sense that the work-crew leaders quickly became aware that we were willing to function and learn in ways they had not anticipated. Our presence on the work sites enabled the foremen and foreladies to show us the kinds of things they were doing and the various projects in which their youngsters were involved. Similarly, it gave us a chance to begin to know many of the boys and girls on the crews and to become acquainted with some of the processes, traditions, and functions of the work-crews themselves. However, more than anything else our coming out to the work sites was perceived as an act of good faith, underlining the fact that there was some substance to our claims of desiring to become acutely aware of and involved in the culture of the work crews. Although the majority of our meetings occurred during the time that the youngsters were involved in the remedial-education component of the program, we were able to get together in several of the other settings (the NECs, the Conte Community School) that played important roles in the overall structure of the program. Each setting we were exposed to and in which we were able to begin to work served the function of providing both the foremen and ourselves with a unique and important learning experience. From our point of view each setting presented us with the opportunity of increasing the scope and degree of our understanding of the work-crew process. Our ability to develop and maintain a helping relationship was predicated on the information made available to us through this direct involvement in the program. The foremen, in turn, perceived our involvement—particularly the fact that our involvement was not a one-shot affair, that it was extended over time and encompassed several different settings—as an indication that we were prepared to function in the ways in which we had said we would like to function. Our words and acts were consistent with the point of view we had presented. We were there, indeed, to work with the foremen and to become as much a part of the program as possible. The port-of-entry problem, at least in this case, had been overcome; and in its place we were able to establish some of the conditions necessary for the development of a working relationship.

The longer we were involved in the work-crew program the clearer it became to us that there were two distinct yet intimately related areas in which we might be able to function in a manner helpful to the foremen and foreladies. The first of these areas involved working with the foremen with both individual and group problems that the foremen felt were adversely affecting the functioning of the work crews. Our primary concern in this area was not only remedial—in the sense that we would deal with problems that had already become apparent—but also preventive—in the sense that we would, on the basis of our knowledge and experience with the crews, attempt to anticipate and deal with areas of potential difficulty. The second of these areas involved the relationship between the foremen (and the work-crew program) and the rest of the CPI apparatus. Here our foci were understanding and working with the existing organizational structure of the agency and being in a position to comprehend the consequences that changes in this structure might have for the foremen and the work-crew program. Here, too, our orientation was basically preventive in nature. Each of these areas presented us with particular kinds of problems; and we attempt, in the following pages, to detail the nature and content of these problems and illustrate the ways in which we dealt with them.

WORKING WITH THE FOREMEN

In our previous discussion of the variables that seem to characterize the foremen as people, we focused much of our concern on the implications each of these variables had on their ability to utilize both themselves and the work setting as agents in the process of therapeutic change. Our major point was that the foremen, by offering themselves to the youngsters as adult role models in an interpersonal relationship, make available to the youngsters a kind of relationship that few of them have ever experienced previously in any continuous or consistent fashion. In this context the commitment, maturity, respect, and concern with which the foremen deal with the youngsters were viewed as important variables that, when combined with the over-all structure of the program, account for much of the behavioral and attitudinal changes observed in the work-crew youngsters.

However, as is often the case in any complex human interaction, those variables that often account for the most dramatic kinds of positive change can also harbor the seeds of potential difficulty. All of us have experienced in different ways the mixed blessing of being in a position to influence and alter the lives of others in significant ways. Our own professional training and experience have indicated the importance that the timing of an intervention and an acute awareness of the means-ends nature of our interactions with clients have on our ability to be helpful in specific situations. In much the same way the qualities of commitment, maturity, respect, and concern are double-edged variables in the therapeutic process. In each instance a fine line exists between the point at which the particular variable facilitates changes that are felt to be therapeutic and the point at which it impedes progress and exacerbates those conditions that are not deemed to be helpful. Thus the quality of commitment may at times result in the perpetuation of a kind of dependency that does not facilitate the development of independence and autonomy. Concern may have much the same result if that concern leads to an overidentification with "the other" to the point where perception and reflection are obscured and impede progress. Similarly, maturity can become an issue when it involves a conflict of values, and respect may bring with it the potential to tolerate behavior that is both repetitive and self-defeating. In each case these variables that define the structure of the interpersonal relationship can result in behaviors that are helpful or harmful, depending on the manner and context in which they are utilized. The major issue involves the degree to which each variable facilitates or impedes our awareness of the nature of the means-ends relationship and our ability to intervene or act at any point in the therapeutic process. This is as true for the foremen and foreladies as it is for anyone else engaged in the helping relationship.

With this in mind we have been meeting with the foremen and foreladies on a regular basis during the time when the youngsters are involved in the remedial-education component of the program. Our meetings have been both individual and group in nature, the focus being to discuss and deal with the particular interpersonal and group problems originating or manifesting themselves on the work crews.

The goal in working with any client in a therapeutic relationship is to help that individual prepare himself for the time when he can leave us and begin to function in an efficient and independent manner. As this is the case—regardless of the theoretical rationale underlying the choice of the particular techniques to be employed in the treatment—the focus is always the eventual termination of the relationship. This same focus is the over-all goal of a youngster's tenure on the work crews. Here it is hoped that after a period of time the youngster will be able to leave the work-crew setting and to begin to participate in a variety of programs for which it is felt the work-crew experience has prepared him. These programs include OJT direct placement, the Job Corps, and various other possibilities.

Because of the nature of these expectations the problem of termination is one that must occupy a good deal of the foreman's attention from the time a youngster enters his work crew. However, as we have already pointed out, the work-crew process is an extremely involved and intense experience for many of the youngsters and foremen in the program. It makes available to many of the boys and girls a relationship never possible in the past, and one that is very difficult to terminate. Consequently, the closer the time comes for a youngster to leave the more likely it is that the foremen will be confronted with behavior patterns that are difficult to understand and cope with in terms of the progress that has been made up to that point. But the problem of separation anxiety is one the foreman must deal with, and the way in which he handles it often determines the degree of success a youngster experiences once he leaves the work-crew setting.

Example 1. Walter, an 18-year-old boy, came into the work-crew program after he had dropped out of high school and "just hung around" for a year. Because he had expressed an interest in woodworking he was placed on a crew that spent much of its time developing skills involved in carpenter's work.

For a long time after his entry onto the crew, Walter was a reticent and angry boy. He would trust no one, least of all his foreman. He often would report late for work and do little else on the work site except what was absolutely required of him. In short his initial attitudes and behaviors were not strikingly different from those observed in several of the youngsters when they first entered the program.

With the passage of time Walter's attitudes and performance on the crew began to change in slow but noticeable ways. He began to show up on time with much greater regularity and began to interact with the other members of his crew. At this point the foreman, feeling that Walter was beginning to "get hooked" on the work-crew process, began talking with him about his earlier behavior on the crew. Their conversations soon took them into many different areas of Walter's past experiences and his hopes for the future. Walter became very close with his foreman and told him of his desire to be a carpenter or to work in a carpenter-like setting.

After having been on the crew for about eight months Walter was made the foreman's assistant. He was put in charge of handing out the work assignments for the day and supervising some of the work that had to be done. Walter had come to be respected by most of the boys on the crew and his own behavior toward them had undergone a dramatic change. He now was not only a fully integrated and involved member of the work crew, but also was viewed as a talented and competent worker who was capable of both teaching and leading other youngsters in their work.

It was at this point that an OJT opening occurred which required a boy with some background in woodworking who was willing to be trained as a carpenter's assistant. The job opportunity seemed tailor-made for Walter. It would give him a chance to earn more money per week and at the same time it would provide him with the training necessary to further his own vocational objectives. The foreman told Walter about the OJT possibility and the boy seemed delighted by the entire idea. He spoke enthusiastically about his prospects and said he was ready to leave that day. This, however, was not possible because the job called for him to start in two weeks.

A few days after the conversation between the foreman and Walter concerning the OJT placement a change seemed to occur in the youngster. He suddenly began to show up late for work and seemed to be less and less concerned with both his duties as assistant foreman and his work on the crew. As the time of his leaving the crew for the OJT assignment drew nearer Walter's behavior more and more began to resemble the behavior he had shown during the first few months he had been on the crew. He began to withdraw and become strangely silent and distant from the foreman. His work had almost completely disintegrated and he started to talk about the fact that he really might not want to be a carpenter after all.

The foreman was quite concerned about this turnabout in Walter's attitude and behavior, and he began to wonder about the wisdom of letting Walter take the OJT placement that had become available. We got together and spoke about the kinds of changes that occurred and the different ways in which we could understand these changes. Much of our time was spent discussing the different ways in which Walter was trying to prove to the foreman that he was not ready for a job and, even more important, how he seemed to be telling us that he might be afraid to leave the work-crew setting. We talked of how, at times, it appears as if "we do our work too well" and make the youngster so dependent on the work crew that he feels that if he leaves the setting he automatically and permanently severs all ties with the other boys on the crew and with his foreman.

The foreman sat Walter down and spoke to him about many of the things we had discussed in our attempt to understand his behavior. He asked Walter how he felt about the OJT opportunity and the youngster, after some attempts to avoid the question, responded by telling the foreman that: "If I had my way I'd screw the job and just work here for twenty dollars a week." The foreman countered by reviewing with Walter the changes that had occurred in him from the time he had come onto the crew until the present, and how a good part of this change accounted for the fact that he, rather than any other boy, had been recommended for the OJT placement. He went on to indicate clearly his intention not to let Walter use his OJT placement as a way of cutting himself off from all the people he knew at CPI; he said that he expected him to keep in touch in very specific and concrete ways. Walter reacted to all that the foreman said as if the foreman had anticipated some of the things that he was feeling. The longer they spoke the easier it became for Walter to talk about his own feelings with respect to leaving the crew and the foreman. He had, indeed, conceived of his departure as signaling the end of what had been for him a most gratifying and therapeutic experience. He was through with his recent behavior trying to delay or postpone his "graduation" from the program. Once he was able to talk about his ideas and feelings about the situation, and once he knew that by leaving the program he was not entirely losing his foreman, Walter was capable of accepting the OJT program for which he had been recommended.

The day of Walter's departure arrived. Before the foreman allowed him to leave he worked out a schedule with the youngster in which arrangements were made for Walter and the foreman to get together at specific times during the week. After a period of time in which Walter had been functioning on his OJT setting the foreman had Walter over to dinner at his house and used the occasion, among other things, to continue their discussion of Walter's social, as well as vocational progress. Gradually the frequency with which the foreman and Walter got together decreased as Walter became more and more involved in his new program of training. Walter started telephoning the foreman on a weekly and then a biweekly basis. Eventually even these calls decreased. His adjustment to the OJT program was relatively successful and he was offered permanent employment on termination of his training period. Walter's last call to his former foreman was utilized to convey that message.

The phenomenon of "testing behavior" is a frequent occurrence on the work crews. It is behavior that usually occurs during the period when a youngster is new on the work crew and it is characterized by a series of acts in which the boy or girl seems to be testing the limits to which antisocial behavior will be tolerated. However, there is more involved than the mere experimentation with authority. This kind of behavior is very often another way in which the youngster makes manifest his intent to act in the ways in which he has come to view himself. It is behavior in which what we have called the "self-fulfilling prophecy" of an individual's essential irredeemability is actualized. What better affirmation of this self-image can there be than the youngster's elimination from the program?

From the foreman's point of view the difficulty in dealing with this behavior stems from several factors. In the first place the behavior itself is dramatic, disruptive, and often frightening. It occurs at times and in ways that make it difficult to deal with it in anything but a reactive manner. Secondly, the intensity of the behavior has immediate consequences in terms of the functioning of the entire work crew. When it occurs it often disrupts the group process and serves to jeopardize the crew's immediate goals and objectives.

Our focus in working with the foremen around this problem is to help free them from being placed in the unenviable position of having to react to this behavior in ways that are similar to the behavior itself. Because only a part of the testing behavior has as its goal a confrontation with the foreman, our work involves the attempt to understand some of the other purposes this behavior might serve. In this context we are often able to step back with the foreman from the immediate implications of the behavior and view it in terms of what it tells us about the youngster's feelings about himself and others.

Example 2. James, a 19-year-old Negro youngster, entered the work-crew program shortly after his arrival in New Haven from the South. He had lived his entire life in various southern communities until the time his family relocated in New England. James was a tall and extremely heavy youngster who, when angry or annoyed, either physically lashed out at people or succeeded in frightening them half to death by the way he stared at them. At other times he could be a completely engaging and charming boy with a uniquely warm sense of humor.

When James first came onto his work crew he made it evident that he was someone who should be feared because of his unpredictable and frightening behavior. He also made it amply clear that he had no particular use for his "white boss," the foreman. James went about his business in such a way as to prove literally both of these assertions. The proof was in his behavior both on and off the work crew.

During this time James almost continually taunted his foreman and many of the other boys on the crew. His provocative behavior often led to fights or cursing battles with those who happened to be around him when he got angry about something. More often than not these flare-ups occurred during the remedial-education component of the program when all the crews were gathered and when his behavior could be observed by youngsters and foremen who were not directly involved with him.

Because of the serious consequences of his behavior, and because it upset many other people, James was always on the verge of being either suspended or expelled from the program. The foreman tried various ways of controlling or dealing with James' provocative and frightening behavior. He would kid James about it but found that James could not be humored by his "bossman." He would threaten James with exclusion from the program only to find himself confronted with a smile and a statement to the effect that James "could not care less."

The more we talked with the foreman about James the more we realized that by cajoling and threatening James we were only playing into his hands. Either course of action appeared self-defeating. By cajoling him we were only admitting that we were frightened of him and his behavior. By threatening him we were merely bringing to fruition what appeared to be the goal of his testing behavior.

What became obvious was the fact that James *wanted* and *expected* to be thrown out of the program. By observing him in class we saw the obvious delight he took both in taunting or disrupting the teacher and in eventually being asked to leave the class. His fights and arguments with the other youngsters were an obvious invitation to exclusion. Everyone was reacting to James by apparently doing the very things James wanted them to do.

We then talked with the foreman about some of the reasons that might account for James' behavior and what it told us about his ideas about himself. Aside from the fact that his behavior always brought attention to himself, it also appeared as if it were designed to indicate how out of place he was in a situation that was both interracial and remedial. Even more important was our feeling that if we allowed James to force us to remove him from the program we would be helping him perpetuate feelings about himself as an inferior, inadequate, and incompetent person. We felt it was important to confront James with exactly these ideas that we had about him and the nature of his behavior.

The foreman sat down with James and talked with him about the ways in which he felt he was using the work-crew program to reinforce further his own ideas and feelings about himself. The foreman told James he could not go along with him simply because he did not feel that way about the youngster. He emphasized that he knew how important this behavior was for James and that yet it would not change things. The foreman complimented James on the apparent success of his plan but went on to tell him that this behavior, because it did not frighten him, could not impel him to kick James off the crew. The only way James could escape from his "white boss" would be to graduate from the crew and get ready for a job.

James reacted to all this with obvious concern, some amazement, and what appeared to be a good deal of relief. For a short time thereafter he continued his provocative and disruptive behavior. But each time the foreman dealt with it by calmly telling James that he knew what James was up to and "how tough it must be to face the fact that people might like you." James' provocative behavior gradually diminished in both intensity and duration. The less prevalent it became the more James began relying on his humor as an attention-getting device; and because of the engaging character his humor had it served to bring people closer to him and to bring him closer to other people.

Coupled with the eventual extinction of most of James' assaultive and alienating behavior was his greater involvement in the work aspects of the program. He became a competent, albeit uneven, worker. More important, however, was the fact that James began talking with the foreman about his feelings about himself in relation to his ideas concerning Negroes and whites. The closer James became to his foreman, the more able he was to use the foreman as a sounding board for feelings he had rarely shared with anyone, much less a white man.

During the ensuing weeks James' performance and behavior on the crew was stabilized and no longer created difficulties for himself or others. When the Job Corps became available the foreman recommended him for the program. According to later reports he had adjusted successfully to the Job Corps and was doing well.

The achievement of adulthood and the development of a realistic sexual identity are universal problems confronting all adolescents. The work-crew youngsters are no different from any other boys and girls in their need to evolve and identify with a relevant adult role model. For many of the work-crew youngsters the foremen and fore-ladies are the people to whom the boys and girls turn in the hope that they will provide them with a meaningful conception of adulthood. However, the process of developing a relevant image of adulthood is significantly influenced by the criteria of maturity which, on the basis of past experiences, the youngster brings with him on his quest. For many of the work-crew youngsters the criteria for adulthood have been erected on foundations that are limiting and often self-defeating. The more circumscribed the youngster's concept of what it is to be an adult, the more difficult it is for the work-crew leader to provide the kinds of experiences that will be helpful to the youngster.

For many of the boys in the program the areas of physical strength and domination have attained the status of being the most important aspects of a meaningful masculine identity. As it is one of the only concrete yardsticks of masculinity available to them, its achievement often becomes the sine qua non of malehood on the work crews. Because of its isolation from other equally important but unavailable aspects of adulthood, undue pressure is often placed on the foreman to respond in terms of this limited definition of the adult male role. As this is the case, the focus of some of our work with the foremen must involve the search for alternate ways in which the youngsters can become aware of the various and different aspects of maturity that combine to form a more meaningful picture of the adult male.

Example 3. The amount of time spent doing actual work on each work site varies with the foreman's judgment of what has to be done and his perception of the general atmosphere pervading the crew on a particular day. Although a certain amount of specified work needs to be accomplished it is up to the foreman to determine how and when that work can best be done. If, for example, the crew is working particularly well on a given day the foreman may decide that his youngsters have earned an additional period of respite in which they may participate in other kinds of activities of a leisure nature. He may also shorten a work day if, for some reason or other, he feels that something is interfering with the boys' ability and willingness to work. The kinds of things the boys do on the crew if they are not working is a matter the foreman and the youngsters often decide together. Because of the youngsters' interests in sports and other physical activities they often use these periodic breaks to kid, horse around, or play different games with the foreman.

Shep, an 18-year-old boy, seemed to take his breaks very seriously. He would look forward to the times when the crew was allowed to kid around with the foreman in a variety of ways. The foreman of Shep's crew was a man who also enjoyed these periods and saw them as a way in which his boys could let off a good deal of steam and get rid of some of their extra energy. He, too, was a man of considerable size and strength who enjoyed athletics and he often used the breaks to improvise different kinds of sports and games.

As time went on Shep began taking the lead in terms of suggesting the kinds of things the crew might do during its break time. He invariably wanted to use the time to wrestle and rough-house with the other boys on the crew and, particularly, the foreman. The foreman and the boys often consented to Shep's wishes and the boys would have wrestling matches with each other, with the over-all winner "meeting the foreman." Shep, himself an extremely strong and agile boy, often would beat the other boys and gleefully would challenge to "take on the old man."

Despite Shep's obvious physical superiority over the other youngsters, the foreman was an extremely powerful and knowledgeable wrestler and so was always able to pin Shep or make the boy give up. After each of these bouts Shep would become somewhat sullen and quiet, vowing "to get the old man" the next time around.

Shep's behavior continued to become more and more provocative. The thought of beating his foreman in wrestling began to appear obsessional and it occupied more and more of his time and behavior both on and off the work site. Not only would he constantly challenge the foreman on the work site, but he would also use the remedial-education setting as a place to taunt and try to bully him. The foreman, in turn, became quite concerned about Shep's behavior. He began to feel threatened by it and viewed it as Shep's attempt to dominate and take over the crew. His only recourse was to make sure that whenever they wrestled he would win, and in that manner maintain his control of the crew and the respect of the other youngsters.

Because the situation did not seem to be getting any better, and in view of the fact that we also had seen the disruptive quality of Shep's behavior toward the work-crew leader, we began meeting with the foreman to discuss Shep's pattern of relating to the foreman. What bothered the foreman most was that, despite Shep's aggressive behavior, he suspected the boy had a great deal of affection for him. We spoke with the foreman of how important it appeared to Shep to be able to conquer the foreman and what this potential conquest might mean for the boy. The foreman knew much of Shep's background and informed us that the boy had often spoken to him of how his father had beaten him and other members of his family. The more we discussed the matter the more we both felt that physical conquest had much to do with Shep's notion of what it meant to be a man, and that his current relationship with the foreman—independent of its symbolic intrapsychic meaning—was a way in which Shep was testing his manhood in a situation that was relatively safe. We also felt that the singular manner in which Shep was defining masculinity on the work crew in the long run was not going to be particularly helpful in enabling the boy to develop a meaningful and well-differentiated model of the adult male role.

The next time the work crew took one of its breaks Shep, as usual, wanted to wrestle. Although most of the other boys seemed to have had enough of that kind of horseplay they consented to follow the pattern established by Shep. When it came time for Shep to wrestle with his foreman, the boy vowed to finally pin him. They wrestled and the foreman, after something of a struggle, allowed him to win. Shep was beside himself with joy although, as he later admitted, he didn't think the foreman was trying as hard as he usually did. When the wrestling was over the foreman went over to the boy and asked him if his win really made him feel like a big man. The boy answered that it did and the foreman proceeded to talk with him about some of the other ways in which Shep could prove his manhood and maturity. Both Shep and his foreman decided that it might be a good idea to have a group discussion about what everyone thought manhood involved. At this discussion the foreman, after eliciting some of the boys' ideas, spoke of responsibility, respect, and concern as some of the other attributes of a man who has really grown up. He tied these abstract notions to the kinds of behaviors that typified maturity on the crew; behaviors such as punctuality, doing a day's work for a day's pay, and being able to deal with boredom, repetition, and many of the other things that characterize the work setting.

The discussion started that day led to subsequent meetings in which the boys began to talk in greater depth about many of their ideas and feelings about masculinity and the male role. As for Shep, his tormenting and antagonistic behavior soon subsided. Without ever actually talking about some of the reasons behind his previous behavior, the behavior itself became less and less a part of his activities on the work crew.

As we have already pointed out, members of the Clinic staff function in several of the different settings that comprise CPI's activities in the inner-city area. Our being in these settings often makes it possible for us to have information concerning a youngster which has been accumulated from many different sources, and to use this information as a basis for establishing individually oriented programs within the context of the work-crew setting. However, even if this information does not lead to the development of a particular kind of work-crew emphasis with respect to a specific youngster, it does enable us to discuss a youngster's problem with the foreman *before* the youngster ever comes onto the work crew. From the foreman's point of view this information can be helpful in preparing him to deal with some of the areas that might become a problem in working with the youngster.

However, as we have already indicated, the wealth of information concerning a youngster often affords us the opportunity of trying to do things that are generally unavailable to a clinical setting that functions in a traditional manner. One example is the establishment of a work-therapy program whose processes and goals involve different individuals who are in a position to coordinate their efforts closely and to collaborate continually with each other on an almost daily basis. The therapeutic effects of such an arrangement with a youngster are difficult to gauge at this point, but it is certainly an arrangement that is made more feasible when the participants in the program have access to and observations on the different settings involved in the therapeutic process. It therefore becomes a program in which individual therapy is not perceived, either by the youngster or the counselor, as an hourly event divorced from other significant areas in which the youngster functions.

Example 4. Della's entrance into the work-crew program was preceded by a meeting almost unprecedented in terms of the number and variety of agencies that were represented and participated in the discussion. All of these agencies (CPI, The Visiting Nurses Association, city welfare, family service, juvenile court, social service, Elm Haven Concerted Services, Aid To Dependent Children, homemaking service, and a host of individuals representing the medical and psychiatric professions) had, in one degree or another, been involved with Della and/or her family. As each agency related the content of its involvement it became increasingly clear that Della had for a long time been shopping around and pitting one agency against another in terms of the nature of the services she expected and wanted from each of the resources available. This was important information in view of the fact that Della was now involved with CPI to the extent that she was asking for admittance to the work-crew program.

Della was described as a pretty, charming, and bright 17-year-old girl who had a way of manipulating many situations to fit her purposes. Thus after giving birth to an illegitimate child she had been able to get the VNA to take over a major role in caring for the child although she was quite capable of doing so. Social service and family service related a similar tale in which Della appeared to have been able to intimidate the family in such a way as to free herself from all responsibilities in the home. Her ability to do this was related to the manner in which she utilized whatever psychiatric and psychological evaluations had been done on her to frighten her family into excessive indulgence of her behavior. The lever she used to achieve these ends was an equivocal diagnosis of organic epilepsy made at a time when she developed seizures in school. Subsequent psychological work-ups raised the possibility that these periodic seizures were related to situations in which Della, via her seizures, could manipulate a series of events and extricate herself from potentially difficult situations.

Although the agencies realized the success with which Della had used them in ways they did not like to see themselves being used, the consensus was that Della was, indeed, an emotionally unstable youngster in need of immediate help. Part of this feeling was based on the realization that the lengths to which Della had gone to manipulate others might be taken as an indication of the degree of anger and resentment she felt about herself and others. Although she was frightened of and had refused psychiatric treatment she used the threat of again becoming pregnant as a means of obtaining whatever agency support she could get. The general consensus of those present was that the opportunity of finally getting together and of sharing information had been important in getting a more complete picture of the girl. The decision was made to coordinate all agency contacts with Della through her participation in the work-crew program. More important, however, a plan was evolved whereby Della's being given what she wanted, namely, participation in the work-crew program now would be made conditional on her adherence to and responsibility for a program in which several people were collaborating closely. Our role in the program was to coordinate and keep open the channels of communication between those people actively involved in the treatment process. We functioned in the following manner:

We met with the forelady and counselor who had been assigned the task of taking major responsibility for Della's program. The over-all plan of the program was severalfold. First, Della's involvement in the work-crew program was to be made contingent on her accepting an ongoing counseling relationship with one of the CPI counselors. Second, the forelady and the counselor would be in constant communication about Della and the things she was doing both on the work site and in the counseling sessions. Third, the counselor would make weekly visits to the work-crew site to observe how Della was functioning. Finally, Della would be informed, from the very beginning, of the reasons for this unique arrangement and the means by which it would be implemented and evaluated. The rest of our meeting was devoted to a detailed discussion of Della, her history, and the kinds of ways she might try to manipulate even this situation. In this context we spoke of how the forelady might deal with the possibility of Della actually having a seizure on the work crew, or how she might handle Della's initial hostility to the work-crew leader and the other youngsters.

A meeting was then arranged between the forelady, the counselor, Della, and ourselves. At this meeting the plan and the reasoning behind the plan were explained to Della. She was made acutely aware of the fact that each of the people present would be intimately and continually involved in sharing their ongoing impressions and observations about her. We informed Della of our wish to be of help, but that this help now would necessitate her own participation in the over-all program. Della was both furious and frightened by the prospects of the program. She was also somewhat overwhelmed by it and we spent a good deal of time repeating it for her and reassuring her. After a while Della calmed down and considered what action she might take. After giving it some thought she agreed to go along with it. She actually seemed somewhat relieved at the thought of finally having some direct structure and limit placed on her behavior. She left the meeting and began her involvement in the work-crew program in a somewhat hesitant but thoughtful manner.

Although there are currently 18 work crews in the program, no two crews are exactly alike. Over a period of time each work crew develops a "tone" all its own. Similarly, each work crew has a group history, process, and set of traditions unique to itself and not replicated in other crews with other foremen. The tradition or tone of a crew is dependent on several factors including the nature of the work it is involved in, the personality of its foreman, and the length of time the boys have been together. The process by which a work crew finally becomes a truly functioning and integrated unit occurs over a period of time, but it is a process that inevitably results in a work crew characterized by its own relatively stable expectations, responsibilities, and obligations. Once this has occurred life on the work crew becomes much less ambiguous and much more secure for those youngsters who have contributed to, and have been absorbed by, the group process.

However, as in any functioning social unit, the newcomer is at a distinct disadvantage. What is a haven of security for others is for him an arena of doubt. Before he can become a part of the group he must, if not accept, at least learn its traditions, values, and orientation. Depending on the nature of the group and the newcomer this learning process can be a period of time filled with loneliness and anxiety. The pride a group takes in its own distinctiveness often can lead to its own self-encapsulation and a guarding of itself from the potential impact of an outsider or intruder. When this occurs many of the long-range goals of the work-crew experience are undermined, and the old-timers as well as the newcomer inevitably suffer.

Because of the nature of our contact with the work crews we are often in a position to appreciate the distinctive and unique character of each crew without being so involved in the group process as to find it difficult to step back and appraise it in a more objective and detached manner. The foreman does not always have this luxury of time available to him for, as we have pointed out, his responsibilities and concerns are more than those existing in many other jobs. We, therefore, can serve a useful function by sharing with him some of our observations about the structure of his work crew and the implications of this structure for some of the youngsters who are encountering difficulty.

Example 5. The formation of a work crew is dependent on several conditions, including the selection of an appropriate foreman, the choice of a relevant work site, and the processing of a group of youngsters. As this is the case, several of the work crews were already functioning at the time we became involved in the program, whereas others came into existence subsequent to the time during which we began to function as consultants.

One of the work crews formed after our inclusion in the program was led by a particularly energetic and enthusiastic foreman. The dedication he brought with him to his crew was in no small measure the reason for its success. He was able, in a relatively short time, to instill a distinct spirit into his youngsters and to transform them from a group of reluctant individuals into an integrated and functioning unit. With the passage of time their relationship with the foreman became a warm and close one and was characterized by the number and variety of activities that they would partake in as a unit both on and off the work site. Soon the youngsters began referring to themselves as "Jim's boys" and the foreman viewed his crew as "my team."

As is inevitably the case, one of the original members of the group left the work crew. He was one of a number of boys comprising the first contingent of youngsters going to the Job Corps. His leaving the crew left room for one additional youngster, and, with the large group of boys waiting to become part of the program, this vacancy was soon filled.

The new member of the crew was a rather shy and retiring youngster. He was a boy who experienced himself as an inadequate, stupid, and timid person; and his style of dealing with these feelings was to withdraw and isolate himself from people until such time as he felt it safe enough to approach them hesitatingly in an indirect manner.

When the new boy entered the crew the foreman introduced him to the other boys and gave him a brief run-down of the crew's activities and responsibilities. He showed him the kinds of things the other boys were doing and told him to watch the others until he had a better idea of how the work was to be done. The foreman hoped that it would not take long before the new member became acclimated to his new surroundings.

The other boys on the crew, after going through the motions of introducing themselves to the new member of the group, paid him only cursory notice. He was not included in their private talks or plans and was clearly tolerated but nothing more. They went about their business as if nothing had happened to the crew. Although not openly hostile to the new boy they made it amply clear that he was a "substitute for the real cat who left the crew." The new member of the crew reacted by withdrawing more and more into the periphery of events. He eventually became mute and sullen but "kept his place" on the crew. The foreman was somewhat concerned about the boy's isolation but felt that the situation would change with the passage of time. Also, because the boy was not a behavior problem and did not cause trouble on the crew the foreman did not want to push the issue or make a mountain out of a molehill.

Things did not improve with the passage of time. The foreman then sat down with the boy to try to find out what was bothering him. By this time approximately two weeks had gone by since the new boy had entered the group and he reacted to the foreman's attempt to find out what was wrong with little more than a mute response. Shortly afterwards he began staying away from work for days at a time. Although this did not seem to bother the other members of the crew, it did bother the foreman and we began to talk about the situation.

In discussing the boy's problem with the foreman we focused our attention on two aspects of the situation. The first was the amazing success with which the foreman had been able to solidify his initial crew in such a short period of time. In this context what appeared to be most important was the enthusiasm with which the foreman approached his work and the kinds of things he was able to do with his energy and commitment. The foreman readily agreed with our observations and volunteered that part of his effort was due to his desire to prove himself to the other, more experienced foremen in the program and to be recognized as one of the group. He spoke of this in terms of his wanting to fit in with the other foremen. It quickly became apparent to the foreman that there was a parallel between his previous situation and the one that confronted the new boy when he was placed on the crew although they reacted to the situations in very different ways. We then were able to discuss a second aspect of the situation, that aspect involving the spirit that characterized his crew, how it came about, and why the other boys seemed to be defending it so vehemently against the new boy. In this manner we were able to discuss their apparent reluctance to let anyone not originally associated with the group have "a piece of the action" or to share what they had come to feel was the fruit of their labor.

The foreman confronted the remaining members of his crew with some of the things we had discussed. He went further, however, by pointing out some of the realities of life in terms of the new situations they would have to face once they left the crew. By giving them a chance to voice their feelings he was able to create the conditions under which they could finally talk about their ownership of the crew and how this was not a sharable property. The foreman then recounted their own histories on the crew and compared it with his own history as a foreman. The boys began to see his point and evidenced a good deal of guilt about their role in the situation. The foreman shared their guilt and told them his feelings and ideas about the matter. Together they evolved a plan on how to deal with the situation, not only in the present instance, but in future situations involving the entrance of a new member into the crew.

The next morning, because the new boy had not shown up for work, the foreman and the kids drove to his house on their way to the work site. They found the boy at home and literally dragged him out of bed, got him to get dressed, and made him come to work. The boy was, to say the least, surprised and overwhelmed by their behavior.

Once the crew arrived at its work site the foreman again brought up some of the questions that had been discussed the previous day. It was a discussion in which all the boys, even the new boy, talked about some of the ways they felt about the crew, the original member who had left, and the new boy who had entered. The foreman then assigned the new boy to one of the other members of the crew. It was to be his major responsibility to show the new boy the ropes, although it was understood that everyone was to be involved in the process. The newcomer was somewhat leery about the arrangement but agreed to give it a try.

The next few days were exciting both for the newcomer and the other boys on the crew. The new boy began to feel more and more a part of the work crew. He was included in all its activities and became significantly more relaxed and more verbal with the passage of time. For the other boys on the crew the experience was one in which they were being called on to help some one else in much the same fashion as they were originally helped by the foreman when they first came onto the crew. In a fairly short time the crew was once more a totally functioning unit. Once the foreman felt there was no longer a need for the kind of plan he had introduced he called another work-crew meeting. At this last session it was decided that when the situation arose involving the entrance of another new boy onto the crew it would be the current new boy's job to take the primary responsibility of seeing to it that the transition period was handled in a smooth and helpful manner.

Often our involvement with the work-crew leaders involves nothing more than giving the foremen and foreladies what might be called the authoritative support to do the kinds of things they really want to do but are hesitant about doing alone or before consultation. It is, nevertheless, an important function from two points of view. First, it provides the foreman with the opportunity of talking over with someone some of the things he feels should be done with a youngster. The foreman's involvement with a youngster often takes him into areas and situations somewhat removed from the work-crew setting, which usually involve the family or some agency that has had contact with the youngster. His willingness and ability to get involved in these different areas does not occur in the absence of some anxiety and doubt. It is completely understandable that these feelings should occur, for they are almost inevitably contingent on the responsible assumption of the helping relationship. The second function, then, of authoritative support is that it makes available to the foreman someone with whom he feels comfortable enough to share these realistic anxieties.

Being a foreman is, in many ways, like being a teacher. It can be a lonely kind of job, especially when it involves the foreman in areas in which the ground rules are unknown and in which he has had very little past experience. Having grown up in a particular neighborhood does not automatically make working in that neighborhood any easier than working in an unfamiliar setting. This is especially true when the foreman becomes involved in doing things he feels have been done traditionally by people in other professions and with other kinds of preparatory training. The fact that he often can do these things in ways that make him just as helpful, if not more so, as people with other kinds of backgrounds is of very little comfort to a foreman embarking on a task that, no matter how appropriate he feels his involvement may be, fills him with apprehension. The opportunity of having someone to talk with about these feelings often helps free the foreman to act in as helpful a manner as he possibly can.

Example 6. Skip was a 16-year-old boy who came into the work-crew program shortly after the death of his mother. His father had passed away when the youngster was four. Before his entrance into program it had been decided that Skip would live with the older of his two married sisters. Although Skip's initial weeks on the crew were characterized by his sadness and depression, he was able to develop a warm and close relationship with his foreman. Much of this was due to the foreman's ability to support Skip during this period of mourning.

Skip's depression did not diminish with the passage of time. He often came to work looking as if he had spent a sleepless night. On these days he would remain tense and withdrawn for the entire time on the crew. His work was inefficient and characterized by a good deal of daydreaming behavior. He rarely brought his lunch to work and never seemed to have enough money to buy lunch.

The foreman became more and more concerned about Skip and began to buy him lunch. After a few days Skip began to tell the foreman some of the reasons for his unhappiness. It appeared that from the time Skip moved in with his sister and her husband life had become a series of endless trials. He felt neither wanted nor accepted in his new home. The only reason he had been placed there was because it had been his dying mother's wish to have him live with his eldest sister who was childless. Because the two sisters had not been on speaking terms for some time the decision was made without discussion or consultation among the members of the family.

Skip told his foreman that his older sister had forbidden him to visit his other sister for the duration of the time he lived in her home. Skip did not like this sister and hated her husband. The feeling was entirely mutual. The youngster told the foreman that he had to sleep on a bed with no mattress in the kitchen, and that his brother-in-law took his weekly check as his payment for room and board. Skip went on to tell his foreman that he really wanted to live with his other sister and her family but that he was afraid to go and see her because of his brother-in-law's threats to "break him in half" if he ever found out about it.

That same day the foreman accompanied Skip home after work to see the situation for himself. He found it much as Skip had described. He saw the mattressless bed and was able to observe the negative quality of the family's interactions with the boy.

The foreman returned with Skip the next day and brought up the possibility that Skip might live with his other sister and her family. The sister said she would "like nothing better" but that she would not be seen in the same room with her sister and her sister's husband. Rather than inquire as to the reasons behind the animosity that existed between the sisters, the foreman was content with the knowledge that a transfer was possible.

We got together with the foreman because of his desire to discuss the circumstances surrounding Skip's living conditions and the possibility of changing them. The foreman felt that such a change was absolutely necessary, but he had some misgivings about acting as an intermediary between two warring factions in a family. He felt that the role he would have to play in order to effect the change was, to say the least, a difficult one and that it might be better done by someone who had more of a background in work that involved family relations. The foreman was particularly anxious because of the stakes involved and he felt that any mishandling of the case could result in dire consequences both for the boy and for his relationship with the youngster.

We shared the foreman's concern about Skip and agreed on the apparent necessity of changing his living conditions. We disagreed, however, with the foreman's feeling that he might not be the one best qualified to handle the transfer. In this context we shared with him our own periodic feelings of doubt and anxiety concerning the psychotherapeutic situation. We spoke of how the decision to intervene in the life of another human being was almost always fraught with anxiety and doubt, and of how the foreman—no less than anyone else involved in a helping relationship—was confronted with these decisions every day on his crew. It appeared to us that in the present situation the foreman was probably the best person to attempt to effect the change in Skip's living arrangements. He knew the situation and had a better understanding of the individuals involved than anyone else. Although we agreed with the foreman that there was always the chance of failure, we felt that his relationship with Skip was a large part of the reason for the problem being brought up in the first place.

The foreman handled the problem of Skip's transfer beautifully. He visited Skip's other sister and her husband and found, as Skip had said, that they would love to have the boy come and stay with them. Although they had younger children in the home they were more than happy to double them up in one room in order to provide Skip with a room of his own in the event that he came to live with them. They felt that whatever money Skip earned at CPI was his, although they felt—and Skip agreed—that he should contribute five dollars a week to the household. The foreman then visited the home where Skip was currently quartered and the people reaffirmed their desire to get Skip out of the house. The foreman did all this without ever mentioning the two parties involved and without ever putting them in the position of being in the same room with each other. When the day arrived for Skip to move from one household to the other it was the foreman who helped Skip transfer his belongings. The transfer was effected smoothly and quickly.

Skip's behavior on the crew showed immediate improvement. His depression quickly subsided and he showed up eager and ready to work each day. When he came to work in the morning he carried his lunch in a lunch box, a gift his new family had given him.

Most of the results of a foreman's day-in and day-out contacts with his youngsters are not immediately discernible. The changes that occur in a youngster take place over a period of time. This is true not only of his behavior but also of the specific work-crew goals of getting him a job, having him decide to go back to school, or sending him off to the Job Corps. By and large, the foreman's work with his boys is far from dramatic, and it is often difficult for him to perceive the immediate results of his labors. The less observable the changes in a youngster with the passage of time, the more frustrated the foreman can become, and the more he can begin to question his effectiveness in working with the youngster. This questioning of his effectiveness—a self-questioning essentially no different from the kind that occurs in other, clinical settings—often can influence the degree of involvement and motivation a foreman brings with him to the work-crew situation. It is difficult to maintain a high level of motivation when the pay-off or feedback, in concrete terms, is so comparatively small and so slow in coming.

Because of the conditions described above much of our work with the foreman and foreladies is supportive in nature. Our ability to function in this manner is predicated on the foreman's perception of us as people who can share with him the sum of the frustrations and difficulties inherent in almost any relatively long-term remedial or therapeutic situation. However, again our ability to be helpful, albeit in a supportive manner, is based on the fact that we can offer the foreman some perspective on a problem from which it is difficult for him to take distance. He is constantly on the front lines; we, most often, are not. What he often needs is someone to listen seriously to some of his gripes; gripes he does not want to share with his fellow foremen and which he feels he cannot share with the administration.

Example 7. Kirk was a 17-year-old boy who had been on the same work crew with the same foreman for about nine months. When he first came onto the crew he was a somewhat reticent and angry youngster who did not make friends easily and who quickly got into several fights. In a relatively short time, however, he developed a fairly close and stable relationship with his foreman. Although Kirk got along well with his foreman his relationships with the other boys on the crew showed no appreciable change. He was constantly challenging them both verbally and physically, and this provocative behavior often would lead to fights. His work was extremely poor, although his attendance was quite good.

As the months passed Kirk's behavior changed very, very slowly. Most of his assaultive behavior disappeared but he remained a fairly provocative young boy. Although he stopped fighting with his fists, his verbal barrages showed no signs of diminishing in either intensity or duration. His work became tolerable but remained well below the foreman's expectations.

When the Job Corps became available Kirk, despite his foreman's objections and cautioning, applied for membership. He was turned down because those on the evaluating committee did not feel he was ready for the experience. For a short while thereafter Kirk again became physically aggressive as he had been when he first joined the crew. Although he soon leveled off again, it was at this point that the foreman began to doubt his over-all effectiveness with the boy.

When we met with the foreman to discuss Kirk the foreman was quite depressed and pessimistic about the boy's future. He felt that he had tried just about everything with the boy but that the youngster was still unemployable and not appreciably different from the way he had been the first day he came into the crew, some nine months before. The foreman felt that all his work had been in vain and wondered about the wisdom of maintaining Kirk in the work-crew program. Even more important, he began questioning his own effectiveness as a work-crew foreman.

We agreed with much the foreman had to say about Kirk. Although we tried to point out some of the areas in which the boy had improved, we too felt that the changes in Kirk's behavior were not as discernible as those that had occurred in some of the other boys. We tried to place the discussion of Kirk in the context of comparing his nine months of participation on the work crew to his 17 years of life before entering the program.

We could well understand some of the foreman's feelings of depression. They were not unlike some of the feelings we had exprienced in clinical work and we shared these experiences with the foreman. The longer we spoke the more able the foreman was to understand the nature of his own depression and the manner in which it was influencing his evaluation of his abilities, independent of the situation involving Kirk.

One of the immediate goals of the work-crew program is to provide the youngsters with the conditions under which they can begin to *talk* about their problems and feelings rather than act them out in ways that are often antisocial and self-defeating. Although we view this as one of the primary aims of the group experience, it is certainly not one of the goals explicitly stated in any description of the work-crew program. Nevertheless, the foreman's ability to create the conditions of mutual trust and confidence are of paramount importance in making it possible for a youngster to verbalize, rather than act out, his difficulties. It is for this reason that we have worked continually with the foremen and foreladies in the area of the various ways in which they can foster this talking out of problems, be it in a one-to-one or group context.

However, once these conditions have been created, problems in communication still can occur. Once the youngsters feel comfortable enough to bring up many of the questions and feelings that they are conflicted about they often confront the foremen and foreladies with areas whose content is often avoided in most situations. This is particularly true when the boys and girls begin to talk about their attitudes, feelings, and concerns involving the area of sex. Often this area is brought up in the context of a youngster seeking the specific information that would help him answer some of the questions about sex that have been puzzling him. Under these conditions there are generally few problems involved. Most of the time the foremen and foreladies handle their youngsters' questions by using the questions as vehicles for setting up a learning situation that is both concrete and relevant to the needs and interests of their boys and girls. If the foreman does not know a specific answer he often joins the youngsters in an answer-gathering adventure that may take the crew into situations (e.g., the library) that are fairly new and unexplored areas of life for many of them.

Sometimes, however, the questions asked are not informational ones. They may be questions of opinion, of right and wrong; questions that are often a matter of the foreman's values, attitudes, and ideas concerning the area of sex. Although we may view the problem of sex as essentially no different from any other value-laden area of life, the work-crew leaders may experience the problem differently and hesitate to impose their values—values that are acknowledged to vary from individual to individual—on the youngsters. The areas of gray involved in questions of sex, religion, personal ethics, and their own unresolved conflicts, often make communication more difficult when a youngster is asking for specific advice and guidance. The conflicts and dilemmas created by these questions are often great enough to result in a kind of avoidance behavior that is helpful to neither the youngster nor the foreman.

Because we often meet with the foremen and foreladies as a group we have the opportunity to explore many of the issues that have led to breakdowns in the communicative process between the foremen and the youngsters on their work crews. Because these group meetings are weekly events we often have the chance to deal with these issues in an ongoing and developmental manner. Things do not have to be decided, one way or the other, in any one session. The sessions give the foremen and foreladies an opportunity to share their feelings and ideas about an area of common concern in a setting that is informal and nonevaluative. Regardless of their decision as to how to handle a problem, for example, of sex, their decision has at least been predicated on a relatively full and open interchange of ideas and feelings. This situation in and of itself is a helpful one, for foremen, no less than teachers in the school system, need the opportunity to sit down with their coworkers and discuss areas of mutual concern.

Example 8. During the course of one of our regular foreman's meetings one of the foremen lightheartedly brought up an incident that had occurred on his crew during the week. It involved one of his youngster's asking him how many women he had "put away" before he had gotten married. The foreman had admitted that he did not feel terribly comfortable answering the boy's question and had inquired as to what prompted the boy's curiosity. Since the question was originally asked at a time when the entire crew was together in one spot it soon involved all the other boys. The more they spoke about it the more involved the boys became in the topic of discussion. What soon emerged were a host of questions the boys had concerning the timing and morality of premarital and extramarital sexual intercourse. The foreman found himself in a personal quandary as to how, if at all, to answer the boys' questions.

Several of the other foremen and foreladies at the meeting reacted in very different ways. One of the foremen felt that the entire line of questioning was improper and out of place. His feeling was that questions of this nature were out of the foremen's area of responsibility and more properly left to the parents. Another foreman felt the questions were reasonable and should be answered directly. His feeling was that premarital and extramarital relations were basically wrong and that it was the foreman's duty to tell this to his kids. A third foreman felt that the question was a relevant one but disagreed in terms of what he felt was the second foreman's black and white views on the matter. One of the foreladies, after making her position known, felt that she had no right to dictate to her girls on a matter of personal morality. Another foreman did not want to make his views public but agreed that each kid had to work out his or her own system of morality.

The foremen and foreladies returned to the question at the next meeting. We asked them how the question of sex was basically different from any other area of concern that the youngsters brought up. Using this question as their point of departure the foremen and foreladies began discussing the various kinds of problems they had to deal with simply because they had not been dealt with at home or because the manner in which they had been handled by the parents had not proved particularly helpful to the youngster. These areas included aggression, trust, respect, responsibility, and a host of other matters involving values, ethics, and standards of a personal nature. The more they shared their ideas and experiences the more they came to feel that sex, like so many of the issues they dealt with on the crews, was a relevant part of their work.

At our next meeting the work-crew leaders began to talk about how to handle questions involving sex. Our role at this meeting was to coordinate and maintain the focus of the discussion. We suggested that the first step in dealing with these kinds of questions involved an appreciation of the fact that something motivates a youngster to bring the problem up in the first place and that the rapidity with which the other crew members pick up the problems might be a reflection of the fact that they too have concerns and feelings about it. The foremen then went on to point out several things. One of these was that the youngsters' asking them—as opposed to anyone else—these questions was an indication that the youngsters trusted them more than they did other people. Another variable brought up was the possibility that the youngsters were trying to find out what kinds of people the foremen really were and how closely they approached them in terms of their values and attitudes. The foremen and foreladies felt that these were all important variables to take into consideration when questions involving sex, or anything else for that matter, were brought up. They decided that because many of them had differing views on the matter it was only fair to label their views, at least as far as the youngsters were concerned, as opinions reflecting their own personal values and attitudes. In this manner they felt that they need not avoid the issue and yet could maintain their own personal commitment to a value system.

WORK WITH THE FOREMEN IN THE CONTEXT OF THE OVER-ALL STRUCTURE OF CPI

The reader is by now well aware that the foremen and the work-crew program comprise only a part of the total CPI program for the inner-city area. Events and changes that occur in other facets of CPI's program inevitably affect the organization and functioning of the work-crew program and, conversely, changes in the nature and content of the work-crew program have consequences for the other aspects of CPI's program.

This is not only true for the relationship between the work-crew program and the rest of CPI's activities; it is also true of the work-crew program itself. The work-crew program is not, by any means, a homogeneous structure. It is composed of two distinct yet interrelated parts: the work-crew and remedial-education components of the program. Even this does not describe adequately the degree of differentiation in the program. The host of individuals (foremen, foreladies, teacher, supervisors, and coordinators) who combine to form the program's personnel are, in one way or another, different kinds of people whose attitudes and behaviors affect those around them.

One of the advantages of being consultants, albeit in the relatively nontraditional manner we have described, is that it affords us the opportunity of viewing the work-crew program both in its own terms and in the context of its relationship to the processes and goals of the overall CPI program. The fact that we are not totally immersed, on a day-to-day basis, in any one aspect of the program makes available to us that luxury of time and uninvolvement so necessary if we are to gain a broader perspective of events. Our interactions with the foremen, coupled with the information and observations available to us from the other CPI settings in which we are involved, often enable us to form a more differentiated and objective picture of the important, though subtle, changes that occur in the program. These changes—or the absence of these changes—have consequences for both the personnel in the program and the program itself.

Because our focus in working with the foremen is preventive as well as remedial we view an important aspect of our functioning as involving the awareness and anticipation of potential areas of difficulty. These difficulties may arise in many different settings, but, because of the interrelated nature of the various aspects of CPI's program, they almost inevitably have consequences, in one way or another, for the work-crew program. Part of our function is to deal with them before they reach the point of becoming the kinds of problems that necessitate interventions of a remedial nature.

We are not always successful, to be sure, but our failures themselves constitute an important learning experience in that they help us to become more acutely aware of and sensitive to the traditions, dynamics, and processes that characterize the subcultures of community organizations. Because of the preventive aspects of our work with the foremen and the work-crew program we have had to become extremely sensitive to the often subtle changes that occur in individuals and organizations as they grow and develop in different ways. This growth and development produces changes not only in the setting, but also in the self-images, aspirations, and needs of the individuals who occupy that particular setting. The problems that this growth produces—problems of communication and organizational structure—are often not as readily apparent to someone who is caught up in these changes as they are to someone who is not. As neither foremen nor members of CPI's administrative staff we are often in a position to appreciate, and to deal with in a preventive manner, some of the consequences of changes for the work-crew program, its foremen, or other aspects of CPI's organization. This is what we refer to when we say that part of our function has as its focus the foremen and foreladies in the context of the over-all structure of CPI.

The fact that the supervised work experience and the remedial-education experience are both component parts of the same work-crew program does not automatically mean that they are experienced as such by the members who are predominantly involved in one or another of these two settings. Because the teachers and foremen in the program share, or should share, a concern for the welfare of their youngsters does not mean that they inevitably share an accurate understanding of each other's problems and difficulties in trying to help the youngsters in the program. The lack of meaningful contact between teachers and foremen can often result in the phenomenon of working at cross-purposes with respect to a particular youngster.

There are many reasons to believe that close cooperation and communication between foremen and teachers do not result inevitably from the fact that they are part of the same program. These reasons involve, among other things, the kinds of people they are, the differences in their backgrounds, and the structure and content of their interactions with the youngsters. With respect to these variables it may prove helpful to the reader if we briefly restate some of the facts in the situation. In the first place, there is a great difference in the amount of time the teachers and foremen spend with the kids in the program. The teachers see them only for about four and one-half hours during the week, whereas the foremen are with them for much longer periods. Second, the conditions under which the foremen and teachers interact with the youngsters are different. The foremen are with them in a much more loosely and informally structured situation than is the case in the classroom. Third, because of the conditions under which the youngsters originally came into the program (e.g., the fact that most of them are school dropouts), it is a reasonable inference that they have some very specific, usually negative feelings about the classroom situation, feelings they may not have, at least to the same degree, about the work setting. Finally, most of the foremen and foreladies are only high-school graduates and some have not completed even secondary-school education, but the teachers, on the other hand, are either in college or have already completed their college education. Some, in fact, are teaching in the program while pursuing postgraduate work. All these factors seem to mitigate against the assumption that teachers and foremen inevitably and immediately form a close working relationship.

However, there are other, more general, problems to consider, problems of which the above differences are only symptoms. They involve the amount of information that is lost or remains unavailable to both foremen and teachers as long as they are—whatever the reasons—unable to communicate with each other or share their experiences. The people who suffer most from this set of circumstances are not the foremen and teachers; they are the work-crew youngsters in the program. The conditions that contribute to the decrease of communication between personnel seem to reside in the insulation that grows between departments when their definitions of each of their functions become exclusive rights to be guarded and defended. The definitions inevitably become narrow and eventually result in the erection of minor kingdoms between which there is little communication or the sharing of experiences.

Example 9. From almost the first day we became involved in the work-crew program we were aware of the different ways in which the youngsters perceived and reacted to the work-crew and remedial-education components of the program. By and large whatever positive feelings they had towards their work-crew experiences were counterbalanced by their almost universally negative feelings toward the remedial-education program. It was not hard to become acutely aware of these differences because some behavior problem almost always occurred during the time in which the boys and girls were in their classes. The severity of these problems varied, but they almost always involved the necessity of a boy or girl being excluded from the classroom situation.

The problems created or exacerbated by the remedial-education program were general in nature. They affected the youngsters, the teachers, the supervisors, and the foremen.[1] The youngsters did not like the program for a variety of reasons. Some could not tolerate the classroom situation; others disliked the content of the material or the ways in which it was presented to them; and still other just plainly disliked the teachers. The teachers found teaching a difficult and extremely unrewarding task. They felt that they were spending more of their time dealing with behavior problems and policing their classrooms than in teaching the material. The foremen were upset because their youngsters' behavior problems were placing them in the position of acting in ways that were not helpful in maintaining the kind of relation-

---

[1] These problems are well depicted in the previous chapter in the narrative description of a particular boy's day on the work crew.

ship with the youngsters that they felt was, in the long run, therapeutic. The supervisors were unhappy because the almost daily outbursts were occupying more and more of their time and leaving them less time to deal with problems of planning and individual supervision.

There were many reasons for this lack of meaningful contact between foremen and teachers, and these reasons were explored at a number of our meetings with the foremen. In the first place, the foremen had many feelings about the value and content of the remedial-education component of the program, especially in terms of the attitudes with which it was being administered. They felt that the way in which the program was being administered was only recreating the kind of classroom situation the youngsters in the past had experienced as intolerable and with which they previously had been unable to cope. They also felt that the kinds of things they were being taught were essentially unrelated to the youngsters' interests, skills, and aspirations. The longer we met, however, the more the foremen began talking about some of the things that bothered them personally about the program, things that had little to do with the content of the program itself. The foremen were acutely aware of the educational gulf that separated them from the teachers. They had many feelings about the ways in which they were perceived by the teachers in general, and the coordinator of the remedial-education program in particular. Once the foremen were able to express these feelings it became easier to deal with them within the context of the group sessions.

We then were able to turn our attention to other variables in the situations. We began talking about the fact that neither the foremen nor the teachers had an adequate appreciation of the kinds of things the others actually did with the youngsters or, indeed, the different ideas they had about the nature of the youngsters' difficulties. The foremen knew little about the day-to-day problems the teachers faced and the teachers knew even less about problems the foremen were confronted with on the work sites. Although both might, in different contexts, be dealing with the same youngster, neither had an adequate understanding of the youngster's behavior in the two different situations.

The foremen thought that it would be helpful if the teachers were able to come out with them to the work sites to observe the kinds of things that were being done there. They felt that circumstances (the discipline problems involving the boys and girls in the classrooms) had forced them to begin functioning in the classrooms but that teachers had never had the opportunity of observing the youngsters on the work sites. They felt this might begin to help both the teachers and the youngsters. They also felt it might be mutually beneficial if the foremen and the teachers had an ongoing opportunity to compare their observations and ideas concerning the youngsters and the different aspects of the program.

The teachers were approached and presented with some of the ideas that had been discussed. They felt that some sort of communication would be helpful to them and they had many questions they would like to ask the work-crew foremen. The possibility also was brought up of the foremen actually helping the teachers to teach some of the material that they felt was relevant to the youngsters.

The format for a monthly meeting between foremen and teachers was then set up. Classes were to be suspended for one day at the end of each month. This time, was to be used by the foremen and teachers to meet as a group to discuss whatever problems they felt to be important in dealing with the youngsters in the work-crew program. It was hoped that the meeting also might serve as a means of getting the foremen and teachers closer together and of giving them a chance to get better acquainted with each other's mode of functioning.

Success, in much the same manner as failure, can lead to problems; and, as in the case of CPI, a social-action program can become the victim of its own accomplishments. This is especially true when the success of an organization mirrors the directions taken in domestic policy by the national government. Under these circumstances external pressures are brought to bear on the organization, not because it has failed in its goals, but because it has demonstrated its ability to attain them. This is particularly true when the organization suddenly finds itself in the position of having to fulfill an immediate and pressing need that emanates from Washington, and to fulfill this need in a limited amount of time. Under these crisis conditions actions occur in an atmosphere of tension and pressure; and though these actions may serve to fulfill the immediate requirements of the situation they may have long-range effects on the organization and its personnel which are not in its own best interests. The air of panic that grips an organization when it is called on to function without being given the time or the opportunity to plan an adequate and comprehensive mode of operating is difficult to describe. Things become chaotic and disorganized; feeling are hurt; and people who previously felt themselves to be important or needed suddenly find themselves to be expendable. However, once the crisis lifts the effects of the actions taken during the crisis situation linger on. What often remains is a problem between the organization and its personnel; a problem that has inherent in it many potential difficulties that could, if not dealt with, ultimately affect the agency's ability to function.

What we have described is a situation in which what happens to an organization as it responds to external pressures has consequences for individuals and programs that were in existence long before the crisis situation ever occurred. The work-crew foremen and the work-crew program fall into this category.

A great deal of the enthusiasm that the foremen brought with them to their work, as well as the commitment they felt for the work-crew program itself, was in no small measure a reflection of the enthusiasm and commitment communicated to them by those in the higher echelons of CPI's organization. They were perceived to be—and eventually experienced themselves to be—individuals with a unique and far-reaching responsibility in the CPI program. For many of the foremen and foreladies this was probably one of the first times in their professional lives that they experienced themselves to be in a position of social responsibility where their contribution to the welfare of others became a tangible and recognized commodity. As this is the case it is not difficult to understand the pride, commitment, and concern with which they approached their work.

The feelings that the foremen had about themselves and their work at CPI were built up over a period of time. These feelings, however, and the kinds of things these feelings enabled them to do on their work crews, are the variables most susceptible to change as a consequence of the organizational chaos that often accompanies a crisis situation. Part of our work, therefore, is predicated on an understanding of, and sensitivity to, these kinds of changes and the effects they have on the foremen and their work crews.

Example 10. The initial Job Corps selection and evaluation process was, in many ways, a very shattering and all-too-sobering experience for the work-crew foremen. The genesis of the problem was CPI's history of success as a community action program.

When the Job Corps ceased to be an idea and became a reality, CPI, in recognition of the work it had already accomplished in the community and because it already had the apparatus and the population necessary for selecting and providing candidates for the program, was chosen as one of the settings for the processing of Job Corps youngsters. Washington's needs were simple and clear-cut: CPI was to select, evaluate, and process the 20 youngsters who would comprise one of the first contingents of Job Corps candidates. What made life difficult was that this task had to be accomplished in a period of days so that initiation ceremonies and departure dates could take place as scheduled. During that brief period of a few days CPI focused most of its attention and personnel on the selection and processing of the youngsters. The work-crew program provided a ready source of potential candidates, so it was understood that most of the youngsters would come from its ranks.

A plan was quickly developed to accomplish the task that Washington had placed in CPI's hands. The foremen were to have a major role in the selection and processing procedures. Before a youngster could be evaluated several pieces of data were necessary. First, the youngster would have to want to join the Job Corps and his foreman would have to feel that he was ready for the experience. Second, before a youngster could be processed it was necessary to have some additional information such as a medical examination and police clearance. Third, the youngster would have to go before an evaluating board for a final determination of his eligibility and appropriateness for the program. Since it was realized that this could be an extremely anxious experience for a youngster, it was felt that his foreman should accompany him and remain with him during the board's evaluating procedure.

Because of the pressures of time very few aspects of the original plan were actually put into practice. The foremen were given the responsibility for getting the medical and police data. Consequently, they were removed from much of the evaluating process and could not accompany their youngsters on their appearances before the board. Similarly, whereas formerly the foremen were to recommend only those boys they felt were ready for the program, CPI's need to be sure that 20 appropriate youngsters would be available for the program forced the organization automatically to process almost all the youngsters in its work-crew program. Consequently, many youngsters were processed—and had their hopes raised—who could not possibly qualify for the program. The entire procedure was a hectic and uneven one, with people often duplicating each others' functions and working at cross-purposes. However, to the credit of everyone involved, the job was finished, and finished on time.

Despite the fact that the selection and evaluation process was completed the foremen were left with a legacy of bewilderment, disappointment, and disillusionment. These feelings resulted from their experience of having been divorced and isolated from the process of selecting and evaluating the youngsters for the program. Although, and particularly because some of their own youngsters were the candidates, they neither were consulted or included in the evaluation procedures.

Aside from their own feelings about the matter, the manner in which things had been handled left both them and the work-crew program with a host of problems. First, because many boys were processed who could not qualify for the program, the foremen were faced with the problem of having to deal with the feelings of disappointment that a large number of youngsters would have, feelings the foremen felt could have been avoided. Second, the general exclusion of the foremen from the selection procedure left them with a minimal amount of information regarding the reasons for the acceptance or rejection of their youngsters. Unable to determine these specific reasons, the foremen felt themselves ill-prepared to deal with the feelings of the youngsters who did not qualify. Finally, the psychological implications of the foremens' feelings of exclusion were difficult to estimate. Certainly they were hurt and upset, and these feelings persisted for some period of time.

As consultants to the work-crew program we had to work with the foremen's feelings as well as help them to deal with their youngsters' feelings. We felt that their experiences of what had happened were not only important in the present situation, but that they had implications for their functioning in the future. Consequently, we felt it important that the administrative and supervisory staff of CPI be acutely aware of what had happened and its implications for the organization. As this was the case, and as Job Corps evaluation procedures would occur at periodic intervals in the future, it seemed appropriate that we attempt to have the situation clarified and explained to the foremen as explicitly as possible.

Meetings then were set up between the foremen and those administrative and supervisory personnel who were in a position to explain and clarify the situation in terms of what had been planned as opposed to what had actually happened. At these meetings the foremen were made acutely aware of the variables which affected the initial Job Corps selection and evaluation process. They were "included in" on some of the problems CPI was confronted with and the reasons for the actions taken in response to these problems. Finally, the foremen once more were apprised of the role they would play in any future Job Corps selection procedures.

We already have touched on the fact that a good part of the reasons accounting for the foremen's involvement with, and ability to be helpful to, the youngsters in the program could be traced to their experience of CPI's direct involvement with and interest in them as foremen. Their willingness to extend themselves into the non-work-crew areas of their youngsters' lives could occur only if and when the foremen experienced this self-extension to involve behaviors and talents that others judged them to be capable of. Put another way, the foremen's orientation toward their work mirrored the orientation and philosophy that CPI adopted toward them. In its ideal form, CPI's attitude toward its own personnel should be essentially no different from, and indeed, completely consonant with, its aims and goals for the community it serves.

It is important for the reader to understand that, for the most part, this was a new experience for the foremen. Their previous working experiences were by and large very different in character, especially in terms of how they perceived and were perceived by the boss. Changes in attitudes come slowly. Consequently, one of our functions as consultants to the foremen involves us in the process of reinforcing the foremen's newly emerging feelings that the agency is often able and willing to support them in what they believe to be the legitimate scope of their responsibilities to the youngsters.

Example 11. A short time after the first contingent of youngsters left for the Job Corps the foremen and their supervisors began receiving letters of a disquieting nature from their former work-crew boys. Some of the boys were disillusioned and disappointed by the camps as they found them. Although they had been given an idea about what the Job Corps was (through speeches and films), they felt that there was a great difference between what they had expected and what they had found. These letters, written mostly to the foremen, created a great deal of concern about the likelihood that the boys would remain in the Job Corps and about the relationship between the way in which the program originally had been presented to them and their current difficulties.

Because of CPI's lack of direct information concerning the situation, the work-crew coordinator and supervisor paid a visit to the Job Corps camp. The camp was located on a mountain in Maryland. When they returned they shared their information and observations with the foremen. Although the manner in which they briefed the foremen was helpful, the foremen still felt the need to have more direct, firsthand information about the situation. Because of the varying nature of the accounts of the camp that had been written by the youngsters to their foremen, the consultant also felt the need for additional information.

The foremen planned to make a trip to the Job Corps camp. Without inquiring into the possibilities that the agency might finance their trip, they were prepared to pool their resources, jump into one of the foremen's cars and go down to Maryland to visit their former work-crew boys.

The consultant felt there was a legitimate reason and need for the foremen to make the trip to Maryland. He too wanted to see and evaluate the situation.

After discussing the matter with the foremen the consultant raised the question as to why they had not tried to determine if the organization itself would help to finance their trip. (Foremen do not earn a great deal of money, and the financial burden of a week-end trip to Maryland is not one they can easily bear.) As it turned out, the foremen never seriously entertained the possibility that they might be financed to make the trip. They felt that such trips were paid for only when made by the "higher-ups" in the organization. The consultant believed that this point of view reflected their lingering doubt about themselves, their role, and how they were perceived by the "higher-ups" in the organization. A frank and open discussion on the matter was held.

The foremen and the consultant made inquiries about the matter to those in administrative positions in CPI. Both the director of the organization and the coordinator of the work-crew program felt that the proposed foremen's trip was necessary and important. Arrangements were made quickly for CPI to assume complete financial responsibility for the trip. The director offered them his official CPI station wagon for the trip so that they would not have to use their own cars. Each foreman and the consultant were given adequate money for the trip.

On their return from Maryland the foremen felt that they had a much better understanding of the situation. They also felt quite good about the manner in which the organization had responded to their request for assistance. They were then asked to draw up a list of their observations and recommendations, a task they accepted wholeheartedly.

The youngsters served by CPI are not the only ones who change as a function of their association with the work-crew program. The foremen and foreladies also change, and change in dramatic and significant ways. Indeed, one of the most interesting aspects of our relationship with the foremen is the opportunity we have had of observing these changes.

Although individuals were originally hired to become foremen or foreladies largely on the basis of the coordinator's impression of the kinds of people they were, it is clear that despite whatever kinds of people they had been, many have changed as a function of being work-crew leaders. These changes have occurred over time, but they have occurred, nevertheless. The direction of these changes is of great interest and note, especially to those who view behavior as a function of the interaction between what an individual brings with him to a situation and the dynamics of the setting itself. As this is the case, a description of some of these changes and the reasons for them might prove helpful to the reader.

The kinds of changes that occurred—or, in some cases, the kinds of changes that did not occur—varied from foreman to foreman. Generically, however, the changes involved differences in the ways the foremen came to view themselves in terms of their talents, abilities, and potentials. These changes in the foremen's self-images or self-concepts were based on their concrete experiences of the kinds of things they were capable of accomplishing once they were accorded the responsibility and the respect that few of them ever had experienced in the past. Their growth as individuals was clearly a function, not only of the kinds of people they were, but of the ways in which they were perceived by others and the content of the responsibilities with which they were able to cope. It is difficult to minimize the changes that occur in an individual once he is placed in a situation or a setting whose dynamics, traditions, and goals facilitate behaviors that have enduring effects on his self-concept, self-image, and value system. When we say that many of the foremen "grew" as a function of being foremen within the CPI setting we mean that their views of themselves and their outlooks about the future changed. Many of the foremen no longer saw themselves as static individuals, but began experiencing themselves as people of specific worth, as people who had a future as well as a past, and as people who made a difference in the lives of those they came into contact with.

The basis for this often newly reawakened self-awareness of worth and importance in the foremen resided in the value system of that particular subculture, CPI, of which they became a part. In a sense, the foremen's identification with and assimilation of the traditions, goals and dynamics of the setting in which they worked played a large part in the changes that occurred in them as human beings. For some, as in the example below, the changes were clearly dramatic and almost immediately observable.

Example 12. While being interviewed for his job one of the potential foremen, after hearing about the kinds of youngsters he would be dealing with, felt compelled to share some of his feelings with the work-crew coordinator. Although he wanted the job he felt it would be only fair and honest to inform the coordinator about some of his prejudices about Negroes. He told his interviewer, in as frank a manner as possible, that he had not had many satisfactory relationships with Negroes, and that he rarely had wanted to associate with them or have much to do with them. He went on to tell the coordinator some of the ideas he had about Negro youngsters and what he felt they were and were not capable of doing or learning.

The work-crew coordinator was somewhat taken aback by the way in which the potential foreman was speaking and the things he was saying. What impressed him, however, was that the man was telling him these things in an attempt to be honest and forthright with him, and that he was not hiding his feelings in order to secure a job for himself. It was for these very reasons that the work-crew coordinator decided to hire him as a foreman.

The new foreman, after a short period of orientation, was given his own crew and placed out at the VA hospital. There were both Negro and white boys on his crew.

The foreman threw himself into his work with a great deal of energy. He viewed the job as a challenge and was determined to try to do all he could to help his youngsters. Much of his enthusiasm was generated initially by the things he saw the other foremen doing and the ways they felt about their jobs and their boys.

In a relatively short time the foreman's energy and dedication began to pay off. He had succeeded in establishing a close relationship with many of his youngsters and they were responding to this by beginning to shape up and become a well-functioning unit. The better the foreman got to know his boys the more their behavior (work attitudes and work habits) changed in a positive direction. This was true of both the Negro and white boys on the crew.

The foreman began seeing his boys as individuals, each of whom had his own particular problems, strengths, and weaknesses. Their behavior on the crew and their emergence as individuals in the eyes of the foreman were important variables in enabling him to change some of his own feelings and ideas about them. The longer he knew the boys and the closer he got to them the more differentiated his view of them became. In the process the foreman was forced to reexamine some of his own feelings, particularly those he originally had about Negro boys.

In the course of time the foreman's feelings and attitudes about Negroes underwent a significant change. The nature of his own relationships with his Negro youngsters was the cause of these changes. The entire experience was an extremely meaningful one for the foreman and he felt he wanted to share them with the work-crew coordinator. He did this and in the process was able to examine some of the bases for his original feelings about Negroes in a more objective manner. Similarly, he was able to talk about some of his experiences as a foreman that led him to change his feelings and ideas about Negroes.

Most of the time the changes that occur in the foremen become observable only over a longer period of time. There is something about being a foreman, perhaps something inherent in the helping relationship, that enables the individual to take stock of himself in ways that were heretofore almost impossible. Once this reappraisal occurs, and once the foreman is able to appreciate the kinds of things he is capable of doing, his feelings about himself and his potential change.

As consultants to the work-crew program, we are often acutely aware of these changes, for we have been in the position of watching them occur over a period of time. It becomes part of our function, then, to transmit these observations to those who are in a position to evaluate these changes and to use them in ways that are beneficial to the individual and the organization. When an individual changes— especially when that change involves personal growth and self-awareness—his aspirations change. Whereas he may have experienced himself in the past to be an individual with very limited talents and no future, he may now begin to perceive himself as a man with usable skills and definite potential, particularly with the CPI setting. Unless the administration is made aware of the wealth of talent—on many different levels—that it has available to it in terms of its existing personnel, that talent may never be recognized and used for the benefit of the individual or the agency. Consequently, we have used our roles as consultants to impress on the administration the wisdom of maintaining a policy of hiring and promoting from within whenever such action is appropriate. From the foremen's point of view the results of such a policy are that they become increasingly aware that they themselves are not in dead-end positions. We have also felt it appropriate to urge CPI to contemplate the advisability of broadening the experience and training of its current personnel so that, when possible, the market value of its own foremen increases as a function of their association with the organization. What this involves is a step on the part of CPI to acknowledge its ongoing interest in the development and future of its foremen. Even more important is the feeling that this creates in the foremen that they, as individuals, are as much a concern of the organization as are the youngsters with whom they are involved.

PROBLEMS OF GROWTH AND THE ROLE
OF THE CONSULTANT

When an organization grows as rapidly as CPI has grown, and especially when its growth is spurred by the domestic policy of the national government, an organization-personnel situation is created which has inherent in it many potential problems that ultimately may affect its functioning. This is true of all rapidly growing organizations, whether public or private in nature and whether they are primarily involved in production or service. Just as growth and expansion have their effects on the organization and its personnel, so too do they have consequences for its consultants.

It is important, at this point, that we again stress that our interest and concern about the effects of growth on an organization stem directly from the fact that we have not functioned as consultants in the traditional manner. We cannot view the internal and external changes that occur in the settings in which we are involved through the eyes of the disinterested observer. We have a definite stake in the organizations with which we are involved because our mode of functioning, no less than our personal and professional orientations themselves, has dictated that we become an integral part of the setting. As this is our position, and as we are fully aware of the dangers involved in such an orientation, we have been acutely aware of the importance of viewing from many different aspects the changes that have occurred in CPI as it has grown. One of these aspects concerns the effects of this growth on the organization itself and the consequences of this growth for the manner in which its personnel function. Another aspect is the implication that this growth has for the manner in which we function.

The changes that occur in an organization as it grows from infancy to adulthood have been described by different writers in different contexts. What most writers have agreed on is that an organization's growth often results in changes in the means-ends nature of its mode of functioning. Whereas at point *A* in time the predominant goal may have been to get the job done (the job being defined as whatever set of circumstances caused the organization to be founded in the first place), at point *B* in time there occurs a shift in emphasis toward the *process* by which that goal is accomplished. This shift in the means-ends relationship may or may not be a subtle one, but it appears to characterize some of the changes that occur in an organization as it grows, matures, and begins to consolidate and solidify its internal structure. Under this set of conditions, questions of procedure and a more structured definition of specific responsibilities become the more immediate focus of the organization's personnel. The rationale for this change in focus is understandable and, at times, essential. The larger an organization becomes and the more areas it becomes involved in, the less likely it is that its previous free-swinging orientation can be helpful in getting the job done. Similarly, the bigger an institution becomes the more difficult it is for people to maintain a closeness with the different settings in which they previously were intimately involved. Power must be delegated and areas of responsibility must be defined clearly. The missionary zeal and fervor of its personnel, though by no means eliminated or significantly diminished, must now be tempered and focused on the variables of internal organization and cohesiveness. In the process people inevitably become removed from the big picture and questions of personal advancement and mobility become more important than they might have been in the past. The atmosphere of the organization changes, and these changes in tone have consequences for the behavior and attitudes of the organization's personnel as well as the functions of those of us involved in the organization as consultants.

In essence then, growth is a mixed blessing for, if not properly channeled and understood, it actually may lead to a decrease in the organization's internal cohesiveness and result in a diminution of its effectiveness as a social agency concerned with human renewal. Perhaps the first symptom of such a process is that an individual begins to feel as though others in the organization no longer understand or have direct access to his problems and questions, or that the channels of communication previously available to him have become cluttered and limited.

In general terms the greatest problem of growth from the point of view of the foremen has been the gnawing experience that channels of communication have become constricted and that the organizational structure has become more rigid and essentially unyielding and unresponsive to their observations and suggestions. This feeling of being further and further removed from the dynamic process that originally set CPI apart from other community-action programs has specific consequences for the ways in which the foremen function and how they perceive themselves as individuals within the CPI complex. The most damaging consequence is that much of their original enthusiasm—founded on their being able to begin to perceive themselves differently than they had in the past—begins to wane and become muted. Under these conditions their job becomes just that, a job.

As consultants we, too, become affected by what growth produces in an organization. We can perceive the nature of whatever changes occur because we are involved in the setting in a manner in which we are confronted with these changes in terms of our own functioning and because of our relationship with the program as a whole. To some extent our function as consultants is to be acutely aware of these effects, in human terms, on the efficiency and self-image of the foremen and to continually communicate our observations to those in the organization who have the authority to alter this potentially irreversible and threatening situation. Often this may bring us into some conflict with those in positions of power. Questions of policy and the legitimate scope of our authority come into play. Our own positions in and relationships to the organization become questions of concern and doubt. Whatever the consequences, however, part of our role remains that of informing and communicating our observations of what growth and change implies for the functional efficiency and long-range goals of the organization as a community-action program.

Chapter 20

CPI: An Attempt at Evaluation

Any attempt to evaluate CPI must start from the recognition that it is' a relatively new type of community agency that in its very short life has undergone rapid growth and change and undoubtedly will continue to do so.[1] It is hard to anticipate the effects of ever-increasing federal legislation and financial support on the structure, scope, and atmosphere of such a community agency. Hungry social agencies, like hungry individuals, do not all respond similarly to sudden affluence. We are not partisans of the state of hunger, but we cannot be uncritical enthusiasts of the effects of success and/or affluence on agencies and individuals. By definition success refers to a past accomplishment and is no secure basis for predicting future achievements. The danger of success is that it can alter the perception of self and work so that judgment is seriously impaired, that is, the individual or agency may look back over time and see a continuous line of progress, oblivious to the fact that after their initial successes they became less and less consistent with their original purposes.

It is because CPI is a new type of community agency, the success or failure of which can have profound effects in the community, that an attempt at evaluation is necessary. However profound our respect for its past achievements and supportive of its present functioning and future goals, we cannot and should not avoid an attempt at a critical evaluation. This should not be taken to mean that what follows is critical in the sense of being only adverse and damning, but rather as an attempt to weigh the pros and cons, the possibilities and pitfalls, the hopes and the realities. We may anticipate what follows by stating that it is in the nature of a critical appreciation.

A note of caution to the reader is perhaps appropriate at this point

---

[1] By the time the manuscript for this book was completed the scope of CPI's program had increased markedly from the time we began writing. This kind of growth brings many problems and serves to emphasize some of the criticisms we make later in this chapter.

538

in order for him to avoid errors of overgeneralization about what we have said and will say about CPI. Essentially the caution is that CPI is most unusual in its accomplishments among community action programs; it is probably not representative of such programs and this should set limits on the applicability of our attempt at evaluation to other programs around the country. As Bebout has said in his foreword to Farrell's (1965) report on CPI:

This report should be an inspiration to people in many other communities, for the work of Community Progress, Inc., has already proved to be a model for community-action programs under the Economic Opportunity Act in many places. At the same time, it may give some readers a sense of frustration as they wonder just how many elements in the New Haven equation must be put together in order to achieve a similar result in another community. There can be no doubt that luck, purpose, and commitment, articulated and translated into action by dynamic local leadership, are essential. But let any citizen in another city who wonders how these local ingredients can be assembled ask how many people a generation ago would have picked New Haven as the city most likely to lead the country in the demonstration of the potential in both the physical and the economic and human aspects of urban renewal.

It may well be that CPI is sufficiently unusual so that whatever we have to say about its significance may, to an undetermined extent, be an overgeneralization.

THE DEMONSTRATED NEED

CPI was brought into existence because of a lack of attention to and adequate services for the inner-city population. It set out to develop new programs and services and, wherever possible, to stimulate existing agencies to change and expand their services to this population. It is fair to say that CPI set out to be a model of innovation and experimentation that older, more tradition-bound agencies could follow. These goals have been achieved. There are very few agencies whose organizations and programs have not changed because of CPI's existence. These changes have not always been gracious. Resistance is not only a characteristic of an individual. But CPI's persistence and successes were effective in dissolving much of this resistance and it did not take long before "everybody wanted to get into the act." At the beginning, CPI essentially went it alone. Today it probably looks with nostalgia at the past when outside forces of resistance strengthened it in the belief that it was on the right road. The schools, a host of state agencies, a variety of social agencies, psychiatric clinics, and other mental-health agencies, practically every city agency, and various parts of Yale University are related in one way or another to some CPI program.

That CPI had funds to initiate its own programs and to enable other agencies to expand and change their programs was certainly a factor contributing to its important role in the community. However, equally as important as its funds (which were far from adequate or unlimited) was the stimulant of CPI's own programs that provided concrete and visual evidence that new services were being provided in new ways to the inner-city population. This was the challenge that existing agencies could not avoid, however pessimistic they were about the permanence and success of the new ventures. If CPI's programs were in the nature of competition to existing agencies, it is likely that it would have accomplished little even with more money at its disposal. But the fact was—and this came to be recognized—that CPI was in its own programs providing services that were valuable additions to the resources of the community. Professional life in the community has not been the same and there are very few who would deny that much of the change has been for the better.

In Chapter 1 we stated the opinion that CPI can be viewed as one of the first and most comprehensive community mental-health programs in the country even though it did not view itself in these terms and the traditions they connote. Aside from the fact that its target population represented a large part of the community, the basic aim of CPI was to influence and change the lives of people in whatever settings they were found: home, school, work, and neighborhood. That CPI chose the vocational area as its major means for changing lives represents an approach markedly different from that of the mental-health fields. In adopting this approach CPI has demonstrated several things that can have, or should have, a salutary effect on the thinking and practices of mental-health workers.

1. It has demonstrated the necessity of placing services where its target population lives, the first manifestation of the belief in adapting services to the needs and characteristics of those we wish to help.

2. It has shown the importance of actively recruiting and even pursuing those for whom we wish to provide service.

3. Although aware that unemployment or the lack of vocational skills are symptoms of personal and social factors, CPI has demonstrated that by attacking these symptoms it is possible to bring about a degree of vocational competence and changes in self-attitude that are stabilizing forces in the life of the individual. Put in another way, by

upgrading vocational competence it has upgraded personal and social competence.

4. In the case of the older adolescent (the work-crew type of boy) CPI has shown how the prevocational setting can be used for preventive and therapeutic purposes in addition to its manifest vocational aims.

To the mental-health worker it is, of course, no surprise that in implementing its programs (particularly the NEC and work-crew programs) CPI encountered the gamut of individual psychopathology. What should be the occasion of serious reflection among mental-health workers is that *CPI encountered and worked with these individuals long before they would ordinarily be encountered in the state hospital or outpatient clinic (in that small number of instances where they would find their way to a clinic)*. As important is the fact that a number of these individuals have been helped by the focus on the vocational area, and it is this fact that cannot be too strongly emphasized—a reminder that there are many ways and settings in which help can be meaningfully and effectively rendered. CPI is not a mental-health facility, but can there be any doubt that it is in the mental-health business? It may well be that the greatest contribution of CPI and other CPI-like organizations is that over time they will force the mental-health fields to review their past parochialism in thinking and action and take steps to change their training programs and modes of service. This is not to suggest that these fields should perform a kind of professional somersault but rather that they should confront themselves with two obvious facts: as presently constituted they reach a narrow segment of our population; and as they move out into the wider community they will have to devise new ways in new kinds of settings if they are to make a significant contribution.

THE CPI PROFESSIONAL

CPI is constantly under pressure to demonstrate the efficacy of its programs. This pressure, generated both from within and without CPI, has had some unfortunate consequences. At this point we wish to direct attention away from the effects of program on clients and direct it to what we call the "CPI professional." As we tried to make clear in previous chapters, CPI consists of people who, with relatively few exceptions, have never engaged in this kind of work before. This is obviously true in the case of work-crew foremen and neighborhood workers but it is only slightly less true in other CPI positions. Even where the title of the position (e.g., job developer, work-crew supervisor, director of manpower, community coordinator) suggests the need of past training, the fact is that these positions were developed in an agency that by its existence and goals would not or could not set great store on formal qualifications. It was implicit (perhaps explicit) in the thinking of those who started CPI that new ground is not to be broken by hiring those who ploughed and reploughed old ground. This is not to say that CPI disregarded previous training, but rather did not weight it highly. In any event, the great majority of those who work (or have worked) for CPI are discharging responsibilities quite in contrast to their previous work history.

It is no small contribution on the part of CPI to have demonstrated that there are many individuals who, despite little formal training and a modest degree of schooling, can be extremely effective in difficult face-to-face and group-management situations. CPI's belief that its staff could rise to the occasion, and the evidence that this belief was being in some measure successfully realized, were the foundations that allowed the staff to maintain the belief that *their* clients had more potentialities than appearances and formal background would suggest. CPI has done for many of its staff what the staff has done for many clients, that is, has made opportunities available and provided the necessary personal support to transform the lives of people. Transformations are not necessarily good in themselves but in the case of many of the CPI staff this transformation has had the following characteristics: a vast increase in knowledge about the community, a kind of newly found awareness that they had interpersonal skills that were in demand, and a sense of mission heretofore lacking in their lives. It is no exaggeration to say that by virtue of the opportunities provided them many of the staff now possess a degree and kind of experience that would enable them to move into positions of greater responsibility within CPI and in scores of similar agencies around the country. It has to be emphasized that before many of these individuals came to CPI their daily lives reflected little of the capacities and competencies they later demonstrated.

It is in the nature of things that, because monies are made available to help clients, there is the expectation that evaluation of the help should be defined in terms of changes in clients. This would be an incomplete evaluation in the case of CPI, because CPI had to achieve with its staff what it wanted its staff to achieve with the clients: to look beyond paper qualifications, degree of schooling, and outer appearances in judging the opportunities of which the clients might take advantage.

It has long been recognized that the number of mental-health workers is and will continue to be inadequate to meet existing problems, and that the mental-health fields will have to consider seriously how effectively to use the subprofessional individual in a more broad attack on the over-all problem. Frequently the term subprofessional is used to refer to a college-educated individual who either lacks any degree of professional training or a minimum of such training. The term has always referred to those who perform services only under the supervision of a fully trained person. The achievements of the work-crew foremen, neighborhood workers, and others in CPI are heartening evidence of how broadly the term subprofessional must be defined and how independently and effectively these individuals can function.

THE CLIENTS

The reader who is familiar with research on the effectiveness of psychotherapeutic techniques is agonizingly aware of how difficult it is to define or evaluate success or failure. Do we rely on what a patient says about how he feels, or what the therapist says? Should we evaluate the degree of change in light of the severity of the problem or the patient's condition at the beginning of therapy? How do we discern and evaluate a transient as opposed to a more sustained change? Should we evaluate change in terms of what the therapist hoped to accomplish? Is termination of treatment by the patient to be considered a failure even though there is reason to believe that some change took place, albeit a "flight into health"? Is the recurrence of problems after therapy an indication that the therapy was ineffective? These and other questions point up the methodological and theoretical problems that beset those who are concerned with the evaluation of the helping process. Anyone attempting to evaluate CPI's programs not only runs up against these problems, but others as well. For example, unlike the psychotherapist who brings to his cases a long period of training, CPI had to initiate new programs in new settings without much, if any, tradition on which to depend. In the several years of its existence CPI has been in a learning situation, but not a learning situation containing characteristics conducive to maximum effectiveness. The manner in which federal agencies develop programs and give financial support does not given an organization like CPI time to think, plan, or reflect. Support tends to be given for relatively brief periods of time with renewal depending not only on congressional actions but on the demonstration that the organization has been successful, an approach that too frequently results in emphasis on numbers, the meaning of which is either unclear, misleading, or irrelevant.[2]

[2] In no small measure some of CPI's problems and deficiences reflect certain

It also has to be borne in mind that CPI's own programs (as distinct from those carried out by other community agencies but with some CPI support) have required, as in the case of the NEC, working cooperation with other agencies, and having secured such cooperation, implementing it on an operational level. This has been far from easy. Regardless of the sources of difficulty, they did not work in favor of a high success rate, regardless of the criteria of success.

In short, even if we were clear about the criteria of evaluation, and assuming that there were funds and appropriate personnel, we might ask if such an evaluation would not be premature. But we do not raise this question with any intent of suggesting that an attack on the problem of evaluation be bypassed or postponed, but only to emphasize that any evaluation must be viewed in the context of a short history, the difficulties in pioneering, and, in the absence of traditions and previous experience, the need to forge traditions and programs.

Our role with CPI was in no sense a research one, although one of the major reasons we have worked with CPI is our research interest in the problem of introducing change into ongoing social systems. We saw ourselves in the role of learners as well as helpers. In the chapters devoted to CPI we have endeavored to describe the complexity of the human problems with which CPI is faced, the ways in which it is meeting them, and the personnel involved. Although these descriptions were necessary in order to make our role meaningful in certain CPI programs, they were perhaps more necessary to convey to the reader the fact that evaluation of these programs will be far from a simple matter. It is precisely because the CPI-type of agency is likely to be-

---

of the self-defeating characteristics associated with the governmental programs, for example, money *must* be spent before the end of the fiscal year; time for planning is viewed as a subversive thought or the unrealistic thinking of the academic mind; grants are usually made for no more than a year and frequently less than that; records must be kept that serve as a basis for grant renewal—the amount of needless paper work stupefying in extent and the administrative regulations developed in Washington often mystifying as to rationale and intent. These characteristics would be more tolerble if the problems to which they frequently give rise had consequences only for the CPI executive staff who are "pros" when it comes to working with governmental agencies. But their consequences inevitably affect all employees, creating uncertainty in them as well as anger, as we have seen firsthand on numerous occasions. Action programs should give rise to action, and the attack on social problems cannot be expected to wait until the appropriate research has been done. But when speed of action becomes an end in itself we run the risk of "problem creation through problem solution." It is our guess that CPI has not been as adversely affected as have other programs in other communities because of the merited faith of CPI employees that their executive director will find ways to protect them and their programs from "the people in Washington."

come a permanent part of the urban community that evaluation cannot be postponed. Its potential for service is too great to allow it to develop uninfluenced by careful and meaningful research.

We have in the previous pages expressed our obvious respect for what CPI stands for and what it has accomplished. In the pages that follow we endeavor to focus on certain aspects of CPI's organization, orientation, procedures, and relationships that have or can have a limiting effect on its ultimate contribution. Certain of these aspects stem from the defects of virtues, others seem to reflect a limitation in perspective, or a tendency to oversimplify and gloss over, while still other aspects are manifestations of a lack of help from parts of the community that potentially have much to offer to CPI. When an agency like CPI succeeds it is indulging superficiality to heap praise on it because, embedded as it is in the community, it cannot succeed solely by its own efforts. Similarly, when a CPI fails, we cannot blame it alone.

THE NEED TO BE CORRECT

There can be no doubt that the impact of CPI and the rapidity of its growth reflect the fact that its initiators were in positions or close to the sources of political power on the local, state, and federal levels. CPI represents an unusual blending of courage, farsightedness, and the power to act, a blending not present in other than a few community-action programs. When we consider the population to be served, the diverse social institutions (school, welfare agencies, private agencies, etc.) to be affected and changed, and the sources of funds, it was inevitable that CPI would have to work through or be related to vehicles of political action and power. To expect this to be otherwise when we are in the business of introducing meaningful change into a community requires a conception of the community which is divorced from the realities of community organization. In the case of CPI such an expectation was truly unrealistic when we consider that those who conceived of and initiated CPI were important political figures with a sense of social mission.

As soon as an agency becomes involved, even indirectly, in the political arena its presentation of its thinking and problems to the public tends to reflect the need to persuade and influence, a need that can result in glossing over of problems and keeping difficulties and failures hidden; it becomes necessary to present the agency as if it were moving inexorably ahead with a minimum of difficulty and a maximum of success. This tendency is understandable—there *are* adversaries waiting to gloat over failure and willing to preside over its demise—and is not peculiar to agencies involved in the political arena. *However, it is the tendency to gloss over problems and to inform incompletely that originally allowed the community to ignore the problems of the inner city and ultimately required that a CPI come into existence.* To the extent that CPI makes the same error, it helps perpetuate public ignorance of the severity of the problem and the fantastic complexity of required solutions (Hersey, 1964).

CPI does not have the funds to do other than a small fraction of what needs to be done or what it would like to do. But the problem is only secondarily a financial one. The problem is of a scope and complexity requiring thinking and rethinking, innovation and evaluation, community organization and social-agency reorganization, professional training and services, changes in attitudes and time perspective—and these are only part of what is involved in approaching the problems of the inner-city population. CPI is aware that what it is doing is far from adequate. It is also aware that its own programs are not unqualified successes and that its failures are not only because of inadequate resources but also because of limitations of staff, inadequate planning, various community resistances, and the consequences of the requirement to improvise and act quickly. However understandable CPI's public stance has been, it is our opinion that its need to appear correct and as an adequate answer to the enormity of the problem sets the stage for later public disillusionment by creating the impression that the war is about to be won. We have been struck time and again by how ill-informed the community is about what CPI is up against—the tendency on the part of the educated public to assume that what is being done is adequate to the problem.

It is perhaps unfair to ask CPI to assume the task of educating the community. Precisely because it is inevitably related to the sources of political action and power it is unrealistic to expect it to expose all of its problems to the public, there being a part of that public all too ready to use such materials for *its* political purposes.[3] But the problem

---

[3] The Cahns (1964) have written very cogently about the philosophical, psychological, and tactical implications of the relationships between war-on-poverty programs and the existing political and social agency structure. Their discussion stems from their experience with CPI but it has much more broad significances as the following quotation suggests:

". . . Comprehensive action programs, devised by professionals and accepted by the dominant social, political, educational, and economic institutions are simply a majority consensus on how to solve certain social problems. To date the silence of the poor has deprived us of a major relevant source of information and insight. We have paid for the lack of this information in other social experiments—public

remains: CPI exists because of the past failure of the community to recognize the scope of the problems of the inner city, and its ultimate success will depend in large part on how good a job it does in deepening public awareness of the enormity of the problems.

THE PROBLEM OF RESULTS

Related to the previous discussion is CPI's presentation of the results of its programs. For purposes of the present discussion we focus on the work-crew program, perhaps CPI's most distinctive and pioneering venture.

CPI's concern with, and interest in, the concrete results of its work-crew program are both understandable and debatable. As an agency involved in human renewal, social action, and hard-core rehabilitation, it is often under attack from sources in the community that do not share its philosophy, views, or objectives. At the same time it receives its funds and support from both public and private sources. Friend and foe alike have a stake in the concrete results achieved (or not achieved) by CPI. Both supporter and detractor want specific information made available to them for their own purposes and evaluations. This is as true for the results of the work-crew program as it is for every other program organized, conducted, or coordinated by CPI.

The information desired is clear and simple. They want to know, in specific numbers, how many work-crew youngsters received direct job placements, how many returned to school, how many entered the

---

housing, urban renewal, welfare programs—in large part because we have not taken steps to assure that the censorial power was effectively vested in the people who were the subjects of such experiments. Token approval, acquiescence, and resignation have been eagerly equated with meaningful citizen participation. In doing so, we, as a society, have deprived ourselves of the only form of validation yet devised for a majority consensus—critical scrutiny and dissent by those with a different perspective. The need to avail ourselves of the views of the poor and to promote and subsidize the articulation of their felt needs and grievances becomes all the more critical in the context of comprehensive planning and monopoly power, where the commitment of resources is greater, the sources of dissent more readily silenced, and the scope of potential error increased many fold. Thus, the civilian perspective requires that the promotion of neighborhood dissent and criticism be an avowed goal of the war on poverty, that its organizational structure make provision for the establishment of groups and institutions with the independence, power, and express purpose of articulating grievances, that the natural incentives to absorb, stifle, or undermine dissenters be countered with the creation of incentives to nurture, promote, and heed criticism, and that the elimination of poverty be understood as comprehending spiritual as well as physical subsistence and as involving the assurance of civic as well as economic self-sufficiency."

intermediate work training program, how many have been sent out on on-the-job-training positions, how many have quit the program, how many are in jail, and so on. Although motivated by different interests, each interested party wants to know the same kinds of things, and to know these things in numbers. The significance.of these criteria can be seriously questioned. For example, returning to school may in a particular case represent a step that gives the individual another opportunity of which he can make productive use. In another case the return to school may be of dubious significance and can lead to another series of failures reinforcing a variety of crippling self-attitudes. In some instances placement on a job has had far from a stabilizing effect on the individual because he was not ready, or because it simply was not a good job, or because of a host of personal and interpersonal considerations. Moving a boy from a work crew to the intermediate work-crew program may not represent progress so much as a means of holding a difficult youngster by giving him a higher rate of pay. The fact that a number of CPI boys went to the Job Corps could be viewed with satisfaction, except that a large percentage of them left the Job Corps and returned to the community. (Our personal knowledge of one Job Corps center and its problems prevents us from concluding that the boys who returned to the community had failed.) In short, numbers reflecting sheer movement of youngsters from one setting to another have limited significances in the absence of other information.[4]

In much the same way that a statistical description of the work-crew youngsters (Chapter 17) offered little by way of helping us to understand the individual circumstances in any one case, so can a purely statistical evaluation of the work-crew program mask and hide effects that are as important as, if not more so, than the number of youngsters who are graduated from the program and go on to full-time employment. If we take seriously CPI's orientation that the primary function

---

[4] For example, getting youngsters to return to school is a highly prized criterion for the success of the work-crew program. Unfortunately, however, a fair number (probably around 50%) of those who return to school soon drop out again. In a number of these cases of re-dropouts we can question the wisdom of having persuaded the youngsters to return to school. Although CPI personnel are well aware of those aspects of the school culture that contribute to a youngster dropping out of school, they tend to underestimate the significance and strength of these aspects when attempting to persuade a youngster to return to school. The important point, however, is that knowing the number of youngsters who return to school is, in the absence of other information, of limited significance. We may argue that if 50% of those returning to school remain in school, there is reason for satisfaction. There is reason for satisfaction only if we assume that being in school is in and of itself a productive experience—and this is precisely the assumption that has to be recognized and studied.

of the work-crew program is *not* to find jobs for its youngsters but to provide them with a remedial experience in living, then it becomes relevant to view personality and attitudinal change, independent of vocational placement, as the most important variables to be studied in any attempt to understand and/or evaluate the program. But it is a much harder and more involved process to describe attitudinal changes than it is to count the number of jobs or on-the-job-training placements garnered by work-crew graduates. And if it is true that attitudinal change is the most important and long-term product or goal of the program, then the tendency to confine our evaluation to an enumeration of placements becomes an effort to evaluate the effectiveness of the program along dimensions for which the program was not originally organized. We might also argue that unless we conceive of these youngsters and their problems as having grown and developed in a societal vacuum it becomes important that we view the social, economic, and political structure of the larger community as a context to be scrutinized in terms of its role in the subsequent experience of the work-crew youngster.

We believe that CPI would agree with much, if not all, of what we say about the significance of the statistics they have collected. The fact remains that CPI has not presented the problem in the frustrating complexity with which they have experienced it. We sense the tendency among some in CPI to believe that a candid and complete presentation of failures and successes would not be comprehended by some and would be seized on by others as evidence of bungling, stupidity, and the worst manifestations of misguided do-goodism. They are undoubtedly correct in having such anticipations but the answer surely does not lie in avoiding discussion.

CPI exists because of its recognition that poverty is not merely the result of an economic process. It is a political, social, and psychological process that destroys the young before they can live and the aged before they can die. It is a pattern of hopelessness and helplessness, a view of oneself as static, limited, and irredeemably expendable. The most frightening aspects of poverty are not the lack of jobs but the destruction of people. It places the stamp of futility on a young life that has not been lived. Poverty, in short, is a condition of being in which the past and future meet in the present—and go no further. Under these conditions—and with specific reference to the work-crew youngsters—we are confronted by individuals whose attitudes and self-concepts, whose experiences of the world, and whose experiences of themselves must become and remain the primary focus of concern. Consequently, a superficial numerical evaluation of the work-crew program must be viewed as merely one, and possibly the least important, basis of assessing the effects and implications of the program on the lives of its youngsters.

THE PROBLEM OF SUPERVISION

Important ingredients in CPI's success include missionary zeal, the selection of untrained but unusually effective people (particularly among work-crew foremen and neighborhood workers), the recognition accorded these individuals by the top leadership of CPI, and the fact that new services are being provided in such a way as to meet needs of the target population. Particularly in the case of the NEC and work-crew programs, the personnel are in the business of helping and influencing the lives of people. Essentially they are clinicians, doing the best they can on the basis of whatever they know to help people who come to them with problems. Although there are levels of responsibility and each individual is responsible in an administrative sense to someone else, it would be stretching matters quite a bit to say that these individuals have the benefits of supervision, if by supervision we mean that the details of an individual's work are carefully gone over by someone of superior experience and knowledge. In Chapter 15 we discussed CPI's apprehensive attitude toward the tendency on the part of certain professional fields to emphasize intensive supervision of staff and to view with something akin to shock the use of nonprofessionals to perform important interpersonal functions.[5] But,

---

[5] Gordon (1965) has written incisively about the problems surrounding the use of subprofessionals in the antipoverty program. In the concluding section in his paper he says the following, with which we fully agree:

"As I see it, the development of subprofessional roles involves both a lowering and a raising of traditional standards. The establishment of specific subprofessional roles affords an economy of training which many will see as a lowering of professional standards. On the other hand, the inclusion of these roles within the professional structures, as suggested above, requires that the fully qualified professional develop new and more advanced skills than those which are currently included in his repertoire. In this sense, we have a call for higher standards. There are those who criticize Project CAUSE and other similar programs as an attack on professional standards. I believe this to be a short-sighted view which implies a refusal on the part of the professions to adapt to the current needs, with the standards-enhancing implication of such an adaptation. The appeal to standards is traditionally the socially accepted defense against disturbance of the established status quo. Segregation in the neighborhoods has been defended by reference to standards of neighborhood care and upkeep; the exclusiveness and hegemony of medieval guilds was defended by reference to craftsmanship standards; the segregation of school children has similarly been justified. I see little use for high and restrictive standards for professional treatment

as we indicated, CPI had no problem to face in this respect because it could not recruit these professional people, in part because it was a markedly atypical kind of agency to most professionals and, perhaps, because the apprehension was made manifest.

A good argument could be made for the contention that much of CPI's contribution reflects freedom from the complex issues surrounding supervision, professionalization of functions, interprofessional relationships, and the inevitable problem of preciousness (Chapter 23). Although we clearly support such a contention, we in no way maintain that there is not a need for closer supervision of and help for those performing clinical functions. This is an opinion we offer not only on the basis of our experiences in CPI settings but on the basis of felt needs expressed by many of their personnel. It could not be otherwise when we consider, as we hope we have made clear in previous chapters, that the clients CPI serves run the gamut of social, personal, and intellectual pathology. In describing our role with CPI we illustrated at the same time the problem of and need for supervision. However, the help our clinic can give, or has given, is far from meeting the felt needs of CPI and even farther from the needs as we see them.

In its very early years CPI was a relatively small collection of individuals whose contact with each other was frequent and whose knowledge of each other's work was extensive. This acted as a kind of support for and control over those who were most untrained and unsophisticated in the processes of help and their knowledge of community organization. Put in another way, in those early years almost everybody was focused on the task at hand, developing and rendering service, and all other matters were relegated to a secondary significance. It is only a slight exaggeration to say that everybody (from top management down) knew something of each client, either by personal knowledge or because everybody talked to each other frequently about whom they were seeing and what they were doing. But as CPI grew in size and scope, togetherness became a victim, a not unfamiliar consequence of organizational growth, be it in a setting like a university, or a hospital, or a business. As a consequence, those personnel who needed guidance most tended to receive less and less of it, formally and informally. Whereas previously everybody was concerned in their

---

if, because of those standards, treatment is completely denied to those needing it. And the data clearly indicate that effective and appropriate treatment is being denied to the disadvantaged youth of today. While such denial may not be willful or intended, its reality testifies that opposition to an expansion of appropriate services in the service of a defense of standards is in the interests of maintenance of the Establishment rather than in the interests of those needing help."

thinking and action with service, the consequences of growth robbed service of its exclusive focus as matters of organizational and administrative concern came to the fore. Ironically, the situation was not helped by the fact that the most clinically effective individuals were deservedly moved into higher positions and those who took their places were, as a group, not as effective. This should be no surprise, in our opinion, considering that those who grew up with CPI, however untrained and uneducated many may have been, were an unusually effective and mature group of people. It is no criticism of CPI to say that as time went on they chose less well, but we cannot avoid the conclusion that CPI has not been as aware as it might be of this selective factor and has not recognized that it must take steps to provide help and supervision for its newer workers. By help and supervision we mean at least two things: the focus of supervision is on the details of the worker's thinking, knowledge, and decisions in relation to those he serves; and the supervisor is acutely aware of the difference between telling someone he is right or wrong—or simply telling him what to do—and aiding the individual to gain an increased understanding of the complexities and pitfalls of the helping process. Let us illustrate our point with the following instance.

Example 1. A boy had recently graduated from high school, although this was via the special class for the mentally retarded. He came to one of the Neighborhood Employment Centers and after going through the process was placed on a work crew in a greenhouse. Because of the pressure of the number of cases it was decided to put him on the work crew before bringing him up for discussion at the disposition conference, there being no apparent reason for postponing the work-crew placement. In the course of presenting his information about the boy one of the staff casually noted that the boy was said to have petit-mal seizures. This was not reacted to by any of the staff.

We deliberately chose this example because epilepsy is not a condition of which the psychological consequences for the individual and all those in touch with him are fully appreciated by many professional people (e.g., the school child described on page 105). It is not perversity on our part that forces us to say that the ignorance of the NEC staff about epilepsy conceivably could have more beneficial effects for the boy than if the staff had that kind of experience that too frequently results in responding to the epileptic so as unwittingly to produce more problems than are solved. But we are not advocates of ignorance and there is no denying that this case points up the problem of lack of training and supervision. Fortunately the clinic consultant was at the conference and took up the complexity of the problem in some detail, but he did not consider what he did in the nature of supervision because he did not inquire about why the problem was overlooked (or by whom) or follow through on the details of how the problem would actually be handled and by whom. That the clinic consultant was helpful is beside the point, which is that there is a need for CPI personnel in contact with clients to have available to them a kind of help and supervision that increases their sophistication and makes for more effective service.[6]

But where is CPI to get such help? It is somewhat glib to say that it has not made a serious effort to recruit help from the mental-health professions. CPI would welcome such help and, in our case, has encouraged us to help in any way and to whatever extent is possible. Neither CPI nor we ourselves initially had a clear idea about our usefulness, and there was explicit recognition of this. Aside from the fact that our services have cost CPI very little money, it may well be that the most important facilitating factor in our relationship was our unquestioning acceptance and support of CPI's goals and program—a degree of acceptance not ordinarily encountered by CPI in its relationships with the professional community.

It is our opinion that CPI has to become more explicit than it now is about the type of professional help it needs, regardless of whether such help comes from outside of CPI or becomes part of its own structure. In light of its responsibility to the goals of its programs, and in order to preserve its distinctiveness, CPI and not the professional person will have to define roles. This last comment will not sit well with most mental-health workers who are not used to having their roles defined by nonprofessional people. What has to be recognized is that the CPI-type of agency is unfamiliar to the mental-health worker and there is a real danger that, confronted with the unfamiliar, he will transform it to that which is familiar and in the process unwittingly subvert the purposes of the agency. There is an apprehensiveness and suspicion of the mental-health fields on the part of CPI which, though very understandable and realistic, may be hampering CPI's awareness of the extent to which it needs and could use these fields. Perhaps, more importantly, CPI will have to recognize that for its own sake and purposes it

---

[6] Lest the reader erroneously conclude from this example that the handling of this case by CPI workers is typical, we would express the opinion that, though it is more frequent than we would like (or CPI is aware of), it is far less frequent than critics of CPI would have us believe. We, of course, cannot generalize our opinion to CPI-type agencies in other communities.

will have to take on the responsibility of influencing and changing the mental-health fields just as it has done with other fields and professions in the community parochially insulated from the wider world.

ORGANIZATIONAL PROBLEMS

CPI has grown fast, very fast, and this growth is far from an unmixed blessing. From the standpoint of its personnel, particularly those who joined CPI in its early stages, this growth opened possibilities for advancement of which many could take advantage because of the policy of promoting from within the ranks. This, among other reasons, engendered a high degree of good morale that was, however, in part diluted by two factors. The first, to which we have already alluded, is that the replacements for those who advanced were as a group not of as good caliber. We do not pretend to understand well why this happened. That it happened is something of which many are aware, and this clearly has dampened spirits. A partial answer probably resides in the haste with which programs have had to be instituted. Another part of the answer undoubtedly is that political, and therefore irrelevant, considerations in hiring are by no means absent, although to view CPI as a major dispenser of favors for appropriate political affiliation or activity would be an incomplete and unfair characterization. Another factor, one that is easy to overlook, is that CPI's growth has taken place during a period of great economic prosperity, and the kind of person CPI would like to attract has opportunities for employment that pay more than CPI has to offer. Whatever the reasons, CPI has not chosen as well as it did in its early stages of growth. This in itself would not be serious if it were not for the second factor which has affected morale.[7] We refer here to the fact that although no one knows better than the CPI administrators who the weak people in the organization are, there is an unwillingness, or an inability, or a misguided chickenheartedness that prevents firing these people. In fact, there is a tendency to solve such problems by promotion! It may very well be that the kinds of people who are motivated to start a CPI, to devote their lives to the problems of the inner-city population, are not individuals who are temperamentally able to fire people. As one CPI leader said in a discussion of the difficult problems

[7] We should make clear our opinion that at the present time the level of morale in CPI is good although at a level discernibly below what it earlier had been. This is perhaps another way of saying that when morale starts at an unusually high level the chances of its dropping are greater than those for maintaining or exceeding that level.

he was encountering within the organization, "You know, I sometimes think that it may be that those people who can get something like CPI going may not be the kinds of people who can see it through."

Perhaps more important than anything we have thus far said is that CPI's growth has given rise to an array of parts, functions, and sections that is not only bewildering to those within and without the organization but a source of a growing feeling of isolation in the individual staff member. Whereas earlier everyone knew and interacted with everyone else, and everyone's focus was how to serve people, this is no longer the case. How to communicate within the organization, to whom to communicate, who has responsibility for what—these are now increasing sources of concern as individuals seek to recreate or rescue an earlier state of affairs. It occurred to us that what we thought we saw happening was a kind of projection of our own feelings; that is, we have been aware that we could not keep up with CPI's growth and that we had increasing difficulty understanding the relationships among its parts and the bases for certain actions and decision. We have reassured ourselves that our perceptions are not in the nature of a projection and that our view was felt by many of the CPI staff.

But, it could be argued, the criticisms offered in this section are not peculiar to CPI but are general characteristics of fast-growing organizations. It probably would be said by some that organizations, like human beings, are characterized by stages of birth, accelerated growth, maturity, decline, and death. We are not prepared here to affirm or deny the validity of such positions because the more important question is whether such positions, which may be correct in the abstract, are being used as excuses for inaction where in fact remedial action is possible. It is true that we will die, but that does not excuse living in a way that facilitates an early death, unless that is precisely what we want. Recognition of what is or may be inevitable is a necessary but not sufficient condition for controlling the pace of processes or stages.

We have attempted to present what we consider to be the most important and pressing problems of which CPI needs to be increasingly aware, and about which some action will have to be taken. Some of these are issues of attitude, others of practices, and others of perspective. The CPI-type of service agency is here to stay. That it has made and will make mistakes should be no occasion for surprise. The ultimate degree of success that this type of agency will enjoy will depend on a number of factors, three of which we consider of crucial significance. The first is recognition by the mental-health fields that this type of agency is struggling with people and problems that the mental-health fields have tended to ignore. Second, there will have to be recognition that this agency is meeting these problems with a commendable degree of success in new settings and with personnel not found in the traditional mental-health setting and, in fact, lacking the training and educational qualification for a job in the mental-health setting. Third, and perhaps most crucial, the mental-health worker cannot approach this type of agency or its personnel with anything resembling the attitude of "bringing culture to the primitives," that is, with that attitude of condescension that, before CPI, tended to characterize the approach of social agencies to the poor. It will have to be a meeting of equals who, despite different backgrounds and appearances, recognize and respect each other's talents. Just as the anthropologist comes to the study of a foreign culture with a desire to learn and understand—to control his own biases stemming in part from growing up in a different culture—so will the mental-health worker have to approach the CPI-type setting and organization.

PART IV

NEW HAVEN REGIONAL CENTER

Chapter 21

Introduction

As we indicated in Chapter 3, the involvement of the Psycho-Educational Clinic in mental retardation reflects long-standing interests of some of the staff members. In fact, as we tried to make clear, it was our earlier clinical experience in settings for mentally retarded children that forced into our awareness the importance of focusing on the public-school setting in terms both of its inadequacies in handling the retarded child and his family and its potential for a productive preventive orientation to many of the problems associated with the presence of a retarded child in a family. In addition, this experience in mental retardation made it abundantly clear that the mental-health professions (among others) would have increasingly to concern themselves with the interrelationships of mental retardation, the school setting, and the complex of problems found in our inner-city areas. It is not surprising, therefore, that these interrelationships defined the scope of the problems and dictated the nature of the settings in which our Clinic would become involved.

It was fortunate for us that at the time our Clinic started we had the opportunity to become related to a new type of facility for the mentally retarded, the New Haven Regional Center for the Mentally Retarded. The concept of the Regional Center combines several aims: (1) to eliminate the need for building large and expensive institutions, primarily residential in nature; (2) to place the facility in a geographical area that contributes the greatest number of retarded children; (3) to utilize, wherever possible, existing community resources so that duplication of services is kept to a minimum; (4) to provide a variety of educational, vocational, and recreational programs that would help parents maintain the child in his own home. The thought and experience giving rise to the concept of the Regional Center are essentially similar to those that after World War II influenced the Veterans Administration to put its new hospital facilities in large population centers and in relation to university programs, whereas previously the facilities, as in the case of institutions for the retarded, tended to be built in isolated areas.

Aside from long-standing interest and the challenge of the Regional Center concept, there were several compelling reasons that made us establish an intimate relationship with this new facility. In the remainder of this chapter we discuss these reasons in an attempt to convey how our involvement with this facility reflected the basic purposes and philosophy of our Clinic.

Because of our interest in the culture of educational settings and processes of change we seized the opportunity to affiliate with the Regional Center before it even existed as a physical plant or as an organization having a staff or program. Our affiliation began at the point when all that was known was that there was to be a Regional Center. Clearly, we had the unusual opportunity to observe the birth and growth of a new educational setting, and to observe and study the fantastic complexity of the interactions among such variables as plans, programs, personnel, hopes, state regulations, community actions and reactions, politics, professional attitudes, and a host of other factors. The fact that this setting was to give expression to a new concept of service in the community—to depart from the traditional way of locating institutions and organizing services—made the opportunity more intriguing than if it was a new institution developing in the context of established traditions. The opportunity, however, was made more compelling because there was the real possibility that our Clinic could influence the development of the Regional Center in ways our past experience in this field indicated as necessary and desirable (Sarason, 1959).

At the time this book was submitted for publication the Regional Center was just about ready to open its doors and to become a full-fledged educational and clinical facility. Consequently, what we have to say about our involvement with the Regional Center will have a somewhat different character from that of the previous sections of this book. However, our relationship with the Regional Center has already been of a kind and depth to allow certain conclusions to be presented, particularly in regard to processes of change.[1]

In our description and discussion of CPI we attempted to make

[1] Beginning in September, 1964, more than a year before its formal opening, the intake conference of the Regional Center, as well as a variety of other planning meetings, were held at our Clinic. From that point on our staff was intimately involved in the Center's beginning activities, including those of a clinical nature, as will become clear in later pages.

clear that the distinctive and innovative features of that organization reflected the fact that its leadership did not feel bound to tradition. Put more positively, the leadership had decided that to achieve its goals it would have to move in new ways. It was largely because of this attitude, and all it implies, that we were able quickly to carve out service roles that heretofore had not existed in the organization. It is easy to overlook, however, that the speed with which we became involved with CPI was due also to the fact that the boldness, flexibility, and pioneer attitude of the leadership were shared by most of the lower-echelon people. In other words, the leadership not only led but it imbued all others with an attitude toward change which facilitated our own involvement. *This is in marked contrast to the school setting in which top leadership may desire to change and innovate but cannot or do not imbue a similar attitude in those below them.*

There are marked similarities between CPI and the Regional Center. The director of the Regional Center was not indigenous to the field of mental retardation, he was not bound by the orientation and practices of other facilities concerned with the problem, he knew the community in a most intimate way, and he chose staff not on the basis of length and quality of training but in terms of their ability to try anything giving promise of being helpful. It must be emphasized that it was not only a matter of a certain type of leadership, because that type of leadership is sometimes associated with the tendency to *impose* a way of thinking and acting. What characterized CPI and the Regional Center was that such imposing of views was rarely necessary, and this is perhaps what differentiates them from most of the school settings.[2] It may well be that the contrasts between CPI and the Regional Center, on the one hand, and the school setting, on the other hand, stem in large part from the fact that the school setting is obviously older, more insular, and, therefore, more tradition-bound so that the problems facing bold leadership (in those infrequent instances where it exists) are indeed formidable. There are three factors that prevent overemphasis on the variable of newness. First, CPI and the Regional Center both had the formidable job of introducing change into a variety of community settings, including the schools. A "community" is not an easy thing to change, as both organizations have found. Second, we have come across a few instances in which the newness of a school did give rise to the type of climate characterizing CPI and the Regional Center, but this was short-lived and soon settled into the traditional mold. Third, since the beginning of our work in the

---

[2] It is not by chance, as will be seen later, that CPI, the Regional Center, and our Clinic were able in short time to develop some joint programs.

schools, we have witnessed a number of attempts to introduce change where initially there was an approximation to the climate necessary for matching intent and action but in almost all instances the change was drastically diluted. Newness of enterprise is by no means a guarantee that the desire to innovate will be sustained or successful. What seem to be necessary are ideas that galvanize, leaders who lead and support, and an acute awareness that the price of success is eternal vigilance, that one always "runs scared." In our experience these characteristics are at a premium in clinical as well as other types of settings.

We are not presenting CPI or the Regional Center as paragons of organizational virtue. Our discussion of CPI in Chapter 20 indicates that it has and will have serious problems. Where the Regional Center will be several years from now is hard to say.[3] Although they are relatively young, they have been and will continue to be for us a splendid laboratory for studying processes of social change.

---

[3] In an article we consider to be among his most important statements—an article not read and reread with the frequency it merits—Freud (1964) takes up the problem of how the analyst must protect himself against tendencies that rigidify and insidiously damage his outlook and practices—considerations that led Freud to suggest that analysts ought to be re-analyzed every several years. His discussion is, in our opinion, highly relevant to the problems of social organizations and their tendency to be smug about what they are doing, and, as a consequence, to be blind to the fact that they are no longer responsive and sensitive to their original goals. Gardner (1965) has succinctly and beautifully put the same problem in terms of organizations and is contained in his concept of "educating for renewal":

"I have collected a great many examples of organizations or institutions that have fallen on evil days because of their failure to renew themselves. And I want to place before you two curious facts that I draw from those examples. First, I haven't yet encountered an organization or institution that *wanted* to go to seed or *wanted* to fall behind in the parade. Second, in every case of organizational decline that I know anything about, there were ample warning signals long before trouble struck. And I don't mean warning signals that only a Monday-morning quarterback could discern. I mean that before trouble struck there were observers who had correctly diagnosed the difficulties to come.

Now if there are plenty of warning signals, and if no organization really wants to go to seed, *why does it ever happen?* The answer is obvious: eyes that see not, ears that hear not, minds that deny the evidence before them. When organizations are not meeting the challenge of change, it is as a rule not because they can't *solve* their problems but because they won't *see* their problems; not because they don't *know* their faults, but because *they rationalize them as virtues or necessities.*"

FOCUS OF PRESENTATION

In subsequent chapters our major goal is to convey a point of view about the mentally retarded child and his family which is shared by the Regional Center and ourselves. Although the physical facilities of the Regional Center were not yet finished at the time this book was being completed, the Center had for one year the responsibility of accepting and evaluating new and old cases that ultimately would enter its different programs. In discharging this responsibility it was inevitable that problems would arise, decisions would have to be made, and actions of a clinical nature be taken. Consequently, our Clinic not only was in a consultant or planning relation to the Regional Center but also participated actively and extensively in clinical roles. Wherever possible, we have drawn on this case material to illustrate our point of view. But it should be kept in mind that our major focus in what follows is on a way of thinking and its implications for programs with preventive and clinical orientations.

Chapter 22

The Problem of Scope

Elsewhere (Sarason, 1959) the peripheral status of mental retardation to the mental-health professions has been discussed in some detail. By peripheral we refer to several things. First, examination of training programs in the mental-health professions reveals that, with rare exception, students learn little about mental retardation, that it clearly is not a field those professions view as central or important to their core. Second, despite hope and knowledge to the contrary, the retarded individual still tends to be viewed as one whose primary problem is reflected in a low IQ, as if the IQ were an etiological factor explaining the personality and behavior of the retarded child.[1] Third, those in the psychiatric setting (in instances where they accept the retarded child as a referral—by no means frequent) think and act in relation to the retarded child rather differently than they do toward the nonretarded child, in terms of therapeutic involvement, parent counseling, clinical optimism, and the serious use of personality theory. To those who have had a sustained clinical experience in the field of mental retardation, its stepchild relationship to the mental-health professions has long been inexplicable and a source of despair. The fact that mental retardation, in theory and practice, confronts us with every important problem facing the mental-health professions has obviously been no bar to its exclusion from whatever is the focus of these professions.

One of the major reasons for this state of affairs reflects not only attitudes and ignorance within the mental-health professions, but also the long-standing tendency within the field of mental retardation to view the retarded child as *the* problem, educationally, or clinically. Put in another way, the retarded individual is *the case;* he is the one

[1] Our experience in a wide variety of schools does not support those who are of the opinion (or nurture the hope) that the lives of many children in special classes have not been affected primarily by the fact that they obtained a low score on an intelligence test.

who has been almost the sole object of clinical attention and all others with whom he lives have been of secondary significance. This is, of course, in marked contrast to child-guidance theory and practice in which *the family* tends to be regarded, so to speak, as the clinical case. In mental retardation, as in so many other medical-clinical problems, the focus of attention has been the one who is "sick." We do not imply that less attention should be paid the retarded child. We do wish to emphasize, however, that when we take seriously the concepts of primary and secondary prevention, it forces us to recognize that the retarded child is part of a family that he has affected and which in turn has affected his development (Sarason, 1964). In short, we are dealing with a number of individuals whose lives have been affected in diverse ways, and these ways far more often than not have had interfering effects (Carver, 1956; Farber, 1959, 1960). We present below two cases, by no means atypical, that illustrate how narrow a concept of clinical help can be if its sole or primary focus is the retarded child.

Example 1. The Regional Center received a letter requesting it to consider placement for a nine-year-old mongoloid girl. The letter, written by the child's mother, was clear, concise, and very specific with respect to the nature and content of the service being requested. The letter stated that the child had been placed at birth in a nursery school some distance from New Haven. Because of the child's current age (she was now older than the other children at the nursery) and the lack of adequate training facilities (the nursery was not equipped to deal with mentally subnormal children) the nursery had suggested that the parents seek placement in a different setting, one that had the necessary facilities and programs to meet the training and educational needs of the child. The letter went on to state that the child was thought to be "trainable," and ended with the hope that the new Regional Center would be able to "do a great deal for her progress."

The referral was by no means atypical: a parent was asking for a particular type of service (in this case, institutionalization), and had furnished the type of information she felt would facilitate the Regional Center's deliberation and planning. The staff of the Regional Center set about its business by having the parents sign the customary release forms so that the staff could secure the appropriate records concerning the situation and begin its preliminary investigation.

The preliminary investigation yielded a picture of the situation that was somewhat at variance with, and certainly more complicated than, the picture communicated by the parents in their letter of referral. What emerged was the picture of a situation that for nine years had been filled with great personal and familial anxiety, doubt, guilt, fear, and all those variables that interact to produce a conflict-ridden family. What follows is a summary of the situation in terms of its history or development, and a description of the situation as we experienced it.

The parents, a couple who had known each other for many years before their marriage relatively late in life, felt that they would like to start a family as soon as possible. The wife's subsequent pregnancy was marked by a great deal of physical and emotional difficulty. After a long and arduous period of time in delivery the wife gave birth to a female child who immediately was diagnosed as mongoloid. Because of the difficult delivery and the mother's weakened condition she was not conscious that she had given birth to a defective child. The father, himself quite shaken by the knowledge, did not wish the mother to be informed of the situation until she was physically strong enough to handle it. He therefore requested that the doctor not inform his wife of the situation "for a few more days." Through some misunderstanding, the father's wishes were ignored and the mother was made aware of the circumstances surrounding her newborn child that same day. Her reaction was almost catastrophic. Her extreme disappointment and emotional upheaval resulted in an intense period of despair, anguish, and feelings of inadequacy. The mother suffered what was described as a nervous breakdown, characterized by suicidal preoccupations and a complete rejection of her child. Arrangements quickly were made to place the child in a nursery, the same nursery in which the child was residing at the time the Regional Center received the parents' request for institutionalization.

Because of the mother's emotional condition and frame of mind following the birth of the child, the family doctor (not the doctor who had ignored the father's wishes at the hospital) suggested that the couple try to have another child as quickly as possible. He made this suggestion with the idea that it would help the wife to overcome her feelings of inadequacy and despair, and —at the same time—would prove to her that she could have a normal baby. The wife became pregnant shortly thereafter and delivered a normal baby boy less than a year after the birth of her mongoloid child.

Despite the birth of the new child the mother's feelings about her mongoloid child remained essentially unchanged. She would not allow the mongoloid child (then about a year old) to be brought into the home under any conditions, and she devoted all her available time to the rearing of her newborn son.

During the succeeding years a family pattern was established. On the average of once a month the parents would take a trip to the nursery where they had placed their daughter. On these days (usually a Sunday) they would leave their son with a trusted relative, one of the very few people aware of the situation. They would visit their daughter at school, bring her additional clothes and sweets, often take her for a ride in the car, and then return to New Haven, pick up their son, and take him home. The son was never told of the existence of his sister and she was never brought to the home. When the son became old enough to begin asking questions regarding his parents' periodic trips he was told that they were "going for a ride and would be back in a few hours." Throughout these years the family doctor—possibly because he was aware of the mother's emotional difficulties and past history with respect to her mongoloid daughter—kept reinforcing the mother's feeling that the son should be kept unaware and uninformed of his sister's existence. Whenever the problem came up it was resolved in terms of waiting "until he is old enough" to understand before making him aware of the facts.

Although the parents maintained contact with their daughter and made no attempt to sever their relationship or abrogate their formal responsibilities toward her, they had very little information concerning her growth and development. They did not know if she could dress herself, were unaware that she was toilet trained, and had no knowledge of the degree of speech development or learning that had taken place since the time of her placement at the nursery. Their contact with the child was confined to periodic visits and phone calls to find out "if there is any improvement since the last visit."

The regular intake conference of the Regional Center took place with the benefit of the additional information that had been gathered during the preliminary investigation. After a review of the essential material now available, several variables emerged that appeared to be particularly salient. First, there was the variable involving the attitudes and behavior of the mother. We found ourselves most impressed with the degree and duration of the mother's conflicts concerning her mongoloid daughter, and the amount of anxiety and guilt she must have experienced about her feelings toward the child. Second, there was the factor involving the "normal" sibling in the family. What concerned us here were not only the kinds of questions (both verbalized and unspoken) he might have about the situation, but also the degree to which his parents' conflicts had affected his own growth and development. Because of the nature of the variables that appeared to be outstanding, and because of the kinds of questions these variables raised, it was the group consensus that the case might be handled best by one of the psychologists working with the Regional Center. It was decided, therefore, that he should assume the primary responsibility for handling the case.

The day after the intake conference we telephoned the family in the hope of arranging a home visit, through which we could establish contact with the family and begin to explore the problems and possibilities of the situation. The telephone conversation (with the mother) began on a discordant note. She failed to see the reason for our call, and felt that the entire situation was outlined clearly in her letter to the Regional Center and in the information she had given us access to through her signing of the release form. From her point of view the request for institutionalization was clear and would be the only plan of action she would accept. She was quite suspicious of our reasons for calling her and felt that we might be utilizing her and her husband's difficulties as a sort of teaching situation or trial case for interns in psychology. She reiterated her physician's advice that her eight-year-old son be kept out of the situation, and she used this reasoning as a basis for her refusal to allow us to visit the home. She did not want her son around whenever there was the slightest possibility that mention would be made of her mongoloid child. On our part, we explained to the mother that our request to visit the home was a standard procedure which the Regional Center had adopted with respect to most of its cases, and that it had nothing to do with a trial case or any purpose other than making it easier for the Regional Center to work more closely with the family in developing and implementing the most appropriate program for everyone concerned. We told her that we understood her feelings about not wanting to involve her son and that we would be happy to schedule our visit at a time when both she and her husband were at home and their son was either away at school or involved in some other activity that kept him away from the home. At this point the mother's anger and suspiciousness appeared to wane, and soon were replaced by a feeling closely akin to relief, relief that we were indeed interested sufficiently in her problem to make available to her a staff member who was willing to come to the home at a time and in a manner that would make the situation as comfortable as possible. We then arranged to visit the home at a time (8:30 A.M.) after the son had left for school and before the husband left for work.

At the appointed time and day we arrived at the home just in time to join the parents over a cup of coffee and to discuss the situation around the kitchen table. The home was a modest but extremely pleasant one, located in one of the better sections of town.

Even before we began to discuss the case itself the mother felt compelled to apologize for her behavior over the phone. In her apology she conveyed very many of her anguished and guilt-ridden feelings concerning her daughter in a direct manner. In the process she quickly became very tearful and hardly could speak. Her husband, a mild-mannered but extremely strong and supportive person, immediately comforted her and continued the discussion while his wife regained control of herself.

We then became more involved in a discussion about the parents' request and the ways in which the Regional Center could be of help. We indicated our understanding of the situation, but also pointed out that the philosophy of the Regional Center is such that we could not guarantee anonymity to the parents because we could not promise to keep the daughter removed from the resources of the area (schools, recreation centers) or from the facilities (religious and social institutions) that existed in the community. We also discussed the fact that there had never been an adequate developmental and psychological assessment of their daughter so that we were unable at this point to state that she was trainable or educable (a distinction of which the parents were unaware). At this point we indicated the variety of things mongoloid children could learn (reading, vocational skills, etc.) under appropriate conditions and with the help of trained personnel and specialized programming. The longer we discussed the situation the more attentive the parents became and the less prone they were to chronicle the years of torment and anguish they had been through.

The discussion then turned to their concern about when and how their son would be informed of the existence of his sister, the conditions under which he would find out, and the possible consequences and effects it would have on him. In discussing their son the parents were remarkably frank and concerned about his current status independent of the situation concerning his sister. What quickly emerged was a picture of an eight-year-old boy who was not as normal and healthy as we might have believed. Although describing her love and devotion ("My whole life is concerned with him.") for her son the mother was quick to point out that he was a "very troubled boy" who kept to himself a good deal of the time and had very few friends. The father saw his son as a somewhat effeminate youngster who spent too much of his time reading and talking with adults and elderly relatives. The mother agreed with much that the father said and added that the young boy was asking more and more questions concerning their "Sunday afternoon trips" and recently had asked her whether or not he was an adopted child. They were, in short, extremely concerned about their son and his development. All we felt we should do was to point out the fact that children are extremely sensitive to these things, that they do have questions, and that these questions do not appear to become less potent with the passage of time.

Turning once more to their daughter the parents made it clear that even if she were placed at the Regional Center they would not want to bring her home until she had become "more of a person" and until they had been able to inform their son of her existence and prepare him for the situation. We agreed with the parents and told them that the Regional Center was acutely aware of the difficulties involved in the situation and was prepared to offer whatever help was possible both in terms of preparing their daughter for a more active involvement in the community and in helping them deal with the issue of how and when to prepare their son for the situation. At this point we attempted to be as concrete as possible in terms of the variety of programs that were and would be available at the Regional Center to help them with their problem. We described the development of the sibling groups, parent groups, and other programs whose aim it was to help the parents and siblings of mentally subnormal individuals deal with the problems that confronted them and their families. We also indicated our intention of involving them in whatever plans and programs might be developed with respect to their child and her education and training.

Toward the end of our meeting the parents appeared genuinely interested with the possibilities and programs we described. Although still quite frightened and skeptical, they agreed to think about the things we had discussed. They wanted to know if our presence in their home was a "one-shot affair" or if we were prepared to see them again or as often as they felt necessary. We told them that we would work with them for the entire period of time during which they felt it necessary and helpful. Before leaving we set up a second appointment with them and left the phone number where they could get in touch with us if there was anything they wanted to talk about before our next meeting. The next meeting was set up for the next week at the same time.

A day before our next scheduled meeting we received a phone call from the mother. In a very hesitant and apologetic manner she informed us of her and her husband's decision to put off their request for institutionalizing their daughter at the Regional Center. She told us they had discussed the situation and had decided to investigate other placement possibilities. Although she did not sound confident about their decision and was extremely thankful for our concern and attention, she nevertheless felt it would be wiser to seek a different placement. After informing us of their decision the mother seemed hesitant about terminating the conversation, so we asked her what factors had influenced their decision. Almost as if she were betraying a confidence she told us that after speaking with us she and her husband had felt it important that they consult their family doctor, the man who "has done so much for us through the years." The doctor was quite opposed to the ideas we had discussed and the suggestions we had made. He felt it was not the appropriate time to involve their son in the situation; that the wife was still too emotionally weak to become involved again in a potentially traumatic situation; and that it was best to postpone the type of program and planning that we had discussed. The mother felt he was correct in his judgment and was withdrawing her application for immediate placement. Before hanging up she asked us if she could contact us again if she and her husband were to change their minds. We told her that we would be available whenever she wished to discuss the matter again.

At our next intake conference we informed our colleagues at the Regional Center of the results of our home visit and of the ensuing telephone conversation with the mother. We all were concerned about the situation, not only because of the results and consequences for the mongoloid child (her future treatment, education, and training), but because of our findings with respect to the parents and the "normal" child. It appeared that the family doctor was the primary agent in influencing the parents to seek placement elsewhere, so we discussed the appropriateness of exploring with him the reasons and bases for his feelings and decisions. Our concern was not solely one of attempting to influence him in the situation, but to apprise him of our findings and perceptions of the situation with respect to the parents and sibling as well as the institutionalized child. We felt it appropriate to involve our own medical staff member in whatever liaison and discussions we could establish with the family doctor.

Although the parents have currently withdrawn their request for institutionalization at the Regional Center, we do not consider the case closed. At the time of this writing we are in the process of establishing a meeting between ourselves (and our medical staff member) and the family doctor—a meeting we hope will lead to a fuller exploration of the variables, problems, and possibilities of the situation.

Example 2. One of the earliest requests for institutionalization reviewed was an old case involving a family that had long petitioned to have a child removed from the home and placed in residence elsewhere. The case involved a young girl—now 12 years of age—who was "markedly mentally retarded" and who had disturbances of balance as a result of postencephalitic cerebral palsy. The girl had contracted encephalitis at the age of one, after which she was found to have regressed in her physical and mental abilities. In the years that followed the family made periodic attempts to have the child institutionalized or otherwise removed from the home. We have termed these attempts "periodic" because they occurred in a rather sporadic fashion. A review of previous records indicated that each of these attempts—often separated by months—were "emergencies," but that in each instance the apparent precipitating crisis would wane and the family would withdraw its insistence for immediate placement. The family's history of petitions also indicated that the parents, although requesting placement, would often specify conditions of placement (the absolute necessity of speech therapy and physiotherapy) that made placement a more difficult process. Although the child's name had been placed on the waiting list for the state training school in Connecticut, the admission pressures under which the training school was laboring made it rather unlikely that she would be admitted in the very near future. In summary, the family was well known to many of the staff members of the Regional Center. Many of them had had to become involved with the family, in one way or another, during one of the many crises that characterized the family's petitions for placement.

Soon after the Regional Center began its weekly deliberations concerning the disposition of cases brought to its attention, it was confronted with another of the family's crisis situations. In a series of telephone calls to various members of the staff, the mother clearly stated her belief that she was at her "wits' end," and that, unless the Regional Center acted quickly and decisively to remove her daughter from the household, it would have to bear the burden of responsibility for whatever events were to follow. There followed a brief letter from the family doctor that indicated his deep concern for the health and well-being of the woman, and his opinion that a good deal of her current difficulties were "precipitated by the care of her mentally retarded child." At approximately the same time a call was received from the husband advising the Regional Center that his wife had started acting "very strangely"; that she was now insisting that their daughter not call her "mother," but address her by her first name; that she was not eating her meals with the rest of the family (the father, daughter, and a male sibling two years older than the daughter); and that she had approached an attorney concerning the possibility of obtaining a divorce.

Although the staff members of the Regional Center had been through somewhat similiar crises involving this family, the nature and degree of the current difficulties led the Center to refer the case to one of the members of its staff who was familiar with the family and its problems and who had had previous experience with the situation. She immediately made a home visit and returned with a report that confirmed the degree of familial disorganization and indicated that it was even greater than previously described. She found the mother in a state of great emotional upheaval, and described her as wanting "to do in" both herself and the daughter.

Because of the nature of the difficulties, and because of the suicidal and homicidal threats that had become prominent features in the situation, the staff felt it was appropriate and necessary for one of the psychologists to become involved in the case. However, because of our relative inexperience with the family itself, it was deemed important that we be introduced to the case and to the family by a staff member who had had extensive experience with the family. It was decided, therefore, that we would make a joint home visit so we could familiarize ourselves with the situation and establish a relationship with the family.

At the time of our visit we found the situation somewhat less dramatic than we had expected, but essentially unchanged. The mother, although not nearly as hysterical as she had been during the preceding days, was clearly distraught and depressed about the situation in general, and about her own existence in particular. When we visited the home only the mother and daughter were in the house. The father was at work and the older son had not returned from school. The home, a neat and tidy place, quickly assumed the appearance of an arena in which the mother and daughter clearly emerged as contestants in an ongoing struggle for domination, a struggle in which the daughter obviously had the upper hand. The longer we remained in the house the more impressed we became with the efficiency with which the daughter had conditioned the mother to fulfill her every command and wish. Time after time the daughter would request something (a glass of water, a change of channels on the TV) in such a nagging, rasping, and repetitive fashion that the mother eventually would do whatever was necessary to mollify her child. No sooner would she placate one of her child's demands than the child would demand something else. The result was something like a human elevator; the mother would jump up and down to fulfill her daughter's demands. We little wondered that she was both physically and emotionally exhausted.

Throughout the time we were in the home the mother kept us aware (by saying to us each time she got up and sat down, "Can't you see what I have to go through for that child?") of the tremendous pressures under which she was functioning, and the lack of help she was receiving from the other members of the family. She felt especially hurt and enraged by her husband, who she felt had done nothing but make her life more painful and difficult. She wanted freedom from a situation in which she felt enslaved and which she experienced as endless and hopeless.

In a little while the older son (14 years old) returned from school; although we were told that he had a "warm and wonderful" relationship with the daughter, he completely ignored his sister when he entered the house. With little more than a hesitant and cursory glance at us he immediately went up to his room. Throughout this time the daughter attempted to dominate the situation and constantly sought to have everyone's attention focused solely on herself. She appeared to giggle at her mother's difficulties and laughed at her whenever her demands were met. She was friendly and inquisitive toward us and constantly sought to engage us with repetitious questions. At every point, however, she appeared intently interested in and aware of everything that was going on and was being said in her presence.

Because of our feeling that the mother indeed did need some sort of immediate help we offered to take her daughter into the Regional Center's day program, as a temporary solution until the Center became available for residence cases or until the family could find a more permanent solution to the situation.[2] As part of the day program we promised the mother that we would arrange to have her daughter picked up at approximately 8:30 A.M., taken to the setting where the day program was being conducted, and then brought back in the afternoon. We also told the mother of our desire to do a more formal intellectual and emotional evaluation of her daughter, an evaluation that would be helpful in determining the kind of placement and program most appropriate for her daughter. In addition we suggested the possibility that the mother might find it helpful if we could get together with her to discuss the situation under less harassing and difficult conditions. We suggested that the most appropriate way of doing this would be for the mother to accompany her daughter to our Clinic, and for us to spend part of our time evaluating the child and part of our time talking with the mother. The mother seemed quite relieved and reassured by the suggestions we were making and the immediate programs we were offering. She decided instantly to accept the threefold program as we had described it. Her daughter would enter the day program immediately; the child would be seen for an extensive evaluation; and the mother would meet with us to discuss in greater detail the problems and conflicts of the situation.

As we left the home—and as we later reported to the rest of the staff—we agreed that the situation appeared to be much more complex than we had believed on the basis of the referral question. This should not be taken to suggest that we in any way doubted the difficulties that the handicapped child was creating in the family in general, and for the mother in particular. It was clear that, for one reason or another, both the mother and the child had conspired to make life virtually unbearable for the mother. What troubled us were the less obvious and certainly less discussed variables in the situation. First, it appeared that the older male sibling was a particularly troubled youngster who appeared to shun any and all contact with the mother and the daughter. He seemed fearful, angry, and certainly in need of help. Secondly, we wondered about the nature of the relationship between husband and wife, and the degree to which their own interpersonal problems were contributing to the conflicts and difficulties of the current situation. Our over-all impression was that we were not dealing with a family whose problems would be alleviated significantly or reduced by removing the daughter from the home. We felt that we were confronted with a situation in which the request for institutionalization was only one of a multitude of variables and problems that had resulted in a socially and emotionally disorganized household.

With the daughter safely involved in the day program the mother indeed was able to experience a certain amount of freedom for at least a portion of the day. Consequently, when she appeared for her first appointment with us she was in considerably better spirits. Her step was a bit more lively; she was

[2] The day program is a program of education, vocational training, and recreation conducted by the Regional Center at a local school that was donated for this use to parents of mentally subnormal children, adolescents, and adults.

well-groomed; and she dressed "fit to kill," as she put it. Each time the mother brought the daughter to the Clinic we spent a few minutes testing the child (she had a very short attention span and quickly tired of the "games" we were trying to play with her) and the remainder of the time speaking with the mother while the child was having milk and cookies in an adjoining room. We met this way for a total of five sessions.

Each of our sessions with the mother appeared to have one general and recurrent theme: the mother virtually never mentioned her daughter, but, rather, spent the entire time talking about her relationship with her husband. The more she spoke of their difficulties the more convinced we became of the overriding importance of their conflicts in setting the stage for the recent crisis situation that we previously had been led to believe was solely confined to the daughter. The marital problems she discussed (the husband's chronic infidelity, her increasing isolation and exclusion from the family process and a "life of my own," etc.) were of long duration and had developed over a considerable period of time. At each of these sessions the mother often became extremely emotional but could begin to see the effects of her relationship with her husband on her behavior with her daughter. It appeared that these sessions constituted the first real opportunity this woman had to discuss the variety of problems with which she had been grappling for a long, long time.

When the mother arrived for our third session she was attired in a white uniform and was virtually beaming. She immediately told us of her having secured a part-time job as a receptionist for an elderly doctor whose office was located in her neighborhood. She was using the time during which her daughter was involved in the day program to "get out from under" and to begin "living again." She felt that she now had the opportunity to get out of the house, earn some money, and begin to meet "new and interesting people." She felt that in getting a job her entire emotional frame of mind had improved considerably, and that she was better able to deal with the problems at home. She felt "refreshed" after a day's work, and began to look forward to the return of her children and husband to the home.

Our remaining sessions with the wife were devoted to a more concrete discussion of the variety of programs available to her and her family now that they all could take a step back and view their problems in a context relatively free of the all-too-frequent pressures emanating from their crisis situations. We then were able to point out the relationship between her requests for institutionalization and the periodic "coming to a head" of a variety of other familial problems. The wife began to talk about these situations and appeared a bit more receptive to working with us to develop a meaningful long-range program for the entire family. In this context she was able to begin to visualize the possibility of placing her daughter at the Regional Center for only a part of each week rather than on a permanent basis. Coupled with this program for her daughter she saw the relevance and necessity of both herself and her husband becoming involved in an ongoing counseling program that the Regional Center would be offering for the parents of mentally subnormal children. Finally, she was able to begin to speak of her son's needs for some type of therapeutic intervention, the type of intervention that would be possible through the formation of sibling groups (therapeutic and discussion groups for the brothers and sisters of mentally subnormal children) at the Regional Center.

In essence, our contact and involvement with this case went far beyond the referral question with which we initially were confronted. The final program that was evolved was one in which the entire family could take part. What had begun as an emergency petition for the institutionalization of a child wound up as a cry for help on the part of an entire family.

It should be emphasized that these cases, stemming from our work with the Regional Center, are by no means atypical. If an entire book could be devoted to a detailed description of each of the cases referred to the Regional Center in its first year of operation (before its physical plant was built), we would only observe variations on a theme. In each case the lives of individuals other than the retarded child have been adversely affected and will continue to be so affected if attention is not directed toward them.

The point we are making is by no means new. The problem resides in recognizing the scope of the problem and implementing it appropriately in practice. Basically what is required is a commitment in practice to a combination of the clinical and preventive approaches, but, unfortunately, the training of clinicians underexposes the student to the ways in which the clinical setting can and must be used to help others than the "patient."

From the start of our relationship with the Regional Center there was complete agreement that each family was to be the case and that in the disposition of a case it would be routine to make explicit the service goals set for those members of the family who were in need of help. Some idea of how we attempted to implement this can be seen in the case material presented above. Because the Regional Center did not have its full complement of staff—and would not have it until the Center actually existed in a physical sense—it was not always possible to implement our conceptions as fully as possible. To the extent that we were able to do it, several important consequences became apparent. First, this approach quickly convinced those clinical psychologists on our staff who heretofore had had little or no exposure to mental retardation that commitment to a family involved them in problems that in principle differed in no way from those they had encountered in the psychiatric setting. Second, these same individuals began to see the significance of *looking for problems* with the aim of determining when and how to intervene to prevent them from becoming more serious and, in some instances, to prevent certain problems from even developing (a point to be taken up in the next section). Third, implementation of this approach led to a degree of "clinical optimism" not ordinarily encountered in settings that focus primarily on the retarded child for whom what can be done is frequently limited.

THE PREVENTIVE ORIENTATION

As soon as we view the family as the focus of attention, it quickly becomes apparent that we have the opportunity either to prevent certain kinds of problems from occurring or restricting the scope of the adverse effects of a problem that has already developed. For example, in the cases presented above many of the problems manifested in these families conceivably might have been prevented or discernibly diluted in their effects if there had been a more sophisticated awareness or anticipation of family dynamics as well as a deeper feeling of clinical responsibility to all those who might have been affected by and in turn affected the retarded child.

It says something about the psychological training of professional people that in its first year of operation the Regional Center had referred to it three neonates whose parents were advised not to take them home but to institutionalize them immediately. This type of recommendation is by no means infrequent, particularly among physicians. There can be no question that such a recommendation is *intended* to solve and prevent family problems. Aldrich (1947–48) in an article entitled "Preventive medicine and mongolism" states:

> The difficulties faced by the mothers of these children are, in many respects, more serious than those faced by the child. Because the mongolian is so incompetent in the ordinary technics of living, his mother soon becomes a complete slave to his dependency. As a result, she devotes all of her time to his necessary care, neglecting her other household duties, her other children if there are such, and inevitably, her husband. The effect of all this is that all other satisfying areas of living are blotted out and that she becomes enmeshed in an almost hopeless entanglement of emotional ties to the mongol. From the practical standpoint, a potentially useful citizen is removed from social intercourse. It is a clinical fact that few such mothers have subsequent children.
>
> In many instances, the father is placed in a very trying situation. When the realization gradually seeps into his consciousness that all is not well with his child, he may notice also that his wife is becoming so engrossed with her baby that she is losing touch with him and all his areas of interest—that she has no time either for his affection or for the outside recreation they used to enjoy together. If he faces facts and tells her his fears, she often feels that she and her child are being attacked and responds with a defensive emotional storm. If he says nothing, they usually drift apart slowly. Many separations and divorces follow the birth of mongolian idiots.

The other children in afflicted families suffer from a social stigma which they and their playmates sense but often do not understand. With passing years, as the mongol becomes less and less acceptable in the neighborhood groups, his brothers and sisters refuse to bring other children into the house, of necessity play elsewhere and are obsessed with a feeling of family shame no matter how unjustifiable it may be. Few situations are worse for household morale or for that of the children.

There is an economic element in this situation also. When parents finally realize the deficiencies of their child, they often begin a hopeless round of visits to doctors and clinics near and far, spending all of their savings and often borrowing up to their capacity in the vain hope of finding a cure. It is a sad commentary on human nature to note that not infrequently they encounter people who promise much and slowly drain the family's resources in fantastic and useless methods of treatment.

There is only one adequate way to lessen all this grief, fortunately a measure which most experienced physicians will agree to, and that is immediate commitment to an institution at the time of diagnosis. But this procedure is difficult to accomplish if the mother has had the child under her care for any prolonged period. She becomes so necessary to the child and so attached to him that she cannot give him up. Therefore, it becomes highly important to make the diagnosis as early as possible. Fortunately this can be done in more than 90 per cent of the cases on the day of birth. I am outlining here a technic which has been found successful in accomplishing separation of newborn mongols from the family, in the hope that it may help others in meeting this tragic situation.

Aldrich then goes on to describe the following recommended procedure:

1. When the diagnosis has been made in a newborn the mother is told that the baby is not strong enough to be brought to her at present and that he must remain in the nursery for a few days.

2. Next, the father is asked to meet the physician immediately, bringing with him any close relatives who are available in the neighborhood. At this conference, the nature of the problem is explained in detail, emphasizing its seriousness, the fact that no one is to blame, that future babies will be normal and that immediate placement outside the family provides the only hope of preventing a long series of family difficulties.

It may be advisable, in many instances, to enlist the aid of the clergyman closest to the family. This has been of great help to me several times, for often the pastor will be familiar with the unfortunate sequence of events which accompanies the birth of a mongol and may have dealt with such disrupted families in his church. He is often eager to prevent any repetition of such tragedies.

3. If the father and close relatives of the family can be made to accept outside placement as the solution of their problem, the physician and the husband, backed up by the family decision, report the whole situation to the mother.

She is asked, not to *make* the decision, but to accept the one which has already been made by the close relatives. This has the advantage of tending to prevent the quite natural feelings of guilt which might otherwise plague her after surrendering the child to another's care.

4. Having obtained unanimous family permission, the physician must arrange for immediate placement of the infant. In some states this can be done through public agencies without delay. In others, a boarding home placement for the interval is necessary until the delays incident to commitment and finding institutional vacancies have been overcome.

Our own experience, illustrated by *Example 1*, strongly suggests that Aldrich's orientation and procedure frequently create problems in members of the family that seriously interfere with their personal lives.

As might be expected, the two hospitals referring the neonates to the Regional Center conveyed the impression that the families would disintegrate almost immediately if the infants were not "put away." However, the orientation of the Center does not permit passive acquiescence to referrals, but rather focuses on the possible consequences of institutionalization on the family, the problems that might be solved in an immediate sense, and the problems that might develop in the future. In two of the three cases it turned out that the family was by no means eager for institutionalization, felt impotent to cope with the professional advice offered, and in general was depressed and bewildered. In each of these two instances the Regional Center—by discussing the problem with the family, helping them prepare for the child's homecoming, participating in the homecoming, and arranging for subsequent help in the management and care of the infant—was able to adjust the child in the home in a way that satisfied the need in these families to participate actively in the care and development of the child, a need expressed as clearly by the siblings as by the parents. In the case of the third neonate institutionalization was necessary less because of any unusual familial reactions than because the child required a type of medical care and supervision not possible at home.

The solution of problems by removal of the mentally retarded individual occurs in contexts other than those already described. One such context involves the public agency. A variety of public agencies often become involved in the process of attempting to deal with the disorganizing effects of mental subnormality on a family, especially the multiproblem family. As is well known, these agencies (e.g., state welfare, city welfare, juvenile court) are usually understaffed and overworked, and are all too often placed in the position of having to make decisions about and plan programs for a family on the basis of limited and incomplete information. The agency often must assume the responsibility for an entire family and, in doing so, must be faced with the problem of providing extensive service with only limited resources. Under these conditions it is not surprising that the agency should attempt to meet its obligations to the distressed family by trying to isolate and eliminate the most obvious cause of the family's problems. By focusing attention on that variable considered to be prepotent in the situation the agency attempts to act in such a manner as to minimize the amount of dislocation suffered by the family and to maximize the remedial effects of its intervention.

The quest for the most parsimonious solution that characterizes the ways in which many agencies approach problems is in no way very different from the tactics employed by others (professionals, families) when they are confronted by the problems usually associated with mental subnormality. In much the same manner as the family often tries to remove and separate the troublesome member from the rest of the family unit, agencies often attempt to remove what they consider to be the primary cause of the difficulty. The underlying assumption in both cases is the same. By removing the most obvious source of the difficulty the family as a whole will benefit, become less disorganized, and begin to employ more adaptive modes of functioning. However, as we already have indicated, the quest for quick and easy solutions are often symptomatic of a lack of understanding of the complexities of the situation. The following example is a case in point.

Example 3. The Regional Center was requested by the juvenile court to become involved in a case in which the question of primary concern was whether or not a mother of six children was mentally retarded. The referral question was specific and quite clear, if the mother was found to be mentally subnormal the state could act quickly to separate her from her children. The reason for the referral was equally clear. The juvenile court had a good deal of evidence leading them to question the mother's intellectual functioning with respect to her capacity to deal effectively with her six children.

The mother, a Negro woman, 27 years of age, had long ago become known to both the welfare department and the juvenile court. For some time the family had been on state aid (Aid to Dependent Children) and, consequently, had been the responsibility of the welfare department. Similarly, the two oldest of the six children (ages 10, 9, 7, 4, 2, and 1) already had been involved in difficulties with the law, and so had come in contact with the juvenile court.

The family situation had been, for some time, a difficult one, and recently had deteriorated to a point that the juvenile court felt to be perilous in terms of the health, safety, and welfare of the children. The father recently had been arrested for stealing a car and currently was in jail. During the routine interrogation following his arrest it was discovered that he was a fugitive from justice, that he had escaped from a prison in Florida where he was serving another sentence for robbery. Following his escape he had come north and had married the woman for whom an intellectual evaluation was being requested. He never informed her of his past, and she had no knowledge of the situation until the police explained it to her. It appeared that, in all probability, the husband would have to return to Florida to complete his previous sentence after he finished serving his current sentence. In any event, it appeared that the father—who had been unemployed for several years before his arrest— would be unavailable to the family for quite some time to come.

Although the father never had been able to secure and hold down a job for any period of time he was of some help to the mother in terms of caring for the children. During the period following his arrest the family situation had deteriorated significantly. The children were not attending school with any regularity; visits to the home had resulted in observations of general chaos and disorganization; the younger children were not being fed or clothed properly; and the older children were running wild, disobeying the mother, and staying away from the home for long periods of time.

Under these conditions the juvenile authorities felt that they had to step into the situation. They were concerned over the health and welfare of the children and the mother, and felt that only by removing the children from the home could they begin to provide for their needs and at the same time alleviate the pressures under which the mother was functioning. When they approached the mother with this suggestion she became almost hysterical and threatened to run away with her children before she would allow anyone to separate them from her.

Because psychological examination was being requested it was decided that the Psycho-Educational Clinic would take primary responsibility for the case. Before scheduling the client for testing, however, we were able to meet with the case worker from the juvenile court. The case worker, a competent, sensitive, and dedicated woman, was quite concerned about the prospects that the mother and her children would be separated. She felt that this "solution" was not a solution at all, but that it would create more problems than it would solve. She clearly indicated her desire that our evaluation concern itself with much more than just "an IQ number," and that we utilize our time with the client to evolve as comprehensive an impression of the case as possible. We agreed with her feelings and informed her of our intention to do just that, and of our desire to work closely with the juvenile court in developing as helpful a plan as possible. We arranged to see the client the following day.

The next day, when the case worker brought the client to the Clinic, the mother appeared to be a frail and petrified woman who looked and dressed much younger than her stated age. She approached the testing situation in a markedly frightened, tense, and bewildered fashion, but was acutely aware of the fact that she was in a "head clinic." Before we could begin testing she anxiously informed us that her "mind is OK and I don't need a mental test." Every word she said was spoken in an apprehensive and tremulous manner. Throughout the period of evaluation she remained extremely frightened and obviously intimidated. She never was able to relax, and her nervousness was manifested in an almost continuous eye tic. Our written observations stated that we "rarely had seen such an obviously frightened and anxious person, a person who is so obviously alone and intimidated by the world around her."

The formal testing results failed to establish whether or not the woman was mentally subnormal. In view of the client's emotional state at and during the time of testing, it was almost surprising that she performed as well as she did. Her performance itself was marked by a great intra- and intertest variability—the type of scattered, sporadic, and uneven performance often associated with an extreme degree of anxiety. With this in mind it was our feeling that, were it not for the almost debilitating effects of anxiety and tension, the client might have performed at a higher level.

More than anything else, we were struck by the fact that we were confronted by a woman who appeared to be so totally alone and isolated, who was being called on to maintain a home and children during a period in her life when she was most vulnerable to the interfering effects of prolonged and realistic anxiety. This fact, coupled with her obvious devotion to her children, led us to feel it was necessary to explore ways, other than removal and separation, in which the situation could be handled.

We shared our findings and our feelings about the case with the juvenile court case worker. She concurred with much that we had observed and described to us just how alone the client and her children really were. From her information it appeared that the woman had no family or friends in the housing project in which she lived, or indeed, in the entire New Haven area. She was alone and friendless, separated from her husband, and isolated from any meaningful contact with the community of which she was, nominally, a part. Whatever homemaking and child-rearing skills and talents she possessed were being undermined and rendered useless by the loneliness and anxiety that engulfed her.

The more we discussed the situation the more we found ourselves emphasizing the psychological, emotional, and social variables that had become predominant factors in the situation. No longer were we talking about "intelligence" or "mental subnormality" as the prepotent variables to be considered in deciding what to do or what to suggest.

Pursuing this line of inquiry we soon found ourselves thinking in terms of what we could put into rather than take away from the situation in order to help both the mother and the children. We began thinking about the possibility of placing someone in the home on a continuous and regular basis, to assist the mother in the day-to-day management of the house and the children. In considering this possibility we were fully aware that the most important factor was not selecting someone who was merely an efficient and competent homemaker, but choosing the kind of person (a mature, stable, and accepting woman) who was willing and able to develop a relationship with the client;

who could be a friend; and who could be supportive as well as function in an instructive manner. In short, we were looking for someone capable of reducing the client's apparent loneliness, of being her friend as well as her helper.

The case worker quickly thought of a person she felt would be "perfect for the job." The woman the case worker had in mind was someone she had met when the woman and her children were themselves the case worker's clients. She described the woman as a mature, gracious, and extremely giving person, capable of exhibiting great strength as well as great gentleness. She lived in the same housing project as the client, and was anxious to "get off relief" and become financially independent of the welfare department. The case worker felt this woman would be the most appropriate person to go into the home as a homemaker.

The case worker contacted the potential homemaker and explained the entire situation to her. The woman was extremely anxious to become involved in the situation and saw it both as a chance to help another human being in distress and as a way of getting off the relief rolls herself. Because of the urgency of the situation the woman, rather than waiting for the city welfare department's red tape to evaluate and process her into the homemakers' program, immediately began to visit the home and to establish a relationship with the client.

In a relatively short time (approximately three weeks) the situation began to change, and to change in a dramatic fashion. The client began to relax a bit and became much more communicative. The house began shaping up again, and the children were attending school and eating regularly. The homemaker began taking the client out of the home, introducing her to some of the other tenants, and showing her the best places in town to obtain bargains. Between the two of them they worked out a budget for the home and began redecorating parts of the apartment. The client began looking forward to the almost daily visits of the homemaker and started to assert herself more strongly in the home. More than anything else the client had—perhaps for the first time—a real friend, another person in the world with whom she could talk, laugh, trade stories, and share problems. The client began to "live" and her children began "living" with her. The entire home situation, although by no means completely transformed, began to get better.

After a few weeks the homemaker contacted the juvenile case worker and informed her that the welfare department had turned down her application to become a paid homemaker. She was angry, hurt; she could not understand why she should have been turned down. We investigated the situation and found, to our dismay, that the welfare department—at least in terms of the homemakers' service—had a policy of not hiring onto their staff people who were their clients. It appeared to be a curious and cruel paradox. On the one hand, the welfare department was working toward the goal of getting their clients off the relief rolls and into gainful employment. On the other hand, they could not bring themselves to hire their own clients and thereby hasten the process whereby they could become self-sufficient. Although we tried to work out an arrangement with the welfare department our efforts were of no avail.

We then visited the homemaker and discussed the situation with her. We could understand her anger and disappointment and told her so. We also investigated and reviewed with her the changes that had occurred in the client's home and life ever since she had entered the household and had become a factor in the situation. We asked her, as a personal favor to us while we investigated other possible sources of income for her, to continue her association with the client and her family. Being the kind of person she was, she agreed to maintain the relationship with the client.

At approximately this time one of the projects connected with Community Progress Incorporated was initiating a homemakers' service that would divide the city into areas requiring a homemaker's service and would then assign a homemaker to that region. We contacted the director of the program and clearly informed him of the situation and described the qualities of the woman who currently was volunteering her services in the client's home. He was quite impressed with her credentials and arranged an immediate interview. His feeling at the conclusion of the interview was that the woman would be perfect for the program. He promised to contact her as soon as the program started and guaranteed a staff position for her. The program was scheduled to start in approximately three months.

The volunteer homemaker was delighted with the results of the interview. She said that during the period between then and the initiation of the program she still would investigate other job opportunities. She also promised, however, to maintain her contact with the client and the client's children. She felt that the client had benefited from their relationship and would continue to benefit from the friendship that had developed between them. There was little to do but agree with her, and add our thanks.

We have attempted to indicate that from the standpoint both of a clinical and preventive orientation it is necessary to enlarge the scope of the problem of mental retardation. Perhaps more important than emphasizing the scope of the problem—an emphasis that is not new with us—is our attempt by means of case material to demonstrate how we have tried to translate such an emphasis into practice. In the next section, which is concerned with the siblings of retarded children, we are concerned with another aspect of the same general problem of scope.

SIBLING GROUPS

Some of the case material already presented and other clinical data obtained in our work with the Regional Center indicate that the personality and functioning of the siblings of retarded children frequently reflect adjustment problems stemming from the degree and nature of the retarded sibling's conditions, his role in the family, and their attitudes and behavior to him. The processes by which the normal sibling may be affected are undoubtedly varied and the kind of systematic research necessary to a better understanding of the problem is yet to be done. In order to gain a better understanding of the problem and ultimately to develop a research program that would evaluate hypotheses about the effects on siblings and the efficacy of clinical and preventive procedures, a pilot study was undertaken.[3] This project was an eight-week nursery school for ten younger siblings of known retarded children. There were numerous difficulties in obtaining reliable estimates of intelligence from this group, but it was apparent from many hours of observations and some formal testing that at least seven were operating at a mildly or moderately retarded level. Further, observations of the children suggested that at least four had some degree of emotional disturbance that interfered with their ability to function in a nursery school situation. Two others were socially grossly inadequate with age mates. Not all of the problems of these children are necessarily the result of having an older retarded sibling in the family. The children come predominantly from culturally and financially disadvantaged families, so that some difficulties unrelated to the siblings' retardation were expected. However, there were clear indications with at least several of the children that the retardate in the family was a significant contributing factor.

Example 4. A little four-year-old girl, Betty, had an eight-year-old sister who was retarded and also grossly deformed. At least several times a day Betty tried to leave the playroom to go see her sister in another program in the same building, despite attempts by the child-care workers to restrain her from going. (Later it was decided to permit her to go and to accompany her in an attempt to help her with the problem.) She would arrive at the door of her sister's classroom, stop, and become suddenly extremely apprehensive and want to go back. The deformed child would see Betty and come running over to hug her. Betty would then try frantically to keep from being touched by the child. This entire sequence was repeated several times each day. At other times Betty cried and said she did not want to go home. Her response to questions suggested she was frightened of seeing her sister and being with her. This girl responded in a retarded and disturbed manner with adults and with peers. The fact that the sister's deformity and retardation was a taboo subject in the home and could not be easily discussed made it seem all the more frightening and dangerous to a small child trying to understand. The fact that this sibling

[3] We are indebted to Dr. Frances Kaplan for the case material in this section. She is the member of our Clinic who is conducting exploratory observational and therapeutic studies of siblings of retarded children.

was physically deformed probably made Betty's reaction more dramatic. However, the underlying concerns seemed very similar to those of children with siblings who are retarded with no physical deformities.

Two additional cases from other sources illustrate the need for further study of siblings.

Example 5. Cindy, a ten-year-old girl, was brought to the Regional Center because of "bewildering behavior." She was considered retarded and had been in a special class for retarded children in the public-school system. She was exhibiting a variety of peculiar behaviors, and also seemed totally unable to learn certain kinds of things. For example, she could not add 7 and 8, although she could read at approximately a fifth-grade level. The most relevant bit of historical data is that she has a twenty-year-old, severely retarded brother who has been institutionalized for many years. When the parents walked into the playroom for their first interview, the mother commented about the one-way vision mirror, "Oh, yes I know about these. We saw these when David went to the institution." By this and many other remarks, she made it clear that she viewed the situation with Cindy and her severely retarded son as nearly identical, despite the fact that Cindy could read and write, speak like an adult, etc. Cindy herself was quite aware of her mother's view of her. In that first interview, as the mother described some of the problems they had with the girl, she burst out, "you want to send me away!" Over several months of individual therapy with Cindy, the conviction grew in the therapist that Cindy could not learn because she felt she was not supposed to learn. She had been designated by the family as being like David and thus she could not or should not do many of the things he was not able to do. As this was discussed with her, she substantiated it in many ways. It is too early in the treatment to know if this child and the family can view her as different from her brother, and thus free her to grow and learn. There is little doubt that his retardation, and its effect on her and the parents' attitudes towards her, have enormously complicated her development.

Example 6. A final illustration is the case of a young adult who has been having a great deal of difficulty on her job. She failed in a rather mediocre college, although she gives the impression of being moderately intelligent. She then did poorly on her job and was given a simpler assignment. Over the past months, she has demonstrated that regardless of how elementary the task given her, she will manage to fail in it, although it is obvious she has the intellectual capacity for the jobs. She is the twin sister of a moderately retarded girl and she prides herself on being the constant companion and mentor of the sister. Without knowing a great deal more, we can only speculate at the dynamics of her difficulty. However, it seems apparent that her identification with her twin is in some way rendering her unable to perform at an appropriate level. We can predict that in treatment she will have to deal with her own fantasies that she is also retarded and/or somehow responsible for her sister's plight.

These are only a few of the numerous examples that became apparent once we began to focus on the problem of siblings. The clinical evidence overwhelmingly supports the contention that this is a group that needs attention. If the concept of preventive mental health is taken seriously, it seems imperative to consider siblings in the initial planning with the family when a retardate is identified and when preventive programs are being initiated.

In this chapter we have attempted to illustrate and discuss the crucial necessity of viewing mental retardation in terms of clinical and preventive approaches. Enlarging the scope of the problem has implications not only for current practices but for training as well. One of the serious obstacles to the attainment of a broadened view of the problem is the tendency of a particular profession to view the problem from its restricted vantage point, a tendency all too often reinforced by the formal structure of helping agencies. In the next chapter we focus directly on this obstacle and suggest an approach that may reduce its seriousness. It is our hope that, at the very least, our experience and suggestions may give rise to a discussion and review of the relation between formal structure of helping agencies, on the one hand, and their quality of service and degree of innovative tendency, on the other hand. Clinicians have tended to be far more imaginative in their work with patients than in their relations with each other.

Chapter 23

Professional Staff and the
Problem of Preciousness

In Chapter 2 we briefly discussed the tendency of mental-health professionals to view their technical skills in very precious kinds of ways, that is, to overestimate the differences in skills among the professions and to underestimate the communalities. This is an understandable tendency, perhaps inevitable, given the nature of training programs. As we said in Chapter 3, it is certainly not our view that all boundaries among the fields should be broken down. Each field does have a core of distinctiveness, and this should be both recognized and treasured. It is one thing, however, to say that each field has a distinctive core of skills and it is quite another thing to say that *everything* a particular profession does is either distinctive or not, in part at least, learnable by the other professions in the settings in which they work together. The history of the child-guidance movement is a clear example of how professional preciousness was gradually dissipated, particularly in the face of the pressure of waiting lists. This dissipation was not always accomplished gracefully or smoothly, because having to alter a conception of professional distinctiveness can be experienced as something akin to a "narcissistic wound." The fact is that even if professional preciousness is not a problem, the unmet mental-health needs in our society confront the mental-health professions with serious questions about the appropriateness of the existing pattern of services and the inadequate numbers of graduates from existing training programs, factors about which Albee (1963, 1964) has written cogently and eloquently.

Within a clinic, usually because it is a relatively small social system facilitating interprofessional contact, professional preciousness tends not to be the problem it is in the larger institutional setting. Our earlier experiences in relatively large institutions made it clear that the pattern of staff organization was both a symptom and a cause of professional preciousness that had some unfortunate consequences. Typically, an institution for the retarded is made up of several "empires": social service, medical, psychological, educational, cottage life, vocational, and others. This pattern of staffing, by no means peculiar to institutions for mentally retarded children, tends to have the following consequences:

1. Each of the departments is a little (or big) enclave within which there is far more communication than between departments.

2. Each department tends to view problems of policy and change primarily in terms of effects on its functioning, status, and role so that it has difficulty viewing problems in terms of larger issues.

3. The possibility that those in one department will truly understand the functions and problems of those in another department is drastically reduced.

4. The broadening of knowledge and skills of those within a department tends to occur within very narrow limits.

5. Each department has a responsibility for a "piece of the child," a tendency conducive neither to a comprehensive view of the child nor of the institution's program.

6. Cold and hot wars can develop when one department perceives that another department is performing something similar to its functions. Such conflicts, unfortunately, tend to be complicated by considerations other than those reflecting preciousness.

These kinds of experiences and considerations led us to suggest to the Regional Center a rationale for staff functioning that had three aims: (1) to make explicit in the process of interviewing and hiring personnel the problems of professional preciousness and the need to combat them; (2) to maximize the amount of experience of professional staff with *all* aspects of the program of the Regional Center; (3) to provide a means whereby each of the professions could help those with different professional training gain experience in certain aspects of its traditional functions.

In its most simple form our suggestion was that *everybody would engage in similar activities*. By "everybody" we referred to social workers, physicians, psychologists, speech therapists, educators, and rehabilitation workers; by "engaging in similar activities" we meant that, to a certain extent at least, each of these people would take complete responsibility for a case shortly after the initial contact with the Regional Center was made and would continue such responsibility as long as the case was appropriate for the Regional Center. In other words the speech therapist would do more than speech therapy, a physician would do more than examine children and handle medical problems, a social worker would do more than visit homes and be concerned with extra-Center problems, and an educator would be concerned with more than the child in a school program.

The sense of our suggestion can be understood more clearly if we describe how it is implemented in practice.

1. All cases referred to the Regional Center are brought up for discussion at a conference of several hours duration. The professional staff is present at this conference, so that a dozen or more people may attend.

2. After the available information on a case is presented and discussed the question is routinely raised as to who should assume full responsibility for the case. "Full responsibility" means that, from that point on, the staff member assigned to the case is responsible for handling all problems, arranging for whatever subsequent procedures are deemed necessary, supervising the transition of the case from the community to any of the Regional Center programs (residential or day care), and staying with the case for as long as it is in a Regional Center program.

3. The staff member responsible for a case can call on the services of any other staff member depending on the kinds of problems encountered and the information needed. However, and regardless of the number of other staff members called on, the "responsible" staff member is the one who coordinates these services and works with the family. In other words, from the standpoint of the family there is one staff member with whom they have primary contact and to whom they can come at any time.

4. The assignment of a case is determined by what the conference considers to be the most important features of the case, that is, those features, questions, or problems that will require understanding and solution if an appropriate program for that family is to be developed and implemented. For example, in a fair number of cases a variety of state and community agencies has been involved with a particular family so that it is clear it will require on the part of the staff member a degree of knowledge of and experience with the practices and traditions of these agencies that will allow him to be of maximum help to the family at the same time that interagency relationships are kept smooth, a task requiring exceptional skill. In these instances a social worker is assigned to the case. In a number of cases where the major questions center around the degree of speech and hearing possessed by

a child and/or the family's understanding of and response to such problems in their child, the primary responsibility for the case is given to the speech therapist. There have been cases in which the conference has decided that the major problem is whether a problem in mental retardation is involved, or whether it is some kind of psychological disturbance in the child and the family. In these instances the clinical psychologist may be given responsibility for the case. Later in this chapter we describe in detail an instance in which the physician was given responsibility for a case. The important point here is that responsibility for a case—handling all aspects from the initial home visit to and after the point when the child is settled in a program—is not predetermined by professional labels.

5. The staff member responsible for a case is expected to bring it back to conference whenever a policy question has come up or when the staff member feels in need of some sort of guidance from the conference. The guidance of the conference is not, however, viewed as a substitute for the individual help and guidance a staff member may require of other staff members. We must emphasize that it is explicit in this process that each staff member has an in-service training responsibility to other staff members, and the failure to seek or to give such training is a serious matter.

6. When the staff member has decided tentatively about a program for child and family he brings the case back to conference. He presents his "prescription," that is, his answers to the following kinds of questions. When should the child be entered into a program? Is this a child who will experience separation difficulties when brought to what is for him a new physical and social setting? Should the child be brought several times for short visits to the Center before exposing him to full-time residence or day-care program? Will either of the parents experience separation difficulties? Is it indicated that the responsible staff member go to the home and actually participate in the transition to the Center? If the child is entering the residential program, in what living unit should he be placed and what should personnel in this unit know about the child, for example, feeding habits, food preferences, toilet habits, special behavioral characteristics, parental expectations and attitudes? [1] Into what training program should the children go? Should the parent be invited or strongly urged to become part of a parent group and, if so, which parent group and what should the

---

[1] Anyone who has worked in institutions for young or handicapped children is aware that it is by no means infrequent that the difficulties encountered by children (and the cottage or hospital personnel responsible for his care) in the weeks after admission are due to ignorance of personnel about the answers these questions provide.

group leader know about the parents? The answers to these and other questions constitute the prescription the staff member responsible for the case develops and brings to the conference.

There are advantages, dangers, and problems in giving this degree of responsibility to staff members whose training has not formally prepared them to assume the degree of responsibility described. The pros and cons of this approach to staff functioning are taken up later in this chapter. At this point we present the first case in which this approach was used, a case in which a physician initially assumed full responsibility. The dramatic consequences of the physician's going into the home (rather than the social worker, as would traditionally be the case) are by no means typical but this case did serve to highlight for the staff the potential fruitfulness of the approach.

THE CASE OF JOE

Joe, four and a half years of age, was one of many children on the waiting list of the State Office of Mental Retardation. Those children on the list who were in the greater New Haven area became the responsibility of the Regional Center. One year before the Center was scheduled to open, the Center's skeleton staff and members of the Psycho-Educational Clinic began the task of reviewing each case for which it would need to provide services. Initially, those cases considered by the State Office to be "emergencies" were reviewed. Joe was not on the emergency list but the following letter from the mother caused his case to be taken up:

I do hope that arrangements for Joe will be made as soon as possible. You see my two-year-old son is now at G. Hospital where he underwent open-heart surgery and when he comes home from the hospital (about the second week in November) I'm so afraid he will push him down as he's done in the past. My mother was here helping me but last Thursday Joe pushed her down, fortunately she was near a chair, as she is in a brace herself. Of course, she went home the next day, because she was afraid Joe would go for her again. I can't get anyone to stay with me because of him. I would feel terrible if the little one should get hurt because of Joe after all he has gone through.

Do hope something can be done at once. Thank you.

Sincerely yours,
Mrs. W.

Enclosed in this letter was the following report of an examination recently conducted by an agency concerned with young retarded children.

Joe is a four-and-a-half-year-old child who was born on April 22, 1960. The mother states her pregnancy with Joe was uncomplicated save for a two-day illness following a flu shot at seven months gestation. Three weeks prior to delivery she had insomnia and vague abdominal pains. The labor and delivery were considered normal. Birth weight was 11 lbs. 4 oz. Joe cried and breathed immediately and had no neonatal difficulties. He has gained and grown well. In January, 1962, he is said to have had an upper-respiratory infection and was hospitalized for four days after a febrile convulsion. Joe has had frequent accidents as follows:

April 4, 1961: Laceration of scalp after telephone pulled over on himself.

July 30, 1962: Burn of right hand.

September 18, 1962: Dropped on head on sidewalk from shoulders of 12-year-old sibling.

May 27, 1963: Joe fell from a window, two stories, approximately 40 feet, to ground below. He sustained a large hematoma of the left fronto-parietal area and was hospitalized for observation for possible cerebral concussion. Skull X-rays at this time revealed no fracture.

July 14, 1963: First and second degree sunburn of shoulders. Developmental landmarks recalled by the mother reveal that Joe sat alone at 10 months, walked alone at 20 months and fed himself with a spoon at one year. He has never had any words.

The family includes two brothers (fifteen and two and a half years of age) and a six-and-a-half-year-old sister. The parents' ages are father 45 years, mother 35 years. They are all in good health.

Mr. and Mrs. W. became concerned about Joe's development at around the age of two years when he still had no functioning language. He was taken to see a physician in D. who sent them to a speech therapist and then to Dr. Y. H. at S. B. It was the impression of Dr. Y. H. that Joe may never talk but he did not give any ultimate prognosis.

At the age of three and one half years Joe was seen at the Y.C.C. The parents made four visits.

Joe was accompanied to the examination by his mother. He is an attractive, robust, active boy who related poorly to both the examiner and his mother. He often laughed inappropriately and was often provocative in the way he refused the test materials. He squirmed in his chair and on the laps of both mother and examiner in a masturbating fashion. He was able to sit for moderate periods. Occasionally he turned to the mother or the examiner, crawled into their laps in an impersonal way, and no affect in the relationship could be detected. He did not seem to discriminate between his mother and the examiner. Because of his deviant relationships and disinterest in toys no formal evaluation could be done. The following are some observations of his behavior.

Gross Motor Development: bases at the 21-month level with scattered successes up to the 36-month zone. He jumps from a low chair to the ground but does not climb stairs alternating feet. His activity was moderate. His gait and gross motor movements were well coordinated. Tempo of movements was normal. During the examination there were unusual motility patterns noted. He had frequent outbursts of gross motor activity such as sudden and impulsive moving away from the table and frequent attempts to leave the room. He could easily be returned to the table by moving to him and directing him back. He also had bizarre hand movements when he would raise his hands above his head and shake or wiggle them. He also frequently held his hands over his ears for no apparent reason. He also could be made to whirl himself about by merely touching his head and starting to rotate him.

Adaptive: behavior in this area is delayed and the quality of performance is poor. He had little drive and investment in the materials. He was most interested in the top. While the top would spin he would place his face very close to it as if entranced by it. He used the puppets and dolls in inappropriate ways. He was easily distracted and often wandered about the room aimlessly. He could not be induced or persuaded to initiate any of the examiner's activities and often seemed involved or preoccupied with his own inner thoughts. He never protested the removal of toys.

Language: no words were produced during the examination and none are reported by the mother. She feels that he may questionably understand "bye-bye." He only makes grunting or squealing sounds. He never seemed to understand simple directions, although he did respond to voice and bell sounds. Hearing does not seem to be a problem.

Personal-Social: development here is very deviant. He does not imitate and in fact avoids contact with people. Although he climbs onto people's laps he does not look at people and does not do this in order to form a human contact.

Impression: Joe's development is deviant and delayed in all areas. In addition to his absent language, the most prominent aspect of his behavior is his inability to form a meaningful relationship with people. Other characteristics of his behavior include inappropriate and bizarre play and laughter, bland affect, and outbursts of bizarre motor activity. Both from the history and from our observations, Joe seems to fit into the category of children with a diagnosis of childhood psychosis, otherwise known as atypical or autistic development.

From the history it appears that from a very early age Joe was not relating well to people and already preferred to be alone. Also from the history it appears that in many ways the parents and particularly the mother, withdrew their attentions from him because of his failure to respond to them. At this point we can only say that his symptoms are severe and his development markedly delayed.

At four and a half years of age Joe is uncontrollable at home. He is completely disobedient, very destructive of property around the house, has no apparent sense of danger and needs constant supervision. He often defecates and wets on floors, eats dirt, sand, soap, and dirty dish water.

He has a poor appetite and sometimes will go without food for several days at a time, except for drinking milk. He does not talk, has aggressive tantrums, and is adversely affecting his younger brother who is now copying his bizarre behavior. Joe takes off his clothes and runs into the street where he is in danger of being hit by an automobile. The parents feel they can no longer handle him at home and desire outside help, preferably to place him in a state school. This family needs immediate help!

Although there would be no institutional facilities for many months to come, there was obviously a need to learn more about the situation and to see what possibilities for help could be developed. Discussion of the case centered around several questions. First, what understanding did the family have about open-heart surgery, that is, did they have the popular notion, usually untrue, that the child with open-heart surgery is to be treated in a most gingerly fashion and spared any kind of upset or stress—a notion that usually raises more problems than it solves? Was the younger sibling's return from the hospital the real reason for the request to have Joe removed from the home or was it an excuse? In light of our lack of knowledge of this family, could we assume that Joe's behavior was not a significant reflection of how he had been handled in the context of family living? What did we know of how the older brother and sister were affected by and responded to Joe? In short, our concern was not only Joe but his hospitalized brother and his older siblings, that is, both preventive and clinical in substance. When the question arose as to who should take primary responsibility for the case it was clear to all that this was an instance in which the physician was most appropriate. For one thing there was the question of the hospitalized child's condition and the family's understanding of it—questions the physician could answer more quickly and appropriately than any other staff member. If the social worker or psychologist took responsibility, they could not handle these issues as quickly, and any advice they could give to the parents (by virtue of a discussion with the physician before and after their home visit) would understandably not carry the weight of medical authority. It was true that the physician might not discern familial interactions and attitudes in as sophisticated a manner as other types of professionals but this was something of which staff and physician had to be aware and handle by individual supervision as well as by the vehicle of the conference.[2] It was agreed that this case seemed particu-

[2] This statement is somewhat unfair to the pediatrician who was given responsibility for the case because he was recognized by all to be an unusually sophisticated observer of psychological events and relationships. As we discuss later, the success of our approach to staff functioning depends initially, and perhaps

larly appropriate to test the idea that the nature of the case would determine who would assume responsibility.

In the course of his initial home visit the physician came to the conclusion that Joe might very well have lead poisoning (pica): "He has eaten and still eats plaster, paint off his toys, and dirt when he plays out in the back yard (up to an estimate of one quart a day according to his mother). He has never had a blood analysis for lead determination. . . ." The physician learned that Joe spent most of his time (when not attending, on a half-day basis, a nursery-school program run by parents of retarded children) in a third-floor attic where he had a swing and several toys. On the way to see the attic the physician noticed several holes in the wall and when he commented about them the father blandly said they were made by Joe, picking and eating plaster. The physician measured an area three feet by eight feet that Joe had completely stripped of plaster. According to the father Joe had picked at the cracks, day by day, eating the plaster. That something should be done to prevent this from happening apparently never occurred to the man. At this point the physician began to wonder about the relationship between Joe's "accidents" and the bland, naive unawareness and lack of concern that characterized the parents, the father somewhat more than the mother. Related to this was the possibility that to an undetermined degree Joe's behavior was a reflection of how he had been perceived and handled in the family. The following are excerpts from the physician's observational report:

Mrs. W. talked in a quiet way about Joe's behavior. When his bus arrived she ran down the stairs, talked with driver before letting Joe out. There was a short tussle with Joe (he tried to eat dirty snow) and then mother carried him up the stairs. . . . He walked through the room ignoring visitors and sister. Mother was showing us his doll and suddenly ran to find Joe. He had removed his outer clothing and was sitting in his underwear, in the middle of the big bed in a room where his brother, Keith, was sleeping in another bed. Mother brought him out and handed him his pajamas. He puts on the slipover top and the pants with little difficulty. (He wears the pajamas with feet attached because he won't keep slippers or shoes on.)

Joe went to the pantry (usually kept locked) and brought out Nabiscos. He opened refrigerator and removed a half-gallon pitcher of water from which he attempted to drink but mother got there in time to pour water into a glass. Joe climbed on lower drawer of refrigerator, removed one item in order to get at the hot-dogs, removed one, found a frying pan, placed the

---

primarily, on how well we select personnel. As in so many other problems, the battle is more than half won if we know how to select appropriately for the tasks to be performed.

hot-dog in it and turned on the gas flame. Mother covered the dish. Later Joe started to remove the cover—mother quickly said, "Joe, that's hot!" He pulled down his sleeve and used it as a holder. Mother cut up half the hot-dog into small pieces and handed Joe a fork. He started to spear the large piece which mother then removed. . . . He disappeared and mother said, "We are now going to the bathroom." When he returned he found a bottle, hunted through the drawers by the sink (mother said he was looking for a brush with which to wash the bottle), eventually gave up the search, brought a quart of milk and filled the bottle very carefully to the very top without spilling a drop. He then screwed on the nipple (Joe uses a bottle with a nipple because the mother is afraid he'd steal the younger sibling's nipple if his was taken away.) and disappeared for a few minutes. . . .

Joe later went to the pantry and came back with a long-handled fork on which he speared a slice of bread. He tried to turn on the gas but only the inner ring lit. He then went to mother, put the fork in her hand, led her to the stove and indicated that she should blow on the gas flame.

A blood-lead determination was quickly done and it was found to be abnormally high. In light of the length of time he probably had the condition, and the brain damage lead poisoning can cause, we clearly were dealing with a many-faceted case in which no one factor was the cause.

It is, of course, conceivable that if a nonphysician staff member had visited the home the possibility of lead poisoning might have been raised. The fact is that when this case was brought back to conference it became apparent that no other staff member was as sensitive as the pediatrician to the possibilities of lead poisoning. Needless to say, the nonmedical staff's sensitivity to the problem was markedly increased by virtue of discussion of the case and subsequently one staff member spotted another case. It should also be said that although Joe had on different occasions been examined by a variety of medical and non-medical specialists, they had always seen him in *their* setting and not Joe's. That the observations of Joe in his home suggested a degree of potential above that indicated in early reports is not surprising if we assume that behavior is, in part, a function of setting.

The pediatrician was able to determine that the family had many misconceptions about the younger sibling's open-heart surgery and communicated to them that their degree of anxiety, while understand-able, was unjustified and not a basis for asking that Joe be removed from the home. There was no doubt that the mother's desire for Joe's removal had different motivations of which her concern for the safety of the younger sibling was only one. The knowledge that Joe did have lead poisoning and that there was no place to which he could be sent were realities that made the question of removal an academic one.

What could be done? The first step, of course, was to bring Joe for a stay in the local hospital to begin the de-leading process. But it was clear that we were far from understanding the child and that terms like atypical, autistic, and brain-damage were descriptive designations that were not helpful in planning action. Parental behavior was indeed strange, to what extent we could only guess. The pediatrician's home observations suggested that the boy was not "as bad" as early reports indicated. It was decided that a staff member would attempt to establish a therapeutic relationship with the boy with three questions in mind. Could anyone establish and maintain a personal relationship with Joe? Could anyone get a clearer picture of family organization and functioning? Would it be necessary to remove Joe from his home when the Regional Center's residential facilities were opened?

Because the Regional Center did not at that time have the staff to provide clinical service over a period of time, one of the Clinic's members was asked to work individually with Joe. The choice of this staff member was determined by several factors. He was a teacher who had little formal psychological training and had taught only for a brief time. He had a good deal of camp experience, both as counselor and director. He had a special interest in mental retardation and it was everyone's opinion that he could handle the assignment under supervision. In other words, just as the initial assignment of the pediatrician (rather than the social worker) proved fruitful, so the assignment of this educator to establish a therapeutic relationship with a very difficult, nonverbal child in order to answer some important questions could be equally instructive. Actually, we had no choice because there was no one else who could devote himself to Joe. We took advantage of the situation to test our skepticism about the tendency to approach the "who does what to whom" problem in terms of professional labels rather than individual potential or competence.

There was one other reason to pursue little Joe that went beyond any of these considerations, and this had to do with the need to begin developing at the Regional Center a tradition combining: awareness of the limitations of diagnostic labels; recognition of the potentially misleading character of hospital-, or clinic-, or office-based observations; and the presence of the attitude that a child's written past should be viewed as a challenge to courage and ingenuity rather than a determinant of categorical thinking and unimaginative actions. Joe was considered a good case with which to begin the tradition.

What follows are the notes the therapist wrote after each contact. They have not been changed in any way except when the goals of disguise dictated changes or omissions.

DECEMBER 9, 1964

This morning I went to the hospital to meet Joe. Dr. R. (who discovered that Joe had been ingesting lead) and I found him in the large day room sitting alone on the floor watching television. Joe is all that Dr. R. described, very big for a four-year-old, and extremely handsome. He walks, however, with a peculiar gait, legs spread wide apart (Dr. R. said he didn't notice this when he visited the home. It is possible that this is a recent development due to the injections in the buttocks the boy had been receiving).

I attempted to engage Joe in some activity and, although I found this very difficult to do, I felt that he understood all that was taking place. I finally involved him by talking off my watch and letting him listen to it tick. I expanded the bracelet and placed it on his wrist, took it off his wrist, and put it back on mine. I then gave him the watch and he expanded the bracelet and handled it in several different ways. With repeated encouragement and direction on my part he eventually put it on his wrist. With continued efforts, I was able to get him to place the watch back on my wrist. The whole process evolved over a period of about 20 minutes and I was impressed with the fact that Joe could understand and was able to attend to a task for an extended period of time.

I also attempted to engage him in a game of ball, but was not successful. I was surprised when ten minutes later he picked up a ball from the table (similar to the one I was bouncing) and articulated the word b---a---l---l---l. Joe had spoken his first word a week earlier when he said "mama" to his mother during her visit to the hospital.[3]

Joe spent most of the morning walking around the room in a peculiar, bizarre manner, occasionally sitting down to watch TV. He did not interact with any of the other children and it was only after I was there for over an hour that I was able to get his attention (after repeated efforts). He appears to know much more than his behavior would indicate and his avoiding me seemed to be deliberate. This is a child who, on the one hand, doesn't speak, shakes his head with his eyes rolling around in a crazy way, but who, on the other hand, was able to find the toilet 20 yards down the hall, defecate, flush the toilet, and return to the room. Dr. R. will speak to the mother to inform her of my interest in working with Joe. He will emphasize the lead variable as a possible important contributing factor to Joe's behavior in order to alleviate any possible guilt and feelings of inadequacy. If she

[3] It will be recalled that Joe had been described as nonverbal, and doubt had been expressed about whether he would ever talk.

is interested, Dr. R. and I will visit the home during the week and I'll set up my first session with Joe as early as is feasible.

DECEMBER 16, 1964

I visited with the family at their home and I set up my first appointment with Joe for January 2nd.

Mr. and Mrs. W. were prepared for our visit and had not only tidied up the house but were also dressed for the occasion. Joe recognized me but ignored my attempt to communicate.

JANUARY 2, 1965

I saw Joe at the Clinic for the first time this morning. He screamed and cried as he entered the building but immediately calmed down as he began to look around this new environment. He did not relate to me at all while we explored the building but appeared to be very curious about what was in the building.

He and I eventually entered our classroom (observation room) and I showed him how the two-way mirror worked and explained that people may be interested in observing us from time to time. Though he appeared interested in the way the mirror worked, I think it was more of a puzzle to him than anything else.

We spent most of the time getting to know each other. Joe walked around the room with that peculiar limbering gait of his and would sometimes move on all fours, in a monkey-like fashion. Occasionally he would roll his head from side to side and voice some Tarzan-like sounds.

He spent the first 10 or 15 minutes of the session drawing a series of scattered lines in a very random manner on the blackboard. He knew how to use an eraser and would erase what he had done when he ran out of space on the board.

I made an attempt to join him at the board by drawing a circle and asking him if he could draw one too. He paid very little attention to me or to the circle I had drawn and continued to play by himself. I repeated my request but he did not desire to be interested.

My next attempt to interact with him took place when I took some clay and made several clay figures (a head and a body). Joe picked up the clay and put it down hard on the table but again refused to join me. He then became interested in the light switch and turned it on and off several times. He returned to the blackboard and drew a circle (I requested this about 10 minutes earlier.).

At this time Joe decided to go home. He tried to reach his hat and coat (on top of the locker) but could not since it was so high. He then attempted to reach it by finding a chair that he carried over to the locker but again it was too high.

At this point I gave him the coat. He asked me to put it on but I refused. He did it himself. He then motioned for me to join him but I continued to play with the clay models so he closed the lights and left the room. (I sat there with the clay and listened for where he'd go and what he'd do.)

He went downstairs, then returned to the second floor, went to the third floor, going from room to room and eventually (about 15 minutes later) joined me in our room. I was still at the table molding the clay and when he came in I asked him to turn on the light (he did). He then came to the table and pulled up some clay and rolled it against the table. I asked him to take off his coat and join me. He complied with this request but only remained at the table for about a minute or so.

His next move was to go into the corner of the room and play with the blocks. He made a vertical pile of some long blocks and knocked them down when they were about a foot high. He returned to the board for a minute or two, wandered around the room in an aimless way, and we soon prepared to leave. He put on his coat (although he first asked me to put it on for him) and zippered it (I started the zipper).

We left the building and as we walked to my car Joe decided to sit down in the driveway. When I asked him to come along, he refused. I left him sitting there and walked on towards my car and in a few seconds heard his scampering feet chasing after me.

I invited him to sit in the front seat but he climbed over it into the back of the car. I opened the back door and invited him into the front (with a struggle) and tried to keep him there (with a struggle, as he kicked and screamed) but eventually I let him scamper into the back of the car where he immediately calmed down.

Joe always rides in the back of his mother's car, and on one occasion much to her dismay he had opened the window and was hanging by his feet outside of and parallel to the body of the car with his hands along the molding. Needless to say, she was upset and since then always brings another party along to control Joe.

Joe did not attempt to open my window but was interested in the passing scenery and also cared to feel the wind from my open window rushing against his face. He became very excited when we passed a park on C. Street and so I stopped the car to take him for a walk. I held his hand but he bolted and ran off to a pond about 75 yards in the distance. (He looked back to see what I would do.) There was a three- to four-foot chicken-wire fence supported by metal posts surrounding the pond, and there was a collection of ducks scattered about and quacking just inside of the fence.

Joe decided to join the ducks and again he looked back to observe my reaction as he began to climb over the fence. I made no attempt to stop him but debated about what I could say to his mother if he decided to go swimming.

He caused quite a commotion with the ducks as he walked among them (ignoring them) and I soon helped him back over the fence. (He came willingly.)

We found some bread that we fed to the ducks but Joe was not that interested. (I was surprised because I thought that the ducks had excited him when we passed by in the car.)

We returned to his house where I spent an hour talking with Mrs. W. about the things Joe does at home. We discussed some of the possible reasons for his behavior and some concrete ways in which Mrs. W. and her family can work in order to change his behavior.

Some of the Issues Discussed

1. Joe undresses as soon as he comes home and refuses to wear clothes in the house.
2. He drinks from a bottle with a nipple on it.
3. He makes toast over the open fire in the stove, holding the bread with a fork.
4. His use of knives.
5. Joe's banging on the gas stove whenever he does not get his way.

To illustrate the nature of our discussion I'll elaborate on two of the issues. Mrs. W. would not allow Joe to use a knife and never told him why. The other children, however, were allowed this privilege (with the exception of the younger sibling who is two and a half). We talked about this and Mrs. W. agreed to let Joe use a blunt knife. Joe immediately took the knife and cut an apple into even quarters and then into even eighths before eating it.

The question of Joe making toast on the fire came up and again I pointed out that everyone else in the household makes toast this way (the toaster is broken) and no one has ever told Joe why he should not be allowed this privilege. Mrs. W. explained that she was afraid he would burn the bread and himself. We let Joe toast the bread over the fire and the boy did a perfect job on both sides and then turned off the gas stove, although not completely.

I explained to Mrs. W. how she could teach Joe to toast bread in this way under controlled conditions, or how she could teach him to discontinue this practice. We discussed why she might want to put a stop to the practice entirely or why she might want him to learn how to use a gas stove safely.

I spent a good deal of time generalizing some basic learning principles and told Mrs. W. that I would spend an hour with her each Saturday, as well as with Joe, and that she should make notes of any questions she may want to ask.

My focus during this session was to provide Joe with the opportunity to explore what I and the Clinic were all about. I deliberately reached out to him by attempting to involve him in various activities. I wanted to show him that I was interested in being his friend. I also made clear that there were certain things Joe would be allowed to do but there were others which he could not do. I did not allow him to go home until I decided it was time. However, I did not force him to sit in the front seat of the car. I eventually will not allow him to sit in the back seat but only after I establish a "trust relationship" and more definite lines of communication.

JANUARY 9, 1965

The Joe who came to the Clinic this morning was not the frightened, crying boy of January 2. He smiled and appeared quite comfortable in his surroundings.

He came into the classroom with some candy in his hand. He took off the wrapper and dropped it on the floor. I asked him to pick it up and put it in the basket and with some encouragement he complied with this request. He removed his jacket and gave me the remainder of his "goodies" to put away for him (I had asked him to do so.). He then went to the blackboard and drew several well-defined circles. (His circle last week was a poor one.) I have spoken with both his mother and teacher and wonder if they had worked with him since I saw him last.[4]

Joe was a very different boy this morning and I was able to involve him in several activities. We spent most of the morning sitting by the mirror (Joe in my lap) identifying some parts of the body. I touched Joe's face, hair, ear, and hands and asked if he would touch mine. I directed his hands when he did not do so (I articulated each of the parts as well). We spent a good part of the session (about twenty minutes) focusing on the body parts in front of the mirror. I then sketched

---

[4] Joe was attending a preschool nursery organized and run by parents of retarded children. As we made clear in Part II, whenever we work individually with a child at the Clinic we also work with the teacher and child in the school setting.

a face with eyes, ears, nose, and mouth on the blackboard. Joe drew several circles.

I also worked with him in a couple of cooperative tasks by building blocks, asking him to help me clean the room and having him open and close the light when we entered and left the room.

As we were leaving the building I stopped to talk with M.L. and Joe suddenly became upset. He started to cry and paid no attention to my attempts to soothe him. He broke away from me and ran upstairs. I waited downstairs, and he soon joined me at the door.

Joe also became upset when we arrived at his house and found ourselves locked out. In both instances I felt that his fear was genuine and that he was not consciously attempting to manipulate his environment.

Mrs. W. and I talked once again about Joe's behavior. In spite of last week's discussion she has still made no attempt to take him off the bottle. She did take Joe to a party, however, and reported that he didn't cause too much trouble.

Mrs. W. asked me why Joe does not like strangers or anything that is new. I asked her what she meant. She said, "I can't get him to wear any new clothes until I dirty and wash them several times." In relation to his fear of strangers, she is always afraid he'll start to scream and cry in strange places and so she never takes him anywhere. Taking him to the party this week was therefore a big step for her.

I reiterated what I told her last week: until we begin to expose Joe to new situations as well as make clear to him what is appropriate behavior and what is not, he will never learn. I pointed out that Joe will not change his behavior overnight and that she must persist in her attempts to change him. Furthermore, she should expect a strong reaction to any change that she attempts to initiate.

I encouraged her to attempt two things during the coming week: to take him off the bottle and to keep him clothed until he is ready for bed.

JANUARY 26, 1965

Joe missed the next two sessions because of illness and poor driving conditions as a result of a snow storm. I continued my contact with the family by speaking with them on the phone. They have not taken a stand to take Joe off the bottle or to keep him clothed.

I also visited the school setting and discussed Joe's behavior with the teacher. He is in a classroom with four other nonverbal kids and the members of this group do not relate to each other at all. I encouraged the teacher to reach out to Joe and attempt to involve him in activity. I explained that unless we do this there is no reason to expect that he will ever begin to interact with people.

JANUARY 30, 1965

Joe seemed quite happy as he entered the Clinic and although he had missed two sessions he was able to find the classroom. After he took off his coat he went to the blackboard and drew several circles and squares with a series of parallel lines within their boundaries.

I drew a triangle and asked him if he could do the same. He understood my question but proceeded to draw some more squares. I repeated the question and illustration but Joe again drew a square. We left the blackboard and went over to the mirror. I touched his hair and said "Hair." I had him touch mine and I repeated, "Hair." We did the same for the hands, ears, nose, and face.

I had a great deal of difficulty in keeping his attention except for about two minutes of this 10-minute lesson. During those two minutes the whole mood of the lesson seemed to change. Joe had a quiet, serious, attentive expression on his face and he repeated the word "Hair,"

At this time I decided to take him downstairs for some food in the kitchen. For some reason he became very frightened at the kitchen door, bolted, and ran upstairs. I was very interested in what he would do, so I remained in the kitchen and prepared a plate of cookies and two cups of tea (there was no milk available). About seven minutes had lapsed since he left the kitchen and I proceeded upstairs with the food. Joe was walking around naked, his clothes strewn on the floor with the pants, underpants, and socks completely wet. (He had put them in the bathtub.)

I told him to put on his top (which was dry) and he seemed pleased to comply. In fact he wanted to put on the wet clothing too and started to scream and cry when I wouldn't let him. We then placed his wet clothes over the hot air vents to dry, took our food, and went into the classroom (which fortunately was quite warm). Joe continued to scream and cry and it looked like I was in for a storm. He spent the next half hour screaming, crying, and stamping on the floor until he was literally "blue in the face." He seemed disappointed that I wasn't upset. (I sat quietly sipping tea, after I finished my cup I drank his.)

At this point (after 45 minutes or so) he became more angry and proceeded to take the room apart. He threw eight to twelve pieces of chalk on the floor, the brush from the blackboard, and several blocks from the corner. Although he was angry at me, until this time he did not strike out at me directly. He finally did hit me, I held him off, he pushed me, pulled me, and threw blocks at me (I'd stop him each time). At first he directed his blows at my feet and legs, then he deliberately focused on more sensitive areas.

After about an hour and three-quarters of this, he settled down. His anger lessened in duration and the time span between each outburst became greater. I then directed him to pick up the material he had scattered about the room. I manipulated his hand for the first two pieces of chalk and he returned the rest on his own. We did the same thing for the brushes and blocks until they were back in their proper places.

I then offered him a cookie (he refused), asked him to turn off the light (he did), and we went to get his clothes. I helped him dress, and took him to the bathroom where I washed his face and gave him some paper to blow his nose. We left for his house and he was the Joe of old, quiet and smiling.

Joe took off his clothing as soon as we entered the door and I quickly briefed Mrs. W. to stage the "battle of the clothes immediately." It lasted for about 15 minutes and Joe kept them on. Mrs. W. and I talked about what happened at the Clinic and she explained that he follows this pattern at home but she has never staged a battle. I told her that I thought of her when I took this stand realizing full well that it was much easier for me to do this since I had only Joe to think about and attend to. I also told her that even under those circumstances it was difficult and that I was concerned and upset to see this child carry on as he did. However, I was determined to show him in a firm but gentle way that there was a will stronger than his.

I told her I did not know why he was upset but I wanted to make clear that he could not put on his clothes because they were wet. I also made clear that he could not always do as he pleased. I strongly suggested that now was the best time to continue the "battle of the clothes." I told her that it would be difficult but that if she persisted it would make life much easier in the future. I also explained the disservice she does to the youngster by not taking a stand and setting limits. That is, she influences his behavior not only by what she does but by what she does not do.

FEBRUARY 6, 1965

Joe was extremely cheerful this morning as he entered the Clinic. He took my hand and we went upstairs to our classroom. Joe turned on the light, smiled at himself in the mirror, and took off his coat and hat. His first few minutes in the room were very baby-like. He walked almost on all fours and at times went into a world of his own as he'd roll his eyes and head around. With some encouragement he quickly changed his behavior, went to the blackboard, erased the writing that was there, picked up the chalk, and drew some almond-shaped designs.

I invited him to join me by the mirror and we continued our body-part game. I had to work to keep his attention and he frequently became frustrated and began to masturbate.

I concentrated on his hair, nose, ears, and face by touching them (repeatedly) and encouraging him to touch mine. I repeated these words many times and asked Joe if he could touch my hair, etc. With some verbal encouragement on my part he did touch my hair. He also said the words hair, mirror, me, and mine although they were sometimes difficult to make out.

He got a big kick out of my telling him that he wanted to be a baby and didn't want to grow up. I told him several times that he was a big boy now.

We left the mirror for the blackboard and I let Joe draw as he pleased for a few minutes and then I drew a triangle, erased it, drew two sides of a triangle and asked Joe to finish it. He did.

The next time I did this he refused to draw the third side as a straight line and joined the open ends with a semicircle. We had a battle over this point for about 10 minutes and he kept drawing a semicircle, I'd erase it and draw a triangle, erase that, draw two sides and ask Joe to complete it. He'd draw a semicircle in joining the open ends. During this interaction he'd sometimes erase my triangle, or the two sides, and put up his own design. He would also cover his ears at times when he didn't want to listen to me. He refused to complete the triangle.

We left the board for the blocks in the corner. He had put several blocks on the floor and was just starting to play with them when I asked if he'd like to play with some toys in the cupboard. He was delighted with this idea and smilingly approached the cupboard.

At this point I challenged him by asking him to put his blocks away first. He refused to and chose the alternative by playing with the blocks. I should not have presented him with this situation because it was unfair, however it was interesting to note that no matter how much he wanted to play with the toys from the cupboard, he refused to let me have my way.

Joe built a well-balanced wall with small blocks that did not fall until it became quite high. While searching for more blocks he came across a block that was shaped like a gun and he held it as such. While holding it he said "gun" (and looked surprised by what he said) and came over to hand it to me. I took it and hid, out of sight, until he approached me. I came out of hiding and said "pshaw, pshaw."

I gave him the gun, he went to the mirror, pointed it at himself and said, "bang, bang." I praised him each time he spoke and he seemed delighted.

Joe then returned to the blocks and I announced that we should get ready to go home. I asked him to put the blocks away and he did. He put on his coat and hat, I started his zipper and he zipped up the coat.

We left the building and drove to his house. Mrs. W. was occupied when we entered their house and Joe started to undress. His older brother put his clothes back on but in a short while Joe was wearing his pajamas.

Mrs. W. told me that they have not consistently controlled his behavior. The younger sibling chose this moment to give her a battle by refusing to pick up his banana peel from the floor (she stood over him until he did).

I told her that this is exactly what Joe does in the extreme. I praised her for handling the younger sibling so beautifully in this situation and encouraged her to treat Joe the same way. Since she had her hands full I left their house and told her I'd call Sunday evening.

FEBRUARY 7, 1965

I just spoke with Mrs. W. to offer her some more support with Joe. Mrs. W. still doesn't fully understand the need to be consistent with Joe or the importance of working to get him to relate to others. She just recently made the first real attempt to get him off the bottle and did so by telling him that I took it for the babies in the Clinic. I asked her why she said this and she told me that she felt this is something he would accept. I explained that it would have been more fruitful to have told him the truth, but I don't think it meant much to her.

We then talked some about Mrs. W.'s feelings regarding Joe and she filled in some more pieces in his relationship with her. Apparently she and Joe just never had any relationship until September of 1964, when he started school. Until then he had never sat in her lap. Most recently she finds Joe communicating much more. In fact, during the past week he played *with* some children who came to visit their home.

Mrs. W. recognizes Joe's ability to turn people off when he so desires. We again talked about the need to involve him in household activities and to treat him as any other child.

Yesterday I went to observe Joe in his school and to continue in my attempt to establish a relationship with his teacher. I wanted to demonstrate my interest to her and I wanted to understand more about her program and the children in the classroom. I felt that only in this way could I effectively influence Joe's school program.

I described to Mrs. S. the January 30th incident at the Clinic and explained why I did what I did. I told her that she too must decide what she will and will not allow Joe to do. I explained the importance of not only explaining to him the reason for not allowing him to do something but also the need to reward him for doing that which is desirable. We also discussed her program in general.

She has a group of difficult children and asked for help in understanding and programming for them. I told her I would bring in a list of suggestions for materials that may be of help, along with a curriculum guide and agreed that she had her work cut out for her.

Joe came in, noticed me, and smiled. He took off his coat and placed it on the correct hook.

Mrs. S. gathered the children around their table, took Joe and steered him around the table while singing a good-morning song. His hand was directed to shake the hand of each youngster although most of the energy for the entire process came from Mrs. S.

Mrs. S. had no planned program for the youngsters and they all went their independent ways. Joe played with some blocks for a few minutes and then went to the center of the room where he rubbed his penis in masturbatory fashion against a pole. He did this by circling the pole several times in a very inconspicuous manner.

There is almost no equipment in this classroom and Mrs. S. limited her teaching to working with the children in a one-to-one relationship with the focus for that day on getting them to write and having them trace the letters of their name. (From what I can gather it is a strictly academic-oriented program.) The physical-education instructor opened the door and told Mrs. S. that he'd be ready for her class in about three minutes time (until now he had never taken the entire class at the same time).

The class walked from their room through the kitchen into a large-sized room that had been prepared as a gym. Its equipment was limited to two boards elevated a half foot off the ground, supported by blocks.

The two instructors took each child individually and helped him walk the board. This was quite frequently interrupted by the other children removing dishes from the shelves, taking milk or other goodies from the refrigerator, or running out of the room.

Joe had no trouble on the board and took to the ladder that was placed very poorly against the window sill. Another youngster, crawling underneath, upset it and Joe came tumbling down. He began to cry and went to hit the other boy. I explained it was an accident and he quickly calmed down. The physical-education instructor had him climb the ladder again.

In a conversation with the physical-education instructor after class (over some orange juice) he talked a good deal about the need to understand the "nature and needs" of these children. However, he had some very set ideas about their parents, their problems, and what they needed.

Our conversation was interrupted for a minute or two by one of the other teachers who informed the physical-education man that the "mess" had been cleaned up. Apparently a child had defecated on the floor and this is something that the physical-education instructor can't tolerate.

I could not see Joe today because I was ill, but spoke with Mrs. W. on the phone. I told her of my visit yesterday with Joe at school and asked how things were progressing at home. In the course of our conversation about Joe's activities she told me that he most often wears a blanket (it can be any blanket) over his head, and has been doing this for quite some time now. He covers himself with it while on his swing, when watching television, while walking around the house, and when he goes to bed.

I asked her if she has ever observed him masturbate. She told me that she has observed him masturbating for several months now. She could not tell me if there was a pattern to when he masturbated.

I asked if he ever rubs his penis against her leg or body. She described how each evening Joe and the two other young siblings lie down with her when it is time for bed. Joe *always* fights for and maintains the position next to her. It is here when she feels he tries hardest to communicate with her. I advised her not to discourage Joe's desire to get close with her and suggested that she attempt to reach out to communicate with him during these instances.

Mrs. W. then told me that yesterday evening she did not lie down with the children but instead took a belt and told them to stay in bed or else. The three-year-old ventured out, was struck by the belt, and returned to bed crying. Joe, however, persisted in his attempts to leave the bed and was beaten quite brutally by Mrs. W. He seemed to enjoy being beaten and Mrs. W. seemed to enjoy beating him. She told me that he is black and blue from the beating he took.

Mrs. W. told me several other troubling things in the course of our conversation.

1. He is still isolated in the attic and is apparently eating plaster again.

2. He is isolated in the small enclosure of their back yard.

3. Billy, the oldest sibling, has some strong feelings about Joe and apparently is quite mean to the child. He frequently hits him in a vicious manner.

The conversation with Mrs. W. uncovered a good deal of pathology in the woman that I did not know existed. I will visit their home later this week.

FEBRUARY 16, 1965

I very briefly spoke with Mrs. W. this evening to arrange for a visit to her home. She told me that she was fit to be tied because of Joe's activity earlier in the day. Apparently he went for a walk on the street in his pajamas while she was visiting (for only a few minutes) with the downstairs neighbor. The police brought him home while she was still with the neighbor.

The other incident had just occurred. He upset a bowl of scalding sauce all over the floor. The bowl had been resting on the top of the refrigerator and it is a puzzle to Mrs. W. how Joe didn't burn himself.

I told her I'd be out to visit tomorrow afternoon and that we would talk about many of the incidents she described.

FEBRUARY 17, 1965

I arrived at the W.'s home at 3:45, probably about 20 minutes after Joe had come home from school. Mrs. W. was not home and Joe was being looked after by his 13-year-old brother, Billy, who had stayed home from school because of a cold.

Joe, who was already dressed in pajamas, greeted me with a smile. I asked Billy if he had tried to keep Joe's clothes on and he replied, "He always takes them off anyway." He told me about yesterday's incidents and we talked about why they may have occurred. After explaining the why's of Joe's behavior to Billy and how he could help (I've done this before) I encouraged him to help get Joe dressed. Joe was beside me on the couch trying to do a headstand and he started to cry and scream when Billy told him he was going to dress him. I touched Joe's bare feet as he brushed against me and they were quite cold, his nose was running as well. The room was a temperature of about 60–65°.

Billy finally got Joe dressed and I asked Joe if he'd like to go for a walk. He went for his coat immediately but I asked Billy to get him a sweater to put on underneath. He brought a blue one and remarked,

"My mother knit it for him, but he would never put it on." Joe refused the sweater so I took off my coat and said that we couldn't go anywhere without it. He cried for a few seconds and let Billy help him put it on as it was a tight fit to get over his head.

We went downstairs to their backyard and Joe started to play on the swing. This was interrupted when Mrs. W. drove up with the two other children and an older lady. Joe ran over to the car and climbed in the back seat. He wanted to go for a drive. We eventually returned to the yard and as the kids played on the swing I talked with Mrs. W. It is interesting to note that her first remark was, "You must have been here when he arrived home because he's dressed." I told her what happened and she was astonished to hear that Joe was wearing that blue knitted sweater.

In a short while Mrs. W. and the other siblings went upstairs and Joe and I went for our walk. We went through a park that is located about a block from their house and played a game of chase. (He'd run and I'd chase him—up and down the park.) We had a good time and it was a game, Joe wasn't running away.

I took him to the corner store for an ice-cream cone and then we headed for the center of town. All this time he walked quietly at my side, babbling at a rapid pace. I'd talk to him every once in a while and he appeared to understand a good deal of what I'd say. He did comprehend my statement about going to the store for ice cream by his quick change of direction and sudden smile as we headed across the park. As we walked I'd stop to look in the windows and point out the various displays to Joe. He wasn't attentive, however, and preferred to keep walking.

About an hour later we returned to the house and entered through the front door without any argument on his part. This is the first time I entered this way with Joe because he has always headed for the back entrance. Mrs. W. told me that some neighbor had seen us downtown and called to report that she had never seen Joe walk so peacefully.

Mrs. W. and I talked about Joe and I repeated the same pitch about how to handle him and help him grow. I also talked to her about the beating she gave him, and what happens when he is left alone in the cold attic or back yard.

Joe by this time was in his pajamas and I encouraged Mrs. W. to dress him. She did so and asked Billy to keep an eye on him. Billy was preoccupied with the television and Mrs. W. dressed Joe about four or five times in the next hour and a half. Mrs. W. explained that Billy often helps out and she hates to ask too much of him so she preferred to tend to Joe this afternoon.

She related how difficult it is to carry the family by herself. Her husband doesn't contribute much support (financial and other) and does not help at all with Joe or with any of the other children. She told me that she had to work part-time because they needed the money and that she has not had an evening out since the last meeting of parents at the school about a month ago.

Mrs. W. went into the details of their old house on Main Street and how Joe had been confined indoors and rejected and neglected most of his childhood. They lived on the fourth floor and the stairs were very steep and with the other kids it was difficult to take Joe for walks, etc. Billy was very good to Jeanne, who is a year older than Joe, and frequently took her for walks but for some reason would never take his brother.

I do not feel that Mrs. W. is "putting us on" but I do feel that she needs some very strong guidance in the handling of her family. I also feel that there is some reason why Joe has been treated differently from the start. I do not know whether she is capable of following directions or rather strong enough to carry them out. The younger sibling is very spoiled and with Joe, the other children, and a seemingly unhelpful husband, it's a difficult chore.

I will meet with the husband next week after I see Joe. I will also consider spending a couple of afternoons a week at their home, to offer more support to Mrs. W. It is clear that we must focus on helping this child in the home and in the school if we are to at all influence his behavior. I've arranged to meet next week with the program director of Joe's school to talk about Joe's school program.[5]

(The next 10 sessions have been omitted because the notes repeat themes and observations already discussed, for example, the increasingly close relationship between therapist and child, the inability and even unwillingness of the family to change their view of and reaction to Joe, and indications of behavioral change. Notes on further sessions are also omitted when they simply repeat material.)

APRIL 24, 1965

Joe came in today grinning from ear to ear. He chased up the stairs to the classroom, took off his coat, picked up a piece of chalk and began writing his name. He wrote a E P H to begin with and became very angry seemingly because he knew it was incorrect. He erased it

---

[5] The program in which Joe was involved had just been taken over by the Regional Center and various changes in and additions to the program were being contemplated.

and started over again, finally after repeating this process several times he eventually wrote JOSEPH.[6] I rewarded his efforts by making a swing with my hands and giving him several turns. This is the first time that he did not request me to write his name for him.

I then took the chalk and wrote the word MAMA and articulated it for him. He beamed and giggled in an ecstatic kind of way and pressed his head very tightly against the board. He traced the word with his fingers very carefully. He erased the word and traced it with the chalk.

I then put the word PAPA on the board. He did not react to it at all but traced it just the same. (Mrs. W. later told me they refer to the father as Dada, never as Papa.)

I wrote DADA and again he showed clear signs of recognition but did not have the ecstatic reaction of before. Joe erased this word, traced the letters over the faint lines, erased it again and rewrote it.

I then printed the letter J and he started to whine, pulling at my hand.

I erased it and wrote the word HAIR. I articulated the sound and touched his hair. He recognized the word, erased it, and without being able to see the faded letters wrote HVIQ. I rewarded him (as I had done for each previous word) by swinging him in the cradle of my arms.

He then indicated he wanted to leave the room and I followed him upstairs to the bathroom.

I met D.C. on our return to the room and asked him to join us. A few minutes later he came in, Joe grinned, and shyly came over and hid his face in my chest. He then became very affectionate, placing his arms around my neck and cuddling closely. He made clear that I was his, and his alone. *This is the first time he has not been frightened by a stranger.*

D. left the room and Joe returned to the board and wrote DADA

---

[6] It is perhaps necessary to remind the reader that although this child is being presented in this chapter to illustrate a point of view about staff functioning—in this case the use of a staff pediatrician and an educator—it is also intended to illustrate the dangers of accepting case descriptions and diagnoses based on observations made in settings (e.g., office, clinic) in which a representative sample of behavior and social interactions is not likely to be obtained. In our experience the discrepancy in Joe's case between what we observed in the home, school, and our Clinic, on the one hand, and the contents of the reports from other agencies, on the other hand, is not infrequent. In our view, attitudes toward staff functions should not, perhaps cannot, be considered independent of how we think about effecting change in those we serve.

(traced it), erased it, and again wrote HVIO for HAIR (without tracing it) and articulated the word at the same time.

I erased the word on the board and wrote JOSEPH, DADA, MAMA. He turned on a grin as wide as his face, erased MAMA, and doodled on the board drawing some pictures and printing some unfamiliar symbols.

I asked him to clean up the area around the board and we left the building. Once outside I made a dash for my car, he laughed, and came running after me.

The ride home was quiet and interesting. He gazed out the window, opened it when I asked, but hid his head when I told him it was getting cold and requested that he close the window. Joe was extremely responsive throughout the session and indicated an understanding of the meaning of the various words and their relationship to the symbols on the blackboard.

I briefly told Mrs. W. what Joe had accomplished and her mouth opened in a disbelieving way. She was pleased that he recognized the word Mama. Her sister who was visiting was pleasantly surprised and in our short conversation it became clear that Mrs. W. had described Joe to her as hopeless.

Mrs. W. told me she had a difficult time with him the other day when she tried to keep him dressed, and after a half hour struggle gave up. I told her that a feeble attempt did no good and would only indicate to the child that he is in control. The sister acknowledged this immediately and then we chatted about Joe's birthday party, Easter, etc. and I excused myself, telling Mrs. W. I'd have a conference with her on the phone early next week.

APRIL 29, 1965

I spoke with Mrs. W. this evening. She was quite upset and complained about how difficult Joe has been lately. Mrs. W. said she was so angry this evening that she almost threw him out of the window.

The two things that bother her most seem to be:

1. The lack of support (moral and physical) from her husband.
2. Her inability to control Joe while others seem to be able to do so.

Mrs. W. brought up the question of institutionalization again and I told her this is something we may want to do when the Regional Center becomes available. However, we have several months before this becomes a possibility and until then it's important to work with Joe at home as well as at school.

I invited her to the Clinic to observe my session with Joe. I also told her that I would bring up the question of institutionalization with the Regional Center and would like to meet with her and Mr. W. sometime next week to discuss Joe.

MAY 3, 1965

I had a conference with Mrs. W. this morning with a major focus on her ambivalence in working with Joe.

We talked about her inability to handle the youngster and I confronted her with her feeling of inadequacy because of this inability (particularly when she sees that others can handle him). Mrs. W. presented a very rational argument about why it was more difficult to control him in the home when there are many other things to contend with. I agreed with her and brought out how it is far easier for me to work with him when I can focus 100% of my attention on him and him alone. We discussed this at great length as well as the situation at school.

We then came back to her relationship with Joe, acknowledging that it is difficult, but how she does the youngster a disservice by not setting limits. I took her back to September, 1964, and we looked at his development from a longitudinal perspective. She pointed out what he did not do then that he does now and was amazed at how he has progressed. I pointed out again and again the situation where she became involved and how this has helped to change his behavior. Mrs. W., then started bringing out a number of examples where she has seen change:

1. The fact that he is now affectionate.
2. That he puts on new clothes.
3. That he can play in the yard without the need to lock the gate.
4. That he interacts with other children, etc.

Mrs. W. then brought up her husband and his lack of involvement with the family. She told me they have been separated several times and she twice filed for divorce. She described him as never being home or ever doing anything with the children. He once took the older boy to New York to see a parade and they watched it from a TV in a bar. She described Mr. W. as denying that there is anything wrong with Joe and continually telling her that handling the children is her responsibility and that it is not his fault if she can't do her job well.[7] For ex-

---

[7] The fact that Mrs. W. observed the school and Clinic working effectively with Joe compounded the feeling of inadequacy she already had because of what her husband continually told her.

ample, yesterday Mr. W. came home at 6:00 P.M. and announced to the family that they'd go to the park. On the way Mr. W. talked about the law which said that a husband can stay in the home as long as he continues to support it. Mrs. W. asked him if they could discuss it at another time but he continued with the one-way discussion. Mr. W. decided that they should go to his sister's house instead of the park and when they arrived he left the family with the sister, not returning until 9:00 P.M.

I empathized with Mrs. W.'s difficulty and brought out the ramifications of the situation insofar as it affects her and her relationship with the children. I pointed to instances where she has been angry at Joe and hit him quite hard and even enjoyed it. I cited instances where she did a disservice to the youngster by depriving him of various things for no other reason than because she was angry.

We discussed these feelings and why it is important that she be aware of them. We also discussed that she is in a very difficult situation and her reaction to many of these things is a normal one. However, while it is important that she realize this, it is also important that she make a serious attempt to control her behavior when working with her children.

I told her that one of the things I could do would be to see her once a week at the Clinic. I brought out the point that it is understandable how she may want to talk about many of her feelings. She agreed.

We then discussed the question of institutionalization and considered it as being a very strong prospect, but that the reality of the next few months is what we should attend to now. I left her with a task for this afternoon re Joe and told her I'd call to find out how successful she had been. I also told her I wanted to think about how we might be able to involve the husband.

I called Mrs. W. as arranged and she excitedly said, "I kept his clothes on until 8:00 P.M."

Joe gave her quite a battle, upsetting his soup bowl and the pot of soup, but she kept them on.

MAY 4, 1965

I just spoke with Mrs. W. who took Joe for a haircut *to a strange barber* which is a bigger feat than taking him to their regular barber. Taking Joe to the barber has been a traumatic experience in the past. To take him to a strange barber was a marvelous accomplishment for Mrs. W. He carried on while they waited for a chair but Mrs. W. told him he was getting a haircut come hell or high water. Joe eventually settled down and enjoyed the haircut. He said the word "barber" several times.

Mrs. W. then treated him to an ice cream and a soda and took him outside in the yard to play, before and after supper. He helped clean up the yard when they were through playing. In the house Joe wanted to undress and take a bath but Mrs. W. said not until 8:00 P.M. He carried on, bit her, and tore the buttons off her blouse but she told him that he had to wait until 8:00 P.M.

At 8:00 P.M. she gave him permission to get undressed and take his bath.

I'm going to mail her a medal.

NOTE: Her reason for trying so hard was because I was good enough to spend my time with her. That *she* should try *for Joe* wasn't the motivating factor.

MAY 7, 1965

I just spoke with Mrs. W. and she was delighted with her progress re Joe. It rained today and this has always presented a problem in the past, since Joe would battle to play outside. The battle today lasted an hour but he stayed indoors. He also kept his clothes on without much discussion until it was time for him to take his bath.

MAY 8, 1965

Mrs. W. brought Joe to the Clinic a half hour earlier than usual and I found them waiting outside as I drove up. He was crying but calmed down when I approached the door. He was dressed in a very smart looking red sport coat that he had refused to wear since an evaluation two years ago, but put it on today without an argument. Mrs. W. was delighted with this, as well as with being able to drive Joe to the Clinic without any assistance (a first since the episode when he hung out her car window).

Joe was very attentive this morning and I worked more closely with him than I usually do. We worked together at the blackboard for about 25 minutes and for the first time I structured the entire session. I corrected his errors and continually rewarded him for his work. He loves to swing in the cradle of my arms and each time he'd write a letter or word correctly I'd give him a ride.

After his visit to the bathroom we returned to the room and I allowed him to do as he pleased. He played with the toy cash register and we made a game out of opening and closing it. He spent the next few minutes exploring the room. He approached the air conditioner and was disappointed that there was no breeze (he remembered the breeze from last week). I showed him how to turn it on and he put his face close to the fan to feel the air. He was quite ecstatic over this and seemed to derive an abnormal amount of satisfaction from the breeze. It seems to me that he may be associating this with the breeze from the swing in the attic, in their yard, and at the school. He was truly in rapture over the sensation to the degree that his eyes became glass-like.

The ride home was uneventful. He sat quietly when I asked him to stop leaning out the window, and closed and opened the window appropriately, at my request.

I spent a half hour talking with Mrs. W. who seemed more alive than ever before. She was delighted with the medal I presented her (a tea bag pinned to a card stating "a cup of tea for a deserving mother"). The barricade set up in the house to prevent Joe from going downstairs is now removed.

MAY 10, 1965

This morning I had my second conference with Mrs. W. at the Clinic. She is slowly becoming excited with her effectiveness in handling Joe. On Sunday she took the children to their grandmother and everyone remarked how differently Joe acted. They were there for several hours and he did not act up at all. All were elated when he picked a dandelion and gave it to his grandmother at his mother's request. There is no doubt that Mrs. W. is seeing the payoff for having taken this consistent stand.

We spent most of our session discussing her and the relationship she has with her husband and his relationship with the children. Mrs. W. took me back 15 years and described in detail the nature and extent of the man's pathology. One of the incidents described involved Mr. W. consistently being absent from work, on Mondays telling the employer that his wife was sick and he had to help out at home. His story was so convincing that the employees took up a collection and a representative brought it to the W. home on Saturday morning. Mrs. W., of course, was fine, and Mr. W. disappeared for a week.

She cited a number of similar incidents, quarrels, etc. In all those incidents involving the children Mrs. W. covered up for the husband. For example, a few weeks ago he was released from the hospital after being ill for two weeks and Mrs. W. went to pick him up. The children were all waiting expectantly but Mr. W. refused to go home until he could spend a few hours in the bar. Mrs. W. told the children that the doctors had to take some additional tests and picked the husband up two hours later.

From what she has told me (and the floodgate really opened today) the description of her husband does not sound good. However, it seems worth an attempt to contact him and discuss his relationship with the children and wife. I think it might bother him if he knew that they will soon know the truth about him. I also think that he has reached a point where he is afraid to try to be a father for fear of failure and needs to be confronted with this hypothesis.

I made the first point because for all that he has done, Mrs. W. has always covered up and he has never felt any embarrassment. Coupled with this he is concerned with what the children and others think of him. For example, he dressed up in a new suit when Dr. R. and I visited the home several months ago. He puts on a front for his bar mates, friends, and his wife when discussing the children.

He tells his wife there is nothing wrong with Joe and that he could teach him to talk in a week. He also does not feel the youngster is different in any way.

It I can reach his conscience by confronting him with his fear of failure and the truth about his relationship to his children then I think this household will really undergo a dramatic change.

MAY 11, 1965

I just spoke with Mrs. W. and things seem to be coming along well. Yesterday she took Joe to a neighbor for a visit. He sat quietly at the table for a half hour or so and drank some water that his mother gave him. He soon began to explore the house and found a box of cereal. The neighbor told him he could have it. Joe emptied the contents of a bowl on the table, filled the bowl with cereal, and said, "milk." Needless to say Mrs. W. and the neighbor were surprised. He finished one bowl, filled another, and said "more."

Mrs. W. was delighted with his behavior. "He behaved just like a normal boy," she said.

Today Mrs. W. gave Joe a chair to paint. He had a ball and did not paint anything but the chair. Mrs. W. is seeing to it that Joe continues to keep his clothes on. He has also made only one attempt in the past two days to jump from the bureau.

MAY 15, 1965

Joe was very attentive for the hour and a half we spent at the Clinic. He worked at the blackboard for about 45 minutes of the time (with very few interruptions or digressions). He loves to write and now knows many letters but becomes confused when he tries to write a word. He frequently gets mixed up with the sequence of letters or with

what letters belong in the word he writes. He does, however, understand the relationship of the word, the object it represents, and the
written symbol.

On the way home we had a small crisis. My car was parked at a
garage three blocks away. I explained this to Joe but with no avail. He
cried all the way to the garage and did not stop until he climbed into
the vehicle.

The family (other children and Mrs. W.) greeted me with open
arms. The young girl had drawn some flowers for me and Mrs. W. had
a cup of tea waiting (with a carefully selected jingle attached to the
bag). "A good listener is not only popular but he learns while he listens." She bought the Salada tea bags especially for the jingles. (I gave
her one as a medal two weeks ago.) She also baked a pie for the occasion. I am beginning to have more than a very special meaning for
Mrs. W. and I better start to prepare her for the separation.[8]

Mrs. W. reports that Joe makes no attempt to remove his clothing
and is not biting or fighting her as much as he did during the past two
weeks when she took her stand.

He interacts with the neighbors in their yards and today used the
words "cookie" and "school" appropriately without any cues.

MAY 17, 1965

I had my third conference at the Clinic with Mrs. W. today. It is
quite clear to her that change has been taking place and she is very
proud of her effectiveness in the situation. I pointed out to her that
not only is she more aware of and involved with Joe and his needs but
her attitude towards the other children has changed as well.

I have not yet been able to arrange for a meeting with Mr. W. and
don't know if one will ever develop. However, I have discussed with
Mrs. W. what she can try to do. I described Mr. W.'s behavior as similar to Joe's in many ways. Mr. W. refusing to take responsibility,
lying, drinking, and staying out in his own world. I told her that I
didn't know how much we could change him but insofar as he influences the children, I felt we should take a stand. For example, on Saturday Mrs. W. came home from shopping at 5:00 P.M. and Joe was on
Mr. W.'s lap dressed in his pajamas. Mrs. W. asked why he was not in
clothes and her husband replied that it was close to his bedtime. Mrs.
W. did not want to rock the boat at this point and left the room. Joe
was grinning from ear to ear for having been able to win his battle.

Until now Mrs. W. has always defended her husband in front of

---

[8] The therapist was going to be away for seven weeks in the summer.

the children by lying for him, etc. I told her that it is time she took a stand. I told her to tell him that unless he begins to carry out some responsibility insofar as the children are concerned (i.e., show them what it means to have a father), then she will start to treat him as if he has no responsibility. In the case described where Joe was in his pajamas, she might want to insist that Joe get dressed irrespective of what his father has said. Furthermore she should make it perfectly clear to him that one day he will be faced with the situation where he has no family to look to. His oldest son doesn't respect him at this point and the other children will soon react to him in the same way.

I also discussed preparing Joe for my leaving in June.

MAY 26, 1965

Mrs. W. is working very well with Joe. On Monday she took him and the other siblings to the beach after school was out. They had driven Mr. W. to work and since it was a warm afternoon decided to go to the ocean. Joe had been restless in the car because of the traffic congestion, etc., and when they finally arrived at the beach he wanted to take off his clothes. Mrs. W. wouldn't allow him to and so he urinated in his pants. She removed his underpants but made him keep on his shorts. They fought for a while but he ended up keeping them on.

That evening Mrs. W. took Joe, the other siblings, and a neighbor's child to watch Billy (the eldest son) play baseball. She brought a pad and pencil along for Joe and taught him to write my name. He enjoyed the ball game and called his brother's name when Mrs. W. encouraged him. He also said my name for the first time. Mrs. W. asked him to say my name and he repeated it after her very clearly.

She is quite enthused.

Tomorrow Mr. W. is scheduled to visit.

I had a discussion with several of Joe's teachers this morning. The physical-education instructors who have consistently attempted to involve Joe with the group are reaping the fruits of their efforts. Joe does not wander away from, but participates with, the group.

MAY 27, 1965

I was surprised when Mr. W. came to the Clinic for our scheduled conference today. I pushed him against the wall in order to get him here and was not too certain that he would come.

I introduced our session with a 10-minute presentation on his children (not only Joe) and their development. I cited example after example of events in their lives that Mr. W. did not share with them. I cited example after example of inappropriate behavior on the part of the children.

Mr. W. spent the next 20 minutes reacting to this, and telling me what he does do for the household and with the children. It was very clear that he had a minimal amount of involvement with the children. I pointed this out to him and discussed what it might be like for a child not to have a father. We also discussed what a father might feel like not knowing the pleasure of helping his children to grow.

Mr. W. told me that his father died when he was only a year old. He admitted that he didn't know what it was like to have had a father but that he would have liked it. He then admitted that his children are spoiled and haven't been treated as well as they could have been.

We discussed how things could be different. I told Mr. W. that it wasn't easy to be a father and that he would have to work at it. His task for the week is to try and teach Joe to play ball, spend a few minutes each day talking to the other siblings, and to get the children to clean up their toys and put the house in order before they go to bed. He also promised to discuss the children with his wife and how they could better work together.

I plan to see him in two weeks time to discuss his progress. I told him it would be hard work and that he shouldn't expect changes to occur overnight. I will speak with Mrs. W. to get her to reinforce my discussion with Mr. W.

MAY 29, 1965

Joe was very attentive for the first part of our session. He showed a remarkable retention ability when he wrote OOKIE for cookie after seeing it for a few brief seconds. We had a grand time with words and he continues to enjoy working at the blackboard.

He had a glass of milk and some cookies and although he was receptive to a snack once before, he approached it very differently this time. He ate the food immediately and drank the milk with two big gulps. The last time I brought him some food he let it sit there for almost a half hour (and not because he wasn't hungry).

For the last part of our hour Joe turned me off and played by himself. I gave him some block letters to play with but he didn't want me to participate. He was very aware of my presence and his turning me off was deliberate. When we were cleaning up before leaving I asked him to collect the chalk on the floor but instead he rolled some additional chalk from the blackboard to the floor. He picked it up when I told him to.

I told him that I would be leaving in a few weeks but that I would be coming back in a short while. I told him I'd send him a card to show him where I'll be staying. I don't know how much he understood.

Before we left the building, I prepared him for my new car and told him that he'd have to be careful in it. He cried very briefly when he saw it but seemed to enjoy riding in it. He sat on the seat and put his feet up only once or twice fully aware of what effect this would have on me.

At their home he wanted to play on the swing but since it was raining I brought him inside.

JUNE 5, 1965

Joe was his usual cheerful self at the Clinic this morning. He still enjoys writing on the blackboard and this morning he showed me a new word that he learned "Happy." He also said it.

After twenty minutes of activity at the board I took him over to the mirror, placed him on my lap, and talked to him. I discussed his "spitting" at home and why he shouldn't do it. I also told him how happy I am with what he has learned. I again told him that I would be leaving for the summer but would return and continue to see him. I think he understood the message re the spitting and acting out behavior as well as how pleased I am with his progress; I am not too sure about his understanding my coming departure.

We then went to the cupboard and Joe selected the magnetic letters and placed them on the table. He wrote nonsense words for about ten minutes and then I told him we were going to play a game. I gave him the four letters and asked him to write MAMA. He did. I gave him the letters for the word COOKIE and asked him to write it. He placed them as follows: C OOKIE. He became restless at this point and so I let him do as he pleased.

I turned on the air conditioner since it was getting warm and Joe was attracted to it immediately. He was ecstatic over the breeze and became a very different child. His behavior was quite bizarre as he moaned, jumped, and rolled around the room shaking his head, walking on all fours, looking at the mirror unaware of my presence. In about five minutes he became aware of me once more and stopped. I took him back.

JUNE 12, 1965

I just spent my last morning with Joe before leaving for the summer. Mrs. W. brought a Father's Day card for me with Joe's picture on the cover. Joe presented me with the card grinning from ear to ear.

We went upstairs, entered the room, Joe turned on the lights and almost immediately began to write on the board. He wrote several letters, left the board, approached the mirror, looked at his reflection and then at mine. He babbled at his reflection and returned to the board.

I went over to him and told him I was going to show him how to write a new word. I wrote the words BYE BYE and he recognized it. Then I told him that I was going bye bye and that I would return. I wrote my name, and then BYE BYE.

He wrote my name but would not write BYE BYE or anything else. He was unresponsive for most of the remainder of our session. I continually reached out to him but he did not respond.

His behavior was very peculiar and somewhat disjointed. I did not know whether this is a reaction to my telling him I was going away or whether it was symptomatic of something else.

I took up the going away issue with him again, reiterating that I would miss him, and that I would be back.

Joe continued to act peculiar and refused to become involved in any activity. He would not even write his name.

When he returned from the bathroom he took the board with the magnetic letters out of the cupboard. He lined all the letters up and I told him I wanted him to write a word. I took the letters of his name and separated them from the group. I asked him if he knew what they could say. He pushed them aside. I wrote JOSEPH with them. He spit at the letters and threw them on the floor. He picked them up with some reluctance when I told him to, but refused to do anything with them.

I told him I didn't understand what was bothering him and asked if he was angry because I was going away. He didn't react to my statement and I repeated I didn't understand what was bothering him. We prepared to leave the Clinic and he tidied up the room, closed the lights, and we went downstairs. He was exceedingly quiet and well-behaved in the car. He took in the breeze by the window and kept his feet off the seat when I asked him to. At their home he ran into the back yard, grinned at, and playfully pushed his sister who ignored him and came running to me. Joe went to the swing.

I went upstairs, had some tea with Mrs. W. and accepted two cards, one from Jeanne and one from the younger sibling. I woke Mr. W. up and asked him what he's been doing with Joe. He hadn't been doing too much and I confronted him with the facts. I told him if he didn't accept this responsibility Joe will always be lacking.

Mrs. W. took my picture with Joe and I said goodbye. I'll see Mrs. W. at the Clinic on Tuesday.

Joe's case is illustrative of a number of things, for example, the need to be skeptical of previous findings and observations without falling into the trap of cynicism; the importance of seeing child and family on their home grounds; the productive effects of direction and support of parental actions, when they are deemed appropriate and necessary; and the importance of correlating and using first-hand knowledge gained in one setting (e.g., Clinic) with that obtained in other settings (e.g., home, school), a procedure basic to the rationale employed in our work in the public schools. However, for our present purposes Joe's case is of primary significance for discussion of the view toward staff functioning presented earlier in this chapter.[9]

The consequences of using professional staff in ways unfamiliar to them, and for which their training did not directly prepare them, are not always as dramatic as in the case of Joe. Also, the fact that the Regional Center had not yet opened its doors prevented us from experiencing all the problems that might come up when a variety of professional personnel are given responsibility for a case beginning with the first home visit and continuing through and beyond adjustment of the child to a day care or residential program. In short, our discussion of the advantages and limitations of our view toward staff functioning is based on pilot experiences in a situation (i.e., preparing to open an institution) that, while conducive to innovation, is not exactly conducive to systematic exploration. But we think the issues involved are of such importance as to justify reporting our view of our experiences.

ADVANTAGES

When we look at each staff member not only in terms of his professional label but also in terms of competencies and potentialities that are not necessarily discernible from the label, our views about and practices in hiring personnel undergo marked change. We do not view the psychologist only in terms of diagnostic testing or psychotherapy, or the physician only in terms of physical examinations, medication,

[9] It is interesting to note, as we pointed out in Chapter 20, that one of the most distinctive contributions of CPI in its inner-city programs involved innovation as to who was hired to perform important staff functions, e.g., neighborhood worker and work-crew foreman. As will be seen later in this chapter, the Regional Center (like CPI) has not always been viewed positively by the professional community, precisely because of the Center's approach to the "who does what to whom" kind of question. It is hardly surprising that in certain quarters of the professional community the Psycho-Educational Clinic is viewed with suspicion because its type of staff, orientation, and work settings are markedly atypical for a helping agency.

and hospital affairs, or the teacher as one whose responsibilities are confined to a classroom and school building, or the speech therapist as one who works only with those having speech problems, or the social worker as one who focuses only on work with the family. It goes without saying that we look closely at training and competency in relation to what is distinctive in each field. In addition, however, we look for interests and potentialities that suggest that the individual could learn to assume skills more or less common to the work of all who help others, for characteristics and special competencies that maximize communalities rather than differences among the various professional fields. The process for achieving this begins at the point of hiring. As we shall see later, not everyone looks kindly at an attempt to stress what is or could become common to the different professions.

The most immediate advantage of our view of staff functioning is that it provides each member with opportunities to experience and be responsible for total service to a family. Rather than seeing problems only within the context of the practices and skills of a single profession, staff members are able to gain a more realistic picture of the complex and changing interrelationships among presenting problems, diagnostic evaluations, program planning, and the processes of implementation. Because program planning and implementation require a knowledge of existing and proposed programs as well as relationships with personnel from other fields, the staff member gains a perspective not ordinarily attainable when he works only within the confines of his own profession or department.

One of the consequences of what the staff member gains by assuming responsibility and performing functions usually thought to be in the province of other professionals is that to the extent that staff members attain flexibility of role the agency has more people to call on as conditions require. If the Regional Center had been forced to assign responsibilities to staff members strictly in accord with their training and professional label, it would have hardly rendered any service in the period before its full professional staff had been hired and its facilities ready to open. In fact, even if the Regional Center had at a very early stage its full complement of staff, the pressure of intake of new cases as well as the need to review old cases were sufficient to have created a long waiting list for social-casework service if, as is usually the case, it had been social workers who were solely responsible for home visits, collection and coordination of relevant information, and the rendering of whatever help was necessary and available.[10]

[10] The traditional approach to staff functioning is seen in the following quotation from an article on psychiatric aspects of mental retardation (Menolascino, 1965):

As we pointed out in Chapter 21, the concept of the Regional Center embodies the aim of bolstering existing programs and helping to develop new programs in the community, that is, the Regional Center has not come into existence in order to facilitate the termination of ongoing programs in the community. *To achieve these aims requires a staff that knows the community in the sense that it is knowledgeable about available services, and is involved in the community in the sense that it represents the agency to certain families in the community. A community-oriented staff is not one that spends most, if not all, of its time away from the community and inside the walls of its own facility. A community-oriented staff is not one that experiences its problems in its institutional setting and rarely has the opportunity to see how the problems manifest themselves in their natural setting. A staff cannot be community-oriented if because of its own physical isolation from the community or lack of commerce with it, it knows only its own programs and has little interest in adding strength to programs other than its own. A community-oriented staff member is not one who talks only with people in his field, be they in his agency or elsewhere in the community.*

One of the most interesting and encouraging aspects of the implementation of our view about staff functioning was (with some notable exceptions) willingness, if not eagerness, on the part of individuals to engage in the venture and to assume the responsibilities involved, to be constantly aware of the help they would require and to be prepared to give help to others in regard to their own fields. We hardly need to emphasize that successful implementation of this approach depends in large measure on the seriousness with which the in-service training features are faced and handled. Our approach is not merely one of "spreading the work around" or equalizing levels of responsibilities because of some abstract conception of professional equality. It is also *not* part of our approach that everyone should be doing the same things in equal degree, but rather that all professional staff should, to some extent at least, share similar responsibilities.

There is no doubt in the case of the Regional Center that implementation of our approach resulted in more cases receiving more serv-

---

"Treatment considerations begin with the initial contact with our social worker, where the presenting problem is discussed; parental expectations from the evaluation are explored; and legal releases are obtained to allow for collation of data from previous medical records, evaluations or other significant contacts." The possibility that the first contact need not be with—and on ocasion *should* not be with—the social worker is never raised or discussed. We consider it symptomatic of the problem of preciousness that questions about staff functions are rarely raised and true attempts at innovation amazingly rare.

ice more quickly than if the more traditional mode of staff functioning had prevailed. But what about quality of service? We must face squarely that for a period of time each staff member performing unaccustomed duties or assuming an unfamiliar degree of responsibility will probably not render the quality of service that a more experienced staff could render. With adequate supervision, however, this differential should decrease. It is our impression, and it would be our prediction, that if this approach is implemented well it results in a professional growth of staff and in an interstaff relationship that makes for better service to the individual. In judging an institution or program we routinely ask about the quality of service to its clients; that is, to what extent have they changed in the desired direction? *It is our contention that an equally important question—the answer to which bears on quality of service to clients—concerns the opportunities for staff to grow, professionally and personally, in desired ways.*

We make no claim to have given our approach to staff functioning an adequate or extensive test. We do have sufficient experience with this approach to be able to say that the principles involved are worthy of further study. Parochialism of view and experience, shortages of professional personnel (now and in the foreseeable future), interprofessional conflicts and hostilities, the effects of institutionalization on staff (as well as patients) are but some of the considerations that should put a premium on innovation in and critical re-examination of existing practices.

LIMITATIONS

When we give people a degree of responsibility and/or ask them to discharge certain functions for which their training does not directly prepare them, we clearly run the risk of diluting quality of services and creating confused professional identities. When the welfare of patients is at stake we do not lightly tamper with the existing order. It may very well be a limitation of our approach that it requires for its successful implementation a degree of professional responsibility and of clinical sophistication, as well as a commitment to training, that are infrequently found in combination in one setting. Unfortunately, however, our experience suggests that where this combination is found the desire to innovate or the response to the innovations of others tends in the first instance to be weak and in the second instance violent or indifferent but rarely neutral. We cannot expect professional preciousness to be overcome or studied in settings in which adherence to the existing order is a source of satisfaction.

Even where there is agreement among staff, as there was in the case of the Regional Center, to view staff functions in the way we have described, we must expect that, when confronted with the realities inherent in change, some individuals will prefer to stay within a familiar tradition. This, of course, can present problems among staff, particularly if the difficulties are not verbalized. It is our experience that the more the staff members can verbalize problems, questions, and reservations about staff organization the more opportunity we have to discuss fundamentals: the significance of shortages in the different professions, the implications of a community orientation for staff functioning, the constricting effects of complete departmentalization of staff on professional growth, etc. However, we cannot deny that what at one time appeared to a staff member as a worthwhile experiment can become at a later time an intolerable situation toward which there is little likelihood of a change in attitude. Such changes in attitudes are to be expected and respected, but not accepted at the cost of impairing staff organization and efficiency. We consider this type of situation a limitation of our approach because it puts an additional burden on those in positions of leadership to be vigilant and sensitive to what is going on and to be prepared to take decisive action—characteristics in short supply among those who are in positions of leadership in mental-health settings (perhaps in short supply among leaders in other types of settings).

In and of itself innovation is neither good nor bad. When innovation becomes an end in itself, a way of achieving distinctiveness and recognition, or a way of denying that tradition has anything to offer, it is likely to be short-lived in time and space. But innovation can be short-lived precisely because it requires an attitude toward change and experimentation, a search for rather than an avoidance of possibilities of growth and development, a kind of self-scrutiny which discriminates between issues of ideas and status, the capacity to entertain the possibility that what has been done may not be right, and confronting the fact that truth is an elusive commodity the possession of which allows certain people to avoid any further need to change or question. The nature of training in the mental-health and educational professions tends to extinguish—or at least not to reinforce—those characteristics necessary for productive innovation and this imposes a restriction on what we may hope to accomplish.

The opportunity we had at the Regional Center to try out ideas about staff functions and organization is rare, primarily because we were part of the Regional Center almost from its conception and because it had a director who on his own came to see the need for innovation. We have not spent this chapter on our ideas and experiences in relation to staff functioning because we have hard data about the effectiveness of our efforts or because we are completely secure in our feelings that we are correct. Our major aims have been to indicate the severe limitations of traditional patterns of staffing, to illustrate how this worked in a particular case, to make clear some of the pros and cons of our approach, and, most important, to convey to the reader our conviction that we are raising some legitimate and important questions that for too long have gone unraised and unstudied. If our impressions or intuitions are correct, we have raised questions that in the course of training and practice have occurred to many people in the different professions concerned with problems of help, be it help in a Regional Center for the mentally retarded, in a state hospital, a mental-hygiene clinic, or in a school. In some ultimate sense it is less important if in this chapter we have posed the right questions and given the right answers than if we helped start or continue a discussion about the characteristics and sources of professional preciousness and their consequences for the professional individual, for those whom he is supposed to serve, and for the larger issues surrounding the serving of the public welfare.

In the present chapter we have discussed our approach to the use of professional staff at the Regional Center. In the next chapter we describe a pilot program concerning the training and utilization of non-professional individuals, a program involving the three major settings with which our clinic is affiliated.

Chapter 24

The Regional Center, CPI, and the Schools

The contents of this chapter might well have come in previous sections of this book because they describe some experiences that initially grew out of problems, ideas, and events involving CPI and the schools. We present it at this point because as the nearness of the opening of the Regional Center approached we realized what a central role the Regional Center could play in a projected training program involving adolescents from the inner-city areas. The significance of this chapter lies less in the experiences to be described than in the possibilities it suggests and in the demonstration of how different community settings can be meaningfully useful and related to each other if there are people who intimately know and are part of each of the settings.

THE INITIAL EXPERIENCES

One of the Clinic staff participating in a panel interview at a disposition conference at a Neighborhood Employment Center met a young Negro, about 17 years old, who was very impressive in personal manner. He had dropped out of high school because he did not find anything of value to him in school and he wanted apprenticeship training in working with horses.[1] The NEC staff agreed to try to

[1] We are not sure what it signifies, if indeed it signifies anything unusual, that interest in horses was a major one for several boys coming to the Neighborhood Employment Center; they wanted employment involving work with horses. As we pointed out earlier, the NEC takes the interests of boys seriously, however remote the satisfaction of such interests may be. In one case an on-the-job training situation with a veterinarian was arranged with splendid results. In the case of the young man we present above there was a tendency among one of our Clinic staff to view the boy's interests as strange, amusing, and probably of no depth. He made it his business to talk to the boy and came away with the statement: "He knows a lot about horses, their breeding and care. He has read a lot about them. It's still not clear to me how he came by this interest but come by it he has."

find a placement for the young man and, in the meantime, the Clinic consultant agreed to use the young man as a clerical assistant on a research project so that he would be placed on the work-crew payroll until the apprenticeship could be developed. The young man carried out his duties with impressive intelligence and efficiency. He would be assigned a job and his supervisor would not hear from him again until the job was properly and promptly completed.

The young man was working at that job for about three weeks when one of our staff at one of the inner-city schools encountered a problem in clinical management. A schizophrenic child in a first-grade classroom had been referred for evaluation to a child psychiatrist because his behavior seemed to be gradually becoming much worse. The teacher had indicated that he was a docile enough child but in his confusion he would wander around the room interfering with other children. He frequently provoked other children to hit and bite him. Discussion with the teacher revealed that her problems with the boy came when she could not be face to face with him in the classroom, and when her group went to the basement lavatory. She had considerable question about whether it was at all reasonable to try and maintain him in a public-school classroom, particularly because she had several other children who were both disturbed and disturbing. The psychiatrist, in considering possibilities for working with him, mentioned that during his training he had once "specialed" such a child in a nursery-school situation, and he wondered about the possibility of finding a special for this child. At that point the idea was born of using our young man as an assistant to the teacher.

The consultant discussed the idea with the teacher and the principal and, finding that both were receptive, discussed the assignment with the young man. A luncheon appointment was set up with the young man and the teacher to discuss how he would work with that child and with other children in the class as necessary. It was emphasized that the young man was to work strictly according to the teacher's direction, and that the consultant would remain in an advisory capacity only. The young man started and on his second day, when the teacher saw the consultant in the school building, she ran up to him saying, "Don't you dare take him away! He's made all the difference!"

No sooner was it clear that he was working out very well indeed, than other members of the Clinic staff requested his services, and we began to seek a second person to perform the same duties.

At this point the Regional Center took over a nursery-school program for retarded children that had been run by a parent group in an old school building. As a result of taking over the program, staff could be added and these were the individuals with whom both young men worked. The second young man worked in this setting for two weeks before being placed in a public-school setting.

It was our feeling that we wanted to get some experience with these young men in various settings, that the teachers would be more comfortable if the young men were in their classrooms only part of the time, and that their value might be greater if they were not present the full time. Although the following list of activities they performed may seem very long, let us emphasize that these activities were performed in a variety of settings and that we do not differentiate between the activities of the two. They functioned primarily in special and lower-grade classes.

During the time a teacher was occupied with her reading groups, each young man would patrol the room, helping children with their work and squelching boisterousness or restlessness that threatened to get out of hand. In some situations, the teachers permitted the young men to work with a small group of children, for example, overseeing a reading group. In other situations the teachers allowed them to read to the whole group, to tell stories, and to demonstrate art work.

Each young man often accompanied a group to recess periods and supervised a group of boys in the lavatory. One man supervised a small group of children during recess period, giving the teacher a well-deserved break. In still another situation, during recess, the young man stayed with the difficult child, either engaging him in a game or helping him to participate.

Both young men served as assistants when a class went on a trip. They accompanied the class and helped to supervise the group. They were particularly valuable in this service; teachers called several times to ask for them to act in this capacity. One of the young men accompanied a group of children on the school bus to and from the summer session for special-class children. The difference his presence made was apparent in the aggression and excitement reported on the bus in the few days he was absent.

Both young men did individual work with children in and outside of the classroom. In the classroom, they would engage individual children at their seats, or in a corner of the room, and help them with assignments in reading and arithmetic, or help and encourage them in completing seat work. Often they would take the children outside of the room for periods ranging up to a half hour and tutor the children in given areas. The focus was always on schoolwork, but the young men showed a great sensitivity in their awareness of manipulation from children, flagging interest, the need to be noncritical, and the need to be very encouraging. The work was supervised closely by either the consultant or the classroom teacher, but certain teachers gave the boys some initiative in preparing material and both showed creativity and ingenuity in the work they did themselves.

Some of the notes the young men kept at our request may give something of a feeling for how they responded to the teaching situation and how they understood the teaching situation. The typed notes are reproduced exactly as they were handed in.

The first time I came to the class they gave me a warm welcome. They thought that they could do anything they wanted to do. But I fooled them. T. was the first one to try, he came to me and said Mrs. N. lets us go to the bath room, when ever we have to go, can I go. I said no T. you, have to, wait for the right time we will all go to gether now go sit down. T. when he does his work is slow at first but when he has, a goal to strife for he can get the work done. Like for instance, I told him to look at the clock and see if he can get finished before, the big hand moves to a surtain number and he well do it fast, and neat. To day T. set his own time before I got to him.

E. is T.'s best frinds they are allways to gether. one that I in joy working with he looks like a little professor, has glasses that are to big for him they hang over and under, his ears he realy is a sight, and the normel things he dose . . . will alone make you love him, he is slow doing his work, but he gets it done a little sloppy perhaps but done.

A. To day I asked him to be good in reading class, and he was better than good he was perfect. He still is sloppy but, he was good he really tryed his best.

G. Still gives me trouble, she asked if I would sit, with her and help just help her and not the rest of the class, To quote her——teacher sit and help they can call Mrs. N., if they need help. I told her that Mrs. N. was very busy, and I was there to help Mrs. N., and the class, not just G! G. likes to grab your arm and pull until you give her your, undevided attion, then she is happy. The class has clamed down some I guess they are getting used to me. When ever they get bored with the same routine I try and get something now like pictures or books or other materials I may bring in class. There are A few who try to get away with things but I stop them;. Going down to the bathroom used to be A bedlem but now I have A new, sistem I used for A couple of days now it has worked, down in the hall leading to the bathroom I have the boys line up, they all line up like they are in the army. Then I pick A mounitour, to pass out the towels and someone to stand out in the hall, and watch the rest of the boys while I am in side watching the other boys.

D. has been absent for three weeks straight and has a lot of work to make up. But he's to slow and the future work will pile up.

He daydreams a lot and his work gets done slowly. After a lot of proding he gets his work done, and he always looks sleepy but he's realy alert.

The following incident occurred when the first young man was given the assignment of escorting an eight-year-old boy to school each morning. The boy had a tendency to cut school or to get into trouble on the way to school each morning. Once he was safely in the school building, his teacher could work effectively with him. Our preventive approach led us to see if we could avoid trouble for this boy. His note is reproduced in full to indicate his intuitive grasp of interpersonal relationships:

Johnny has to be shone who is boss, and that you are a little stronger than he is or he try to run all over you, he thinks that, no one is his boss and so he can do anything he wants to do. The day after I met him he told me that he could run fast so I said I don't believe you, he said I can run, then you have to chase me, I said No Johnny you run, and i'll give you a heard start, we raced and I won, but in sted of passing him I picked him up while he was still running, after that I had no more trouble out of him. With Johnny you must always talk with a stern voice, but only when you talk about what he can or cannot do.

The second young man was equally effective in working with an extremely disturbed child in a public-school classroom during the regular school day. Although the boy himself said that he experienced only a little tension, the unusual, even unique nature of the situation cannot be overstated. Here was a 17-year-old Negro high-school dropout working in an all white suburban public-school classroom, specialing a severely disturbed schizophrenic child. The following is a summary that B. wrote of his experience:

What I though of the work
And the people I worked with

From the very first day that Dr. L. and I went to the HS school. And I was introduced to the principal and M.'s teacher, and M. I could see that I would like working with them and there surroundings. All though I wasn't there very long and din't get to know them very well, I could see they were very nice people there. And ready to help any one in need of help.

And not knowing very much about the work, but having some idea. There I was working with a little boy, that seemed to never to be able to get up on his own two feet.

M. and I became very good friends. With M. and I working together every day, gave me a chance to learn some of his ways and habits.

One of his habits was putting things in his mouth. And he also had a habit of looking off around the room, when you were trying to teach him.

(Here's something of important, although M. would be looking off and around the room, he would know some of what you were talking about.)

When it was time for work in the morning just after recess period, we started on having him try to print his hame. We would work on that for about ten or fifteen minutes. Any longer than that he would start to tire. Then I would switch over to what he liked mosted of all, and that was reading. Now and then there were a couple of words that he didn't know. When he got tired of that he would start to call one word another word, and get confused.

In playing, he does have the ability to play. If M.'s with a group of children in a game, he'll just stand and look and look around. And soon find something to put in his mouth. Now if you were to take him and play with him alone, and show him what you want him to do. He has the ability to play.

M. seemed very slow at some things, and then again if he liked it a little faster. But even I would say that he has improved.

And I don't think that he's the only one that's learned something. I liked what I was doing very much.

The last line is revealing of the therapeutic benefits of being the helper in a helping relationship. Rieff and Reissman (1964) have pointed to the therapeutic aspects of the role of indigenous worker and our experience thus far bears out their observations fully. Both young men seemed to have benefited personally from having responsible positions and functioning in a cooperative relationship with authority figures. Others who know them speak about a distinct change in their manner, in their general mood, and in their dress.

We may note that the project was not undertaken lightly and that the principals and teachers who agreed to participate in this experiment were indeed bold. Here was a clear break with tradition in a setting not noted for the ease with which traditions are broken. Actually word did get around the school system and some teachers and supervisors expressed considerable apprehension and opposition to the experiment. Some of the teachers in two of the buildings knew the young men. One of the young men had a reputation in the lower grades as a "hellion," and later was seen as a typical smart-aleck, negativistic dropout. As both young men proved themselves, the resistance changed to pleasure. Teachers expressed a great sense of satisfaction in seeing the young men do so well.

Testimonials are always suspect but we cite these reports from teachers to round out the picture of what our assistants accomplished. In addition to the notes and letters, it should be noted that in one class the teacher presented one young man with a gift and a letter of thanks from each child in the class. In another situation, the last day of class was devoted to a birthday party for the young man, and the teacher gave him a gift.

One of the young men also functioned as an assistant in the Regional Center's program. There is no better way of describing his functioning than to quote these excerpts from the teacher's notes:

During the lunch period it was obvious to me that he must have had previous experience working with children, as he showed much insight to the problems and needs of each child. I found him performing tasks in enforcing self-help with various individuals without my having to bring it to his attention. Part of Tuesday's lesson dealt with the family concept—touching on such questions as who makes up a family and the role that each member plays. This morning L. brought in word and picture association cards depicting different members of a family—mother, father, brother, sister, baby, etc. He worked with the class as a whole for a period of half an hour and then proceeded to take two of the children aside and work individually with them, stressing the small-big concept and reviewing the picture cards. It should be stated that L. planned this activity entirely on his own.

[During a lesson] Steven began his usual heavy breathing and negative answers.[2] Without much difficulty L. explained to him that he would have to stop if he wanted to continue working. Steven, who has showed much enthusiasm in working with L., stopped and they continued.

The following letter describes the teacher's view of the young man functioning as an assistant in a first-grade classroom in the public schools.

L., an eighteen-year-old school drop-out, began work in my classroom as a non-professional aid in early April. He came for an hour and a half three times a week.

The class consisted of thirty-two active, difficult first graders, many of whom suffered from emotional disorders. My primary need for L.'s help was in the area of assistance in keeping two-thirds of the class quietly occupied while I worked with the other third in a reading group. Although I provided seat work, the children were frequently unable to function alone and the changing of the groups contributed further distraction.

L. seemed to grasp very quickly what was required of him. He moved quietly *and with purpose* from child to child, giving help, suggesting additional activities, settling arguments between children, and, throughout, offering encouragement and warmth. Although he seemed particularly empathetic to certain children, he was aware that the *whole* class was anxious for his attention. For a few children who craved the contact with a functioning, adult male figure, he provided, I believe, a most meaningful, unforgettable experience.

L. is not a fully mature, experienced teacher, capable of leading a group alone. However, I do believe he possesses a sensitivity, a flexibility, and a warm charm that makes him an asset with children.

The following letter was written by the first-grade teacher in the suburban public school where one of the young men specialed a schizophrenic child.

I found B. to be a friendly, cooperative boy. He was extremely neat and clean at all times. He seemed interested in all children, eager to learn, and

---

[2] Steven is a very tense and rigid youngster who has a tendency to wheeze and breathe heavily when excited.

open to suggestion. I definitely feel he has a future in dealing with children in some capacity.

As regarding M., B. handled him very well. M. responded well and seemed to enjoy working with B. However, I did find that M. would masturbate furiously when B. would leave.[3] I wonder if perhaps a prolonged period of time of individual attention is too much of a strain for M. It seems he would do better with individual attention given in smaller doses.

For my own personal views, I find the only drawback in such an arrangement (teacher-helper) is the distraction it causes in the classroom. B. worked very quietly and yet the children, especially this type of class, were distracted. This was the only disadvantage I found. Otherwise I feel B. served a very useful purpose.

Principals in the several public schools also had favorable reports to make. One principal was outspoken in his satisfaction with the responsible way in which the young man reported to him each day when he entered and left the building. In other instances we had to say "no" to some requests for help because we felt the principal might have been expecting the young man to take on too much responsibility in the situation. In some situations irregular attendance by one of the young men, and a tendency toward what seemed to be overconfidence, led to some very minor problems. These comments were the most serious of the criticisms that we heard from anyone about the young men. With the rare exception that the teacher felt a young man was occasionally too harsh with some children, there was never any real question raised about their work with the children. When this sort of issue came up, the consultant encouraged the teacher or the principal to take the matter up directly with the young man, and the consultant would discuss the issues in individual supervisory sessions.

The use of these young men in an assistant capacity is not an unmixed blessing. Our experience is quite limited, and we were extremely fortunate in our selection of the first young man. Others who followed seem equally capable in their work with children. However, not all of the boys have the same level of motivation or initially the same sense of responsibility toward the job. It is our impression that the importance of the work with a child and the sense of being useful and helpful to another person do a great deal toward helping the young man develop a sense of responsibility to the job, but it is also clear the job requires close supervision. Anyone entering into such a program may have to anticipate a certain amount of anxiety and dis-

---

[3] This child frequently would masturbate furiously whenever his attention was not fully occupied by his teacher. His behavior after B. left the classroom is not unusual for him.

appointment in the attitudes of the young men toward the job, although we have had no untoward incidents in relation to children. If the job is supervised closely enough, and if the supervisor is sufficiently supportive of the young men (a great deal of personal praise and encouragement seems necessary) it seems that considerable improvement in attitudes toward the job responsibilities can be expected.

Anxiety may in part stem from the consultant's biases, and it persists even when the anxiety proves unfounded. For example, although the consultant had a great deal of confidence in the young men, and although he was aware they were in a closely supervised situation, each time he received a telephone message to return a call concerning one of the boys, he felt a twinge of concern that something disastrous had occurred. As it happened, each message only served to renew confidence in the person. For example, once a teacher called to ask permission to have a young man come at a time other than his usual time to accompany the class on a trip. On another occasion, the young man called to inform the consultant he was requested to change his schedule by the supervisor in one of the settings. Another time the young man called to indicate he was out because of illness.[4]

MANPOWER NEEDS

All available estimates of the potential of schools and universities to turn out enough trained manpower to meet current demands for mental-health services indicate that the job cannot be done. Moreover, even if the numbers of people in training were doubled and tripled, it is highly unlikely that current and future demands would be met adequately. The trend in the field is toward developing preventive approaches that help maintain individuals in normal social settings with a minimum of disruption in their lives and those of others. The public schools have a vitally important role to play in such programs because everyone passes through them and because the full therapeutic and

---

[4] It is interesting and perhaps instructive to note that the first time a criticism of these young men was presented to us we reacted with some apprehension as if our doubts (and the more hostile doubts of others outside the Clinic) about what we were doing were receiving confirmation. Our anxiety was considerably reduced when we became aware that the criticisms made of these young men were precisely those which over the years we came to make and expect of our interns in clinical psychology. The same behavior in very similar situations is interpreted differently depending on whether one is a graduate student or a school dropout on a work-crew assignment—a difference in interpretation that bears the hallmark of prejudice.

preventive significance of a good educational program is being given ever-increasing recognition.

Along with the increasing emphasis on preventive approaches, we are beginning to see increasing use of the subprofessional, working under close supervision, carrying out some of the day-by-day tasks of working with other people.[5] In mental hospitals, in institutions for the retarded, and in residential treatment centers for children, attendants have long carried extensive responsibility for day-by-day patient care. We see increasing use of volunteers as companions for both adult and child patients. In social-service agencies and in community-action programs we see increasing use of the indigenous worker in a variety of capacities. Camps have long been familiar with the use of adolescents and young adults as counselors and junior counselors with considerable responsibility for the day-by-day care of younger children. Untold millions of parents have entrusted the care of their children for varying lengths of time to adolescent baby sitters.

The use of the subprofessional, working under supervision, has a long history in the human-relations field. Moreover, there is increasing recognition that human-relations tasks require personal characteristics that are not easily acquired through formal education. Responsibility, warmth, sympathy for others, the ability to feel for another person and yet maintain objectivity in judgment are characteristics that are desirable but not necessarily "trained in" by formal education. There is, in fact, some suggestion that a formal educational program, with its emphasis on verbal conceptual skills, may in some instances screen out those who may be naturally intuitive and sensitive individuals. If we accept the premise that personal characteristics are the overriding consideration for successful performance in human-relations tasks, then it becomes obvious that the selection, training, and supervision of the subprofessional or the assistant become vital.

THE PROJECTED PROGRAM

At the time of this writing five boys and seven girls have been selected from the CPI work-crew program for our projected program. All of these late adolescents are Negro. Experience with these boys and

[5] Unfortunately, the book *New careers for the poor* by Pearl and Riessman (1965) did not become available until after the present book was ready for publication. We can here only recommend this book to the reader desiring an extended and thoughtful presentation of the problems and potentials in programs geared, in Pearl and Riessman's phrase, to the "nonprofessional in human service."

girls suggested that many have the ability to gain excellent rapport with other people, and some seem to have a high degree of skill in relating to others. Many come from large families where they have had experience and responsibility for younger children from the time they themselves were very young. It is typical of poorer families (Negro and white) with many children that older children are given a great deal of responsibility for the care of younger ones. Children from poorer circumstances have had to share a great deal with others in their family, and in consequence many have tended to develop a tolerant attitude toward the problems that others have. Further, those who themselves have experienced restlessness, uneasiness, and some difficulty in learning may be able to appreciate similar problems that a child may be having in his learning experience.

There are other reasons for selecting the young Negro. First, from the point of view of the young person, he may be motivated toward a career he would not ordinarily consider. There are steady, responsible, reasonably well-paying positions for attendants in institutions. Typically, turnover is high in these positions because they tend to obtain people by default, so to speak.[6] Some, of course, may be sufficiently motivated and capable to want to further their own educations. Second, it is important for both white and Negro youth to experience Negroes in positions of responsibility. Such youngsters provide models for others and tend to be a corrective for the stereotype of the Negro as capable only of holding down menial positions. Third, it has been our experience that once the young Negro experiences himself in a posi-

[6] The job of "attendant" has not been considered an important position and this attitude has in the past been reflected in low salary and poor working conditions—a situation that helps explain the sad conditions in many institutions. This is undergoing rapid change, however, as the strategic importance of the position has become increasingly recognized. For example, a year before the Regional Center was due to open the director arranged for a tuition-free night course for prospective attendants to be given at a local college. It was indeed surprising to see the number and variety of people who came regularly to the course, which was concerned with the nature of mental retardation, problems in management of children, and the Regional Center's program. From those who attended regularly the Regional Center was able to recruit a number of excellent prospects for jobs as an attendant. It needs hardly to be added that choosing Negro youngsters for our pilot project in no way reflected a view that they were appropriate *because* the jobs into which they would be placed would not require a high level of skill and understanding. On the contrary, it was the view of the Regional Center and ourselves that the program involved the acquiring of a good deal of psychological knowledge and skill that would allow the youngster to look forward to positions of differing levels of responsibility.

tion in which he feels he is doing important work, and in which he receives respect, he is willing to devote himself to the position because he finds he is helping himself as much as he is helping others.

The youngsters we have selected have had several months of experience on CPI work crews. They were selected by their work-crew foreman or forelady and the Clinic staff connected with CPI activities. They have shown ability to take responsibility, to relate well with their peers as well as to those in authority. Initially they will be assigned to work in the Regional Center once its own facilities are available. They will work there under the close supervision and observation of the Regional Center staff as well as those Clinic members involved in Center activities who work in close cooperation with the Regional Center staff. If they seem to relate well to the children and to the adults in the setting, they will then be given further responsibility for individual children or for a small group. Subsequently, they will be given additional work in the school setting.

The youngsters will be under the direction of classroom teachers or recreation supervisors and will be expected to be aware that, for the sake of their learning as well as for the benefit of children with whom they work, they must be open to direction and criticism. The staff of the Psycho-Educational Clinic will stay in close touch both with the youngsters and the classroom teacher. Regular group discussion sessions with Clinic staff will be scheduled and recorded. These sessions will serve both as a form of supervision and as a method of teaching these young people.

SIGNIFICANCES

In the beginning of this chapter we stated that there were two significances to the contents of this chapter. The first of these concerns the possibilities in the use of highly selected, late-adolescent, inner-city individuals as aids in the education or care or management of others. There seem to be a number of individuals in the inner-city population who possess characteristics that allow them in appropriately supervised settings to render services that discernibly increase the likelihood for these settings to more effectively achieve their goals. For example, it will be recalled that we noted the numerous and morale-shattering management problems encountered by teachers in inner-city schools, a discussion hardly necessary for anyone with even minimal experience in these schools. Our experience suggests that the youths in our projected program can be of great help in such schools. This type of assistant does not eliminate the need for professional help in those instances where such help is indicated or available, but it is only realistic to state that professional help is and will be in pathetically short supply.

It is easy to anticipate a variety of problems: the reluctance of the school to accept the youths, to recognize their role by creating positions and budgeting for them, to use them appropriately, and to view them not in terms of labels but in terms of their potentialities and actual performance. There may well be problems stemming from what these experiences mean to the youths involved, for example, unrealistic vocational or financial expectations. But these anticipations should serve as cautions on how to proceed and the degree of vigilance to be exercised, and not as barriers to action. Some of these anticipations are those that caused many professionals to view CPI's work-crew and Neighborhood Employment Center programs as dangerous ventures potentially harmful to the clients served and the type of staff employed. Such forebodings cannot be dismissed but they should not serve as obstacles to responsible innovation.

The second significance of the contents of this chapter—and in our opinion more important than the particular project described—lies mainly in demonstrating how certain community facilities can come into a relationship with each other so that the goals of each are more likely to be achieved. The schools, CPI, the Regional Center, the Psycho-Educational Clinic—these are settings that became meaningfully related to each other in a way that gave substance to the idea of cooperation. Ordinarily community agencies come into relation with each other around problems that have already developed and that involve questions of interagency practices and areas of responsibility. Too frequently the felt need for cooperation reflects still another need to maintain the independence and boundaries of each of the agencies. This is not to say that these are not legitimate needs but rather to emphasize that it tends to result in a kind of cooperation not conducive to truly integrated action programs (a situation familiar to anyone knowledgeable about the relations among departments of a university). The significance of what we have described in this chapter is that we were able to facilitate a degree of relationship among several agencies, in large part because we were related to each of them in a way that allowed us to make clear to them how their self-interests required an integrated program. By being part of each agency setting we were able to see problems and possibilities that otherwise we would not have perceived.

As we shall see in the concluding chapter, "getting into the community" is a problem with which a number of mental-health workers are grappling. As we see and have experienced it, the problem is not only where to go in the community but the nature, scope, and depth of involvement. As we have indicated earlier, to the extent that the mental-health worker stays within the bounds of the traditional consultant role—in one or even several community settings—he limits the degree to which he can effect change within and among different community settings.

Chapter 25

Toward Studying, Understanding, and Serving the Community

This book has been primarily concerned with descriptions of our Clinic's activities in the four settings in which we work: the elementary schools, different parts of the local community-action program, the New Haven Regional Center for Mental Retardation, and our own Clinic. In describing what we do and discussing the various considerations entering into our actions we have been guided by the opinion that, at this stage of knowledge and experience in the field, our most important obligation was not to prove anything but to report as faithfully as possible what we experienced in our efforts to develop what was for us a new way of functioning in new kinds of settings.

At the present time community mental health is beginning to occupy the center of the professional stage, if only because huge sums of federal money are now available for community mental-health programs. This book represents not only an attempt to describe our approach to the community but also to express some of our strong concerns and criticisms of community mental-health programs, particularly as these programs are (or may be) restricted to practice in the hospital or clinic setting, require their clients to come to a setting familiar to the professional person, are primarily, if not exclusively, clinical in nature, as contrasted to the preventive orientation, depend on one or another form of psychotherapy as the major vehicle of help, and are embedded in a vague network of ideas that attempts to view programs as falling logically and traditionally within the jurisdiction of a particular field. We did not offer these criticisms lightly, and this book attests to the importance we attach to the recent efforts to develop community mental-health programs. That we disagree with many of these efforts, and hope that what we have done is not to perpetuate the old in the guise of the new, does not obscure in our minds—and should not obscure in the mind of the reader—the crucial necessity to avoid premature closure on such questions as how and where such programs should be organized, under what auspices, and with what services. Clearly, of course, we prefer our rationale and approach to those we have seen elsewhere, but this does not blind us to the newness and complexity of the problems and the likelihood that we are far from seeing the problem as a whole.

It is our opinion that a question that should precede those involving services and orientation is how we conceptualize and understand the complexity we call a community. What is meant by the oft-repeated phrase "getting into the community"? A community is a fantastically complicated set of related and unrelated activities, groups, and functions with varying traditions, purposes, and goals. What criteria do we have, or what criteria may be developed, by which to judge how good a grasp we have of this complexity? The knowledge a politician has of his community is different from that possessed by the mental-health worker. Is the former knowledge unnecessary for the mental-health worker who wants to "go into the community"? The knowledge a clergyman has of the neighborhood he serves is rarely known by the mental-health worker. Is this type of knowledge a luxury or a necessity for the community mental-health worker? If we were to asks groups of mental-health workers, sociologists, and anthropologists to define the concept of a community, would we be surprised if the definition of the mental-health workers were discernibly more narrow and incomplete than the definitions of the anthropologists and sociologists? If we let the three groups loose in a community with the task of studying it in their own ways, would the final report of the mental-health workers be of the depth of those of the other two groups? We have no doubt that sociologists and anthropologists would deny that they have *the* answers to questions about how to study, understand, and conceptualize the modern community. Our point is not that they have the answers, but that their fields have had a longer and more sophisticated concern with understanding and studying communities than the mental-health fields. Whereas mental-health workers talk about the community in ways that suggest oversimplification and narrowness, the anthropologist and sociologist at least have an understanding or appreciation of the complexities, and are realistic as to the distance we have to go until we have a meaningful conceptual statement of this thing we call a community. The problem is not made any easier by the fact that communities differ among themselves. New Haven, Bridgeport, Waterbury, Stamford—these are the "large" cities in Connecticut, and yet what knowledgeable person would deny that these communities, albeit similar in many respects, differ markedly on a number of dimensions? Are these differences irrelevant to how to get into the community and the types of services to develop for different groups? But we cannot answer these questions until we have a more adequate conceptualization to and appropriate methodologies for grasping the complexities of a community. We must raise serious doubts about the competency and interest of the mental-health fields for the task at hand. Competency to work with and theorize about the individual patient—and this is the core of training programs in the mental-health fields—does not establish competence when the community becomes, so to speak, the patient or object of concern.

When we deal with the individual patient we are constantly engaged in a diagnostic and prognostic process in which alternative hypotheses and tactics are considered. It is our impression that planning for community mental-health programs proceeds with a minimum of consideration of alternative ways of proceeding, and this unwittingly reflects two things: the weight of tradition and its constriction on the range of possibilities to consider, and, perhaps more important, the failure to recognize that theories and procedures appropriate to the individual are not necessarily appropriate to programs designed to service a community. The result tends to be that community mental-health programs become larger versions of what has already existed. More people get more service but this does not constitute serving the community, unless we are content to define the community simply in terms of who *comes* for help, a group that may overlap with but certainly does not include those who *need* some form of help. The challenge to community mental-health programs is not the individual who is willing and able to come for help. The challenge to these programs is threefold: those *individuals* who need help but cannot or will not take initiative to get it; those *situations, settings,* or *forces* in the community that produce or set the stage for the development of problems; and the kinds of *actions* that can be taken to prevent problems.

The Psycho-Educational Clinic is *not* a community mental-health program. As the early chapters of this book indicated, there were a number of interrelated reasons for the development of the Clinic, and one of those reasons was to have a vehicle whereby we could become more educated about this complexity we call a community. Before the Clinic existed our view of the community was a function of the traditional psychiatric setting in which we worked in diverse ways, and we were aware of the limitations on scope that these settings imposed. It was this awareness that helped us to decide we had to develop services and work in settings that, for us at least, were completely or relatively new. This was not done in a vacuum of theory, but neither was it done with theoretical clarity or security. We should not (and we did not) break lightly with our own traditions. There is nothing inherently good about new experiences. We ventured forth in the hope that our failures and stupidities would not be of catastrophic proportions but rather would be productive of learning and, together with our successes, would lead us to ask and formulate the right questions. We were aware that we were an extremely small group of people—at no point were there more than five full-time staff members, four interns in clinical psychology, and two part-time people—and that our potential contribution would have to reside in how clearly we presented our thoughts and actions and the stimulation value this presentation might have in the field at large.

There is one conclusion to which we have come that needs to be presented at this concluding point in the book. To study and understand the community with the intent ultimately of serving it will require a type of personnel that now does not exist. Cultural anthropology, sociology, psychology, psychiatry—each of these fields has a distinct and co-equal contribution to make, but none of them alone combines the knowledge, theories, and skills necessary on the one hand, to study and understand *and,* on the other hand, to serve. The nature of training in these different fields prevents the student from attaining the kind of overview necessary for the kind of development in theory that forces re-examination of existing facts and practices and leads to new knowledge and actions.

The problem in the future is how to train students so that what now to us are separate fields will in the minds of students be viewed as a single body of knowledge, theories, and methodologies that are "naturally" organized *because* of the nature of the problems involved. Studying, understanding, and serving the community will require knowledge, perspectives, and conceptualizations that will make the present boundaries among the fields artificial barriers, the significance of which will be as relics of past parochialism. It will no longer be "psychology in the community" or some other field in the community but a designation that more adequately reflects the widened scope of those involved.

We are fully aware that changing training programs is (like changing a university) a task to be undertaken only by those who need to indulge their masochistic tendencies. It is not by chance that, in the mental-health fields at least, university training programs tend to be the last places in which new ideas and practices are seriously incorporated. This is as true in regard to community mental-health concepts and practices as it was once true for psychoanalytic theory and therapy, group-therapy procedures, and certain diagnostic devices. What should be centers of innovation are frequently the strongest defenders of the existing order. The problem, be it in training programs or going into the community, remains that of how to introduce change into ongoing social systems. The solution will in large part depend on how well we understand these social systems in their terms.

References

* Albee, G. W. *Mental health manpower trends.* New York: Basic Books, 1959.
* Albee, G. W. American psychology in the sixties. *American Psychologist,* 1963, 18, 90–95.
* Albee, G. W. *Manpower for mental health.* Address delivered to Columbus, Ohio, Mental Health Association, 1964a.
* Albee, G. W. A declaration of independence for psychology. *Ohio Psychologist,* 1964b (Presidential address).
Aldrich, C. A. Preventive medicine and mongolism. *American Journal of Mental Deficiency,* 1947–48, 52, 127–129.
* American Psychological Association. *Training in clinical psychology. The matter from several perspectives.* A report by the Education and Training Subcommittee, Corresponding Committee of Fifty, to the Executive Committee Division of Clinical Psychology. March, 1964.
* American Psychological Association. Committee on the scientific and professional aims of psychology. *American Psychologist,* 1965, 20, 95–100.

Barker, R. *One boy's day.* New York: Harper Bros., 1951.
Beach, F. A. The snark was a boojum. *American Psychologist,* 1950, 5, 115–124.
Bebout, J. A foreword to the CPI story. In G. Farrell, *A climate of change: the New Haven story.* New Brunswick, N.J.: Urban Studies Center (Rutgers Univer.), 1965.
Bower, E. M. Primary prevention of mental and emotional disorders. A conceptual framework and action possibilities. *American Journal of Orthopsychiatry,* 1963, 33, 832–848.
* Brown, M. Form follows function—psychologists in broadening roles. *Comprehensive Psychiatry,* 1965, 6, 274–281.

Cahn, E. S., & Cahn, J. C. The war on poverty: a civilian perspective. *Yale Law Journal,* 1964, 73, 1317–1352.
Caplan, G. Beyond the child guidance clinic. *Working Papers in Community*

---

* Starred references are those considered particularly relevant to the recent changes in thinking about the nature and purposes of training in clinical psychology in particular, and the mental-health fields in general.

Mental Health, Department of Psychiatry, Harvard Medical School, Vol. 2, No. 2.

Caplan, G. General introduction and overview. In G. Caplan (Ed.), *Prevention of mental disorders in children.* New York: Basic Books, 1961.

Carver, J. *The reactions of the parents of severely retarded children at a state training school.* Unpublished doctoral thesis, Yale University Library, 1956.

Clark, K. B., & Plotkin, L. *The Negro student at integrated colleges.* New York: National Scholarship Service and Fund for Negro Students, 1963.

Community Progress, Incorporated: *Work-crew follow-up report.* December 1964. (270 Orange Street, New Haven, Connecticut.)

Cutler, R. L. A research evaluation of an action approach to school mental health. Research evaluation of a school mental health program. *American Journal of Orthopsychiatry,* 1961, 31, 339–346.

Dentler, R. A. Dropouts, automation and the cities. *Teachers College Record,* 1964, 475–483.

Eisenberg, L., & Gruenberg, E. M. The current status of secondary prevention in child psychiatry. *American Journal of Orthopsychiatry,* 1961, 31, 355–367.

* Eisenberg, L. If not now, when? *American Journal of Orthopsychiatry,* 1962, 32, 781–791.

Farber, B. Effects of a severely mentally retarded child on family integration. *Monographs of the Society for Research in Child Development,* 1959, 24, No. 2.

Farber, B. Organization and crisis! Maintenance of integration in families with a severely mentally retarded child. *Monographs of the Society for Research in Child Development,* 1960, 25, No. 1.

Ferman, L. A., Kornbluh, S. L., & Haber, A. (Eds.) *Poverty in America.* Ann Arbor. University of Michigan Press. 1965.

Freedman, M. K. Perspectives in youth employment. *Children,* March–April, 1965.

Freud, S. Analysis terminable and interminable. In *Complete psychological works of Sigmund Freud* (Standard Edition). London: Hogarth Press, 1964.

Gardner, J. W. Educating for renewal. *Occasional Papers.* American Association of Collegiate Schools of Business, 1965, No. 101.

Glazer, N. The grand design of the poverty program. *New York Times Magazine,* Feb. 27, 1966, p. 21.

Gordon, J. E. Project Cause, the Federal anti-poverty program, and some implications of sub-professional training. *American Psychologist,* 1965, 20, 334–343.

Gordon, S. Are we seeing the right patients? Child guidance intake: the sacred cow. *American Journal of Orthopsychiatry,* 1965, 35, 131–137.

Gray, B. Child guidance clinics: characteristics of its population, its patterns of servicing and outcomes. *Working Papers in Community Mental Health,* Department of Psychiatry, Harvard Medical School, Vol. 2, No. 2.

Hassler, F. R. Psychiatric manpower and community mental health: a survey of psychiatric residents. *American Journal of Orthopsychiatry,* 1965, 35, 695–706.

Hersey, J. Our romance with poverty. *The American Scholar,* 1964, 33, 525–536.

Heyder, D. W. A contribution to overcoming the problem of waiting lists. *American Journal of Orthopsychiatry,* 1965, 35, 772–778.

Hill, K. T., & Sarason, S. B. A further longitudinal study of the relation of test anxiety and defensiveness to test and school performance over the elementary school years. *Monographs of the Society for Research in Child Development,* in press.

* Hobbs, N. Mental health's third revolution. *American Journal of Orthopsychiatry,* 1964, 34, 822–833.

Howe, L. P. The concept of the community: some implications for the development of community psychiatry. In L. Bellak (Ed.), *Community psychiatry and community mental health.* New York: Grune and Stratton, 1964.

* Joint Commission on Mental Illness and Health. *Final report: action for mental health.* New York: Basic Books, 1961.

Journal of the American Academy of Arts and Sciences (*Daedalus*). *The Negro American.* Fall, 1965.

Kipfer, J. F. A research evaluation of an action approach to school mental health. Introduction to the action research project. *American Journal of Orthopsychiatry,* 1961, 31, 320–323.

Leon, R. L. Maladaptive interaction between Bureau of Indian Affairs and Indian clients. *American Journal of Orthopsychiatry,* 1965, 35, 723–728.

* Los Angeles Society of Clinical Psychologists. *A history of the professional and social issues confronting psychology.* A special supplement. Los Angeles: Los Angeles Society of Clinical Psychologists, June, 1965.

McNeill, E. B. A research evaluation of an action approach to school mental health. The school mental-health program. *American Journal of Orthopsychiatry,* 1961, 31, 332–338.

May, E. *The wasted Americans.* New York: Signet Books, 1964.

Menolascino, F. J. Psychiatric aspects of mental retardation in children under eight. *American Journal of Orthopsychiatry,* 1965, 35, 852–861.

Meyer, H. J., Borgatta, E. F., & Jones, W. C. *Girls at vocational high: an experiment in social-work intervention.* New York: Russell Sage Foundation, 1965.

Morse, W. C. A research evaluation of an action approach to school mental health. The mental hygiene dilemma in public education. *American Journal of Orthopsychiatry,* 1961, 31, 324–331.

Passow, A. H. (Ed.) *Education in depressed areas.* New York: Bureau of Publications, Teachers College, Columbia Univer., 1963.

Pearl, A., & Riessman, F. *New careers for the poor. The non-professional in human service.* New York: The Free Press, 1965.

Powers, E., & Witmer, H. *An experiment in the prevention of delinquency. The Cambridge–Somerville youth study.* New York: Columbia University Press, 1951.

* Raimy, V. (Ed.) *Training in clinical psychology.* New York: Prentice–Hall, 1950.

Rieff, R., & Riessman, F. *The indigenous nonprofessional.* New York: National Institute of Labor Education, 1964 (mimeographed).

Roe, A. (Ed.) *Graduate education in psychology.* Washington, D.C.: American Psychological Association, 1959.

* Rossi, A. M., Klein, D. C., Von Felsinger, J., & Plaut, T. F. A. A survey of psychologists in community mental health: activities and opinions on education needs. *Psychological Monographs,* 75, 1961.

Sarason, S. B. *Psychological problems in mental deficiency* (3rd Edition). New York: Harper, 1959.

Sarason, S. B. Teacher training and the mental health professions. In A. J. Solnit and S. A. Provence (Eds.), *Modern perspectives in child development.* New York: International Universities Press, 1963.

Sarason, S. B. Some aspects of the brain-behavior problem. *Boston University Journal of Education,* 1964, 147, 53–61.

Sarason, S. B. The school culture and processes of change. The Brechbill Lecture, University of Maryland, School of Education, January, 1966.

Sarason, S. B., Davidson, K. S., & Blatt, B. *The preparation of teachers: an unstudied problem in education.* New York: John Wiley, 1962.

Sarason, S. B., Davidson, K. S., Lighthall, F. F., Waite, R. R., & Ruebush, B. K. *Anxiety in elementary school children: a report of research.* New York: John Wiley, 1960.

Sarason, S. B., Hill, K. T., & Zimbardo, P. G. A longitudinal study of the relation of test anxiety to performance on intelligence and achievement tests. *Monographs of the Society for Research in Child Development,* 1964, No. 98.

* Shakow, D. Seventeen years later: clinical psychology in the light of the 1947 committee on training in clinical psychology report. *American Psychologist,* 1965, 20, 353–362.

* Strother, C. (Ed.) *Psychology and mental health.* Washington, D.C.: American Psychological Association, 1956.

Taylor, D. (Conference Chairman). Education for research in psychology. *American Psychologist,* 1959, 14, 167–179.
* Thompson, A. S., & Super, D. E. *The professional preparation of counseling psychologists.* Report of the 1964 Greystone Conference. New York: Bureau of Publications, Teachers College, Columbia Univer., 1964.
* Tryon, R. C. Psychology in flux: the academic-professional bipolarity. *American Psychologist,* 1963, 18, 134–143.
Tuckman, F., & Lavell, M. *Attrition in psychiatric clinics for children.* Public Health Reports, Public Health Service, April, 1959, 74, No. 4, 309–315.

White, M. A., & Harris, M. W. *The school psychologist.* New York: Harper & Bros., 1961.
* Wirt, R. D. (Conference Chairman). *Professional education in clinical psychology.* Report of the Conference on Professional Education in Clinical Psychology, sponsored by the Graduate School of the University of Minnesota, 1964.

Appendix

Teacher-Discussion Groups

The formation of the teacher-discussion groups is discussed on page 292. Each of the first two transcripts to follow is of groups conducted by a different Clinic staff member (CSM) and observer (OBS). The last two transcripts are of two consecutive meetings of a group conducted by a third staff member and observer. Except as required for purposes of anonymity, the transcripts are exactly as given to us by the stenotypist. We view these transcripts as integrally related to the chapters of Part II of this book. In those chapters we give scores of examples of the problems confronting or referred to us in our work in elementary schools. In most instances our descriptions of these problems are from our particular vantage point, and not those of others in the situations; it is *our* description of problems, and not those of teachers. The significance of these transcripts is the degree to which they confirm and illuminate our assessment of the problems we encountered. Perhaps their greatest significance is the light they shed on aspects of the school culture.

GROUP I, SESSION 3

TEACHER 3. I have an interesting experience to relate to you. Starting tomorrow I will be permanently in the third grade. I have been teaching the fifth grade at School B, and the third-grade teacher is a man, and he and I have been slowly—we started out with an hour a day, and then afternoons —we have been switching classes. He takes the fifth, and I take the third, and tomorrow we are going to switch completely. And there is a difference; there is such a difference in the children that, well, it is just hard for me to analyze it completely why there is such a big difference between the fifth and the third graders.

For instance, the fifth graders, I could say to them, "Let's go out to recess" and that is the time that they want to sit down and read a book. They are just obstinate, I guess you would say. I know they have all kinds of inner conflict, and all of this is coming out, but it is going to be changed. It will be different.

csm. You worked from the third—

teacher 3. From the fifth to the third. And of course the man is very happy to have the older children. He was very unhappy with the younger children himself, so it really worked out beautifully.

obs. Which group is obstinate, the older ones?

teacher 3. Yes, they are all right if any man comes into the room. The fellow who washes the windows was in one morning, and the children snapped to attention, and they did what they were told. But for instance, this afternoon I was in the fifth grade, and one of the boys, he constantly and continually kept yapping at something, and I kept telling him, "Philip, sit down and do your work," and he didn't. Everyone else was doing their work except for this one little boy, so I didn't want him to aggravate the others.

So I said, "All right, Philip, let's go." So he walked out of the room with me, and outside of the room he said, "I ain't going." And I said, "Philip, let's go."

I started walking again, and he wouldn't come, and I walked back to him, and I said, "Philip, we are going." There was no response. He just stood there.

So I wasn't going to wrestle with him. I think it is below what I am supposed to do. I don't think I'm supposed to be wrestling with him. Besides, he was a pretty big kid. So I stepped into one of the classrooms where there was a big man teacher. The sixth grade it was. He came out, and all this man teacher had to do was say, "All right, Philip," and the child snapped to and away we went. Nothing to it. And that is what I am changing.

teacher 12. So you feel that physical strength is the key?

teacher 3. Well, there is something there. They realize that I can't go up and wrestle with them. I can't even hold them, which I have tried to do. I can, but it takes all my strength, and I feel I am not there to struggle with them. But they don't ever attempt such a thing with a man, because I think subconsciously they know that that man is capable of just laying them on the ground if necessary. And just with the physical appearance of a man, it seems that it is all right. The strength is present. I don't know. I am too close to the situation really to get an idea of what is actually going on.

But I don't think this is going to be the case in the third grade, and the man is so happy to come up to the older children, so I think it is going to be much nicer.

teacher 4. I have kind of found it is any outsider, anyone unfamiliar to them, that has this ability to create more of an impact on them, because they have tested their limits long enough with you, and what they can get by with. With an outsider it is so new.

teacher 3. I agree.

TEACHER 4. If you say, "She says do this," or "He says do this," they usually follow through.

TEACHER 3. I do agree, but even so, I was continually going to the principal's office, and I was going out of my mind, and I said, "What am I to do?"

He said, "What do you want of these children?"

I told him that I wanted them to mind, and I was convinced that it was something I was doing, as to why they weren't minding.

TEACHER 12. You were from a relatively suburban type school, weren't you?

TEACHER 3. Yes.

TEACHER 12. Perhaps in the transition you carried with you some ideas about discipline that didn't apply here, and your lenience perhaps—I mean it was lenience to them—it had to be tested and tested and tested, and it was probably very difficult for you to come from a stamp of lenience to more and more discipline, because they see the lenient side of you, it is pretty hard for them to respect anything else.

TEACHER 3. I think you are probably right, that there was such a difference between the two groups of children. It really threw me.

TEACHER 12. Did you feel you could do it differently or better, if you came in again now, knowing about the children—

TEACHER 3. Yes, this has really been a learning situation. I don't see how anybody could not come in and learn something from it, and more or less I am getting a second chance with these third graders. I will come in with them the way I should have with the fifth graders. I could stay in the fifth grade for the rest of the year, but Mr. K. wants the change, and I don't feel as though I am really accomplishing too much with the fifth graders with the situation as it is. So there is no reason not to change, and I think it is going to be a better situation for all the children involved.

TEACHER 12. Would you be willing to trade to the fifth grade next year?

TEACHER 3. Oh, sure, I am willing to try anything. Probably next year I will ask for the fifth grade, perhaps. It all depends. I have always taught fifth grade, and it seems to me we should switch around with grades because we might find we like something a little differently. But if we keep on in the same grade, you never have an opportunity to find out that maybe there is another grade that you would prefer.

TEACHER 12. How do you feel the children are reacting to this kind of switch?

TEACHER 3. It is mixed. Some like it, and some don't.

TEACHER 12. I had a funny experience with Mr. K's class—I don't remember whether I told this—on a field trip. I thought they were lacking a female, mother figure, and they hung on to me, and I dragged them around the field trip, and I just wondered if you were getting this same response?

TEACHER 3. I get a good response. I don't let them get too close anyway.

TEACHER 12. I just wondered if you found girls, especially, happy about the change.

TEACHER 3. I do think so. A couple of the little girls sat right down and made me cards, welcoming cards, and about how they want me to be their best friend, things like that that I could never get out of the fifth graders. So you are probably right on the whole, the girls will enjoy it more.

TEACHER 12. How do the rest of you feel about that? Do your girls react with you more than the boys?

TEACHER 4. Mine do, but I think it is just the personality.

TEACHER 12. Do they come more and kind of look up to you?

TEACHER 4. In a way, yes, because they are more expressive of their feelings. They come out more openly.

TEACHER 12. Do you think it is that, and not the fact that you represent an image of a mother or an adult female?

TEACHER 4. I had never really thought of it in comparing the two different sides of it. It is interesting.

TEACHER 5. I know that when I read the children stories, we have sharing time, I will sit on the piano bench or in a chair, and I have them feeling my legs.

TEACHER 12. All of them, or just girls?

TEACHER 5. Boys also.

TEACHER 12. They like the touch?

TEACHER 5. Yes, the touch. They love my red coat. It is sort of wooly, and they like to feel it. And sometimes they pull the little things out and make little balls. But it is amazing, I have a few boys who will come over to me at playtime, and they go like this to me (indicating stroking motion). I have one boy in particular, he is more interested in doing this to me than in playing. He could be there the whole time.

It is funny, but children about this age like to have very close feelings to people, and they like this touching business. I don't mind it. Or they come around and stroke your hair. I don't mind this, though. I don't think a teacher, especially teaching young children, should mind this if it is not overdone, you know.

TEACHER 7. I think a lot of it might be just the texture, and I am looking at your coat, if that is your coat—

TEACHER 5. Yes, they like that.

TEACHER 7. A lot of them haven't had these different textures, any experience with them.

TEACHER 12. Do you think that is it?

TEACHER 7. I think that might be part of it.

TEACHER 12. It sounds like Harlow and the cloth monkey experiment, the tactile feel of things.

TEACHER 5. They like the fuzzy feeling, things like this sweater. We were making Halloween hats today, and I feel like a kitty, but they like to do that. Every day, if I am sitting there, somebody, whether it be a boy or a girl, will be feeling my legs, with the stockings. I think it is the nylon.

TEACHER 4. I got that in first grade. I think it is because your legs are different from theirs. You have something on them that looks different. I think that was the thing with nylons. It used to drive me nuts.

TEACHER 5. Yes.

TEACHER 12. But you mentioned that you didn't let them get too close to you.

TEACHER 3. I like to keep them in their seats when we are working. That is what I meant about not being too close.

TEACHER 4. When I go to the playground, I don't like to fight about who is going to hold her hand or the teacher's hand.

TEACHER 3. I don't know if this is related, but in the fifth grade I have a pronounced abundance of thumb sucking.

TEACHER 4. I do. Well, it is third, but I still do have it in third.

TEACHER 3. I have it in fifth, and it is very open. Both boys and girls. In fact, I have more boy thumb suckers then girls. If they are disturbed at anything, in goes the thumb. Or if they have a problem they can't quite figure out, in goes the thumb.

TEACHER 7. Well, at least you know when.

TEACHER 3. But in working with other children I had not seen that before, and that surprised me. I thought it was very interesting. I don't know what the theory is on thumb sucking. Is there something to thumb sucking?

CSM. Did you not see it in the third grade at all? Was it just something in the fifth?

TEACHER 3. I saw it in the third grade, but not that pronounced. Maybe it is just that group of children, but when I taught other fifth graders, I had never seen it, and such an abundance of it.

CSM. The only thing I can think to say is the kid probably is not getting very much—I don't know if I mean this or not, but let me say it, and then I will say I don't believe it. I will tell you what it is before I tell you that I don't believe it.

Originally, kids apparently suck because they want to get some kind of milk or water, and you would think that a thumb is a lousy substitute, and isn't producing much. On the other hand, it is also certainly true that kids suck just to suck. Even if it is something that is not producing any kind of nourishment, they will suck—

TEACHER 3. Like a pacifier.

CSM. Yes. In young kids there is apparently a need to suck for gratification that comes from sucking. There also seems to be a lot of individual situations that you people would know about better than I would such as with the kids that you have in the fifth grade still doing it. Others seem to give it up very much younger.

TEACHER 4. Isn't it a lot perhaps just habit? My third grade even, could be just a plain habit they have of subconsciously sticking their thumbs in their mouths.

CSM. What do you mean, a habit? I am not sure I understand the question.

TEACHER 4. Like somebody sitting here tapping their fingers, and not realizing they are doing it. But this child, instead of tapping fingers, if they are bored or if they have a problem, instead of tapping fingers, they suck their thumb. I have heard it connected a lot with their insecurity. It is like a baby that has a blanket when it is little, and needs that blanket, and another child may need the security of the thumb sucking. I don't know. It is interesting.

CSM. Can you see a way that would produce security?

TEACHER 4. No.

TEACHER 12. Sure.

TEACHER 3. Sucking the thumb, again it would be to me the same as touching, feeling things.

TEACHER 12. It is associated with the nipple and security, and so this may be sort of—

TEACHER 4. That is true.

TEACHER 12. —sort of latent, you know, to turn to some means of security. Even though it gives no satisfaction, either security-wise or nutrition-wise, it is sort of a leftover.

TEACHER 3. I think it is interesting, also, that it is so open. The boys weren't ashamed that they sucked their thumb. I have made comments about it. For instance, if I called on someone, and they weren't sucking their thumb, I would say, "Will the boy who is sucking his thumb . . ." but nobody paid any attention, and he didn't either.

I wasn't trying to get a reaction particularly on it, but I just thought it was very interesting. It was just as though it were very fine and accepted by all.

TEACHER 12. Do either one of you, CSM, or OBS, know if there has been any study about Negro or white children sucking their thumb, as far as mother discipline goes? Obviously children don't suck their thumb because the mother stops them, and they put things on the thumb.

TEACHER 5. And those are the children that suck it more.

TEACHER 3. I thought a child had to break himself of thumb sucking.

TEACHER 5. They do.

TEACHER 4. My sister sucked her thumb, but not in public. The minute she was in bed, she sucked her thumb, and that was up until about the fourth grade, but not in public, because mother had tried to break her of this, and she was ashamed of it, but at night she put her thumb in her mouth.

She was always a happy child, of course I was only five years old, and I wasn't a child psychologist trying to figure out why my little sister sucked her thumb.

TEACHER 3. I thought it was so interesting that it was so accepted.

OBS. Do you notice anything about the kids who do it, as opposed to the kids who don't?

TEACHER 3. Yes, and they are different, so I could not draw any conclusions from that either. One little boy does it, and he is pretty good discipline-wise, and he is a pretty good student, one of the better ones anyway.

And then there is another one, and all he is capable of doing is copying from somebody else, and he copies pretty well, but that is as far as he goes. About the second day of school, he was talking, and I thought I was going to lay down the law, and I said, "You stay after school," and I excused everyone else, and he was sitting there, and he got up and said, "I'm going home," and he went.

So they are the two extremes.

TEACHER 4. The two that suck their thumb in my class are the two that are, I would say, most withdrawn, very quiet, soft spoken, and basically insecure, I would say. But I only do have the two.

CSM. There are two things that we seem to be noticing about thumb sucking, which are two very interesting general questions about everything and everybody, I am sure. One of them is why is it that under certain kinds of conditions, some of us go back to earlier ways of dealing with the world, ways in which we used to deal with the world at an earlier time? And the other question is: When things get rough out there, do we go back to the one place that may still be safe ourselves?

The thing that makes me think of that is that, as you say, the kids were withdrawn, which I read to mean that they don't have a great deal of contact with the teacher or the other students, and they are getting it with their own body. I wonder if that is the same thing as the other question of kids going back to an earlier time in their lives when there was the nipple and the pacifier.

TEACHER 3. I thought it was pretty well established that there was always a human escape mechanism of going back.

CSM. Not just in kids.

TEACHER 3. No. That brought to mind, it didn't register with me at first, but one little boy was at my desk doing his arithmetic today, and he kept complaining, "I can't do it, I want to go back to third grade."

TEACHER 7. There is one thing about my kids, they certainly can't go back any further than they already are, and some of them have stayed there. I really feel sorry for them. I have one little boy, and he will be seven years old next month, and if you were to divide them in good, poor, and then below par, he is below par. And it is really sad.

TEACHER 12. Hasn't he been placed in a special class for this?

TEACHER 7. They don't place them in the special room until they are in the first grade.

TEACHER 4. Is this his third year in kindergarten?

TEACHER 7. Second. I thought he was in third year, but it is only his second year. I look at some of the ages of my kids, and they must be going on three years in kindergarten.

TEACHER 3. When I was checking the register, and had to put in how many years the children already were in school, and these were fifth graders, and the normal age is nine and ten. Half of my class is in that category, and half are older children, and I have to have these children, and they are not good students. They have been in school seven years, and it really shocked me. I looked at the record, and I couldn't believe it. But this city, I guess, is very good about kindergarten and the reading-readiness and then first grade—

TEACHER 4. Yes, it is a great help. When I was going over my register, those who had that year of reading-readiness are not always the better students, but because mentally they maybe were not able to be in, you know, the best group in reading, but they were the children who were ready to work. They weren't in there to mess around and find other diversions from what the rest of the group was doing. They were in there working. It was an interesting kind of mental survey that I made of it. I was kind of thankful that they had that extra year.

TEACHER 7. I think it is really good in that—well my children when you don't know the difference between a cow and a horse—maybe it is because I lived for a couple of years on a farm—but you know a cow and a horse, and these kids just haven't had the experience.

I am beginning to wonder if some of them have even been to the center of the city. If all they have ever been in is a car and a bus, and they're living right along the river—I think it is the Q. River—and they have never been on a boat to go along the river. It isn't that they are below average. They just haven't had enough experiences to meet first-grade activities and a lot of them haven't had the experience. It is just a physical experience. Some kids have crayons at home, but these kids don't have these things at home, so naturally when they come to kindergarten, they aren't too good at holding a crayon, and things like that.

TEACHER 12. What does a year of reading-readiness do for children who have not had experience in the world?

TEACHER 7. In kindergarten, like my kindergarten in the morning, which is in a rather—I don't know what you want to call it—poor district, instead of going into a reading-readiness program, I will probably just keep giving them experiences that a lot of children might get in nursery school, or some of them just get at home playing, learning how to socialize and things like that. I will go into general things like farm animals, and just reading books to them, and they get something through singing songs, and they are working through their coordination with large blocks and puzzles. They will have experiences that many children have before kindergarten if they have puzzles at home or magazines. It is a great deal to have a magazine in the home, no matter what kind it is.

TEACHER 12. You think you can give to the children some sort of perception of their environment through books?

TEACHER 7. Just add to it. I don't profess to be able to get everything in there, but it will help these children who, if they were placed in the first grade, just don't have the muscle coordination, and they haven't had the sociability, you know, with other children.

Some of these mothers—one kid said to me he had spent the whole night outside, and it was cold, and the mother didn't bring them in until ten o'clock. They haven't got the direction. They came to me, and when I said sit down, they weren't quite sure whether I meant it or not. If these kids did go into first grade, some of them will definitely not be ready. They have been on their own. They have had no direction really that a lot of mothers will give their children. And they will be ready for the experiences like reading, reading-readiness which is sort of like half kindergarten, and they will still have things like puzzles and play period. And like midway, or maybe the beginning, they will begin reading-readiness. If these kids don't know the difference between a circle and a square, which some of mine don't, how can you teach them how to make letters, and if they don't know how to hold a crayon?

TEACHER 3. Have you ever speculated on taking these children you now have, and assuming that many of them will not achieve a great amount of success in school, but they will be able to go on and get through school, how they will treat their children as parents? Obviously their parents have never had the opportunity of such a thing as reading-readiness. Have you ever speculated on the ultimate goals of such a program as reading-readiness? What do you think it will help?

TEACHER 7. If society doesn't say, "You are nineteen and just getting out of high school," as in some parts of the country, it is all right. To be a year behind isn't the best, but with some of them going into reading-readiness, they won't have that sense of failure. I have three or four kids now, and they will just sit there and scribble. They can't make a circle, and naturally they are going to have some sense of failure, I think, unless they are really immature, and this won't give them quite as much. And a lot of times all they need at this stage is that they can mature so that one year will mean the difference between, you know, staying back maybe in the second or third grade, or not staying back at all.

TEACHER 3. Do you think it would help to take them at four years old, rather than five?

TEACHER 7. Well, I have nineteen who have been in prekindergarten. This was last year through the Ford Foundation, and then six who are repeating.

TEACHER 4. Why take them at four if they don't have the coordination at five?

TEACHER 3. If they are not getting it at home, you can give them the crayon, so they can be practicing at four years old.

TEACHER 4. And rather than holding them back in the same grade in the same school, prekindergarten or nursery school would be more beneficial, and they can see themselves moving up.

TEACHER 7. This group of children that I have is a group that has all been together in nursery school or prekindergarten, in kindergarten, first, second, and maybe third. This group is going to stay together, and they are going to see how it works out through three or four years.

TEACHER 4. They were selected?

TEACHER 7. Yes. They have other kids who have gone to the prekindergarten which are now separated, and they are in with children who have not gone to prekindergarten, and they will all go through.

TEACHER 5. I think the prekindergarten program is very good. A friend of mine is teaching there, I think in the S. Street area, and I think it is very good for these children because they could just come to school with absolutely no direction, and when you meet the parents you know why. When you speak to the parents for just milk money or just something very simple, you know why these children have no direction. You know why their speech is so poor, because their parents' speech is so poor. Half the time these children are never spoken to, and if they are it is in English that is very, very poor. Many of the parents in my area have come from the South, and unfortunately, educating the southern Negro has been a very, very—they have done a very poor job, and so most of them have quit school, and their education is very, very limited, and so they have these children, and some of them can't even speak English. It is English, but they don't speak it very clearly, and the children come to school, and they mumble.

TEACHER 4. Last night, at our teachers' meeting, since our school has a lunch program, they are trying to get the children back, to come back fifteen minutes earlier to school, and they will dismiss them fifteen minutes earlier. So they said we will send a notice home to the parents of the younger children, and one teacher raised the point, will they please put a clock on it to point to the numbers so the parents will know what time it says.

It gets really difficult when you have no cooperation from home, and they cannot feed into any background that you try to set up in school. They cannot reinforce it. Let's not say feed into it. That was interesting to me.

TEACHER 5. We had a PTA meeting last Tuesday night, and it was interesting. We are a K-4 school, and we have around 500 students in the school. I have 26 in the morning and 26 in the afternoon. I won the banner with eight parents, and so I had the best turnout. So you can imagine some rooms just had no representation at all, there wasn't one parent that showed up.

But they are very quick to come if this child didn't get milk for some reason. They are very quick to criticize. It is amazing. I had a mother come today and say, "Why didn't my son get milk?" She sent the milk money in on a Monday, and it should have been on Friday. They are so quick to criticize, but not quick to come and listen to what is going on.

And our principal finally said, "If we are going to have a PTA, we are going to need a better turnout." It was very, very bad, no cooperation from the parents at all.

TEACHER 7. I had one mother who called up the school and wanted to know why her daughter had only gotten a half a bottle of milk. I went and looked in my little book and found out that her daughter had never really brought milk money anyway, but she called the school to find out why her daughter only received a half bottle. I had three children absent who had paid for milk, and rather than have it spoil, I gave them a half bottle. And I thought oh, boy, such parents I need to have.

csm. Let me see if I can understand what this conversation has been about, if I can give it any kind of order for myself and hopefully for all of us. It seems to me, if I understand it correctly, that we have been talking in a way about growing up, that, or maybe growing up and going down depending on what the circumstances are. We began with Teacher 3 considering some of the interesting differences between teaching older kids and teaching younger kids, and kind of from there we have been talking about such things as growing up, giving up old ways, and like who doesn't give up thumb sucking, and who doesn't give up childish kinds of things like petting the teacher instead of learning, and things like this.

And then the conversation went to a very interesting notion, it seemed to me, which is for kids, I suppose primarily, and maybe for all of us in a way, who helps us grow, and what kind of help do we need from the outside to grow, because there has been a lot of talk about how the kids are going to learn and develop if their parents don't help them at home. Can we help them in the school with reading-readiness programs? And it interests me particularly because it is so much the problem I am sure teachers have tremendously, of time to help kids grow up, and trying to learn what the children's own developmental limits are. Is that a meaningful term? How far have they developed, and how far can they be brought with your help? And then it is interesting even for the rest of us, like new teachers in a brand-new situation, often feeling like kindergarten kids, or new psychologists, or new anything in that terrible moment when any brand-new situation comes along: The first year of teaching, the first problem with the principal, the first problem with the child who refuses to obey. And the tendency is to go back to an earlier way of coping, and how do we grow up? Who helps us to find ways of coping with this? Who is our reading-readiness teacher?

teacher 12. Is this what you are suggesting that we turn to, or is this your question that you are throwing out—

csm. I am saying that this is what I kind of heard being discussed about the question of how people grow up, what their limits are, who helps them. This is mostly for kids, but I was wondering if that generalizes for everybody.

teacher 3. Who grows up—what was that again? Are you throwing out a question?

csm. I don't know. I am sure I don't know.

teacher 3. I wasn't sure whether you were just summing up what we had discussed before.

csm. Yes, I was saying what I had heard in the conversation.

teacher 3. Another side of this thing that I would like to bring up, and I don't know the solution, but it is beginning to bother me. Take a group of underprivileged, underdeveloped—whatever you want to call them—children, and take them today. Take for instance, my fifth graders, who have been helped with prekindergarten, kindergarten, reading-readiness, and they are still not performing on the fifth-grade level—they are not, and you have to face facts once in awhile—they are not performing at the fifth-grade level. They are doing perhaps better than they would have without prekindergarten and reading-readiness. They are progressing, this group of children slowly.

Then let's take another group of children over here in suburbia. These children are going along and for the past three years, I think it is, they are being introduced to such things as modern math, and these children are being introduced to it, and it is being included in their curriculum. These suburban children progress right along, with these new things that are coming along.

These children down here that we are working with, they are going to be able to read and write and to do regular arithmetic. Then when they all come down here to where, let's say, they all meet in the job line, which more or less everybody is going to have to come down to, these underprivileged and underdeveloped kids are still always going to be behind, and I do not see how in the world they are ever going to really catch up.

TEACHER 4. They aren't.

TEACHER 3. I guess that's right, but it is so hard, you know, to accept.

TEACHER 4. It is hard to accept, and it is frustrating.

TEACHER 3. Yes.

TEACHER 4. The children's abilities range so differently, and I think from the city where you get your concentric rings leading out, like your poor people, and going out to the suburban areas. They come from better families and so your schools are going to have to go along with the type of experiences and the type of intelligences, and I suppose the parental cooperation. The taxes in those areas are more expensive, so we don't have that much to work with, which is quite obvious. It is unfortunate that they can't provide them with these things, but yet you can't bring everyone, you know, to one level.

TEACHER 3. That's right, and it is a good thing that we need all kinds of people. For instance, they want people for certain jobs with lower intelligence quotients, because anyone else couldn't stand there and do what they have to do.

TEACHER 7. But you don't want everyone working in an assembly line.

TEACHER 3. True, but it stands to reason that you don't want everybody to come up to the—I guess what I am really concerned about is the Negro person and Puerto Rican, and I separate them. First of all, the Puerto Rican has to learn English if they're going to live in this country. I don't like to see the Negro person as a group always down here, because there are some Negros who have the ability and the capability of going just as far as anyone else in the world, and yet they are kept back in this group.

TEACHER 4. This is what frustrates me. I have Negro and white in my class who are way above and over the intelligence of the others. The majority of mine are working at the two level in all areas, but I have two or three that are ahead of them, and perhaps could go into fourth and manage. And they are having to suffer along with my other say 28 out of the 32, because they cannot always be stimulated and challenged.

They have special classes for those who are retarded, and I haven't found a special class for those who are gifted—not gifted but—

TEACHER 3. Have the potential.

TEACHER 4. Yes. These kids come from a project area, and their parents have not been successful or perhaps, in what we call a middle-class line of work and success. But these children were endowed with an intelligence that offers them a challenge and the ability perhaps to go to college and bring themselves above this level. But if they have to follow these students through the school system, they will never reach it.

TEACHER 3. School L. has classes for those children, but it is an after-school program and called a junior-achievement school. The people who work with them are all voluntary, and I am sure the women are quite capable and all, but still it is this after-school thing, and it just pains me, because we could do the same thing in the schools that all these other programs are doing. And we could have one thing, and that is homogeneous grouping.

TEACHER 4. Within a certain range.

TEACHER 3. It will always be within a certain range, and as long as you don't restrict ability, I can't see why the school systems fight homogeneous grouping. You have it in your classes anyway. They want three reading groups, high, medium, and low. They stress three reading groups or more, and I just cannot see any real hope for the American educational system unless we can begin to encourage such things as homogeneous grouping. It seems to me that maybe homogeneous grouping does have a bad name, but let's redefine it and work with it a little.

TEACHER 4. I give each of my three levels arithmetic, spelling, and reading at different levels, so therefore I am having to cut from other areas, and I am having to cut them on time, but my low group cannot possibly spell the words that the other group can spell, so it is unfair to either one. It seems frustrating to have to hold back some at a level and try to bring up others who get frustrated because they can't reach the level.

TEACHER 12. Are the parents the main source of resistance?

TEACHER 5. No.

TEACHER 12. Who is it?

TEACHER 4. Resistance to what?

TEACHER 12. To homogeneous grouping.

TEACHER 3. I don't think school systems encourage it on the whole.

TEACHER 4. They think it is good to have this child down here stimulated by this child up here because the child up here is achieving at this level, and the other child sees that and thinks maybe he can reach up to that level. Well, sometimes the gap is so great that they think, "The heck with it, I couldn't care less, why even try?"

That is the kind of attitude that I have in four or five.

TEACHER 3. But I just cannot see—it seems to me they could have a far better school system and far better educational system if they would encourage homogeneous grouping, and of course it isn't going to be perfect, but as long as you have that mobility where you say that we made a mistake with this child, and this child should be in this group and that group and then move him, I just can't see any evil in it.

TEACHER 4. I see the point that with parents that don't really care what their child is doing in school, as with most of our schools, and they probably wouldn't care if the children had homogeneous grouping, and they wouldn't be as opposed to it. But in a suburban area you get these middle-class areas and they push the children all the way through school, and if you tell them their child is even in the middle group in homogeneous grouping, they say forget it.

TEACHER 3. Then when does the school board or superintendent, when should they run the schools, and when should the parents run the schools?

TEACHER 7. Don't they have something already? I know like if they have two first grades, they will have a high first grade and a low first grade. Maybe that isn't the best, but I think it is something when you consider they don't have enough teachers for the small group, and I think you will admit it is a smaller group that are either above average or below.

TEACHER 4. I think they try.

TEACHER 7. And by switching some kids, I have four or five that can go directly on to first grade without reading-readiness. That is going to help them. Maybe they will catch the material faster than some of these other kids who have been in reading-readiness and now are in first grade, but they also will be behind and in other areas, and they will if you understand what I mean—almost in essence, some of these children who are ready, are going to be skipping a grade.

I am the one who says whether they go into reading-readiness, first grade, or stay in kindergarten.

TEACHER 3. And they are skipping what?

TEACHER 7. Skipping a year of reading-readiness, and going to first grade. I think that is the understanding I have. I am not sure about this. I haven't talked to the principal now or whoever you talk to, because it obviously isn't the end of the year yet, and most of the people are not concerned with it.

But I think there are some who could go on to first grade, and I personally won't keep any kid in reading-readiness when it is going to be wasted.

TEACHER 4. I am at School C right now, but my children are bussed from an outside area. It will be a K through four. That will be one of each grade, so they have to take all the children in this area.

TEACHER 7. I think it is only possible in the larger schools where you have two teachers teaching first grade and two for second grade and so on. When you don't have the money or space, there is nothing to do.

CSM. Do I understand that one of the problems you are talking about, is on one hand that there are the advantages of homogeneity in that the slower kids don't hold the faster kids back, but on the other hand, the problem is that homogeneity means something like consigning the lower group to always being the lower group, whereas mixing them up, though it does disadvantage the faster kids who are held back, as I understand what you said, you get stimulation somehow by mixing them up? Is that the conflict?

TEACHER 4. It seems to be according to the authoritative opinions given on the subject.

TEACHER 12. I disagree. I don't know.

CSM. You disagree that that is the conflict we were discussing?

TEACHER 12. No, I just disagree with the theory.

CSM. I didn't even know that I stated the theory. I was just discussing what I thought I heard was a conflict. But I think we ought to quit. It is five o'clock. Why don't you raise it next week?

TEACHER 12. All right.

(Whereupon, at 5:00 P.M., the meeting was adjourned.)

GROUP II, SESSION 6

CSM. Where do you want to begin?

TEACHER 7. No problems. (Laughter) They are all against me. See what they are doing?

CSM. They are lined up, aren't they?

TEACHER 3. She did that on purpose, to be different. What do you do when you have to make up your own report card? I'm serious. I have to make up a report card that is suitable for the children to understand and the parents to understand, and the social worker to understand. We decided at our last meeting that regular report cards really weren't fair.

I had promised my kids—they kept bugging me for report cards, or something, you know, so they could say, "Well, what am I doing?" Because they are improving in some ways, in some areas.

So they want, you know, to be able to show this on a report card. This is the problem. If you have got two kids at first-grade level in some areas, and in other areas they are functioning like on third- and fourth-grade level, and then you have got another kid who functions on fifth- and sixth-grade level in all areas, and one who functions on fifth- and sixth-grade level in most areas but on a third- and fourth-grade level in another area, you can't tell the kid, "Well, you are doing F work when you are supposed to be doing sixth and seventh grade," this kind of thing. But they are doing their work. They have learned some new things.

TEACHER 7. How about S, X, and checks? But you have to let them know the level where they are.

TEACHER 3. Then there's another problem in terms of teasing from the group. I had one kid once who said he didn't want to have his words in a workbook that I had because it was a baby's workbook. But he can't spell difficult words. He is on a second-grade level. He didn't want to take it.

He said he would do spelling if I could write them out, and he would take them and do the spelling, and he would learn them for the test that I gave him, but he didn't want to take the book because he was teased. And they have a pretty good system of teasing out there.

TEACHER 10. That's the one thing, you know, that bothers me about report cards, like A, B, C, D, or F, or S, X, or whatever system you use. Here the parents are getting the report, and they are seeing just a letter or a number, but it doesn't really mean anything to them.

Where I came from in New York, I only did my student teaching there, but the report cards are such, for example, that in reading you mark them excellent, satisfactory, fair, or poor. There are four categories. But then there is a box next to it where the teacher can, and does, and is required to make comments, you know, to let the parents know via the report card just how the child is standing. So it is not just a letter. There is more to it.

Whereas when I first got these report cards a few weeks ago, when they were first brought to my room, I know I sent them home, and they had the letters on them, but that was it.

TEACHER 7. Did that include anything else?

TEACHER 10. Next time, I will sit down and write a note to the parents. But I did try to encourage the children to have the parents come in. I have had a number lately, and I am having a number of parents come up for conferences, so we can talk and discuss these things. But I find these report cards practically worthless in one respect.

CSM. Because you think it isn't communicating anything to the parents?

TEACHER 10. Yes. I mean, what does an A or B mean? I had more or less the same problem. Here the child was on a second-grade reading book, and you know, they would be doing the work required of them on this level. But say it wasn't the level that they should be at. Well, I wasn't as generous. I gave him a B-plus. I didn't give them good marks, even though they were working, because I felt that they should—well, especially this first report card, that they should realize that I expect a lot more of them, and I want them to work. So I didn't give such great marks, for the most part.

CSM. How do you know this is being communicated either to the child or to the parent? What you are saying is that you are going to be tough the first marking period because you want them to know that you expect a lot of them.

TEACHER 10. Before I gave the report cards out, I spoke to my children for about 20 minutes. I told them how I marked, and on what basis, and so forth. Today was a hectic day, because we had a play in the classroom. But I will spend the rest of this week and part of next week having individual conferences with each child, and discussing their report card with them, and showing them how they can improve. So in this way, I know it will be communicated to them.

As far as the parents, next time I hope I will get to write the parents notes, or I might send a Ditto letter home to the parents telling them that I am available on such and such days for conferences to discuss the child's work with them.

TEACHER 3. Do they have anything in the system where it is compulsory for the parents to try and see teachers during the year?

TEACHER 10. Nothing at all.

TEACHER 3. In Town M. where I taught, every report card, you would get two days where the children would be home, and during that time you had to schedule conferences with the parents, and they sent out postcards, and the parents had to return the postcards with the time when they could come. And you made every effort to see the parents. It was really good. The report cards went home, but the parents then had to come in and have a conference with the teacher, as to how the child was functioning.

It was a mass scheduling that had to go on, because some of the parents would have about five or six children, and how were they going to get to see all the teachers? You would have to plan to do them first, in the general schedule, or master schedule, and then you would fit in the other parents at the times that you could see them. I distinctly remember sometimes going to school at seven o'clock because some parents had to go to work, and the only time they could come was early in the morning, and things like that. It paid off.

TEACHER 5. We just had this American Education Week, and the parents were supposed to come in. I had exactly three parents out. So they didn't come to see me. Monday I started going to see them. I sent little notes home, and I called. In some places, mama went across the street, or to the store at the hour I was scheduled to come. So it worked out beautifully. They don't want to see me.

CSM. How many came, did you say?

TEACHER 5. Three.

TEACHER 10. I had four.

TEACHER 5. I said, if they don't want to see me, I will go and see them. I think there is an awful lot that can be learned from a home visit, an awful lot. For example, I learned that one of my little boys is from a home where there is no father, and he is one of 13 children. The older children go to school here and there, and they come home and help out mommy. I had been screaming and shouting at this little boy for a long time, trying to force him into doing his work. I found yesterday that he just has a problem, and there is nothing that he can do about it himself.

It is a problem for which he is not responsible. This certainly helped me to understand him a bit better. I won't use the same methods that I have been using with him. The communication between the teacher and the home and the parents and school is important.

TEACHER 10. There was something I always wondered about, a teacher going into the home. I could never quite make up my mind how I felt about that, whether or not it was correct.

TEACHER 5. Well, correct or not, I did it. I went to the home. First I went home and put on my sneakers, my sweater, an old dress that didn't mind anyone spilling soda or anything on it, because I didn't know what to expect. Like a good salesman, I dealt with them on their level. I saw five Monday, and I saw four yesterday, and two were not home. Like a salesman, I went in.

I took their folders with me, and just talked with them. I certainly have a great deal more insight and understanding of the children. I told my principal beforehand that I was going to do this. So he said, "Well, if you are ambitious and want to—it's not required—but you may do so."

OBSERVER (OBS). Did the parents respond to this?

TEACHER 5. Well, some were very nice after they saw I wasn't coming in to see how many webs were in the corner, you know, this sort of thing. Some didn't like it at first. They kept their foot in the door, "Yes, Miss 5," and we just talked and talked. Eventually, with tactics here and there, they let me in. But some did object.

TEACHER 10. How did they react, those that objected?

TEACHER 5. Very nervously. "I'm fixin' to go to the store. Forgive me," that sort of thing. I said, "I will come back another day. Could we arrange it now?" They saw that I was determined, and they just let me talk. I found this in about two cases.

Also, I found that one of my little boys—I didn't realize it before—but his mother speaks Italian, and his father speaks fluent German. I didn't know this before. Sometimes he said, "Miss 5, what did you say? What did you say?" He has a language problem, and I didn't know this beforehand. This will help. No one, of course, told me that he was from this type of home, but now I found out.

TEACHER 6. Do you have records where it says what language is spoken at home, about the family?

TEACHER 5. It is in the pack. I have never read the packs, because I don't like to read the packs and build up this stereotyped idea about the children.

TEACHER 6. But that would also give you a lot more insight.

TEACHER 5. That is true. I haven't read them.

TEACHER 6. Because many of them even have health problems.

TEACHER 5. I did read those, yes.

TEACHER 6. And family problems.

TEACHER 5. I have just glanced through the yellow packs. But I did read the medical records. I have been a victim wherein the permanent record card has been read, and they build up these peculiar ideas. I have read about this. I don't know, sometimes you are influenced by what others say, and have a tendency to believe it. For this reason alone, I didn't, deliberately.

TEACHER 10. I also didn't look at the reading records and marks that previous teachers gave, but I did look at the top of the yellow card, where it has a note if the parents are divorced, or if there is a foreign language spoken in a home, or when the child first entered school. I noted that, whether they were left back, things like that, so I would know the age of the child, and things like that.

TEACHER 5. In the beginning of the year I submitted a little questionnaire. I didn't know, I didn't find out who was divorced. But I was concerned about, "Have you repeated a grade?" And I found out that much. But as far as scrutinizing those completely, I didn't.

CSM. What feeling do you have about the home visitation? You indicated you weren't sure whether—you know.

TEACHER 10. That the parents can resent it. I don't know if it is the teacher's place to go and enter into the personal life. The teacher should make herself available, and should try to see a parent because, of course, you can learn a good deal. But I don't know, I really don't believe it is the teacher's place to take the step and walk into the home, go into the home.

TEACHER 5. Well, I certainly let them know beforehand.

TEACHER 3. What do you do in a case when your parents don't take the initiative, and it is imperative that you do see the parent? Because the parent has a very definite influence upon the child. You sort of can be counteracting each other as to what you are trying to achieve in the classroom situation, even in terms of a kid's attitude about school. This can come from a parent. In other words, some parents say, "Oh, well, he is getting by. Okay, that's it." Or they may say, "I was like this when I was a little boy. You have a behavior problem." And the parent is really taking pride in the kid acting up. What do you do then?

You have to sort of help the parent see it.

TEACHER 10. Right. But if you have this type of a situation, you know, your first step would probably be to write to the parent, or try to contact the parent, or phone. If this doesn't work and the parent is going to resist this, then I think that would probably be the same type of parent that would resent your coming to the home to speak to them.

TEACHER 3. But how are you ever going to break that? How are you going to get the parent on the side of the school, or get them halfway, or partially interested in the school? Because school is something every child has to go through, and it takes up an awful lot of time. The sooner you start altering the attitudes toward this, and get cooperation from the home, and get sort of like a joint effort, you get a better reaction.

TEACHER 10. True, I agree with you. In the case where you are meeting resistance, I don't know if the teacher going into the home is the answer.

TEACHER 3. What I am speaking of right now is: all right, if this isn't the answer, what is? What is another method of handling it, or who handles it, or what? Because you just can't leave it there.

TEACHER 10. I know. That's the problem. Maybe somebody else has a suggestion.

CSM. Isn't the question, under what conditions would one want to visit the home? What reasons would one have for wanting to visit the home? For example, why did you decide that you were going to visit the home?

TEACHER 5. To help me understand the children a bit better. And I like to see my parents. And they deliberately—well, not deliberately—but they didn't come. I had mimeographed a letter that one of the older teachers had, inviting them in September. And still the excuse is, "I work all the time. I have to hire a babysitter." So I made it convenient.

I sent notes home stating that I was coming. In some cases I called. But it was merely to have a better understanding of the child, to help me in some cases understand why the child behaves as he does.

CSM. Why do you think so few parents came during American Education Week?

TEACHER 5. I don't know. I am very sincere in it. I don't know.

TEACHER 3. I would say, offhand, an average parent probably is not really interested in American Education Week. You take the title "American Education Week," and what does it mean to a parent?

You work all day long. "My kid goes to school. All right, he's getting an education. That is what education is, my kid going to school, making sure he has something in his stomach, some clothes on his back, he is clean and neat."

This is all he can give. What are you going to do when you go there? You are going to sit and listen to a couple of recitals, or something like this, and some kind of an assembly program. This is a stereotype that I am sort of coming out with. But this would be my reaction if I were a parent. I would be more interested in just seeing the teacher, finding out how my kid was doing, and having a chance to sit down and talk about my child. This is what I am interested in.

TEACHER 10. In my school, American Education Week, as such, wasn't played up. It was sent home, you know, "Come to school, and you can visit your child's classroom, see the class in action," although it wasn't the fact that it was American Education Week. And still I only had four parents come. I would say almost half the children in my room, probably both parents work. Or in the case where a number of parents are divorced, and the child is living with the mother, and the mother is working. A few of them have sick children. One boy, his mother has two children and a sick infant at home. There were problems like that also. But I know there were more that could have come that didn't. It is an apathetic feeling that I feel some of these parents have.

TEACHER 7. I know every teacher in our school had at least half of the enrollment, the parents of the enrollment of their children. I know I had fourteen mothers out of my eighteen children. A lot of them stayed almost the whole day to watch the class. Now, I don't know if this is because I have a lower grade, first grade, where a lot of them are interested, "How do they begin reading? How do they begin arithmetic?" There was a tremendous—I don't know the word—interest, enthusiasm for what was going on. Maybe it is because of the neighborhood.

I don't know whether the people encourage school for these children.

CSM. What school are you in?

TEACHER 7. School W.

CSM. Would that differ from the other ones?

TEACHER 7. A little. I have a middle-class, a lower-middle Italian neighborhood. It is near the end of town.

CSM. Is it likely that your school draws, in terms of social class, differently than the others?

TEACHER 7. I think a little higher.

CSM. I wonder what that means, though. You know these parents come and your parents don't come.

TEACHER 7. Maybe as a community, school is more encouraged.

TEACHER 10. I can look back to my own school days. If my mother or father would have gone to school and heard I wasn't behaving or wasn't doing, you know, what I should, if I was sitting during arithmetic and drawing or anything like that, I would have gone home and I would have gotten it. This wouldn't have stopped. My parents would have sat over me until I did what I was told, and until I got a better report.

Now, I have some children, and this one mother came to school in the beginning of the year, and there was a discipline problem. Her son could do no wrong. Her son William? No, absolutely not. And she has two children, one in each of the fourth-grade classes we have. She defends these children. They just can't do anything wrong. There are a number of other parents like that. There is just not the same feeling. If you speak to them as a teacher, and you want to cooperate with them and help their child do better, it doesn't work when you are up against such a wall.

CSM. You see, I am wondering whether, in fact, your parents are apathetic, whether they are really uninterested. I am wondering if there aren't—

TEACHER 3. Do you think they are embarrassed, in that they are not on the same social status or social level as the teacher, as the school? They don't have the pretty clothes to wear to school that they see the teacher in, and it shows them up. Also, there is the fact that you can't speak English properly.

CSM. It is very interesting that before Miss 5 went, she said she changed her dress and put on her sneakers; which is another way of saying, "I am going to try to put them at ease, and not to accentuate the obvious differences between me and them."

TEACHER 5. An "A" today.

CSM. I am just wondering if it is more than mere apathy. For the most part, you are drawing from a population where the parents are relatively uneducated, where their experiences in school were by no means happy ones, where it was a situation of relative failure and frustration for them. Why should it be easy for them to come to school? Let's ask that question.

Just imagine a situation where, you know, it is your child going to school. Would you feel any embarrassment, any hesitation about going to school to talk to the teacher, and the like? Why should they feel any differently? Why should they look upon the teacher and the school as a place to which they can comfortably come, and a place where they are unreservedly welcome?

TEACHER 3. Because their past has told them that school is not this kind of a place, in part. If their experiences have been unfavorable, they already don't like school, and they already have some notion of what teachers are like, having been a student, and having been picked on, or made to feel uncomfortable; and they realize that they have had the report card, and maybe their report cards weren't that good. So they realize there is a gap. That is one element.

And some teachers do have a way of pointing out the difference, not in a pleasant manner. They are sensitive already, and it only takes it a little bit deeper. Maybe with one teacher a generalization can be made from that.

Maybe they have made an effort and really didn't feel welcome. This is a possibility. Some teachers just don't really—it's a job, and that's it, and they don't want it. They want the kids to behave, and to learn, but they don't want to be bothered with anything else, if they can help it.

OBS. What you are saying, in a way, is that if you are going to work with the parents, in some sense, as well as the kids, that you have to not only understand the kids, but understand the parents.

TEACHER 3. I think in some cases that is true.

CSM. What do the schools do to make these parents comfortable about school?

TEACHER 7. Why is that important? I realize the importance, but they also have something to offer. I think there is more of a problem, the fact that the parents have been made uncomfortable for some reason, and therefore are uncomfortable for their children. I don't know how to word it, but you keep coming back to, "Why has it been made uncomfortable?" Whereas our problem is, "How do you get them into the school to overcome this, overcome their uncomfortable feelings, to get them in there and forget their feelings and take an interest in the children, and sublimate what happens to them?

CSM. I agree. That is the question. You are assuming that they are uninterested. I am just saying, why do we assume that they are uninterested? It may be true. Certainly, for some it would be true. But why do we assume that they are not interested in what is happening to their kids?

TEACHER 3. Well, like American Education Week, not very many of them showed up. In a sense, they haven't come to the school, or when they were invited they didn't come, or they have never come on their own to find out what is going on. Some of them might come after the report cards, I don't know. This would be the reason why you would say they are not interested, because you haven't seen them.

CSM. What about P.T.A. attendance? Is it true that very, very few of the parents in your classes show up for P.T.A.?

TEACHER 5. Well, we had a P.T.A. meeting last week sometime. I had exactly five parents out of a class of 29. I think that was a very poor attendance for 29 children.

TEACHER 7. I had 17 out of 18.

OBS. Miss 5 describes going to the home and seeing things that were going on, and she was able to understand some of the kids better, and in some sense felt that she had to change her approach with them, not to do what she had been doing, but sort of take into account some more things she learned about them, and try to deal with the kids and to do what she has to do in a slightly different way.

I wonder if perhaps the same may not be true of the parents. The ideal way would be to kind of just sit and wait for them to come and talk. In cases where this works, this is fine, and there is no reason to think about other ways. But when it doesn't work—just like when you know more about a child, you think of different ways to try to approach him. Perhaps the same could be true of the parents.

CSM. I suppose I am raising the question whether it isn't a little too easy, whether it isn't an easy out to say, "The parents are uninterested," whether in fact we have done as much as we could to determine whether in fact they are that much uninterested.

When do parents hear from school? The one situation that a parent can count on hearing from the school is when something goes wrong. If things are going okay, the chances are you will not go out of your way to tell a parent that things are fine, and that you are gratified, and they should know this.

You may do it via a report card, but one doesn't go out of one's way to tell a parent something good in the same way that we do when we have something bad to communicate. Let's say you have Jimmy sitting in your class and Jimmy is doing fine. You take your sixth grader, the kid is reading on the sixth-grade level. So I would ask the question, "Have you gone out of your way when you became aware of how well this kid was doing, to make it your business to tell this to the parent?"

Or is it the situation that you thank God that you have got this kind of kid in your class, and you don't have to worry about him? (Laughter)

TEACHER 5. Well, the moment the parent found out that he had had the Metropolitan Achievement Test, she came to find out, how well was he doing? So I didn't have the opportunity to do it. He was from the home on the right side of the tracks.

But this is very true. I think, as a whole, in our school—I will speak about our school because I don't know what is going on in the others—I think that is a very good generalization. When a child is doing well, we don't mention it. It is only when the bad things occur that we make it known, make sure the parent gets it. And this too could bring on attitudes on the part of the parents.

TEACHER 7. I don't know if you have it, but isn't it usually the children who are doing well, it is their parents who show up for the P.T.A., who show up for American Education Week?

TEACHER 3. That's right.

TEACHER 5. Yes.

TEACHER 7. The parents of the children who do well come, and the children who are doing poorly, or are having some trouble, they don't come.

TEACHER 6. I have exactly that.

TEACHER 7. I sort of remember from when we went to school, the same thing.

CSM. You mean there aren't any kids that are doing well, who come from families that do not visit, do not attend P.T.A.?

TEACHER 3. Occasionally, there are some; but the majority of parents that you do see at the P.T.A.—we used to have like classroom helpers and stuff like that—these are the parents where the children are functioning fine. They have a few problems, you know, general problems in learning how to do something new, but they catch on, not too many behavior problems. They are more or less the child that the teacher is glad to have.

csm. You know, a thought just occurred to me. Let's go back to some of our earlier sessions. I want to pick up the business of your seeing the transcripts of those earlier sessions, but we will take that up later. Earlier, essentially you were describing problems that you were running into with administration. Let's just group it that way. You were more or less saying, "Look, who the hell is interested? Who is really putting out for us? What about this? What about that?"

You know what it added up to, that you were alone, and there wasn't anybody who was really interested in what was happening to you and what you needed, and the like.

In a sense, I kept asking the question, "Well, why do you take it?" You remember, I was asking that question. The answer was kind of, "When you are up against a stone wall, there are so many concussions you are willing to subject yourself to."

I am wondering if this is not true for a lot of parents that we are discussing now. I mean, given their own lives in relation to these schools, their previous experiences with the schools, whether they don't start off with the assumption —for which in many cases there may be good grounds—"What is the sense in getting involved and getting mixed up in this?"

You know, it is a very uneven battle to begin with. Now, I am sure that if we had sessions like this for the administrators, they would be talking a great deal about what they really want the teachers to do and to feel and to think, and what have you. If we could read what you say and what they say, it is as if you are dealing with two different worlds, and yet there may be appropriate motivation on both sides.

Somehow or other, they cannot talk to each other. This was basically what was coming out in these early meetings. In terms of what you were experiencing, and whatever it was that they were experiencing, whatever frames of reference they had, somehow or other there wasn't a meeting of minds.

What I am asking is, may this not be the case as between yourselves and the parents that you are dealing with? I could ask the question, "Why should it not be comfortable for you to say outside of here what you said inside of here at this meeting earlier? Why can't you go to the superintendent, or why can't you go to whoever is the supervisor in your district, or why can't you go to your principal and say the things that you said here?"

What you were describing was a situation in which people could not talk to each other. We are dealing with a very similar situation here. Maybe we are dealing with this kind of a situation.

Now, I don't want to appear to have prejudged the issue, that is to say, that in fact parents are very interested, that they are not apathetic. I am, you know, merely raising the question, "Let's look at ourselves."

I can give you a personal example which I may have mentioned before, and which the obs, being in our department, can testify to. Several years ago the graduate students in our department made it clear finally to us that the only time that a student in this department ever heard from us was when we had sometime bad to say to him. And it was absolutely true. If they were doing all right, you know, they didn't need any special reward, and encouragement and motivation. But if he got a call from the director of graduate studies, he knew damn well that this was not going to be tea and cake.

So it is not that I am taking sides here. I just feel that it may be a more complicated issue. Or I am asking, is it possible that it can be a more complicated issue.

TEACHER 10. This is making me do a little bit of thinking. I can look back and see where I have gotten notes from parents regarding why a child was absent, or some such thing, and the notes have been grammatically incorrect. You know, from the note, it was easy for me to tell that the parent had gone just so far in education. I can see why then, in this case—when we were younger, as students we looked up to the teacher, and the teacher was somebody up there whom we were afraid of. These parents probably in many cases still, you know, to a large extent put the teacher up on a pedestal, and feel very funny about coming and showing themselves to a school teacher, and not being able to hold a conversation, or something like that. They feel very inhibited, to a large extent.

CSM. I often wonder about the schools in which you people are. Not only is it tough for a lot of them to write, but I sometimes wonder whether they can read some of the things that are coming home. It would be an interesting little study just to find out how many of them can really read a report card. I don't know about this city's report card. I have seen some report cards elsewhere that require a fair level of vocabulary in order to comprehend it. Some of these report cards look like railroad timetables.

TEACHER 5. As a rule, when there is a note to go home, I always explain it to them, because I have wondered this myself. I always tell them what it is about. I took a blank report card yesterday, before I issued the others, and explained it to them.

TEACHER 3. When I send the kids to the office, which I do—my two nonreaders don't know the difference. They have to have passes whenever they go anywhere. They have a pass which says, "Has permission to go." So when I am sending them, I cross it out and say, "Is being sent," and I also write on it what it is. There are two children that can read. They would read it. So what I do, I state exactly what has happened, because I am working on them. "This is what has happened—let's face the fact—on why you are being sent." They know exactly what I am going to say. Sometimes I will call over there, and they are present when I say it.

So that if there is a misunderstanding about what happened in the situation, then we can at least let all sides know, so we don't have a pitting of people. This is something you have to be very aware of. Children play people off against each other, and they have done this. So this is what I have to do.

I read it off to them. Sometimes they go, when they just have to do their assignment. They can't work in a classroom situation. This is stated.

But there is no difference between "Has permission" and "Is being sent." It is sort of vocabulary too. It is a regular pass that I send with them, because I know they can't read it. It is better that I read it to them than let another child read it to them.

The child might say, "Oh, no, I didn't do that." But if I am there, I can defend my position and what I perceived. One thing I have been thinking about right now is what you pointed out about how we were looking at administrators, and then the problem we were having in terms of trying to communicate with them, and getting in their shoes. Then you raised the point about putting myself in a parent's shoes, and how I would accept a teacher; and what could I do sort of to help a parent want to come to school and see me.

I think this is something that would need practice, you know, in terms of more or less helping me to feel more comfortable in this kind of a situation. One thing that does help is having friends that are parents who have to go to the P.T.A., and talking with them. I think this does help.

TEACHER 7. I am looking at it very negatively. You said, "What do you have to lose?" You were referring to us, as teachers, in our relationship to administrators, as to what parents have to lose or gain in relationship to the teacher.

As teachers, we are working under politics and every other kind of pull that there is. I think that is probably why we are afraid, because you are new, you are inexperienced. You will get your experience, and we are afraid to open our mouths.

But what does a parent have to lose in their relationship to the teacher, except possibly how they see themselves in relation to the teacher?

TEACHER 3. That is pretty important. The way they perceive themselves.

TEACHER 7. But I think that is where it is a little bit difficult to make the comparison, where we, as teachers, are afraid to do that to administrators.

TEACHER 3. What do we have to lose? We have a job to lose.

TEACHER 7. All right, it is important to us.

TEACHER 3. Their child is important to them. They have got to live with them for how many years?

TEACHER 7. That is what I am saying. They have more to gain than to lose. I don't know that we can compare the situation.

TEACHER 3. Can they lose the feeling that, "I don't understand my child. I am helpless in taking care of my child. I don't know how to help him in school. This is an area I can't do anything with."

TEACHER 7. I think that depends on how the teacher presents the problem to the parent. I think a big part of that is the attitude of the teacher toward the parent when she sees them.

TEACHER 3. In a sense, this is why I was suggesting, to try and put myself in their shoes. How could I better present myself to fit their needs, so I can either bring them where I want them to be, or whatever.

CSM. Being a parent, I have had some experience in going to my daughter's teacher over the years. Some of you will be experiencing this, so let me tell you about it, particularly because you will be professionals in the area.

One of the first problems I experienced was, "I don't want my daughter to get caught between me and the teacher." I had this feeling that, you know, what happens in school is tremendously important, that the relationship between the child and the teacher makes a big difference. If I have any kind of criticism or any kind of suggestion, how is this going to be taken? Am I going to say it right? Or if she says something to me with which I disagree, if I disagree with it, you know, is she going to feel aggressive or hostile?

I was just amazed, the first time this happened, at all the feelings that this aroused in me, precisely because what was at issue was my daughter, and the fear that I didn't want her to get caught between me and the teacher. It wasn't that the issues were, you know, that difficult. But I was just surprised that this was, for me, a loaded area. I was very concerned about what this teacher thought, what the teacher would say.

So if you say, "Well, what have you got to lose?"—in a sense my major concern was not my pride, but it concerned my daughter. I didn't want to do anything that might, in a negative sense, interfere with what she was experiencing in the classroom.

Now, I have had experience with a wide variety of teachers in different settings. I don't know whether you have had enough experience along these lines, but what I have gotten from other teachers is that the relationship they fear the most, and in which they feel most uncomfortable, is when they are dealing with parents who themselves were teachers.

TEACHER 7. Or any professional people that have had comparable education.

CSM. Yes. That is why I say this is a loaded area, this relationship. Now, if this can happen with well-educated parents, I think there is no reason to believe that, for other reasons, it doesn't happen with less-educated parents, that they can get just as scared, just as fearful.

There it becomes complicated with self-esteem. They don't know if they are going to say things in the right way. They can't write things in the right way. They don't know if they can say it in the right way. So they tend to either shut up, or not show up. So it is important to try to understand that from the standpoint of the parents. The teacher, just as she is for the child, is a tremendously important person, important for them and important for the child. The teacher is an authority person.

I found myself looking at the teacher, in a sense, in the same way that you described the way you looked at administrators. I was very much aware of this. To me it was a very instructive experience.

When you some day will be talking to teachers about your child, particularly because you are professionals in the area, it is not going to be easy, when you become aware that you have a suggestion to make to the teacher.

Now, how do you make it so that you don't make her feel that she doesn't know what she is doing, that she has overlooked something? This is quite a problem. This is why, when you say, "Well, the parents don't come, they are not interested," and the like, it may be too easy just to say that they are uninterested and apathetic. In some cases I am sure that is true.

So it is the old business that when we experience a problem, that we have to learn, in a sense, to look at ourselves and into ourselves to see in what way we contribute to it. Rarely, you know, is it a matter that is all on one side.

As somebody indicated, this is the one area where teachers have to function, must function, and for which they get absolutely no training, and that is, how you talk to parents. This is not a God-given gift. It is not a simple problem.

I have had groups of teachers—and you get it more in the middle-class schools, and I can name the schools—where they said, "My God, if we could avoid having to have these parent conferences, we would all be a lot better off."

TEACHER 3. You know, that's true. They say that in the middle-class schools you have problems with your parents; in the lower-class schools you have problems with the children, because you don't see the parents, and you are just involved with the children. But the other is just the opposite.

TEACHER 10. Conant brings that out in his book, just that point.

CSM. Now I will come to the business of the transcript before we break. We have the transcripts of the first session. We have it for the third but we don't have the second yet. What I wanted to discuss with you is the problem of how we should handle the transcripts. You know, you have all been extremely open in the discussion and on a couple of occasions I have matched your openness by some of the things that I have said. We have mentioned names, places. So what is in the record is, in one sense, extremely personal kind of stuff, which is why we said at the very beginning that this doesn't leave this building.

So the question has come up in my mind as to how we should handle this. If you want, we can give you transcripts of each of the sessions, which you can take home with you. Speaking again very candidly, this scares me a little bit, because things can get misplaced, and the like. But if that is what you want, and this was our original contract, this is the way it should be.

Another thought is that these transcripts are here at the Clinic, and you can read them here any time you want to. This may be inconvenient and this may not be what you want. The other thing would be to give you the transcripts, and then you can bring them back. So they are on file here. Any time you ever want these things, they are available to you.

So I raise this as a question which I think we ought to talk about. Again, it is not a simple kind of issue. I know when we set up these meetings, and the people downtown were talking to me about it, they indicated they would love to see it. I indicated to them that this would be a very short conversation, because they were not going to see it.

In the case of one or two people, I would trust their motivations completely, because they felt that this would give them an idea of what needed to be done in a way that something else wouldn't But I said, "Look, this is the only way it could be set up. If the group says you can see it, then you can see it. But I am not showing it."

For example, Mrs. W. said she would just love to see this thing, but I am not making it available. But that is another issue.

But how should we handle this in terms of the transcripts? What would you prefer?

TEACHER 6. I would prefer, for myself, to bring them home and then bring them back. I think they should be kept in one place. I don't think it is worth it to take a chance of it getting out. And it is more convenient to read it at home than it is for me to come here and read it.

CSM. How do the rest of you feel?

TEACHER 10. Yes.

CSM. Well, that is the understanding. Hopefully next week we will have the second session. We have the first and third meetings, and if we can have the second, that would make three.

We have talked about whatever has come into our minds. Next week I will have here all the transcripts that are available up to that point, and then you can bring them in the week after.

TEACHER 3. Is it possible to pick them up on Tuesday? Because I can't come next week. I am going away.

CSM. Well, let me see if my secretary is here. We may be able to give it to you right now, the ones that we have.

GROUP III, SESSION 3

CSM. I guess we can begin. Why don't you just go on with what you were talking about? *

TEACHER 10. There is not too much union support in the school. There is much more league support.

CSM. What is the difference between the league and the union?

TEACHER 10. The union is affiliated with the AFL-CIO, and the league is affiliated with the National Educational Association and the Connecticut Education Association. In other words, it is nonunion. The union would like to be known as a professional society also.

CSM. I am afraid I don't understand.

TEACHER 10. The league is the nonunion group of teachers, and the union is the American Federation of Teachers, AFL-CIO.

* This was the third session of this particular Teacher's Discussion Group. The last topic discussed at the previous meeting involved the teachers' feelings about their "union," its functions, problems, etc.

csm. I take it that one has greater membership than the other?

TEACHER 10. The league has a far greater membership, but I think the union in some fliers that they have put out have said that their membership has increased threefold since last year. This means nothing.

TEACHER 12. There is some third group of some kind.

OBS. You can individually belong to one or the other?

TEACHER 10. Yes, individually.

TEACHER 12. But your faculty sort of leans one way or the other, and you are highly encouraged to go one way or the other.

TEACHER 10. In general, the administrators in most districts I have seen are against the union in the schools, partly I suppose—well, the union, for instance, in New York City brought about the strike, the teachers' strike, whereas a league—I haven't seen any league that would go out on strike.

TEACHER 9. They are more professional.

csm. Also a little bit more sedate?

TEACHER 12. Apparently we are all leaning towards something like the league—.

TEACHER 9. I didn't get a very good impression of the union at the orientation meeting.

TEACHER 10. At the orientation meeting this man got up and started— it was pretty much sour grapes—he said they hadn't been given a list of the new teachers, so they couldn't send them any material. He apologized very sarcastically for this, indicating that if they had been able to get the information, they could have sent the information, and there would have been more time to read it. He was just boorish.

TEACHER 9. He was fighting for his equal time.

TEACHER 10. Yes.

TEACHER 9. What transpired last week? I wasn't here. What did you talk about?

TEACHER 10. My mind is blank now. We were talking about the pressures on teachers from different areas, pressures from parents—.

TEACHER 12. Which you don't have, and administrators.

TEACHER 10. We were talking about pressures from various kinds of groups, and the feeling of frustration that—well, being powerless in many situations to do very much about different things.

TEACHER 12. We talked about values, trying to transmit values to the children, trying to get them to do something because it is good, not because you get a star.

By the way, my principal is extremely interested in what is going on here. Every time I walk in on a Friday I have to give a report.

TEACHER 9. My principal doesn't even know about it.

OBS. What kind of thing does she want to know?

TEACHER 12. I told her we were talking about pressures last week, and she wanted to know what kind of pressures we talked about. She wanted to know whether we were talking about pressures from principals or higher up. She is very interested. I don't know exactly for what reason she is interested, but she is.

CSM. You know, we made it clear really that as far as we were concerned this was a confidential meeting.

TEACHER 10. Yes.

CSM. And this is away from the school authorities, and here is a principal who is quite interested in what we talk about.

TEACHER 12. I thought that might be interesting to you, and considering what you said at the first meeting. I have to give a full report.

CSM. You really feel you have to give her a full report?

TEACHER 12. I edit some.

CSM. Because really you don't have to say anything if you don't want to, because this is in a sense our own meeting to do with and direct in any way we want to, and actually by our agreement, she doesn't have to be told.

TEACHER 12. Yes, but I have another relationship with her which makes it, you know, sort of necessary in a way.

CSM. It is like with the union. It sounds exactly like the union. In a sense you are given the choice of joining either the league or the union, but you have made it clear that within the school itself at least, there are certainly possibly indirect pressures—.

TEACHER 10. Sometimes I think there is a feeling—I know I have the feeling, I just don't feel a union is professional. I may be wrong in this. This is my own feeling, and I would not join a union. I don't care whether all the other teachers in the school were in it, I would not join the union.

Others feel strongly that the only way to get decreased clerical work and increased salaries, is with the union. But the majority of the teachers, I think, feel that the union is not a professional organization.

OBS. Why?

TEACHER 10. I suppose because of the background, the origins of the labor-union movement, being in nonprofessional groups, in factory workers, and later in blue-collar workers. I am pretty sure this is the reason why.

OBS. It is more a question of guilt by association rather than—.

TEACHER 10. Pretty much so. I think other professional groups have a professional organization, but they are nonunion, such as the American Medical Association and various lawyers' organizations, the engineering societies; they are professional societies. I think the teachers would like eventually to be thought of as a profession. You don't need as much training as you do in law or medicine, but the amount of training is increasing, and I think they would like to feel on the same basis.

CSM. I can understand this, but what I was struck by was in a sense the similarity between in one way being given a choice of a union or a league, which you could decide to join either one depending on how you felt. For example, you feel that it is more professional to be in a league rather than the union, and indeed, your views may be shared by most of the other people, but on the other hand there is also a kind of pressure exerted by the school to become a member of one as opposed to the other.

And here, for example, we have this meeting which I think was clear to the principals and to the other people in administration, that this was a teachers' meeting to talk about what the teachers wanted to talk about, and I think we kind of established this to be our own meeting, and it was a confidential meeting of people. And here is a principal who, either he or she, was really interested. But I think they put you in the position—.

TEACHER 12. Yes.

CSM. —of in a sense breaking our contract, only in the sense that—well, you could talk to her sure, if you wanted to, but I wonder if you would have told her what was going on, or edited what was going on for her if she didn't ask you and if you didn't feel some obligation to this member of the administration.

TEACHER 12. I felt an obligation to tell her, but yet I didn't—you know—I just gave her general things. I certainly didn't go into great detail, but she is very interested.

TEACHER 10. The thing I wondered about after we had left, how did this group come to be formed? Who started it, and what was the purpose in mind?

CSM. I think you must have been at the meeting with Dr. M. in our Clinic, asking for volunteers. So it was whoever signed up, just volunteered for a group. The idea for the group came from our experience in the school where we really found teachers feeling the need and desiring to be able to sit down and talk about their mutual concerns with other teachers and with people interested in the schools. That is where it started.

TEACHER 12. Then why have it here? We do that at lunch.

CSM. Because we felt that here it would be away from the school, that is, away from the administration, and away from the formal structure of the school. In other words, here we don't have to worry, for example, or wonder about an administration person even walking around, whereas in the schools, although we know these talks are held informally over coffee and so on, they still take place in the confines of the school system and the school structure and the administration and supervisors, and I guess we felt it would be easier to talk away from the school.

TEACHER 10. The only problem is that we don't really have that much in common with each other. This seems funny, since we are all new teachers in this city's school system and so forth. There are some apparent common bonds, but when you get right down to things, there aren't too many problems that we share, and even though we do talk out problems that you can—well, you can get a kind of abstract common bond. We are talking about our problems, but it doesn't seem as if it will really get us anyplace other than just rehashing some of the problems. Granted, it sort of gets the problem off your chest, and granted there is a certain psychological value in just talking about a problem, but I think we do talk about these things at other times and I am just not sure exactly what purpose this serves, to be perfectly honest about it.

CSM. Are you asking me or throwing it out to the group?

TEACHER 10. I am primarily asking you since none of the other new teachers could answer it exactly as to the purpose of this. I don't know.

TEACHER 12. In a way, I think, at least I feel, that you could be getting more from us than we are getting from talking. We wondered about this.

Perhaps you are making a study of the frustrations of teachers or something like this, and using this way of getting material.

TEACHER 10. It seemed to us that this would be a perfect opportunity for such a study.

OBS. Yes, like any other association of professional people, but there is no purposeful design. There is another thing that can be read into this. I think the mere association, professional association of psychologists and teachers, who are in the educational profession, can be very useful, and we both can benefit from it just by listening to each other and reflecting about these things. We talked in the beginning of these two professions being too much separated, and think that one purpose can be just the association and the sharing of professional experience between them.

TEACHER 10. It seems to me that it might have been better if we had settled this in the beginning, and at least confined the field to deal with something such as how the psychologist and the teacher can work together. Today we are talking about problems with administration, some things that really don't have much bearing on ways that we can work together, and I think that if this were a little more defined in the beginning, it would be more helpful.

Granted that this is only our third meeting—.

OBS. That is one thing we can find out by associating, because it is really a first experience, I think, for both of us, and you can really find out after having such experience together.

CSM. You said before that there were some things that separated even the teachers here?

TEACHER 10. Yes.

CSM. I didn't understand that.

TEACHER 10. For instance, some of us are working with children who come from a very good background. Others work with children that come from a poor background. And the problems with each one don't go into the other territory. So that—well, I guess you run into that with almost any group, that you are not going to have any common problems or problems common to everybody in a group, but each one has her own particular concerns, and there just don't seem to be that many problems that are common to the majority of the group.

There are, if you put it in fairly general terms. For instance, you can say that there are problems in dealing with administrators. All right, that is a fairly general problem, but when you get down to specifics, they aren't really the same class of problems and it is hard to see any purpose in just talking about them. This is the way I felt anyway. I think it is just sort of a feeling of unrest or dissatisfaction. Maybe it is a holdover with being dissatisfied with the job also.

OBS. You mean dissatisfaction with this type of group?

TEACHER 10. Yes, just in general.

TEACHER 12. It seems to make for a lot of time, considering how many things we have to do in preparation, as I have. In fact, I have to make detailed lesson plans, grading papers, and bulletin boards. Ten hours of time is a lot for something like this, although it is enjoyable, but the pressure of having to come every week for 10 weeks, this begins to weigh on you and you have so many other things that you have to do also.

TEACHER 10. An hour a week out of 168 doesn't seem like such a lot, but sort of not being able to see any real purpose in coming every week—.

TEACHER 12. This is sort of prime time also.

CSM. What kind of purpose would you people have in mind?

TEACHER 10. This is what I am not sure about really, which doesn't help you any.

TEACHER 12. Learning about how to deal with children, learning actual things. When I came the first day, I didn't realize what it was, and I came with pencil and paper and thought it was a lecture and—.

TEACHER 10. Frankly, that is somewhat what I would like. After dealing with kids at a very low ability level—well, there is a challenge to my energy, but not a challenge to my interest, and that is most what I would like. So I think I would like to learn something.

Granted, I am a little tired at the end of the day, but I still would rather learn something than just rehash the problems of the day. I would like to leave them for a while.

TEACHER 12. But on the other hand, you can always say that these in-service training deals, you don't really get much from them. They are a waste of time. If we could have some beneficial learning experience about psychology and children.

TEACHER 10. It is kind of funny that we should want a little more work in some way.

OBS. There is another part to learning, and that is that you really become passive and receptive. One thing that you want to be is passive, and not really active.

TEACHER 10. Not necessarily. Actually, I had expected a different kind of seminar. I studied under a seminar when I went to school, and I enjoyed this kind of situation. You have a large table and a group of eight or ten, or sometimes four or five, getting together and you sort of are fed a certain amount of material for a while and then you start discussing things. The material that is given to you serves as a springboard for discussion. And this is the kind of thing I like very much, so it isn't just passive. I don't like just sitting and taking notes, but I like being given some food for thought and then working over it.

CSM. You would have felt more comfortable if we had had an agenda or assigned readings?

TEACHER 10. Not necessarily. I am not sure exactly. If there had been some sort of certain set topics, not necessarily a lecture—I don't know. This is kind of hard to figure out what we should have had or what we should have. I don't think necessarily reading, although it might have been a part of it. I am trying to think of some topic that might serve as an example.

Can you think of any topic that would serve as something to do with both psychology and education?

TEACHER 12. Discipline. Whenever I discipline a child, I always have a guilty feeling because I don't know whether I am doing the correct thing psychologically, when I am just crushing the child, or is there something else?

TEACHER 10. This idea of ways of dealing with children, I am sort of curious about the effects of various kinds of discipline.

TEACHER 12. Yes, I did a little reading on that in college, and it is extremely interesting, the effects of different discipline, how you can discipline certain types of problems effectively without injuring the child. Sure you could smash him in his seat and tell him to stay there, but this might be doing some terrible damage repeatedly. Whenever I do something with a child it bothers me, because I don't know whether I am doing the right thing, not knowing his psychological makeup. If it effects my end, it is pleasing, but I don't know whether it is doing the right thing in effecting the end.

I am sure there are some fascinating things to find out about that, and I would like to find out.

CSM. Is that what you had in mind?

TEACHER 10. Something like that, yes, and perhaps along the same line, dealing with different kinds of children. There is the aggressive child. Of course, they aren't always one of these, but I do see basic types of children in the classroom.

Thinking back to last year, there were some children—I think one thing I would like to learn more about is that if a child is withdrawn, learn more about different causes for this kind of behavior, and what the teacher can do to bring the child out. You learn some things by experience, but you would like to be able to learn things a little more quickly, and I think we would like to profit from somebody else's knowledge. I am thinking of things to draw a withdrawn child out, or suppress a child that is too aggressive—not exactly suppress—but ways of dealing.

TEACHER 12. And you deal with children in special sessions and can see the results of what we do and tell us how to work with them.

TEACHER 10. I think the idea of behavior is a good one to work on, not just in the sense of behavior as a problem, but I guess I am thinking of behavior as it is used when you talk about behavioral signs or just people's actions or a child's actions, his general makeup, his general psychological makeup. I think that is the sort of thing I would like to work on.

CSM. There are two things that you bring up really. One is your feeling that in some ways our meetings would be more helpful to you if we had a kind of seminar in which we discussed specific problems, and maybe did some reading or maybe did some other kind of research on it, and then we discussed them.

The other thing you bring up, though, is that there are certain questions that you have, which I have a feeling are related to your kids right now—I mean, you have a feeling that you might have a withdrawn child in your class—.

TEACHER 10. Yes.

CSM. —and you might have an overly aggressive child in your class—.

TEACHER 10. Yes.

CSM. —and my feeling is that we do have a group of teachers here, who have been involved in working with these kinds of problems, and we might very well be able to talk about our experiences with these children.

It would seem as though whatever training, for example, you had in dealing with psychological problems or behavioral problems with children, would have conveyed to you in your preparation to become teachers the answers to your questions, but obviously you feel that that isn't so. Maybe the reason is because nobody really does have the answers, and that the answers may possibly come from being able to sit down with other people who are interested in these problems and in the children, and talk about them.

TEACHER 12. Perhaps this would come with a slightly more structured group, with a discussion topic of some kind, rather than just starting with a discussion on something that just happened, a chance question.

CSM. Well, you brought up a question about different kinds of children.

TEACHER 10. Well, I am not sure where to begin on it really. I really wouldn't know where to start on asking about the different kinds of children. It is just that I think that this is one problem all teachers run across, the different kinds of children in the classroom.

CSM. But I have a feeling that behind your question there was maybe a particular child in mind.

TEACHER 10. Well, practically every child in my room, I would like to know a little bit more about how to deal with. The one that usually concerns the teacher first of all is the very aggressive child, because this is the one that usually causes the most problems, at least at the start.

TEACHER 12. How to get a boy who is trying so hard to get attention by all the wrong ways, how can you get him to understand the right ways to get attention. Or a girl that is doing that? This is a problem.

CSM. This is a question, I am sure, that most everyone here is concerned about. I guess that is why we see these kinds of questions that we have as being really related in the group. I am sure that everyone is dealing with that kind of a child.

TEACHER 12. But you just have studied teaching—.

TEACHER 9. Yes.

TEACHER 12. —and I am not really teacher-trained. I was an English major. I am not saying that these people don't know the answers, but perhaps people with ten or fifteen years of experience would have a little more experience than we have.

TEACHER 10. Let's take it from this viewpoint then: What happens when you—let's see—if you are dealing with an aggressive child, and you try a harsh form of discipline, and it just seems to perpetuate the problem, and yet there isn't time to try to work with the child in a gentle, persuasive manner, and the child is so suspicious that he will only distrust you for trying some sort of a kindly approach. What ways are there for dealing with a very aggressive child?

The ways that I have seen, you can either somehow try to ignore the child, which isn't usually possible—it works once in a while, but not too often. Or you can have the child removed from the room or school by suspension or temporarily suspending the child. You can send him to the principal's office, and of course, that removes the problem from your room, but it does nothing toward alleviating the child's problem. We can talk to the parents. We can bring the parents in for a conference with the teacher and the vice-principal and the guidance counselor, and it works for one day, but obviously one conference is not going to solve all the problems that a child has.

So you can holler at the child, which is your first impulse, but of course that does no good. It exhausts you and antagonizes the child and disrupts the classroom. You can try to find something interesting for the child. This sometimes works, but it is sometimes hard to get the child's interest.

You can try to use that old word "motivate," but this again sometimes is very hard. First of all, I find it sometimes hard to motivate myself when I am tired and disgusted with the whole situation, so that if I find it hard to feel intrinsic motivation, then it is very hard to motivate the class in that case. So there is the method of trying to find something to motivate the group or this child in particular.

I don't know—those are the things that come to mind at first hand. You can try talking to a child individually, having a sort of private conference with the child, and this I found sometimes works also.

I am looking, I guess, for more ideas. Sometimes I try all of them. Sometimes it is a matter of trying one after the other.

What sort of ways have you found in dealing with children who are aggressive or disturbed, just some of the general methods? When psychologists work with children, what do they do? When you work with children who have severe problems, what do you do?

CSM. Very often the same kinds of things you have done. But are you talking about a specific child that you have?

TEACHER 10. Right now, no. They are all problems. There is no one child that I can give you as a problem example. There are a lot of them who just have this very aggressive behavior. I can't give you one example. I could, if you would like me to.

csm. Yes.

teacher 10. All right. This one girl came in, and she is more socially mature than a lot of the others. They obviously need to feel more like most people, but she shows it more. She will want to do things like erase the board or give another child a spelling test or something. But when she doesn't get her way, she becomes very disruptive in the classroom. She hits other children and swears, and I don't remember if she is the one—there are children who have drawn filthy pictures on the blackboard and written filthy things. She may have been one of the ones. I don't remember now.

Going into more background about her, she is the oldest of about five children, I think. She does a lot of work at home. There is no father at home and from what she has said, her mother spends the day doing nothing or sleeping. So she is responsible for a lot of things at home, cleaning and so forth.

She has more ability than a lot of the others, but also she can be difficult. She will refuse to do work in the books that the others work with, saying that it is baby work, even though she is having trouble herself. She refuses to work with the books the others use. We have scheduled her for work in the seventh-grade math class, a very low math class, but she has trouble with it, but it is some appeasement. She had sessions talking with the guidance counselor. Her mother has been in twice, I think.

She will just talk out in class, saying anything she feels like, anytime she wants to. She is a class leader, and I have tried to work on this in the conference with the mother and the vice-principal. She can either lead them or set a poor example. In the beginning she set a poor example. I tried to work with the idea of encouragement, saying to her or the mother that she is improving, but she is still a tremendous problem. But she is now setting a better example, and I hoped this would continue to improve. But we finally said that unless she can improve, we would have to suspend her for a certain amount of time, because this seems to have been one way of getting at her.

She knows what is right and wrong because sometimes when the guidance counselor or I have been in conference with her, she will start crying, so she knows what is right and wrong. But she is just a constant troublemaker.

So we have tried all these things. I have worked with her individually in the morning, fifteen or twenty minutes extra work, giving her extra work in the classroom. But the others claim that I am playing favorites. We have tried the parent conference, discussing things with the guidance counselor. All of these things we have tried. I keep on trying, but there just doesn't seem to be any one thing, but the combination of things. There are so many family problems that you don't know where to begin. You can't do anything about the fact that there is no father, and she is responsible for most things, and there is not much you can do about the home situation really.

Very few of the kids have fathers—well, have fathers living with them—.

TEACHER 9. There is a difference.

TEACHER 10. —and there is no record as to whether there is brain damage or not. There is no neurological examination of these kids so I can tell really whether it is emotional or physical. I have a feeling that if we knew that, then we could know a little better the ways of working with the kids.

TEACHER 9. About her not working with the books that were given to the other children, I know a teacher in a special-session class who had this problem with a boy about 17 with a group of kids much younger. So I think he had to be put in this class because there wasn't anywhere else to put him. He refused to work with this book. She got ahold of some books for an older group or college level. He couldn't even read. He was really happy to go back to doing work he was able to do, and he sort of got into it. But you might try giving her some things she will be frustrated at so she might be a little happy to work in a book that she could have some success with.

TEACHER 10. I have given her a chance to do extra reports. We got into a discussion of current events the other day after Khrushchev's ouster. She said she wanted to find out something more about communism. So I said, "All right, if you would like you may go up to the library." In talking about it, they said they wanted to find out, and I don't think they understand the concept of communism, but there are sort of simple ideas you can discuss about this.

So we got some questions together like "What is life like in a country that is ruled by the Communists?", and "When did this begin?" They are fairly general and simple questions. So she got a book out of the library, the school library, on communism, and struggled through it page by page. She asked me to help about words. It gives her a feeling of importance to be able to do this.

I suppose basically it is a matter of trying all these different things at once, but it gets pretty tiring.

TEACHER 9. How old is she?

TEACHER 10. Thirteen.

TEACHER 9. You have only had her a month. It seems that you are doing pretty well.

TEACHER 10. I feel that it is too much to deal with at one time. I know perfectly well I shouldn't expect quick results, but it still doesn't stop me from hoping for them, I suppose.

Do you have any suggestions as to what to do?

CSM. I am very much impressed about how much you care about this child.

TEACHER 10. It was so frustrating. Then the other day she got into a fight with another girl in the homeroom after she had improved quite a bit. She and the other girl were rolling on the floor, pummeling each other, and it was discouraging to see the setback. You work along for a while and it seems to be of no avail.

TEACHER 9. I think one thing that bothers me about my classes, the children think nothing of taking a book and just slamming another child. They do not understand kindness toward one another.

TEACHER 10. Yes.

TEACHER 9. They just don't care what they do to one another, and it is so hard to teach them to care for one another. They care so little for themselves, I feel they don't care. Getting a beating at home is like getting breakfast, if you are lucky enough to get breakfast instead of a beating. So they have no conception of kindness toward one another.

TEACHER 10. Yes, it is heartbreaking.

TEACHER 9. Sometimes I could cry.

TEACHER 10. Yesterday afternoon I was waiting for my husband over at the engineering building near the Far Eastern Institute, and there was a little girl about three or four years old, a little Chinese or Japanese girl, riding a tricycle. She was riding back and forth on the sidewalk, very contented, and all of a sudden she leaped off the tricycle and ran over about 10 feet and started picking up some leaves. She picked up one and very carefully looked at it, and picked up another one, and gathered about four or five of them and ran back to the tricycle and pedaled back very fast to a car, and I guess it was her father waiting in the car, and she handed him the leaves. It really got me, seeing a young child, innocent and happy, enjoying something simple and beautiful. It was just an indescribable feeling, a sort of sadness and longing, not having seen anything like this with these kids in two months, to see a child looking happy and innocent with something simple and beautiful.

TEACHER 9. They seem happiest when they are hitting each other.

TEACHER 10. They are not happy.

TEACHER 9. No, they are not really happy.

CSM. I think we can all understand how you feel. I understand how you feel.

TEACHER 10. But what do you do?

TEACHER 12. Go home and get a good night's sleep.

TEACHER 10. I go home and cook.

CSM. I think a lot of us are concerned with just this thing that you are talking about, and I think this is really the main reason for our sessions, for our meetings, because the example you bring up, and what you find touching about this little girl in running and getting leaves, is in many ways very much like what you described you would like to be able to see.

TEACHER 10. Yes.

TEACHER 12. I had one last week. I think I motivated him for the first time. He wanted a piece of scotch tape, and he hadn't done anything, and we were doing creative writing, and he has a very high IQ, very high potential, and he is the one that his parents don't have any control over at home, and there is disagreemeent as to how they should discipline him, so that nobody has. He is the one that the principal says, "Don't feel bad, no one has been able to work with him yet."

But I got him motivated the other day and it was just an accident. He wanted this piece of scotch tape, and I said, "When you finish your paragraph you may have a piece of scotch tape." That is the first time he has done a paragraph. This is just a piece of scotch tape, and we have all these elaborate motivations.

CSM. You know, this reminds me of what we were talking about before. You know, we have books and books and books about how to motivate children and how to teach children, and you have been exposed to them, to tons of them yourself in your training. I have been exposed to tons of them in my training. And yet the examples we are talking about, these real things that happen, I wonder if there is a seminar possible for it.

TEACHER 10. There is not much that will tell you to use a piece of scotch tape as a motivation

TEACHER 12. I haven't gotten him motivated since.

CSM. But I guess what I do feel is that there are these kinds of things with children that you and we do feel very deeply about, and I think these are the things we can share. It is so frustrating so many times to be confronted with what appears to be a helpless situation, and I guess what seems to keep us going is that once maybe a little piece of scotch tape or a little piece of caring works.

TEACHER 9. I don't know how good this example is, and I don't know whether I made a mistake in doing this or not. There is one girl in my room from a very poor home. Her mother and father are both alcoholics. Right now we do not have a social worker. Both she and her sister were out for a week, and the children were saying that her mother and father were sick, and this means they were having a party for a week, so neither the girl in my room nor the sister in the forth grade came to school.

On the Monday when she came back to school, I said, "Why were you absent?" She said, "Because I didn't want to come to school." I said, "You will have to stay after school. When we play hooky, we have to stay to make up the time." That night it was late, and I decided to take her home. I took her home and waited for her to get into the house, but she was locked out and her parents were not home, and I didn't know what to do. So we left a note on the door and I took her home with me. And my roommates and I took her out to a discount place.

She comes to school in rags. She doesn't have shoes. She wears sneakers with holes. We took her out, and for something like $7 we bought her a dress and shoes, and she was so happy. She wears that dress all week. I know she goes home and washes it out every night, and she shines the shoes. And the shoes were very inexpensive. She never had a pair of shoes, only sneakers that were hand-me-downs before.

This child was such a problem. She is very bright. She is the highest in my room. She got 69 on the Monroe reading test. This is pretty good for the school and exceptionally good because she was in a reading readiness last year and in the low group.

This week the teachers were amazed, because she is so bright and says hello to all the teachers, and she has to show off the dress.

I have promised her that I would take her home on the weekend, and she has permission from her parents. We have decided not to tell the children where she got the dress. I don't know whether it would be a good thing to become so involved as to take her to my home for a weekend. I don't know. Would it? Would this be wise?

TEACHER 10. Offhand I would say not for a weekend.

TEACHER 9. For a day?

TEACHER 10. Possibly for a day or something, or sort of an outing.

TEACHER 12. My idea would be—there is a possibility you have reached this child—could you put her in another class, so she could be in the other class of the same grade, so she won't be in your class, but you can reach her and continue to reach her?

TEACHER 9. No, I wouldn't be able to change her. I know the other teacher wouldn't want her. She is a problem.

OBS. Do you have doubts about taking her for a weekend?

TEACHER 9. I don't mind becoming involved, but I was told by the teachers just not to get involved. I don't think by becoming involved I would have any trouble controlling her. I am afraid what it will do to the other children. She has kept her promise not to tell them very much, and she doesn't say anything because I asked her not to, but if they did find out, would they think anything of it, because she has always had so much less than they did anyway, and now she seemed to have such a little bit, but I don't think they would be jealous. I don't know.

TEACHER 12. What does your principal say about it?

TEACHER 9. He doesn't know. You see, my principal is a fairly old man, and he—I think he has problems of his own, personal problems. I feel very disloyal saying this, but I don't think he is very much interested in the students. I have never seen him talk to a student. If any teacher comes with a problem, he gets very much upset and says, "This is your problem," and that type of thing. He doesn't want to be bothered. So I wouldn't tell him.

And there is no guidance counselor in the school. There was last year, but she was changed to another school. There is no guidance counselor, and no social worker. There is on one, no help for the teacher. And people from CPI aren't particularly concerned with this facet of the child's life.

TEACHER 12. I think it is an extremely interesting situation. I don't know what to do, but I am fascinated by it.

CSM. I tell you that what fascinates me most about it is that I have the feeling—and I have a feeling that I am right—that in all your schooling to become teachers, nobody told you or taught you that this was a method to use.

TEACHER 9. No, but I think in our home life, in church or anything, it is just a natural sort of thing. But sometimes the natural thing is not the thing to do. Or the opinion of some people would be that it isn't a professional thing to do, you know, and they must have their reasons. I would like to know their reasons, and some people told me not to become involved. Why would they say this? There must be a reason, not just for my benefit, but for the benefit of the child. Would there be? Is it going to turn into a detrimental type of activity to do this?

CSM. Aside from what the possible consequences of it are in the future or how you might handle it now, what remains clear to me is that you did something which one might call, if one was very strict, nonprofessional or not from the book, and yet certainly you are confronted with a child which you finally reached, and you don't seem to feel very bad about it.

TEACHER 9. No, I don't feel bad.

CSM. And I guess that is what impresses me most about it. Maybe sometimes it is not so bad to be just human.

TEACHER 10. I think I would lean toward just a one-day type thing. I thought of one thing, but I don't think that will work out too well, doing something on a sort of small group basis. I think it will be better if you kept it confidential.

TEACHER 9. Yes. I think we should for a while.

TEACHER 12. I hate to break this up, but I have to get an absentee ballot notarized before six o'clock.

CSM. Well, all I wanted to close with was that this example sounds very much like what we are talking about, where you saw a girl doing exactly what was so natural for a little girl to do, and it seemed so appropriate, and here is one of our own teachers doing something so natural to do and so appropriate, and it rings the same way. Maybe these are the kinds of things we could keep talking about even without an agenda. So we will meet again next week, same time.

(Whereupon, at 5:00 P.M., the meeting was adjourned.)

GROUP III, SESSION 4

CSM. If it is okay with you people, I would like to pick up on something we were talking about last week, which I found extremely interesting, and we can fill you in on it.

I guess one of the most important things we were talking about, really was how very often it happens that in a sense—well, one of these people here literally almost violated a rule of teaching, and yet I think it satisfied something that we would have done very humanly. And in my mind this raised the whole question of teaching sometimes not quite by the book, but rather in terms of what you think the needs of the child are.

You are kind of unaware of what we were talking about?

TEACHER 1. Yes.

TEACHER 10. We were talking about trying to reach certain very difficult kids in different ways, and mainly, I think it ended up with our talking about ways that we could try to get through to a kid that created serious problems in the classroom. We talked about the standard methods of parent-teacher conferences, talking with the child, various disciplinary measures, all sorts of fairly standard things.

And then Teacher 9 came up with an incident—more than an incident—it is a very complex situation with one little girl that had ability, but she didn't use it very well, She was a serious behavior problem—I think that was the case—and both her parents are alcoholics. She came to school dressed in rags literally, and one time she had been truant for a while because her parents were on a binge, so she was out for a week or so. When she finally came to school, Teacher 9 told her she would keep her after school, and she did.

When the time came to take her home, it was late and dark. She drove her to her home, and no one was at home. The girl had no key, and she had nowhere to go. So Teacher 9 took her home, and she and her roommate gave her dinner and bought her a dress and a pair of shoes in a discount house. She never had shoes, but only sneakers. And she said that this little girl seemed to change so much in her attitude. She became polite to the teachers and started doing her work. This changed her so much, this unusual act of kindness; but she had gotten herself involved with the child, which was sort of in violation of the code, almost. She had gotten very involved, but in so doing had done something very radical for this child in that her behavior changed so.

That was what we finished up on. We were talking about some standard things, and then we went into unusual things like that.

csm. I guess what I wanted to keep talking about was one of the things that Teacher 9 was really concerned about, and that was that on the one hand I think we were pretty gratified as to what happened with this girl, the real change that took place. The way we heard it, or the way I heard it at least, it was almost unbelievable.

But on the other hand, one of the things I think Teacher 9 was wondering about was, first, would there be any further complications of this relationship, and the second thing I think she alluded to, was whether she should tell any of the school administration about this.

teacher 10. She hadn't told anybody. She wasn't sure she was doing the right thing.

csm. What do you think about that? It is a fascinating kind of problem.

teacher 1. I have never had that kind of situation.

csm. What would you do?

teacher 2. I don't know what I would do.

teacher 1. I would tell someone.

teacher 2. Yes.

teacher 1. I think if you have a good principal, you should at least have the principal know.

teacher 10. I don't think she felt that she could tell the principal.

csm. How did she describe the principal?

teacher 10. I don't remember now. We have had many descriptions of cruddy principals. I don't know which one was hers.

TEACHER 1. You could really get into hot water over this if the parents didn't like it.

TEACHER 10. Apparently the parents hardly knew she existed. They just did nothing for her. She wasn't sure what she should continue to do. She had tentatively invited the girl to stay at her house for a weekend, and wasn't sure whether this was right.

CSM. Neither were we.

TEACHER 10. Just so long as the little girl could keep it a secret. To me that would be more of a problem than telling the principal. Even if the principal found out, to me that wouldn't be as bad as if the other children in the classroom found out. How would she explain it? She had on a new dress, and she hadn't told them where she got it, but it is just so long that that kind of thing can be kept.

OBS. Why is it so important that the other kids don't find out?

TEACHER 10. This is an extreme case of favoritism. It is bad enough if you always choose the same kid to do the errand, but doing such a thing as buying clothes for a child and inviting the child to spend the weekend at your place, would be—well, the others would feel—I don't know exactly what the feeling would be, but it would be dissatisfaction, I think, and they would be puzzled by it.

OBS. But what I am wondering is if such things couldn't be explained and discussed with the kids.

TEACHER 1. If they are very young, they would be too small, and they wouldn't understand. To them it is share and share alike.

TEACHER 10. I don't think you could explain that to them.

TEACHER 1. Especially if you had other children in the room that were poor.

TEACHER 10. Yes, and there are others that are poor, though not as poor as she is.

TEACHER 1. And also, you will hurt the child's feelings if you explain what her parents are like. They would tease her and everything.

CSM. Have any of you ever run into this kind of situation where you found yourself in a sense playing favorites, you know, because you felt that at that point or at that time it was something that you wanted to do? Or is that something that never occurs?

TEACHER 10. I think it is an impulse. I have felt sometimes that I would like to do more for a certain child, but—let me think about this a bit more, and you go ahead.

TEACHER 2. I don't know. I think that naturally, instinctively, you like certain children more than others, not really like them, but I don't know—I really like all my children, but you just can't help but pick certain ones for certain things because they are reliable. And I try to make them understand that the reason certain ones are being picked—I don't always pick just the same ones, but there are certain ones that you pick, because then you know that if you send them somewhere, it will be all right. In my third grade, if I can send one of my children to watch the first grade, naturally they will raise their hand to go, and I have told them that when they can take care of themselves in the room, when I can trust them when I am out of the room to behave themselves, then I can trust them to take care of other children. And believe it or not, it is hard for them to realize that I am not playing favorites, even at that age level. That is why I think trying to explain the situation to first graders, would be exceptionally difficult, but I think you don't favor anyone because you like them, but because they are reliable in that sense.

TEACHER 10. There is also a sense of rapport, kinship, something that will click between a teacher and a certain child, and with others it just won't. You can work with them, but there isn't the same sort of feeling.

TEACHER 2. I think also we are only human, and I think also that certain children appreciate things, and others don't, and I think—I don't care who you are, but I think a teacher, she can try and try with a certain child, and in the end there isn't any sense of outward appreciation. Not that you give up, but you put it aside for a while and work on where you do get a bit of appreciation.

TEACHER 10. A little feedback.

TEACHER 2. That's right. Some children show appreciation. They really do. And you can always sense that.

CSM. Also by this kind of unfortunate term, favoritism, the way Teacher 9 told us this incident last week, it turned out really that she was maybe not playing favorites, but certainly paying a different kind of attention to a child who clearly was not the reliable child in the class, and I was kind of wondering if this kind of thing comes up when you might feel for one reason or another that you should direct your attention to the problem child rather than the good child.

TEACHER 10. I have found this. I think, thinking of the matter of playing favorites, this is all part of getting involved with the child, how much emotional involvement you have with the class. I don't feel it is healthy to have too great an emotional involvement with the class, with the children you work with. This I found out through experience when I started working with mentally retarded children in the summer. During the first summer that is all I talked about off the job. I must have been very boring to anyone I talked to. It was exhausting to get so involved.

The second summer I felt less emotionally involved with the kids, and I think I was able to do a better job. I think a certain kind of detachment is healthy. Beyond that, if you get too attached, you can't do a good job.

Now, I think this ties in with this idea of playing favorites. Last year when I taught, the class pretty much agreed that I did not show favoritism. There were a couple of kids that I felt showed their appreciation of my efforts more, and I had preferences for working with certain children, but occasionally some child would say, "You favor so and so," and the others would say, "No, she doesn't."

So I manage to work reasonably equally with some of them. There was one boy that I just somehow could never feel any sense of kinship or any of this rapport with, but for the most part, I was able to sort of favor each one in a different way. For instance, there were a couple of kids with art projects, so I would favor them by letting them work on the bulletin board and projects such as that. I tried to find some way to favor each child. There were only 13 in this class. It was a special class, so you could sort of find areas to let each child show off his efforts and abilities.

This year I am trying to do the same thing. It takes a while to work this out. I find right now that the thing that I have been accused of is letting the kids with behavior problems get away with certain things, and what the others mean, I think, is that I am paying more attention to them necessarily, because I have to keep going over to the desk and saying, "What are you doing on this," or "Have you finished this assignment?" It is just the fact that I am over at the troublemakers' desks more is the reason that I have been accused —not so much now, but a couple of weeks ago—that I let them get away with this.

There are a lot of problems with this sort of thing. Kids don't want teachers to play favorites.

TEACHER 2. Oh, no.

TEACHER 10. And sometimes it is hard to keep yourself from playing favorites. But if you can possibly stay reasonably detached, it will create a better atmosphere, I find, in a self-contained classroom such as the special classroom. I have never taught elementary grades, but I would guess it is the same.

But I find that with a special class, that you have to maintain a certain distance, and you just can't play favorites. You can ruin any spirit in the class there is. There may often be very little, but it can ruin what little there is.

I have found a new way of working with one of the obnoxious kids. He came up and asked if I could keep a record of whether he had been good or not. What the practice is in the school, if a child misbehaves, you write up an index card on him, and the vice principal keeps a record, and he tries to talk to them. He is good with the kids, and the kids have a lot of respect for him. He has a way of reaching most of them.

This kid has been down to the office at least 15 or 20 times. And the vice principal said, "If he starts creating a disturbance, hitting kids, just doing anything, send him down to me, and I will have him standing in the corner." And he has spent several days standing with his nose against the wall, because he has created such a disturbance in the classroom, that he can't stay.

This past week we started keeping a goodness record. Each day he asked me, "Have I been good?" And I would say, "Well, most of the day, but toward the end of the day not so good." But he said, "I have been better, haven't I?"

I kept a record which said good part of the day or good in the morning or something like that.

Today he asked how he had been doing, and I said, "You are getting a little better, there are still places you need a little improvement." And he said, "I haven't been doing anything bad like hollering out."

We decided that the next thing to work on is not jumping out of his seat. We will try that next, and then after that, we will get to his calling other kids names. But one thing at a time.

I wrote this sort of summary. I started this a week and a half ago, this summary report, and said that Dick has improved in the classroom, that his behavior has gotten somewhat better.

I said to the boy, "Why don't you bring this down to the vice principal?" He said, "If I go down, he will think I have been sent down for being bad."

I said, "I will write a note that you have been sent down for being good."

And the vice principal looked at him and said, "Now what have you done?"

He said, "Look at the card." He brought the card down, and the vice principal looked at the card and said, "I've got to shake your hand." The kid broke out into a big grin. The vice principal wrote on the card, "I don't believe this." The kid has improved.

Usually these cards are just used to record bad things. But this thing has proved to be amazing. He is still a troublemaker, but he is a little better.

These odd little things you never hear about in any course, and this seems to be working.

TEACHER 2. I have been doing a similar thing today. In the morning when they come in, I have this good citizenship chart. I have it named that because it is actually working for good citizenship, but actually good behavior is what it is.

When they come in in the morning, before we start our lessons, I have them write on a piece of paper. I cut the paper up for them, and they put on it what they are going to work on for that day. And every day they have to write something different. At a quarter of three they have to stand up and read it to the class, and if they have done it all day, they get a check for that day. And at the end of the week I give them a bookmark.

It has really been working. If the child hasn't been doing that, the children will say, "Oh." And if they put down the same thing on two days in a row, the other children will say, "You did that yesterday."

After a while it gets monotonous, and I don't think you can do the same thing too long, at least not with little children like that, but it is a little better.

TEACHER 10. It sure is trial and error.

TEACHER 2. To know all the ways, though, that is the only thing.

CSM. You know, what you were talking about, you know we have the same kind of concern in psychology, the problem of how close you get to somebody, before you begin to feel that it is obscuring your own vision or your own experience of this person. In a sense we have that similar kind of concern.

But what struck me was, first, that from what you said nobody has ever taught you to do these things, in teacher training, these different kinds of things. And the other thing is that when you describe, in a sense, paying a different kind of attention to each child, and maybe this sometimes brings you to the point of being at one kid's desk more than another kid's, but paying a different kind of attention to each child is not the same thing, I guess, as favoritism.

TEACHER 10. No, it isn't. Just the very fact, though, that if you can pay a different kind of attention to each child, you can find some way to pay attention to the child, it will help to eliminate this feeling that you are playing favorites, I think that is what I was getting at, by trying to find some way in which to favor a child, that it will—it is such an odd word, favoritism—.

CSM. Isn't it?

TEACHER 10. It is one of these words that is over-used.

CSM. I wonder if there is a distinction that we could make that might be helpful, the distinction between—for want of a better word—favoritism, that, and paying a different kind of attention to each child?

TEACHER 1. To me what Teacher 9 did isn't favoritism. I wouldn't put it under that. I really wouldn't. I mean, she just felt that it was necessary to do it, and because of maybe the type of person she is, she wanted to do it. You find some other teachers that just wouldn't want to do it.

I think when they say favoritism, they mean that you have one or two kids that you have do everything, and that is it. You don't run into that so much in the ordinary classroom. This is drilled into your head in college, that you just don't play favorites, and try not to get involved with your children. I know we used to get this all the time, and it is "for your own good that we are telling you all these things," and it is hard not to try to get to each child, although it seems to them as though you are playing favorites, because they don't really understand it, just as we don't understand it. So they say that you are favoring this child or that child.

TEACHER 2. That is the same thing as far as picking on certain children. You don't pick on them because they are favorites. There is not just one, but I would say that half my class gets picked on for errands, and there are some, you can't let them go, because what kind of an example would it be for the other children? It wouldn't be a good example. They can't do it because they don't behave. I have never heard the word favoritism in my classroom.

TEACHER 1. I haven't either.

TEACHER 2. What is the correct meaning for favoritism?

TEACHER 10. I have run across it a lot in the classes that I have worked in. I have a feeling that it is because the kids are so insecure anyway. They have been told all their lives that they don't know anything and are not worth much, so anything they can hang onto, they try to hang onto. I have run across that a lot in classes.

CSM. Then I guess it is easier for us to understand the kind of questions that Teacher 9 had about what she did with this little girl, because in one sense, I think as Teacher 1 made so clear, on the one hand you are really drilled—.

TEACHER 1. Didn't you get that in college?

TEACHER 10. I don't recall that exactly, but I know that I felt this way very strongly.

TEACHER 1. I didn't feel that way when I went in. I wasn't even aware of it when I first went in, but after teaching for a year, I really went back to it.

TEACHER 2. It was exceptionally hard for me because I taught in my own neighborhood, and a lot of these children would come to see me. Two little girls all the time used to come and knock at the back. I taught one year, and the next year we didn't teach, and it so happened I had the same children the second year in between, and they would come and see me and tell me how they were doing in school, and it isn't really favoritism.

TEACHER 10. It is not on your part. It is just that the kids don't understand that the things that you do for one child don't necessarily mean that you are favoring that child. It is the other kids' attitude. It isn't the way you feel. It is what the other kids perceive to be your relationship with the various students in the classroom. They may think that you are playing favorites, even though you are not. You have to be quite careful the way you work with the kids, not to create this impression. At least I have found this.

TEACHER 1. They would be old enough to understand this at least, but they are very sensitive to this feeling that somebody dislikes them or that someone is favoring them or someone else.

CSM. It is kind of like this problem, this question that came up last week. On the one hand it does seem, at least in part of your teacher training that you are exposed to the idea, at least, that it is a kind of bad thing or not a very helpful thing to show favoritism. And yet Teacher 9 in a sense, if you wanted to use that silly term, favoritism, in a sense she pulled away from some of the things she was taught and really went out to this kid. And maybe it is more helpful to think of it in the terms that we were thinking about before, that instead of seeing this as favoritism, really you could see it first as a fairly natural thing to do, and the second thing as maybe showing a particular kind of attention to a particular kind of kid.

TEACHER 10. I think perhaps what she was—I can't really speak for her— but I sort of feel that it is not so much a feeling about her playing favorites, but how to continue trying to help the child without destroying any kind of favorable relationship with the rest of the children. In other words, what can she do about helping the girl, without alienating the rest of the kids if they find out, and they are bound to.

TEACHER 1. What did she say to the child when she did all this? Did she say how she explained why she was buying the shoes?

TEACHER 10. No, she didn't say. She didn't say what she said to her.

CSM. It is too bad that she has illness in her family, or whatever it is. Maybe we can pursue this with her next week.

You brought up another thing, and that is that I think you mentioned that one of the things the kids really don't want, is to have you show a special kind of affection or special kind of involvement with one kid as opposed to another kid.

TEACHER 10. They want you to be basically impartial.

CSM. What I have experienced when I have been in the schools is, for example, something like this. I have to tell you this little thing that I saw, and it happens, I am sure, in all of your classes. It is that there is a question to be answered, and you call on a kid to answer a question, and five other hands shoot up, and you know each one wants to answer the question as if almost hoping that this kid wouldn't answer the question, so that you would call on the boy or girl whose hand is up, so he or she could answer it. And to me it seems a little inconsistent if indeed the kids want to be treated like equals without any favoritism, why should they try so hard to be the best or to answer the question or to get that extra recognition?

These two things—at least from what I have seen—it poses some kind of a problem in understanding it. On the one hand they don't want anybody to be a favorite of the teacher, and they don't want anyone to be unduly in the teacher's attention. And yet on the other hand, they seem—at least in the schools that I have been in, and this has been in many different grades—they all seem to be vying for the teacher's attention and affection and recognition.

TEACHER 1. They want it, but they won't admit it.

TEACHER 2. Subconsciously they want it.

TEACHER 1. Yes.

TEACHER 10. I am not sure that a child wants to be thought of as the teacher's pet. He wants the attention for himself, but in some subtle way perhaps. One thing that I have found out, when you get a flock of hands shooting up, a couple of things that work—I am not sure it is the best—what I do is sometimes call a group of children, and if there are different enough answers, once I get a few of them replying in the same way, the rest will reply in the same way whether they intended to in the first place or not. If the answer is fairly obvious, if I want to wake somebody up, I will call on one child, and say to someone else, "Is that right" or, "What was your answer?" I can get a group of answers before we get the definite answer. It is a small thing, but it does help sometimes.

TEACHER 2. Sometimes you don't have the time to do that.

TEACHER 10. I know.

TEACHER 1. We had a funny instance. They took pictures for the grade teacher—they did it throughout the whole school. They came in and just took candid shots, and then they loaded up the camera, and they took a picture of one girl, and they posed one picture. And evidently the other children didn't notice. But the principal walked in. She was in the room, and she commented on it afterward. And their reaction was that they lost all enthusiasm about this magazine article. They couldn't care less because they felt they were going to use the one girl's picture. It was really funny. Here they go snapping all these candid shots, and it had to be in color, and yet they had to tell them this.

CSM. How did you handle that?

TEACHER 1. The bell rang. It really rang.

CSM. Saved by the bell.

The other thing that came out of what we were talking about, and that I wanted to ask you about, was: have there ever been times in your teaching experience when you really wanted to do something with a child or a group of children—and I don't mean like kicking them out of the door or the window—but you really wanted to do something with a kid that in a sense almost violated what you have been taught to do, or what your teacher training advised you to do, because that is in essence what Teacher 9 was talking about. And I was wondering if this ever did happen, on what basis you would or would not do it.

In other words, I am asking the question not whether or not you really did what you wanted to do, but I am wondering if and when the occasion ever occurred or came about, and on what basis you decided to do something or not to do something. Or was Teacher 9's the only case?

TEACHER 1. I have never had a situation where I could really give a lot of attention to one child or anything like that.

TEACHER 10. I am trying to think of other situations in which there might be some sort of code you might want to break. I can't think of any offhand.

TEACHER 2. I had one child, and I know he didn't get enough food at home. They used to carry their lunch, and I noticed that a lot of the time he would carry cereal for lunch and get milk in school, and the milk he didn't pay for because he couldn't. But it was just never let out. I don't think the other children knew. That didn't present a problem as to why he didn't pay.

But I used to give him cookies. I used to say I wasn't hungry anymore. The class was there, and naturally they are all eating their lunch, but they never said anything. This was in fifth grade, and I think the children knew.

I don't know, it all depends what kind of a class you have. Like here, I couldn't, because most of my children—well, if you have a class where most of them are poor, or where you have more than one, that would probably present a problem. But here the children—I think they felt like me, like they were giving cookies and different things like that. So you know, whether it is right or not, who cares? He needs something to eat; give it to him.

I brought clothes to school, but I have never said whom they were from. You know, I brought clothes, old clothes, and have given them to the principal to give to certain children. But the children never knew that they were from me, or if they were from someone else. The children never knew where from. That could be done in that way. If they knew they were giving this child something because she needed it, they could say that somebody brought it in, and it just fits her. Well then, what did you do with the other children if it fits the other children also? That would present a problem also. But it could be done that way, where the child wouldn't know that it came from the teacher.

TEACHER 10. Indirectly, yes.

TEACHER 1. I can't help thinking about the parents' attitude. Especially if they are alcoholic, sometimes they don't like things like that, and they don't like the people to meddle in their lives, and they consider it that.

CSM. And yet sometimes we don't even ask parents whether or not we should meddle, but we just meddle because something has to be done, if you want to call it meddling. I guess what you mentioned was that you preferred in a sense to break the rules, but anonymously.

TEACHER 2. Yes.

TEACHER 10. I think you tend to go by conscience and try to sneak your conscience around the rules in some way to do what you feel is the right thing to do.

CSM. Like I said before, we have this same kind of thing. In our training there are also certain prescribed do's and don'ts, but I really don't know of any psychologists who, if they were really honest with themselves, haven't said that at times they really didn't understand why they shouldn't do something or why they should do something else. There are times, I think, when simply because, as you put it, because of our own feelings or conscience, we do things that we are told not to do, and we do accept the responsibility for doing them without asking parents and without even telling principals. And I think the two cases are very similar.

I am really curious to find out how it turned out.

TEACHER 10. She had just done this a few days before, I think, so it hasn't gotten very far.

CSM. All we really know at this point is that there was a dramatic change, not only in her behavior, but in her ability to learn.

TEACHER 1. It has its good points and bad points. She is not going to have the same teacher next year.

TEACHER 10. But the change is effected. It may persist.

TEACHER 1. Will it persist?

TEACHER 2. Anything you teach a child, you teach a child something, and yet maybe the next year it might be a different teacher, and there might be a personality clash, and the child is completely different.

TEACHER 1. At six years old, they aren't that stable yet.

CSM. I guess that is the question that is open, you know, as to what she accomplished with this child and whether it is going to be transferred over to another grade and to another teacher and to another situation. But at least I feel that—.

TEACHER 1. For the time being.

CSM. Exactly, at least what she did right here and right now in the school, caused something to happen with this child's motivation, if you want to call it that, or ability or desire to learn.

TEACHER 10. Regardless of whether the change persists, at least for a short time you have given the child a feeling that she can do something or accomplish something. There is some intangible reward for her action. Just the fact that her behavior is reinforced, that may establish more lasting patterns of behavior.

CSM. What about the little boy you described to us today? In a sense, isn't it the same thing? I mean, it isn't a case of taking him home or buying him anything. But what did it involve really from your point of view?

TEACHER 10. A few minutes more each morning. You mean what have I done with him?

CSM. What I am wondering is: How do you see what you have done with him in terms of how he sees it and how he responds to it?

TEACHER 10. I am not sure I know exactly what you are getting at.

CSM. Well, let me tell you. Teacher 9 did something, and what we haven't had time to talk with her about is how she felt the child saw what she was doing as meaning. That is one of the things I hope to be able to talk to her about next week.

But you did something with the boy, and he came over to you and proposed this—.

TEACHER 10. He has been in my homeroom as well as the special class. I have tried, if I have worked with him, to talk with the kid about behavior, about any problems he may have. When he has been in my homeroom, the only way I have been able to keep him quiet often is to talk to him, to try to get him doing something, or just to talk with him about something, just to get him away from hitting another kid, or just to get him involved in something on the other side of the room, and this pretty much came about from that. He finally suggested doing this.

So each morning, I guess each morning he checks the card—I keep it in my desk drawer—and this is just between the two of us. I have suggested to a couple of other kids if they would like to do this, because one had asked about it.

One I asked today, and he thinks he would like to try that also. He has been a troublemaker also.

Basically it involves spending a few minutes with the child, preferably at the beginning of the day, to try to set some kind of behavior for the day. It involves some sort of talk with him and asking him to tell you how he is going to act or how he will try to act during the day. This is just what you were doing—.

TEACHER 2. Yes.

TEACHER 10. —and I try to set some goal for them during the day, and at the end of the day you sort of reinforce that by having them tell you again how they have been. I think it works better if you have them tell you what is right, rather than for you to tell them. Sometimes this is hard to do in the beginning, but this is the kind of thing, to try to work with the child individually. I know it just didn't seem possible, but maybe it is possible—.

CSM. Maybe it is not so hopeless. But really it sounds as if this kid, rather than being involved in other things, he becomes involved with you.

TEACHER 10. He says his other teacher kept him very busy. I have tried to keep him busy. I don't think he realized how busy I have tried to keep him. I have let him suggest things that he feels will help him keep out of trouble. And between his suggestions and mine, it sometimes works. I guess that is about all you can ask for.

CSM. In this case it sounds like we were very lucky to have the vice principal.

TEACHER 10. He is a good man. He is someone the kids realize they can rely on or trust. He is very good. The principal we would be better off without, but the vice principal is very good.

Having somebody else to tell them that this is good and to keep it up, this is very good. For any other kid, his behavior would be terrible, but for him it is good. By any other standards, by comparison with the other kids in the homeroom, he is still obnoxious, but he is a little better than he was.

CSM. I guess what we have talked about really today was an extension of last week: At what point do we as human beings just feel that it is necessary to do something, whether or not we were taught specifically that kind of thing? And I really look toward next week hopefully, if we can talk with her some more about this.

The other thing that was raised just now that maybe we could get into is relations between the teachers and the administration. You mentioned, for example, a vice principal who was someone you feel you can work with, and indeed would like to work with. And on the other hand, you mention a principal whom I have a feeling you—.

TEACHER 10. He is an absolute jerk to put it bluntly. This opinion is held by all the faculty members and all the students, and it is very unfortunate, but it happens quite often, I gather.

CSM. Maybe these are things we can get into next week, because it sounds really fascinating, especially this vice principal. He sounds like a really sensitive guy.

TEACHER 10. He is. He is very good, really very good with the kids. Some kids he can't reach either, but then nobody has been able to reach them, judging from the past records. There has been almost no one to find some way to sort of get to their hearts. You know, there is so much of teaching that is just instinct—.

CSM. Yes.

TEACHER 10. There are things you learn, certain methods, but when it comes down to how you get along in the classroom day to day, it is sheer instinct that gets you through, I think. There are certain methods, certain kinds of exercises that you prepare and certain kinds of lesson plans to prepare, but I think it is just that sort of a feeling that you should do a certain thing or not in many cases, and no one can tell you this.

TEACHER 2. Because every child wants to learn something different.

TEACHER 10. And you can't be told this or get it from books or records or anything else.

CSM. I guess that is all.

(Whereupon, at 5:00 P.M., the meeting was adjourned.)

Index